# Core Text Series

- Written with authority by leading subject experts
- Takes a focused approach, leading law students straight to the heart of the subject
- Clear, concise, straightforward analysis of the subject and its challenges

**Company Law:** Alan Dignam and John Lowry

**Constitutional and Administrative Law:** Neil Parpworth

**Criminal Law:** Nicola Padfield

**European Union Law:** Margot Horspool, Matthew Humphreys MBE, and Michael Wells-Greco

**Evidence:** Roderick Munday

**Family Law:** Mary Welstead and Susan Edwards

**Intellectual Property Law:** Jennifer Davis

**Land Law:** Ben McFarlane, Nicholas Hopkins, and Sarah Nield

**The Law of Contract:** Janet O'Sullivan and Jonathan Hilliard

**The Law of Trusts:** James Penner

For further information about titles in the series, **please visit www.oup.co.uk/series/cts/**

WITHDRAWN

OXFORD
UNIVERSITY PRESS

CORE TEXT SERIES

# Land Law

**BEN McFARLANE**

Professor of Law, University College London

**NICHOLAS HOPKINS**

Law Commissioner for England and Wales and Professor of Law, University of Reading

**SARAH NIELD**

Professor of Law, University of Southampton

OXFORD
UNIVERSITY PRESS

# OXFORD

UNIVERSITY PRESS

Great Clarendon Street, Oxford, OX2 6DP,
United Kingdom

Oxford University Press is a department of the University of Oxford.
It furthers the University's objective of excellence in research, scholarship,
and education by publishing worldwide. Oxford is a registered trade mark of
Oxford University Press in the UK and in certain other countries

© Oxford University Press 2017

Published in the United States of America by Oxford University Press
198 Madison Avenue, New York, NY 10016, United States of America

British Library Cataloguing in Publication Data
Data available

Library of Congress Control Number: 2016960647

ISBN 978–0–19–873532–8

Printed in Great Britain by
Bell & Bain Ltd., Glasgow

# Preface

In the preface to our first edition of *Land Law: Text, Cases, and Materials* we wrote that it was 'somewhat daunting' to add to OUP's well-regarded texts, cases, and materials series. This time, we have also aspired to the extremely high standards of Kevin Gray and Susan Francis Gray, to whom this book is dedicated. We all used and greatly admired their book *Land Law* in OUP's Core Text series, which so ably met its aims to challenge and to inform, and to serve as a companion to their more detailed *Elements of Land Law*. We certainly have not tried to produce a new edition of the Grays' text, as no one could hope to match their distinctive and insightful style. Rather, this book is a wholly new one, and takes its own path in aiming for the same end of challenging and informing the reader.

Our book contains within its own covers full coverage of the core rules, principles, and debates in land law. So, whilst it can be used as a companion to our more detailed *Land Law: Text, Cases, and Materials*, it is also a stand-alone resource. Each chapter of this Core Text is designed to be read straight through as an introduction to the material, or, perhaps, as a recap: the flow of the text is not interrupted by extracts from primary and secondary sources or footnotes, and further details on specific points are always available in our *Text, Cases, and Materials* book. Those familiar with that longer book will need no introduction to the structure used here, based on the content, acquisition, and defences/priority questions. They will also recognize, in Chapter 2, our continued belief that the topic of human rights is important in land law, not least in raising directly some of the fundamental tensions (eg between occupiers, landowners, and creditors) that are often hidden behind the technicalities of the subject. In this shorter book, we have focused on the law of registered land, as now of course the vast majority of titles to land are registered. In seeking to challenge as well as to inform, we have also included a final chapter, Chapter 12, which considers some of the wider issues raised by the current land law rules and which we hope will assist, and even inspire, students writing essays or dissertations on land law topics.

Whilst cooperating closely, we have capitalized on our own research interests in the division of labour: Ben is responsible for Chapters 1, 3, 5.83–5.138, 7.1–7.86, and 12; Nick for Chapters 4, 5.1–5.82, 6, and 11; Sarah for Chapters 2, 7.87–7.137, and 8–10. In addition to a bibliography of sources, each chapter contains suggestions for further reading and self-test questions.

We are very grateful for the feedback provided by anonymous reviewers, and also for those (such as Professor John Mee) who have read and commented on specific chapters.

We are also indebted to OUP in general and Felicity Boughton in particular for their help in bringing the book into being.

*Ben McFarlane, Nicholas Hopkins, Sarah Nield*

Nick Hopkins is the Property, Family and Trusts Law Commissioner for England and Wales, but nothing in this work should be taken as representing the views of the Law Commission.

# Guide to Using the Book

There are a number of features throughout the textbook designed to help you in your studies.

## SUMMARY

This chapter considers leases. Leases can count a
ownership of land for a period. They are very imp
of their homes, and most businesses have leases
how the content, acquisition, and defences ques
there are often both contractual and proprietar
chapter will also consider leasehold covenants. A
or implied promise made by a landlord to a tenar

**Chapter summaries** highlight what will be addressed in each chapter, so you are aware of the key learning outcomes for each topic.

## FURTHER READING

Bright, S, 'Of Estates and Interests: A Tale of Own
    Dewar (eds), *Land Law: Themes and Perspecti*

Lochery, E, 'Pushing the Boundaries of *Dutton*' [20

McFarlane, B, '*Keppell v Bailey* (1834) and *Hill*
    the Common Law' in N Gravells (ed), *La*
    Publishing, 2013).

At the end of each chapter is a list of recommended **further reading**.

These suggestions include book and journal articles, and will help to supplement your knowledge, and develop your understanding of the key topics.

## SELF-TEST QUESTIONS

1   Is there a continuing role for land covenants

2   Are restrictive covenants genuine property
    contract?

3   Restrictive covenants and easements share s
    similarities and differences?

4   What is meant by annexation? Do you think

Each chapter concludes with a selection of **self-test questions**.

These allow you to check your understanding of the topics covered and help you engage fully with the material in preparation for further study, writing essays, and answering exam questions.

# Contents

# Table of Cases

# Table of Legislation

The European Convention on Human Rights is tabled under Sch 1 of the Human Rights Act.

## Statutory Instruments

## EU Directive

# Abbreviations

| | |
|---|---|
| **A1-P1** | Article 1 Protocol 1 of the European Convention on Human Rights and Fundamental Freedoms |
| **AJA 1970** | Administration of Justice Act 1970 |
| **Can J L Juris** | Canadian Journal of Law and Jurisprudence |
| **CCA 1974** | Consumer Credit Act 1974 |
| **CFLQ** | Child and Family Law Quarterly |
| **CLJ** | Cambridge Law Journal |
| **CLP** | Current Legal Problems |
| **COA 1979** | Charging Orders Act 1979 |
| **CONC** | Consumer Credit Sourcebook |
| **Conv** | Conveyancer and Property Lawyer |
| **CRA 2015** | Consumer Rights Act 2015 |
| **ECHR** | European Convention on Human Rights and Fundamental Freedoms |
| **Edinburgh LR** | Edinburgh Law Review |
| **EHRLR** | European Human Rights Law Review |
| **Fam Law** | Family Law |
| **FCA** | Financial Conduct Authority |
| **Fem LS** | Feminist Legal Studies |
| **FLA 1996** | Family Law Act 1996 |
| **FOS** | Financial Ombudsman's Service |
| **FSMA 2000** | Financial Services and Markets Act 2000 |
| **Harv L Rev** | Harvard Law Review |
| **HRA 1998** | Human Rights Act 1988 |
| **IA 1986** | Insolvency Act 1986 |
| **ICLQ** | International and Comparative Law Quarterly |
| **IJCL** | International Journal of Constitutional Law |
| **IJHP** | International Journal of Housing Policy |
| **J Eq** | Journal of Equitable Property |
| **JBL** | Journal of Business Law |
| **JCL** | Journal of Contract Law |
| **JHL** | Journal of Housing Law |
| **KLJ** | King's Law Journal |

| | |
|---|---|
| **L&T Rev** | Landlord and Tenant Review |
| **LASPO** | Legal Aid, Sentencing and Punishment of Offenders Act 2012 |
| **LMCLQ** | Lloyd's Maritime and Commercial Law Quarterly |
| **LPA 1925** | Law of Property Act 1925 |
| **LP(MP)A 1989** | Law of Property (Miscellaneous Provisions) Act 1989 |
| **LQR** | Law Quarterly Review |
| **LRA 1925** | Land Registration Act 1925 |
| **LRA 2002** | Land Registration Act 2002 |
| **LS** | Legal Studies |
| **LTCA 1995** | Landlord and Tenant (Covenants) Act 1995 |
| **MCD** | Mortgage Credit Directive Order 2015 |
| **MMR** | Mortgage Market Review |
| **NILQ** | Northern Ireland Legal Quarterly |
| **OJLS** | Oxford Journal of Legal Studies |
| **S Cal L Rev** | Southern California Law Review |
| **Sydney LR** | Sydney Law Review |
| **TOLATA** | Trusts of Land and Appointment of Trustees Act 1996 |
| **Tru LI** | Trust Law International |
| **Web JCLI** | Web Journal of Current Legal Issues |
| **Yale LJ** | Yale Law Journal |

# 1

# What is Land Law?

## SUMMARY

This introductory chapter explains what topics we will—and what topics we will not—consider in detail in the remainder of the book. In considering the content of land law as a subject, it also tackles the question of why we study land law at all. It sketches some of the wider benefits that can come from considering land law, and also looks at why we consider land separately from other forms of property.

The chapter also introduces some of the crucial questions and key themes that arise in a land law or property law course, and so appear throughout the book. In particular, it introduces three fundamental questions that we will use to understand and structure the often complex rules encountered in land law: the content, acquisition, and defences questions. In doing so, the chapter considers three specific case law examples from which useful wider lessons can be drawn. The chapter also considers the different sources of current land law rules, and emphasizes the importance of the statutory framework established by the Law of Property Act 1925 and the Land Registration Act 2002.

The chapter also looks at the legal definition of land itself: what does it mean, for example, to say that someone owns a piece of land? What rights does such a party have, for example, in relation to objects attached to that land, or found in or on that land?

Key topics explored in this chapter are:

- The focus of land law on private rights to use land (1.1–1.7)

- The special features of land that distinguish it from other forms of property (1.8–1.12)

- The key distinction between personal rights and property rights, and the usefulness of the *content, acquisition*, and *defences* questions in understanding the structure of land law (1.13–1.36)

- The importance of equitable rules and of statute in shaping land law (1.37–1.50)

- The key role played by land registration in modern land law (1.51–1.55)

- The application of the content, acquisition, and defences question to case law examples (1.56–1.79)

- The nature and extent of the rights enjoyed by an owner of land, including possible rights to objects attached to, or found in or on that land (1.80–1.94)

## The Focus of Land Law: Private Rights to Use Land

### Land Law as Part of the Legal Rules Relating to Land

1.1 Land is central to our lives. This was true long before the profusion of television shows about the property market, long before the board game *Monopoly* was invented. In fact, some of the earliest surviving governmental records, dating from the time of the ancient Egyptians, were created to record ownership of land. Perhaps the very first examples in England of what we would now call universities were established by monasteries to train students in the rules governing the acquisition of land.

1.2 It is therefore no surprise that a great variety of different types of legal rules, ranging from those imposing criminal offences to those regulating planning decisions, all touch in some way on our dealings with land. No one book, or undergraduate or postgraduate course, could look at all those different rules. Books and courses on land law or property law therefore focus on one particular part of those rules. This book is no exception. Its focus is on *private rights to use land*.

1.3 By 'private' rights, we mean rights that any of us might acquire: we are not, therefore, concerned with the special powers that a government agency might have to make a compulsory purchase of land. Nor are we concerned with the special public powers, such as to make a grant of planning permission, that can limit the scope of private rights to use land. By focusing on 'rights to use land', we can exclude, for example, the types of claims for damages that someone injured on another's land might bring against the occupier of that land: such a claim is to money, not to a right to use land.

1.4 By choosing such material for this book, we are not, of course, suggesting that other types of legal rule relating to land are unimportant or uninteresting. Nor are we suggesting that the scope of land law is set in stone. For example, even 20 years ago, the topic of human rights was rarely discussed in any book or course on English land law or property law. Even today, it might be claimed that, as the Human Rights Act 1998 is chiefly concerned with placing limits on the powers of public bodies, its operation lies outside the core of land law. It is, however, now clear that, in trying to understand the nature and importance of private rights to use land, we do need to consider the impact of human rights in some detail, and we will do so in Chapter 2.

### Rules Linked by Concepts, Not Just by Contexts

1.5 An important reason for focusing on private rights to use land is that it allows us to study rules that are linked not only by the context in which they apply (dealings with land) but also by their underlying *concepts* (Birks (1998)). In fact, the most fundamental of those concepts underpin not only land law, but property law more generally.

1.6 Let's say, for example, that you are advising a friend who is interested in buying a home. If the transaction proceeds, the purchaser will not be buying the land as such: instead, he or she will be getting the particular *right* in the land held by the vendor. You would therefore need to find out the *content* of that right: does the vendor have a freehold or a lease? The distinction may be crucial as a lease exists only for a limited period, whereas there is no such time limit on the duration of a freehold (**7.28–7.39**). You would then also need to know what must be done in order for your friend to *acquire* the right of the vendor: are there special rules that must be met before your friend can have a binding contract with the vendor? Yes (**4.5–4.31**). Are there further special rules that must be met to perform that contract by ensuring that the transfer of the right from the vendor to the purchaser is completed? Yes (**4.32–4.62**).

1.7 In studying land law, then, you would expect to learn about the *content* of different rights in relation to land, and to learn how such rights can be *acquired*. This will be useful not only in the immediate practical context of advising your friend, but also because some of the key concepts used in land law operate throughout property law as a whole. So, for example, if you are buying a car, it is also the case that you acquire a particular right held by the vendor of the car, and you will also need to know what precisely must be done before you can acquire that right. The idea that rights rather than things are transferred, like the concept of separate *content* and *acquisition* rules, applies not only throughout land law but also across the whole of property law.

## Why Land Law? What is Special about Land?

1.8 One of the benefits of studying land law is that it provides a useful way to study key concepts used throughout property law. This gives rise to the question of why we should study land law as a distinct subject, rather than simply studying property law. The practical importance of land provides one answer, but that practical importance depends on the *special features* of land as a resource. Those special features in turn mean that the legal rules regulating private rights to use land differ in important ways from the legal rules regulating private rights to use other physical resources.

1.9 It has, for example, been suggested that the special features of land include its permanence; the uniqueness of each piece of land, as its physical location can never be shared by another piece of land; its capacity for multiple simultaneous use; its social importance; and its limited availability (McFarlane (2008)).

1.10 Those special features of land as a resource are reflected in the legal rules regulating private rights to use land. For example, we noted that, when buying land, a purchaser needs to know if he or she is acquiring a freehold or a lease. When creating a lease, a freehold owner (call him or her A) in effect, gives ownership of that land to the holder of the lease (call him or her B) for a limited period. This means that B, even before taking possession of the land, acquires a property right in the land: a right that is capable of binding not only A, but also third parties who later interfere or deal with the land (**1.24–1.27**). In contrast, if A owns other forms of property (such as a car), A *cannot* divide up ownership of the property in that way: in such cases, an attempt to create a lease will give B only a personal right against A.

1.11   The ability of an owner of land thus to split up ownership over time can be linked to each of the special features of land. The permanence of land means that, in practice, there is more likelihood that an owner will wish to split up ownership of the land over time; the uniqueness of land, along with its limited availability, provides a reason why the law might want to protect the rights of B, a party with a lease of land, not only against A, but against third parties too; the capacity for multiple simultaneous use of land can be seen in the fact that A can give B possession of the land for a period whilst receiving the benefit of, for example, rent from B; the social importance of land helps to explain why there might be reason to protect B's right to possess land for a limited period more strongly than B's right to use a different form of property, such as a car, for a limited period.

1.12   The special features of land have also been recognized in the European Convention on Human Rights. For example, Article 8 of the Convention states that everyone has the right to respect for '*his home*' and, in the vast majority of cases, the concept of home is linked to the social importance of land. Certainly, as we will see in **Chapter 2**, the courts have recognized the great adverse impact that removal from a home can have on an occupier.

## Types of Private Rights to Use Land: Personal Rights and Property Rights

1.13   We have seen that, whilst a lease of land counts as a property right, a lease of a car does not, and gives its holder only a personal right. This distinction between two types of private right to use land—property rights and personal rights—is fundamental to land law. Indeed, the distinction between the two types of right is fundamental to property law as a whole: this supports the point that, by studying key rules of land law, we can also learn about property law more generally.

1.14   We will look at the distinction between property rights and personal rights throughout the book, and will do so in particular detail in **Chapter 3** (**3.1–3.4**). The importance of the distinction means that it is also worth discussing in this introductory chapter. The crucial practical point is that if B has a personal right against A, that right, by itself, binds only A. A personal right is a right against a specific person. If B instead has a property right, even if that right was acquired as a result of B's dealings with A, that right is capable of binding not only A, but also third parties, such as C. This is because a property right is not simply a right against a specific person, but is a right that relates to something independent of a specific person, such as some land.

**1.15**  To see clearly the distinction between personal rights and property rights, it may be helpful to consider two homely examples:

> *Example 1*: A and B make a contract under which A will, for £20, mow B's lawn.
> *Example 2*: A sells A's lawnmower to B for £200.

In *Example 1*, B has only a personal right against A. The contract gives B a right, which consists of A's duty to B, and that duty is owed to B by *A alone*. If A, for example, were to sell A's lawnmower to C, B would have no right against C that C should now mow the lawn: the duty to mow B's lawn is owed only by A. In contrast, in *Example 2*, the sale transfers A's ownership of the mower to B. B thus has a property right: a right that relates to the mower itself, and so is independent of any specific person. So, whilst B's right was acquired from A, it is capable of binding not only A but also third parties. If A were to make a second sale of the lawnmower to C, for example, B's pre-existing property right would bind C, unless C could make out a defence to B's earlier right (see eg Sale of Goods Act 1979, s 24 for an example of such a defence).

**1.16**  The basic factual pattern of our examples, involving A, B, and C, recurs throughout property law, and is thus very important in land law. In many of the cases we will look at in this book, including those discussed later in this chapter (**1.56–1.79**), there are three key parties. One party, A, owns some land; a second party, B, deals with A, or with the land, and so acquires some sort of right; a third party, C, then acquires either ownership of the land, or some other right in the land, from A. The structure of such cases can usefully be represented in a diagram (see **Figure 1.1**).

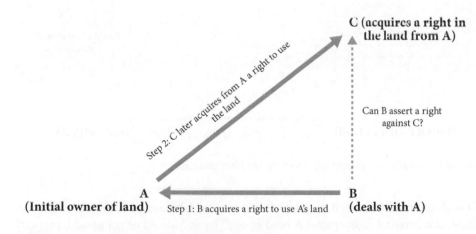

**Figure 1.1**  A common structure for land law cases

In such three-party cases, it is crucial to know if the right held by B, before C's involvement, is a personal right against A (and so binding only on A) or is instead a property right. Crucially, if B's right is a property right, it is prima facie binding on C: in other words, it will bind C unless C has a defence to it.

1.17 The distinction between personal rights and property rights is also important when considering B's position as against X. X is a party who, unlike C, does not acquire any rights from A, but instead interferes directly with the property. Consider a case where X carelessly damages the lawnmower. In Example 1, where A has simply made a contract with B to mow B's lawn, it is possible that X's careless action may cause B some loss: for example, it may mean that A cannot perform the contract with B. Nonetheless, B has no claim against X, as the loss caused to B is purely economic loss (see eg *Cattle v Stockton Waterworks Co* (1875)). In the second example, if the careless damage occurs after A has sold the lawnmower to B, and so at a point when B has ownership of the mower, B does have a claim in tort against X, as X has breached a duty owed to B not to carelessly damage the mower. B's loss is not categorized as purely economic, as B has a property right in the mower, and so the loss flows from an interference with B's property. This shows how the distinction between personal rights and property rights is of great practical importance in the law of torts.

1.18 The basic factual pattern of our example, involving A, B, and X, is also important in property law, and hence in land law. Such cases differ from the A–B–C pattern as X does not acquire any right from A, but instead simply interferes with the property, or with B's use of the property. The structure of such cases can also be usefully represented in a diagram (see **Figure 1.2**).

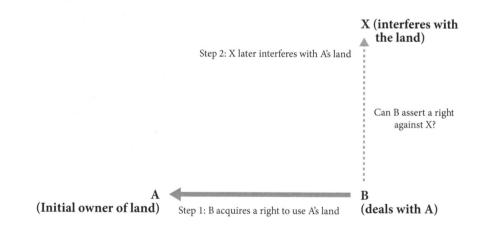

**Figure 1.2** A second important structure for land law cases

1.19 In such three-party cases, it is crucial to know if the right held by B, before X's involvement, is a personal right against A (and so binding only on A) or is instead a property right. Crucially, if B's right is a property right, it may be prima facie binding on X: in other words, it will bind X unless X has a defence to it.

1.20 There are of course many similarities between the A–B–C fact pattern and the A–B–X fact pattern. It is, however, worth distinguishing the two types of case. First, as we will see later in the book (**Chapters 4** and **11**), where B has a property right, there are more defences potentially available to C (the party who acquired a right from A) than to X (the party who acquired no right from A). Secondly, it may be that some types of property right (known as equitable property rights) are prima facie binding on C, but not on X (**3.42–3.46**).

## Personal Rights

**1.21**  The key feature of a personal right is that it can only be asserted against a specific person. Its content is, therefore, always linked to a specific person. So, where A makes a contractual promise to mow B's lawn, B acquires a personal right against A. If A fails to honour the promise, B can sue A, but the contract, in itself, does not allow B to pursue any third party.

**1.22**  Personal rights can be very important in practice in land law: in some cases, B's right to his or her home may be a personal right against A. That will be the case, for example, if B is a lodger occupying a room in A's house. The weakness of such rights, however, lies in their dependence on A. If A asks B to move out of A's house, then B's contract with A may well protect B: B could ask a court for an injunction to prevent A breaking the contract and removing B. B's personal right against A can thus give B valuable protection against A.

**1.23**  The problem for B occurs if, for example, A sells the house to C (ie if A transfers A's freehold or lease of the house to C). If C then asks B to move out, B's previous contract with A does not provide B with any protection against C: that contract gives B only a right *against A* to occupy the house.

## Property Rights

**1.24**  The key feature of a property right is that, unlike a personal right, its content is defined independently of any specific person. The content of the right is instead linked to something, such as a piece of land, that is independent of any particular person. So we saw at **1.17** that, if X, a stranger, carelessly damages B's mower, then B will be able to assert that right against X and sue X for the negligent interference with the mower. It does not matter that there was no prior relationship between B and X. B's property right (ownership of the mower) is defined independently of any particular person, and so can be asserted against X (or anyone else who carelessly damages the property and has no permission from B or other defence to B's property right).

**1.25**  Property rights are fundamental to land law. We saw at **1.22** that, if B is occupying a room in A's house as a lodger, then B has only a personal right against A. If, instead, B is living in A's house, and B's contract with A gives B a right to exclusive possession of that house, or part of it, for a limited period, then B has a lease. We will consider leases in detail in **Chapter 7**. Because of its content, a lease counts as a property right in land. B is therefore in a stronger position than the lodger we considered at **1.22**. If A sells the house to C, even though B has no contract with C, it may be possible for B to assert his or her lease against C. In fact, we can say that B's lease, as it is a property right, is prima facie binding on C: C will be bound by the lease unless C can establish a special reason why he or she is not bound by it. If such a special reason exists, C can be said to have a *defence* to B's lease.

**1.26** When it comes to making a claim against A, provided A is not insolvent, it does not matter if B's right to use land is a personal right against A or a property right in the land itself. It is likely, however, that B will want a right that will endure even if, for example, A sells the land to C. A claim for damages against A may be a poor substitute for such a right, given the uniqueness of each piece of land, and the possible social importance to B of using the land itself. The special features of land may make it particularly important for B to show that he or she has a property right in the land, rather than a mere personal right against A.

**1.27** This does not mean, however, that we should expect land law to be particularly generous in allowing B to assert a right against a third party such as C. In fact, the special features of land can also be used to argue against such protection for B. The limited availability of land, along with its uniqueness and social importance, are important factors here. If it were easy for parties such as B to acquire property rights in A's land, so that pieces of land quickly became burdened by such rights, it would then be difficult for A to sell that land, or for C to acquire land that C would then be free to use for C's own purposes. Certainly, as we will see in this book (see in particular **Chapters 4** and **11**), the desire to promote the marketability of land has long been recognized by land law. It was an important motivation of two of the most significant statutory interventions in land law: the Law of Property Act 1925 and the Land Registration Act 2002 (**1.47–1.55**).

## Property Rights: Three Key Questions

**1.28** It is therefore clear that, when considering private rights to use land and, in particular, property rights in land, the land law system has a very difficult balance to maintain. On the one hand, the uniqueness and social importance of land may provide a good reason for protecting B's right to use land not only against A (the current owner of the land) but also against C, a party later acquiring a right in the land from A. On the other hand, the limited availability of land means that care must be taken in ensuring that land remains freely marketable, and if it is too easy for enduring burdens to be imposed on land, this will interfere with potentially important uses that C might make of the land.

**1.29** This tension between the needs of B and of C is evident when considering each of the three questions that determine the operation of property rights in land: the *content*, *acquisition*, and *defences* questions.

## The Content Question

1.30   The classification of a right as personal or proprietary depends on its *content*. So, for example, it is the different content of their rights that explains why a lodger in A's house has only a personal right against A (**1.22–1.23**), whereas a party with a lease in A's house has a property right (**1.25**). As we will consider in more detail at **7.28–7.39**, B has a lease only where he or she has a right to exclusive possession of particular land for a limited period. As far as the balance between B and C is concerned, the law looks to the content of B's right in determining whether or not B's right counts as a property right and is thus prima facie binding on C.

1.31   There are some rights which count as property rights in land, but not in other forms of property. For example, if A owns land and gives B a right to exclusive possession of that land for a limited period, B acquires a lease: a property right. The agreement between A and B thus gives B a right that is capable of binding third parties. In contrast, we saw at **1.10** that if A owns some other form of property (such as a car) and gives B a right to exclusive possession of that property for a limited period, this does not give B a property right: the agreement between A and B gives B only a personal right against A. The special features of land are thus reflected in the fact that the list of permissible property rights in land is longer than the list of such rights in other forms of property. As we will see in **Chapter 3**, however, the list is still relatively short. In particular, a key principle of land law (often referred to as the *numerus clausus* or 'closed list' principle) is that A and B cannot simply decide to create a new type of property right. A and B can, between them, decide on the content of B's right to use A's land—but that right will count as a property right only if its content matches that of one of the rights on the list of recognized property rights in land (**3.47–3.50**). In that way, the land law system can maintain some balance between the desires of B and of C.

## The Acquisition Question

1.32   Special rules regulate the *acquisition* of property rights in land, and B must satisfy such rules in order to show that he or she has in fact acquired such a right. For example, it may be that A is willing to give B a right to exclusive possession of A's house for a limited period, and so B's right will have the content required of a lease. We still need to know, however, what the parties must do for B to acquire that property right.

1.33   In framing acquisition rules, a balance can again be drawn between the needs of B and of C. B's preference may be that the lease can be acquired as quickly and informally as possible, by a mere oral agreement between A and B; in some relatively rare cases, that is indeed possible (see Law of Property Act 1925, s 54(2), discussed at **7.61**). The fear for C, however, is that B might then be able to acquire a property right—a right prima facie binding on C—in circumstances that make it very difficult for C to discover that right. The risk then arises for C that he or she may buy A's land, and be bound by B's lease without having realized that this would happen, and without having taken account of that burden when deciding what to pay A. As a result, the general position is that, to acquire a property right in A's land, B must show that certain formal steps (such as the use of a written contract, a deed, or the recording of B's right on a central register) have been complied with (**4.32–4.62**).

## Priority and the Defences Question

**1.34**   We have seen that there is a good reason why B might wish to show that he or she has a property right in A's land rather than a mere personal right against A: a property right in land is prima facie binding on C, a party later acquiring a right in A's land. As we noted at **1.15**, however, it may be possible for C to establish a *defence* to B's pre-existing property right. When considering the operation of property rights, it is therefore vital to take into account the possibility that C may establish such a defence.

**1.35**   For example, in a case where B and C have competing property rights in relation to particular land, it is often said that there is a dispute as to 'priority': we need rules to tell us whether it is B, or C, who should be free to exercise his or her property right in the land. The starting point is that the property right that was acquired first in time will prevail: this is good news, of course, for B. This is where, however, the concept of a defence comes in: even if B's property right arose before C's property right, it may be possible for C to take priority by having a defence to B's earlier property right. This does not mean, of course, that it is necessarily B who is the claimant in court and C who is the defendant: for example, in *Williams & Glyn's Bank v Boland* (1981), which we will examine at **1.63–1.70**, the bank was the claimant, as it wanted to get possession of the land from Mrs Boland. The bank, however, had acquired its property right in the land *after* Mrs Boland had acquired her property right, and so, to take priority and thus win, the bank needed to show it had a defence to Mrs Boland's pre-existing right. On the terminology used here, the bank was thus C, and Mrs Boland was B, as her right arose before the bank's right (Mrs Boland had acquired her right because of her dealings with Mr Boland, the registered owner of the land: Mr Boland was thus A). The idea of a defence to a pre-existing property right, therefore, is that it gives a means for C to take priority, and thus win, even if B's property right arose before C's property right.

**1.36**   The possibility of a defence provides another means for land law to balance the positions of B and of C. In particular, it offers a means to isolate situations in which C is, relative to B, particularly deserving of protection. As we will see in **Chapters 4** and **11**, for example, a prominent defence (the 'lack of registration' defence) rests on a combination of factors: C's having given value to A in return for acquiring a right in the land; C's having ensured that C's right is noted on a central register; and B's having failed to have B's right noted on that register. At **1.56–1.79**, we will see how the content, acquisition, and defences questions can be helpful when examining three important land law cases. Before we can start looking at those cases, however, we need to outline the impact on land law of two very important sources of rules: equity and statute.

# The Impact of Equity

**1.37**   Equity, when used to refer to a source of legal rules, refers simply to those current rules that are based on rules initially developed in particular English courts: the courts of Chancery. Originally, at least, those courts were regarded as having more flexibility and broader discretion than their common law counterparts, and were thus in a position to mitigate some of the harshness of the common law rules, by providing a form of 'safety valve'. In some ways, the equitable rules applied today reveal those original characteristics: for example, as we will see in **Chapter 5**, B may acquire an equitable property right in land even if he or she has not complied with the strict formality rules governing the creation of a legal property right in land. It would be a serious mistake, however, to think that equitable rules are simply based directly on discretion: indeed, some of the most complex and technical parts of English law (such as the law of trusts) are entirely creations of the courts of Chancery.

**1.38**   The former existence of those Chancery courts means that in land law, as in other areas of law, it is possible to distinguish between common law rules and equitable rules. In fact, in land law, the distinction is particularly important. Not because equitable rules are based simply on discretion; rather because, when we look at each of the content, acquisition, and defences questions, we will see that property rights based on equitable rules (equitable property rights) operate differently to those property rights based on common law rules (legal property rights). Whilst it may well seem strange that a single jurisdiction such as England ever had separate courts of common law and of equity, that arrangement has thus left an important legacy in land law.

## Equity and the Content Question

**1.39**   There are two kinds of property right: legal property rights and equitable property rights. They share a key feature which distinguishes them from personal rights: their content is not linked to a specific person, and so it is not the case that they can be asserted only against that person. If B acquires an equitable property right in relation to A's land, that right, like a legal property right, is prima facie binding on C, a party later acquiring a right in the land from A.

**1.40**   We will consider the differences between equitable property rights and legal property rights in more detail at **3.35–3.46**. As far as the *content* question is concerned, the most important point for present purposes is that the list of equitable property rights in relation to land is longer than the list of legal property rights in land. Consider a case, for example, where A is a freehold owner of land, but A holds that land on trust for B. In such a case, A is under a duty to use his or her rights as freehold owner for the benefit of B. B has no legal property right in the land, as the content of B's right does not match that of any of the recognized legal property rights in land. Yet, hundreds of years ago the courts of equity developed the protection available to B, the beneficiary of a trust, so that

B was allowed to assert his or her right not only against A but also against some third parties who acquired a right in the land from A. That was the case even though the trust initially depends on a duty owed by A to B. That development continued until the point was reached when it could be said that B's right under the trust was prima facie binding on C, a party later acquiring a right in the land from A. B could then be said to have an equitable property right: a right that could be asserted against parties other than A. So, whilst the content of B's right as a beneficiary of a trust means that it does not count as a legal property right, it can count as an equitable property right, and is therefore prima facie binding on C.

## Equity and the Acquisition Question

1.41 Equity also provides additional means by which a property right may be acquired. Of course, where B relies solely on one of those means of acquiring a property right, B's right can only be an equitable, as opposed to a legal, property right. So equity does not provide additional means by which B can acquire a legal property right; but, as the means by which an equitable property right can be acquired are different from those by which a legal property right can be acquired, equity does provide additional means by which B can acquire, from A, a right that is capable of binding C. In many—but not all—cases, those means of acquiring equitable property rights do not require the same level of formality as is generally demanded before a legal property right can be acquired.

1.42 For example, consider a case in which A and B, cohabiting partners, live together in a home, and A is registered as the sole freehold owner. As the registration is in A's name only, B has no legal right of ownership. It may still be possible, however, for B to show that A holds that freehold on trust for A and B (that was the case, eg, in *Williams & Glyn's Bank v Boland* (1981)). Such a trust gives B an equitable property right in relation to A's land. It is possible for B to acquire a right under a trust without the need for registration. Indeed, it may be possible for B to acquire a right under a trust even if there have been no formal dealings between A and B at all. If (eg as in the *Boland* case) B has paid part of the purchase price of A's freehold, that conduct of B may give rise to a trust. The doctrine of proprietary estoppel (**5.93–5.138**) provides another equitable means of acquiring rights in relation to land, and may apply even if there have been no written dealings between A and B.

1.43 A link can be drawn between the existence in equity of a longer list of equitable property rights and of a wider set of means by which property rights can be acquired. The basis of equitable property rights (as noted by eg Smith (2005)) is a particular type of *duty* being owed by A to B. Where such duties exist, an equitable property right can arise. This means that, when seeking to show that he or she has acquired such a right, B's principal concern is to show that A has come under such a duty to B. As a result, all the different means by which A can come under a duty to B (eg the existence of a contract; a proprietary estoppel; A's commission of a wrong against B etc) are, in principle, means by which B can acquire an equitable property right.

1.44   That does not mean, of course, that if A is under a duty to B, B will necessarily have an equitable property right. In most cases, the fact that A is under a duty to B simply means that B has a personal right against A. That is the case if, for example, A is under a duty to pay B a sum of money, or to perform a service for B. The crucial question is as to the content of A's duty. If A's duty instead relates to a *specific right* held by A (such as A's freehold of land), then B may have an equitable property right: B's right can be attached to something (eg A's freehold) that is independent of A. This means that it no longer needs to be seen as a personal right, as a right dependent on A (1.14). The key aspect of a trust, for example, is that A is under a duty to use a *specific right* for the benefit of B: where that right of A is a property right in land, such as a freehold, B's right is then prima facie binding on anyone later acquiring A's property right.

### Equity and the Defences Question

1.45   We have seen that the rules of land law aim to achieve some sort of balance between the competing desires of earlier users of land (such as B) and later users of the same land (such as C). So far, the contribution of equity to land law seems to have been very one-sided: by acknowledging a longer list of property rights, and of means by which property rights can be acquired, equity has favoured B rather than C. A crucial point, however, is that, if B has an equitable property right rather than a legal property right, there is a longer list of defences that C may be able to use against that right.

1.46   We will consider such defences in detail in **Chapter 11**. The simple point to make here is that if B has an equitable property right, the fact that such a right is somewhat easier to establish than a legal property right is mitigated by the fact that it is also easier for C to establish a defence against that right than against a legal property right. In that sense, then, equitable property rights are weaker than legal property rights. We will consider this point further at **3.35–3.46**, and will also see an example of its operation in practice at **1.71–1.77**.

## The Impact of Statute

1.47   One of the features of land law, certainly when compared to other parts of property law, and also to contract law and the law of torts, is the great importance of parliamentary intervention in shaping the current rules. Land law is emphatically not a subject that you can hope to study without reading, and engaging with, statutes.

1.48   The Law of Property Act 1925, for example, was part of a set of legislation, introduced from 1922–5, which greatly simplified land law. When introducing part of that legislation into the House of Lords, Lord Birkenhead, the Lord Chancellor, recounted how, when studying property law as a law student at the end of the 19th century, he had been appalled at its complexity and had vowed that he would one day ensure that it was over-hauled. To this day, students of English land law have much to thank him for.

**1.49**  For example, the very first section of the Law of Property Act 1925 clarifies the content question in relation to legal property rights, by setting out a clear and short list of the permissible legal property rights in land. Rights with more complicated content (such as a right to have exclusive possession of land only for the duration of someone's life), for-merly capable of counting as legal property rights, were relegated to the status of equit-able interests, and could take effect only under a trust. Such changes were of great benefit to third parties, such as C, later dealing with the land, as section 2 of the Law of Property Act 1925 goes on to recognize that C may have a straightforward defence to rights under a trust of land (**1.71–1.77**). The first two sections of the Act thus have an important im-pact on the content and defences questions.

**1.50**  As far as the acquisition question is concerned, sections 52, 53, and 54 of the Law of Property Act 1925 are very significant as they contain the basic formality requirements that must be satisfied if B is to acquire either a legal or equitable property right in land. We will consider those rules in detail in **Chapters 4** and **5**. Of course, statutory interven-tion has continued, and section 2 of the Law of Property (Miscellaneous Provisions) Act 1989 now sets out the formal requirements that must be met before A and B can con-clude a contract for the sale or other disposition of a property right in land.

## The Importance of Registration

**1.51**  The most important recent land law statute is undoubtedly the Land Registration Act 2002. It took on the role formerly played by the Land Registration Act 1925, and sets out the key rules applying to dealings with registered land.

**1.52**  In our earlier example, where you are advising a friend who plans to purchase a house from A, the overwhelming likelihood is that A's right in the land, a freehold or lease, will be registered: that is, recorded on the central register maintained by Land Registry. More than 24 million such legal titles to land are thus recorded, and together they account for nearly 88 per cent of the land mass of England and Wales. Land which is unregistered is usually land that is infrequently dealt with: if A does wish to transfer to B an unregistered freehold, for example, then section 4 of the Land Registration Act 2002 states that the transfer of A's right to B can be completed only by registration.

**1.53**  The permanence of land, and the uniqueness of each piece of land, makes registration possible: it means that, if C wishes to acquire a right in relation to a particular plot of land, it will be easy for C to identify the relevant title in the register. The desirability of registra-tion lies chiefly in its ability to provide certainty as to which parties hold which rights in land and thus to promote the security and marketability of land (O'Connor (2003)). This can be seen in the effect of the 2002 Act on the acquisition and defences questions.

**1.54**  As for acquisition, various sections of the Act (such as ss 4 and 27) establish a basic rule (to which there are some exceptions, eg for leases of seven years or less) that, if B wishes to acquire a *legal* property right in registered land, B must ensure that he or she is registered as holding that right. It is never the case, however, that B needs to register in order to acquire an *equitable* property right in relation to land. As for defences, various sections of the Act (such as ss 29 and 30) establish a basic rule (to which there are some important exceptions, such as the overriding interests set out in Sch 1 and Sch 3 to the Act) that, if C acquires a legal property right in registered land for value, C will have a defence to any pre-existing property right of B that is not recorded on the register. This defence, based on B's lack of registration, is particularly important when considering the impact of a pre-existing equitable property right on C. The basic position is that, if B's equitable property right has not been protected by means of an entry on the register, then, if C later acquires a legal property right in the land for value, C will have a defence to B's right, unless B was in occupation of the land.

**1.55**  We will of course examine these rules in much more detail elsewhere in the book, especially in **Chapters 4** and **11**. For present purposes, it is important to note not only the effect of the provisions of the 2002 Act, but also the philosophy behind that Act. When setting out the draft Bill that led to the Act, the Law Commission stated that its fundamental objective was that: 'the register should be a complete and accurate reflection of the state of the title of the land at any given time, so that it is possible to investigate title to land on line, with the absolute minimum of additional enquiries and inspections' (Law Commission (2001), para 1.5). It is true that the Law Commission's plans depended on the introduction of a general e-conveyancing system, allowing for transactions with land to take place entirely online, and such a system is not yet in place. Moreover, we will see at various points in this book (in particular when discussing overriding interests: **11.34–11.62**) that the 2002 Act is far from comprehensive in requiring registration as a condition for B's right to be protected against C. Nonetheless, the Law Commission's statement does emphasize that, as far as the balance between B and C is concerned, registration rules can be very important in providing C with protection against the risk of acquiring land and then discovering that he or she is bound by a hidden legal or equitable property right of B.

## The Structure of Land Law: Three Examples

**1.56**  In this introductory chapter, we have seen that this book, like most land law and property law courses, will focus on private rights to use land. In considering such rights, the distinction between personal rights and property rights is crucial. In examining if B has a property right, we need to consider both the content question and the acquisition question; and to see if B can assert a property right against a particular third party, C, we also need to consider the defences question. In looking at each of those three questions, we must of course be aware of the impact of equity—in particular the possibility that B may have an equitable property right—and of the impact of statutes—in particular of the Law of Property Act 1925 and the Land Registration Act 2002.

**1.57**    The best way to demonstrate these general points about the operation of land law is to consider some specific case law examples. Our present purpose is not to understand all the details of those cases: we will return to examine specific points of detail later in the book. It is rather to show how a focus on the content, acquisition, and defences questions can assist in grasping the basic structure of the rules of land law.

**1.58**    *National Provincial Bank v Ainsworth* **(1965):** Mr and Mrs Ainsworth lived together in Hastings, Sussex. Mr Ainsworth was registered as the sole holder of the freehold. After the marital relationship had broken down, Mr Ainsworth moved out of the house. Acting without the knowledge of his wife, he borrowed some money from the National Provincial Bank. This was done as part of a mortgage deal: his debt to the bank was secured by giving the bank a legal property right (a charge) over the land. The content of that right was such that, if the loan was not repaid, the bank had the right to take possession of the land, sell it, and use the proceeds to meet the outstanding sums due under the loan (for discussion of mortgages, see **Chapter 8**). So, when Mr Ainsworth failed to repay the loan, the bank sought to remove Mrs Ainsworth from the property, so that it could sell the house with vacant possession.

**1.59**    The facts of the case fit into the classic A–B–C structure: Mr Ainsworth (A) is the legal owner of the land; Mrs Ainsworth (B), through her dealings with A, then acquires a right to make some use of the land; the bank (C) is the third party that later acquires from A a competing right to make some other use of the land (see **Figure 1.3**).

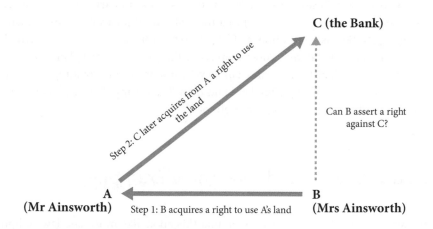

**Figure 1.3** *National Provincial Bank v Ainsworth*

**1.60**    The crucial question for the court was whether Mrs Ainsworth had any right that she could assert against the bank. She could not claim that she had acquired any direct right as a result of the bank's own conduct, so she needed to show that the right she had acquired through her dealings with Mr Ainsworth was binding on the bank. As a result, she had to show that her right was not a mere personal right against her husband, but was rather a legal or equitable property right, and so prima facie binding on the bank.

**1.61** In the Court of Appeal, Mrs Ainsworth was successful. In the House of Lords, however, she was not. The two courts differed in their approach to the *content* question. The Court of Appeal held that equity imposed a duty on Mr Ainsworth, having left the matrimonial home, to 'provide the wife with a roof over her head'. The correlative right of Mrs Ainsworth, a 'deserted wife's equity', was found by the Court of Appeal to be capable of binding the bank, as it was, in Lord Denning's words, a 'right to remain in the matrimonial home'. It was also held that the bank, which was aware of Mrs Ainsworth's occupation of the home when it acquired its charge, had no defence to her right.

**1.62** The House of Lords, in contrast, held that the content of Mrs Ainsworth's right was such that it was only a personal right against her husband, and so was not capable of binding the bank. The defences question was therefore irrelevant: as Mrs Ainsworth had no right that was capable of binding the bank, there was no need for it to establish any defence. Lord Wilberforce, for example, pointed out that Mr Ainsworth's duty was simply to provide some accommodation and support for his deserted wife, and so Mrs Ainsworth 'has no specific right against her husband to be provided with any particular house, nor to remain in any particular house'. As a result, her right was not a right in relation to any specific piece of land. Moreover, its content was not independent of her relationship with her husband: in its very nature, the right depended on his duties as a husband, and so the right could not sensibly bind a third party such as the bank. The Court of Appeal had therefore been wrong to say that Mrs Ainsworth had a 'right to remain in the matrimonial home': rather, Mrs Ainsworth had a right *against Mr Ainsworth* that *Mr Ainsworth* support her, and provide her with *some* accommodation. That right, in its content, clearly depended on Mr Ainsworth and so it was a personal right. As a result, it could not bind the bank. The bank was therefore free to exercise its legal property right, as holder of a charge, by requiring Mrs Ainsworth to vacate the land.

**1.63**    *Williams & Glyn's Bank v Boland* **(1981):** Mr and Mrs Boland lived together in Beddington, Surrey. Mr Boland was registered as the sole holder of the freehold, but Mrs Boland had contributed some of the money used to purchase the freehold. Mr Boland ran a building company with his brother. To support that business, and acting without the knowledge of his wife, he borrowed some money from Williams & Glyn's Bank. This was done as part of a mortgage deal: the debt to the bank was secured by giving the bank a legal property right (a charge) over the land. As in the *Ainsworth* case, the bank thus had the right, if the loan was not repaid, to take possession of the land, sell it, and use the proceeds to meet the outstanding sums due under the loan. As in *Ainsworth*, when the loan was not repaid, the bank sought vacant possession of the land, and so attempted to remove Mrs Boland.

**1.64** The facts of the case again fit into the classic A–B–C structure: Mr Boland (A) is the legal owner of the land; Mrs Boland (B), through her dealings with A, then acquires a right to make some use of the land; the bank (C) is the third party that later acquires from A a competing right to make some other use of the land (see **Figure 1.4**).

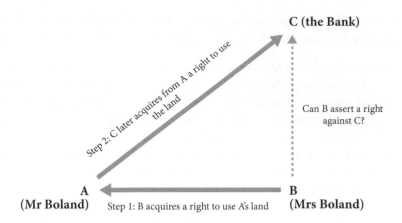

**C (the Bank)**

*Step 2: C later acquires from A a right to use the land*

Can B assert a right
against C?

**A**
**(Mr Boland)**   Step 1: B acquires a right to use A's land   **B**
**(Mrs Boland)**

**Figure 1.4** *Williams & Glyn's Bank v Boland*

**1.65**  The crucial question for the court was whether Mrs Boland had any right that she could assert against the bank. She could not claim that she had acquired any direct right as a result of the bank's own conduct, so she first needed to show that the right she had acquired through her dealings with Mr Boland was a legal or equitable property right, and so prima facie binding on the bank.

**1.66**  At first instance, the bank won; but in each of the Court of Appeal and the House of Lords, Mrs Boland was successful. As far as the *content* question was concerned, the case was critically different from *Ainsworth*. Mrs Boland did not attempt to assert a 'deserted wife's equity', or any other right arising purely because of her status as a spouse. Rather, she argued that she had an equitable property right in relation to the land, as Mr Boland held his freehold on trust for both himself and for her. A right arising under a trust is a recognized equitable property right: in such a case, A's duty is not simply a duty to act in a particular way (such as Mr Ainsworth's duty to provide Mrs Ainsworth with *some* accommodation), it is rather a duty that relates to a specific right of A: in this case, Mr Boland's freehold of the land. As a result, if a trust could be established, Mrs Boland's right would then be linked to her husband's freehold, and so would be prima facie binding on a party, such as the bank, later acquiring a right from Mr Boland, as the bank's right would then also depend on that freehold.

**1.67**  Mrs Boland also had to satisfy the *acquisition* question, by showing that a trust had indeed arisen. She was able to do this because, unlike Mrs Ainsworth, she had made a financial contribution to the purchase price of the freehold held by her husband. As that contribution was not made by way of a gift or a loan, it gave rise to a trust, under which Mrs Boland acquired a share of the benefit of the freehold (**5.13–5.72**).

**1.68**  As Mrs Boland was thus able to pass both the content and acquisition tests, her right was an equitable property right and so prima facie binding on the bank. This meant that (unlike in *Ainsworth*) the *defences* question had to be considered: could the bank establish a defence to Mrs Boland's pre-existing equitable property right? If so, it

would be free to assert its own right to possession, arising under the charge g
it by Mr Boland.

**1.69**  A particular question arose concerning what can be called the 'lack of registration' defence. At the time, the relevant provisions were those of the Land Registration Act 1925. The basic approach of that Act, as applying to a pre-existing equitable interest under a trust, was retained by the 2002 Act: C, when acquiring its legal property right for value, will be able to rely on the lack of registration defence *unless* B was in 'actual occupation' of the land at the relevant time. At first instance, it was held that, when the bank acquired its charge, Mrs Boland was not in actual occupation (in the sense of the term as used in the relevant provision—s 70(1)(g) of the 1925 Act) as she had then been living in the home *with her husband*, and such occupation would not alert the bank to the risk that Mrs Boland might have her own independent property right in the land. Each of the Court of Appeal and the House of Lords, however, rejected that interpretation of the term 'actual occupation', finding instead that Mrs Boland fell within the plain meaning of the statute, as she was in fact occupying the land, albeit with her husband, when the bank acquired its charge. As a result, the bank could not use the 'lack of registration' defence against Mrs Boland's equitable property right; and, on the facts, no other defences were available to the bank.

**1.70**  As a result, Mrs Boland did therefore have a pre-existing equitable property right that bound the bank. As we will see at **6.85–6.126**, however, this does not mean that, in practice, a party such as Mrs Boland will be able to continue living in the home for as long as she wishes. The bank, as holder of the charge, has a legitimate interest in selling the home so that it can have access to the share of the proceeds of sale available to its debtor, Mr Boland. If such a case were to arise today then, under another important statute, the Trusts of Land and Appointment of Trustees Act 1996, the bank can apply to court for an order that the property be sold. The mere fact that a beneficiary of a trust, such as Mrs Boland, does not consent to the sale will not persuade a court to deny the bank's request, as otherwise the bank could be prevented indefinitely from exercising its right to receive the value of the debtor's share of the property. When the sale occurs, however, a beneficiary of a trust such as Mrs Boland, in contrast to a party such as Mrs Ainsworth, will at least be entitled to a share of the proceeds of sale, with the size of that share depending on the size of his or her beneficial interest under the trust.

**1.71**  ***City of London Building Society v Flegg*** **(1988):** Mr and Mrs Flegg lived with their daughter and son-in-law, Mr and Mrs Maxwell-Brown, in Gillingham, Kent, in a property appropriately named Bleak House. The Fleggs had sold their own home in order to contribute to the purchase price of Bleak House. Only Mr and Mrs Maxwell-Brown were registered as the joint holders of the freehold of Bleak House. The Maxwell-Browns later ran into financial problems and, without the knowledge or consent of the Fleggs, borrowed some money from the City of London Building Society. The debt to the society was secured by giving it a legal property right (a charge) over the land. As in the *Ainsworth* and *Boland* cases, when the loan was not repaid, the society sought vacant possession of the land, and so attempted to remove the Fleggs.

**1.72**    The facts of the case again fit into the classic A–B–C structure: the Maxwell-Browns (A1 and A2) are the joint legal owners of the land; the Fleggs (B1 and B2), through their dealings with A1 and A2, acquired a right to make some use of the land; the society (C) is the third party that later acquired a competing right to make some other use of the land (see **Figure 1.5**).

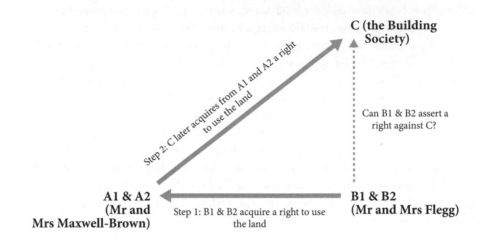

**Figure 1.5**  *City of London Building Society v Flegg*

**1.73**    The crucial question for the court was whether the Fleggs had any right that they could assert against the society. They could not claim to have acquired any direct right as a result of the society's own conduct, so they first needed to show that they had a legal or equitable property right that was prima facie binding on the society.

**1.74**    The Fleggs lost at first instance: that judgment was reversed by the Court of Appeal, but reinstated by the House of Lords. It might seem surprising that the Fleggs lost, given the earlier success of Mrs Boland. It is true that, as in *Boland*, the Fleggs satisfied each of the content and acquisition questions. As a result of their contribution to the purchase price of Bleak House, they had an equitable interest under a trust of the freehold held by the Maxwell-Browns. That right was, therefore, prima facie binding on the society. Moreover, as the Fleggs, like Mrs Boland, were in actual occupation of the land, the society could not establish the 'lack of registration' defence provided by the Land Registration Act 1925.

**1.75**    The problem for the Fleggs, however, was that the society could rely on a *different* defence. Whilst their actual occupation of the land prevented the society from invoking the lack of registration defence, it had no impact at all on the operation of that other defence. The defence, which we will examine in more detail at **11.70–11.89**, is the overreaching defence recognized by section 2 of the Law of Property Act 1925. That defence is key to the structure of the 1925 Act, as it gives C a relatively straightforward way to avoid being bound by an interest arising under a trust of land. It is a defence in the sense that it can be used as a means for C (a party acquiring a later property right) to take priority over B

(a party with a pre-existing property right): as discussed at **1.35**, it can of course
in a case, such as *Flegg*, where it is C, the party with the later property right, w
claimant in the particular court proceedings.

**1.76** A peculiarity of the statutory overreaching defence, clear from its requirements as set out
in section 27 of the Law of Property Act 1925, is that where C acquires its right in the
land in return for paying money, C can establish the defence only if that money is paid
to at least two trustees of the land (or to a trust corporation). In a case such as *Boland*,
where A holds a freehold on trust for B, and so C pays money only to A, C cannot, therefore, make out the statutory overreaching defence. In a case such as *Flegg*, in contrast,
where A1 and A2 hold a freehold on trust, and so C pays the money to A1 and A2 jointly,
the defence *can* be made out.

**1.77** As a result, in *Flegg*, the society was free to take possession of the land, and then to sell
the freehold without giving any of the proceeds of sale directly to the Fleggs. If the value
of the land was eaten up by the debt owed to the society, then the Fleggs' only recourse
would be against the Maxwell-Browns: one of their duties as trustees was to account to
the Fleggs for their share of any money raised through dealings with the land (such as
the money provided by the society). In practice, however, such redress was unlikely to
assist the Fleggs: the Maxwell-Browns had almost certainly spent the money lent by the
society and, given their financial difficulties, they would not be in a position to restore
those funds.

## Evaluating the Examples

**1.78** There are a number of useful lessons that can be drawn from our examination of the
decisions in *Ainsworth*, *Boland*, and *Flegg*. First, there are some specific lessons that we
will return to later in the book. For example, the concept of an 'overriding interest' is very
important in registered land (**11.34–11.62**): an overriding interest is a property right
in land that cannot be defeated by the 'lack of registration' defence. Where C acquires
a right in A's land, any property right held by a person who was in actual occupation of
the land when C committed to acquiring C's right will count as an overriding interest.
A comparison between *Ainsworth* and *Boland* demonstrates the key point, often overlooked by students, that B's actual occupation of A's land *alone* does not give B an overriding interest: B also needs to have a legal or equitable property right in that land. If, as
in *Ainsworth*, B has only a personal right against A then that right cannot bind C, even if
B was in actual occupation of A's land. Similarly, a comparison between *Boland* and *Flegg*
demonstrates another key point, again often overlooked: even if B's actual occupation is
coupled with B's holding of a legal or equitable property right, that does not mean that
C can have no defence to B's right. Rather, whilst an overriding interest is immune from
the lack of registration defence, it may still be vulnerable to a *different* defence, such as
the statutory overreaching defence used by C in *Flegg*.

**1.79** Secondly, there are some more general lessons that can be taken from a comparison of
the three cases. For example, the fact that different courts disagreed about the result in

the same case (eg the Court of Appeal and House of Lords reached different outcomes in *Ainsworth*) shows that land law cases often raise very difficult issues, and that each of B and C may be able to put forward a persuasive argument. In *Boland* and *Flegg* the results differed because, in the latter case, C had paid the money it lent to A1 and A2, rather than just to A. This shows that the resolution of these difficult disputes may sometimes turn on seemingly technical details. The point is that, in trying to resolve the acute tension between the wishes of B and of C, the land law system has adopted a carefully structured set of rules, focused on the concept of property rights, and the content, acquisition, and defences questions. As we will consider further throughout the book, it is of course possible to disagree with the outcomes that the rules produce, but it is first necessary to understand how those outcomes are reached.

## Defining Land: The Extent of Ownership

**1.80**   What does it mean to say that B owns land? As we have seen so far in this chapter, the focus of land law is on private rights to use land. To be described as an owner, B must have a property right in the land: a right that is defined independently of a specific person, and so is capable of binding anyone who interferes with the land. To understand B's position as owner, we therefore need to examine the *content* of B's property right.

**1.81**   There are two forms of legal property right in land that involve powers of ownership: the freehold and the lease. In simple terms, a freehold confers ownership of land without a limit of time, whereas a lease involves ownership of land for a limited period. To understand B's rights, we therefore need to define what we mean by land.

**1.82**   The importance of defining land can be seen in the following two case examples.

> **Star Energy Weald Basin Ltd v Bocardo SA (2010):** X drilled diagonally from the surface of neighbouring land to get to oil located directly underneath the surface of B's land. B did not have any property right in the oil itself—by statute such rights are vested in the Crown—but it claimed that, as it was a freehold owner of the land, X had committed the tort of trespass by entering, without permission, the space underneath the surface of the land. The Supreme Court found in favour of B: the ownership conferred by its freehold thus extended to at least the depth at which X had drilled.

> **Kelsen v Imperial Tobacco Co (1957):** B, who had a lease of a shop, obtained an injunction forcing X to remove a large sign that projected into the air space above the shop.

**1.83**   It is therefore clear that B's rights, as an owner of land, extend both below and above the surface of the land itself. This point is captured in an old Latin maxim: *cujus est solum, ejus est usque ad coelum et ad infernos* (whoever owns the soil also owns to the sky and to the depths). As pointed out by Lord Hope in *Bocardo*, however, the maxim (referred to by Lord Hope as a 'brocard') should not be applied literally. In *Bernstein of Leigh (Baron) v Skyviews & General Ltd* (1978), for example, it was held that X did not commit a trespass simply by flying an aircraft high above B's land. Whilst B's property right certainly allows B a significant degree of control not only over the land itself, but also over the space above and below the land, there are inherent limits on the content of that right, even before we take into account special statutory rules such as the restrictions on B's use of oil or gas under the land, or the privileges conferred on operators of aircraft under the Civil Aviation Act 1949. A balance must be struck between the claims of the party with a pre-existing property right and the freedoms of others.

## Defining Land: What Objects Does the Land Include?

### Objects That Become Part of the Land

1.84   If B has a freehold or lease of land, B's ownership rights will extend to, for example, crops or other plants growing on the land, but this does not of course mean that B owns everything that might be found on that land: B has no claim to the coat of a dinner guest, for example. Such independent objects are known as *chattels*: tangible things that can be owned but which are not land. It is, however, possible for an initially independent object to lose its separate identity and to become part of the land, and thus part of B's ownership: in such a case, the object can be said to accede to the land as a fixture: it loses its independent identity and is no longer a chattel, but is instead part and parcel of the land.

1.85   The process by which an object can lose its separate identity and become part of the land is apparent in the following example.

> **Elitestone Ltd v Morris (1997):** Mr Morris lived in a wooden bungalow on land owned by Elitestone Ltd. He wanted to claim that he had a lease of the bungalow and so qualified for statutory protection. Elitestone argued instead that the bungalow was not part of the land, but was an independent chattel, and so Mr Morris did not qualify for the statutory protection. The bungalow had been built on the land using, for example, timber frame walls which, when brought onto the land, were of course independent chattels. The House of Lords held that the wooden bungalow was 'part and parcel of the land' and so was not an independent chattel: it was therefore possible for Mr Morris to have a lease protected by statute. Two key factors were identified: the extent to which the bungalow was physically attached to or integrated with the land; and the purpose for which it had been thus attached.

1.86   In the case of a standard house built on land, for example, the extent of attachment is such that the house clearly becomes part and parcel of the land: the bricks and so on used to construct it lose their independent identity as objects capable of being owned separately from the land. In the absence of such significant attachment, however, it may still be *possible* to reach the same result, by looking at the purpose of the attachment, as stated by Blackburn J in *Holland v Hodgson* (1872):

> *Thus blocks of stone placed one on the top of another without any mortar or cement for the purpose of forming a dry stone wall would become part of the land, though the same stones, if deposited in a builder's yard and for convenience sake stacked on the top of each other in the form of a wall, would remain chattels.*

**1.87**    A useful contrast to *Elitestone* is provided by the following case.

---

**Tower Hamlets LBC v Bromley LBC (2015):** The dispute concerned ownership of a valuable Henry Moore sculpture, 'Seated Draped Woman', which had for a long period been sited on a housing estate in Stepney, East London. The sculpture had been bought in 1952 by the London County Council (now defunct and so represented by Bromley) and it had never transferred away its ownership. Tower Hamlets, however, claimed that, as it owned the land on which the sculpture was sited, its ownership rights extended to the sculpture itself, as it had become part of that land. Applying the tests in *Elitestone*, Norris J rejected that argument: although the sculpture had been present on the land for a long time, that did not mean it had become part of the land. The crucial point was that, in contrast to the bungalow in *Elitestone*, the sculpture 'could be (and was) removed without damage and without diminishing its inherent beauty. It might adorn or beautify a location, but it was not in any real sense dependent upon that location.'

---

**1.88**    As it happened, this finding that the sculpture remained an independent chattel did not in the end prevent Tower Hamlets from establishing that it had a better right to the sculpture than Bromley but it established that claim in a different way: by showing that, as it had had possession of the sculpture without Bromley's consent for a sufficiently long period, the Limitation Act 1980 had extinguished Bromley's right to the sculpture. Tower Hamlets' success, however, did not depend on showing that the sculpture had become part of its land.

## Objects Found On or In the Land

**1.89**    B's freehold or lease does not, by itself, give B any property right in all objects on B's land: B has no claim to the coat of a dinner guest. What is the position if a small object falls from the guest's coat pocket and is lost down the back of B's sofa? As the object has clearly not become part and parcel of B's land, B cannot claim to be entitled to it on that basis. The object retains its independent identity and so the basic position is that the dinner guest retains his or her ownership of it. It may be, however, that the object is found only some time later, and the dinner guest cannot be traced, or does not come forward to claim it. In such a case, if the object was found by X, a later dinner guest of B, then does B, by virtue of his or her freehold, have a better claim to the object than X?

**1.90**    The first point to note is that X, by taking possession of the object, does acquire a right to it. The doctrine of *relative title* is a key part of property law: although X is not the 'true owner' of the object, X's right to possession will be protected against anyone who cannot show that he or she has a better property right to the object than X. The basic test as to which of two such property rights is 'better' is that the earlier property right will win. So B would need to show that he or she acquired a property right to the object *before* X found it and took possession of it.

**1.91**  It is reasonably clear that, if B argues that, simply as an owner of land, he or she acquired a right to the object as soon as it was lost on B's land, that argument will be rejected (see eg *Hannah v Peel* (1945)). The mere fact of the object being lost on B's land does not give B a property right in the object. There are, however, three types of situation in which it has been suggested that B can acquire a property right that would prevail over the rights of a different party later finding the lost object. As we will see, none of those suggestions is very convincing.

**1.92**  First, in *Parker v British Airways Board* (1982), Donaldson LJ suggested, in obiter dicta, that, at least where B occupies a building, B can acquire a property right superior to the finder by showing that, before the object was lost, B had 'manifested an intention to exercise control over the building and the things which may be upon it or in it'. He also stated that B is 'under an obligation to take such measures as in all the circumstances are reasonable to ensure that lost chattels are found and, upon being found, whether by him or a third party, to acquaint the true owner of the finding and to care for the chattels meanwhile'. It should be noted that, on this view, B's right stems not simply from his or her ownership of land, but from his or her occupation of it. It places great weight on B's intention to assert control over particular property. It is, however, hard to see why such an intention alone should give B a better right than a party who did in fact find, and take possession of, the object.

**1.93**  Secondly, again in obiter dicta in *Parker v British Airways Board*, Donaldson LJ suggested that, if the finder is a trespasser on B's land, then 'public policy' demands that B should have a better property right in the object than the finder. It is however difficult to find authority for that proposition and, in a later decision—*Costello v Chief Constable of Derbyshire* (2001)—the Court of Appeal in fact held that a party who had possession of a stolen car had a better right under the general law to that car than the police force that had seized it. This suggests that (where the 'true owner' is not known) disputes can be decided on the simple basis of which of the two competing parties first took possession of the object, even if the first possessor is a wrongdoer.

**1.94**  Thirdly, in *Waverley BC v Fletcher* (1996), Mr Fletcher, on a visit to a public park owned by the council, used a metal detector and then dug up a medieval gold brooch that lay about nine inches below the surface of the land. The Court of Appeal held that the council, as a result of its ownership of the land, had a better right to the brooch than Mr Fletcher. It was noted that, as Mr Fletcher did not have permission to use his metal detector and then dig for property, he was a trespasser. Emphasis was also placed on the fact that the brooch was not simply on the land, but rather had been found under the surface, and it was stated that: 'Where an article is found in or attached to land, as between the owner or lawful possessor of the land and the finder of the article, the owner or lawful possessor of the land has better title.' Again, however, this analysis is difficult to support. It is true that it is possible for an object to lose its identity and become part and parcel of B's land (1.84–1.88). In such a case, however, the 'true owner' of the object, who lost it on B's land, would also lose his or her property right in the object. The suggestion in *Fletcher*, however, is that the location of the object under the surface simply means that B has a better property right than the finder, not that B also has a better right than the party who lost the object in the first place. It is hard to see the logic of that position: if the object has retained its independent identity, so that it could be claimed by the 'true owner', then why should the rights of B vary according to whether or not the object was found under the surface of the land?

## FURTHER READING

Dunn, A, 'National Provincial Bank v Ainsworth (1965)' in C Mitchell and P Mitchell (eds), *Landmark Cases in Equity* (Oxford: Hart Publishing, 2012).

Goodhart, A, 'Three Cases on Possession' (1929) 3 CLJ 195.

Hickey, R, *Property and the Law of Finders* (Oxford: Hart Publishing, 2010), ch 2.

Hopkins, N, 'City of London Building Society v Flegg (1987): Homes as Wealth' in N Gravells (ed), *Landmark Cases in Land Law* (Oxford: Hart Publishing, 2013).

Howell, J, 'Subterranean Land Law: Rights Below the Surface of the Land' (2002) 53 NILQ 268.

Smith, R, 'Williams and Glyn's Bank Ltd v Boland (1980): The Development of a System of Title by Registration' in N Gravells (ed), *Landmark Cases in Land Law* (Oxford: Hart Publishing, 2013).

## SELF-TEST QUESTIONS

1    What are the special features of land? Can you explain how those special features might influence particular land law rules?

2    What is the key difference between a property right and a personal right?

3    How might each of the content, acquisition, and defences questions be relevant when advising a party as to his or her rights in relation to land?

4    The *Ainsworth* and *Boland* decisions each concerned the rights of a wife occupying her home against a bank, where the bank had acquired rights in the land without the knowledge or consent of the wife. Can you briefly explain why the results in the cases were different? And can you briefly explain why the result in *Flegg* differed from that in *Boland*?

5    What problems would arise if it were indeed the case that the rights of an owner of land extended indefinitely in a column stretching both above and below the surface of the land?

6    Are there any convincing reasons why an owner or occupier of land should have any rights in relation to an object found on that land? Do any different reasons apply if the object is found below the surface of the land?

# 2 Human Rights

## SUMMARY

This chapter considers the impact of human rights upon property relations focusing on Article 1 Protocol 1 and Article 8 of the European Convention on Human Rights which has been incorporated into our domestic law by the Human Rights Act 1998. In order to fully appreciate the relatively recent influence of human rights upon property relations, the chapter provides a background to the particular jurisprudence of human rights reasoning before considering the import of Article 1 Protocol 1, in protecting possessions, and Article 8, in requiring respect for the home. When considering Article 8 the chapter focuses upon repossession of the home. Article 14 (protection against discrimination) and Article 6 (right to a fair trial) are also considered in outline. The chapter finally offers a brief insight into the impact of human rights in the development of property relations.

Key topics explored in this chapter are:

- Adjudication under the Human Rights Act 1998 (**2.6–2.23**)
- Vertical effect (**2.24–2.29**)
- Horizontal effect (**2.30–2.41**)
- Article 1 Protocol 1 (**2.42–2.65**)
- Article 8 (**2.66–2.92**)
- Article 14 (**2.93–2.94**)
- Article 6 (**2.95–2.97**)
- Impact of human rights (**2.98–2.101**)

## Introduction

2.1   A property lawyer might at first sight be sceptical about the need to consider the impact of human rights upon land. Often human rights are considered in the context of public law rather than private law of which land law forms part. However, human rights permeate our entire legal system and land lawyers cannot ignore the fundamental rights enshrined in the European Convention on Human Rights and Fundamental Freedoms (ECHR). As such, human rights demonstrate an interaction between the state, representing the interests of society as a whole, and rights enjoyed by and between individual citizens. Human rights in this context thus touch upon the ethical dimensions of land law and the role it plays in our society. Although all human rights are inherently enjoyed by persons rather than being attached to land, they do encompass rights enjoyed by all persons and we will see in this chapter that certain protected human rights can operate to affect the relations between people and land. In addition, certain domestic legislation, for instance the Equality Act 2010, which prohibits discrimination against certain groups by both public and private entities, for instance in the sale, letting, or mortgaging of land, is also patently human rights-based. In this context, they demonstrate an interaction between personal freedoms and property rights. We have thus chosen to include a chapter on how human rights can affect land law at an early stage in this book although this chapter will benefit from rereading when you have a greater grasp of land law. An appreciation of the effect of human rights on land law presents a challenge—as Gray has observed 'land law and human rights have never seemed particularly natural bedfellows' (Gray (2002) at 211). The challenge lies in the need first to explain how human rights' reasoning operates within private law. We can then move on to consider those human rights that have a particular impact on land law and the challenge they present to the aims of clarity and certainty that have traditionally dominated land law. It is then hoped that you will be able to appreciate some of the human rights-based questions that can arise as we consider these property rules in the rest of this book—we will point out where they arise.

2.2   The ECHR was born out of the human rights abuses of the Second World War and the advance of communism. Its object is to set out the freedoms that are considered central to human life in a democratic society. As such, the values it espouses are not a radical departure from the traditional principles upon which property law has been founded and upon which it has developed over centuries. For instance, Magna Carta set a bulwark against the arbitrary dispossession of property by the Crown and the great 18th-century thinkers across Europe prompted a renewed articulation of essential social and civil liberties. In the legal context, Blackstone called for the 'sacred and inviolable rights to private property' even in the face of public necessity unless full recompense was given. Likewise, we have seen that in *Entick v Carrington* (1765) the inviolability of property against unsanctioned entry has long been upheld and has spawned the time-honoured sentiment that 'an Englishman's home is his castle' (for a further consideration of the origins of human rights, see Gray (2002) and Allen (2005)). Nevertheless, the content of the rights enshrined within the ECHR is not set in the past, for the ECHR is conceived as a living instrument enabling rights to evolve over time as societies develop.

2.3   The particular Convention rights upon which we will concentrate in this chapter are Article 1 Protocol 1, which guarantees the peaceful enjoyment of a person's possessions, and Article 8, which guarantees the respect for a person's private and family life and his or her home. Other protected rights are also significant in governing relationships with land including Articles 10 and 11 which guarantee freedom of speech and assembly and as such may impact upon the ability of individuals to access land in order to exercise these fundamental rights. For instance, the 'Occupy' political protest movement has asserted such rights (see Lees (2013)). It is also significant to bear in mind the impact of two further rights. First, there is Article 6, which guarantees the right to a fair trial in the determination of civil rights and obligations including property rights and, secondly, Article 14 prohibits discrimination in the enjoyment of Convention rights including Article 1 Protocol 1 and Article 8. It is thus said to be 'parasitic' in the sense that it is dependent upon another Convention right rather than prohibiting discrimination per se. It is the Equality Act 2010 which provides the main bulwark against discrimination and it too may be a domestic source of human rights protection.

**2.4**  Article 1 Protocol 1 and Article 8 are both qualified rights in the sense that the guarantee they afford is not absolute and an infringement with a particular right may be justified on specific grounds. There will thus be two fundamental questions when victims allege a breach of their human rights. First, is the right engaged in the sense that it falls within the terms of the guaranteed right and if so, secondly, is the infringement justified? The Strasbourg Court has developed a formula to examine whether an infringement is justified which we will consider at 2.11–2.23.

**2.5**  Since 1953, when the ECHR was ratified, victims may bring a case before the European Court of Human Rights (the Strasbourg Court) alleging a breach of their rights secured under the ECHR but only if they have exhausted their remedies before their domestic courts. The Human Rights Act 1998 (HRA 1998) has incorporated the rights enshrined in the ECHR into our domestic law (see HRA 1998, Sch 1). Thus a victim now can directly raise a human rights issue before the domestic courts. However, to do so he or she will need to establish that the HRA 1998 provides a route by which a domestic court or tribunal is able to consider the human rights compatibility of our law and/or the conduct of our public bodies. The operation of the HRA 1998 has triggered considerable debate amongst public lawyers primarily because it affects the separation of powers and this delicate balance between the sovereignty of Parliament and the judiciary as well as judicial oversight of administrative actions. You no doubt will have considered these questions in your study of public law but it is useful to briefly remind ourselves of the salient issues to fully appreciate the impact of human rights upon property law. Indeed, property-related cases have helped shape current thinking.

## Adjudication Under the Human Rights Act 1998

**2.6**  The HRA 1998 incorporates the ECHR into domestic law by placing certain duties upon our courts in the adjudication of disputes. First, the courts, and other public bodies, are under a duty as far as it is possible to read and give effect to legislation (whenever enacted) in a way that is compatible with Convention rights (HRA 1998, s 3). The court's powers of statutory interpretation are thus expanded beyond their traditional role of divining the intention of the legislature. Section 3 enables the court to modify a legislative provision to achieve human rights compatibility although the courts will stop short of adopting a meaning which would effectively amend the statute because it is inconsistent with the fundamental thrust of the legislation that is subject to scrutiny (see *Ghaidan v Godin Mendoza* (2004), *McDonald v McDonald* (2016)). Where a court decides that it is unable to use its powers of statutory interpretation to achieve compatibility, it cannot overrule the statute but it may issue a declaration of incompatibility whereupon the government may decided that it needs to amend the offending legislation utilizing a fast-track procedure (see ss 4 and 10). Thus, all the property-related legislation should comply with human rights standards and litigants can question its compatibility regardless of whether their dispute is with a public body or private person.

**2.7** Public authorities are required by the HRA 1998 to act in a manner which is compatible with the ECHR (s 6). The courts and tribunals fall within the definition of a public authority and so they too must act in a human rights compatible manner. The difficult question is to determine the nature and extent of the court's obligation in this regard. We have already seen that they must interpret legislation in a compatible manner and courts should also exercise any discretion they enjoy in line with human rights norms.

**2.8** An issue that has attracted considerable debate is the extent of the court's obligation to interpret and develop the common law in a compatible manner. This is a particularly important question for property lawyers given the diverse and intertwined sources of the property rules. Whilst legislation is a growing source—just look at the **Table of Legislation** at the beginning of this book—the common law remains a vital component either in itself or as the foundation upon which a statute has been built. As Lord Walker observed in *Birmingham CC v Doherty* ((2008) at [100]) the common law is like 'a patch of grass in the middle of a motorway junction' such that 'it would be unrealistic, and productive of error, not to look at the whole picture'. It could also be arbitrary since it is largely a matter of history or chance whether or not a particular rule is derived from statute or the common law. The issue is particularly pertinent to the extent to which the relations between private parties are influenced by human rights norms, the so-called horizontal effect, which we will considered further at **2.30–2.41**.

**2.9** The HRA 1998 calls for legislation to be interpreted, and for public bodies to act, compatibly but how do we determine what is human rights compatible? The final arbiter of human rights compatibility is the Strasbourg Court, comprising the Chamber (with a number of divisions) and the appellate Grand Chamber; and section 2 of the HRA 1998 requires our domestic courts to 'take into account any judgment, decision, declaration or advisory opinion' of the Strasbourg Court. We thus need to engage with cases decided by the Strasbourg Court to understand when the law is or is not compatible.

**2.10** The court's duty under section 2 does not require our domestic courts to follow Strasbourg decisions as a matter of strict precedent but it creates an obligation to give practical recognition to the principles laid down by the Strasbourg Court (*Kay v Lambeth LBC; Leeds CC v Price* (2006)). It is evident that our highest courts have not always relished this task where it has found itself at odds with the Strasbourg Court. A dialogue between the two courts may result through the judgments of cases that have proceeded to the Strasbourg Court, until a clear and consistent line of authority from Strasbourg results (see *R v Horncastle* (2010)). One such dialogue was conducted over the compatibility with Article 8 of mandatory rights to possession of the home by a public authority with the final Strasbourg message accepted by the Supreme Court in *Manchester CC v Pinnock* (2010)—a decision we shall explore when considering Article 8. However, where the Supreme Court does not believe that a clear and consistent line of authority has yet emerged from the Strasbourg Court, it will adopt its own interpretation of compatibility (*McDonald v McDonald* (2016)). If the losing victim disagrees, they can start a dialogue by pursuing an appeal before the Strasbourg Court.

## The Justification Formula

**2.11**  We have noted that the human rights with which we are concerned as property lawyers are qualified and thus an infringement may be justified. The primary focus in a human rights-based challenge is thus often upon whether an infringement is justified. In addressing this question, the Strasbourg Court has developed a tried and tested formula which their judgments will follow. Our domestic courts will also look to this formula with appropriate modification to reflect their different constitutional and adjudicative position (see eg *R (on the application of N) v Lewisham LBC; R (on the application of H) v Newham LBC* (2014)). It is thus important to become familiar with this methodology before we see how it operates in the context of the particular human rights that relate to land.

**2.12**  An interference will be justified if it is *in accordance with the law* AND *in pursuit of a legitimate aim* within the qualifications set out in the relevant Article AND is *proportionate* in striking a fair balance between the legitimate aim and the interference of the individual's human rights in issue. The Strasbourg Court acknowledges that states enjoy *a margin of appreciation* in formulating the legitimate aim and the means adopted to achieve that aim since states are more familiar with local conditions. Whilst the margin of appreciation is an inappropriate concept for our domestic courts to adopt in assessing compatibility, we find a similar approach in what has been called '*the deference*' or '*weight*' the courts show both to the legislative decisions of Parliament and the administrative decisions of public bodies. This *deference* or *weight* seeks to capture the appropriate constitutional responsibilities and expertise of judiciary, Parliament, and administrative bodies. We now need to examine each of these concepts in a little more detail.

### In Accordance with Law

**2.13**  An interference must be lawful within the laws of a state to meet the requirements of the rule of law. It is for a state to determine its own laws but the Strasbourg Court has set minimum qualitative demands that a law should meet. Laws should not be arbitrary and should be 'accessible, precise and foreseeable in their application' (see *R&L, SRO and others v The Czech Republic* (2014) at [113], see also *Prokopovich v Russia* (2005), *Pelipenko v Russia* (2014)).

2.14 Law is widely defined in a substantive rather than a formal sense. It can include written law in the form, for instance, of legislation and regulatory measures, and unwritten law including case law (see *R&L, SRO and others v The Czech Republic* (2014)). In respect of case law, the Strasbourg Court has also set a base qualitative standard in requiring the courts to demonstrate clear and rational reasoning from a sound evidential base. Weakness in this regard may also be of weight in the proportionality balance (*Kryvitska and Kryvitskyy v Ukraine* (2010)).

## Legitimate Aim

2.15 An interference must be made for a legitimate purpose that serves the appropriate qualification set out in the Article. Thus under Article 1 Protocol 1 an interference must be in the public and general interest and under Article 8 an interference must be necessary in a democratic society to address a pressing social need, for example the economic well-being of the state or because it protects the rights and freedoms of others.

## Proportionality

2.16 Although proportionality is a well-established concept within European jurisprudence, it is relatively new to English law. At its heart is the search for a fair balance between the interests of the community at large in qualifying a human right and the protection of the individual's rights that have been infringed. It asks whether the ends justify the means. The following case neatly illustrates this balance.

> **Rousk v Sweden (2013):** Mr Rousk's home was sold for €186,000 following enforcement proceedings to recover his unpaid taxes. Whilst it is clear that enforcement against a taxpayer's assets is a proportionate means to serve the legitimate aim of the efficient recovery of taxes in the public interest, the Strasbourg Court found that the sale of Mr Rousk's home was disproportionate in the circumstances and, accordingly, a violation of Article 1 Protocol 1 and Article 8. The reason was that by the time of the sale Mr Rousk's outstanding tax bill stood at just €800—a better, and proportionate, way to recover this small sum should have been pursued rather than forcing the sale of Mr Rousk's home.

2.17 Perhaps the most insightful consideration of the concept of proportionality in domestic jurisprudence was made by Lord Reed in *Bank Mellat v HM Treasury (No 2)* ((2014) at [68]–[76]) in which he makes several pertinent observations before advancing a structured approach to proportionality. Lord Reed notes that the Strasbourg

Court often approaches proportionality in a 'relatively broad brush way' but that the intensity of their examination of proportionality varies according to the context and the different Articles under consideration. Thus, for instance, under Article 1 Protocol 1 the focus is generally upon the burden the public interest places upon the individual victim whilst under Article 8 there may be more nuanced policy considerations at stake to determine what is necessary in a democratic society. Lord Reed goes on to note, that in the light of our different legal tradition, the approach of common law jurisdictions (including our own) differs from that of the Strasbourg Court in preferring a more structured analysis. This common law approach to proportionality is described by Lord Reed (at [74]):

1. *Whether the objective of the measure is sufficiently important to justify the limitation of a protected right;*

2. *Whether the measure is rationally connected to the objective;*

3. *Whether a less intrusive measure could have been used without compromising the achievement of the objective;*

4. *Whether, balancing the severity of the measure's effect on the right of the persons to whom it applies against the importance of the objective, to the extent that the measure will contribute to its achievement, the former outweighs the latter ie whether the impact of the rights infringement is disproportionate to the likely benefit of the impugned measure.*

**2.18**  The first two stages are threshold tests which are generally relatively easy to pass. The focus is thus often on the latter two stages which have been described respectively as 'relative proportionality'—in assessing alternative measures—and 'overall proportionality'—in looking to an overall costs–benefits assessment (see Hickman (2010)). These stages reflect proportionality operating at two levels of intensity. First, there is the fair balance to be struck between the relevant Convention right and the legitimate interest to be advanced. Here it is the law itself that is in issue in defining the balance between the severity of the interference and the legitimate aim and the particular means employed to achieve that aim. For instance, an infringement may be disproportionate where there is an alternative and equally effective means of achieving the legitimate aim which does not interfere with an individual's human rights, or at least does so in a less severe fashion. Secondly, there is the proportionality of the interference upon the victim since no individual is expected to bear an excessive burden when his or her human rights are infringed in the pursuit of a legitimate aim. It is here that the individual victim's particular circumstances may be relevant.

**2.19**  Determining whether or not an infringement is proportionate calls for procedural safeguards to enable an independent judicial body to make that assessment (*Connors v UK* (2005), *McCann v UK* (2008), *Kay v UK* (2012), *Manchester CC v Pinnock* (2010)). It is in fact these procedural safeguards that have proved most problematic in deciding the compatibility of possession proceedings with Article 8 which we will consider later in this chapter.

## The Margin of Appreciation and the Strasbourg Court

**2.20** Lord Reed noted in *Bank Mellat* that 'the principle of proportionality is indissolubly linked to the concept of the margin of appreciation' (at [71]). In assessing proportionality, value judgments need to be made to decide whether a fair balance has been struck. Whilst it is ultimately for the court to make that assessment, it is recognized by the Strasbourg Court that an individual state is generally in a better position to decide its society's needs and the best means of meeting them given the local conditions. The Court thus acknowledges that states enjoy a measure of discretion through the concept of a state's margin of appreciation. An example of the operation of the margin of appreciation is found in the following case.

---

*James v UK* **(1986):** The Duke of Westminster owned a significant number of houses in prime areas of London which were let on long leases. The Leasehold Reform Act 1967 gave the lessees a right to acquire the freehold reversion for a sum below their market value. The Duke objected and eventually brought his complaint before the Strasbourg Court based upon an interference with the right to the peaceful enjoyment of his possessions under Article 1 Protocol 1. The Strasbourg Court accepted that his rights had been infringed but found that the infringement was justified in pursuit of the legitimate aim of the public interest. The Court accepted that the UK legislature was in a better position to assess what was in the public interest within the UK. The Westminster Parliament's decision to enact legislation which rebalanced the rights of lessors and lessees under long leases in pursuit of what they judged to be 'greater social justice in the sphere of people's homes', fell within the UK's margin of appreciation as it was not 'manifestly without reasonable foundation'.

---

**2.21** The test of 'manifestly without reasonable foundation' adopted in *James v UK* is clearly wide. However, it is equally clear that the width of the margin of appreciation will differ according to the impugned Article and the context in issue. The Strasbourg Court in *Connors v UK* (2005) at [82] noted that:

> This margin will vary according to the nature of the Convention right in issue, its importance for the individual and the nature of the activities restrictive, as well as the nature of the aim pursued by the restrictions. The margin will tend to be narrower where the right at stake is crucial to the individual's enjoyment of intimate or key rights.

In the sphere of social and economic rights, as opposed to civil and political rights, the Strasbourg Court has suggested that the margin is wide. Such social and economic rights might include planning measures or housing or welfare provision (see *Connors v UK* (2005)). A wide margin of appreciation has generally been adopted in the context of an Article 1 Protocol 1 infringement. Whereas when Article 8 is in issue the margin tends to be narrower particularly where the nature of the interference is severe. Whether or not a state remains within its margin of appreciation is also crucially dependent upon the existence of procedural safeguards which we have already noted are also an important element within proportionality (see *Kay v UK* (2012)).

### 'Weight' and the Domestic Courts

2.22   The margin of appreciation is a concept within Strasbourg jurisprudence but a similar concept is apparent in the domestic context where the courts give deference to the political decisions of Parliament, in formulating and enacting policy, as well as the decisions of administrative bodies charged with the implementation of such policy. The Supreme Court dislikes the label of 'deference' and prefers instead to adopt the concept of the court giving due *weight* to the views of primary decision makers with the explicit role and expertise to make an appropriate judgment (see *Huang v SS for the Home Department* (2007) at [16] per Lord Nicholls). The central concern is to maintain the appropriate constitutional balance between Parliament, the administration, and the courts in the face of the courts' new role under the HRA 1998 as adjudicators of human rights compatibility.

2.23   The HRA 1998 requires the courts to delve into matters of policy in assessing whether or not a law is human rights compatible or a public body has acted in a human rights compatible manner. This is a new role which calls, to a greater extent than hitherto, for some consideration of the legitimacy of policy aims as well as the proportionality of the means employed to implement those aims (see eg the comments of Lord Nicholls in *Wilson v First County Trust Ltd* (2003) at [61]–[63]). Nevertheless, in areas of social and economic policy, particularly where public expenditure is in issue, the courts have been reluctant to interfere with these policy choices (and their legislative design) or indeed the administrative decisions of those bodies responsible for the practical face of those policies. For instance, the courts have tried to steer clear of questioning the policy shaping the complex web of ever changing legislation and administrative guidance governing housing policy (see eg *Kay v Lambeth LBC* (2006), *Manchester CC v Pinnock* (2010), *McDonald v McDonald* (2016)).

## Vertical Effect

2.24   The responsibility to respect human rights falls primarily upon public bodies and the HRA 1998 provides that all public authorities are under a direct duty to act in a human rights compatible manner (s 6). This duty is known as vertical effect because a victim of an infringement by a public authority has a direct cause of action so that he or she can bring proceedings against a public authority or may defend proceedings brought by such an authority (s 7). Where breach of a section 6 duty is established, the court may grant such remedy as it deems 'just and appropriate', which may include the award of damages or a declaration that the act is unlawful (s 8).

### Public Authorities

2.25   It is clearly thus important to know what is meant by 'a public authority'. A functional distinction is made between a 'core public authority' and a 'hybrid public authority' (see s 6(3)(b) and *Aston Cantlow and Wilmcote with Billesley Parochial Church Council v Wallbank* (2004)). A core public authority is required to comply with Convention rights in the performance of all of its functions because it is a public authority 'through and through' (per Lord Hope in *Aston Cantlow* at [35]). It is relatively easy to spot a core public authority, for instance a local authority is a core public authority and required to act in a human rights compatible manner when conducting all its business including as the landlord of the social housing it provides.

2.26 A hybrid public authority is only required to act in a human rights compatible manner when it is discharging functions of a public nature. It is not so constrained when performing a private function (s 6(6)). A twofold assessment thus determines the human rights responsibilities of a body that is not a core public authority. First, does it qualify as a hybrid public authority because some of its functions are public in character? If so, and secondly, is the act or omission in question a public function? These functional tests are not always easy to divine and their Lordships have sometimes come to different views (see eg *Aston Cantlow and Wilmcote with Billesley Parochial Church Council v Wallbank* (2004), *YL v Birmingham CC* (2008), *London Quadrant Housing Trust v Weaver* (2010)). Yet the distinction is crucial particularly when many traditional public services have been outsourced to private providers.

2.27 An example of interest to property lawyers is the provision of publically subsidized housing which at one time was controlled almost exclusively by local authorities but is now largely made available through regulated private housing providers including housing associations and charities. The Court of Appeal considered the issue in *London Quadrant Housing Trust v Weaver* (2010) when the question arose as to whether London Quadrant was exercising a public function when it terminated the private tenancy it had granted to Mrs Weaver. London Quadrant accepted that it was a hybrid public authority but argued that it was exercising a private function in terminating Mrs Weaver's tenancy. The majority of the court decided that London Quadrant was exercising a public function and was thus subject to a duty under s 6 to act compatibly—although Rix LJ gave a robust defence. The majority held that, although made in exercise of a private contractual power, the termination of Mrs Weaver's tenancy was so bound up with the public functions of London Quadrant as a housing provider that it was impossible to separate the two. The public functions of London Quadrant arose from the fact that its activities were partly funded from the public purse and it worked in close harmony with the local housing authority to discharge the local authority's statutory housing obligations and was subject to regulation to that end. Moreover, the court viewed the provision of subsidized housing to meet the needs of the less well-off as a typical governmental function. It thus also appears that the majority of the court believed that London Quadrant had been correct in accepting that it was a hybrid public authority.

2.28 A public authority, or hybrid public authority, will have a defence to a claim that it is in breach of its section 6 duty where it could not have acted differently because it was under an obligation to act as it had done (s 6(2)(a)). For instance, when a law is declared incompatible, it may take some time before the incompatibility can be addressed, yet the public body is still obliged to go about its business and discharge its statutory responsibilities. They may thus have no alternative but to continue to act pursuant to an incompatible provision.

2.29   A defence is also available under section 6(2)(b) where a public authority is acting 'to give effect to or enforce' an incompatible provision. The application of this latter defence has caused some difficulty where a public authority has relied upon an incompatible power or discretion, for instance to claim possession from one of its tenants, when it could have acted differently either by not seeking possession at all or by relying on an available compliant power. The better view is that the defence is not available in these circumstances when the public authority is not discharging a duty as such but exercising its management powers, upon which it may or may not choose to rely (*Manchester CC v Pinnock* (2010) at [93]–[103] per Lord Neuberger, *Birmingham CC v Doherty* (2008) per Lord Mance but see Lord Hope at [38]–[40]).

# Horizontal Effect

2.30   A critical issue for land lawyers is the extent to which human rights may impact upon a dispute between private individuals. Unfortunately, it is complicated issue. It is clear that the HRA 1998 does not operate to confer a direct cause of action between private individuals. Unlike public authorities, private individuals are not subject to a statutory duty to act in a human rights compatible manner. But it is equally clear that human rights can affect the relationship between private individuals and a breach of a protected right may be raised in the context of other proceedings—for instance, by questioning the human rights compatibility of the law governing the dispute. Leigh has distinguished several ways in which private parties may be affected by Convention rights—it is helpful to adopt his categorization (Leigh (1999)).

## Direct Statutory Horizontality: section 3 of the HRA 1998

2.31   We have already noted that the courts are under a duty to interpret legislation in a human rights compatible manner and this duty applies as much to legislation governing the relations of private parties as public bodies. Indeed, the leading case on this section 3 duty, *Ghaidan v Godin-Mendoza* (2004) concerned a dispute between private individuals. We will see throughout this book that there are other occasions when statutory provisions effecting the relations of private individuals have been similarly challenged.

## Public Liability Horizontality

2.32   In examining vertical effect, we saw that a private body may be characterized as a hybrid public authority, because of the public functions it undertakes, and that when carrying out such functions, it will be subject to a duty to act in a human rights compatible manner under section 6 of the HRA 1998.

## Intermediate Horizontality

2.33   Under Strasbourg jurisprudence, intermediate horizontality encompasses the possibility that a state may be responsible for the conduct of private parties. This responsibility may arise because a state has sanctioned a private party to act in a way which results in a breach of a Convention right. For instance, in *Lopez Ostra v Spain* ((1995), the Spanish government was held responsible for a breach of Article 8 caused by environmental pollution from a chemical plant conducted by a company to whom the government had granted permission to operate. In a similar vein, a state may be held responsible for the legal or procedural framework it constructs which governs the rights and liabilities of private parties (see eg *JA Pye (Oxford) Ltd v UK* (2008), *James v UK* (1986), *Zehentner v Austria* (2011)).

2.34   There are indications that the Strasbourg Court may be prepared to press these positive state obligations further. Contrasting the Strasbourg Court decisions in the following two cases illustrates this development.

> ***Di Palma v UK* (1986):** Ms Di Palma disputed the amount of the service charges she had contractually agreed to pay under the long lease of her flat. She refused to pay the disputed charges and her private landlords exercised their express right to forfeit her lease. The Strasbourg Court refused to entertain her case, based upon an alleged breach of Article 1 Protocol 1 and Article 8, because the dispute arose from a private agreement.

> ***Mustafa & Tarzibachi v Sweden* (2011):** Mustafa and his wife, in breach of their lease from a private landlord, erected a satellite dish on the outside of their flat so they could receive media broadcasts in their native language. Their landlords, in reliance of their rights under the lease, terminated the lease and sought possession. Mustafa and his wife alleged that such action breached their right to freedom of expression under Article 10 and also respect for their home and private life under Article 8. The Strasbourg Court agreed that Mustafa and his wife's human rights had been violated. The termination of the lease to remedy a comparatively minor breach was disproportionate. This decision was based upon Article 10 rather than Article 8.

2.35   Both cases involved the exercise of private contractual rights to terminate a lease but the difference in the approach of the Strasbourg Court is striking. The cases were decided on the basis of different Articles but their different approach is not readily explicable on this basis. Article 1 Protocol 1, Article 8, and Article 10 are all qualified rights and thus subject to the same justification process. Article 8 was also raised in *Mustafa & Tarzibachi* but the Court, having found a violation under Article 10, did not consider the further alleged violation of Article 8—an approach which is not unusual where more than one violation is alleged. A plausible explanation may lie in the changing attitude of the Court in interpreting the ECHR as a living instrument. In their decision in *Mustafa & Tarzibachi* the Court described what would appear to be their current approach to intervention in private party relations in the following terms (at [33]):

> Admittedly, the Court is not in theory required to settle disputes of a purely private nature. That being said, in the exercising the European supervision incumbent on it, it cannot remain passive where a national court's interpretation of a legal act, be it a testamentary disposition, a private contract, a public document, a statutory provision or an administrative practice appears unreasonable, arbitrary, discriminatory or, more broadly, inconsistent with the principle underlying the Convention.

2.36 However, the Supreme Court in *McDonald v McDonald* (2016) preferred to continue to follow the approach of the Strasbourg Court in *Di Palma* in declining to interfere with an exclusively private contractual relationship as regulated by statute. They believed that *Mustafa & Tarzibachi* can be explained on the basis that the violation arose because the Swedish government had failed to enact legislation to sufficiently protect freedom of information under Article 10. However, protection of that right (or indeed the right to respect for the home under Article 8) might only effectively be accomplished by enacting legislation which interferes with the parties' freedom of contract by prohibiting the termination of a private lease which would disproportionally interfere with an individual's rights under Article 10. All in all, the Supreme Court's explanation is not convincing but has some support from the recent case of *Vrzic v Croatia* (2016).

2.37 A state's positive duties to protect individuals from threats to their Convention rights by private parties are more prominent where a victim is perceived as vulnerable. Particular vulnerability may arise because a person is of poor physical or mental health (eg *Zehentner v Austria* (2011)), or is underage or of advanced years (eg *Bjedov v Croatia* (2012)) or because he or she belongs to a minority ethnic or cultural group subjected to discriminatory treatment (eg *Connors v UK* (2005), *Yordanova v Bulgaria* (2012), *Winterstein v France* (2013)). Such vulnerability may call for a state to provide for distinct treatment to address the vulnerability in question and/or vulnerability may weigh more heavily in the proportionality balance. The Equality Act 2010 provides a domestic example of the distinct treatment of vulnerability.

2.38 The following case illustrates the need to provide distinct procedural protection to address mental vulnerability even in the face of such hallowed property values as certainty, the efficient payment of debts, and the protection of the bona fide purchaser.

> ***Zehentner v Austria* (2011):** Ms Zehentner suffered from a severe mental illness. She failed to pay for some repairs to her home when she was taken into hospital for treatment. Her creditors obtained a judgment debt against her which was subsequently enforced by the sale of her home after Ms Zehentner failed to object within the strict time frame required by the Austrian enforcement process. The Strasbourg Court found a violation of both Article 1 Protocol 1 and Article 8 in view of the failure to provide adequate procedural

> safeguards which would have enabled Ms Zehentner to respond despite her mental condition. The importance of such safeguards to protect the mentally vulnerable from the loss of their possessions and/or home outweighed the efficient enforcement of judgment debts by private litigants and the certainty of the ownership afforded to a purchaser under a judicial sale.

The positive obligation of a state to provide adequate procedural safeguards has been of growing prominence and we will see how this obligation has been formulated in the context of both Article 1 Protocol 1 and Article 8.

## The Courts and Remedial and Procedural Horizontality

**2.39**   The courts in the conduct of the proceedings before them and in the award of remedies to resolve a dispute is subject to a duty to act compatibly with Convention standards under section 6 of the HRA 1998 regardless of whether the parties before them are public or private bodies or individuals (*McDonald v McDonald* (2016)).

## The Courts and Indirect (or Direct) Horizontality

**2.40**   The final possible impact of the HRA 1998 upon private parties also flows from the court's duty to act in a human rights compatible manner under section 6. The focus here is on the extent to which a court is required to observe human rights norms when adjudicating private rights which may involve balancing different private parties' human rights. A further focus may be on how the courts, in resolving a dispute between private parties, develop the common law which governs those parties' relations including their property relations. A fair amount of academic ink has been spilt over this issue. At one end of the debate are those who argue that the courts are under a duty to develop the common law to provide private parties with a direct action to safeguard their human rights, whilst at the other end of the debate are those who suggest that the court's obligations under section 6 are indirect and restricted to interpreting existing common law rules in a human rights compliant manner. The strength of the court's obligations under indirect horizontal effect is also the subject of academic debate—is it only weak in requiring the court to give weight to Convention norms or strong in imposing a duty to interpret the common law in accordance with the ECHR?

**2.41**   Commentators often point to the development of the tort of misuse of private information as evidence of the court's acceptance of their section 6 obligations to develop private common law in accordance with Convention rights. However, in *McDonald v McDonald* (2016) the Supreme Court, in considering their duties under section 6, drew a distinction between tortious relationships 'where the legislature has expressly, impliedly or through inaction, left it to the courts to carry out the balancing exercise' and 'a contractual relationship in respect of which the legislature has prescribed how their respective Convention rights are to be respected' (at [46]). *McDonald* concerned a private tenancy agreement in which the tenant questioned whether section 6 required the court to consider the proportionality of her eviction upon the exercise of the statutory right to possession enjoyed by her private landlord. We will consider this important case in more detail when considering Article 8. Suffice it to say at this point that the Supreme Court did not accept that section 6 required them to consider the proportionality of Ms McDonald's eviction from her home:

> [t]o hold otherwise would involve the Convention effectively being directly enforceable as between private citizens so as to alter their contractual rights and obligations whereas the purpose of the Convention is … to protect citizens from having their rights infringed by the state. (At [40].)

## Article 1 Protocol 1

**2.42**  Reaching agreement on the protection of property rights proved more difficult than the other human rights contained in the ECHR. It thus did not form part of the initial Convention rights but is found in a separate protocol. The first and important point to note is that Article 1 Protocol 1 (A1-P1) does not provide a right *to* property but a right *of* property. Its aim is to protect existing possessions and not to ensure that individuals enjoy sufficient resources to sustain life. A1-P1 is qualified and thus dispossession or control over the absolute nature of ownership may be justified in the public or general interest. Thus, for instance, land may be compulsorily acquired for road or rail building or the provision of other public services or utilities or for preservation of the natural or built environment. Common controls of possessions include planning controls or controls to ensure public health or environmental protection. Gray has noted that '[w]e live in an age of unprecedented regulation … with the consequence that the landowner's user rights are potentially cut back by a plethora of regulatory controls' (Gray (2002) at 218). Accordingly, he observes that the tension between an absolutist and relativist view of ownership has in the modern age swung inevitably towards the relativist view where ownership is qualified by pressures of 'social accommodation, community-directed obligation and notions of reasonable user' (Gray (2002) at 221–2). A1-P1 personifies this balance.

**2.43**  The protection of possessions found in A1-P1 is found in the three limbs contained within its wording (*Sporrong and Lonnroth v Sweden* (1983)). First, there is a protection of the peaceful enjoyment of possessions. Secondly, there is the prohibition against the deprivation of possessions save in the public interest and then only in accordance with domestic law and the principles of international law. Thirdly, there is protection against arbitrary controls over possessions which must be justified in pursuit of the general interest. Although these three limbs are distinctly articulated in A1-P1, it is clear that they are connected. The second and third limbs, relating to deprivation and control respectively, are instances of interferences with the peaceful enjoyment of possessions comprised within the overarching first limb, and the Strasbourg Court will look first to see if there is a breach of the second and third limbs before considering (if necessary) whether the first limb is engaged (*James v UK* (1986)). Thus, a deprivation in the public interest or a control in the general interest will not constitute an unjustified infringement with the peaceful enjoyment of possessions under the first limb (*James v UK* (1986)). A violation based solely on the first limb is less common—but see *Sporrong and Lonnroth v Sweden* (1983).

## What is a Possession?

2.44   As A1-P1 protects existing possessions it is important to understand what constitutes a possession for these purposes. Possessions have an autonomous meaning in Strasbourg jurisprudence and thus are not constrained by domestic definitions (*Beyeler v Italy* (2001) but note *Ker v Optima Community Housing Association* (2013) at [36] per Patten LJ). The Strasbourg Court has adopted a wide meaning of possessions. Clearly, property estates and interests in land fall within the concept as do other accepted categories of property rights that fall outside the scope of this book, including personal and intellectual property rights as well as choses in action arising from a contractual or tortious claim or from statutory entitlement. What is less clear is whether an expectation of the receipt of a possession in the future will constitute an A1-P1 possession. The strength in terms of enforceability of the expectation may provide a guide. For instance, an expectation of receipt of an inheritance will not qualify since a will or the rules of intestacy take effect from the testator's or the deceased's death (*Marckx v Belgium* (1979)). However, in the case of an expectation upon which a victim has relied to their detriment to support an estoppel, it might be argued that the victim enjoys an immediate, though inchoate, possession (see **Chapter 5**). There is even some support for the proposition that a legitimate expectation that cannot for some reason be met may constitute a possession (see *Stretch v UK* (2004) and *Pine Valley Developments Ltd v Ireland* (1992) followed in *Rowland v Environment Agency* (2003) but note *Ker v Optima Community Housing Association* (2013)).

2.45   In this book we explore the content of proprietary estates and interests which we need to bear in mind when determining what constitutes a possession in land. For instance, we will see that a leasehold estate must be held for a term certain and thus a limitation which defines that certainty will be an inherent part of a lease possession rather than a deprivation or control. Likewise, an existing covenant, easement, or other interest to which a freehold or leasehold estate is subject will define the possession rather than constitute an external interference or control. The following three cases illustrate this insight into the nature of land as a possession.

*Sims v Dacorum BC* **(2015):** Mr and Mrs Sims jointly held a periodic tenancy of their home from Dacorum BC. Their marriage broke up and Mrs Sims, in order to obtain alternative social housing, served a notice terminating the joint tenancy leaving Mr Sims a trespasser. He was subsequently evicted by Dacorum. Mrs Sims was entitled to bring the tenancy to an end without the knowledge or consent of Mr Sims by virtue of a term in the tenancy agreement or alternatively was entitled to rely on the common law rule in *Hammersmith &*

*Fulham LBC v Monk* (1992). The Supreme Court found no interference with Mr Sims' possessions represented by his joint tenancy which they held was inherently defined by the right of his wife to unilaterally bring the joint tenancy to an end.

---

***Aston Cantlow and Wilmcote with Billesley PCC v Wallbank* (2004):** Mr and Mrs Wallbank owned Glebe Farm which was subject to an ancient, and generally little enforced, liability to contribute to the costs of repair to their local church. This liability had been imposed because land on which Glebe Farm was built had once belonged to the church. Pursuant to this chancel repair obligation, the Wallbanks were required to pay a little over £95,000. They objected on the grounds that this chancel repair liability was an unjustified control over their possessions contrary to A1-P1 but the House of Lords disagreed. They held that this liability was part and parcel of their ownership of Glebe Farm—it defined their possessions.

---

***Horsham Properties Group Ltd v Clark* (2009):** The Clarks had bought their property with the help of a mortgage but they had fallen into arrears. Their mortgagees, through receivers they had appointed, sold the property which, by the terms of their mortgage, they were entitled to do without having to go to court. The Clarks tried to argue that their rights under A1-P1 had been infringed but the court decided that their mortgagee's powers were part of the mortgage itself to which the Clarks had agreed.

---

**2.46**  A different view may be taken if a new burden upon existing ownership is created—or, rather, imposed. Thus, a burden or adverse right which arises by independent acquisition—rather than dependent acquisition to which the grantor has agreed—could constitute an interference with the rights protected by A1-P1. There are two prominent forms of independent acquisition. First, there is adverse possession by which a squatter may acquire freehold ownership which we consider in **Chapter 4**. The Grand Chamber of the Strasbourg Court has held that adverse possession is an interference of A1-P1 but an interference which, subject to certain controls, may be justified (*JA Pye (Oxford) Ltd v UK* (2008)). Secondly, there is prescription by which a person's use of the land of another for a limited purpose without the owner's consent may create a presumed easement—see **Chapter 8**. Its human right compatibility has not yet been tested but is likely to be found to be justified in the public interest.

**2.47**  If we look at the other side of the coin, a right appurtenant to an estate in land is not generally viewed as a separate possession but it forms part of the possession to which it is attached (*Antoniades v UK* (1990)). For example, an easement or right to the benefit of a covenant forms part of the dominant land, and the rent and other covenants that a tenant gives in a lease are not a separate possession but form part of the landlord's reversionary estate. Likewise, the covenants that a landlord gives are an indivisible part of the tenant's leasehold estate.

**2.48**  The inherent definitional articulation of a property estate or interest is thought to stop short of encompassing the effect of the legal rules that regulate the enjoyment of that possession as opposed to shaping its content. Goymour suggests that to find otherwise would strip A1-P1 of any meaning (Goymour (2006)). For instance, to say that land ownership is inherently defined by the legislative rules which enable a state to compulsorily acquire land in the public interest, would strike at the very heart of the peaceful enjoyment of possessions with which the Article is directly concerned and there has certainly been no suggestion that this is the case.

## When is A1-P1 Engaged?

**2.49**  To answer this question we need to look more closely at the three limbs within the Article. Following the approach of the Strasbourg Court, we will look initially at the second limb (deprivation of possessions) and third limb (controls over possessions) as examples of interferences with the peaceful enjoyment of possessions, before looking briefly at this overarching first limb.

**2.50**  A deprivation of possessions generally encompasses a transfer or shift in ownership. Examples include the compulsory acquisition of land (*Howard v UK* (1987)), the nationalization of an industry or business (*Lithgow v UK* (1986)), or the confiscation of the proceeds of crime (*R v May* (2008), *R v Waya* (2013), *R v Ahmad* (2014)). Often the transfer is to the state or a state agency but it need not be so. It may be to another private individual where the deprivation is sanctioned by legislation (see eg *James v UK* (1986)).

**2.51**  We have to be careful, however, in distinguishing what might appear to be a termination, disposal, or transfer of ownership and the inherent nature of the possession itself. We have noted already that a lease as a possession is defined by the term for which it is granted—see **2.45**. A fixed term tenant is not deprived of his or her lease when the term expires nor will a periodic tenant be deprived of his or her lease when a notice is served bringing the lease to an end. Likewise, a right of re-entry leading to forfeiture of the lease is conferred upon the landlord as an express term of the lease (*Di Palma v UK* (1986)). A more difficult question is whether a power of sale conferred upon a trustee or mortgagee is a deprivation or control rather than part of the content of the trust or mortgage itself. Goymour suggests that the answer may depend on whether the power of sale is expressly agreed, and thus defines the possession, or is implied by statute and thus statutorily imposed (Goymour (2011) at 281–4). However, the High Court in *Horsham Properties Group Ltd v Clark* (2009) drew no distinction between an expressly conferred and statutorily implied power of sale. It drew comfort from the fact that section 101 of the Law of Property Act 1925 was conceived as a word-saving default rule reflecting the commonly agreed express mortgage terms.

**2.52**  We have already noted that controls over property are numerous and, it seems, ever increasing. Planning controls dictate how an owner can develop their land which may be further constrained where a property is of architectural importance or lies within a conservation area. A landowner may be required to allow public access to his or her land under the Countryside and Rights of Way Act 2000 or be under an obligation to conserve land because of its ecological and environmental importance. Controls may not just be public in nature but affect the relations of private individuals. For instance, rent control and security of tenure legislation may dictate when landlords can recover possession from their tenants and how much they can charge by way of rent. Indeed, throughout this book we explore controls over land ownership and land use.

2.53   A difficult question arises in distinguishing between a control and deprivation of possessions. Although both are the subject of A1-P1, the distinction is of import when we come to consider the proportionality of these interferences because compensation is generally required to justify a deprivation of a possession. On the one hand, what might appear at first sight to be a deprivation may be construed as a control of possessions whilst, on the other hand, a control of possessions may be so invasive as to amount to a de facto deprivation.

2.54   A particularly pointed example of the former boundary is found in the case of adverse possession when the Grand Chamber of the Strasbourg Court decided in *JA Pye (Oxford) Ltd v UK* (2008) that the extinction of the paper owner's title resulting from adverse possession was a control of possessions rather than a deprivation (see **Chapter 4**). The Grand Chamber decided (in effect) that the Limitation Act 1980, in extinguishing the landowner's title, and the consequent provisions of the Land Registration Act 1925 were administrative measures to bring the legal evidence of land ownership into line with the de facto possession of the land by a squatter who could no longer be evicted and had thus acquired their own title.

2.55   The point at which a regulatory control becomes so invasive that it constitutes a de facto deprivation is notoriously difficult to identify (see Gray (2002)). Various formulations have been advanced. For instance, in *Fredin v Sweden* ((1991) at [45]) the Strasbourg Court talked of the control needing to deprive the owner of 'all meaningful use of the properties in question' and in *Baner v Sweden* ((1989) at [5]) they drew a distinction between controls which redefined the content of the property right as opposed to expropriation of the substance of the property right. Whilst in *Matos e Silva, LDA and others v Portugal* ((1997) at [85]), the Strasbourg Court declined to find a de facto deprivation where 'all reasonable manner of exploiting the property had not disappeared'. Thus, although a control may deprive owners of the freedom to use their land as they might wish, it should not amount to a deprivation within the second limb if they are able to derive some remaining utility from the land.

2.56   An interference which does not fall within the second and third limbs as a deprivation or control may nevertheless be an interference with the peaceful enjoyment of possessions.

*Sporrong and Lonnroth v Sweden* (1983): The victims owned land which was earmarked for development and the authorities issued expropriation notices. However, these notices were never enforced but the victims' ability to deal with their land was so blighted that the court held that the notices constituted an unjustified interference with the peaceful enjoyment of their possessions.

In accordance with its overarching character, the first limb also exerts an influence against which a deprivation or control is measured (see *Matos e Silva, LDA and others v Portugal* (1997), *Chassagnou v France* (2000)).

## When is an Interference Justified?

**2.57**   We need to apply the justification formula that we examined in **2.11–2.23** in determining whether the interference is in accordance with the law and fulfils a legitimate aim as defined by the Article which is nevertheless proportionate in striking a fair balance.

**2.58**   The interference must be sanctioned by domestic law (*R&L, SRO and others v The Czech Republic* ((2014)). The domestic law must also meet the fundamental requirements of the rule of law and should be certain, accessible, foreseeable, and provide adequate procedural safeguards to enable the victim to question the compatibility of the measure. An example of a violation on this basis is found in the following case.

> ***Hentrich v France* (1994):** Mrs Hentrich bought a property in Strasbourg. It was alleged by the tax authorities that the price she declared she had paid for the land was inaccurate to evade the payment of tax—it seemed very low. The tax authorities exercised their right of pre-emption to force Mrs Hentrich to sell the property to them for the declared price with an uplift of 10 per cent and the costs of the purchase. Mrs Hentrich claimed that this action deprived her of her possessions in breach of A1-P1. The Strasbourg Court agreed because the manner in which the right of pre-emption had been exercised failed to satisfy the requirements of lawfulness and proportionality. The right of pre-emption as applied in Mrs Hentrich's case was unlawful because, although it served the aim of combating tax evasion, it had been applied in an arbitrary and selective manner and, furthermore, Mrs Hentrich was afforded no opportunity to challenge the tax authority's action, including their estimation of the value of the property.

**2.59**   The legitimate aims of an infringement are stated in the terms of A1-P1; namely, that a deprivation of possessions should be 'in the public interest' and a control of possessions should be 'in accordance with the general interest or to secure the payment of taxes and other contributions or penalties'. There is not thought to be any distinction between the public and general interest and it is clear that under A1-P1 states enjoy a wide margin of appreciation in deciding what is in the public or general interest and in formulating measures to address that interest. A state's decisions will be respected unless they are 'manifestly without reasonable foundation' in the sense that no reasonable government would have come to a similar decision in the circumstances (*James v UK* (1986)).

**2.60**   The transition of states in Eastern Europe from communist regimes, with widespread state-owned and regulated housing, to democratic states, in which market forces predominate, has necessitated fundamental reform of their property rules. These dramatic changes have triggered a number of complaints from property owners and tenants alike in the rebalancing of housing policy through reform of rent control and security of tenure measures. In considering these complaints, the Strasbourg Court has emphasized the wide margin of appreciation that states enjoy in managing this challenging transition (see *Hutten-Czapska v Poland* (2007), *Bitto v Slovakia* (2014), *Berger-Krall v Slovenia* (2014), *Statileo v Croatia* (2014)). Similar rent control and security of tenure legislation has also been challenged in other jurisdictions where, again, the object of these measures has been found to fall within the state's margin of appreciation (*Lindheim v Norway* (2015), *Gauci v Malta* (2011), *Aquilina v Malta* (2015)). Indeed, it is rare given the wide test of 'manifestly without reasonable foundation' for an interference not to fall within a state's margin of appreciation. The real focus is generally upon the proportionality of the interference.

2.61  In assessing proportionality the courts will need to decide whether a fair balance has been struck between the public or general interest to be advanced and the individual's A1-P1 rights. For instance, in *Hutten-Czapska v Poland* (2007), although the housing legislation in issue was found to be within the Polish state's margin of appreciation, the Grand Chamber decided that it did not strike a fair balance in the difficult task of protecting the property rights of landlords whilst affording tenants adequate residential security. It found that the legislation, in trying to transform the country's housing supply, placed a disproportionate burden on landlords who could not repossess their property or recover a fair return on their property investment.

2.62  There is a recognition that targeted regulation in seeking to advance the public or general interest may benefit the community of which the victim forms part. This indirect benefit may offset to a degree the burden placed upon the individual victim. Thus, there is increasingly evident an element of social obligation inherent in land ownership, for instance within planning controls or conservation regulation, that a landowner is expected to shoulder (see eg *Fredin v Sweden* (1991), *Pine Valley Developments v Ireland* (1991), *Matos e Silva, LDA and others v Portugal* (1997)). The balance is tipped where the individual victim is called upon to bear too onerous a burden. Although all the circumstances must be taken into account in determining proportionality, particularly prominent in this inquiry are two issues: first, the availability of compensation and, secondly, the adequacy of procedural safeguards enabling the victim to question the proportionality of the interference.

2.63  A1-P1 does not expressly include a right to fair compensation but it is clear that where the interference constitutes a deprivation of possessions under the second limb of the Article the payment of compensation is expected in order to assure proportionality (see eg *Holy Monasteries v Greece* (1995), *The former King of Greece v Greece* (2001), *Mago v Bosnia and Herzegovina* (2012)). Only in exceptional circumstances will the absence of compensation be justified (*James v UK* (1986)). It is not just the fact of compensation that is significant but also its amount. Although fair market value is a guide, it is not guaranteed. Below market compensation may be justified where the public or general interest to be advanced by the interference seeks to achieve a rebalancing of economic interests or greater social justice (*James v UK* (1986)).

2.64   The payment of compensation is not so important in the proportionality of control of possessions under the third limb (*JA Pye (Oxford) Ltd v Pye* (2008)). The question of whether or not an interference is a deprivation or control of possessions is thus an important distinction that can be difficult to rationalize (see Gray (2002)). The lack of compensation can lead to greater scrutiny of other factors within the proportionality inquiry, in particular the weight of the public or general interest and the procedural safeguards available to the victim (*JA Pye (Oxford) Ltd v Pye* (2008)).

2.65   The process by which a person is deprived of his or her possessions or by which controls over possession are imposed is an important aspect of proportionality. A person should be afforded an opportunity to question the interference and its proportionality before an independent body. *Zehentner v Austria* (2011) provides an example of this concern. The fact that Ms Zehentner was unable to participate in the judicial enforcement proceedings which led to the sale of her home, because of her incapacity coupled with the relative small debts that this sale recouped, was significant in the finding of incompatibility. The process by which a dispossession or control is effected should also be relatively expeditious so that a landowner is not left in a state of uncertainty as to his or her position (*Matos e Silva, LDA and others v Portugal* (1997), *Sporrong and Lonnroth v Sweden* (1983)).

## Article 8

2.66   Article 8(1) guarantees a right to respect for an individual's private and family life, his or her home, and correspondence. This guarantee is not absolute but may be infringed in pursuit of the legitimate aims set out in Article 8(2), namely 'the interests of national security, public safety or the economic well-being of the country, for the prevention of disorder and crime, for the protection of health or morals, or the protection of the rights and freedoms of others'.

2.67   The ambit of the Article is thus wide and the range of circumstances in which Article 8 has been employed is correspondingly diverse, from defences to deportation to claims to adequate social care. Our focus will, however, be upon the right that the Article affords to respect for the home given the obvious connection between the physical manifestation of home as a shelter and the land upon which it is built. At the outset, it should be noted that Article 8 does not confer a right to a home nor does it impose upon a state a general positive duty to meet an individual's housing needs given the resource implications such a guarantee would involve (*Chapman v UK* (2001)). There is some recognition that a state may owe a limited positive duty to facilitate the family life of particularly vulnerable victims, including assistance in securing suitable accommodation (*Marzari v Italy* (1999), *Yordanova v Bulgaria*

(2012)), but the focus of our attention is upon the negative protection afforded to an individual's existing home.

## When is Article 8 Engaged?

2.68    Home has an autonomous meaning within Strasbourg jurisprudence as a place of residence with which an individual has 'sufficient and continuing links' (*Gillow v UK* (1989), *Buckley v UK* (1997)). This test has been consistently applied both in cases before the Strasbourg Court and by our own domestic courts. The important point to note is that this test is not dependent on the victim having a legal right to occupy and it is this absence which forms the basis for the challenge that Article 8 presents to established property rules—particularly in the context of possession proceedings which have traditionally been determined according to who has a better legal right to possession. The disconnect with property rights thus admits the possibility that those whose legal right to possession has been lost, or indeed those who never had a legal right to possession, may claim to have a home and enjoy the guarantees afforded by the Article. For instance, a tenant whose tenancy has been terminated or a family member who never enjoyed or acquired a legal right to possession, may nevertheless have a home within the meaning of Article 8 (Nield and Hopkins (2013)). The significance of property rights falls to be considered when examining if an infringement with respect for the home is justified under Article 8(2) which expressly gives weight to the 'rights and freedoms of others'.

2.69    The nature of 'sufficient and continuing links' is not easy to pin down (Buyse (2006)). They connote an emotional and psychological attachment to a physical space. In *Connors v UK* (2005) the Strasbourg Court described the links as: 'Rights of central importance to the individual's identity, self-determination, physical and mental integrity, maintenance of relationships and a settled place within the community.' These concepts resonate with the home values explained by Lorna Fox O'Mahony within the concepts of home as identity (reflecting one's personality and sense of self), territory (as a private place to express oneself and find sanctuary), and a social and cultural expression (as an expression of status and place within the community)—see Fox (2006).

2.70    A more definitive description has not developed largely because sufficient and continuing links are easily found. Actual occupation of a residence for a period of time will be the norm, although absence may not be fatal if merely periodic or temporary (compare *Gillow v UK* (1989) and *Zabor v Poland* (2014)). It is only on the odd occasion when there is just fleeting occupation that 'sufficient and continuing links' have not been forged (*Manchester Ship Canal Developments v Persons Unknown* (2014)—short occupation by protestors, *Leeds CC v Price* (2006)—occupation for a few days, *O'Rourke v UK* (2001)—occupation of a hotel room for less than a month).

2.71    The right guaranteed by Article 8 is respect for the home. Respect has wide connotations and may encompass negative protection against direct state interference from, for instance, police powers of entry and search (*McLeod v UK* (1998), *Keegan v UK* (2007)), compulsory purchase (*Howard v UK* (1987)), and planning and residency controls

(*Buckley v UK* (1997), *Gillow v UK* (1989)). In these latter contexts, an infringement may be combined with the infringement of peaceful enjoyment of possession under A1-P1 when the victim has a proprietary interest in the home.

**2.72** In addition, Article 8 may give rise to a positive obligation for a state to ensure that a private individual or body has respect for a person's home. Here we find intermediate horizontal effect. For example, states have been found to owe a duty to prevent individuals committing anti-social behaviour (*Moreno Gomez v Spain* (2005), *Oluic v Croatia* (2010)) or domestic violence (*Case of B v Moldova* (2013), *Eremia v Moldova* (2014)) and companies committing environmental pollution (eg Heathrow and Gatwick airports in *Powell and Rayner v UK* (1990) and *Hatton v UK* (2003)), large construction projects (eg road construction in *Khatun v UK* (1998)), or industrial undertakings (eg a chemical plant in *Lopez Ostra v Spain* (1995)).

**2.73** Although respect under Article 8 is a nuanced concept which recognizes varying degrees of interference, we will concentrate upon the interference presented by repossession of the home; both because repossession presents the clearest interface with property rights and repossession is recognized as one of the most obvious and serious interferences with respect for the home (*Connors v UK* (2005), *McCann v UK* (2008), *Kay v UK* (2012)). In this respect, an imminent threat of repossession, rather than the immediate act of repossession, is sufficient but the loss of a right to possession leaving the occupier a trespasser may not be a sufficiently proximate threat (*Cosic v Croatia* (2011), *Sims v Dacorum BC* (2015)).

## When is Repossession Justified?

**2.74** We again need to apply the justification formula examined in **2.11–2.23**. The grounds for repossession must be sanctioned by law and be in pursuit of one of the legitimate aims set out in Article 8(2). In the context of repossession, the common legitimate aims are 'the economic well-being of the country' and the 'protection of the rights and freedoms of others'. Article 8(2) further requires that these aims are necessary 'in a democratic society' which is generally taken to require that the grounds of repossession address a pressing social need.

**2.75** A pressing social need is without doubt the provision of adequate housing in the formulation of which states will enjoy a margin of appreciation. The Strasbourg Court in a number of appeals from UK repossession cases has articulated the nature of states' margin of appreciation and its interface with proportionality (see *Connors v UK* (2005), *McCann v UK* (2008), *Kay v UK* (2012)). There is also considerable case law from other jurisdictions which adopt this common approach. The Strasbourg Court acknowledges that generally states enjoy a wide margin of appreciation in spheres such as housing, which play an important role in welfare and economic policy, and that a state's judgment in articulating that policy in the light of local conditions will be respected. However, it has stated, given the inherently personal nature of the rights protected by Article 8, that the scope of the margin of appreciation under Article 8 will depend on the context and may be narrower depending on 'the extent of the intrusion into the personal sphere of the victim' (*Connors v UK* (2005)). Given that repossession is one of the most serious interferences with respect for the home, it is no surprise to find that the Strasbourg Court has been clear and consistent in its demand for states to observe certain safeguards in formulating rights to repossession of the home. In so doing, they have signified that 'a home' as a physical asset is distinct from other land and deserving of protective treatment that calls for a consideration of proportionality.

2.76    The Strasbourg Court's attention is directed at the procedural safeguards afforded to the home occupier. It has consistently held that:

> Any person at risk of an interference of this magnitude [ie loss of home] should in principle be able to have the proportionality of the measure determined by an independent tribunal in the light of the relevant principles under Article 8 of the Convention notwithstanding that, under domestic law, his right to occupation has come to an end. (Kay v UK *(2012).)*

It took a little time for our domestic courts to hear and accept this message (see *Harrow LBC v Qazi* (2004), *Connors v UK* (2005), *Kay v Lambeth LBC* (2006), *McCann v UK* (2008), *Doherty v Birmingham CC* (2008), *Kay v UK* (2012) discussed in Nield (2011) and Goymour (2011)). However, after a lengthy dialogue they finally did so in the leading case of *Manchester CC v Pinnock* (2010) which was closely followed in the conjoined decisions in *Hounslow LBC v Powell; Birmingham v Frisby; Leeds CC v Hall; Salford CC v Mullen* (2011).

2.77    It is important to note that the Supreme Court's acceptance in *Pinnock* of the need for an independent tribunal to assess the proportionality of an eviction was expressly limited to possession proceedings brought by a public authority—the vertical effect of the HRA 1998. Subsequently, in *McDonald v McDonald* the Supreme Court rejected the horizontal application of such safeguards in possession proceedings brought by a private landlord when it is necessary to balance the A1-P1 rights of the landlord and the Article 8 rights of the tenant. The decision is to be appealed to the Strasbourg Court and thus we must wait and see if the Strasbourg Court agrees.

*McDonald v McDonald* **(2016):** Mr and Mrs McDonald in trying to secure permanent accommodation for their mentally vulnerable daughter, Fiona, bought a house with a mortgage from Capital Homes Ltd. They rented the home to Fiona and used her housing benefit to meet the mortgage instalments. Unfortunately, Mr and Mrs McDonald fell into arrears and Capital Homes appointed a receiver who, acting as agent for Mr and Mrs McDonald, gave notice to end Fiona's tenancy and applied for possession upon a mandatory ground—namely, section 21 of the Housing Act 1988. This ground afforded the court no discretion as to whether or not to grant the possession order once they were satisfied that the necessary termination notice had been served. Fiona argued that despite this mandatory ground for possession the court, in pursuance of their duties under section 6 of the HRA 1998, were required to consider the proportionality of the possession order evicting her from her home. In the light of expert evidence of the likely effect of the eviction on her mental state, she argued that making an order would be disproportionate and thus a violation of respect for her home under Article 8. The Supreme Court disagreed.

**2.78** The Supreme Court in *McDonald* was not convinced that there was clear and consistent Strasbourg case law calling for a proportionality review in possession proceedings by a private landlord or owner. Instead, they looked to the parties' contractual tenancy relationship as regulated by section 21 of the Housing Act 1988—the clear policy of which was to remove security of tenure to encourage private landlords to enter the private rental market. They thus refused to conduct a proportionality review pursuant to their duties under section 6 of the HRA 1998. They said:

> It is not open to the tenant to contend that article 8 could justify a different order from that which is mandated by the contractual relationship between the parties, at least where, as here, there are legislative provisions which the democratically elected legislature has decided properly balance the competing interests of private sector landlords and residential tenants. (At [40].)

Nor would they have done so if required to interpret the compatibility of section 21 of the Housing Act 1988 pursuant to section 3 of the HRA 1998.

**2.79** The Supreme Court's judgment in *McDonald* was directed at the private relationship between landlords and tenants under a particular form of statutory regulated tenancy predominant in the private rental sector—the assured shorthold tenancy. However, the judgment must have implications for other forms of private property relationships relating to the home where repossession is in issue; for instance, when a mortgagee seeks possession against a mortgagee. It is evident that the Supreme Court will be most reluctant to allow Article 8 to trigger a change in established property rules, particularly when those rules have been the subject of recent and considered review by Parliament. We will see in **Chapter 8** that that has not been the case in relation to the mortgage relationship, although current regulatory and legislative policy reflects some elements of proportionality in allowing the home owner time to pay. The possible influence of Article 8 thus cannot be ruled out.

## Proportionality in Home Repossession

**2.80** We have noted the requirements of proportionality in striking a fair balance between the legitimate aim and the impact of an interference upon an individual victim's Convention rights. Where rights to possession are in issue, the legitimate aim is generally to protect the rights of the landowner. In the case of a social landlord, the legitimate aim is also the discharge of its role in the management of social housing; for instance, in allocating scare resources or controlling the anti-social behaviour of tenants of social housing for the benefit of other tenants or the wider community (see *Manchester CC v Pinnock* (2010), *Hounslow*

*LBC v Powell* (2011)). The call for procedural safeguards looks both to evaluate the proportionality of the legal rules governing such rights to possession and also the impact of those rules upon the particular occupier having regard to his or her particular circumstances. In this context, therefore, proportionality operates at two levels of intensity.

2.81    Whilst our highest courts were content to accept that the proportionality of the law was a legitimate object of scrutiny (see *Kay v Lambeth LBC* (2006), *Doherty v Birmingham CC* (2008)), they were more reluctant to accept the need for proportionality in the impact of those rules upon the occupier's individual circumstances. The Supreme Court finally did so in *Manchester CC v Pinnock* (2010). Their reluctance springs from the fact that to do so acknowledges that Article 8 gives rise to a human rights protection of the home beyond the realm of domestic property rights. This so-called 'human property right' requires a right to possession of a home to be proportionally exercised in the light of the individual occupier's personal circumstances with an independent tribunal making the necessary judgment as to proportionality (see Bright (2013) and Nield (2013a)). However, following the Supreme Court's decision in *McDonald*, this 'human property right' is largely enjoyed only by social housing tenants rather than having wider horizontal effect. Should the Strasbourg Court come to a different conclusion to the Supreme Court when it hears the appeal in *McDonald*, its decision could recognize this 'human property right' for all home occupiers.

2.82    The Supreme Court has been at pains to keep this 'human property right' within very strict bounds. Although Lord Neuberger in *Pinnock* disliked use of the term, varying degrees of the word 'exceptional' have been used to describe the likelihood of a disproportionate outcome and, indeed, there are very few reported cases in which an Article 8-based claim has been upheld. One reported case is:

---

**Southend-on-Sea BC v Armour (2014):** A local authority sought to repossess the home of Mr Armour on the grounds of his anti-social behaviour. Mr Armour suffered from Asperger's syndrome and depression and had been disruptive. However, he had managed to satisfactorily control his behaviour for over a year before the repossession hearing. In the light of Mr Armour's improved behaviour, the judge decided that it would be disproportionate to evict him—a decision the Court of Appeal refused to overturn.

---

2.83    A disproportionate result is more likely where the occupier is particularly vulnerable; for instance, because of old age, physical or mental disability, ill health, or because he or she is part of a minority cultural community whose way of life places them at some disadvantage and thus particularly adversely affected by eviction and subsequent homelessness. The Roma or traveller community is one such cultural group. This reflects the growing trend in Strasbourg jurisprudence to recognize a positive duty upon states to protect the vulnerable (see Peroni and Timmer (2013) and *Connors v UK* (2005), *Bjedov v Croatia* (2012), *Yordanova v Bulgaria* (2012), *Winterstein v France* (2013)). Lord Neuberger in *Pinnock* acknowledged that such vulnerability will weigh in the proportionality balance and, in *Armour*, the mental ill health of Mr Armour was a factor.

2.84   In contrast, distressing circumstances that are not associated with, and would not be exacerbated by, the eviction will not be relevant (*Corby BC v Scott* (2012)). The circumstances also need to go beyond the norm. For instance, in *Thurrock BC v West* (2013) the plight of a young family with children who faced homelessness after their eviction from a home they never had a right to occupy, was not disproportionate. Other relevant factors include the availability of other support, for instance the offer of alternative accommodation and the basis upon which the eviction is sought (see *Kay v Lambeth LBC* (2006) at [38] per Lord Bingham). In short, all the circumstances are relevant and Lord Bingham in *Kay v Lambeth LBC* (at [38]) suggested that the judgment of proportionality should be left to the experience of the county court judges, who usually hear possession proceedings affecting the home.

2.85   It must also be borne in mind that proportionality does not necessarily call for a refusal to make a possession order at all. Such a response looks dangerously close to recognizing a right to a home since, by refusing to allow a landlord to evict, that landlord will be required to allow the tenant to remain in their home. Accordingly, those circumstances are likely to be rare indeed (*Pinnock* (2010) and *McDonald* (2016)). Proportionality is more likely to be achieved by merely giving the occupier time to find alternative accommodation or suspending the possession order until some future event, for instance the victim's recovery from an illness (see eg Housing Act 1988, s 89).

## Procedural Safeguards

2.86   A disproportionate eviction may be rare but the implications of proportionality may be far-reaching because of the need for a process to determine proportionality. The Strasbourg Court has emphasized the importance of procedural safeguards as a critical element of the margin of appreciation when states formulate the legal framework conferring a right to possession (see *Connors v UK* (2005), *Zehentner v Austria* (2011), *McCann v UK* (2008), *Kay v UK* (2012)). An evaluation of proportionality calls for both a judicial process before an independent tribunal and sufficient discretion within the jurisdiction of that tribunal to be able to consider proportionality. Legal frameworks which confer a mandatory right to possession are problematic. Here the occupier has no defence to the claim for possession and the court no, or very limited, discretion to refuse or delay an order for possession—let alone consider proportionality.

2.87   Most possession proceedings against secure tenants of a social housing are not mandatory but allow a court to consider proportionality both through the requirement for a court order for possession of a dwelling house in the Protection from Eviction Act 1977 (s 3) and in the statutory discretion of the court to consider the reasonableness of the eviction (Housing Act 1985, s 84). The leading cases of *Pinnock, Powell, Sims*, and *McDonald* were problematic because they all concerned mandatory rights to possession enjoyed by a landlord against a tenant. In the public sector tenancies at issue in *Pinnock, Powell*, and *Sims*, the Supreme Court read in to the relevant legal rules a discretion for a court to consider the proportionality of the eviction, in pursuance of their duties under sections 3 and 6 of the HRA 1998. However, in the private sector tenancy case of *McDonald*, the Supreme Court indicated that, if they had thought that proportionality was required, they would have issued a declaration of incompatibility under section 4 of the HRA 1998 rather than reinterpreted the statutory rules.

**2.88**  Mandatory rights to possession are also in issue where the victim does not have a right to occupy, for instance because they are squatters. They remain trespassers until, through the rules governing adverse possession, they acquire a legal right to possess. In *Yordanova v Bulgaria* (2013) and *Winterstein v France* (2013) the Strasbourg Court found a breach of Article 8 following the eviction by state authorities of squatters. Both cases concerned Roma gypsies and travellers who had unlawfully occupied the land for many years. The unlawfulness of their occupation was no bar to the engagement of Article 8 nor an automatic justification for eviction. Their eviction should also be proportionate. Given that the victims were a vulnerable community whose distinct culture and way of life had led to discrimination, the states had a positive duty to facilitate their way of life, for instance by demonstrating that they had tried to provide acceptable alternative living arrangements particularly for those members of the community most at risk including the young, old, and sick.

**2.89**  These decisions throw some doubt upon the human rights compatibility of the summary process for the eviction of squatters established by *McPhail v Persons Unknown* (1973) because the court has no discretion to consider proportionality. The House of Lords offered differing obiter dicta comments on this question in *Kay v Lambeth LBC* (2006) and subsequently Sir Alan Ward in *Malik v Fassenfelt* (2013) provided a dissenting critique of the rule, although again as obiter. It is evident that after *McDonald* (2016) a proportionality defence is likely only to be available when the landowner is a public authority and even then the unlawfulness of the occupation will be a very weighty factor. The likelihood of an eviction of a squatter being found disproportionate is thus slim indeed (*Birmingham CC v Lloyd* (2012)).

**2.90**  The need for a process to assess proportionality of an eviction by a public authority is clear but what sort of process is adequate and where does the burden of proof lie? On this latter question the Supreme Court in *Pinnock* decided that in the normal course proportionality is to be presumed and it is for the occupier to raise the issue and to prove the circumstances that would render an immediate eviction disproportionate. This burden will be reversed if the proportionality of an eviction must be established under the Equality Act 2010 because the occupier proves that their eviction is discriminatory. In these circumstances, a structured approach to proportionality is required (*Akerman-Livingstone v Aster Communities Ltd* (2015)).

**2.91**  The Strasbourg Court has stated that the proceedings themselves need to be sufficiently substantive for the courts to be able to thoroughly examine the relevant factors to evaluate proportionality. Establishing grounds for repossession, as well as their proper exercise and enforcement, may take a number of stages. For instance, within some regulatory frameworks a social landlord's decision to evict may be subject to an internal review which can subsequently be questioned by the courts whether within the scheme of the legislation or through judicial review. In these circumstances, the whole of the process is considered (*Manchester CC v Pinnock* (2010), *R (on the application of N v Lewisham LBC; R (on the application of H) v Newham LBC* (2014)). Once a possession order is made, it may need to be enforced where the occupier refuses to vacate their home. Proportionality should be raised (if at all) during the possession proceedings themselves since enforcement proceedings, in which the court is merely concerned to regulate the timing and execution of a possession order that has already been made, are inadequate (*Paulic v Croatia* (2010), *Buckland v UK* (2013)).

**2.92**  The adequacy of traditional judicial review upon *Wednesbury* grounds has been the subject of considerable conjecture given that the courts would have limited ability to investigate contested facts that are likely to be at issue within proportionality (see *Lambeth LBC v Kay* (2006), *Doherty v Birmingham CC* (2008), *Kay v UK* (2012)). However, in view of the demands of the HRA 1998, judicial review has undergone a period of evolution to accommodate the demands of a human rights-based challenge to a public authority's decision making. As a result, the indications are that a human rights-based judicial review of a local authority's decision to evict should now provide the adequate safeguards to accommodate proportionality (*Manchester CC v Pinnock* (2010), *R (on the application of N) v Lewisham LBC; R (on the application of H) v Newham LBC* (2014)).

## Article 14

**2.93**  The target of Article 14 is discrimination but it is not a free-standing protection against discrimination. The Equality Act 2010 provides domestic protection against discrimination. Article 14 is directed against discrimination in the enjoyment of other Convention rights. It is necessary for another Article to be engaged before Article 14 can be invoked where the justification operating under the host Article operates in a discriminatory fashion. It is thus parasitic in nature but can provide effective protection as illustrated by the following case:

> **Ghaidan v Godin-Mendoza (2004):** Mr Godin-Mendoza was in a homosexual relationship and lived with the tenant of a flat of which Mr Ghaidan was the landlord. After his partner's death, Mr Godin-Mendoza claimed to be entitled to succeed to a protected tenancy under Schedule 1 paragraph 2(2) to the Rent Act 1977. This provision entitles a person who lived with the tenant 'as his or her wife or husband' to succeed to the tenancy following the death of the tenant. Mr Godin-Mendoza asserted that the statutory provision acted discriminately against homosexual partners and was thus a breach of his right to respect for his home under Articles 8 and 14. The House of Lords upheld his claim and, in performance of their duty under section 3 of the HRA 1998, read into Schedule 1 paragraph 2(2) an extension of the right to succeed to a protected tenancy in favour of same-sex partners.

**2.94**  In *Ghaidan v Godin-Mendoza* Baroness Hale outlined the overlapping steps required to establish an unjustified infringement of Article 14. First, the facts must engage one or more Convention rights. Secondly, a difference in treatment in the protection afforded by the right must be established between the victim and other individuals in an analogous situation. Thirdly, the difference in treatment is objectively unjustified and, finally, the difference in treatment must be based upon one or more of the grounds set out in Article 14. Article 14 provides that the basis of prohibited discrimination are 'any ground such as sex, race, colour, language, religion, political or other opinion, national or social origin, association with a national minority, property, birth or other status'. Thus, although the grounds of discrimination are widely cast, they will generally relate to the personal status of the victim.

## Article 6

**2.95**  We have already seen that within A1-P1 and Article 8 there is a concern with procedural safeguards in the overall justification for a breach of the relevant Article. In addition, Article 6 requires due process in the determination of civil rights and obligations, including property rights and duties. This process calls for a timely, fair, and public hearing before an independent tribunal. The whole process is the subject of scrutiny under Article 6 so that an internal determination of a civil right is acceptable provided that the outcome may be appealed or reviewed by an independent tribunal; for instance, by judicial review where a decision made by a public authority is in question (*R (Alconbury Developments Ltd) v SS for Environment, Transport and the Regions* (2003)).

**2.96**  A civil right or obligation is an autonomous concept in Strasbourg jurisprudence and encompasses those rights and obligations that are in essence private rather than public. The line between private and public rights is not easy to draw and is not necessarily distinguished by the public character of one of the protagonists. For instance, planning controls and the compulsory purchase of land, although within the administrative control of a public body, are civil rights within the meaning of Article 6.

**2.97**  Article 6 has demanded a rethink of a number of traditional self-help remedies including both a landlord's rights to exercise distress for unclaimed rent and to peacefully re-enter premises without a court order to forfeit a lease. We will look at how these remedies have been tamed to comply with Article 6 in **Chapter 7**.

## The Impact of Human Rights

**2.98**  We started this chapter by noting that land lawyers cannot ignore human rights, but what difference do human rights make to how we view property rights? Allen suggests that there are two possible reactions to explicitly incorporating human rights into our property framework. First, that there is unlikely to be any change because human rights values are already embedded in our fundamental attitudes towards property.

Alternatively, human rights may have a greater impact by offering an explicit process by which property rights can be balanced between competing interests through the search for the proportionate achievement of a legitimate aim within the justification formula (see Allen (2005)).

2.99   It is clear that our domestic courts are keen to limit the impact of human rights upon private property rights. They wish to maintain the relative certainty of established rules and thus to resist the discretion and consequent uncertainty that proportionality entails (Howell (2007), Walsh (2015)). Furthermore, the courts have no appetite to scrutinize, and possibly upset, sensitive socio-economic policy beyond their proper constitutional remit. The implementation of policy through the law reform process is not, however, always seamless or logically. Property lawyers do not have the luxury of sweeping away what seem to be unsatisfactory rules well past their sell-by date. The law relating to property must be developed piecemeal and prospectively to avoid upsetting established rights and obligations. It is where anomalies and gaps occur within this evolutionary process that human rights may have most to offer and in the remainder of this book we will try and identify opportunities where human rights might provide an incentive for change.

2.100   Article 8 is the primary candidate as a game changer. Under pressure from Strasbourg, it requires us to rethink our approach to the protection of residential security within the home. It divorces home from property rights, raising the possibility of a human rights-based protection of the home derived from the occupier's connection to their home and their vulnerable status. Furthermore, this protection changes the dynamics of repossession from a positive vindication of property rights to a violation of the human right to respect for the home which must be objectively justified in meeting a pressing and proportionate social need. In so doing, home is afforded recognition as an asset of particular significance to the enjoyment of human values and dignity. The process demands of proportionality signal an inching away from clean-cut mandatory rules governing repossession (at least by a public authority) to admit the opportunity for the exercise of discretion to strike the necessary fair balance in the light of an individual's circumstances. Although it will be rare to find an Article 8-based protection, the required procedural safeguards inevitably shape the rules governing possession with a consequent impact upon the substantive content of proprietary interests themselves. We have seen this impact in relation to mandatory rights to possession by a public authority through the vertical effect of the HRA 1998. These emerging dynamics will be more far-reaching should private property relations be redrawn through horizontal effect. The signs are that our domestic courts are ready to repel such a challenge, and indeed they have done so in *McDonald*, but they may yet be required to rethink if Strasbourg takes a different view when hearing the appeal in this important case.

2.101   A1-P1 may be less dramatic in its impact. Indeed, Goymour noted that, at the time of her writing, no violation of this Article had been successfully upheld (Goymour (2011)). The influence of A1-P1 may rather lie in its interface between private rights and public interest and the explicit recognition of the social obligation inherent within property ownership (see Gray (2002)).

# FURTHER READING

Allen, T, *Property and the Human Rights Act 1998* (Oxford: Hart Publishing, 2005).

Bright, S, '*Manchester City Council v Pinnock* (2010)' in N Gravells (ed), *Landmark Cases in Land Law* (Oxford: Hart Publishing, 2013), ch 11.

Cowan, D, O'Mahony, L, and Cobb, C, *Great Debates in Property Law* (Basingstoke: Palgrave Macmillan, 2012), ch 8.

Goymour, A, 'Property & Housing' in D Hoffman (ed), *The Impact of the UK Human Rights Act 1998 on Private Law* (Cambridge: Cambridge University Press, 2011), ch 12.

Gray, K, 'Land Law and Human Rights' in L Tee (ed), *Land Law: Issues, Debates, Policy* (Cullompton: Willan, 2002), ch 7.

Nield, S, 'Article 8 Respect for the Home: A Human Property Right' (2013a) 24 KLJ 147.

Nield, S, 'Strasbourg Triggers Another Article 8 Debate' [2013b] Conv 148.

Nield, S, 'Thumbs Down to Horizontal Effect' [2016] Conv forthcoming.

Nield, S and Hopkins, N, 'Human Rights and Mortgage Repossession: Beyond Property Law Using Article 8' (2013) 33 LS 431.

# SELF-TEST QUESTIONS

1   When is an interference with the qualified human rights in A1-P1 and Article 8 proportionate?

2   What do we mean by vertical and horizontal effect?

3   How do A1-P1 and Article 8 respectively define 'possessions' and 'home'?

4   Why are mandatory rights to possession problematic in human rights terms?

5   Is there such a concept as a human property right?

# 3 Personal Rights and Property Rights

## SUMMARY

This chapter first considers property rights in land. Such rights form one of the key building blocks of land law. Their importance lies in the fact that, unlike personal rights, they can bind third parties. This chapter therefore focuses on the *content* question: does the type of right claimed by B count as a property right? To answer that question, we will need to distinguish between different types of property right. The most important distinction is between legal property rights, on the one hand, and equitable property rights, on the other. As we will see, this distinction is crucial not only when considering the content question, but also when looking at the acquisition and defences questions.

The chapter then goes on to explore personal rights that may allow a party to make a particular use of land. It focuses on licences to use land and contrasts their operation and effect with those of property rights in land. We will see that, whilst the distinction between property rights and personal rights may seem technical and abstract, it is in fact of great practical importance, and can, for example, determine the strength of a party's rights in his or her home.

Key topics explored in this chapter are:

- The distinction between personal rights and property rights (**3.1–3.15**)

- The structure of the Law of Property Act 1925 and the *numerus clausus* ('closed list') principle (**3.16–3.34**)

- The distinction between legal property rights and equitable property rights (**3.35–3.53**)

- The content of legal estates and legal interests in land (**3.54–3.59**)

- The content of equitable interests in land, including equitable interests under a trust (**3.60–3.68**)

- The nature of licences and the controversy over the status of the contractual licence: is it merely a personal right or should it count as a property right in land? (**3.69–3.91**)

# The Distinction Between Personal Rights and Property Rights

## The Basic Distinction

**3.1**   What is the difference between a personal right and property right? It might sound like the set-up to a joke, but the question in fact introduces the single most important point in land law. And failing to understand the answer is no laughing matter, as it often leads to failure in land law exams. The answer is that if B has a personal right against A, that right, by itself, binds only A. A personal right is a right against a specific person. If B instead has a property right, even if that right was acquired as a result of B's dealings with A, that right is capable of binding not only A, but also third parties, such as C. This is because a property right is not simply a right against a specific person, but is a right that relates to something independent of a specific person, such as some land (**1.24–1.27**).

**3.2**   We can see this point by returning briefly to the examples given at **1.15**:

> *Example 1*: A and B make a contract under which A will, for £20, mow B's lawn.
> *Example 2*: A sells A's lawnmower to B for £200.

In *Example 1*, B has only a personal right against A. The contract gives B a right, which consists of A's duty to B, and that duty is owed to B by A alone. If A, for example, were to sell A's lawnmower to C, B would have no right against C that C should now mow the lawn: the duty to mow B's lawn is owed only by A. In contrast, in *Example 2*, the sale transfers A's ownership of the mower to B. B thus has a property right: a right that relates to the mower itself, and so is independent of any specific person. So, whilst B's right was acquired from A, it is capable of binding not only A but also third parties.

**3.3**   As we noted at **1.17**, the distinction between personal rights and property rights is also important when considering B's position as against X. X is a party who, unlike C, does not acquire any rights from A, but instead interferes directly with the property. Consider a case where X carelessly damages the lawnmower. In Example 1, where A has simply made a contract with B to mow B's lawn, it is possible that X's careless action may cause B some loss: for example, it may mean that A cannot perform the contract with B. Nonetheless, B has no claim against X, as the loss caused to B is purely economic loss (see eg *Cattle v Stockton Waterworks Co* (1875)). In the second example, if the careless damage occurs after A has sold the lawnmower to B, and so at a point when B has ownership of the mower, B does have a claim in tort against X, as X has breached a duty owed to B not to carelessly damage the mower.

**3.4**  The distinction between personal rights and property rights is also of great practical importance in land law. We saw at **1.58–1.62** that, in *National Provincial Bank v Ainsworth* (1965), the House of Lords permitted the National Provincial Bank to remove Mrs Ainsworth from her home as her right in relation to the home was only a personal right against Mr Ainsworth, and so was not capable of binding the bank. At **1.63–1.70**, we contrasted that case with *Williams & Glyn's Bank v Boland* (1981): there, the House of Lords denied the bank an order for possession and so permitted Mrs Boland to remain in her home, at least temporarily. The crucial point was that, unlike Mrs Ainsworth, Mrs Boland's right counted as an equitable property right, and so was capable of binding not only her husband but also a third party, such as the bank, who had acquired a right from her husband. This shows that important practical consequences can turn on the seemingly technical question of whether a right is a personal right or a property right.

## Two Kinds of Third Party

**3.5**  The facts in each of *Ainsworth* and *Boland* fit in with a common pattern for land law disputes: one party, A (Mr Ainsworth/Mr Boland) owns some land; a second party, B (Mrs Ainsworth/Mrs Boland) deals with A, or with the land, and so acquires some sort of right; a third party, C (National Provincial Bank/Williams & Glyn's Bank) then acquires either ownership of the land, or some other right in the land (such as a security right) from A. It is crucial to know in such cases if the right B acquired from A is a personal right or a property right. The structure of such cases can usefully be represented in the diagram we first encountered at **1.16** (see **Figure 3.1**).

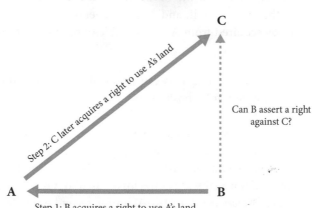

C

Step 2: C later acquires a right to use A's land

Can B assert a right against C?

A ⟵ B

Step 1: B acquires a right to use A's land

**Figure 3.1**  A common structure for land law cases

**3.6**  Disputes can also arise, however, where the third party, X, does not acquire any right from A, but instead simply interferes with the land, or with B's use of the land. The structure of such cases can be usefully represented in the diagram we first saw at **1.18** (see **Figure 3.2**).

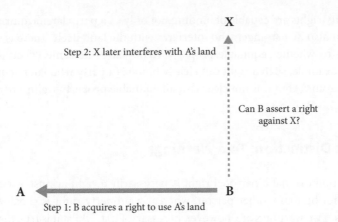

**Figure 3.2**   A second important structure for land law cases

**3.7**  In such cases, the distinction between personal rights and property rights is, again, crucial. This can be seen by considering the following case.

---

***Hill v Tupper* (1863):** The dispute concerned the hiring out of pleasure boats on the
Basingstoke Canal. The canal company (A), owners of the canal, gave Mr Hill (B), an 'exclusive' permission to hire boats out on the canal. Mr Tupper (X), who ran a pub on a bank of
the canal, then also started to hire out boats on the canal. The question was whether B could
prevent X from doing so, and obtain damages from X for the loss caused to B's business. The
Exchequer Chamber held that B's contract with A gave it only a personal right against A, and
not a property right in the land (the canal). This meant that, even though X's actions may
have interfered with B's business, B had no claim against X. Instead, B's only possible claim
was against A.

---

It is possible, of course, to have a property right to make a particular use of someone
else's land (a right of way is an example) but the content of the particular right claimed by
Hill meant that it did not, for example, meet the content requirements for an easement
(those requirements will be discussed in **Chapter 9**). Of course, if X was putting boats
on the canal without A's permission, then A, as owner of the canal, could sue X. If A had
given X such permission, or if A refused to sue X, B could then sue A for a breach of the
contract to give B an 'exclusive' licence; but B's only right was against A, not against X. In
a general sense, it could be said that X, in the absence of any permission from A, had no
right to put boats on the canal; but that does not mean that B can sue X, as to make such
a claim, B has to show that *B* (and not only A) has a right against X.

**3.8**  The decision in *Hill v Tupper* can be contrasted with a case such as *Star Energy v Bocardo*
(2010) (**1.82–1.83**). In that case, the claim of Bocardo (B) succeeded: B had a freehold,
a recognized property right in the land and, by drilling and extracting oil from beneath the surface of that land without B's permission, Star Energy (X) committed the
tort of trespass against B. It did not matter that X was a stranger: B was the registered
freehold owner of the land and so had a legal property right in the land. It is clear that

legal property rights are capable of binding not only C, a party later acquiring a right in the land, but also X, a stranger who interferes with the land itself. There is some doubt, however, as to whether equitable property rights have the same effect: as shown by *Boland*, for example, such a right can clearly bind C (a party who later acquires a right in the land from A) but it is not clear that all equitable property rights are also binding on X (**3.42–3.46**).

## The Basic Distinction: Two Warnings

**3.9**   The crucial point is that a personal right is necessarily a right against a specific person and so cannot bind any other person, whereas a property right is capable of binding third parties. Two warnings are, however, necessary. First, whilst it is true that a personal right cannot *in itself* bind a third party, this does not mean that B will necessarily lose against C or X in a case where B initially has only a personal right against A. This is because it may be possible for B to assert a *different* right directly against C or X.

**3.10**   For example, consider a case where A makes a contractual promise to mow B's lawn on a certain day for £20, and X then persuades A to breach that contract and instead mow X's lawn for £50. If it can be shown that X knew of the contract between A and B, and also knew that A's conduct would be a breach of it, and that there was no justification for X's action, X will be liable to B for the tort of procuring a breach of contract. In such a case, the existence of B's personal right against A does have *some* effect on X. Nonetheless, B is not directly asserting that personal right against X: B is not claiming that X is under any duty to mow the lawn. Rather, B is asserting a *different* right against X. Such a new, direct right arises as a result of X's conduct and is thus distinct from B's personal right against A. The possibility of asserting a new, direct right may, however, give B some limited protection against a third party even where B's initial right is only a personal right against A. That is the first warning: the fact that B has a personal right against A does not necessarily mean that B will lose against a third party (**3.83–3.86**). In general, however, it is very difficult for B to show that he or she has acquired such a new direct right: for example, no such right arises from the mere fact that C buys land knowing that B has a personal right against A in relation to the land, and intending to stop B exercising that right (see eg *Midland Bank Trust Co v Green* (1981): **11.6–11.7**).

**3.11**   The second warning is the converse of the first: the mere fact that B has a property right in land does not necessarily mean that B will win against a third party, even if B had that property right before the third party's involvement. This is because the third party may have a *defence* to B's pre-existing property right (**1.34–1.46**).

**3.12**   For example, we have drawn a contrast (**3.4**) between *National Provincial Bank v Ainsworth* (1965) and *Williams & Glyn's Bank v Boland* (1981): in the former case, B had only a personal right against A and so was not protected against C; in the latter, B had an equitable property right in the land and that right bound C. It is, however, also possible to draw a contrast between *Boland* and *City of London Building Society v Flegg* (1988) (**1.71–1.77**). Mr and Mrs Flegg, like Mrs Boland, had an equitable property right in the land before the charge in favour of the bank was created. As a result, their right was prima facie binding on the bank. This, however, is where the *defences* question comes in. The bank was able to show that it had a defence to the equitable property right of Mr and Mrs Flegg, and so was not bound by that right: in other words, the bank took priority. The particular defence used in that case, the overreaching defence, will be examined in detail elsewhere (11.70–11.89). Overreaching is simply one example of a defence, and the important point for present purposes is that the possibility of a defence means that it would be a mistake to think that a property right binds *all* third parties. It can rather be said that, if B has a property right in the land, whether it is a legal or equitable property right, it will be prima facie binding on C, a party later acquiring a right in the land. If B has a *legal* property right in the land, it will also be prima facie binding on X, a stranger later interfering with the land; the position regarding equitable property rights and strangers is not so clear (3.42–3.46).

## The Practical Importance of the Distinction

3.13  The two warnings just given do not undermine the basic distinction between personal rights and property rights. In land law, there is still a great advantage to B in showing that his or her right counts as a property right rather than as a personal right. It is true that, even if B has only a personal right against A, it may still be possible for B to show that he or she has a new, direct right against C or X. It is equally true that, even if B has a property right in the land, it may still be possible for C or X to show that he or she has a defence to B's right. The crucial difference, however, is that if B has only a personal right, it is for B to show that C or X has acted in such a way as to give B a new, direct right, and it will usually be *very* difficult for B to establish this. Whereas if B has a property right in the land, it is for C or X to show that he or she has a defence to B's pre-existing property right, and it will usually be difficult for C or X to establish that.

3.14  A good example of the practical importance of the distinction between personal rights and property rights is provided by the case of A's insolvency. If B has only a personal right against A, B usually has no special protection if A goes into insolvency, and so will, for example, have to settle for receiving only a proportion of any money due from A: by definition, A will have insufficient assets to meet all of the debts owed by A. In contrast, if B has a property right in land held by A, that right will be protected: A's insolvency officer, like any third party acquiring property from A, is prima facie bound by B's property right. This is why, for example, lenders (such as the banks and building societies in cases such as *Ainsworth, Boland,* or *Flegg*) often insist on acquiring a property right in A's land (such as a charge) to secure any debt owed by A. A personal right against A is only as good as A, and so depends on A's continued solvency; a property right, in contrast, is only as good as the property, but as land often holds its value well, and is very easy to find, a property right in land is often an excellent form of security.

3.15  The distinction between personal rights and property rights is important not only for lenders, but also for individuals occupying land as their home. This point can be seen clearly by considering the different outcomes in each of *Ainsworth* and *Boland* (3.4).

It can also be seen in the debate as to whether a contractually binding permission to use another's land (a contractual licence) counts as a property right in land (3.78–3.82). That debate is far from being purely technical. It may be that B's only right in relation to his or her home consists of such a licence, given by A, the owner of the land. If B's right counts as a property right, it will therefore have some permanence and durability as it will be prima facie binding not only on A, the current owner of the land, but also on C, a party later acquiring a right in the land.

## Property Rights: The Content Question

**3.16**  Our focus so far has been on the different *effects* of property rights, on the one hand, and personal rights, on the other. In a specific case where B acquires a right from A, we also have to know how to tell if that right counts as a property right, and so is capable of binding someone other than A. This requires us to address the *content* question (1.30–1.31).

### The *Numerus Clausus* Principle

**3.17**  The first, and most fundamental point, is that A and B cannot make B's right a property right by simply declaring it to be one. In *Hill v Tupper* (3.7), for example, A gave B an 'exclusive' right to put boats on A's canal, and it may well have been the case that each of A and B intended B to have a property right in the canal, capable of binding X as well as A. Such intention, however, cannot, by itself, turn B's right into a property right. The status of B's right is instead determined by the *content* of B's right: A and B can determine the content of B's right, but it is then for the law to decide if a right with such content counts as a property right. In *Hill*, the content of B's right was such that it did not count as a recognized property right (it did not, eg, meet the content requirements of an easement—those requirements are discussed in **Chapter 9**) and the court was unwilling to extend the existing list of property rights to include a right such as an exclusive permission to make a particular use of A's land.

**3.18**  It should come as no surprise that A and B alone cannot decide that B's right counts as a property right. After all, the key effect of such rights is that they can bind third parties, and so the existence of B's property right has consequences for parties other than A and B. Given those consequences, it would be odd if A and B (who may of course have no reason to take into account the interests of others) could simply choose to create such burdens for third parties. The courts' control over the content of property rights thus reflects the obvious principle that A and B, by means of a contract, cannot impose a burden on C or X (McFarlane (2011)).

**3.19**  The idea that the content of property rights is limited is well known in civilian legal systems. In such jurisdictions, it is often referred to as the *numerus clausus* (ie closed list) principle. It is, however, also a part of common law systems (see eg Rudden (1987),

Merrill and Smith (2000)). Indeed, in England and Wales, it has been given statutory force in relation to land by sections 1 and 4 of the Law of Property Act 1925. Whilst section 1 provides a list of the types of right that can count as legal estates or legal interests in land, section 4(1) instead imposes a freeze on the development of new types of equitable interest in land, stating that: 'after the commencement of this Act (and save as hereinafter expressly enacted) an equitable interest in land shall only be capable of being validly created in any case in which an equivalent equitable interest in property real or personal could have been validly created before such commencement' (for discussion, see Briggs (1983)). As a result, only Parliament can add a new type of legal or equitable property right in land to the list of such rights.

**3.20**  This control over the content of property rights is fundamental to the operation of land law, as it means that the types of burden that can be imposed on land are carefully limited. This point is particularly important given the permanence and scarcity of land, and also its social and economic importance (**1.8–1.12**). The fact that A happens to be a current owner of land does not mean that A can then decide to impose any idiosyncratic type of burden on that land by giving B a right and declaring that right to be a property right. Rather, B's right will be capable of binding third parties only if its content is such that it appears on the list of recognized proprietary rights. In England and Wales that list was, in effect, approved by Parliament in the Law of Property Act 1925.

**3.21**  As we saw in *Hill v Tupper* (**3.7**), this control over the content of property rights can protect strangers such as X who might interfere with A's land. It is also, of course, important in protecting third parties such as C who might later acquire A's land, or a right in A's land. This can be seen in the following example, also discussed at **10.15**.

---

*Rhone v Stephens* **(1994):** Land formerly in A's common ownership was divided into a house and a cottage. One of the bedrooms of the cottage lay beneath the roof of the house. A sold the cottage to B. A later sold the house to C. When A sold the cottage to B, A promised, for himself and future owners of the house, that the part of the roof of the house above the cottage would be kept in 'wind and watertight condition'. It thus seems clear that A and B each intended that B's right would be a property right, capable of binding future owners of the house. The House of Lords, however, held that the promise gave B only a personal right against A.

---

The decision of the House of Lords was based on the content of B's right. A negative promise (eg a promise *not* to use land for commercial purposes) is, in certain circumstances (**Chapter 10**), capable of counting as a recognized property right: the restrictive covenant is on the list of equitable interests in land. A's promise, however, was of positive action: as a result, it was not capable of binding future owners of A's land. If A had instead granted B a lease and made the same promise, the position would have been different, as A would then have been B's landlord, and positive promises made as part of a landlord–tenant relationship are capable of binding later parties who take on the role of landlord or of tenant (**7.87–7.136**). As the House of Lords confirmed in *Rhone*, however, in the absence of such a landlord–tenant relationship, a positive promise is not capable of binding future owners of A's land. As a result, A cannot impose an enduring positive burden on such future owners.

3.22 The recognition of a limited list of permissible property rights in land makes it relatively simple to answer the key question of whether B's right, in any particular case, is a property right or a personal right. The starting point is that B's right will be merely a personal right against A, and so will not be capable, in itself, of binding a third party. If B wishes to show that the right is in fact a property right, B will need to show that the content of B's right matches the content of a recognized type of property right in land. To do so, B must identify a particular type of property right in land and then show that the content of B's right is such that it falls within the definition of that type of property right. For example, the lease is a recognized type of property right in land: see section 1(1)(b) of the Law of Property Act 1925. If B can show that he or she has acquired a lease in relation to A's land, B's right will then be capable of binding C, a party later acquiring the land from A. To do so, however, B must show that the content of his or her right falls within the definition of a lease. A lease consists of a right to exclusive possession of land for a limited period (**7.8–7.39**). If, therefore, the right that B acquired from A is only a right to make a specific *limited* use of A's land, such as a right to share use and occupation of the land with A, it cannot be a lease, as it does not give B a right to exclusive possession of the land.

3.23 This approach to identifying property rights means that, if you want to be able to advise people accurately as to their rights in relation to land, you have to know: (i) the list of permissible property rights in relation to land; and (ii) the content requirements of each of those types of property right. An important part of success in land law, therefore, consists of learning the requirements of the different types of property right—just as, for example, an important part of success in criminal law consists of learning the requirements of different types of criminal offence. So, for example, in **Chapters 7–10**, we will discuss the content requirements of leases, security interests, easements, and covenants.

3.24 It should be remembered that the content question is only one of the questions that you need to consider if advising someone as to their rights in relation to land. It may be, for example, that the right that A has promised to give B is a right to exclusive possession of land for a limited period, and so is capable of counting as a lease. That, by itself, does not mean that B necessarily has a lease, however: the *acquisition* question also needs to be considered. For example, to acquire a legal lease of registered land of a duration of more than seven years, B will need to have registered that lease (**7.62**). Moreover, even if B has satisfied both the content and acquisition questions, if B wishes to enforce that property right against C, the *defences* question needs to be considered: C may have a defence to B's pre-existing property right.

## Identifying Property Rights: No General Test

3.25 The approach taken to the content question helps to explain why land law has a reputation as a technical subject. In deciding if B's right counts as a property right, we do not go back to first principles and ask, for example, if B deserves to be protected against parties other than A. We need to look instead at the list of recognized property rights in land, and the content requirements of each of those types of right. It would be a mistake, therefore, to think that there is an overall, general test that can be applied to determine if B's right counts as a property right.

3.26 In *National Provincial Bank v Ainsworth* (1965), the House of Lords decided that Mrs Ainsworth's right (a 'deserted wife's equity') did not count as a property right, and was purely a personal right against her husband, Mr Ainsworth (**1.58-1.62**). As a result, that right could not bind the National Provincial Bank, and Mrs Ainsworth could not resist the bank's request that she give up possession of her home. Whilst the Court of Appeal had reached a different result, the case was, on the law as it then stood (see **12.19-12.20** for discussion of the current position), relatively straightforward. The 'deserted wife's equity'—a strange sort of right invented by the courts—was, on any view, dependent on the relationship of husband and wife that existed between Mr Ainsworth and Mrs Ainsworth. The right consisted of liabilities that Mr Ainsworth was under to his wife, and it is very difficult to see how a stranger, such as the bank, could come under such liabilities to Mrs Ainsworth. Indeed, as Lord Wilberforce pointed out, Mr Ainsworth was not under any duty to allow his wife to continue to occupy the current family home: he simply had to provide her with *some* accommodation. As a result, Mrs Ainsworth's right did not provide her with a claim to any specific land: it was clearly a right against a specific person, rather than a right imposing a burden on something (such as specific land) independent of any specific person. It was therefore no surprise that the 'deserted wife's equity' was not on the list of recognized property rights in land. Indeed, whilst the House of Lords did not make this point, it seems that, in allowing the right to bind a third party, the Court of Appeal was guilty of ignoring the statutory limit on the types of property rights in land imposed by sections 1 and 4 of the Law of Property Act 1925 (**3.19**).

3.27 In *Ainsworth*, Lord Wilberforce summed up the clearly personal nature of Mrs Ainsworth's right by stating that: 'Before a right or an interest can be admitted into the category of property, or of a right affecting property, it must be definable, identifiable by third parties, capable in its nature of assumption by third parties, and have some degree of permanence or stability. The wife's right has none of these qualities, it is characterized by the reverse of them.' This statement draws an important link between the effect of a property right (it is capable of binding third parties) and the content of such rights. For example, it would clearly be unjust if a third party could be bound by a right even if the third party had no chance of ascertaining that such a right existed.

3.28 It is important to note that Lord Wilberforce simply stated some general, *necessary* requirements of a property right: features that are shared by all of the rights currently recognized as property rights in land. He was not setting out a list of *sufficient* conditions, and so was not stating that a right will be a property right merely because it is definable, identifiable by third parties, capable in its nature of assumption by third parties, and has some degree of permanence or stability. This can be seen by returning to *Rhone v Stephens* (1994) (**3.21**). A's promise that A and future owners of A's land would keep a roof in wind and watertight condition did *not* give B a property right, even though it gave B a right with each of the four features identified by Lord Wilberforce in *Ainsworth*. B therefore had only a personal right against A and so it was only A, and not C, who was under any duty to B to keep the roof in a particular condition. The point is that there is no general, overall test for identifying a property right. We need rather to see if the content of B's right matches the content of any recognized property right; in *Rhone*, B's right did not, as it imposed a positive burden on A.

## Evaluating the Current Approach

**3.29**  We have seen that the current approach to identifying property rights, which requires the content of B's right to fall within the content of a recognized property right, is deeply embedded in land law and has received the approval of Parliament (**3.19**). It can be justified both in terms of principle and efficiency. As for principle, it merely reflects the general position that A and B do not have a general power, simply by making an agreement between themselves, to impose burdens on third parties. As for efficiency, it can be seen as limiting the information costs imposed on such third parties, by restricting the types of right which a third party dealing with land has to look out for (Merrill and Smith (2000)). It also lowers the information costs for courts when resolving disputes as, rather than having to address the very difficult question of whether, in principle, B's right is worthy of protection against third parties, the court can instead simply look to the list of recognized property rights, and the content requirements of each such right.

**3.30**  It is, nonetheless, possible to criticize the current approach. Such criticisms can also be made on the basis of both principle and efficiency. As for principle, it can be argued that it is arbitrary for the law to insist that B's right can count as a property right only if it features on a pre-existing list of such rights: such an approach lacks the flexibility to accommodate particular rights which may in fact be especially worthy of protection against third parties (Gray and Gray (2003)). Moreover, the approach may lead to complexity and a lack of transparency if a court, wishing to allow B's right to bind a third party even though it is not in fact on the list of recognized property rights, strains the content requirements of one of those recognized property rights to include B's right. It is also the case that (as in eg *Rhone v Stephens* (1994): **3.21**) the current approach may lead to the intentions and plans of A and B being frustrated. As for efficiency, it can be argued that as long as there is a defence allowing C to take priority over a pre-existing but unregistered property right of B, there is no good reason to prevent A imposing an idiosyncratic burden on A's land, as the potential costs of such a burden on third parties will simply be reflected in the price of the land (Epstein (1981–2)). Moreover, the current approach obliges parties to enter into complicated and inefficient transactions in order to achieve indirectly some of the consequences that would flow from recognizing B's right as a property right (Rudden (1987)). In a situation such as that arising in *Rhone v Stephens*, for example, it may be that A would instead grant B a lease of the cottage, so that A's duty to maintain the roof would then be capable of binding future owners of A's land, as such owners would be in a landlord–tenant relationship with B, or parties later acquiring the cottage from B.

**3.31**   The Supreme Court's decision in *Berrisford v Mexfield* (2012), discussed at **7.34-7.39**, provides some support for such criticisms. The basic problem for B in that case was the rule that, to count as a lease, B's right to exclusive possession must be for a term: that is, for a limited period. On the face of it, it seemed that A and B's intention that B should have a property right, a key part of their transaction, would be defeated by the fact that no such limited period had been set by the parties. The Supreme Court, however, avoided the apparent unfairness of denying B a property right by employing a complicated manoeuvre which led to B being regarded as having acquired a lease with a maximum duration of 90 years, even though the parties' agreement made no reference to such a limit.

**3.32**   Whilst it is important to be aware of such criticisms, it seems that the current approach can be justified. First, the arbitrariness of the approach is in fact part of its appeal. An arbiter, after all, is someone who has to make a decision, and the rule that B's right will be proprietary only if it features on the list of such rights provides an efficient means for a court to make that decision, and hence for a third party dealing with particular land to judge if B's right is capable of binding him or her. An analogy can be drawn with bouncers controlling access to a particularly exclusive area of a club and denying entry to anyone not on the list that they have been given: their job would be much more difficult if they were instead asked to evaluate, in each particular case, if a person were worthy of admission. It should also be noted that it remains possible for Parliament to add to the list of recognized property rights in land: the Law Commission, for example, has recommended allowing a positive covenant made between freehold owners, such as that in *Rhone v Stephens*, to count as a property right (**10.53-10.55**). It is therefore possible for the list of property rights to be expanded, prospectively, if a truly deserving case is discovered.

**3.33**   Secondly, it would be dangerous to place too much weight on registration requirements as a means of protecting third parties from idiosyncratic burdens imposed on land by A. In particular, given the limited availability of land, there are good reasons for limiting the burdens that a current owner may place on a particular piece of land, even if such burdens are easy to discover. The courts have also rejected the idea that a right of B, whatever its content, can bind C simply because C acquired the land with knowledge of B's right (see eg *Keppell v Bailey* (1834)). Moreover, whilst the lack of registration defence may sometimes operate to protect C, a third party later acquiring a right from A, from an unregistered property right of B, it does not currently provide any protection to X, a stranger interfering with the land.

**3.34**   Thirdly, whilst it is possible to criticize the practical implications of decisions such as *Rhone v Stephens* or *Berrisford v Mexfield*, those complaints are better seen as objections to the specific content requirements of particular types of property right, rather than as reasons to depart from the very concept of having a fixed list of property rights. Those complaints, if justified, can be met by statutory changes to the specific rules in question and so do not call into question the wider basis of the current approach to identifying property rights in land.

# The Distinction Between Legal Property Rights and Equitable Property Rights

**3.35**   Land law provides a very good example of the need to distinguish between rules based on those originally developed by common law courts, and rules based on those originally developed by courts of equity (**1.37–1.46**). Certainly, it is crucial to distinguish between legal property rights, on the one hand, and equitable property rights, on the other. Each type of property right is capable of binding third parties, and so differs from a personal right. Yet there are also important differences between legal property rights and equitable property rights.

## The Effect of Legal Property Rights and of Equitable Property Rights

**3.36**   It is possible to organize the different types of right encountered in land law into a hierarchy, based on the usefulness to B of each type of right (see **Table 3.1**).

| | |
|---|---|
| Legal property rights | *Capable of binding C* |
| Equitable property rights | |
| Personal rights | *Binding only on A* |

**Table 3.1**  A hierarchy of rights

**3.37**   Personal rights are at the bottom of the list, as they are binding only on A. In contrast, each of an equitable property right and a legal property right is capable of binding a third party. There are two reasons, however, for which B would in general prefer a legal property right.

**3.38**   The first reason is the clearer of the two and relates to the *defences* question. It is always possible that a third party may be able to establish a defence to B's property right: such a right is only prima facie binding on the third party. The clear general position is that it will be far harder for the third party to establish such a defence if B has a legal property right rather than an equitable property right. This is true throughout property law. For example, consider a case where B owns a bike, and the bike is stolen by X, who then sells it to C. C buys the bike from X in good faith, honestly believing that X was the true owner. B can still assert his or her pre-existing legal property right in the bike against C: C's bona fide purchase is no defence to B's legal property right (see eg *Farquharson Bros v King* (1902)). Compare the case where T, a trustee, holds legal title to a bike on trust for B. T, in breach of trust, then sells the bike to C. C again buys the bike in good faith, honestly believing that T was the true owner and without any reason to suspect that the bike was held on trust. In such a case, C's bona fide purchase *does* give C a defence against B's pre-existing equitable property right (see eg *Pilcher v Rawlins* (1872)).

3.39    We will discuss the defences question in more detail in **Chapter 11**. It is vital to note that the general bona fide purchaser defence has, to a very large extent, now been eliminated from land law: it is of relevance only in relation to unregistered land, and then only where B has one of the relatively small number of equitable property rights that cannot be registered as a land charge. Land law, however, preserves the basic point that it is far harder for C to have a defence to a legal property right than to an equitable property right. In registered land, for example, if B has a legal property right, such a right will almost always be binding on C. It is often the case that, in order to acquire a legal rather than an equitable property right in the first place, B will be required to register: registration, as we will see in **Chapter 4**, is often a requirement for the acquisition of a legal property right. In some cases, however, B is able to acquire a legal property right without registration: one example occurs where B is granted a lease of seven years or less (**4.51**); another where B acquires an implied, rather than an express easement, over A's land (**9.31–9.50**). In such cases, even if B fails to enter a notice on the register protecting that legal property right, it will almost certainly still bind C, a party who later acquires, for value, A's registered estate in the land. In contrast, if B has only an *equitable* property right in relation to A's land, and B does not protect that right by means of a notice on the register, that right can bind C, a party who later acquires, for value, A's registered estate in the land, *only* if B was in actual occupation of the relevant part of A's land when A made the disposition of the land to C.

3.40    The case of *City of London Building Society v Flegg* (1988), which we discussed at **1.71– 1.77**, provides another example of the greater vulnerability to defences of an equitable property right in land. In that case, Mr and Mrs Flegg, the parents, held a right under a trust. Such an equitable property right is vulnerable to a statutory overreaching defence, arising under section 2 of the Law of Property Act 1925: that defence applies to some (but not all) equitable property rights, but applies to no legal property rights (**11.70– 11.89**). If Mr and Mrs Flegg had instead been holders, with their daughter and son-in-law, of the legal title to the land, the building society would not have been able to take advantage of that overreaching defence.

3.41    So, whilst the general bona fide purchaser defence no longer applies in land law, it is clear that, in land law as elsewhere in property law, equitable property rights are more vulnerable to defences than legal property rights. This provides a sufficient reason, as far as the effects of such rights are concerned, to distinguish legal property rights in land from equitable property rights in land. There is a second reason, also concerning the effect of such rights, to make that distinction. It is, however, more controversial.

3.42    The second reason concerns the impact of equitable property rights on strangers, such as X, who interfere with A's land without acquiring any right in that land. *Hill v Tupper* (1863) provides an example of such a case (**3.7**). There is a strong argument that equitable property rights, unlike legal property rights, are *not* in themselves capable of binding such a third party (McFarlane and Stevens (2010)). Of course, even on this view, equitable property rights are still stronger than mere personal rights, as (like legal property rights), they are prima facie binding on C, a party who later acquires a right in the land from A. On this view, however, whilst legal property rights are prima facie binding on any third party, equitable property rights are more limited, as they can bind C (a party acquiring a right from A) but not X (a stranger who acquires no right from A). It should be emphasized that this second reason, if correct, has nothing to do with defences: the argument is not that X has a defence to B's equitable property right, but rather that X has no need for any defence, as B's right is not in any case binding on X.

3.43    It can be argued that this difference in effect between legal property rights and equitable property rights depends on their different nature. A legal property right in land can be seen as a right in the land itself, so that it is prima facie binding on anyone (C or X) who later interferes with that land. In contrast, an equitable property right can be seen as a right in relation to A's right in the land, so that it is prima facie binding on C (as C later acquires either A's right, or a right that depends on A's right), but is not capable of binding X (as X acquires no right from A). On this view, a legal property right in land is a right that burdens the land itself, whereas an equitable property right is instead a right that burdens A's right in the land. Each right can thus be defined independently of A (and so is more than a personal right against A); but whilst the legal property right relates to the land itself, the equitable property right relates instead to A's right in the land.

3.44    This model of equitable property rights has attracted some academic support (see eg Edelman (2013)). One of its attractions is that it sees equitable property rights as different in nature from legal property rights, and so helps to explain why certain types of right can operate only as equitable, and not as legal, property rights. It also seems to fit well with the nature of a very important equitable property right: the right of a beneficiary of a trust. This is because a trust depends on A holding a *specific right* on trust for B. For example, in a case such as *Williams & Glyn's Bank v Boland* (**1.63–1.70**), it would be inaccurate to say that Mr Boland held the land itself on trust for himself and his wife; rather Mr Boland held his *freehold* on trust for himself and Mrs Boland. Moreover, the idea that an equitable property right does not bind a stranger such as X has support from the case law (see eg *The Lord Compton's Case* (1587), *Leigh & Sillivan Ltd v Aliakmon Shipping Ltd* (1986)) and (as noted by eg Swadling (2013)) must be true of at least some equitable property rights. For example, B can acquire an equitable property right where A makes a contract to sell A's freehold to B: it is easy to see how such a right of B can affect C, a party later acquiring A's freehold (C can also be made to transfer the freehold to B), but it is hard to see how it might affect X, a stranger who acquires no right from A.

3.45    Nonetheless, the idea that equitable property rights are fundamentally different in nature from legal property rights has been criticized (see eg Gardner (2013), Penner (2014)). It is certainly true, for example, that one particular type of equitable property right in land, the restrictive covenant (**3.21** and **Chapter 10**), has been allowed to bind strangers such as X. More recently, in *Shell UK Ltd v Total UK Ltd* (2011), the Court of Appeal permitted beneficiaries of a trust of land to bring a claim against X, a stranger who had carelessly damaged the land, provided that the trustees of the land were also joined to the action. The analysis in that case is, however, somewhat confused. Indeed, it is significant that the Court of Appeal regarded the case as one involving the recovery by the beneficiaries of pure *economic* loss: in other words, it was not seen as a case where the beneficiaries sought to recover damages for an interference with their own property, and so the beneficiaries were *not* given the same type of protection as the holder of a legal property right.

3.46    Whilst it is important to be aware of the ongoing debate as to the nature of equitable property rights, it is useful to bear two points in mind. First, even if you do not agree with the view that equitable property rights are fundamentally different from legal property rights, the longer list of defences available against such rights means that it is in any case crucial to distinguish them from legal property rights. Secondly, the debate is generally concerned not with changing the law, but rather with putting forward the most satisfactory account of the existing law, so, in many cases at least, it may simply be a matter of personal taste as to whether you prefer to regard an equitable property right of B as a right that burdens a right of A, or to see it instead as a right that burdens the land itself.

## The Content of Legal Property Rights and of Equitable Property Rights

3.47    The list of permissible legal property rights in land is determined by section 1 of the Law of Property Act 1925 (LPA 1925). As a result of the special features of land (1.8–1.12), the list is longer than the list of permissible legal property rights in property other than land. It is, however, still a short list. It does also include profits, rentcharges, and rights of entry, but those are not included in Table 3.2 as they are, generally, of less practical importance and so are not considered in any detail in standard land law courses.

| Freehold | Ownership of land without limit of time | Estates in land |
|---|---|---|
| Leasehold | Ownership of A's land for a limited period | |
| Charge | Right to the value of A's right in land if a secured obligation is not performed | Interests in land |
| Easement | Right, benefiting some other land, to make a particular, limited use of A's land | |

Table 3.2  Principal legal estates and legal interests in land

3.48    The table adopts the terminology of section 1 of the LPA 1925 by dividing the list of legal property rights in land into estates in land (set out in s 1(1)) and interests in land (set out in s 1(2)). The simplest way of understanding the difference between estates and interests is that the former confer on B ownership rights in the land, either for a limited period (the lease) or for a period without a time limit (the freehold). In contrast, an interest in land does not give B ownership of that land, but rather allows B to make some specific, limited use of that land (**3.58**).

3.49 Once section 1(1) and (2) of the LPA 1925 have set out the list of legal estates in land and of legal interests in land, section 1(3) then states that: 'All other estates, interests, and charges in or over land take effect as equitable interests.' It is worth noting that the LPA 1925 thus denies the possibility of there being an equitable estate in land: whilst legal property rights in land are divided between legal estates and legal interests, any equitable property right in land must be an equitable interest in land.

3.50 As noted at **3.19**, section 4(1) of the LPA 1925 does not draw up a list of permissible equitable property rights in land, but rather prevents the recognition of any new forms of such right. This means that we need to look to the law as it then stood to compile a list of equitable interests in land. Disregarding any such interests of limited practical importance (such as equitable profits), the following list can be drawn up (see **Table 3.3**).

| Rights under a trust | A holds a freehold or lease on trust, and B is one of the beneficiaries of the trust | Rights arising under a trust |
|---|---|---|
| Estate contract | A is under a duty to transfer a freehold or lease to B | Rights based on legal property rights |
| Option to purchase | If B exercises the option, A is under a duty to transfer a freehold or lease to B | |
| Right of pre-emption | If A decides to sell, A is under a duty to offer B the chance to buy A's freehold or lease | |
| Equitable lease | A is under a duty to grant B a lease | |
| Equitable charge | A is under a duty to grant B a charge | |
| Equitable easement | A is under a duty to grant B an easement | |
| Equity of redemption | A, a mortgagee, is under a duty to B as B may discharge the mortgage by performing the secured duty | Other equitable interests |
| Restrictive covenant | A is under a duty to B not to make a particular use of A's land, and that duty benefits B's land and is intended to bind future owners of A's land | |
| Mere equity | B has a power to acquire a property right in A's land by eg setting aside or rectifying a transaction | |

**Table 3.3** Principal equitable interests in land

**3.51**   The table identifies three basic forms of equitable interest in land (building on the analysis of Swadling (2013)). First, equitable interests arising under a trust (such as the equitable property right of Mrs Boland: see **1.63–1.70**). Secondly, equitable interests modelled on recognized legal property rights (such as an equitable easement). Thirdly, other equitable interests, independent both of trusts and of recognized legal property rights (such as the restrictive covenant). In relation to registered land at least, it may be possible to add another interest, the 'estoppel equity', to this third category—but there is some controversy about the nature of such a right (**5.133–5.134**).

**3.52**   It is in any case clear that the list of equitable interests in land is longer than the list of legal estates or interests in land. Moreover, as we will see in **Chapters 4** and **5**, there are means of acquiring equitable interests that do not apply to legal estates or interests. For example, consider a case in which A makes a contractual promise to give B a right of way over A's land. Unless and until B is registered as the holder of that easement, B will acquire no legal interest in the land (see the Land Registration Act 2002, s 27(2)(d) and **4.56**). B can, however, acquire an equitable interest in the land, by means of an equitable easement, at an earlier stage, and without any registration: the principle allowing B to acquire such an interest depends on A's being under a duty to B to grant B the easement, not on the grant in fact having occurred (see eg *McManus v Cooke* (1887) and **5.76–5.92**). Of course, however, B should not be satisfied by merely having acquired such an equitable interest: if A does grant the easement and B goes on to register and thus acquire a legal easement, B will gain at least two advantages. First, B's legal property right will be easier to assert against C, a third party later acquiring a right from A, as it will be less vulnerable to defences than an equitable interest. Secondly, by registering and acquiring a legal property right, it will be easier for B himself or herself to make out a defence to any equitable interest that may previously have arisen in relation to A's land. In addition, whilst it is clear that a legal easement can be asserted against X, a stranger later interfering with X's land, it is far from clear (**3.42–3.46**) that an equitable easement can be asserted against such a stranger.

**3.53**   It can therefore be suggested that, whilst it may well have been illogical for English law to have contained the two separate court systems of common law and equity, the distinction between legal property rights and equitable property rights can be defended, on the simple basis that, whilst it may be easier for B to show that he or she has an equitable property right, such rights provide B with fewer advantages than a legal property right. Additionally, if the analysis set out at **3.42–3.46** is accepted, the distinction can also be defended on the basis that equitable property rights are of a fundamentally different nature to legal property rights, as they impose burdens not on any specific physical thing, such as land, but rather on a specific right held by A.

## Legal Property Rights: Estates in Land

**3.54**   Section 1(1) of the LPA 1925 establishes that there are only two types of legal estate in land: the freehold (referred to in s 1(1)(a) as 'an estate in fee simple absolute in possession') and the lease (referred to in s 1(1)(b) as 'a term of years absolute'). The content of each of these can be defined by reference to the idea of ownership (see Harris (1996) and, on the freehold, Douglas (2013)): a freehold confers ownership of particular land without a limit of time; a lease gives ownership of land for a limited period.

**3.55**   The position under the LPA 1925 is far simpler than under the previous law, much of which is still effective in common law jurisdictions such as Ireland and the states of the United States. Under that previous law, there was a far wider selection of possible legal estates in land. This was because of the doctrine of estates, which allowed ownership of land to be dealt with in potentially quite complex slices of time (Birks (1998)). It was, for example, possible to create a legal estate which consisted of B's having a right to possession of the land in the future, only if a particular event (such as the death of A without male heirs) occurred. The existence of such legal property rights not only limited the freedom of A to deal with the land, but also caused problems for a third party such as C who wished to acquire rights in the land from A. The LPA 1925 simplified things greatly, by ensuring that any such complex arrangements would have to take effect in equity, with B acquiring only an equitable interest under a trust. The existence of such equitable interests can still limit A's freedom to deal with the land, but the great advantage to a party such as C is that it is far easier for C to have a defence to such rights: as we noted when discussing the *Flegg* case (**1.71–1.77**), the overreaching defence provided by section 2 of the LPA 1925 (**11.70–11.89**) means that C may have a defence to B's equitable interest under a trust of land even if B is in occupation of the land, and even if C is aware of B's equitable interest under the trust.

**3.56**   The historic doctrine of estates retains some very small influence in relation to the freehold. Under that doctrine, there was in fact no such thing as an estate giving B ownership of land forever: a fee simple was rather a grant of land to 'B and B's heirs'. If, in the future, there was no heir of B to take the land, the estate would end and the land would go (by 'escheat') to B's superior lord. This reflected a feudal model of land-holding: the rights held by B and B's heirs were always potentially subject to the rights of the superior lord. On that feudal model, the rights of B and B's heirs in relation to the land depended ultimately on their relationship to the superior lord. The law has, of course, long since moved on from this feudal model. This particular form of escheat was abolished by statute in 1925: if B, a freehold owner, now dies and no one is entitled to receive B's property, B's land (and other property) goes to the Crown. It is, technically, still possible for escheat of a freehold to occur (Williams (2015)), for example where a foreign company holding land is dissolved. As a result, whilst it is reasonable, for almost all practical purposes, to regard a freehold as giving ownership forever, it is technically still accurate to view it as an estate that has no inherent time limit, but lasts for as long as there is a party to hold it.

**3.57**   It is worth noting that the lease, the second form of legal estate permitted by the LPA 1925, is not itself a product of the historic doctrine of estates. Rather, a lease was seen initially as involving a purely personal relationship between A and B, and came gradually to be recognized as a right prima facie binding on any third party interfering with the land. It is, however, possible to think of the lease as an estate, in the sense used by the Law of

Property Act 1925, as one of the fundamental content requirements of a lease is that it confer on B a right to exclusive possession of land: and, as noted by Lord Templeman in *Street v Mountford* (1985), if B has exclusive possession, he is 'able to exercise the rights of an owner of land, which is in the real sense his land albeit temporarily and subject to certain restrictions' (7.8–7.27). Of course, a lease may exist for only a short period and if A has a freehold and gives B a lease of, say, six months, we would naturally think of A as, overall, the owner of the land. The key point of a lease is that, nonetheless, during those six months, it is B who has the right to exclusive possession of the land and is, in that sense, the owner of the land *for that period*. The importance of a right to exclusive possession of land, and hence of ownership of land, was emphasized by Lord Hoffmann in *Hunter v Canary Wharf* (1997), where he stated that exclusive possession is the 'bedrock of English land law'.

## Legal Property Rights: Interests in Land

3.58   The difference between a legal estate in land and a legal interest in land is clear when considering the easement. If B has, for example, a right of way over A's land, B cannot in any meaningful sense be seen as the owner of that land. Indeed, if the right claimed by B amounts to a claim to have exclusive possession of any part of A's land, it *cannot* be an easement (see eg *Copeland v Greenhalf* (1952): 9.24–9.28). If B wants to have a property right involving exclusive possession, B cannot claim an easement but must instead show that he or she has a lease or a freehold. The difference is important as the means by which B may acquire a lease or freehold are more limited than the means by which B may acquire an easement: for example, an easement, unlike a lease or freehold, can be acquired by prescription (9.51–9.59).

3.59   The difference between an estate in land and an interest in land is somewhat less clear when considering a legal charge over land. Overall, in the standard case where A buys land with the help of a mortgage from B Bank, it is clear that we would not regard B Bank as the owner of that land. Technically, however, the rights of B Bank are defined by reference to the rights of a party with a lease (see the LPA 1925, s 87(1)), and the lease is of course an estate in land. Nonetheless, as will be seen in Chapter 8, much of the law of charges is concerned with ensuring that B's charge functions purely as a security right, thus giving B a limited right rather than the open-ended powers that characterize ownership, and so it is no surprise that a legal charge is regarded as an interest in land rather than as an estate in land.

## Equitable Property Rights: Rights Under Trusts

3.60   The Law of Property Act 1925 ensures that many attempts to divide up ownership of land over time must take place behind a trust (3.55). For example, if A, a freehold owner, wants to ensure that B1 has the benefit of the land for B1's life, with B2 having the benefit from that point onwards, A needs to set up a trust. A can, for example, transfer his or her freehold to trustees (T1 and T2) to hold on trust for the benefit of B1 during B1's life, then for the benefit of B2. It is crucial to note that the trust divides up the *benefit* of ownership, but does not divide up ownership itself: the freehold remains intact and is held by the trustees. This important point is confirmed by section 6(1) of the Trusts of Land and Appointment of Trustees Act 1996, which states that: 'For the purpose of exercising their functions as trustees, the trustees of land have in relation to the land subject to the trust all the powers of an absolute owner.' Indeed, where T1 and T2 hold a freehold on trust for B1 and B2, neither B1 nor B2 has an estate in the land: instead, each has an equitable interest, arising because of the duty of the trustees to exercise their powers of ownership for the benefit of B1 and B2.

3.61 It is important to note the difference between the creation of a lease and the creation of a trust. If A, a freehold owner, grants B a legal lease of the land, A can be seen as carving out a slice of A's ownership and transferring that slice to B: for the period of the lease, B has a right to exclusive possession and is, in effect, the owner of the land (3.57). In contrast, where a trust is set up, there is no such carving out: in our example, A transfers his or her freehold, intact, to T1 and T2 to hold on trust. The right to exclusive possession of the land is thus held by T1 and T2. The existence of the trust means that T1 and T2 are under a duty to allow B1 and B2 the benefits of that right, but it does not change the fact that the ownership of the land is vested in T1 and T2, not B1 and B2. As an Australian judge once put it: 'An equitable interest is not carved out of a legal estate but [is] impressed upon it' (*DKLR Holding Co (No 2) Ltd v Commissioner of Stamp Duties* (1982)).

3.62 It is also important to remember that, as we have seen already, where B has an equitable interest under a trust of land, a special defence is available to C, a party later acquiring a right in the land from the trustees. That defence is the overreaching defence provided by section 2 of the LPA 1925, which was successfully used by the building society in *City of London Building Society v Flegg* (1988): **1.71–1.77**. The overreaching defence will be examined in more detail at **11.70–11.89**.

## Equitable Property Rights: Rights Based on Legal Estates or Interests

3.63 In some cases, the content of an equitable interest in land is based on the content of a recognized legal estate or legal interest in land. The possibility of B's having such an equitable interest depends on the fact that the rules as to the *acquisition* of equitable interests differ from the rules as to the acquisition of the corresponding legal estate or legal interest. An equitable interest can arise where A is under a duty to transfer a property right in land to B, or to grant B such a right, even if no such transfer or grant has yet occurred (**5.87–5.92**). In such cases, of course, B must show not only that A is under a duty to give B a right, but also that the content of that right matches the requirements of a recognized legal or equitable property right. So if, for example, A is under a duty to give B a right that does *not* amount to exclusive possession of land for a limited period, B cannot claim to have an equitable lease.

3.64 Where A is under a duty to transfer A's existing legal estate in land to B, we might expect, by reason of analogy to the case of an equitable easement, that B would be regarded as having an equitable freehold, or equitable lease. In such a case, however, B's equitable interest is said to arise under an *estate contract*, although the principle allowing B to acquire such a right is indeed the same as in the case where A is under a duty to grant B an easement. A related case occurs where, instead of coming under an immediate duty to transfer A's estate to B, A instead gives B an option to purchase that estate at some point in the future. Such an *option to purchase* also gives B an immediate equitable interest, as B is in a position to demand that A's estate be transferred to B. It is also possible for A to give B a *right of pre-emption*: in such a case, B does not have the option of forcing the sale to B, but A does promise that, if and when A decides to sell the land, A will first offer to sell the land to B. There was some controversy as to whether a right of pre-emption counts as an equitable interest (see eg *Pritchard v Briggs* (1980)) and section 115(b) of the Land Registration Act 2002 ends that controversy, in relation to registered land at least, by clarifying that such a right is indeed capable of binding C, a party later acquiring a right in the land from A.

## Other Equitable Property Rights

3.65 There are some cases in which B's equitable interest does not arise under a trust, and its content does not correspond to that of a legal estate or legal interest. For example, some centuries ago, the courts recognized that, where B held an estate in land, but then transferred that estate to A to hold as security (eg for the payment by B of a debt owed to A), B had an equitable interest in the land known as an *equity of redemption*. This interest reflected the fact that, although B no longer held the estate itself, B could require the return of that estate by A (eg by paying A the secured debt), and, as A had acquired the estate purely for the purposes of security, A was not free to use the land entirely as A wished. Nowadays, a mortgage of land does not involve B transferring an estate in the land to the lender: rather, B keeps the estate and instead grants A a legal charge over the land. Technically, then, B's rights could be explained as depending on B's retained estate, rather than an equity of redemption, but, as we will see at **8.29–8.31**, the concept of an equity of redemption continues to play a role in the modern law.

3.66 A more recent addition to the list of equitable interests in land is the *restrictive covenant*, which gradually hardened into an equitable property right in the second half of the 19th century. We will examine the content of this right in detail in **Chapter 10**. It arises where A comes under a particular type of duty to B, but does not depend on A being under a duty to grant B a recognized property right. An example occurs where B sells part of B's land to A and makes A promise, on behalf of A and future owners of A's land, that the part of the land sold to A will not be used for commercial purposes. If it can be shown that this promise benefits B's retained land, it is capable of binding not only A but also parties later acquiring a right in A's land. An important part of the current test for the content of a restrictive covenant is that A's promise must be a negative one: that is, it must be one that can be performed without any positive action or expenditure of money by B. This limit, and the practical inconvenience it may cause in a case such as *Rhone v Stephens* (1994: **3.21**), has led the Law Commission to suggest that Parliament should add to the list of *legal* interests in land by creating a new legal property right, known as a 'land obligation', which is capable of imposing both negative and positive burdens on future owners of A's land (see Law Commission (2011) and **10.56–10.59**).

3.67    The *mere equity* is included in the list of equitable property rights set out in **Table 3.3**. Such a right arises where, for example, B has transferred a property right to A, but has a power (eg because of an innocent misrepresentation by A) to set aside that transfer, or to rectify the transaction. In the period before exercising such a power, B can be said to have a mere equity. Such a right is more than a mere personal right against A, as it is capable of binding C, a third party who later acquires that same property right from A. Outside the context of land law, a mere equity is, however, distinguished from a full-blown equitable property right, as, unlike such a right, it is vulnerable to a particular defence: that of a bona fide purchaser for value from A of an *equitable* property right (*Phillips v Phillips* (1861)). In registered land, however, such an additional defence may not be available to C against a mere equity, as section 116(b) of the Land Registration Act 2002 seems to confirm that such a right operates like a standard equitable interest in its effect on a party later acquiring rights from A. This means, of course, that a mere equity is prima facie binding on C, but C may be able to establish a defence: such as the lack of registration defence, or the statutory overreaching defence (*Mortgage Express v Lambert* (2016)).

## Property Rights in Land: Conclusion

3.68    It is important to know the list of legal and equitable property rights in relation to land, as those rights are key building blocks of the land law system. In seeking to balance the position of B and of C, for example, the location of the boundary between personal and property rights is critical. As a result of its special features (**1.9–1.10**), including its capacity for multiple, simultaneous use, the list of property rights in land is longer than that applying to other forms of property: it includes, for example, the lease, easement, and restrictive covenant. The charge is also capable of existing as a legal interest in land, whereas that is not the case for other forms of property. The list is still, however, relatively short and, crucially, B's right can only be recognized as a property right if, in its content, it falls within the definition of one of those rights. Perhaps the most recent sustained attempt to have a new type of right recognized as a property right was carried out by the Court of Appeal, led by Lord Denning, from the 1950s to the end of the 1980s, when attempts were made to allow contractual licences to bind third parties. As we will see at 3.78–3.82, that attempt was unsuccessful.

## Personal Rights: The Licence

3.69    The term 'licence' simply means permission: something which 'makes an action lawful which, without it, had been unlawful' (*Thomas v Sorrell* (1673)). In land law, it is used to refer to cases where B has permission to make some use of A's land but does not have a recognized legal or equitable property right (such as a lease or easement) in A's land. It is thus the core example of a case where B has only a personal right against A.

3.70    The consequences of a licence being only a personal right of B against A are clear in *National Provincial Bank v Ainsworth* (1965): 1.58–1.62. Mrs Ainsworth's 'deserted wife's equity' meant that she had permission to occupy the former matrimonial home, solely owned by her husband, and that she may well have been able to prevent her husband from removing her from that property. It was, however, only a personal right against Mr Ainsworth, and so did not bind the bank, which was free to assert against her the right to possession of the land it had acquired as a result of its legal charge over the land. In contrast, in *Williams & Glyn's Bank v Boland* (1981), whilst Mr Boland was the sole legal owner of the land, Mrs Boland had more than a mere permission to occupy: she had an equitable interest in the land, under a trust, and that right was capable of binding the bank.

## Types of Licence

3.71    The simplest form of licence is known as a *bare licence*. It arises where B has permission to make some use of A's land, but there is nothing to prevent A simply revoking that permission. If B, a dinner guest at A's home, makes an ill-advised comment over dinner, A is free to require B to leave without any dessert. In such a case, of course, it would be wrong to say that B *immediately* becomes a trespasser as soon as he or she is asked to leave: having been invited onto A's land, B is entitled to a reasonable 'packing-up period' before he or she can be regarded as a wrongdoer (Hill (2001)).

3.72    It is worth noting that if B has a bare licence, but is in sole possession of A's land, the fact of that possession can give B a legal property right: such a right can therefore be asserted by B against X, a stranger later interfering with A's land. In such a case, however, it is not the licence that binds X: it is rather the legal property right (a freehold) that B has acquired through the fact of B's exclusive possession of the land. Indeed, that fact gives B a freehold even if B is in possession of the land without A's permission (4.88–4.136).

**3.73**   Of more interest are cases where B has a licence, and A is under a duty to B not to revoke B's permission to use A's land. Such a duty might be imposed by a statute, in which case B can be said to have a *statutory licence*. For example, following the decision in *Ainsworth*, Parliament intervened to give some protection to B in relation to B's occupation of a family home belonging to B's spouse. The relevant modern provisions, which also apply to civil partners, are sections 30–33 of the Family Law Act 1996 and are discussed at **12.19–12.20**. Whilst a basic right of occupation is conferred on B in such a case, a court has relatively wide powers to exclude or restrict B's right, taking into account, for example, the housing needs and resources of A and B, and of any 'relevant child'. Significantly, B's right to occupy is capable of binding a third party, such as a bank acquiring a charge over the land from A, but *only* if B's right has been entered on the register. Even if B is in actual occupation of the land, that occupation will not make up for a failure to protect the right through registration, and the right will not bind C. Whilst statutory licences are thus limited to specific contexts, there is no such limit on the scope of either (i) a *contractual licence*: such a licence exists where A's duty not to revoke B's permission to use A's land arises as a result of a contract; or (ii) an *estoppel licence*, which exists where A's duty instead arises as a result of proprietary estoppel (**5.93–5.125**).

## Contractual and Estoppel Licences: Effect on A

**3.74**   In a case where A is under a duty to B not to revoke B's licence, there are two possible types of response to an actual or threatened breach of that duty by A. First, B might claim damages from A, with such damages aiming to place B, as far as possible, in the position that B would have been in had A's duty been performed. Each piece of land can be seen as unique, however, so it may well be that damages will be an ineffective means of protecting B's right to make some use of A's land. The second type of response may therefore be relevant: B can instead claim that A should be compelled by a court not to revoke B's permission. In *Verrall v Great Yarmouth Borough Council* (1981), for example, the Court of Appeal upheld an order that A had to perform its contractual duty to allow B to make use of A's land for a political meeting. An award of damages was regarded as inadequate, given the disruption to B's plans that would be caused by having to find an alternative venue for the meeting.

**3.75**   Perhaps surprisingly, it was thought at one point that this second type of remedy, which involves specific protection of B's licence, should never be available. The reasoning (apparent in eg *Wood v Leadbitter* (1845)) was that, as B has no property right in A's land, A should be free to control the use of that land and so could not be prevented from breaching the licence and simply paying damages to B. The flaw in that reasoning, of course, is that whilst the non-proprietary status of a licence is crucial in assessing its effect on a third party such as C, it should make no difference to the impact of the licence on A.

## Contractual and Estoppel Licences: Effect on X

**3.76** As noted at **3.72**, when considering the bare licence, if B is in exclusive possession of A's land, the fact of that possession gives B a legal property right capable of binding X (a stranger who later interferes with A's land). B's protection in such a case depends on the legal freehold that B acquires through possession, and not on any licence that B may have from A.

**3.77** In some recent cases, however, the courts have extended the protection available to B against a stranger such as X. In those cases, it has been accepted that, even if B has not yet taken exclusive possession of A's land, if B has a right against A to take such possession, that right alone can give B a claim against X. This trend can be seen in the following example.

---

*Manchester Airport v Dutton* **(2000):** The National Trust owned some land neighbouring Manchester Airport. It gave the airport a contractual licence to go on to part of the land to cut down trees there, so as to prepare for the building of a new runway. Before the airport could enter the land, environmental protestors occupied it with the intention of protecting the trees. The airport applied for an order for possession, requiring the protestors to leave the land. Of course, the National Trust itself could have sought an order against the protestors, who were on the land without its permission, but it may well have been the case that this would have been an unpopular move. By a majority, the Court of Appeal granted the airport the possession order. In a powerful dissent, Chadwick LJ noted that the decision overlooked the previously crucial distinction between cases where B in fact has gone onto land and taken exclusive possession of it, and cases where B simply has a contractual right against A to take such possession.

---

The basic point in favour of Chadwick LJ's dissenting position (also supported by Swadling (2000)) is that it is hard to see why a contract between A and B, which does not give B a lease or any other recognized property right, should be capable of giving B additional rights against a third party such as X. Nonetheless, the majority's position has received some significant judicial support (such as from Lord Neuberger in *Mayor of London v Hall* (2010)) on the basis that the law should protect B against X if B is 'entitled to use and control, effectively amounting to possession, of the land in question …'. The difficulty here is as to the word 'entitled': where B has a personal right against A under a licence, it is possible for B to be entitled to some benefit (eg possession of land) *as against A*, without that meaning that B thereby has an abstract entitlement, good against the rest of the world, to the same benefit. In *Hill v Tupper* (**3.7**), after all, B was entitled as against A to run an exclusive business putting boats on A's canal, but that in itself did not mean that B had a right against X.

## tractual and Estoppel Licences: Effect on C

### The Contractual or Estoppel Licence Itself Cannot Bind C

**3.78**  The basic position in relation to contractual licences is now very clear: a contractual licence is not a legal or equitable property right in land, and so cannot, in itself, bind C, a third party later acquiring a right in A's land. This position is confirmed by two decisions of the House of Lords.

---

***King v David Allan* (1916):** Mr King (A) owned land. He entered into a contract with David Allan & Sons (B), giving B a right to display posters on the wall of a cinema to be built on A's land. The Phibsboro Picture House (C) then acquired a lease of the land, including the cinema, and C refused to allow B to display the posters. B therefore sued A for breach of contract. A argued that B had suffered no loss, as its right to display the posters was in fact binding on C. The House of Lords rejected that argument, finding that the contract between A and B created 'nothing but a personal obligation' and so could not itself bind C.

---

As we have seen (**1.58–1.62**), the House of Lords in *National Provincial Bank v Ainsworth* (1965), in holding that Mrs Ainsworth's 'deserted wife's equity' did not bind the bank, also confirmed that B does not acquire an interest in land simply because A is under a duty to B not to revoke B's licence.

**3.79**  Some doubt was, however, caused by a series of decisions in which the Court of Appeal, at the urging of Lord Denning, sought to avoid the clear authority of *King v David Allan*, and, later, of *Ainsworth*, and held that a contractual or estoppel licence could, in itself, bind C. Those decisions were, however, based on flawed reasoning.

**3.80**  In *Errington v Errington* (1952), for example, Denning LJ applied the same mistaken logic, analysed at **3.75**, that had once led the courts to find that, as a contractual licence is not a property right, it cannot be specifically enforced against A. Denning LJ's essential argument was that, as later authorities had since held that a contractual licence can be specifically protected against A, this meant that such a right had been added to the list of equitable interests in land. As Lord Wilberforce pointed out in *Ainsworth*, however: 'the fact that a contractual right can be specifically performed, or its breach prevented by injunction, does not mean that the right is any the less of a personal character or that a purchaser with notice is bound by it: what is relevant is the nature of the right, not the remedy which exists for its enforcement'. In fact, Lord Denning made the same error in the Court of Appeal in *Ainsworth*: there he assumed that, as Mrs Ainsworth could prevent her husband from removing her from the land, she therefore had an abstract right to stay in occupation. The better conclusion, however, is that Mrs Ainsworth had a right *against her husband* that he not remove her from the land; such a right could not then bind a third party. Lord Wilberforce might also have pointed to the statutory restriction on the recognition of new forms of equitable interest imposed by section 4(1) of the Law of Property Act 1925 (**3.19**).

3.81   After the House of Lords' decision in *Ainsworth*, the Court of Appeal, again led by Lord Denning, adopted a different approach. In *DHN Food Distributors Ltd v London Borough of Tower Hamlets* (1976), it was held that, where B has a contractual licence that can be specifically enforced against A, B acquires an equitable interest in A's land by means of a constructive trust. We will consider constructive trusts in detail in **Chapter 5**. Like any trust, a constructive trust involves the beneficiary, B, having an equitable property right: a right capable of binding a third party. So, if a specifically enforceable contractual licence gives rise to such a trust, then B immediately acquires a recognized equitable interest in A's land: a right under a trust. There is, however, no basis for saying that the mere fact of a specifically enforceable contract gives rise to a trust. It may do where the contractual duty of A is to transfer A's freehold or lease to B (**5.87–5.92**). In the case of a licence, however, A is under no duty to give B a recognized property right: A's duty is simply a duty not to revoke B's permission to use the land. It is therefore no surprise that, in *Ashburn Anstalt v Arnold* (1989), the Court of Appeal confirmed that: 'we prefer the line of authorities which determine that a contractual licence does not create a property interest. We do not think that the argument is assisted by the bare assertion that the right arises under a constructive trust.'

3.82   It is also possible to find decisions of the Court of Appeal recognizing an estoppel licence as an equitable interest in land (see eg *Williams v Staite* (1979)). Those decisions were, however, made in the period when that court also regarded a contractual licence as an equitable interest. Given that it is now clear that a contractual licence gives B only a personal right against A, it seems clear that an estoppel licence should be treated in the same way (Battersby (1998)). The fact that A's duty not to revoke the licence arises as a result of an estoppel, rather than as a result of a contract, provides no reason for thinking that the licence should receive better protection against third parties. Of course, there may be cases where B has permission to occupy A's land, and also has the benefit of a proprietary estoppel claim which can only be satisfied by A's granting B a recognized property right in A's land (such as a lease or an easement). In such a case, B will have an equitable interest in A's land, arising through estoppel, but that interest is separate from B's licence: it depends on the fact that the estoppel, on the facts of the particular case, requires A to do more than merely allow B permission to make some use of A's land, and instead requires A to grant B a recognized property right (**5.124–5.134**).

## B May Acquire a New, Direct Right Against C

3.83   We noted at **3.10** that, even if B has only a personal right against A, this does not necessarily mean that it will be impossible for B to assert a right against C, a party later acquiring a right in A's land. The personal right itself will not assist B against C, but it may be that B has a *different*, new right that can be asserted against C, arising as a result of C's own conduct. This possibility is important to bear in mind when considering contractual licences.

**3.84**   When considering *King v David Allan* at **3.78**, we saw that, if A gives B a contractual licence for a particular length of time, and then sells the land to C during that time, and C refuses to honour the licence, A will be liable to B in damages. Depending on the reduction in price that C may demand as a result, it may therefore be in A's interest to require C, when buying the land, to honour B's licence. The simplest solution in such a case would be for A to insist on C's making a direct contractual promise to B: if such a promise were made, B would then have a new, direct right against C. Nowadays, the parties might also take advantage of the Contracts (Rights of Third Parties) Act 1999, to allow C to make the promise as part of the contract of sale with A, but to give B a right to enforce that contractual promise.

**3.85**   Even before the 1999 Act, however, the courts recognized that a promise made by C to A, when acquiring land from A, could be enforced, in certain circumstances, by B.

---

*Binions v Evans* **(1972):** The trustees of the Tredegar Estate (A) owned a cottage, which was occupied by Mrs Evans (B). A made an agreement with B allowing B to remain in the cottage for the rest of her life. A later sold the land to Mr and Mrs Binions (C), making C promise that C would continue to allow B to occupy the cottage for as long as she wished. As a result of that promise, C paid a reduced price for the land. The Court of Appeal held that C's promise, although made only to A, gave B a right against C: Lord Denning MR stated, surely correctly, that: 'it would be utterly inequitable for [C] to turn [B] out contrary to the stipulation subject to which [C] took the premises'.

---

The principle applied in such a case seems to be a reasonable one: it has been argued, for example, that the same principle can also explain the *Pallant v Morgan* equity (**5.78-5.82**). As the Court of Appeal has more recently emphasized, the principle can operate only if C has indeed made a promise to give B a new right and has thus 'undertaken a new obligation' (see *Lloyd v Dugdale* (2002) and *Chaudhary v Yavuz* (2013)).

**3.86**   In *Binions v Evans*, and in other decisions discussing the principle in that case, it was stated that, where the principle applies, B's right against C arises under a constructive trust. This suggests that, even if C has merely promised to allow B to continue to use the land under a licence, B thereby acquires an equitable interest in the land. Such a result would be very strange, however: B's initial licence with A is merely a personal right, and the new, direct right B has acquired against C has exactly the same content as that licence (McFarlane (2004)). Moreover, the initial licence arises in a contract between B and A, where B has given consideration; it would be very odd if B could acquire a stronger right as a result of the same promise being made in a contract between C and A, for which B has provided no consideration. The better view, therefore, is that if C has merely promised to allow B's licence to continue, then any new, direct right that B acquires against C as a result of that promise can amount to no more than a licence, and so must be only a personal right of B against C.

## Licences and Leases

3.87  It is worth pausing to ask why it was that the Court of Appeal, under Lord Denning's direction, made such efforts to have a contractual or estoppel licence added to the list of equitable interests in land. It can be suggested that the answer lies in the approach that the court, again at the urging of Lord Denning, developed in the same period when deciding on the content test for a lease. As we will see at **7.42–7.43**, the Court of Appeal's 'revolution' (to adopt the term once used by Lord Denning himself) involved departing from the orthodox position that if B has a right to exclusive possession of A's land for a limited period, then B has a lease, even if A and B had intended to give B only a personal right against A. The motivation for this revolution was that, if B did have a lease, legislation then curtailed A's right to regain possession of the property at the end of the agreed period of the lease (**7.4**). If a court thought that such an outcome was unsatisfactory, the only way to avoid it was to regard B as not in fact having a lease. As a result, in many cases where B would previously have been regarded as having a lease, and thus a recognized legal property right capable of binding C, the Court of Appeal's new approach meant that B only had a licence.

3.88  The motivation behind that new approach, however, was simply to deny B the additional statutory protection available if B were held to have a lease; it was not to deny B protection against a third party acquiring A's land during the period in which A was contractually bound to allow B possession of the land. As a result, it seems that the Court of Appeal, although regarding B as having merely a contractual licence, did not wish to deny B all the advantages of a lease. The second part of the 'revolution' was, therefore, to regard a contractual licence as an equitable interest in land and thus capable of binding C.

3.89  As we will see at **7.8–7.15**, the House of Lords in *Street v Mountford* (1985) rejected the first part of Lord Denning's revolution, and reinstated the orthodox position that, if A has given B a right to exclusive possession of A's land for a limited period, then B has a lease even if A intended only to grant B a personal right. Once this occurred, the central part of the motivation for recognizing contractual licences as equitable interests disappeared. It is therefore no surprise that, since the confirmation in *Ashburn Anstalt v Arnold* (1989) that a contractual licence is only a personal right, there has been no further challenge to that position. In fact, to complete the picture, Lord Denning would probably be happy enough with the current law, as the statutory protection available to parties with a lease has been severely reduced by Parliament, and so the concern which motivated the first part of his revolution has also, to a very large extent, disappeared.

## Licences: The Future

**3.90** Two main points flow from the analysis of the relationship between the law of leases and of licences at **3.87–3.89**. First, there is the specific point that the main motivation for adding contractual and estoppel licences to the list of equitable interests in land—the need to protect a party with a right to exclusive possession of land for a limited period—is no longer relevant, as such a party is now recognized as having a lease. Secondly, there is the more general point that, in considering whether any specific type of right should be added to the list of proprietary rights in land, it is important to bear in mind the wider structure of land law, and the other forms of protection available to a holder of such a right.

**3.91** For example, it might be thought that the case for recognizing a new type of equitable interest is at its strongest when B's licence is the only right which B has in his or her home. Certainly Article 8 of the European Convention on Human Rights recognizes the importance of the right to respect for B's home (see **Chapter 2**). In *Manchester CC v Pinnock* (2011), the Supreme Court accepted that Article 8 may provide a restriction on the freedom of a local authority to remove B from its land, even in a case where B has no property right in that land. On the one hand, this may seem to lend support to the idea that at least some contractual or estoppel licences (those under which B occupies his or her home) are worthy of additional protection; on the other hand, it could be said to demonstrate that the real concern in such cases is B's loss of a home, and that the weight of B's right to a home can be evaluated directly, on the facts of the particular case, without the need for it to be recognized as a property right that is *always* capable of binding a third party. Similarly, the fact that B, in a case such as *Binions v Evans* (see **3.85**), has been protected against C through the recognition of a new, direct right might on the one hand be seen as recognizing the importance of B's licence; equally, however, it can show that B can be protected against C in a suitable case without the need for Parliament to extend the list of equitable interests in land.

## FURTHER READING

Bright, S, 'Of Estates and Interests: A Tale of Ownership and Property Rights' in S Bright and J Dewar (eds), *Land Law: Themes and Perspectives* (Oxford: Oxford University Press, 1998).

Lochery, E, 'Pushing the Boundaries of *Dutton*' [2011] Conv 74.

McFarlane, B, '*Keppell v Bailey* (1834) and *Hill v Tupper* (1863): The *Numerus Clausus* and the Common Law' in N Gravells (ed), *Landmark Cases in Land Law* (Oxford: Hart Publishing, 2013).

Moriarty, S, 'Licences and Land Law: Legal Principles and Public Policies' (1984) 100 LQR 376.

Swadling, W, 'Property' in A Burrows (ed), *English Private Law* (3rd edn, Oxford: Oxford University Press, 2013), 4.114–4.128.

# SELF-TEST QUESTIONS

1    What is the key difference between a personal right and a property right?

2    What is the *numerus clausus* principle?

3    Why might a party prefer to have a legal property right rather than an equitable property right?

4    If B has only a personal right against A, an owner of land, does that mean that B will never have a good claim against C, a party later buying A's land?

5    What is the strongest argument for recognizing a contractual licence as a property right in land? What is the strongest argument against doing so?

# 4 Registered Title and the Acquisition of Legal Estates

## SUMMARY

This chapter considers how legal estates in land are created and transferred. The formal creation and transfer of estates involves three distinct stages; contract, conveyance, and (in most instances) registration. Where registration is required, legal title is not obtained unless and until registration takes place. The majority of land in England and Wales is now registered and that which is not yet registered will become registered the next time one of a number of dispositions take place, including the sale or other transfer of the land. The chapter considers the principles that lie behind registration of title and examines the content of a registered title. Finally, the chapter considers how title to land can be acquired informally by adverse possession or 'squatting'.

Key topics explored in this chapter are:

- Contracts for sale of land (4.5–4.31)
- Creation and transfer (4.32–4.37)
- Registration (4.38–4.62)
- The content of a registered title (4.63–4.87)
- Informal acquisition of a legal title: adverse possession (4.88–4.131)
- Adverse possession and the criminalization of residential squatting (4.132–4.136)
- Human rights and adverse possession (4.137–4.139)

## Introduction

4.1 This chapter is concerned with both the acquisition question and the content question in relation to legal estates. Legal estates can be acquired both formally and informally, with informal acquisition taking place through the law of adverse possession. The chapter first considers the formal acquisition of a legal estate, which is subject to particular statutory requirements. In most cases (with the exception only of short leases), formal acquisition of a legal estate now requires registration on a central register of title maintained by Land

Registry. The rules governing registered titles are contained in the Land Registration Act 2002 (LRA 2002). That Act addresses the acquisition, content, and defences questions in respect of registered land. We consider the provisions of the Act in respect of the acquisition and content questions in this chapter, while its provisions in respect of defences are considered in **Chapter 11**. After considering the formal acquisition of legal estates, we discuss the content of a registered title, to understand what it means to be the registered proprietor of a legal estate in land. Central to the content of a registered title is the idea that title is 'indefeasible'. That is to say, that once registered a title is guaranteed and a proprietor cannot be removed from the register even if it transpires that, as a matter of general law, he or she was not in fact entitled to the estate. We consider the extent to which a registered title is indefeasible in the light of case law on the effect of fraudulent transactions. Finally, the chapter explains how legal estates can be acquired informally through adverse possession.

## Formal Acquisition of Legal Title

**4.2** The formal acquisition of legal title can be divided into three stages: contract; creation, or transfer; and registration. Not every instance of formal acquisition will follow each of these stages. Legal title may be transferred without there being a contract. For example, title may be transferred on a sale even though the parties have not in fact entered a binding contract, or the transfer may be by way of gift. Registration is not required in the case of short leases. It is convenient, however, to use the three stages as a structure for our examination of formal acquisition, not least as a typical conveyance or sale of a home will follow each of these stages. The same three stage process may be followed whether the conveyance of land involves the transfer of an existing legal estate (eg the transfer of a freehold or assignment of the existing term of a lease) or the creation of a new one (eg the grant of a new lease).

- *Contract*: the vendor and purchaser enter a contract for sale of the legal estate (whether freehold or leasehold). The purchaser usually pays a deposit.

- *Creation or transfer*: the contract is executed by the vendor transferring title. This stage is commonly referred to as 'completion', and is the stage at which the outstanding balance of the purchase price is paid and the purchaser takes possession of the land.

- *Registration*: after completion, the purchaser applies to be registered as proprietor of the estate. Legal title does not vest in the purchaser until registration. Registration may take place some weeks or even months after completion or transfer.

**4.3** Although legal title does not vest in the purchaser until registration, contracts for sale of land are recognized as being specifically enforceable. That means that in the event of a breach the court will order the performance of the contract, rather than simply award damages, as long as there is no bar to the award (such as undue hardship, impossibility, or inequitable conduct on the part of the person seeking the award). As soon as there is a specifically enforceable contract, the purchaser acquires equitable rights in the land. A specifically enforceable contract for sale of land itself is a property right, known as an 'estate contract'. Additionally, a constructive trust, known as the vendor–purchaser constructive trust (discussed at **5.83–5.86**) arises on the entry of a specifically enforceable contract and continues until registration. Under the trust, throughout that period of time, the vendor (seller) holds the legal estate on trust for the purchaser (**Chapter 5**).

4.4   It will be apparent from the foregoing description that the formal acquisition of legal title is heavily regulated. Each stage of a transaction is subject to its own statutory requirements. The effect of these requirements is that land is more difficult to deal with than many other types of property. In part, these requirements reflect the uniqueness and importance of land. But formality requirements also serve a functional purpose (Birks (1998)). Property rights in land are invisible; one cannot see a freehold or leasehold estate. Formality requirements make property rights visible by providing a record of them. They also serve an important 'cautionary' role (Law Commission (1987)) in giving people cause to reflect before entering into transactions that involve complex rights and obligations. Finally, they provide an important evidentiary function and protection against fraud (Law Commission (1987)).

## Contracts for Sale of Land

4.5   In this part of the chapter we look at the requirements for a valid contract for sale of land and the effect of non-compliance with those formalities. The formality rules governing contracts for sale of land are complex as they perform a crucial role in determining when a vendor and purchaser have legally committed to the sale of land. The law needs to provide a careful balance between, on the one hand, preventing people from unintentionally entering legally binding obligations and, on the other, ensuring that people cannot escape bad bargains that they have freely entered into. We first consider what the requirements for a valid contract for sale of land are and how those requirements have evolved. We then consider the types of contracts that are governed by the formality requirements. We discuss the two different ways in which a contract can be created to comply with the statutory requirements (using a single or two separate documents). We then turn our attention to what happens in cases of non-compliance. We see how doctrines of rectification and collateral contract may be used to establish the existence of a valid contract and, finally, we examine the possible use of proprietary estoppel to establish a non-contractual claim.

4.6   The requirements for a valid contract for the sale or other disposition of an interest in land are provided by section 2 of the Law of Property (Miscellaneous Provisions)

Act 1989 (LP(MP)A 1989). Under that section, for a contract for sale of land to be valid it must:

- be in writing;

- incorporate all the terms the parties have expressly agreed (by setting out the terms or by reference to another document) either:

  - in a single document signed by both parties; or

  - in each of two documents signed by one of the parties and exchanged.

The LP(MP)A 1989 is based on recommendations of the Law Commission in its Report No 164, *Transfer of Land: Formalities for Contracts for Sale etc of Land* (1987). The Act replaced the previous formality requirement contained in s 40 of the Law of Property Act 1925 (LPA 1925). The 1989 Act has been considered to mark a change in phil-osophy from previous legislation, focusing attention on the written contract. As a re-sult, case law under the previous legislation may no longer be authoritative (*Firstpost Homes Ltd v Johnson* (1995)). The 1989 Act has proved controversial in a number of respects. Recurring concerns have been that the Law Commission's report and the le-gislation (which differs from the draft Bill annexed to the report) have failed to consider the consequences of the changes, and may enable parties to escape from what appears to be a clear bargain. Writing extra-judicially, Lord Neuberger (2009) provided a damning indictment, '[n]ow that the Law Commission, by needlessly meddling, Parliament, with misconceived drafting, and the courts, through inconsistent decisions, have had their wicked ways with section 2, we are worse off than we ever were with section 40'.

**4.7** Section 2 governs all contracts entered into on or after 27 September 1989. It differs from section 40 of the LPA 1925 both as regards the formality requirements specified and the consequences of non-compliance. As regards the formality requirements, under section 40 there was no requirement for a contract to be in writing; it was necessary only for it to be *evidenced* in writing. In contrast, section 2 of the LP(MP)A 1989 requires the contract to be in writing. This difference has a direct effect on the consequence of non-compliance. Under section 40 of the 1925 Act, a contract that was not evidenced in writing remained valid, but was not enforceable by action. Under section 2 of the 1989 Act, no contract exists unless and until formality requirements are fulfilled. There is no concept of a contract being valid, but unenforceable.

**4.8** The principal significance of the difference in the effect of non-compliance between sec-tion 40 of the LPA 1925 and section 2 of the LP(MP)A 1989 is the abolition by section 2 of the doctrine of part performance. That doctrine (for which specific provision was made in the LPA 1925, s 40(2)) enabled the court to order specific performance of an oral contract if there was a sufficient act of part performance by the claimant (*Steadman v Steadman* (1976)). Essential to the application of the doctrine was the fact that, under section 40 of the LPA 1925, an oral contract was valid. Without a valid contract, there is nothing in relation to which specific performance can be ordered. The uncertainty created by the doctrine was identified by the Law Commission as one of the key defects in the operation of section 40. Its effect was that 'an oral contract for sale can readily and unilaterally be rendered enforceable and the provisions of section 40 left to beat the air' (Law Commission (1987)). It was considered a 'blunt instrument for doing justice' (Law Commission (1987)) where formality requirements have not been complied with. Its abolition was therefore a key recommendation in the Law Commission's report. Although nothing in the terms of section 2 of the LP(MP)A 1989 expressly abolishes the doctrine, no such provision is necessary. Its abolition was recognized by the Law Commission as inherent in the requirement for a contract to be in writing. The abolition of the doctrine has generally been given effect by the courts (*United Bank of Kuwait v Sahib* (1997)), although its abolition was doubted in *Singh v Beggs* (1996) and by Swann (1997) and the doctrine has continued to attract some support (Griffiths (2002)).

4.9  Under section 2, the written contract may take one of two forms: a single document signed by both parties; or separate documents signed by each party and exchanged. The document—or each document, in the case of an exchange—must contain all of the terms expressly agreed by the parties. The terms may be contained in the signed document—or documents, in the case of exchange—or be contained in a separate document that is incorporated by reference. Four main issues arise for discussion:

- the contracts to which section 2 applies (4.10–4.12);
- the possibility of contracts by correspondence (4.13);
- the concept of an exchange (4.14–4.15); and
- the definition of 'signed' (4.16–4.17).

## Contracts to Which Section 2 Applies

4.10  Section 2 of the LP(MP)A 1989 applies to all contracts for the creation or transfer of an interest in land. For the section to be applicable, the contract must have the purpose of disposing of land. The section does not apply to contracts which have land as their subject matter, but do not have a disposing *purpose*—even if the contract has the *effect* of disposing of land. The distinction between contracts with a disposing purpose and those without a disposing purpose, but which may have a disposing effect, is difficult to understand in isolation. A contract in which a vendor agrees to sell land to a purchaser is a clear example of one with a disposing purpose; the purpose of the contract is to dispose of title to land from the vendor to the purchaser. In *Yeates v Line* (2013) section 2 was held not to apply to a compromise agreement reached in a boundary dispute. The agreement had the effect of disposing of land, but this was not its purpose. The purpose of the contract was to compromise (or settle) a dispute between the parties. Section 2 has also been held not to apply to a 'lock-out' agreement, through which a vendor agrees not to negotiate with anyone other than the purchaser for the sale of land for a fixed period of time (*Pitt v PHH Asset Management Ltd* (1994)). Land is the subject matter of a lock-out agreement, but the contract has neither a disposing purpose nor effect. The agreement facilitates negotiations for a sale which, if successfully concluded, will lead to the parties entering a contract for sale of land which will need to comply with section 2.

**4.11**   In *McCausland v Duncan Lawrie Ltd* (1997) it was held that section 2 also applies where parties wish to vary the terms of a contract for sale of land. Unless the variation complies with section 2, the terms of the contract as originally agreed remain enforceable. In that case, the parties had entered into a valid contract for sale of land. An attempt was made to vary the contract in order to change the completion date, but the variation did not comply with section 2. As a result, the parties' contract remained binding on its original terms.

**4.12**   A specific issue arose as regards the application of section 2 to an option to purchase; a contract enabling the grantee to purchase land on terms specified in the option within a specified time. An option to purchase land consists of two stages: in the first stage, the option is granted; in the second, the option is exercised by the grantee. Following the enactment of the LP(MP)A 1989, Adams (1990) suggested that the exercise of the option by the grantee would need to comply with section 2; an outcome that would run counter to commercial practice and that, Stark (1992) suggested, would give the provision 'seismic effect', by leaving the exercise of options to 'the whim of the vendor'. A matter of weeks after section 2 came into force it was held that while the grant of an option must comply with section 2, the exercise of an option is a unilateral act (*Spiro v Glencrown Properties Ltd* (1991)). As such, the exercise of an option does not involve entry into a new contract and no question of compliance with section 2 arises.

## Contracts by Correspondence

**4.13**   Under section 40 it was possible for a contract for sale of land to come into existence through correspondence between the parties—the correspondence providing the written evidence of the contract required by section 40 of the LPA 1925. Parties could prevent their correspondence from being interpreted this way by indorsing it 'subject to contract'. In its report, the Law Commission (1987) anticipated that contracts by correspondence would remain possible. In *Commission for the New Towns v Cooper* (1995) the Court of Appeal considered that Parliament had gone further than the Law Commission had anticipated and that contracts by correspondence were not possible under section 2. It is clear that correspondence would not meet the requirements for an 'exchange' given in that case (and discussed at **4.14**). However, correspondence may produce a contract where it results in the creation of a single document signed by both parties (Oakley (1995)). Hence, in *Green v Ireland* (2011) the court accepted in principle that a 'string' of emails which contains the (typed) signatures of both parties could create a contract under section 2, although the claim failed on the facts.

## The Concept of an Exchange

**4.14**   As we have seen (**4.6**) a valid contract may be created under section 2 where separate documents are signed by each of the parties to the transaction and are then exchanged.

The concept of an exchange is a formal one, characterized by the parties' mutual intentions as regards the documents and a formal delivery. It was defined in *Commission for the New Towns v Cooper* (1995) in the following way.

- Each party draws up or is given a document which incorporates all the terms which they have agreed, and which is intended to record their proposed contract. The terms that have been agreed may have been agreed either orally or in writing or partly orally or partly in writing.

- The documents are referred to as 'contracts' or 'parts of contract', although they need not be so entitled. They are intended to take effect as formal documents of title and must be capable on their face of being fairly described as contracts having that effect.

- Each party signs his or her part in the expectation that the other party has also executed or will execute a corresponding part incorporating the same terms.

- At the time of execution neither party is bound by the terms of the document which he or she has executed, it being their mutual intention that neither will be bound until the executed parts are exchanged.

- The act of exchange is a formal delivery by each party of his or her part into the actual or constructive possession of the other with the intention that the parties will become actually bound when exchange occurs, but not before.

**4.15**  The manner of exchange may be agreed and determined by the parties. The traditional method was by mutual exchange across the table, both parties or their solicitors being present. Exchange can also take place by telephone (*Domb v Isoz* (1980)) which has become the most common method. Exchange takes place as soon as the solicitors agree during the conversation that it has done so. The contract exists from that point in time, even if paper documents are subsequently physically exchanged. One disadvantage of relying on a telephone exchange, however, is the possible lack of evidence that exchange had taken place in the event of a dispute—although the solicitors should make a written memo of the fact. Alternatively, exchange can take place by post. Where post is used, exchange is sequential and does not take place until the second document to be dispatched has been received or posted (*Eccles v Bryant and Pollock* (1948)).

## The Definition of 'Signed'

**4.16**  To constitute a contract within section 2 of the LP(MP)A 1989, the 'document' or 'documents' in the case of an exchange must be 'signed'. The meaning of both of these terms was considered by the Court of Appeal in the following case.

*Firstpost Homes v Johnson* (1995): An Ordnance Survey plan was attached to a letter that purported to record an agreement for sale of land. The vendor signed the letter and the plan, but the director acting for the purchaser had signed only the plan. It was held that the 'document' requiring signature for section 2 was the letter alone, the plan being a separate document incorporated into the letter by reference. Peter Gibson LJ acknowledged that the identification of the document was 'largely one of first impression', but, on the facts, the 'natural' interpretation was to treat the letter alone as the document. In the absence of the purchaser's handwritten signature on the letter, the question arose whether the requirement of a signature was met by the appearance of his printed or typed name. The purchaser had prepared the letter for the vendor and so had placed its director's name on the letter as the intended addressee (in the format 'Dear Geoff'). It was held that placing the director's name as the intended addressee did not constitute a 'signature'. Peter Gibson LJ indicated that courts had taken a liberal approach to the interpretation of formality requirements under the previous legislation (LPA 1925, s 40; see **4.6**) to enable contracts, including oral contracts, to be enforced. However, he suggested that the 1989 Act has a 'new and different philosophy' from previous legislation and should not be encumbered with 'ancient baggage' Peter Gibson LJ suggested that 'signed' should be interpreted as an ordinary person would understand it—and an ordinary person would not consider writing one's own name on a letter as the intended addressee to constitute signing the document. It should be noted that on the facts of the case the letter would have failed as a contract in any event because it did not contain an obligation to buy.

**4.17**   It is clear, however, that for the purposes of section 2, 'signature' is not confined to a 'wet ink' signature on a piece of paper. As we have seen above (**4.13**) the court has accepted that a contract for sale of land may be formed through a string of email correspondence. What constitutes a signature in the context of an email? It has been held in relation to section 2 that a typed named at the end of an email is a 'signature' (*Green v Ireland* (2011)). In contrast, in a case decided outside section 2, the court held that the name of the sender of an email, which is automatically inserted into the header, was not a signature as it had not been inserted to give the document authenticity (*J Pereira Fernandes SA v Mehta* (2006)). Between these two cases lies a range of possibilities, though the key question appears to be whether the name (or other typed mark) has been inserted in the email by the sender to give the email authenticity.

## Effect of Non-Compliance with Section 2

**4.18**   The effect of non-compliance with section 2 of the LP(MP)A 1989 is that there is no contract (**4.7**). This proposition is fundamental to section 2 and provides the starting point in any case in which the requirements of the provision are not met.

**4.19**   Notwithstanding the apparently draconian effect of non-compliance with section 2, there is a limited period within which the validity of a contract can be raised. In *Tootal Clothing Ltd v Guinea Property Management Ltd* (1992) Scott LJ explained, 'section 2 is of relevance only to executory contracts. It has no relevance to contracts which have been completed. If parties choose to complete an oral land contract or a land contract that does not in some respect or other comply with section 2, they are at liberty to do so. Once they have done so, it becomes irrelevant that the contract they have completed may not have been in accordance with section 2.' The effect of *Tootal Clothing* has, however, proved to be contentious. On one interpretation, it was suggested that *Tootal Clothing* has the effect that 'once all the land elements of an alleged contract have been performed, the remaining parts of the alleged contract can be examined without reference to section 2' (*Kilcarne Holdings Ltd v Targetfellow (Birmingham) Ltd* (2005)). However, this broad interpretation has now been rejected. The Court of Appeal has held, '[t]he proposition that a void contract can, by acts in the nature of part performance, mature into a valid one is contrary to principle and wrong' (*Keay v Morris Homes (West Midlands) Ltd* (2012)). The correct position is that once land has been transferred, the court will not permit the validity of the transfer to be challenged for non-compliance of the contract with section 2. However, non-compliance with section 2 will still prevent the enforcement of any aspects of the parties' agreement that remain executory.

4.20    Beyond the position with executed contracts, the Law Commission (1987) acknowledged the potential for strict formality requirements to lead to injustice. Where the parties have written and signed a document—or documents, in the case of exchange—but the terms are absent or wrong, two possible responses are available.

- The court may find that the parties had entered into two contracts: a contract for sale of land that complies with section 2 and a collateral contract, which is not a contract for sale of land and therefore does not need to comply with section 2 (4.21–4.22).

- The court may order rectification to create a contract that complies with section 2 (4.23–4.25).

Alternatively, rather than seeking to establish a valid contract (or where there is no prospect of one being established, for example through an absence of writing) a non-contractual remedy may be sought. The Law Commission specifically anticipated the doctrine of proprietary estoppel playing a role in this regard, although, as will be seen (4.26–4.31), its application has proved problematic.

## Collateral Contracts

4.21    As we have seen (4.6) one of the requirements in section 2 of the LP(MP)A 1989 is that the contract for sale of land contains all of the terms agreed by the parties. Hence, if a term is omitted, there is no contract, even where there is a written and signed document (or documents, in the case of exchange). However, section 2 does not prevent parties from entering a composite transaction, consisting of a contract for sale of land and other, separate or collateral, agreements. The challenge for the courts lies in distinguishing between those cases where the parties have entered a composite transaction from those in which an omitted term is part of the bargain for the transfer of land. If parties are permitted to 'hive off' parts of their bargain into separate contracts, then the purpose of section 2 is undermined (*Grossman v Hooper* (2001)). However, section 2 is also open to abuse by parties who 'look around for expressly agreed terms which have not found their way into the final form of land contract' in order to escape from a bargain following a change of mind (*North Eastern Properties Ltd v Coleman* (2010)).

4.22    Whether a term is part of a contract for sale of land is ultimately a question of fact: '[t]he question to which section 2(1) requires an answer is whether the written document the parties have signed as recording the terms of the sale or other disposition of an interest in land includes all the terms of such sale or disposition that they have expressly agreed' (*Keay v Morris Homes Ltd* (2012)). For example, an agreement to repay a loan to a third party was held to be collateral to the transfer of a home from one former partner to another on the breakdown of their relationship (*Grossman v Hooper* (2001)). Equally, an agreement for payment of a 'finder's fee' on exchange was held to be collateral to 11 contracts entered into between the parties for the sale of flats in a development (*North Eastern Properties Ltd v Coleman* (2010)). The court was satisfied that the parties had entered into a composite transaction consisting of the purchase of the flats and the payment of the fee. Performance of the land contract was not considered to be conditional upon performance of the finder's fee agreement. Further, the court noted that there were sound commercial reasons why the agreements had been structured so that the finder's fee was not part of the contracts for sale of land. In contrast, the court rejected an argument that a 'works obligation' that required developers to make prompt progress on the construction of a medical centre was collateral to a transfer of land (*Keay v Morris Homes*). The vendors argued that the works obligation was a separate promise the purchasers had agreed to enter into 'if' the vendors entered a supplemental agreement reducing the sale price. The Court of Appeal accepted that on this analysis the works obligation would be collateral. However, the evidence available to the court equally suggested that the works obligation was an express term of the supplemental agreement. However, the case arose on an application for summary judgment in which no determination of the facts could be made.

## Rectification

4.23    Where the parties have reached an agreement, but the terms are not all recorded in the document (or documents, in the case of exchange), or are recorded wrongly, the court may order rectification, with the result that the document then satisfies section 2 of the LP(MP)A 1989. The possibility of rectification is specifically referred to in section 2(4), which confers on the court discretion to determine the time at which the contract comes into being. The purpose of the discretion is to enable the court to take into account the possible effect of rectification on third parties who enter a transaction between the date of the original 'contract' (void at the time for non-compliance with s 2) and the court's decision to rectify the agreement.

4.24    It is established as a matter of contract law that rectification may be awarded where there is a prior agreement or common intention to contract on specified terms, and convincing proof that the written agreement does not reflect those terms (*Josceleyne v Nissen* (1970)). More controversially, rectification may also be available in cases of unilateral mistake, but only where the party not mistaken has acted unconscionably (*George Wimpey UK Ltd v VI Construction Ltd* (2005)). Unconscionability may arise, for example, through estoppel, fraud or dishonest misrepresentation, undue influence, breach of fiduciary duty, or though actual knowledge of the mistake. It has been suggested, obiter, that unconscionability may also be found where one party suspects the other to be mistaken and intends them to be so, without proof of inducement (*Commission for the New Towns v Cooper* (1995)).

4.25   To date, there is little authority on the use of rectification in relation to contracts for sale of land. The remedy was, however, used where a purchaser had agreed to buy a show flat, the price of which was to include carpets and furnishings (*Robert Leonard Developments Ltd v Wright* (1994)). This term was not included in both written contracts on exchange and the vendor removed the furniture. The contract was executed by the transfer of the lease of the flat and therefore the validity of the contract could no longer be questioned (4.19)—but the purchaser sought damages for breach of contract. The Court of Appeal considered that there was no separate or collateral contract for the sale of the furnishings; it was part of one package for the sale of the flat. Instead, the court held that the contract should be rectified to include the omitted term. In contrast, rectification will be refused where a term is deliberately omitted from the parties' agreement, even where both parties mistakenly consider the document to be a valid contract in the absence of the agreed term (*Oun v Ahmad* (2008)).

## Proprietary Estoppel

4.26   In its recommendations that led to the LP(MP)A 1989, the Law Commission (1987) specifically envisaged that proprietary estoppel would be available in appropriate cases in which the new formality requirements for a contract for sale were not complied with. The doctrine of proprietary estoppel has application in a wide range of circumstances, in many of which (eg promises of a gift or an inheritance) there is no question of the existence of a contract. The doctrine is fully discussed in Chapter 5. In this chapter, we are concerned with a specific point regarding the operation of proprietary estoppel: can the doctrine be invoked by a claimant where a contract has failed for non-compliance with section 2(1) of the LP(MP)A 1989?

4.27   Despite the Law Commission's confidence in the availability of proprietary estoppel, its availability has proved to be contentious. Ultimately, 's 2 has never been used by a court to reject a proprietary estoppel claim' (McFarlane (2014)), but at the same time the courts have not been consistent in their reasoning or provided authoritative answers to key questions (McFarlane (2014)). The ability to invoke estoppel was first called into question in the following case, which has continued to cast a long shadow over the relationship between section 2 and proprietary estoppel.

---

*Yaxley v Gotts* **(2000):** Mr Yaxley, a builder, found a property ripe for redevelopment. He entered an oral agreement, described as a 'gentleman's agreement', with his friend,

Mr Brownie Gotts. The terms of the agreement were that Brownie would purchase the property, and that Mr Yaxley would undertake the redevelopment and manage the building, in return for which he would be given the two ground-floor flats. The property was, in fact, purchased in the name of Brownie's son, Mr Alan Gotts. Mr Yaxley carried out the works, but, following a falling out between the friends, Alan refused to transfer the flats to Mr Yaxley. At first instance, the judge had found that Mr Yaxley could invoke proprietary estoppel and ordered a long lease of the flats to be granted to him. On appeal, the Gotts argued that the agreement with Mr Yaxley was void for non-compliance with section 2(1) of the LP(MP)A 1989 and estoppel could not be invoked to give effect to the void agreement. The Court of Appeal dismissed the appeal and so the remedy awarded by the judge at first instance remained unaltered. However, the ratio for the Court of Appeal's decision is difficult to identify. In particular, it is unclear whether, in the Court of Appeal's judgment, Mr Yaxley's claim succeeded on the basis of estoppel.

Two key issues were central to the Court of Appeal's discussion: first, a 'public policy principle' that estoppel could not be used to render valid a transaction that legislation has enacted is to be invalid; secondly, the scope of section 2(5) of the 1989 Act. That provision contains a saving for the operation of resulting and constructive trusts, but makes no reference to proprietary estoppel. This second issue, in turn, raised the question of the relationship between estoppel and the common intention constructive trust; a type of constructive trust of land discussed in **Chapter 5**. Robert Walker LJ considered that 'in the area of a joint enterprise for the acquisition of land', the concepts of proprietary estoppel and the common intention constructive trusts coincide. On his view, the findings of fact on which the judge found a proprietary estoppel would equally support a claim under a constructive trust, enabling Mr Yaxley to rely on the exception in section 2(5). Beldam LJ suggested that where an interest in land could equally be claimed under proprietary estoppel or constructive trust, it could not be contrary to a public policy principle to allow the claim to succeed under estoppel even though section 2(5) is limited in its terms to constructive trusts. He considered that on the facts equity would impose a constructive trust, but that the judge was entitled to reach the same conclusion through proprietary estoppel. In a brief judgment, in which he concurred with Robert Walker and Beldam LJJ, Clarke LJ agreed that Mr Yaxley's claim should succeed under constructive trust. However, Clarke LJ also accepted that on the particular facts of the case, a claim to proprietary estoppel may not be considered to undermine the public policy principle that underpins section 2.

4.28   The key issue that remains uncertain following *Yaxley v Gotts* is whether a claimant in Mr Yaxley's position succeeds under proprietary estoppel or constructive trust. That point has remained unresolved by subsequent cases (see eg *Kinane v Mackie-Conteh* (2005)).

4.29   *Yaxley v Gotts* is a difficult and unsatisfactory decision. The exact relationship between proprietary estoppel and the common intention constructive trust is difficult to ascertain and is discussed further at **5.135–5.138**. Relying on an overlap between the principles in the context of section 2 appears attractive as it enables the courts to invoke the statutory exception for constructive trusts in section 2(5). But there are conceptual and practical difficulties in utilizing constructive trusts in estoppel cases. It is not apparent, for example, that the remedy in *Yaxley v Gotts*—the grant of a lease—can be explained on the basis of a constructive trust, which is imposed on the basis of a common intention to share *beneficial* ownership. Since *Yaxley v Gotts*, the courts' general attitude to the relationship between proprietary estoppel and constructive trusts has changed, and Robert Walker LJ has recanted from his own view that there are situations in which the doctrines merge or coincide (*Stack v Dowden* (2007)). This shift towards emphasizing the differences between the doctrines has not yet penetrated the case law under section 2.

4.30   As a judge in the Court of Appeal, Neuberger LJ (as he then was) adopted an approach consistent with Robert Walker LJ in *Yaxley v Gotts*. Where a claim to proprietary estoppel was made in respect of a charge which had not been formally executed, Neuberger LJ held that the claim succeeded under constructive trust (*Kinane v Mackie-Conteh* (2005)). For the purposes of his judgment, Neuberger LJ assumed (without deciding) that the claim would fail if the claimant could only establish a proprietary estoppel and not an overlapping claim to a constructive trust. Subsequently, writing extra-judicially, Lord Neuberger has indicated a broader approach to estoppel and section 2. He has moved towards the view that an estoppel claim is not precluded by section 2 even where there is no overlapping constructive trust. Notably, this change appears to have been prompted by a narrow approach to estoppel both generally and in relation to section 2 that was advocated by Lord Scott in *Yeoman's Row Management Ltd v Cobbe* (2008). Giving judgment in that case, Lord Scott commented, obiter, 'My present view, however, is that proprietary estoppel cannot be prayed in aid in order to render enforceable an agreement that statute has declared to be void. The proposition that an owner of land can be estopped from asserting that an agreement is void for want of compliance with the requirements of section 2 is, in my opinion, unacceptable. The assertion is no more than the statute provides. Equity can surely not contradict the statute.' In a discussion of that decision, Lord Neuberger (2009) stated:

> I suggest that section 2 has nothing to do with the matter…[T]he fact that, if there was a contract, it would be void is irrelevant: indeed the very reason for mounting the proprietary estoppel claim is that there is no enforceable contract. I accept of course that it is not open to a claimant to take the unvarnished point that it is inequitable for a defendant to rely on the argument that an apparent contract is void for not complying with the requirements of section 2. But where there is the superadded fact that the claimant, with the conscious encouragement of the defendant, has acted in the belief that there is a valid contract, I suggest that section 2 offers no bar to a claim based in equity.

4.31   There is strong logical force in favour of the view that section 2 should not bar claims to estoppel even where the claim does not coincide with a constructive trust. It is beyond doubt that estoppel cannot be used to enforce an otherwise invalid contract

(Dixon (2005)). But, as McFarlane (2014) explains, 's 2 applies only to regulate the requirements of a valid contract. As a result if [the claim] is based on a different doctrine capable of giving rise to rights... the rule simply does not apply. In such a case, therefore, there is no need for [the claimant] to resort to s 2(5) by attempting to show that his or her claim gives rise to a constructive trust.'

## Creation or Transfer

4.32    Creation or transfer—or 'completion' (4.2)—of the contract serves a different purpose to the contract and is subject to its own formality requirements. The contract creates a legally binding obligation between the parties, which is performed—or in legal terms, the contract is executed—by the vendor creating or transferring the property right. Hence, while the contract requires a mutual act by the parties, its performance is a unilateral act by the vendor.

4.33    The formality requirements necessary for the creation or transfer of the legal right, and their exceptions, are provided by sections 52 and 54 of the LPA 1925. Under section 52 of the LPA 1925, save in exceptional cases, the creation or transfer of a legal right requires the execution of a deed. The effect of non-compliance is that legal title does not pass. The intended recipient of the rights may, however, have a claim in equity. For example, where there is a contract for sale, but section 52 is not complied with, an equitable interest will arise under the doctrine of anticipation (4.3 and 5.76–5.81).

4.34    The most notable exception to the need for a deed is that contained in section 54(2) for short leases. Under that section, no formalities are required to create a legal lease of three years or less, where the lease is granted at market rent, without a premium, and takes effect in possession. It has been held that possession must be immediate (*Long v Tower Hamlets LBC* (1998)). A legal lease that meets the criteria in section 54(2) can be created orally.

4.35    The requirements for a document to constitute a deed are provided in section 1 of the LP(MP)A 1989. That section, like section 2, implements recommendations by the Law Commission (1987). The key requirements under section 1 for a document to be a deed are that it is signed and attested, and that it specifies on its face that it is a deed. The specific need for attestation, explained in section 1(3)(a)(i), is that the document is signed 'in the presence of a witness', who then signs the deed him or herself. This requirement is not met, for example, if a witness who was not present when the party executing the deed signed it, subsequently signs the document. Where a deed appears on its face to comply with the requirement of attestation, the party executing the deed will be estopped from seeking to invalidate it on the basis that attestation did not in fact take place (*Shah v Shah* (2002)). However, estoppel will not apply where non-compliance is apparent on the face of the document; for example, where there is no space for attestation (*Briggs v Gleeds* (2014), *Bank of Scotland v Waugh* (2014)).

**4.36** A deed takes effect when it is 'delivered as a deed' (s 1(3)(b)). Delivery will be immediate if the document specifies that it is 'signed and delivered' as a deed; in other cases, there will need to be a subsequent delivery. Delivery originally denoted a physical act, but the requirement has evolved to relate to an intention to be bound (*Vincent v Premo Enterprises (Voucher Sales) Ltd* (1969)).

**4.37** Establishing an intention to be bound becomes significant where, in the ordinary course of transactions, deeds are prepared and signed in advance of an anticipated completion of creation or transfer. A deed that has been signed, but not delivered, may be classified in one of two ways: as an escrow or as a 'non-deed' (*Longman v Viscount Chelsea* (1989)). Each has different legal consequences. An escrow is irrevocable but does not take effect unless and until the conditions of the escrow (which may include, eg, payment of the purchase price) have been fulfilled. In contrast, a non-deed is a revocable document which has no legal effect unless and until it is delivered as a deed. Whether a document is classified as an escrow or non-deed is dependent on the intention of the party executing the document.

## Registration

**4.38** While the execution of a deed is required to convey or create a legal estate (save in exceptional cases (**4.34**)), in most cases it is not sufficient itself to do so. In most cases registration is required. Registration is required where the legal title being transferred is a registered estate (**4.56**) or where the estate is currently unregistered and the transfer triggers compulsory first registration (**4.51**). Where registration is required, once the deed has been executed by the vendor, the purchaser must apply for registration. Failure to register carries the consequence that legal title will not be transferred (**4.52** and **4.56**). Title remains with the transferor, although, in the case of a sale, it will be held in trust for the transferee under the vendor–purchaser constructive trust discussed at **4.3** and **5.83–5.86**.

**4.39** Registration of title is now governed by the LRA 2002, which repealed and replaced the Land Registration Act 1925 (LRA 1925). The 2002 Act is based on recommendations that followed a joint project of the Law Commission and Land Registry (Law Commission (2001)) ambitiously titled 'A Conveyancing Revolution'. While the Act is a revolution in its own terms, it also marks the latest stage in the *evolution* of registered land, the origins of which can be traced back to the 18th century. Over the course of time, the system has developed from a mechanical means of registration of title, based on the substantive principles of unregistered land law, to an independent system of 'title by registration' (Law Commission (1998)).

**4.40** The LRA 2002 is currently being reviewed by the Law Commission (2016), which published a Consultation Paper on the Act in March 2016.

## The Evolution of Registered Land

4.41    The origins of registration of title lie in the work of a Royal Commission, whose report
was published in 1857. The Commission considered the following question:

> By what means, consistently with the preservation of existing rights, can we now obtain
> such a system of registration as will enable owners to deal with land in as simple and easy
> a manner, as far as the title is concerned, and the difference in the nature and the subject
> matter may allow, as they now can deal with movable chattels or stock? No-one doubts
> that it would be a great benefit to the proprietors of land if they were able to convey it
> with the same facility as the owners of ships or of stocks or railway shares can now assign
> their property in any of them. The questions is, can this be accomplished?—and if so how?

The Royal Commission concluded that registration of title provided the only answer to
this question.

4.42    The provision of a system of registration of title based on the 1857 Royal Commission
report was first provided by the Land Transfer Act 1875. Despite this, even at the time of
the 1925 legislation, registered land was still seen as experimental. The intention was to
operate both registered and unregistered systems for a ten-year period, before adopting
'whichever system should be found more safe, simple, speedy and economic' (Ruoff et al
(1986)). Although no formal decision on the matter was ever taken, the system of registration was gradually extended.

4.43    In replacing the LRA 1925, the primary focus of the LRA 2002 is to lay the foundations for the implementation of electronic conveyancing, or 'e-conveyancing' (Law
Commission (2001)). While e-conveyancing has not yet been achieved (**4.59–4.62**),
the changes made to facilitate its introduction are far-reaching in their own right. The
changes introduced by the LRA 2002 impact, in particular, on the operation of priority rules in registered land (discussed in **Chapter 11**) and on adverse possession of
registered land (**4.121–4.131**).

## Three Underlying Principles

4.44    Registration of title is not unique to English law. Its introduction matched a parallel development in Australia, in the introduction to New South Wales of the Torrens system
of registration, named after its pioneer Sir Robert Torrens. The principles underlying
systems of registered title are identified in a seminal work by Ruoff (1957).

4.45    The first principle, the mirror principle, 'involves the proposition that the register of
title is a mirror which reflects accurately and completely and beyond all argument the
current facts that are material to a man's title' (Ruoff (1957)). Achieving the 'mirror principle' has been a continuous goal of registration of title. Ruoff acknowledged that 'in
this imperfect world the mirror does not invariably give a completely reliable reflection'.

Tension remains, in particular, as regards the balance between the mirror principle and the category of 'overriding interests'—that is, those not entered on the register, but necessarily binding against purchasers. This category of interest is discussed in **Chapter 11**.

4.46    The second principle, the curtain principle, 'provides that the register is the sole source of information for proposing purchasers, who need not and, indeed, must not concern themselves with trusts and equities which lie behind the curtain' (Ruoff (1957)). The 'curtain principle' is ensured through the process of overreaching, whereby (as long as certain conditions are met) purchasers take land free from beneficial interests under a trust. The mechanism is discussed in **Chapter 11**.

4.47    The third principle, the insurance principle, reflects the idea 'that the mirror that is the register is deemed to give an absolutely correct reflection of title but if, through human frailty, a flaw appears, anyone who thereby suffers loss must be put in the same position, so far as money can do it, as if the reflection were a true one. A lost right is converted into hard cash' (Ruoff (1957)). The 'insurance principle' is reflected in the provision for payment of an indemnity, now governed by Schedule 8 to the 2002 Act, for those suffering loss as a result of a rectification of the register (or a mistake, the correction of which would involve rectification), or through mistakes made by Land Registry. It is closely connected to the issue of indefeasibility of title (**4.66–4.83**).

## Voluntary and Compulsory Registration

4.48    When registration of title was first introduced, it operated on a voluntary basis. The Land Transfer Act 1897 was the first to make provision for compulsory registration. Compulsory registration is a two-stage process: first, an area is declared (by Order in Council) to be subject to compulsory registration of title; secondly, title is then registered for the first time on the occurrence of an event that triggers registration. Compulsory registration began in London and spread piecemeal. The last remaining districts were made subject to compulsory registration on 1 December 1990 (Registration of Title Order 1989 (SI 1989/1347)). Hence, title to all land in England and Wales is now either registered or will be registered for the first time on the next triggering event.

4.49    Voluntary registration is possible under section 3 of the LRA 2002. To assist in the completion of the register, financial incentives have been provided by the reduction of fees for voluntary registration (Land Registration Fee Order 2013 (SI 2013/3174), art 2(5)). The Act further encourages voluntary registration through making a registered title qualitatively superior to its unregistered counterpart (Law Commission (2001)), in particular, through its limited vulnerability to claims to adverse possession (**4.121–4.131**).

4.50    It is estimated that nearly 88 per cent of land in England and Wales is now registered, with 24.5 million titles on the register (Land Registry (2016)). The Law Commission (2001) identified 'total registration' as a goal: '[U]nregistered land has had its day. In the comparatively near future, it will be necessary to take steps to bring what is left of it on to the register.' But the recommendations for the 2002 Act did not include provisions to achieve this goal, for which three reasons were given (Law Commission (2001)). First, the Law Commission noted that it would be premature to do so before existing provisions were given the opportunity to work (including an anticipated rise in voluntary registration under the LRA 2002). Secondly, it was felt that the triggers for compulsory registration catch the principal dispositions of land and extension of compulsion beyond this may be heavy-handed. Thirdly, concerns were expressed at further stretching Land Registry's resources following the changes introduced by the 2002 Act.

4.51    The scope of registration of title is outlined in the LRA 2002 (s 2). Compulsory registration under the Act extends to freehold title and leases of more than seven years' duration (LRA 2002, s 2(1)(a), (2)). Leases of seven years or less cannot be registered, although leases of more than three years' duration may be recorded on the title of the estate out of which the lease was granted through entry of a notice (11.27–11.33) as a means of preserving their priority on a transfer of the landlord's estate. Provision is also made in the LRA 2002 for registration of rentcharges, franchises, and profits à prendre in gross, though registration of these rights takes place on a voluntary basis.

4.52    Now that all remaining unregistered land is subject to compulsory first registration of title (4.48), first registration will take place on the occurrence of one of a number triggering events (LRA 2002, s 4). These events include a transfer by sale or gift of a freehold estate or of a lease with more than seven years' remaining duration and the grant of a new lease of more than seven years' duration. Where compulsory first registration is triggered, the effect of failing to apply for registration within the statutory timescale (LRA 2002, s 6) is that the transfer becomes void as regards the transfer of legal title (LRA 2002, s 7). In the absence of an event triggering compulsory first registration, an unregistered freehold title and an unregistered lease with more than seven years' remaining duration can be registered voluntarily (LRA 2002, s 3).

## The Register

4.53    Where a title is registered, it is entered on the register with a unique title number. Information about the title is then recorded in three parts.

- The property register identifies the title as freehold or leasehold, and, in the case of a lease, provides brief details of its terms. It identifies the land by a description, usually the address, and by reference to the official plan. It also lists rights that benefit the title, such as the benefit of an easement.

- The proprietorship register gives the name and address of the registered proprietor(s) and any restrictions on their ability to deal with the land. It may also state the price paid for the title.

- The charges register contains information on registered mortgages and other secured interests, and any other burdens affecting the title: for example, leases, easements, and covenants to which the land is subject.

4.54    On first registration, a freehold estate is registered with absolute, qualified, or possessory title. 'Absolute' title is the usual expectation, and vests the estate in the proprietor subject principally to burdens on the register and overriding interests (LRA 2002, s 11(3)–(5)). 'Qualified' or 'possessory' title may be awarded (respectively) where there is a possible defect in the applicant's title or insufficient documentary proof. Registration is additionally subject to estates, rights, or interests that are excepted from registration in the case of qualified title (LRA 2002, s 11(6)), or are subsisting or capable of arising at the date of registration in respect of possessory title (LRA 2002, s 11(7)).

4.55    Leases may also be registered with absolute, qualified, and possessory titles, which have an analogous effect to those grades of freehold title, with additional provision that they are subject to covenants, obligations, and liabilities in the lease (LRA 2002, s 12(4)). Absolute leasehold is only available, however, where the freehold is also registered or proved to the satisfaction of the Registrar. Where this is not the case, 'good leasehold' title is granted, leaving open a possible challenge against the estate out of which the lease was granted (LRA 2002, s 12(7)).

## Dispositions of Registered Titles

4.56    Once legal title has been registered it is essential that the register is kept up to date. Hence, once a title has been brought onto the register through voluntary or compulsory first registration, subsequent dealings must be completed by registration. It is therefore provided that certain dispositions of registered estates do not operate at law until registration (LRA 2002, s 27). These 'registered dispositions' have a logical symmetry with the type of events that trigger compulsory first registration. Hence, for example, the transfer of a registered freehold or leasehold title (LRA 2002, s 27(2)(a)), and the creation of a lease of more than seven years' duration (LRA 2002, s 27(2)(b)) are included in the list of registrable dispositions. It should be noted that the transfer of a registered lease requires registration even if there is less than seven years of the term left to run. The limitation of registration to leases of more than seven years' duration applies only to determine whether a lease is brought onto the register. Once a lease is on the register it is subject to formalities in respect of subsequent dispositions regardless of its remaining duration.

## The Registration Gap

4.57    As we have seen in this chapter, the completion of a transaction (the transfer or creation of the legal estate) and registration are two distinct stages. Legal title does not reach the purchaser until registration. Inherent in the scheme of registration is the existence of a 'registration gap'—that is, a period between completion of a transfer by execution of a deed and the vesting of legal title by registration. During this period, legal title is held on trust for the purchaser through the vendor–purchaser constructive trust (4.3). But the purchaser remains vulnerable to third party rights arising during this period. Further, as the legal title remains with the vendor, there is a risk that the vendor will undertake further dealings affecting the title. In *Brown & Root Technology Ltd v Sun Alliance and*

*London Assurance Co Ltd* (2001), a tenant (vendor) assigned a registered lease, but the assignee (purchaser) did not apply for registration of title to the lease. This meant that the legal title remained with the vendor, who then exercised a break clause to bring the lease to an end. On the facts, the vendor and purchaser were both part of the same corporate group and by exercising the break clause the vendor was able to release the company from what had become a bad bargain. Hence the vendor's ability to exercise the break clause worked in favour of the purchaser. But on other facts, the loss of the property right may be detrimental to the purchaser. For example, if the companies were unrelated and the break clause was exercised out of spite. Personal remedies may lie against the vendor on such facts although the utility of these is dependent on the vendor's whereabouts and ability to pay. See also *Pye v Stodday Land Ltd* (2016).

4.58    The Law Commission (2016) has considered, but provisionally rejected, legal solutions to the existence of the registration gap, including the possibility of changing the time at which legal title passes to the date of the transfer. The Law Commission has acknowledged that while the registration gap causes practical problems, particularly in the context of leases, practitioners have developed their own solutions in cases where the gap is most likely to cause difficulties. At the time of the LRA 2002 it was hoped that the registration gap would be removed by the introduction of e-conveyancing, under which transfer and registration would occur simultaneously, rather than as separate stages of a transaction. E-conveyancing has not, however, progressed in the way that had been hoped.

## E-conveyancing

4.59    A fundamental objective of the LRA 2002 was to provide the legal framework for the introduction of e-conveyancing. Indeed, the Law Commission (2001) described the provision of this framework as 'the most important single function' of the Act. E-conveyancing was said by Cooke (2003) to have provided the 'magic carpet' that transported the Bill through Parliament by making it politically attractive.

4.60    The goal of e-conveyancing is to enable transfers or dispositions of land to become electronic transactions. The LRA 2002 envisages a scheme of electronic conveyancing in which dispositions would be effected by electronic documents and in which creation and registration would occur simultaneously. The registration gap would therefore be closed. Equitable intervention would also be prevented as instead of a disposition having no effect 'at law' until registration (LRA 2002, s 27(1)), in the scheme of e-conveyancing provided by the LRA 2002 a disposition 'only has effect' on registration; there is no statutory qualification to its effect at law (LRA 2002, s 93(2)).

4.61    Despite its centrality to the 'conveyancing revolution' promised by the LRA 2002, e-conveyancing has remained elusive and in 2011 Land Registry placed work on the project 'on hold'. Land Registry cited three reasons for the decision to do so. First, work towards the planned introduction of e-transfers in 2011 coincided with a downturn in the property market that followed the global economic crisis. Secondly, there remain concerns—albeit doubted by Land Registry—that e-conveyancing will exacerbate the risk of conveyancing fraud. Thirdly, there are unresolved legal issues surrounding the possibility of parties to the transaction delegating their authority to sign to a conveyancer. In particular, there is a concern whether a transaction signed by a single conveyancer on behalf of joint owners will trigger the overreaching mechanism. Overreaching, which is discussed in **Chapter 11**, plays an essential role in transactions involving co-owned land, but is triggered only where the transaction is undertaken by at least two trustees. It is uncertain whether it will apply to a transaction signed by a single conveyancer on the authority of two trustees.

4.62    In its Consultation Paper on the LRA 2002 (**4.40**) the Law Commission (2016) has provisionally proposed reforms to put the development of e-conveyancing back on track. The Law Commission has proposed that the requirement of simultaneous transfer and registration should be removed from the legislation. Whilst agreeing that such a development should remain the ultimate goal, the Law Commission concludes that it is not practical to move straight from a paper-based system to an electronic system in which transfer and registration are simultaneous. The Law Commission considers that removing the requirement of simultaneity will pave the way for enabling the development of electronic conveyancing through the use of more flexible models, as well as allaying some of the practical and legal concerns that have prevented the full implementation of the scheme of electronic conveyancing provided for in the LRA 2002. One consequence, however, is that e-conveyancing will no longer remove the existence of the registration gap (**4.57–4.58**). Under the newly proposed scheme, it will also continue to be possible for equitable interests to arise prior to registration. Finally, the Law Commission has proposed reforms that will ensure that overreaching takes place where two or more trustees collectively delegate their power to sign an electronic conveyance and give receipt for capital monies to a single conveyance.

## The Content of a Registered Title

4.63    As we have seen, in respect of registered estates—freehold titles and leases created for more than seven years—registration is essential in order for legal title to be obtained (**4.56**). We will see in **Chapter 11** that the proprietor of a registered estate is conferred with certain 'owner's powers', which are expressed broadly in the Act as including 'power to make a disposition of any kind permitted by the general law in relation to an interest of that description' (LRA 2002, s 23(1)). Registration therefore operates both to confer title and to determine the powers exercisable in relation to that title by the proprietor.

4.64    In order fully to understand the content of a registered title, however, it is necessary to consider further the effect of registration. The requirement of registration in order to obtain a legal estate can be seen as the 'negative' operation of registration; the requirement says that failure to register means that no legal title is obtained. That is the case even if, as a matter of general law, a person is 'entitled' to the legal estate, in respect of which a deed has been executed to transfer the title to him or her.

4.65   But registration also operates positively; that is, the mere act of registration confers title on the proprietor even if, as a matter of general law, he or she would not be entitled to the title. The most obvious reason why a person is not entitled to a title under the general law is because the transfer has taken place by fraud. The conclusiveness of registration is established by section 58 of the LRA 2002, which provides, in disarmingly simple terms, that 'If, on the entry of a person in the register as the proprietor of a legal estate, the legal estate would not otherwise be vested in him, it shall be deemed to be vested in him as a result of the registration.' As Goymour (2013) explains, section 58 thus confers the Registrar with a 'Midas Touch'; the act of registration confers the proprietor with title regardless of whether or not he or she is entitled to the land.

## 'Conclusiveness' of the Register and Indefeasibility of Title

4.66   The effect of registration is brought into sharp relief when section 58 operates to confer title on a person who is not in fact entitled to the land. The 'conclusiveness' of the register provided by section 58 is qualified by provision made in the legislation for alteration and rectification of the register (LRA 2002, Sch 4). These provisions mean that while the register is conclusive, what the register says can, in specified circumstances, be changed, either by the Registrar or by the court. Most significant amongst these circumstances is provision for the register to be changed in order to correct a 'mistake' (LRA 2002, Sch 4, paras 2(1)(a) and 5(a)).

4.67   Mistake is not defined in the LRA 2002. The essence of a mistake is that 'a change is made to the register but nobody was entitled to procure that change at the moment when it was made' (Cooper (2013)). The classic instance of a mistake is where the register says that one person (B) is proprietor of an estate, but under the general law another person (A) is in fact entitled to the estate. Such a mistake will arise, for example, where A's title is transferred to B by fraud, as a fraudulent transfer has no effect as a matter of general law. A mistake will also arise where A's title is left on the register but, by fraud, a registered charge is created in favour of B (*Swift 1st v Chief Land Registrar* (2015)). It has also been held that registration of a claimant as proprietor of an estate through adverse possession is a mistake if the claimant has not in fact been in adverse possession (or has not been in adverse possession for the requisite period of time) when registration is procured (*Baxter v Manion* (2011), see (**4.127**)).

4.68   An alteration of the register to correct a mistake, which 'prejudicially affects the title of a registered proprietor', is referred to in the LRA 2002 as a 'rectification' of the register. Where the register is rectified—or a decision is made not to make an alteration of the register that would be rectification—the party or parties who suffer loss are entitled to an indemnity (LRA 2002, Sch 8, para 1(1)(a) and (b)). The entitlement to an indemnity in these circumstances reflects the 'insurance principle' (**4.47**); a person who suffers loss as a result of registration is compensated. Land Registry stands for these purposes as an insurer of first resort. A party who suffers loss can claim an indemnity from Land Registry without pursuing those responsible for the loss.

**4.69** When rectification is available, the question whether the register should be changed has become one of the most difficult and contentious issues under the LRA 2002. Much of the case law in which the question has arisen has involved two innocent victims of another party's fraud. The court, through balancing section 58 of the LRA 2002 with provisions enabling rectification of the register, must determine which of the victims is entitled to the land, and which must instead be left to claim an indemnity. The case law can be distilled into two basic fact patterns.

- The first scenario (the 'AB scenario') involves two parties. At the start of the scenario, A is the registered proprietor. A's title is then transferred to B (or a registered charge is granted to B) through fraud. The fraud comes to light only after B has become registered. A then seeks the return of the title from B, or seeks to have B's charge removed from the register. The essence of the scenario is that the person who B was dealing with was not in fact the registered proprietor (A) but a fraudster purporting to be A.

- The second scenario (the 'ABC scenario') involves three or more parties. In this scenario, there is again a fraudulent transfer of A's registered title to B, who becomes registered proprietor. In this scenario, following B's registration, B transfers the land to C or grants a registered charge to C. It may be, for example, that B is buying A's land with finance provided by C as a mortgage lender. The transfer or charge to C is therefore a genuine transaction; C is dealing with B who is in fact the registered proprietor. However, B's registered title is tainted by the fraud in the earlier transaction that resulted in B's registration. Once the fraud comes to light, A seeks the return of the title from C, or seeks to have the title returned from B and C's charge removed from the register.

**4.70** In each of these scenarios a decision must be made whether to restore the title to A, which requires taking the title away from B and/or C, who will then claim an indemnity; or to enable B and/or C to keep the title, leaving A to claim an indemnity. Typically, all of the parties involved are innocent victims of another person's fraud.

**4.71** Whether B and/or C's registered title should be removed from the register is referred to in Torrens jurisdictions as a question of 'indefeasibility' of title.

**4.72** Two general approaches to indefeasibility prevail in systems of registered title. Most Torrens jurisdictions adopt 'immediate indefeasibilty'. Under this system, once B becomes registered, B's title is generally considered secure. Immediate indefeasibility thus provides dynamic security that favours the purchaser's title. An alternative approach is 'deferred' indefeasibility, whereby A's title would be restored to the register if the flaw in B's registration came to light while B was still proprietor. If, however, B had sold the land to C, who was now registered proprietor, then C's title would be secure; C being a step away from the flawed registration. Deferred indefeasibility provides static security, which favours the title of the original registered proprietor.

**4.73**  English law has not adopted either immediate or deferred indefeasibilty. Instead, the approach adopted in the LRA 1925—and carried over into the LRA 2002—was described by the Law Commission as 'qualified indefeasibility' (Law Commission (2001)). In essence, the English legislation favours returning title to A because the LRA 2002 provides that where there is a power to alter or rectify the register, the power must be exercised unless there are exceptional circumstances (LRA 2002, Sch 4, paras 2(3) and 6(3)). However, the preference in favour of A gives way where the other party to the dispute is a 'proprietor in possession'. Rectification is not possible against a proprietor in possession unless he or she caused or substantially contributed to the mistake by fraud or lack of proper care, or it would otherwise be unjust not to rectify the register (LRA 2002, Sch 4, paras 3(2) and 6(2)).

**4.74**  The practical effect of the provisions in the LRA 2002 on rectification is as follows. In a dispute between A and B, the title will be returned to A (in the absence of exceptional circumstances) and B will be left to claim an indemnity unless B has moved into possession. If, however, B has taken possession, then B is a 'proprietor in possession' and benefits from qualified indefeasibility. Rectification cannot then be ordered against B save in the limited circumstances provided by the legislation.

**4.75**  In the AB scenario it is uncontentious to describe B's registration as a mistake. As a result of the fraud, the transfer from A to B is void as a matter of general law. B is conferred with title only through the Registrar's 'Midas Touch' on registration.

**4.76**  The position of C in the ABC scenario is more complex. Once B is registered, then B is deemed to have registered title by virtue of section 58 regardless of any flaw in the underlying transaction. As registered proprietor, B has 'owner's powers', including the power of disposition (LRA 2002, s 26). If B then transfers the land to C or grants C a registered charge, can C's registration be said to be a mistake? If not, then A may have no prospect of recovering the land (unless alteration of the register is available on a basis other than mistake) and neither A nor C (if the register is altered) is entitled to claim an indemnity. Not to classify C's registration as a mistake therefore leaves an innocent victim of fraud without a remedy. However, to describe C's registration as a mistake calls seriously into question the effect of B's registration and, therefore, the claim in section 58 that the register is conclusive.

**4.77**  Courts have struggled to understand C's position and there is some support for the view that C's registration cannot be considered a mistake (*Guy v Barclays Bank plc* (2008)). The undesirable outcome of this interpretation has, however, led the courts to a purposive interpretation of the legislation. There is now no doubt that rectification of the register is available against C, so that in a dispute between A and C either A will recover title and C will claim an indemnity, or C will retain title and A will be able to claim an indemnity. Courts have reached this outcome by suggesting that either C's registration is 'part and parcel' of the mistaken registration of B, or that reversing the mistake in B's registration requires the court to remove subsequent transactions from the register (*Knights Construction (March) Ltd v Roberto Mac Ltd* (2011), *Ajibade v Bank of Scotland plc* (2008)).

## The *Malory* (2002) Problems

4.78   The provisions of the LRA 2002 dealing with alteration and rectification of the register seek to draw a careful balance between the competing claims of parties where entitlement to land is disputed. The provisions play two essential roles. First, they identify the factors that should determine which of the parties should receive title to the land and which should be left to claim an indemnity. As we have seen (4.74), the provisions favour the return of the land to the party divested of title (A) unless the claim is against a proprietor in possession. Secondly, they ensure, through drawing a link between rectification and indemnity, that the party or parties who are unable to keep the land are able to claim an indemnity (4.68). A matter of days before the LRA 2002 received Royal Assent, the Court of Appeal delivered judgment in *Malory Enterprises Ltd v Cheshire Homes (UK) Ltd* (2002). Based on the provisions of the LRA 1925, the judgment contained two ways through which the balance drawn by the provisions on alteration and rectification can be undermined. One of these ways was to say that where B becomes registered proprietor under a fraudulent transaction, B holds the title on trust for A. It has subsequently been held that the decision in *Malory* was *per incuriam* (decided without reference to authority) and wrong on this point (*Swift 1st v Chief Land Registrar* (2015)). The *Malory* trust can no longer be imposed and need not be discussed further.

4.79   The second argument made in *Malory* has not, however, fully been resolved and requires further exploration. This argument focused on the nature of A's statutory right to seek rectification of the register against B. The Court of Appeal held that the statutory right to seek rectification is a property right which, if coupled with A's occupation, is binding on B as an overriding interest (4.45 and 11.37-11.59). If A is in occupation of the land in order to claim an overriding interest, then B cannot be in occupation. Therefore the overriding interest argument may apply only where B is not, in any event, a proprietor in possession. As we have noted, where B does not have that special status, the legislation is weighted in favour of returning the land to A.

4.80   However, it is an established principle that where the register is changed to reflect an overriding interest, the person against whom the change is made (B) is not entitled to an indemnity (*Re Chowood's Registered Land* (1933)). Changing the register to incorporate an overriding interest is not rectification of the register; either because it does not involve the correction of a mistake, or (if it does) because the correction is not prejudicial to B's registered title. B is not prejudiced because B was already bound by the interest. Hence, the overriding interest analysis in *Malory* (2002) also risks undermining the policy balance in the LRA 2002 by preventing B claiming an indemnity. This outcome was prevented in the following case but the solution would not apply in all cases.

**Swift 1st Ltd v Chief Land Registrar (2015):** Mrs Rani (A) discovered that a mortgage had been granted over her home by forgery only when she was served with possession proceedings by the mortgagee, Swift 1st (B) who were registered with the forged mortgage. The forgery meant that registration of the mortgage was a mistake and the register was rectified by removing the charge. Swift 1st then claimed an indemnity from the Registrar. The Registrar argued that no indemnity was payable. Mrs Rani's statutory right to rectify the register was a property right, which bound Swift 1st as an overriding interest by virtue of her actual occupation. This argument failed. The LRA 2002 provides that (Sch 8, para 1(2)(b)):

> *the proprietor of a registered estate or charge claiming in good faith under a forged disposition is, where the register is rectified, to be regarded as having suffered loss by reason of such rectification as if the disposition had not been forged.*

This provision mirrors one contained in the LRA 1925 to overturn a decision made under earlier legislation which held that where the register is changed to reverse a forged disposition, any losses incurred are the result of the fraud, not of the change in the register, and do not attract an indemnity (*Attorney-General v Odel* (1906)). The provision ensures that an indemnity is available in such cases by deeming the losses to be the result of the forgery. The Court of Appeal held that the provision goes further and ensures that an indemnity is available despite the existence of an overriding interest. In this way, the Court of Appeal ensured that Swift 1st were entitled to claim an indemnity, despite Mrs Rani's overriding interest. The Court of Appeal therefore avoided the logical indemnity consequences of the *Malory* argument. But by invoking a provision confined in its scope to 'forged dispositions', the decision leaves open the outcome of a case where the transfer from A to B (or the grant of the mortgage in favour of B) arises from fraud other than forgery; such as a successful claim to '*non est factum*' (a defence that a document is not my deed) where A is tricked into executing the disposition.

4.81 Even though the effect of *Malory* has been substantially curtailed, the decision continues to cast a shadow over the policy balance drawn in the LRA 2002 and has had a significant influence on case law arising under the legislation. In its current consultation paper, the Law Commission (2016) has proposed that the statutory right to rectify should not be capable of being an overriding interest. If enacted, this proposal will mark the reversal of *Malory*.

4.82 In its current consultation on the LRA 2002, the Law Commission (2016) has also suggested a new formula for determining the outcome of claims to rectification of the register. The formula does not purport to provide the outcome in every case. The Law Commission suggests that the complexity of claims means that discretion to determine which of two innocent parties is entitled to the land and which must claim an indemnity is necessary. However, the Law Commission suggests that its formula will settle the principles that determine the outcome in every case.

4.83 Under the proposed formula, the provisions will remain weighted in favour of returning the land to A (who has been removed or omitted from the register by mistake) as long as A remains in possession of the land. The Law Commission retains the special protection for B or C where he or she is a proprietor in possession. B or C's title is protected unless (as under the current law) the party caused or contributed to the mistake by fraud or lack of proper care, or it is unjust not to rectify. However, the Law Commission has proposed the introduction of a 'long stop' so that, after ten years, B or C's title becomes indefeasible. That means that rectification would not be available against B or C as a proprietor in possession ten years from the time of the mistake unless B or C caused or contributed to the mistake by fraud or lack of proper care. In such circumstances, the other party (A) would still be able to claim an indemnity. Where none of the parties are in possession, the Law Commission's proposals favour returning title to A for an initial ten-year period (in the absence of exceptional circumstances). Under the long stop, after ten years the registered proprietor's title would become indefeasible; but again unless the registered proprietor caused or contributed to the mistake by fraud or lack of proper care and without interfering with any claim to an indemnity.

## Informal Acquisition of Legal Title: Adverse Possession

4.84    So far, this chapter has considered how legal estates are acquired through compliance with statutory formality requirements for their creation and transfer. In this part of the chapter we turn our attention to the informal acquisition of legal title through adverse possession of land. Adverse possession has its roots in the concept of relativity of title and the operation of limitation periods. The paradigm case, on which the following explanation is based, is adverse possession by the claimant (C) in unregistered land, of which the title, traced through the title deeds, belongs to the paper owner (PO). In English law, there is no concept of absolute title: title is relative and is based on possession. In a dispute between two parties, the court determines which party has the stronger claim to possession. As soon as C enters into adverse possession, he or she obtains a legal freehold title to the land. C's right to possession is stronger than that of any subsequent possessor, but is vulnerable to earlier claims. Hence, PO can bring an action against C to recover the land, relying on its earlier claim to possession evidenced by the paper title. In other words, in a dispute between the parties, PO has the relatively stronger title. But there is a 12-year limitation period for actions to recover unregistered land (Limitation Act 1980, s 15). If PO does not take action within that time, then its claim is time-barred. Once it has been time-barred, PO's title is extinguished by statute (Limitation Act 1980, s 17). There is no transfer of PO's title to C. Once the limitation period has expired, however, the title that C obtained by the inception of adverse possession becomes unimpeachable by PO (and anyone claiming through PO's title).

4.85    The concept of title being acquired by possession and extinguished at the end of the limitation period makes no sense in the context of registered land, where title is acquired by registration (4.56). A registered title is indefeasible (4.66–4.77) and could not be 'extinguished' for so long as the proprietor is registered as holder of the estate. The LRA 1925 sought to align registered land with the operation of adverse possession in unregistered land. Hence, it enabled title to be acquired automatically in registered land by adverse possession, using the device of a trust to reconcile the extinguishment of a title with registered land principles (LRA 1925, s 75). The LRA 2002 provides a significant departure from the previous law. There is no concept of title being acquired by adverse possession, or of a limitation period at the end of which the assertion of title is automatically time-barred (LRA 2002, s 96 and Sch 6). Instead, adverse possession provides access to a procedure though which the claimant may acquire title by registration. Under the LRA 2002, 'proof of title has been divorced from proof of possession' (Cooke (2003)). While the concept of relativity of title does not have the same significance in registered land as it has in respect of unregistered land (Cooke (2003)), it still provides the foundation of claims to adverse possession (*Parshall v Hackney* (2013)).

4.86    The LRA 2002 has been described as the 'emasculation' of adverse possession (Dixon (2003)) and as making registered land 'virtually squatter proof' (Cooke (2003)). A policy choice has been made to make registered land more secure, at least in part as a means of encouraging voluntary registration (4.49). However, the legislation acknowledges that adverse possession still has a legitimate role to play in a system of registered title. The nature of that role is different from the justification for adverse possession in unregistered land. In unregistered land, where the only documentary evidence of title consists of a set of deeds, adverse possession is needed to facilitate investigation of title (Dockray (1985)). Indeed, facilitating the investigation of title was considered by the Law Commission (1998) to be the 'strongest justification' for adverse possession. In registered land, where title is recorded on a central register, adverse possession plays no role in the investigation of title. Instead, the legitimate role of adverse possession is reduced to settling boundary disputes and ensuring the marketability of abandoned land (Cooke (2003)).

4.87    A claim to legal title through adverse possession under the LRA 2002 consists of two stages. The first stage is the inception of adverse possession, which identifies the time at which a claimant commences adverse possession of land. From the time of inception of adverse possession the claimant acquires legal title to land, but his or her title is vulnerable to that of the registered proprietor, whose superior title can be asserted at any time. The second stage is an application by the adverse possessor to be registered as proprietor of the legal estate. The application can be made after ten years of adverse possession have been completed (4.122). The application triggers a procedure which will have one of two outcomes; either the registration of the adverse possessor as proprietor, or the assertion of the superior title by the registered proprietor to bring the adverse possession to an end.

## Inception of Adverse Possession

4.88    Although limitation periods do not operate in respect of registered titles under the LRA 2002 (4.121–4.127), the date of inception of adverse possession for the purposes of the Act is defined as the date on which a period of limitation *would* run under section 15 of the Limitation Act 1980 (LRA 2002, Sch 6, para 11). Under the Limitation Act 1980, a limitation period begins to run in one of two instances (Sch 1, paras 1 and 8); discontinuance in possession by the registered proprietor, followed by the claimant moving into adverse possession, or dispossession of the registered proprietor by the adverse possessor.

4.89   Discontinuance arises where 'the person in possession abandons possession and another then takes it' (*Powell v McFarlane* (1979)). Discontinuance in *possession* is not demonstrated by discontinuance in physical *occupation*; rather, it is analogous to abandonment of land. Hence, it has been held that 'merely very slight acts by an owner in relation to the land are sufficient to negative discontinuance' (*Powell v McFarlane* (1979)).

4.90   Dispossession arises by 'a person coming in and putting another out of possession' (*JA Pye (Oxford Ltd) v Graham* (2002)). The act of dispossession necessarily entails the claimant moving into adverse possession (*Pye v Graham*). Dispossession need not involve an ouster of the registered proprietor by the claimant to adverse possession. Dispossession arises simply by the claimant establishing that he or she has moved into adverse possession.

4.91   Regardless of whether the inception of the limitation period is based on discontinuance of possession by the registered proprietor or their dispossession, the central requirement is the claimant establishing that he or she has moved into adverse possession. In the context of dispossession, adverse possession follows the registered proprietor's effective abandonment of the land. In relation to dispossession, the fact of the claimant's adverse possession demonstrates that the registered proprietor has been dispossessed.

4.92   Adverse possession must be 'single and exclusive' possession (*Pye v Graham* (2002)). Two or more adverse possessors may jointly be in single and exclusive possession, but the requirement means, for example, that an adverse possessor cannot be in possession concurrently with the registered proprietor (*Pye v Graham*).

4.93   The requirement of exclusive possession has raised a specific question as to whether it is possible to claim adverse possession of part of a building; for example, a room in a house or one flat in a block. It has been accepted that such claims follow logically from the fact that land can be held horizontally (*Ramroop (Sampson) v Ishmael and Heerasingh* (2010)). It must be shown, however, that 'part of the building was capable of being possessed by the claimant to the exclusion of others' (*Ramroop (Sampson) v Ishmael and Heerasingh*). The Privy Council in that case noted that this 'might be relatively easy to plead and prove if the property in question was a self-contained residential flat in a purpose-built block. It might be much more difficult in a building which had slipped into informal multiple occupation with shared facilities.'

## Possession Must Be 'Adverse'

4.94   For possession to be 'adverse', the claimant must be in possession without the permission of the registered proprietor. Permissive occupation is characterized by the presence of a lease or licence. In the context of claims to adverse possession, disputes as to whether a claimant's possession is adverse generally arise in respect of whether the claimant has a licence to occupy. Licences are generally expressly granted by a registered proprietor and can even be unilaterally imposed (*BP Properties Ltd v Buckler* (1988)). If a claimant is already in adverse possession, the effect of imposing a licence is to place his or her possession on a consensual footing and so to bring to an end the adverse possession (*BP Properties v Buckler*).

4.95   Although it is possible for a licence to be implied, the courts will only do so where there is 'some overt act by the landowner or some demonstrable circumstance from which the consent can be implied' (*London Borough of Lambeth v Rumbelow* (2001)). For example, a licence was implied where the claimant to adverse possession and the owner had been in negotiations for the sale of the title (*Colin Dawson Windows Ltd v King's Lynn, West Norfolk* (2005)). The claimant's adverse possession therefore began only after the breakdown of negotiations, which, on the facts, defeated the claim. A more generous approach to the implication of a licence in earlier cases has been reversed by statute (Limitation Act 1980, Sch 1, para 8(4)).

4.96   Possession that begins as permissive may become adverse once the permission comes to an end. Hence, a tenant (*BP Properties v Buckler*) or licensee (*Pye v Graham* (2002)) who remains in possession of land at the end of their lease or licence may from that point become an adverse possessor.

4.97   A person cannot be in adverse possession of land in respect of which they are registered proprietor, even if their registration is a mistake. This principle was established by the Court of Appeal in *Parshall v Hackney* (2013).

---

**Parshall v Hackney (2013):** By an error on the part of Land Registry a small triangular piece of land, described as being under two metres at its widest point and four metres long, that adjoined two properties (numbers 29 and 31) became registered under the titles to both of them. Paper title belonged with number 29 but, following the mistake, the registered proprietors of number 31 had put a chain-link fence around the land and used it (in conjunction with land that was within their title) as a parking space. The land was in Chelsea, where its utility as a parking space gave it a value disproportionate to its size. The registered proprietors of number 31 argued that they had obtained title to the land by adverse possession. The claim to adverse possession failed. The court concluded that in view of the registered title held by the claimant to adverse possession, their possession was 'lawful' and as such it could not be adverse. The claimants were not in possession with the permission of the true owners (the registered proprietors of number 29). The case therefore suggests that possession will not be adverse if it is either with the permission of the registered proprietor or is otherwise lawful. The concept of possession which is lawful but not permissive is unlikely to arise outside of cases of mistaken dual registration of land. Notwithstanding, the case gives rise to the possibility of registered titles being vulnerable to claims where mistakes do not come to light for decades (Xu (2013)). Further, the decision has the curious effect that the claimants to adverse possession, who may have reasonably supposed that the land was theirs, were in a worse position than if they had parked their car on land that they knew did not belong to them.

---

## The Definition of 'Possession'

**4.98**   Possession is to be understood in the 'ordinary sense of the word' (*Pye v Graham* (2002)). It has been defined as comprising two distinct elements (*Pye v Graham*), drawing on *Powell v McFarlane* (1979):

> [There] are two elements necessary for legal possession: (1) a sufficient degree of physical custody and control ('factual possession'); (2) an intention to exercise such custody and control on one's own behalf and for one's own benefit ('intention to possess'). What is crucial is to understand that, without the requisite intention, in law there can be no possession. . . . [There] has always, both in Roman law and in common law, been a requirement to show an intention to possess in addition to objective acts of physical possession. Such intention may be, and frequently is, deduced from the physical acts themselves. But there is no doubt in my judgment that there are two separate elements in legal possession.
>
> In a claim to adverse possession it is necessary to address each of these elements of possession separately, but it should be borne in mind at the outset that the two are closely interconnected. Ultimately, a claimant's acts provide the strongest evidence of his or her intent. Factual possession has been defined as consisting of an appropriate degree of physical control. . . . The question what acts constitute a sufficient degree of exclusive physical control must depend on the circumstances, in particular the nature of the land and the manner in which land of that nature is commonly used or enjoyed.

**4.99**   An intention to possess requires 'the intention, in one's own name and on one's own behalf, to exclude the world at large, including the owner with the paper title . . . so far as is reasonably practicable and so far as the processes of the law will allow' (*Powell v McFarlane* (1979)). An intention to possess does not require an intention to own (*Buckinghamshire CC v Moran* (1990)). Hence, a claim to adverse possession will not fail where the claimant concedes that land would have had to be given back to the true owner, a council, if required for its intended use as a road (*Buckinghamshire CC v Moran*) or by a willingness to place use of the land on a permissive footing (*Pye v Graham* (2002)).

**4.100**   The application of the elements of a claim to adverse possession are illustrated in the following case, which is the leading case on adverse possession in English law.

> **Pye v Graham (2002):** Pye was the registered proprietor of development land that adjoined the Grahams' farm. The land was enclosed by hedges, except for a gate, to which the Grahams held the only key, and a public footpath and highway. Pye had initially granted the Grahams a short grazing agreement to use the land. On the expiry of the agreement, Pye refused a request for renewal, because it was concerned that the existence of an agreement could adversely affect its application for planning permission. The Grahams continued to use the land for their farm, including uses that went beyond the original agreement. Initially, the Grahams continued to seek a renewal of the licence, but their requests went unanswered.

Pye did nothing in relation to the land and the Grahams successfully argued that they had acquired title by adverse possession. Their possession of the land had originally been permissive through the licence, but it became adverse once the licence expired. In relation to factual possession, the Grahams were held to be in occupation of the land with exclusive physical control. Pye was physically excluded by the hedges and by the lack of a key to the only gate. In relation to intention to possess, by continuing to use the land at the expiry of the grazing agreement the Grahams had acted in a way that they knew to be contrary to the wishes of Pye. They had made such use of the land as they wished, including for purposes beyond the scope of the original agreement. In essence, the Grahams had used the land 'for all practical purposes…as their own and in a way normal for an owner to use it'. They had therefore established an intention to possess. Their willingness to enter into a new agreement may have been contrary to an intention to 'own', but was not inconsistent with an intention to possess.

**4.101**  The claimant's acts of possession must be open, but in the absence of deliberate concealment it is not necessary for the PO to be aware of them (*Powell v McFarlane* (1979)). If the PO credibly denies knowledge, the test is an objective one, 'whether a reasonable owner of the plot, paying that due regard to his interests as owner of it which was to be expected of him, would have acquired notice of them and would thereby have clearly appreciated that the squatter concerned was seeking to dispossess him' (*Roberts v Swangrove Estates Ltd* (2007)).

**4.102**  The geographical scope of a claim to adverse possession is not necessarily limited to the extent of the land over which the acts that constitute factual possession have been exercised. The scope of a claim is 'necessarily one of fact and degree' (*Roberts v Swangrove Estates Ltd* (2007)). For example, 'a squatter [who] has occupied a terraced house, has lived in it and has denied access through its doors other than to his visitors, he would, no doubt, be taken to have had possession of the whole house notwithstanding that he failed to prove he had occupied a back room on the top floor. Conversely a squatter who created for himself a small kitchen garden in a corner of a 40 acre field might find, on claiming title as to the whole 40 acres, that all he acquired by adverse possession was a fee simple in the kitchen garden part' (*Roberts v Swangrove Estates*). Possession of part will also constitute possession of the whole where such an inference is reasonably drawn from a 'common character of locality' (*Lord Advocate v Lord Blantyre* (1878–9)).

**4.103**  How to prove intent, and the relationship between intent and factual possession, remains unclear. Intent may be inferred by the claimant's physical acts (*Pye v Graham* (2002)). Conversely, a claim to adverse possession may fail because a claimant's acts of possession are insufficient, in qualitative terms, to establish intent. This was the case in *Powell v McFarlane* (1979) where the claimant's acts were considered to be equivocal, in the sense that they were open to interpretation as demonstrating merely intent to use the land for so long as the owners took no steps to prevent the use. There, the claimant, as a 14-year-old boy, had started to use neighbouring land for the purposes of his grandparents' farm. He had cut hay and made some 'rough and ready' repairs to the boundary fence, so that the land could be used to graze the family's cow. The claimant's age appeared a significant consideration in the decision that he could not establish the requisite intent. It appears, however, that the only way in which Mr Powell could have established intent would have been to show that he had made greater physical use of the land. Slade LJ indicated that little weight would be afforded to self-serving declarations by a claimant as to his or her intent.

4.104    Conversely, intention will be more readily established where the acts that constitute factual possession are qualitatively strong. Hence, where the claimant makes full use of the land as if he or she were the owner, the claimant's conduct is sufficient to establish intent (*Pye v Graham*). The burden then shifts to the PO to provide evidence that points to the contrary. Similarly, it has been suggested that 'unequivocal' acts by the claimant will establish intent, unless the PO can demonstrate otherwise (*Powell v McFarlane* (1979)). Such acts include enclosure, which has been described as the strongest evidence of intent (*Seddon v Smith* (1877), the cultivation of agricultural land, placing and enforcing 'keep out' notices, and locking or blocking the only means of access (*Powell v McFarlane*). Where, however, the claimant's acts are equivocal the claimant will need to adduce additional evidence to demonstrate his or her intent.

4.105    On the face of it, the relationship the courts have drawn between intent and the qualitative strength of the claimant's physical use of the land suggests that, in some cases, intent will be determined by reference to the claimant's acts, while in others, the claimant will be invited positively to prove his or her intent. Given the courts' (understandable) reticence to give weight to self-serving statements by claimants as to their intent, however, it is difficult to know what evidence, other than the claimant's acts, could be adduced. It has even been doubted whether intent is, in fact, a free-standing requirement (Radley-Gardner (2005)) though the weight of the authorities practically puts the matter beyond doubt.

4.106    Claims to adverse possession are assessed on the basis of what the claimant has done (*Purbrick v London Borough of Hackney* (2003)). The fact that the claimant could have done more does not defeat a claim if what he or she has done is sufficient to demonstrate factual possession and an intention to possess. Similarly, acts fall to be assessed on their own merits and not by reference to previous dealings between the parties. Hence, a claim to adverse possession is not precluded where, in the context of previous permissive use of the land by the claimant, the same acts were said by the parties' agreement not to constitute possession (*Topplan Estates v Townley* (2004)).

## The Discredited Rule in *Leigh v Jack* (1879)

4.107    In *Leigh v Jack* (1879) it was held that there is no 'dispossession' of the PO by a claimant whose acts are not inconsistent with the PO's future use of the land. On the facts, the claimant's use of land for storage connected with his business was held not to constitute a dispossession of the PO, because the acts were not inconsistent with the PO's intention to dedicate the land to the public as a road. This approach has been held to be wrong as a matter of law (*Pye v Graham* (2002)). Adverse possession is fundamentally concerned with the intention of the adverse possessor, not that of the PO. Lord Browne-Wilkinson has described the idea that the sufficiency of a person's possession as dependent on the intention of the PO as heretical and wrong (*Pye v Graham*).

## Termination of Adverse Possession

**4.108**  Once a period of adverse possession has commenced, it is terminated if the claimant moves out of adverse possession, whether on his or her own accord or by the execution of a judgment for possession obtained by the PO. In other circumstances, the present period of adverse possession may be terminated and a fresh period begin. That is, for example, the effect of an interruption of the claimant's adverse possession (**4.109**) by the PO or of an acknowledgement by the claimant of the PO's title (**4.110**).

**4.109**  If a claimant's adverse possession is interrupted by the PO, the period of adverse possession comes to an end. If the claimant remains in adverse possession after the interruption, then a fresh right of action is accrued. What constitutes a sufficient interruption to bring a period of adverse possession to an end was considered by the Court of Appeal in *Zarb v Parry* (2012). That case arose from a boundary dispute between the parties. The contested land was found to be in the Zarbs' paper title, but the Parrys obtained title by adverse possession. At one point in the dispute, the Zarbs had physically entered the land, cut down a tree, uprooted a fence post, and started to mark a boundary. The incident lasted for around 20 minutes and ended when the Parrys threatened to call the police. The Court of Appeal held that the Parrys' adverse possession had not been interrupted. The Zarbs were not considered to have retaken possession 'in any meaningful sense'. The Zarbs had embarked on conduct which would have led to them retaking possession if completed, but had been prevented from doing so through the Parrys' intervention.

**4.110**  A right of action that has accrued to the PO on the inception of adverse possession is brought to an end and replaced with a fresh right of action if the adverse possessor acknowledges the PO's title. The date of the acknowledgement of title, therefore, replaces the date of adverse possession as the time from which the limitation period begins to run in unregistered land or the adverse possession is treated as having commenced in registered land. However, only a formal acknowledgement, made in writing and signed by the person making it, is effective (Limitation Act 1980, ss 29 and 30). An acknowledgement of title may consist of an offer to buy property or a defence in possession proceedings to be entitled to a lease, as the defence operates to acknowledge the owner's freehold title (*Ofulue v Bossert* (2009)). An acknowledgement of title generally operates on the date that it is made, so that the fresh cause of action arises on that date (*Ofulue v Bossert*).

## The Effect of Adverse Possession

**4.111**   The effect of adverse possession differs between unregistered land, registered land claims governed by the LRA 1925, and registered land claims governed by the LRA 2002.

### Unregistered Land

**4.112**   Unregistered land displays the purity and simplicity of the operation of adverse possession in a system of relative titles. The general limitation period of 12 years is provided in section 15 of the Limitation Act 1980. Once adverse possession has continued for the 12-year limitation period, the PO's title is extinguished by the operation of limitation of actions (Limitation Act 1980, s 17).

**4.113**   In unregistered land there is no 'statutory conveyance' of the PO's title to the adverse possessor (*Tichborne v Weir* (1892)). The effect of the statute is entirely negative (*Fairweather v St Marylebone Property Co Ltd* (1963)).

**4.114**   The adverse possessor acquires an independent freehold title from the time at which he or she commenced adverse possession. The effect of the limitation rules, combined with relativity of title, is that the adverse possessor's title becomes inviolable by the PO. But the adverse possessor is not a purchaser for value of the land and therefore will be bound by pre-existing property rights affecting the PO's title: for example, the adverse possessor is bound by any easements or restrictive covenants affecting use of the land (*Re Nisbet and Potts Contract* (1906)).

**4.115**   Exceptions to the operation of the 12-year limitation period are provided in a number of special cases, including: the mental incapacity of the PO (Limitation Act 1980, s 28); fraud and concealment on the part of the adverse possessor and cases of mistake (Limitation Act 1980, s 32); acts between parties to a trust of land (Limitation Act 1980, Sch 1, para 9); Crown lands and the foreshore (Limitation Act 1980, Sch 1, paras 10–11).

### Registered Land: Land Registration Act 1925

**4.116**   The LRA 1925 sought to align registered land with the operation of adverse possession in unregistered land. Registered land was subject to the same limitation period. At the end of the limitation period, however, instead of being extinguished the registered title became subject to a statutory trust (LRA 1925, s 75). Once adverse possession had continued for the requisite limitation period, the registered proprietor held his or her title on trust for the adverse possessor.

**4.117**   At first sight, the imposition of a trust appears to be an expedient means of dealing with the fact that paper title and entitlement to the land have diverged (Cooke (2003)). But a trust was not in fact necessary—all that was required was provision for the adverse possessor to apply for registration (Law Commission (1998))—and was a source of confusion. The trust had the potential to confer a windfall on the adverse possessor, by providing a choice of enforcing his or her rights against the land or enforcing personal liability against the dispossessed registered proprietor as trustee (Law Commission (1998)). Further, the consequential imposition of fiduciary duties on the registered proprietor towards the adverse possessor appeared inappropriate (Cooke (1994)).

4.118   A separate issue arising from the imposition of the trust is the nature of the interest acquired by the adverse possessor. In registered land, as in unregistered land, the claimant obtains a freehold title from the inception of the adverse possession. This title is independent from the title held by the registered proprietor. Once the statutory trust was imposed, however, the adverse possessor necessarily had a beneficial interest in the registered proprietor's estate. Therefore, the adverse possessor of registered land appears to have two distinct interests in the land: the independently acquired freehold title and a beneficial interest in the registered proprietor's estate (Cooke (1994)). Statute conferred a right on the adverse possessor, having extinguished title, to apply for registration (LRA 1925, s 75(2))—but it was unclear from the language of the provision which title the adverse possessor should be registered with: the freehold title independently obtained at the inception of adverse possession, or the (existing title) that was subject to the trust in his or her favour (Cooke (1994)).

4.119   It is debatable whether the 1925 Act provided for adverse possession to operate a parliamentary conveyance in registered land. Land Registry's practice was to close the old title and open a new title, of which the adverse possessor became first registered proprietor. The opening of a new title by Land Registry suggests that there was no parliamentary conveyance. Under the LRA 1925 (as in unregistered land cases), the adverse possessor obtained an independent freehold title, although he or she remained bound by property rights affecting the previous registered title (LRA 1925, s 75(3)). The final closing of the registered proprietor's title produced a result analogous to the extinction of an unregistered title. Notwithstanding, however, there was some judicial support for the idea that a parliamentary conveyance took place (*Fairweather v St Marylebone Property Co Ltd* (1963)) and at least one case in which that interpretation was applied (*Central London Commercial Estates Ltd v Kato Kagaku Co Ltd* (1998)).

4.120   The LRA 2002 preserves the rights of adverse possessors acquired under the 1925 Act, but removes the statutory trust (LRA 2002, Sch 12, para 18). The LRA 2002 came into force on 13 October 2003. Under the transitional provisions contained in the Act, a claimant who had completed 12 years of adverse possession on or before 12 October 2003 is entitled to be registered as proprietor of the estate in respect of which he or she is in adverse possession. Under the LRA 2002 there is no doubt that a statutory transfer now takes place.

## Registered Land: Land Registration Act 2002

4.121   The LRA 2002 provides a new scheme of adverse possession. The scheme applies to adverse possessors in registered land who had not completed 12 years of adverse possession on or before 12 October 2003. It marks a clean break from attempting to transplant the operation of adverse possession in unregistered land into registered land. Instead, it takes as its starting point the underlying principle that, in registered land, registration alone confers title, and seeks to provide a more appropriate balance between the registered proprietor and adverse possessor (Law Commission (2001)).

4.122   Under the 2002 Act, there is no concept of title being acquired by adverse possession or of a limitation period barring the assertion of a registered proprietor's title (LRA 2002, s 96). Sections 15 and 17 of the Limitation Act 1980, which provide the 12-year limitation period for an action to recover land, and 'extinguish' title at the end of that period, are disapplied in relation to registered land. Instead, the completion of a minimum of ten years' adverse possession (LRA 2002, Sch 6, para 1) enables the claimant to access a procedure that will result in one of two outcomes: either with the claimant acquiring title to the land *by registration* (not by adverse possession itself); or with the assertion of title by the registered proprietor. Where the adverse possessor acquires title, there is a 'statutory transfer' of the registered proprietor's estate.

4.123   Under the LRA 2002, adverse possession has no effect unless or until an application for registration is made under the procedure contained in the Act (Sch 6). Adverse possession must have been maintained for at least ten years immediately prior to the application (Sch 6, para 1(1)). The general period of ten years is subject to exceptions: in particular, an application cannot be made against a registered proprietor who is incapacitated by mental disability (Sch 6, para 8(2)). Applications relating to Crown foreshore land can be made only after a period of 60 years' adverse possession (Sch 6, para 13).

4.124   Once an application for registration is made, the registered proprietor and other persons specified in the Act (including the proprietor of a charge on the estate) are notified of the application by the Registrar (Sch 6, para 2). The onus then shifts to the registered proprietor to take steps to assert his or her title by issuing a counter-notice requiring the application to be dealt with under paragraph 5. The period that has been provided in which the registered proprietor can do so is 65 business days from the date of issue of the notification (Land Registration Rules 2003, r 189). If the proprietor fails to issue a counter-notice within that period, then a statutory transfer of the estate is effected to the adverse possessor (Sch 6, para 4). The adverse possessor thereby acquires title to the land by registration.

4.125   If a counter-notice is issued, then (save where one of three conditions are met, discussed at 4.128-4.131) the application for registration is rejected. The registered proprietor then has two years in which to commence proceedings for possession of the land (Sch 6, para 6). If no such proceedings are commenced within that period, then the adverse possessor may make a further application for registration (Sch 6, para 6(1)). This application does not instigate a new system of notifications. On making this application, the adverse possessor is immediately entitled to be registered as proprietor of the estate (Sch 6, para 7).

4.126   Registration of the adverse possessor as proprietor does not affect the priority of interests affecting the estate (Sch 6, para 9). An exception is, however, made as regards registered charges. A registered chargee is notified by the Registrar of the adverse possessor's application for registration, and has the same opportunity as the registered proprietor to issue a counter-notice and bring proceedings for possession against the adverse possessor. If a chargee fails to do so, then there is no justification for enabling him or her to enforce his or her charge against an adverse possessor who obtains registration.

**4.127** While the procedure contained in the LRA 2002 confers on a successful applicant an entitlement to be registered, that entitlement presupposes the existence of the underlying claim to adverse possession. The existence of adverse possession is a pre-condition to the right to make an application and of the entitlement to obtain registration if that claim is successful. If it transpires that the claimant was not in fact in adverse possession, then his or her registration is a 'mistake' and the register will be rectified to restore the registered proprietor (*Baxter v Mannion* (2011), see further **4.67**).

## The Three Conditions

**4.128** As noted above (**4.125**) where one of three conditions is met, an adverse possessor's application for registration will be successful despite a counter-notice being issued. The first condition is where 'it would be unconscionable because of an equity by estoppel for the registered proprietor to seek to dispossess the applicant' (Sch 6, para 5(2)). The second condition is where the applicant 'is for some other reason entitled to be registered as the proprietor of the estate' (Sch 6, para 5(3)). These two conditions are both circumstances in which, although the applicant argues that he or she is entitled to the land through adverse possession, in fact the applicant is entitled to the land for another reason. In its current review of the LRA 2002 (**4.40**) the Law Commission (2016) has questioned whether these two conditions should be maintained.

**4.129** The third condition enables the applicant to be registered where the following requirements are met (Sch 6, para 5(4)):

    (a) *the land to which the application relates is adjacent to land belonging to the applicant,*

    (b) *the exact line of the boundary between the two has not been determined under rules under section 60,*

    (c) *for at least ten years of the period of adverse possession ending on the date of the application, the applicant (or any predecessor in title) reasonably believed that the land to which the application relates belonged to him, and*

    (d) *the estate to which the application relates was registered more than one year prior to the date of the application.*

**4.130** This third condition reflects what the Law Commission (2001) acknowledged to be a legitimate conveyancing justification for adverse possession in registered land. The register is not conclusive as to boundaries (LRA 2002, s 60) and therefore there is no conflict with the concept of title by registration to enable adverse possession to be used to settle genuine boundary disputes.

4.131  It has been held that the adverse possessor should take steps to secure registration as soon as he or she learns facts that could make his or her belief as to ownership unreasonable (*Zarb v Parry* (2012)). Hence, while the ten years of mistaken belief does not need to endure up to the date of the application, 'it cannot end more than a short time before then' (Milne (2012)). In its review of the LRA 2002 (4.40) the Law Commission (2016) has proposed that the reasonable belief must not have ended more than six months from the date of the application. The relevant belief is that of the adverse possessor, not of his or her solicitor (*IAM Group plc v Chowdrey* (2012)). The relevant question is whether the adverse possessor 'was reasonable in holding the belief that he or she did in all the circumstances' (*IAM Group plc v Chowdrey*). In answering this question, it is relevant for the court to consider whether the adverse possessor 'should have made inquiries' as to what fell within his or her paper title, but in answering this question the adverse possessor is not imputed with knowledge held by his or her solicitor.

## Adverse Possession and the Criminalization of Residential Squatting

4.132  Adverse possession necessarily involves trespass to land and therefore constitutes a civil wrong. Until relatively recently, the main criminal offences that may be committed by an adverse possessor were those contained in the Criminal Law Act 1977. Under that Act, an offence is committed (in certain specified circumstances) where a person 'without lawful authority, uses or threatens violence for the purpose of gaining entry into any premises' (s 6). A defence is provided where the attempt to gain entry is a 'self-help' remedy being exercised by a 'displaced residential occupier' or a 'protected intending occupier' (definitions of which are contained in the Act). A person commits an offence if he or she fails to leave premises in which he is trespassing on being required to do so by or on behalf of a 'displaced residential occupier' or a 'protected intended occupier' (s 7).

4.133  The use of criminal law as a response to squatting was extended significantly by the introduction in 2012 of a new offence of squatting in residential premises (Legal Aid, Sentencing and Punishment of Offenders Act 2012 (LASPO), s 144). Under the Act an offence is committed where a person is living in, or intends to live in, a residential building, which he or she entered as a trespasser. No exemption is provided for those who entered the building as a trespasser before the section came into force (on 1 September 2012). However, the offence does not extend to those who remain in premises at the end of a lease or licence. The offence was introduced as a means of enhancing the rights of property owners, but its necessity has been doubted and it has been criticized for tackling the symptom of squatting rather than the underlying disease of a lack of affordable housing and homelessness (Cowan, Fox O'Mahony, and Cobb (2012)).

**4.134**  The creation of the offence left open a question whether occupation of land that constituted a criminal offence under section 144 could be used to claim title through adverse possession. This question arose for decision in *Best v Chief Land Registrar* (2015).

---

***Best v Chief Land Registrar* (2015):** Mr Best had entered an empty and abandoned house in 1997, having learnt that the owner had died and her son had not been seen for around a year. Mr Best claimed to have been in adverse possession since that time and had renovated the house with the intention of making it his home. He moved into occupation in January 2012 and in November of that year he applied under Schedule 6 to the LRA 2002 to become registered proprietor. Mr Best's application for registration was refused by Land Registry on the basis that, since 1 September 2012, his occupation had been a criminal offence under section 144. The Chief Land Registrar took the view that a period of adverse possession that constituted a criminal offence could not be used to establish the basis for an application under the LRA 2002. Mr Best successfully sought judicial review of the Registrar's decision.

---

Giving the judgment in the Court of Appeal, Slade LJ explained that Schedule 6 to the LRA 2002 provides a careful balance between protecting registered proprietors from the loss of their title by adverse possession and the public interest in the active use and marketability of land and the positive role that adverse possession plays in this respect. He explained that the provisions of the LRA 2002 have been 'carefully worked out'. The courts explained that LASPO is not intended to draw (or redraw) the balance between these competing interests, but to assist owners of residential buildings in a practical way, particularly by helping owners gain entry when squatters have moved in. Slade LJ explained that the purpose of the Act:

> was to provide deterrence and practical, on the ground assistance for home-owners in removing squatters from their property. Disruption of the law of adverse possession was not mentioned as an intended effect of the provision, nor was it suggested that it was being introduced to try to re-balance the rights of property owners as against those of adverse possessors with respect to the entitlement to be treated as title-holder in relation to property.

The argument advanced on behalf of the Chief Land Registrar was that criminalization makes a critical difference to balancing competing public interests due to the strong public interest in ensuring that people do not benefit from their crimes. Slade LJ established that there is no 'blanket' rule on the effect of illegality, the effect of which has instead been tailored to each context. Slade LJ noted that the Chief Land Registrar's argument would render the title of those registered under the Schedule 6 procedure vulnerable to claims that their title was invalid as their adverse possession involved criminal acts. It would also lead to arbitrary results: for example, years of adverse possession could be prevented from being used to claim title by a few days of occupation, while claims to adverse possession of residential and other property would be treated differently. Therefore, Slade LJ considered that the balance of public policy favoured allowing the adverse possession claim to be accepted by the Registrar.

**4.135**   It should be noted that the outcome of Mr Best's successful application for judicial review was not that he should be registered as proprietor. The decision meant only that his application for registration should be accepted, so that the procedure in Schedule 6 was then followed. In the event, in subsequent proceedings Mr Best's application for registration was challenged by the son of the deceased owner, but his challenge was unsuccessful and Mr Best's claim to registration succeeded.

**4.136**   *Best* does not fully resolve the relationship between the operation of adverse possession and the section 144 offence (Dixon (2014)). Slade LJ's decision leaves open the possibility of some disqualification for illegality being read into Schedule 6. For example, Mr Best had not in fact been convicted of a criminal offence and it may be questioned whether a different view would be taken where the adverse possessor has been convicted of an offence. However, even in such circumstances, the courts may be reluctant to find that the careful balance drawn by the LRA 2002 has been altered in the absence of express provision to the contrary.

## Human Rights and Adverse Possession

**4.137**   Following the decision in *Pye v Graham* (2002) (**4.100**), Pye commenced proceedings in the European Court of Human Rights. It argued that the loss of its land was an infringement of its right of property under Article 1 Protocol 1 to the European Convention on Human Rights (ECHR), for which it was entitled to compensation from the government. The Human Rights Act 1998 (HRA 1998), which incorporates the ECHR into domestic law, was not applicable to *Pye v Graham*, because the cause of action arose before that Act came into force. Hence, a direct action in the Strasbourg Court was the only means through which the human rights argument could be raised. The financial stakes were high, with Pye assessing its loss at £10 million (a sum disputed by the government). The legal stakes were higher, with the legitimacy of rules of adverse possession called into question. The case focused on the operation of limitation periods under the LRA 1925, the scheme applied in *Pye v Graham*, although raised more generally the justification for adverse possession claims in a system of registered title.

**4.138**   In *JA Pye (Oxford) Ltd v UK* (2008), the Grand Chamber of the European Court of Human Rights ultimately rejected Pye's claim by ten votes to seven. This decision reversed that of the ordinary Chamber, in which Pye had succeeded by the narrowest of margins (four to three votes). We have seen, in **Chapter 2**, the different stages of a claim under Article 1 Protocol 1. First, it must be established that the provision of the ECHR is engaged and, secondly, if it is, the possibility of justification must be considered. The Grand Chamber agreed that Article 1 was engaged, and considered the operation of limitation rules to be concerned with the control of possessions, rather than with deprivation. The Court then turned its attention to the possibility of justification. The Court accepted that limitation periods serve a legitimate aim and that even when title is registered it is legitimate for a state to attach more weight to long use of land than to formal ownership. Applying its justification formula, the Court considered that the rule struck a fair balance between the general interest and the interest of the individuals. The absence of provision for compensation in domestic law was not considered significant in the context of limitation rules, while adequate procedural protection was available to Pye to enforce its rights. The Court was not swayed in its conclusions by the extent of Pye's loss and the corresponding gain enjoyed by the Grahams.

**4.139**  Although based on the 1925 Act, it is implicit in the judgment of the Grand Chamber that the operation of adverse possession in unregistered land, and in registered land under the 2002 Act, is also human rights compliant. The Grand Chamber accepted the legitimacy of limitation rules and hence the crucial issue is that of fair balance. The holder of unregistered land enjoys the same level of procedural protection as his LRA 1925 counterpart. The acceptance of the scheme under the 1925 Act necessarily means that the LRA 2002, with its additional protection for registered proprietors, would satisfy this test. This is implicit even in the joint judgment of five of the seven dissenting judges. The Grand Chamber decision in *Pye v UK* (2008) is not technically binding on English courts, but it has since been followed by the Court of Appeal (*Ofulue v Bossert* (2008)). Importantly, the court rejected an argument that the justification for the operation of adverse possession is a matter that arises for reconsideration where a claim is distinguishable on the facts from *Pye v Graham* (2002). The court explained that the margins of appreciation afforded to states means that 'national authorities could *in general* determine the rules for the extinction of title as a result of the occupation of the land by a person who was not the true owner' (emphasis added). For a case to fall outside the margin of appreciation 'the results would have to be so anomalous as to render the legislation unacceptable'.

## FURTHER READING

Cobb, N and Fox, L, 'Living Outside the System? The (Im)morality of Urban Squatting after the Land Registration Act 2002' (2007) 27 LS 236.

Cooke, E, *The New Law of Land Registration* (Oxford: Hart Publishing, 2003).

Cooper, S, 'Regulating Fallibility in Registered Land Titles' (2013) 72 CLJ 341.

Dixon, M, 'The Reform of Property Law and the Land Registration Act 2002: A Risk Assessment' [2003] Conv 136.

Gardner, S, 'The Land Registration Act 2002—the Show on the Road' (2014) 77 MLR 770.

Goymour, A, 'Mistaken Registrations of Land: Exploding the Myth of "Title by Registration"' (2013) 72 CLJ 617.

Jourdan, S and Radley-Gardner, O, *Adverse Possession* (2nd edn, Haywards Heath: Bloomsbury Professional, 2011).

Lord Neuberger of Abbotsbury, 'The Stuffing of Minerva's Owl: Taxonomy and Taxidermy in Equity' (2009) 68 CLJ 537.

Nair, A, 'Morality and the Mirror: The Normative Limits of the "Principles of Land Registration"' in S Bright (ed), *Modern Studies in Property Law: Vol 6* (Oxford: Hart Publishing, 2011).

# SELF-TEST QUESTIONS

1 What contracts are governed by section 2(1) of the Law of Property (Miscellaneous Provisions) Act 1989? Where that provision applies, what is the effect of: (i) compliance; and (ii) non-compliance with the statute?

2 How can a valid contract for sale of land be created using: (i) a single document; and (ii) two documents?

3 Explain the different roles played by contracts for sale of land and deeds. What requirements must be met for a document to be a deed?

4 In what circumstances and in respect of which legal estates is registration of title compulsory? Where registration is compulsory, what is the effect of: (i) registration; and (ii) a failure to register?

5 Advise A in the following circumstances:

  **a** A was the registered proprietor of land. A has discovered that a fraudster impersonating him has transferred his title to B (an innocent party), who is now the registered proprietor.

  **b** A was the registered proprietor of land. A has discovered that a fraudster impersonating him transferred his title to B, who has subsequently sold the land to C. C purchased the land with mortgage finance provided by D. C is now registered proprietor of the land and D has a registered charge. B, C, and D are all innocent of the fraud.

6 What requirements must be met for a person to be in adverse possession of land? Consider, in particular: (i) what is meant by 'dispossession' and 'discontinuance in possession'; (ii) when possession is 'adverse'; and (iii) how 'factual possession' and an 'intention to possess' can be established.

7 A client, S, comes to see you and shows evidence that she has been in adverse possession of registered land for the past ten years. What steps must S take to obtain title to the land and in what circumstances will she be successful in doing so? Will it make a difference to your advice if S's claim to adverse possession is that she has been living in a house?

# 5

# The Acquisition of Equitable Interests

## SUMMARY

This chapter is concerned with the acquisition question: it considers the principal circumstances in which equitable property rights can be acquired. We look first at how a beneficial interest under a trust can be acquired. We consider how express trusts of land are created before discussing the acquisition of beneficial interests through resulting and constructive trusts. In relation to resulting trusts, we focus on the presumed intention trust that arises where a person purchases or contributes to the purchase of land in the name of another. We then consider four types of constructive trust. We begin with the most significant constructive trust arising in relation to land, the common intention constructive trust, which plays a specific role in determining ownership of the home. We then discuss constructive trusts arising under the doctrine of *Rochefoucauld v Boustead*, the *Pallant v Morgan* trust, and the vendor–purchaser constructive trust arising where there is a specifically enforceable contract for the sale of land. As we will see, this final type of constructive trust depends on an important broader principle, exemplified by the decision in *Walsh v Lonsdale*, which we will refer to as 'the doctrine of anticipation'. It can operate to give rise to beneficial interests under a trust, and it can also operate to give rise to other types of equitable interest. We then turn to proprietary estoppel. We will consider the circumstances in which the doctrine can give rise to equitable property rights, and look at its practical importance in protecting those who rely on informal promises relating to land. We also consider the relationship between proprietary estoppel and the constructive trusts.

Key topics explored in this chapter are:

- Express trusts of land (5.10–5.12)
- The presumed intention resulting trust (5.13–5.21)
- The common intention constructive trust (5.22–5.69)
- The doctrine in *Rochefoucauld v Boustead* (5.73–5.77)
- The *Pallant v Morgan* constructive trust (5.78–5.82)
- The vendor–purchaser constructive trust (5.83–5.86)

- The wider doctrine of anticipation (5.87-5.92)

- The requirements of a proprietary estoppel claim (5.93-5.113)

- The effect of a proprietary estoppel claim (5.117-5.123)

- Proprietary estoppel and third parties (5.124-5.134)

- The relationship between proprietary estoppel and constructive trusts (5.135-5.138)

## Introduction

5.1 In this chapter we address the 'acquisition question' in relation to certain equitable interests. We are concerned with equitable interests that arise under a trust and with those acquired through the doctrine of proprietary estoppel. Equitable interests that arise under a trust are also known as beneficial interests. Interests that exist under a trust are necessarily equitable, but not all equitable interests require a trust. For example, restrictive covenants and equitable easements do not exist under a trust. Similarly, a claim to an interest in land through proprietary estoppel does not involve a claim to a trust; the outcome of a successful claim to an estoppel depends on the content of the particular duty that the doctrine imposes on the party with a property right in land. In this way, proprietary estoppel sometimes gives rise to a trust, and sometimes gives rise to a different type of interest. Sometimes the successful claimant does not obtain an interest in the land at all, but (for example) is awarded financial compensation. The different categories of equitable interests are explained in Chapter 3.

## The Different Categories of Trust

5.2 In this chapter we consider the acquisition question in relation to three categories of trust: express, resulting, and constructive. These categories of trust are generally differentiated by their method of creation and, specifically, by the different role afforded to the settlor's intention in the creation of the trust. Neither this classification, nor its basis in the settlor's intention, are universally accepted (see eg Swadling (2011)), but it remains the most commonly adopted scheme.

5.3 An express trust is created by the actual intention of the settlor. Resulting and constructive trusts both arise through operation of law. Both these types of trust take different forms (Chambers (1997), Oakley (1996)) and apply to personal property as well as land. Our discussion is confined to their application in respect of land. The term 'implied trust' is sometimes used to describe any trust that is not express, and both resulting and constructive trusts may therefore be described as types of implied trust, but the term does not have a clear and consistent usage.

**5.4**   In relation to land, the most significant application of the resulting trust is the presumed intention, or purchase money trust. The trust arises where B (the beneficiary) purchases or contributes to the purchase of property in the name of T (the trustee). The trust is imposed through an assumption B does not intend a gift.

**5.5**   Constructive trusts have been described as trusts imposed 'by operation of law *rather than through the express or presumed intention of the owner* of the property to create a trust' (McGhee (2014), emphasis added). Constructive trusts may even be imposed *contrary* to the intention of the owner. In relation to land, one of the most important types of constructive trust is the 'common intention constructive trust' that has been developed to determine ownership of the family home (**5.22–5.69**). As we will see, however, even in this constructive trust, the meaning of intention is contested and it does not always refer to an actual intent held by the parties.

**5.6**   Rather than being imposed on the basis of intent, constructive trusts are said to arise 'whenever the circumstances are such that it would be unconscionable for the owner of property…to assert his own beneficial interest in the property and deny the beneficial interest of another' (*Paragon Finance plc v DB Thakerar & Co* (1999)). While unconscionability can be seen as a common thread that ties all constructive trusts together, care must be taken in understanding the role that it plays. It is never sufficient to argue that a trust should be imposed by the court simply because a person has acted unconscionably. The concept is too ill-defined to operate in that way and such an approach would result in uncertainty and unpredictability about ownership of land; an approach sometimes described in derogatory terms as 'palm tree justice' (**5.24**). Instead, it may be said that the combination of other, more clearly defined, elements that are required for the imposition of a constructive trust in each application of the doctrine collectively establish conduct considered by the courts to be unconscionable. In this respect, as well as being a common thread tying together the different types of constructive trust, it also operates within each type of constructive trust to hold together the specific elements required to establish the trust. In this chapter we consider four types of constructive trusts:

- common intention constructive trusts (**5.22–5.69**);
- trusts arising under *Rochefoucauld v Boustead* (**5.73–5.77**);
- *Pallant v Morgan* constructive trusts (**5.78–5.82**);
- The vendor–purchaser constructive trust (**5.83–5.86**).

A further type of constructive trust, which is imposed where land is transferred 'subject to' property rights in favour of another party, is discussed in **Chapters 3** and **11**, see **3.85–3.86** and **11.93**.

**5.7**   There is continuing debate as to the extent to which individual instances of constructive trust are illustrations of separate principles or may be unified under a single principle. It has been suggested that some of the doctrines of constructive trust discussed in this chapter—trusts arising under *Rochefoucauld v Boustead* (1897) and *Pallant v Morgan* (1953)—together with certain other instances of constructive trust, are illustrations of a unified principle. Three separate suggestions have been made as to a common principle that ties these claims to a constructive trust together.

- The trusts are imposed where property is received after a promise has been made as to its ownership (McFarlane (2008)).

- The trusts are imposed because otherwise the claimant to the trust would suffer a 'reliance loss' (Gardner (2009)).

- The trusts are imposed through a doctrine that enables oral (or 'parol') agreements for a trust to be enforced in order to prevent a specific form of fraud (Allan (2014)).

The idea that these constructive trusts are all united by a common principle has attracted judicial support (*Crossco No 4 Unlimited v Jolan Ltd* (2011)). However, on the present state of the authorities, particularly specific features attributed to individual trusts, recognition of a single principle appears unlikely (Hopkins (2006), Swadling (2009)).

5.8 Even if a single principle unites *Rochefoucauld v Boustead* (1897) and *Pallant v Morgan* (1953) trusts, the common intention constructive trust and the vendor–purchaser trust sit outside any unifying principle. Each of these constructive trusts is better seen as being part of different wider debates. The common intention constructive trust has been devised to determine the legally and socially complex issue of ownership of the home, while the vendor–purchaser trust sits within a broader doctrine of equity called the doctrine of anticipation (**5.87–5.92**).

5.9 All trusts that consist of or include land, are 'trusts of land' for the purposes of the Trusts of Land and Appointment of Trustees Act 1996 (s 1(2)(a)). That Act, which is discussed in **Chapter 6**, deals with the 'content question' in respect of trusts: it sets out the general rights of beneficiaries and duties of the trustees for all trusts of land. The Act draws no distinction between express, resulting, and constructive trusts, except that, where a trust is created expressly, the settlor may make specific provision as regards those rights and duties. The 'defences question' in relation to trusts is considered in **Chapter 11**.

## Express Trusts of Land

5.10 An express trust is one created by the actual intention of the settlor (**5.3**). The creation of express trusts of land is subject to compliance with formality requirements, which require the trust to be 'manifested and proved by some writing signed by some person who is able to declare such a trust or by his will' (Law of Property Act 1925 (LPA 1925), s 53(1)(b)). The effect of the statutory requirement is that while an express trust of land does not need to be created in writing, there must be written evidence of the declaration of trust. In the absence of written evidence, an express declaration of a trust of land is unenforceable.

**5.11** An express declaration of trust that is evidenced in writing in compliance with statutory requirements (LPA 1925, s 53(1)(b)) is conclusive as to the existence of the trust. If the declaration also specifies the parties' respective beneficial shares, it is additionally conclusive in that respect (*Goodman v Gallant* (1986)). Otherwise, the parties' shares will be quantified by the application of resulting (**5.13**) or common intention principles (**5.22–5.69**).

**5.12** Debate arises as to the classification of a trust when there is evidence that the settlor intended to create the trust through an oral declaration but the formality requirement in section 53(1)(b) of the LPA 1925 is not complied with. An oral declaration of trust is unenforceable, but when combined with other evidence, the court may find that a trust has come into existence. It has been suggested that a trust that arises following an oral declaration should be classified as 'express' on the basis of the settlor's intention to create the trust (Swadling (2011)). The alternative view is that a trust of land should be classified as an express trust only where section 53(1)(b) is complied with (Hopkins (2006)). In the absence of compliance with statutory formalities, the trust should be classified as resulting or constructive to invoke the statutory exception for compliance with formalities provided for these trusts (LPA 1925, s 53(2)). Neither approach may be considered entirely satisfactory. It is difficult to describe a trust as having been created expressly when the declaration of trust is unenforceable for non-compliance with statute. Equally, however, it appears unsatisfactory to classify a trust as a type of implied trust (**5.3**) where there has been an express (but unenforceable) declaration of trust. Notwithstanding, it is suggested that the better view is that in the absence of compliance with section 53(1)(b) of the LPA 1925 any trust that arises should be classified as resulting or constructive. Preference should be given to the solution that reflects the statutory scheme over conceptual tidiness.

## Presumed Intention Resulting Trust

**5.13** Where B (a beneficiary) purchases or contributes to the purchase of land in the name of T (a trustee) a resulting trust arises because it is presumed that B did not intend a gift (*Dyer v Dyer* (1788)). The link between the trust and payment of purchase money is reflected in the quantification of shares under the resulting trust. Each party receives a share in proportion to their contribution; hence, for example, say that B contributes 25 per cent of the purchase price of land that is purchased in T's name. Under a resulting trust, B will have a 25 per cent share of the beneficial interest, leaving T with the remaining 75 per cent. This example is illustrated in **Figure 5.1**. The presumed intention resulting trust is also used in some—but not all—cases where property is purchased in joint names to draw an initial presumption of the extent of each party's share where there is no express declaration of the parties' shares. There is one category of case in which, as we consider later in this chapter (**5.72**), it has been held that the presumption of resulting trust no longer applies, and the initial presumption of beneficial ownership is determined using the common intention constructive trust (**5.22–5.69**).

**Figure 5.1**   Sample resulting trust

**5.14**   In a limited number of circumstances, due to the relationship between B and T, no presumption of resulting trust is currently drawn; instead, it is presumed that B did, in fact, intend to make a gift of the land to T and, therefore, that B does not have any beneficial interest in the land despite B's financial contribution. These cases are described as involving a 'presumption of advancement', or a 'presumption of gift'. The relationships to which the presumption of advancement applies were established by the early 20th century and reflect the prevailing views of relationships in which there is a moral obligation for one party to provide for another. Hence, the presumption applies to transfers from a husband to his wife (but not from a wife to her husband, or between cohabiting partners), and from a father to his child. In *Laskar v Laskar* (2008) the Court of Appeal assumed that it would also apply to a transfer from a mother to her child although counsel did not argue for its application on the facts.

**5.15**   The values on which the presumption of advancement is based now appear outdated. Its continuing application on a transfer from husband to wife has met with particular criticism (*Pettitt v Pettitt* (1970)). Although the presumption of advancement still exists in a transfer from husband and wife, it is unlikely to be determinative of the parties' ownership (*Pettitt v Pettitt* (1970), *Stack v Dowden* (2007)). Provision has been made for the statutory abolition of the presumption, but has not yet been bought into force (Equality Act 2010, s 199).

**5.16**   The presumptions of resulting trust and of advancement can be displaced by evidence of the actual intention of B. Where the presumption of resulting trust is rebutted, B does not obtain a beneficial interest in the land despite his or her financial contribution to its purchase. Where the presumption of advancement is rebutted, the land is held on resulting trust for B, who provided the purchase money, despite B's relationship to T.

## Illegality and Resulting Trusts

**5.17**   Particular questions arise in respect of rebutting the presumption of advancement or trust where property has been transferred to T, or purchased in T's name, in order to facilitate an illegal activity. Can an illegal purpose be used to rebut an initial presumption of resulting trust or of advancement? In *Tinsley v Milligan* (1994) the House of Lords espoused a 'reliance principle'. Under the principle, a presumption of resulting trust or of advancement could be rebutted as long as it was not necessary to rely on the illegal purpose in order to do so. In that case, Miss Tinsley and Miss Milligan had both contributed to the purchase of the house that they shared as cohabitees, but the house was transferred into Miss Tinsley's sole name in order to facilitate fraudulent social security claims. Miss Milligan subsequently repented and confessed to the frauds, following which Miss Tinsley moved out of the house. Miss Tinsley then sought possession of the house and argued that she was solely entitled. The initial presumption on the facts was one of resulting trust. A 3:2 majority of the House of Lords held that Miss Milligan could rely on the presumption of trust to establish her shared beneficial ownership of the house because she did not need to plead the illegality in order to do so.

5.18    The reliance principle was subject to significant criticism, reflected in a subsequent Law Commission report (2010). One of the difficulties with the principle is that the outcome of a case may be determined by matters unconnected with the nature of the illegality. In *Tinsley v Milligan*, Miss Milligan succeeded because the initial presumption was one of resulting trust. The outcome of the case would have been different if the relationship between the parties was one to which the presumption of advancement applied—for example, if the parties had been husband and wife and the house had been purchased in the wife's name to facilitate social security fraud. On those facts, the initial presumption would have been of advancement and the husband would have had to plead (ie rely on) the illegality in order to rebut the presumption of gift and establish a resulting trust.

5.19    The Law Commission recommended replacing the reliance principle with a statutory scheme. Under the proposed scheme a beneficiary would be able to retain his or her interest and enforce a trust despite illegality unless the court exercised discretion to deprive the beneficiary of his or her interest. The Law Commission's proposed legislation was not adopted. However, in a landmark ruling a nine-member panel of the Supreme Court has effectively implemented the Law Commission's approach to illegality (*Patel v Mirza* (2016)).

5.20    The approach to take in cases of illegality arose before the Supreme Court in *Patel v Mirza* in the context of a claim to unjust enrichment, rather than a claim to a trust, and so the facts of the case are not repeated here. The Supreme Court held that the reliance rule laid down in *Tinsley v Milligan* should no longer be followed. The key question in cases of illegality is whether enforcing the claim would be harmful to the integrity of the legal system. In answering that question, Lord Toulson, giving the judgment for the majority of the court, identified three matters that the court must consider:

(i)    The underlying purpose of the prohibition which has been transgressed and whether that purpose will be enhanced by denial of the claim;

(ii)    any other relevant public policy on which the denial of the claim may have an impact; and

(iii)    whether denial of the claim would be a proportionate response to the illegality, bearing in mind that punishment is a matter for the criminal courts.

Lord Toulson explained:

> *Within that framework, various factors may be relevant, but it would be a mistake to suggest that the court is free to decide a case in an undisciplined way. The public interest is best served by a principled and transparent assessment of the considerations identified, rather by than the application of a formal approach capable of producing results which may appear arbitrary, unjust or disproportionate.*

5.21   While the approach taken in *Tinsley v Milligan* has therefore been discredited, the outcome on the facts of the case has not been doubted. Lord Toulson noted that even if Miss Milligan had not owned up to her fraud, it would have been disproportionate to have prevented her from enforcing her equitable interest in the property. If she had not been able to do so, then Miss Tinsley would have been left with a windfall. The approach adopted by the Supreme Court, reflecting the Law Commission's recommendations, has the advantage that the outcome of a case is not dependent on whether the initial presumption is one of resulting trust or gift. In all cases, the starting point is that underlying illegality will not prevent a claim to a trust.

## The Common Intention Constructive Trust

5.22   The common intention constructive trust is used to determine ownership of the home. How disputes as to ownership of the home should be resolved has become one of the most practically significant and contentious contemporary legal and social issues. The question raises fundamental issues as to the nature of ownership and the value placed on different contributions—both financial and non-financial—made by parties who share a home. Courts have been required to determine which aspects of a couple's shared lives are relevant to determining ownership of the home, and which are attributable purely to the nature of the parties' relationship. While questions of ownership arise in a number of circumstances (5.23), the leading cases have involved the fallout of relationship breakdown, where parties' claims to the home may be coloured by bitterness engendered by the breakdown of their relationship (*Pettitt v Pettitt* (1970)). Against such a background, the parties' words and conduct become subject to forensic examination by the court to ascertain whether the elements required for a trust subsist.

5.23   There are four key circumstances in which the question of who owns the home arises: when a person leaves the home, for example following a relationship breakdown; on a person's death; when a mortgage lender seeks possession; and where a non-secured creditor seeks to have the property sold to discharge the debt (Law Commission (2002)).

5.24   With one exception, when the question of ownership arises it falls to be determined by the application of property rules. In such cases, the question for the court is what each party actually owns, not what they ought to own. In determining property rights, the court 'does not as yet sit, as under a palm tree, to exercise a general discretion to do what the man on the street, on a general overview of the case, might regard as fair' (*Springette v Defoe* (1993), per Dillon LJ). The exception arises where there is a breakdown of a marriage by divorce or the dissolution of a civil partnership. In that exceptional case, statutory schemes enable the courts to make property adjustment orders between the parties (Matrimonial Causes Act 1973, s 23; Civil Partnership Act 2004, Sch 5, para 2). The statutory schemes are confined in their operation to divorce or dissolution. They do not apply, for example, when the question of ownership arises on the death of a spouse or civil partner, or falls to be determined in a dispute with a mortgagee or creditor.

5.25    Significantly, there is no equivalent statutory scheme applicable on the breakdown of a relationship between cohabitants who live together without having married or entered a civil partnership. There are sound policy reasons for not treating the property rights of cohabitants on the breakdown of their relationship in the same way as the property rights of married couples or civil partners (Law Commission (2007)). Marriage and civil partnership both confer a particular legal status and those who choose to cohabit should have their decision not to enter into that legal status respected. Notwithstanding, the disparity in treatment between spouses and civil partners, on the one hand, and cohabitees, on the other, is at the forefront of dissatisfaction with the operation of property rules. As the Law Commission has noted (2001), current property law is generally accepted as being 'unduly complex, arbitrary and uncertain in its application. It is ill-suited to determining the property rights of those who, because of the informal nature of their relationship, may not have considered their respective entitlements'. The application of property rules is no more adept at dealing with the consequences of the breakdown of a relationship between cohabitees than would be the statutory rules applicable to couples who have married or entered a civil partnership. A bespoke scheme is needed to take into account the particular issues that arise in respect of cohabitees (5.64–5.69).

5.26    Dissatisfaction with the operation of current property rules, combined with frustration at the absence of legislative intervention, have led to an increasing 'familialisation' (Dewar (1998)) of property law doctrines, involving the modification of 'general principles of land law or trusts to accommodate the specific needs of family members' (Hayward (2012)). The process is aptly illustrated by *Stack v Dowden* (2007) in which a majority of the House of Lords, led by the ethos that '"context is everything" and the domestic context is very different from the commercial world' made a policy decision to treat the home differently to other property when determining ownership (Hopkins (2009)). But familialisation raises concerns as to whether the doctrines that result can be described as property at all. Commenting on the development of the common intention constructive trust to determine ownership of the home, Dixon (2012) suggested 'call it family law, call it an exercise of the court's inherent equitable jurisdiction, but, maybe, do not call it property'.

## The Scope of the Common Intention Constructive Trust

5.27    It is important to note that the common intention constructive trust apples only in the absence of an express declaration of trust. An express declaration is conclusive as to the existence of a trust and (if declared) as to the extent of the parties' beneficial interests (*Goodman v Gallant* (1986)). The common intention constructive trust applies where:

- there is no express declaration of trust; and

- there is an express declaration of trust, but not as to the parties' beneficial shares.

5.28   The scope of the trust must now be understood in the light of two landmark decisions: *Stack v Dowden* (2007) and *Jones v Kernott* (2011). In those cases, the House of
Lords and the Supreme Court (respectively) kept distinct two types of case: those involving sole legal ownership and those in which there is joint legal ownership. The separation
of these cases has been strictly maintained (*Thompson v Hurst* (2014)) and arises because
of the different starting point in each type of case (see **Figure 5.2**).

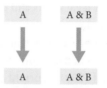

**Figure 5.2**   Starting point in sole and joint legal ownership

- Sole legal ownership: the starting point is that the sole legal owner is also the sole
beneficial owner and so the land is not held on trust. With one exception, the
common intention constructive trust will be used by a claimant who argues that
they are entitled to a beneficial share. If the claim is successful and it is therefore
found that the land is held on trust, the trust will also be used to quantify the parties' shares. The exception arises where the presumption of resulting trust applies
(**5.13–5.16**). There, the claimant will obtain a beneficial share in proportion to
his or her financial contribution through a resulting trust. The claimant will use a
constructive trust only if he or she wishes to claim a larger beneficial share.

- Joint legal ownership: the transfer into joint names is conclusive as to the existence of a trust and the starting point is that the parties are beneficial joint tenants
under the trust. As we see in **Chapter 6**, joint tenants do not individually own
shares, but they can obtain shares by a process known as 'severance'. Through
severance, the joint tenants obtain equal shares. Hence, the effect of this starting point is to give the parties equal beneficial shares. A common intention constructive trust may be used by a claimant to show that the beneficial interest is
held in unequal shares. If the case is a joint ownership case in respect of which the
presumption of resulting trust still applies (**5.13** and **5.72**), then unequal shares
may also be established through a resulting trust.

5.29   Hence, the common intention constructive trust is used to answer two distinct questions.

- In cases of sole legal ownership only, the trust is used to answer the acquisition
question to determine whether a claimant is entitled to a beneficial share. This is
sometimes described as the 'primary question' of the existence of a trust.

- In cases of sole legal ownership (where a trust has successfully been claimed) and joint legal ownership, the trust is used to answer the question of the extent of a claimant's beneficial share. This is a 'secondary question' of quantification of shares.

5.30  Both *Stack v Dowden* (2007) and *Jones v Kernott* (2011) are cases of joint legal ownership. The question for the court was therefore confined to the secondary issue of quantification. It is accepted that the approach to quantification adopted in those cases applies equally to determine the parties' shares in sole legal ownership cases where a claimant has successfully established a beneficial interest (*Abbott v Abbott* (2007), *Jones v Kernott* (2011)). When addressing the secondary question of quantification, the only difference between cases of joint and sole legal ownership is the starting point (5.28). However, the significance of the cases extends beyond quantification and a key issue, that remains unresolved, is the extent to which the approach taken to quantification can and should be carried over to the primary acquisition question (5.54–5.60). As a result, it is necessary to understand the courts' approach to quantification fully to appreciate the issues that now arise in relation to the primary acquisition question. Therefore, this chapter addresses cases of joint legal ownership and quantification first, before considering cases involving sole legal ownership.

## Joint Legal Ownership and the Quantification of Beneficial Shares

5.31  The starting point in a case of joint legal ownership is equal beneficial ownership (5.28). A claimant may use the common intention constructive trust to establish an unequal share. The presumption of joint and equal beneficial ownership is rebutted by demonstrating a common intention by the parties to alter their shares. This common intention may be established by the claimant to have been reached at the date of acquisition or later, which has led to the trust being described as 'ambulatory' (*Stack v Dowden* (2007)). For example, in *Jones v Kernott* (2011) the presumption was held to have been rebutted some time after the breakdown of the parties' relationship when a life insurance policy was cashed in to enable Mr Kernott, who had moved out of the home the couple had shared, to buy a home for himself.

5.32  A common intention to vary shares must be based on the existence of an actual common intention between the parties. Hence, the common intention may be express or inferred, but it cannot be imputed (*Jones v Kernott* (2011), *Barnes v Phillips* (2015)). These terms are discussed further at 5.37.

5.33  The courts have warned that the task of rebutting the initial presumption and of demonstrating a common intention to vary beneficial ownership should not be undertaken lightly. The House of Lords suggested that a claim to unequal shares will succeed only where the facts are 'very unusual' (*Stack v Dowden*). Despite the authority of the House of Lords' decision it is unclear whether such a strong presumption is being maintained (Hayward

(2016)). Further, there is little guidance on the type of factor that make a case sufficiently unusual, although the parties' financial arrangements appear to carry some significance.

---

***Stack v Dowden* (2007):** Mr Stack and Ms Dowden had cohabited for nearly 20 years and had four children. Their home was registered in their joint names but with no express declaration as to their respective beneficial shares. The purchase had been funded from the proceeds of sale of a previous home held in Ms Dowden's sole name, money from her bank account, and a joint loan. While both parties contributed to the discharge of the loan, Ms Dowden's contributions were higher. Throughout their relationship they had kept their financial affairs rigidly separate. The House of Lords held that the facts were sufficiently unusual to depart from the presumption of joint and equal beneficial ownership. The court appears to have been swayed, in particular, by the parties' separation of their financial affairs throughout their long relationship. Ms Dowden was held to be entitled to 65 per cent of the beneficial share.

---

***Fowler v Barron* (2007):** Miss Fowler and Mr Barron had separated after a 23-year relationship. Their home had been purchased in their joint names with the aid of a joint mortgage. However, Mr Barron argued that he was the sole beneficial owner. He had provided the deposit for the purchase and paid the mortgage instalments. Miss Fowler's income was spent on herself and the couple's children as well as holidays and special occasions. The court noted that these were in fact largely expenses for which both parties were responsible. The court held that the facts did not provide a basis for departing from the presumption of joint and equal beneficial ownership. The evidence showed that the couple 'treated their incomes and assets as one pool from which household expenses will be paid'.

---

5.34 Once a claimant has established a common intention to vary beneficial ownership, the question arises as to the basis on which beneficial shares should be quantified. In *Stack v Dowden* the House of Lords held that the quantification of beneficial shares should be addressed by reference to the 'whole course of dealings' between the parties with a view to establishing their common intention. This holistic approach had previously been adopted by the Court of Appeal (*Oxley v Hiscock* (2004)) which had, however, suggested that the purpose of the inquiry was to establish a 'fair' share. *Stack v Dowden* therefore shifts the basis of the quantification of shares from fairness to common intention.

5.35 Only the parties' *common* intention is relevant. In *Fowler v Barron* Mr Barron argued that the home had been placed in the parties' joint names to ensure that Miss Fowler, who was considerably younger than him, would benefit on his death, on the assumption that the couple were still together at that time. He had not appreciated that the effect of joint ownership was to confer an immediate beneficial interest on Miss Fowler. This 'secret intention', which was not communicated to Miss Fowler, had no effect on determining the parties' beneficial ownership. As we have seen (5.33), *Fowler v Barron* is a case in which the court refused to depart from the presumption of joint and equal beneficial ownership.

**5.36**  In a significant paragraph of her judgment in *Stack v Dowden*, Baroness Hale outlined a non-exhaustive list of factors that may be taken into account in order to determine the parties' common intention. She explained:

> *Each case will turn on its own facts. Many more factors than financial contributions may be relevant to divining the parties' true intentions. These include: any advice or discussions at the time of the transfer which cast light upon their intentions then; the reasons why the home was acquired in their joint names; the reasons why (if it be the case) the survivor was authorised to give a receipt for the capital moneys; the purpose for which the home was acquired; the nature of the parties' relationship; whether they had children for whom they both had responsibility to provide a home; how the purchase was financed, both initially and subsequently; how the parties arranged their finances, whether separately or together or a bit of both; how they discharged the outgoings on the property and their other household expenses. When a couple are joint owners of the home and jointly liable for the mortgage, the inferences to be drawn from who pays for what may be very different from the inferences to be drawn when only one is owner of the home. The arithmetical calculation of how much was paid by each is also likely to be less important. It will be easier to draw the inference that they intended that each should contribute as much to the household as they reasonably could and that they would share the eventual benefit or burden equally. The parties' individual characters and personalities may also be a factor in deciding where their true intentions lay. In the cohabitation context, mercenary considerations may be more to the fore than they would be in marriage, but it should not be assumed that they always take pride of place over natural love and affection.*

**5.37**  What was left unclear in *Stack v Dowden* was the meaning of 'common intention'. A common intention may be expressly agreed by the parties (eg *Gallarotti v Sebastinelli* (2012)), inferred or imputed. In *Stack v Dowden* Lord Neuberger explained the difference between an inferred and imputed intention in the following terms:

> *An inferred intention is one which is objectively deduced to be the subjective actual intention of the parties, in the light of their actions and statements. An imputed intention is one which is attributed to the parties, even though no such actual intention can be deduced from their actions and statements, and even though they had no such intention. Imputation involves concluding what the parties would have intended, whereas inference involves concluding what they did intend.*

**5.38**  In *Stack v Dowden* it was unclear whether the parties' common intention as to quantification could be imputed, or if the courts would act only on the basis of an express or inferred intent. Lord Neuberger considered imputing intent to be 'wrong in principle'. However, he delivered a minority judgment in which he concurred with the outcome in the case, but rejected the reasoning of the majority. The majority, led by Baroness Hale, did not directly address the distinction between inferred and imputed intent.

**5.39**  The meaning of common intention, and in particular the role of imputed intent, was addressed by the Supreme Court in *Jones v Kernott* (2011). There, the Supreme Court unanimously held that a common intention in respect of the quantification of beneficial shares may be imputed, but only in limited circumstances. Imputation is permitted in those cases where 'it is not possible to ascertain by direct evidence or by inference what [the parties'] actual intention was as to the shares in which they would own the property'. Hence, the parties' common intention may be imputed in the absence of an express or inferred intent. The Supreme Court divided on the question whether it was necessary to impute a common intention on the facts of the case. The majority considered there was an inferred common intention by the parties that Mr Kernott's interest in a home in which he and Ms Jones had cohabited had crystallized after the breakdown of their relationship at the point at which an endowment policy was surrendered to enable him to buy his own home. On this basis, it was held that Mr Kernott had a 10 per cent beneficial share. The minority reached the same result, but preferred to do so on the basis of an imputed intent.

**5.40**   As we have seen, an imputed intention is one attributed to the parties that they did not in fact hold (**5.37**). The question therefore arises as to the basis on which the courts determine the parties' imputed intention. It appears that the criterion is 'fairness'. In *Jones v Kernott* (2011), in outlining the approach to quantification, Lord Walker and Baroness Hale—citing *Oxley v Hiscock* (2004)—explained that in the absence of evidence of the parties' actual (express or inferred) intent, 'the answer is that each is entitled to that share which the court considers fair having regard to the whole course of dealing between them in relation to the property'. Hence, the criterion of fairness that was rejected by the House of Lords in *Stack v Dowden* (2007) as providing the basis of the quantification of shares (**5.34**) is re-introduced by the Supreme Court in the guise of imputed intent—though confined in its application to those cases where the parties' actual common intention cannot be divined.

**5.41**   The ability to impute the parties' common intention does not provide a route to so-called redistributive justice (*Graham-York v York* (2016)), whereby the courts can simply decide to whom the property should be given and in what shares. The court's inquiry remains directed at ascertaining what each party owns, not what they ought to own (**5.24**).

---

*Graham-York v York* **(2016):** Miss Graham-York and Mr York had cohabited for over 30 years. The question of ownership of the home the parties had shared arose following Mr York's death. The home had been registered in Mr York's sole name. At first instance, Miss Graham-York had successfully established that she was entitled to a beneficial share and the judge quantified her share at 25 per cent. On appeal, Miss Graham-York argued that she should be awarded a 50 per cent share. Miss Graham-York had made some financial contributions to the property, but these appeared minimal. She had also cooked the meals and, jointly with Mr York, had raised one of the couple's two children (the other child lived with his grandmother). The relationship between the parties was abusive and dysfunctional. Mr York is described as 'controlling' and having a 'proclivity for violence', while Miss Graham-York is 'intelligent but vulnerable'. Rejecting Miss Graham-York's appeal, Tomlinson LJ explained that the sympathy she attracted having endured years of abuse 'did not enable the court to redistribute property interests in a manner which right-minded people might think amounts to appropriate compensation'. In determining a fair share, the court's inquiry is confined to considering the 'whole course of dealing between [the parties] *in relation to the property*' (emphasis in the original). Wider considerations about the abusive nature of the parties' relationship could not therefore be taken into account in quantifying Miss Graham-York's share.

**5.42**   Even confined to the parties' dealings in relation to the property, 'fairness' is a nebulous criterion. In *Aspden v Elvy* (2012), the first case in which an imputed intent was used to quantify shares, the court acknowledged that the award of 25 per cent was 'somewhat arbitrary'.

## Sole Legal Ownership

**5.43**   Where there is sole legal ownership, the initial presumption is of sole beneficial ownership (**5.28**). The common intention constructive trust may be used by a claimant to establish a beneficial share under a trust (the primary question, **5.29**) and, if successful, to quantify that share.

**5.44**   The leading case on the application of the common intention constructive trust to the primary acquisition question is *Lloyds Bank plc v Rosset* (1991). There, the House of Lords distinguished two forms of common intention constructive trust.

- Express agreement constructive trusts: these trusts require 'evidence of express discussions between the parties, however imperfectly remembered and however imprecise their terms may have been'. Once an express agreement is established, the claimant must separately demonstrate that he or she has acted to his or her detriment in reliance on the agreement.

- Inferred agreement constructive trusts: these trusts arise where there is no evidence of an agreement between the parties 'and where the court must rely entirely on the conduct of the parties both as the basis from which to infer a common intention to share the property beneficially and as the conduct relied on to give rise to a constructive trust'. In the inferred agreement trust, the claimant's conduct serves the dual purpose of providing evidence of the agreement and of his or her detrimental reliance.

**5.45**   Hence, the common intention of the parties provides the basis of the primary acquisition question, as well as the secondary question of the quantification of the parties' shares. Importantly, however, at the acquisition stage the courts' inquiry is confined to establishing an express or inferred common intention. That means that an agreement to share beneficial ownership must be derived from a common intention that the parties actually held, or are considered to have actually held. A common intention to share the beneficial interest cannot be imputed.

## Express Agreement Constructive Trusts

5.46   The requirement of 'express discussions' (5.44) appears unrealistic in the domestic context. In *Pettitt v Pettitt* (1971) Lord Hodson noted, 'The conception of a normal married couple spending the long winter evenings hammering out agreements about their possessions appears grotesque.' There is a sense of artificiality in the courts' detailed examination of the parties' relationship in the search for evidence of an agreement (*Hammond v Mitchell* (1991)). The description of agreements as 'express' perhaps belies the fact that the doctrine of constructive trust imposes an interpretation on informal discussions between the parties during the context of their relationship. Those discussions may come to have a significance that the parties were not aware of at the time.

5.47   In *Lloyds Bank plc v Rosset* (1991) Lord Bridge accepted as 'outstanding examples' of express discussions cases in which the legal owner had given the claimant an 'excuse' for not putting the property in their joint names (*Eves v Eves* (1975), *Grant v Edwards* (1986)). Lord Bridge suggested that excuses provide evidence of an agreement, because the claimant 'had been clearly led by the *[legal owner]* to believe, when they set up home together, that the property would belong to them jointly'. But the interpretation of an excuse as an agreement is contentious and has attracted competing academic views (Gardner (1993), Glover and Todd (1996), Mee (1999)). More recently the Court of Appeal has emphasized that the interpretation of an excuse is fact-sensitive (*Curran v Collins* (2015)).

> ***Curran v Collins* (2015):** Mr Collins and Ms Curran had been in a long-term relationship, which had included periods of cohabitation in properties that were in the sole legal ownership of Mr Collins. Their relationship was not always a happy one and, after a period of separation, Mr Collins had allowed Ms Curran to move back into their home, the judge finding that he was prepared to 'tolerate' her presence. When the parties' relationship finally broke down, Ms Curran unsuccessfully argued that she had a beneficial interest in the home they shared at the time and from where they had bred and showed Airedale terriers. Ms Curran's claim failed, as there had been no common agreement that she should have a beneficial interest. One of the arguments Ms Curran put forward was that when a previous property had been purchased, she had raised the question of having an interest in the house. Mr Collins had told her that it would be too expensive to put the house in their joint names because two life assurance policies would then have to be funded. The court rejected an argument that this excuse was evidence of a common intention. Reviewing *Grant v Edwards* and *Eves v Eves*, where an excuse had been interpreted as a common intention, Lewison LJ explained that those cases do not establish that an excuse 'necessarily or even usually leads to an inference that the person to whom the excuse is given can reasonably regard herself as having an immediate entitlement to an interest in the property in question'. He identified two differences between the earlier cases and the facts before the court. First, in both the earlier cases the excuse was coupled with a 'positive assertion' that the property would be jointly owned 'but for' the excuse that was given. There was no such positive assertion on the facts of the current case.

> Secondly, in both the earlier cases the parties were living together in the home when the excuse was made. In the current case, Ms Curran had not moved in when the excuse was given and had no intention of moving in at that time. Ms Curran's life revolved around the home that she shared with her mother. Lewison LJ's reasoning, with respect, is not without difficulty. In particular, it may be difficult to distinguish cases on the basis of whether the excuse is coupled with a positive assertion. Notwithstanding, the case highlights the need to consider the facts of each case in the round to determine whether the claimant has reasonable grounds to believe that there is a common intention to share beneficial ownership. As Lewison LJ remarks, 'If one who is not versed in the difference between legal and beneficial ownership asks to be on the deeds and is told "No", the more usual inference would be that they would have understood that they were not to become owners or part owners of the property.' This comment perhaps reflects a disparity between how people think about ownership in their everyday lives and the legal analysis that is superimposed onto their words and conduct.

**5.48** In *Lloyds Bank v Rosset* (1991), Lord Bridge suggested that the express agreement must usually be reached prior to acquisition of the home. Only exceptionally would it suffice for an agreement to be reached at a later date. Applied strictly, this requirement would preclude express agreement trusts arising where the claimant moves into a home already purchased by the legal owner. In practice, post-acquisition express agreements have been accepted without reference to a requirement that the case must be exceptional (*Hammond v Mitchell* (1991)).

**5.49** Once an express agreement has been established, the claimant must show that he or she acted to his or her detriment in reliance on the agreement. Detriment requires 'conduct on which [the claimant] could not reasonably have been expected to embark unless [he or she] was to have an interest in the house' (*Grant v Edwards* (1986)). Direct financial contributions to the purchase of property, which would be sufficient for the courts to infer an agreement to share, would necessarily constitute detriment where there is an express agreement. The court has also accepted indirect financial contributions—where through paying household expenses the claimant frees-up the legal owner's income to meet the direct costs of acquisition—for example, the mortgage instalments (*Grant v Edwards* (1986)). Beyond financial contributions, substantial improvements to property may constitute detriment (*Eves v Eves* (1975)), but not redecoration of a more 'ephemeral' nature (*Pettitt v Pettitt* (1970)).

**5.50** The central difficulty arising from the test of detriment (**5.49**) is that it requires the court to distinguish between conduct that a person may and may not reasonably undertake without a belief that they have an interest in the home. Unfortunately, in drawing this distinction, courts—predominantly presided over by male judges—have tended to resort to outdated stereotypes of what conduct it is reasonable to expect of a man or woman without any belief as to ownership of the home. Because most claimants have been women, the most significant effect of this approach has been the rejection of domestic work and childcare as constituting acts of detriment. It has been suggested that '[t]he use of the stereotype as a norm, from which deviation has to be established, is an almost inevitable consequence of [the test of detriment]' (Flynn and Lawson (1995)).

5.51   For a constructive trust to arise there must be a causative link between the common intention and the detriment. The causative link is reflected in the requirement of reliance. It seems that once the claimant has established the existence of a common intention and his or her acts of detriment, reliance is assumed and the burden of proof shifts to the legal owner to establish that the claimant did not rely on the common intention (*Wayling v Jones* (1993)). In order to discharge the burden it is not sufficient to show that the claimant would have acted the same way if no common intention was reached. Adapting the test of reliance provided in the context of proprietary estoppel (*Wayling v Jones* (1993)) it must be shown that the claimant would have acted the same way even if informed that the defendant would not comply with the parties' initial common intention. As will be seen at **5.106–5.108**, however, the approach adopted in *Wayling* has been criticized.

## Inferred Agreement Constructive Trusts

5.52   In *Lloyds Bank plc v Rosset* (1991) the House of Lords took a restrictive approach to conduct from which a common intention can be inferred. Lord Bridge suggested that:

> direct contributions to the purchase price ... whether initially or by payment of mortgage instalments, will readily justify the inference necessary to the creation of a constructive trust. But, as I read the authorities, it is at least extremely doubtful whether anything else will do.

There is a stark contrast between the narrow range of conduct from which Lord Bridge suggests a common intention can be inferred to determine the primary acquisition question, and the wide non-exhaustive list of factors provided in *Stack v Dowden* (2007) by Baroness Hale as conduct relevant to an inferred agreement in respect of the secondary question of quantification (**5.36**).

5.53   Lord Bridge's judgment has long been the subject of criticism (for a recent example, see Fox O'Mahony (2014)). In *Stack v Dowden* (2007) Lord Walker expressed doubt as to whether Lord Bridge's interpretation of the conduct from which a common intention may be inferred took full account of conflicting views in the previous House of Lords' decision in *Gissing v Gissing* (1971)). He suggested that 'the law has moved on' since *Lloyds Bank plc v Rosset* (1991). In particular, it seems that Lord Bridge cast the net of inferred intent too narrowly by not accepting the relevance of indirect financial contributions (**5.49**). In *Gissing v Gissing* Lord Reid said he saw 'no good reason' for distinguishing between direct and indirect contributions and noted the distinction may be 'unworkable' where finances are pooled into a joint bank account. It is difficult to disagree with the tenor of Lord Reid's judgment that the determination of rights in the home should not be dependent on the happenstance of how a family's finances are arranged. In the light of the divergence in the authorities on the point prior to *Lloyds*

*Bank plc v Rosset*, and the comments in *Stack v Dowden*, it would be a modest extension to accept that an inferred intention could be drawn from indirect as well as direct financial contributions.

5.54   The more difficult and tantalizing question is the extent to which—beyond financial contributions—Baroness Hale's list of factors in *Stack v Dowden* (5.36) could be used to infer an agreement in respect of the primary acquisition question. If it is possible to infer an agreement to share the beneficial interest on the basis of some or all of the criteria given in *Stack v Dowden*, then two consequences follow.

5.55   First, an extension of the *Stack v Dowden* factors would reduce the need for the courts to search for evidence of express discussions for an express agreement constructive trust, and hence remove criticism of the artificiality of this exercise exemplified by the 'excuses' cases (5.47). The broader the range of conduct from which a common intention can be inferred, the less need there is to search for an express agreement.

5.56   Secondly, and most radically, an extension of *Stack v Dowden* would mean that domestic conduct that is not currently considered sufficient detriment in reliance on an express agreement would become relevant to determining the existence of an inferred common intention to create a trust. Such a development may be welcomed. As we have seen, the current approach to detriment has been criticized for its denigration of domestic activities (5.50). The failed claim in *Burns v Burns* (1984) has become a *cause célèbre* to highlight the issue (Cowan, Fox O'Mahony, and Cobb (2012)). There, the Court of Appeal held that no agreement to share the beneficial interest could be inferred by Mrs Burns' 18 years of domestic duties or her contributions to household expenses. Mrs Burns had not contributed—directly or indirectly—to the purchase of the home, but had been 'free to do what she liked with her earnings'.

5.57   To date there is no definitive guidance as to whether the approach to inferred intent in *Stack v Dowden* can be extended to the primary acquisition question. In the light of the precedential value of *Lloyds Bank plc v Rosset* (1991) as a decision of the House of Lords, such guidance could come only from the Supreme Court in a case involving sole legal ownership. However, the current position is a curious one. The same criterion of the parties' inferred common intention can be used both to determine whether there is an agreement to share the beneficial interest (in a case of sole legal ownership) and to quantify the parties' shares (in cases of sole and joint legal ownership). But in determining the parties' common intention, the court is confined to a narrower range of criteria at the acquisition stage than it is in respect of quantification. This divergence of approach means that a claimant whose activities are confined to domestic conduct receives no interest (*Burns v Burns*), but one who has made a small direct financial contribution (to give rise to an inferred agreement) can have their domestic conduct taken into account to quantify their share (*Midland Bank plc v Cooke* (1995)).

**5.58**   There are indications at the highest judicial level of a willingness to extend *Stack v Dowden* to the acquisition question. In *Abbott v Abbott* (2007) a claim to a beneficial interest in a sole legal ownership case was considered by the Privy Council. Delivering the Opinion of the Board, Baroness Hale suggested, 'The parties' whole course of conduct in relation to the property must be taken into account in determining their shared intentions as to its ownership.' As a decision of the Privy Council, however, the case is not binding on English law. Further, the legal owner did not dispute that the claimant should obtain a share of the beneficial interest and the dispute concerned the extent of her share.

**5.59**   Prior to the Supreme Court's decision in *Jones v Kernott* (2011), Gardner and Davidson (2011) expressed the hope that the court would take the opportunity to 'make clear that constructive trusts of family homes are governed by a single regime, dispelling any impression that different rules apply to...the "establishment" and the "quantum" of the constructive trust'. The Supreme Court did not go that far, but in a direct response to Gardner and Davidson, Lord Walker and Baroness Hale noted that, '[a]t a high level of generality, there is of course a single regime: the law of trusts'. Notwithstanding, Gardner appears confident that the criteria for an inferred agreement are the same at the acquisition and quantification stages and has suggested that Mrs Burns would succeed before a modern court (Gardner (2013)). However, in the absence of a clear direction from the Supreme Court, it may be premature to lay *Burns v Burns* to rest (Sloan (2015)).

**5.60**   In a comprehensive review of cases decided since *Jones v Kernott*, Sloan (2015) concludes that there has been only one case—the first instance decision in *Aspden v Elvy* (2012)—in which the outcome of a claim to a beneficial share in a sole ownership case is inconsistent with *Rosset* (1991). There, Mr Aspden successfully claimed a beneficial interest in a property registered in the sole name of his cohabitee, Ms Elvy. The property was a barn, which had originally formed part of a property registered in Mr Aspden's sole name. The barn had been transferred to Ms Elvy a number of years after the couple had separated. Mr Aspden had then made a significant financial contribution to its conversion into a dwelling in the expectation (which never materialized) that the couple would again live together. It is a modest extension of *Rosset* to infer a common intention on the basis of direct financial contributions to the conversion, rather than to the acquisition of the property—more so perhaps when the property originally belonged to Mr Aspden.

## Rejection of Imputed Agreement Constructive Trusts

**5.61**   We have seen above (5.39) that the Supreme Court has held that in limited circumstances when quantifying beneficial shares in a constructive trust the court may impute a common intention between the parties (*Jones v Kernott*). As a result, where a constructive trust has been established, but there is no actual common intention between the parties—whether express or inferred—as to the extent of their beneficial interests, the court may impute an agreement. Hence, at the stage of quantification, the court can attribute the parties with an agreement that the parties did not in fact make. The Supreme Court was clear, however, that imputation is confined to quantification. A common agreement between the parties cannot be imputed in a case of sole legal ownership to establish the existence of a constructive trust. **Figure 5.3** provides a 'roadmap' to constructive trusts, explaining the different forms of common intention that are available at the two stages of acquisition and quantification.

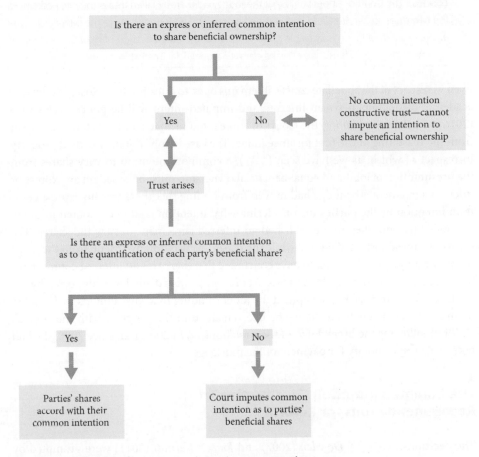

**Figure 5.3**   Roadmap for common intention constructive trusts

5.62    The structure of claims to a constructive trust is complex for courts and lawyers to understand—let alone the parties to the case. It has been left to appellate courts to ensure that the imputation of an agreement is strictly confined to the quantification of beneficial shares (*Barnes v Phillips* (2015), *Capehorn v Harris* (2015)).

*Capehorn v Harris* **(2015):** Mrs Capehorn and Mr Harris were in a relationship for around 20 years. Their relationship was unstable, with periods during which they lived together and periods when they lived apart. When their relationship broke down for the final time, Mr Harris claimed a beneficial share in a property, Sunnyside Farm, that had been purchased in Mrs Capehorn's sole name. She had bought the property from her mother and both she and Mr Harris had operated a business from the home. Following the parties' separation, Mr Harris had remained in occupation. At first instance, the judge found that there was no agreement between the parties to share the beneficial interest, either at the time the property was purchased or at a later date (after the separation) when the parties had discussed their finances and the business, which was in Mrs Capehorn's name. However, the judge then proceeded to impute an agreement that Mr Harris should have a 25 per cent beneficial share in the home, by reason of his contribution to the business. The Court of Appeal held that the judge had thereby fallen into error; she had elided the two stages of the trust and had imputed a common intention to share the beneficial ownership when imputation is available only in respect of the quantification of shares. The Court of Appeal held that Mr Harris had no valid claim to a beneficial interest in the property.

5.63  Even in respect of the appellate courts, it remains open to question how closely the 'overly academic distinction' between inferred and imputed intent will be policed (Hayward (2016)). In *Barnes v Phillips*, the Court of Appeal found that a 'critical step' was absent from the reasoning of the first instance judge. The case involved jointly owned property in respect of which, as we have seen (5.32), a common intention to vary shares from the presumption of joint and equal beneficial ownership must be based on an express or inferred agreement. The judge had moved from finding that there was no express common intention by the parties to considering what intention could be imputed to them. The judge had not therefore established an inferred agreement to vary the shares. The Court of Appeal was satisfied that while the reasoning was 'totally absent' from the judgment, the judge must be taken to have concluded that there was an inferred common intention to vary the shares, which the Court of Appeal was satisfied was supported by the evidence. The Court of Appeal upheld the judge's finding that Miss Phillips was entitled to an 85 per cent beneficial share. She had remained in the property with the couple's children following the breakdown of their relationship in 2005 and, since 2008, she had taken sole responsibility for payment of the mortgage.

## The Common Intention Constructive Trust: Recommendations for Reform

5.64  The decisions in *Stack v Dowden* (2007) and *Jones v Kernott* (2011) were prompted by the absence of legislative intervention determining the property rights of cohabitees. As Baroness Hale explained in *Stack v Dowden*, this is an area where the law has not kept pace with social and economic developments, particularly the significant increase of cohabitation. Further, there is an established divergence between how property rights are *actually* resolved and how many people *believe* that they will be resolved. There is evidence of a widespread 'myth of the "common law Marriage"; a belief, wrongly held, that unmarried couples acquire the same rights as a married couple after a period of cohabitation' (*Stack v Dowden* citing Barlow et al (2001)).

5.65  The Law Commission investigated the possibility of providing a single scheme to determine the property rights of all those who share their home, whether as a married or unmarried couple, as friends, relatives, or for companionship or support. The Law Commission

(2002) concluded that the diversity of situations in which people share homes precludes such a unified approach. Instead, the Law Commission (2007) refocused its attention on the financial consequences of relationship breakdown between cohabitants 'living as a couple in a joint household' who have not married or entered into a civil partnership.

5.66   The Law Commission's scheme is directed at providing financial relief to cohabitants on the breakdown of their relationship. The scheme is based on determining the economic impact of cohabitation by measuring economic disadvantages incurred by the applicant and benefits retained by the respondent. Having done so, the court has discretion to make an order directed at reversing the retained benefit and sharing equally between the parties any remaining disadvantages on the part of the applicant. The order may take the form (amongst others) of the payment to the applicant of a lump sum, a transfer of property, and an order of sale of property.

5.67   The scheme will apply where cohabitants meet specified eligibility criteria. These are that *either* the cohabitants have a child together, *or* they have cohabited for a minimum duration, which the Law Commission recommends is set between two and five years. It will be possible for cohabitants to opt out of the scheme. This must be achieved through a signed agreement between the parties, which 'makes clear the parties' intention to disapply the statute'. Notably, an express declaration of trust will not, without more, constitute such an opt-out.

5.68   If enacted, the Law Commission's scheme will apply in place of determining the parties' property rights under the doctrines of trust discussed in this chapter. The scheme moves the inquiry away from determining the parties' ownership of property, but is deliberately not modelled on existing schemes applicable on divorce or the dissolution of a civil partnership, thus keeping the cohabitation relationship distinct. In situations that fall outside the Law Commission's scheme, ownership of the home will still need to be determined under doctrines of trust. That includes, for example, where the parties sharing a home are not 'living as a couple in a joint household'; where the parties meet that criterion but fall outside other eligibility criteria as a result of the duration of their cohabitation and the absence of children; and where the parties' rights need to be determined in circumstances other than relationship breakdown—for example, in a dispute with a mortgagee or creditor (5.24).

5.69   On 6 September 2011 the government announced that it did not intend to implement the Law Commission's recommendations during the parliamentary term that ended prior to the May 2015 general election. The Law Commission expressed a hope that implementation would follow in the early days of the next Parliament. No such plans have been announced and while there have been attempts to introduce the Law Commission's proposals through Private Members' Bills, to date these Bills have been unsuccessful.

## The Relationship between Resulting Trusts and Common Intention Constructive Trusts

5.70   In respect of the circumstances giving rise to a trust, there is a close relationship between the resulting trust and the common intention constructive trust. As we have seen (**5.13**), a resulting trust arises where a financial contribution is made to the purchase of land in another's name. A financial contribution to the purchase of land in another person's name may also provide evidence of a common intention for a constructive trust. Hence, the same action—contributing to land purchased in another's name—can be used either to establish a resulting trust or a common intention constructive trust. The outcome, however, may be different depending on which trust is imposed. In a resulting trust, the beneficial interest is proportionate to the financial contribution that has been made (**5.13**). In a constructive trust, the beneficial interest may differ from a party's financial contribution and will reflect the common intention of the parties (**5.31–5.42**).

**5.71**   How do we know which interpretation of the payment will be taken on any particular facts? The two types of trust are conceptually different, which is reflected in how the claimant's contribution is analysed under each doctrine. A resulting trust is imposed on the negative basis that the claimant did not intend to make a gift of his or her contribution. A constructive trust is imposed on the basis that the claimant's contribution establishes that the parties had reached a common agreement to share the beneficial ownership. In practice, however, it may be difficult to ascertain which interpretation is most appropriate on the facts. Increasingly, the courts have looked to the outcome of the different types of trust to guide the circumstances in which the application of each type is most appropriate. The flexibility of the constructive trust is preferred in the 'domestic context' (*Stack v Dowden* (2007)) where the property is the parties' home, as contributions other than money are relevant to determining each party's share. The resulting trust is preferred in the 'commercial context' where dealings may be conducted at arm's length and each party's share may be expected to reflect his or her financial contribution. Examples of the operation of the presumed intention resulting trust include the following:

- where a property was bought by a mother and daughter as a 'buy to let' investment (*Laskar v Laskar* (2008));

- in respect of business premises (*Malayan Credit v Jack Chia* (1986));

- where the property is bought as a home, but in circumstances that fall outside 'the ordinary domestic context' (*R v Muzafar and Qurban* (2014)): this comment was made in a case in which a father purchased property in the name of his sons, to provide a home for his daughter.

**5.72**   After initially using a general distinction between the domestic and commercial spheres to mark the likely scope of operation of the resulting and common intention constructive trusts, the courts have now gone a step further. The Supreme Court has held that the presumption of resulting trust no longer applies where a property is purchased 'in joint names for joint occupation by a married or unmarried couple, where both are responsible for any mortgage' (*Jones v Kernott* (2012)). In the absence of an express trust (**5.10–5.12**), beneficial ownership of such homes is determined by the common intention constructive trust (**5.31–5.42**). The presumption of resulting trust remains applicable, and provides the starting point to determining ownership, in respect of other property that falls in the domestic sphere: for example, homes bought by siblings or friends or purchased in the sole name of a spouse or cohabitant. However, the constructive trust is still likely to be preferred in such cases (*Stack v Dowden*).

## Constructive Trusts Arising Under *Rochefoucauld v Boustead*

**5.73**   The doctrine in *Rochefoucauld v Boustead* (1897) stems from the maxim that 'equity will not allow a statute to be used as an instrument of fraud' (Allan (2014)). Where land is transferred on trust, but the statutory requirements for an express trust (**5.10**) are not complied with, a constructive trust is imposed to prevent the transferee from reneging on the trust and seeking to retain the property for him or herself. The paradigm case within the doctrine involves two parties and arises where land is transferred from B (a beneficiary) to T (a trustee), to hold on trust for B. T then relies on the absence of formalities for an express trust of land to renege on the agreement and keep the land for him or herself. An extension to this paradigm is a three-party case, in which land is transferred from X to T, to hold on trust for B, who is a third party to the transfer.

---

**Example of a two-party case—*Rochefoucauld v Boustead* (1897):** The Comtesse de la Rochefoucauld owned coffee estates in Ceylon, but had been unable to pay mortgages on the estates. She transferred the estates to Boustead, who had subsequently sold them. The Comtesse argued that the estates had been transferred to Boustead on trust for her and that the surplus proceeds of sale (after discharge of sums owed to Boustead) should therefore be paid to her. The court doubted that there was written evidence of the trust, as was required under the Statute of Frauds 1677—the precursor to the requirement of written evidence now contained in the LPA 1925 (**5.10**). However, the court held that the Statute of Frauds cannot prevent proof of a fraud and 'It is a fraud on the part of a person to whom land is conveyed as a trustee, and who knows it was so conveyed, to deny the trust and claim the land himself'. The effect of the fraud was to enable oral evidence to be admitted as to the existence of the trust. On the facts, the court was satisfied that the evidence established that the land had been transferred to Boustead on trust in favour of the Comtesse, who was therefore entitled to the surplus proceeds of sale.

---

**Example of a three-party case—*Neale v Willis* (1968):** Mr and Mrs Willis were purchasing a house from a council under the right to buy scheme. There was a shortfall of £50 in their finances to complete the purchase. Mr Willis obtained a loan for that sum from his mother-in-law. The loan was made pursuant to an agreement between Mr Willis and his mother-in-law that the house would be purchased in the joint names of Mr and Mrs Willis. Mr Willis reneged on that agreement and purchased the house in his sole name. When the couple divorced, the question arose as to beneficial ownership of the house. The court held that a constructive trust would be imposed to prevent Mr Willis from setting up the absolute character of the conveyance to himself to defeat the beneficial interest which, on the true bargain, belonged to his wife. The case is notable because, unlike *Rochefoucauld v Boustead*, the agreement to hold on trust was not made between the transferor (the council) and the transferee (Mr Willis), but between Mr Willis and a third party to the transfer (his mother-in-law) who was providing finance for the purchase.

**5.74**   In a two-party case, where the intended beneficiary (B) is also the transferor of the property, it is clear that the constructive trust arises in favour of B. In a three-party case, the intended beneficiary (B) and the transferor (X) are different people and the question arises in whose favour the trust should be imposed. It is suggested that the transferor's claim should *generally* be preferred (Feltham (1987), cf Youdan (1984, 1988)). The purpose of the doctrine is to prevent T's fraud (5.73) and intervention should go no further than necessary to achieve this purpose. B, the intended beneficiary, is a volunteer, and 'equity does not assist a volunteer'. The imposition of a trust in favour of X, the transferor, provides X with a further opportunity to benefit B. Finally, intervention in favour of X does less violence to the formality requirement in section 53(1)(b) of the LPA 1925 (Youdan (1984), Worthington (2006)). There are exceptional cases where intervention in favour of B is justified as the only way to prevent fraud. For example, *Neale v Willis* where the agreement to hold on trust was not made with the transferor (5.73). Further, B's claim may be compelling where X has died and so would not have a further opportunity to benefit B (Hopkins (2000)).

**5.75**   For the constructive trust to arise, it is not necessary that the transfer is obtained by fraud. The fraud arises at the point when the absolute character of the conveyance is relied upon to defeat the beneficial interest (*Bannister v Bannister* (1948)). Nor is it necessary for the technical language of trust to be used in the parties' agreement (*Bannister v Bannister* (1948)). In *Neale v Willis* the agreement stated simply that the house would be taken in 'joint names'. In English law such a transfer necessarily takes effect under a trust (Chapter 6).

**5.76**   The *Rochefoucauld v Boustead* trust is contentious because the fraud consists in denying the trust, which is the very thing that statute—now the LPA 1925—requires to be evidenced in writing (5.10). The classification of the trust may be crucial in its justification. In *Rochefoucauld*, the court classified the trust as express. The trust was one that the parties intended to create and on that basis there is some support for that classification (Swadling (2009, 2011)). But the classification of the trust was discussed in the context of the prevailing Statute of Limitations and the classification of a trust for that purpose is not conclusive (McFarlane (2004)). Although the parties intended to create the trust, the trust was not imposed on the basis of their intent. It was imposed to prevent Boustead's fraud. There is no practical distinction between *equitable* fraud and unconscionability (Hopkins (2004)) and, as we have seen, trusts imposed to prevent unconscionable conduct are generally classified as constructive (5.6). Hence, the better view is that the *Rochefoucauld v Boustead* trust is constructive (Hopkins (2006), Allan (2014)). The trust was classified as constructive by the Court of Appeal in *Bannister v Bannister* (1948).

**5.77**   The doctrine in *Rochefoucauld v Boustead* has been further extended to situations in which X transfers land to T expressly 'subject to' rights in favour of B, where the rights intended to be enjoyed by B have either been proprietary rights that do not generally take effect under a trust (such as an option to purchase in *Lyus v Prowsa* (1982)) or personal rights including a contractual licence to occupy in *Binions v Evans* (1972)). In such cases, the courts have, notwithstanding, held that a constructive trust may be imposed to prevent T reneging on the 'subject to' agreement. The imposition of a constructive trust pursuant to a 'subject to' transfer is considered in **Chapters** 3 and **11,** see **3.85-3.86** and **11.93.**

## The *Pallant v Morgan* Constructive Trust

**5.78**   The *Pallant v Morgan* (1953) constructive trust is imposed, when specific conditions are met, to prevent a party (T) who has acquired land from reneging on an assurance that another party (B) should have some interest in the land. As with the doctrine in *Rochefoucauld v Boustead* (**5.73-5.77**), the trust is triggered by T reneging on an agreement pursuant to which land is acquired and the origins of the trust lie in that principle (Nield (2003)). There is, therefore, a clear conceptual link between these different claims to a constructive trust. However, where a claim is made to a *Pallant v Morgan* trust the agreement must arise in a particular factual matrix (**5.79**).

**5.79**   The *Pallant v Morgan* constructive trust requires three key elements, derived from *Banner Homes Group plc v Luff Developments Ltd* (2000).

(i)   An arrangement or understanding prior to the acquisition of property that one party (the acquiring party) will take steps to acquire property and, if he or she does so, the other party (the non-acquiring party) will have an interest in the property.

(ii)   In reliance on the agreement or understanding, the non-acquiring party does, or omits to do, something which confers an advantage on the acquiring party in relation to the acquisition, or is detrimental to the non-acquiring party's ability to acquire the property on equal terms.

(iii)   The acquiring party, having obtained the property, then reneges on the agreement or understanding.

---

*Banner Homes Group plc v Luff Developments Ltd* **(2000):** Banner Homes (the claimant) and Luff Developments (the defendant) had commenced negotiations for a joint venture for the acquisition of development land. The parties had reached an agreement in principle for the joint venture, but no contract had been concluded, at the time the land was acquired by Stowhelm Ltd, a wholly owned subsidiary of Luff, with Luff providing the purchase money. At the time of the purchase, Banner Homes had every reason to believe that the joint venture would go ahead. However, Luff had received legal advice expressing serious doubts as to the commercial benefit to it of the agreement. Luff did not inform Banner Homes of its doubts, out of concern that Banner Homes would mount a rival bid for the land. Luff decided to withdraw from the agreement shortly after the purchase and subsequently informed Banner Homes of its decision. The Court of Appeal held that the shares in Stowhelm Ltd (as representing the land) should be held on constructive trust for Banner Homes and Luff equally, charged with the payment by Banner Homes of half of the purchase price. This decision, in effect, enforced the parties' joint venture agreement. There was a pre-acquisition arrangement or understanding between the parties that the land would be acquired by a jointly owned company as a vehicle for the joint venture. Banner Homes had relied on this agreement by treating the site as 'out of play', as a potential acquisition in its own right. Their reliance had conferred an advantage on Luff of keeping Banner Homes out of the market as a potential competitor for purchasing the land. It was therefore unconscionable for Luff to seek to retain the property for itself in a manner inconsistent with the parties' agreement.

**5.80** The requirements of the trust have generally been strictly interpreted by the courts, as a result of which the trust has been described as being 'notable for instances of its rejection, rather than its successful application' (Hopkins (2012)). Attempts to invoke the trust have failed where the land in question was already owned by one of the parties to the joint venture agreement (*London & Regional Investments Ltd v TBI plc* (2002)); where there is no agreement that the land would be acquired for the parties' joint benefit (*Kilcarne Holdings Ltd v Targetfellow (Birmingham) Ltd* (2005)); or where the agreement alleged to have been entered into was not an agreement to share the beneficial interest (*Crossco No 4 Unlimited v Jolan Ltd* (2011)). However, it appears sufficient that the parties' agreement anticipates joint ownership of the land, even if the mechanics of how this will be achieved are not addressed (*Baynes-Clarke v Corless* (2010)). A claim to the trust will also fail where the parties' negotiations are conducted 'subject to contract' (*London & Regional Investments Ltd v TBI plc*) or where, without express provision to that effect, there is a mutual intention by the parties not to be bound without a formal contract (*Crossco No 4 Unlimited v Jolan Ltd*).

**5.81** A distinctive feature of the *Pallant v Morgan* constructive trust is that the non-acquiring party's reliance on the agreement need not be detrimental (*Banner Homes Group plc v Luff Developments Ltd*). It is sufficient that the reliance confers an advantage on the acquiring party. In *Banner Homes*, the court left open the issue whether Banner Homes had suffered detriment: it was sufficient to establish the trust that Luff had obtained the advantage it had sought of keeping Banner Homes out of the market.

*Pallant v Morgan* (1953): The parties were neighbouring landowners and land adjacent to both of their properties was due to be sold at auction. Both parties were keen to preserve the amenity value of the adjacent land and appreciated that if they were to bid against each other the only person to profit would be the vendor. They therefore started negotiations as to how they might divide the land if they did not bid against each other. No agreement had been reached at the time of the auction and both parties sent agents to bid on their behalf. Immediately before the auction started, the agents agreed that the claimant would refrain from bidding and, if the defendant succeeded in acquiring the land, part would be sold on to the claimant. The defendant's agent obtained the land with a bid of £1,000, but the defendant then reneged on the agreement. The defendant's agent was authorized to bid up to £3,000,

> while the claimant's agent was authorized to bid to £2,000. On these facts, it is clear that the claimant suffered no detriment, because the land would not have been acquired even in the absence of the agreement—but the defendant obtained an advantage, because the land was acquired for half of the sum that would have been necessary to outbid the claimant. The court decided that the defendant held the land for himself and the claimant jointly, subject to agreement by the parties as to its division. In the absence of an agreement, the court would order the land to be resold.

5.82    The basis of the *Pallant v Morgan* trust remains contested. In *Crossco No 4 Unlimited v Jolan Ltd* (2011) a majority of the Court of Appeal felt bound by authority to hold that the trust is an example of the common intention constructive trust. Etherton LJ, in a minority judgment, considered the basis of the trust to lie in a breach of fiduciary duty. There are problems with both analyses. The *Pallant v Morgan* trust can arise in response to B's gain or detriment (5.81), whereas a common intention constructive trust requires detrimental reliance (5.49). The common intention constructive trust is preferred where a claim to a beneficial interest is made in relation to domestic property, because of the flexibility it confers to recognize that a claimant has obtained a share dis-proportionate to his or her financial contribution. This flexibility may not be apposite in a doctrine developed specifically to apply in respect of failed commercial joint ventures. However, if the trust is based on a breach of fiduciary duty, then there seems no jus-tification for setting the cases apart from others involving such a breach (Yip (2013)).

## The Vendor–Purchaser Constructive Trust

5.83    Consider a case in which B wishes to buy land belonging to A. As we saw at 4.5–4.31, before A's legal estate is transferred to B, the parties will first make a contract: A will promise to make that transfer, and B will promise to pay A. What then happens if A fails to honour that promise? B can, of course, bring a claim for damages for breach of con-tract against A. As we have noted (5.19), however, each piece of land is unique, and so, even if B receives damages from A, B will not be able to use that money to acquire the very thing B was entitled to under the contract: A's land. The basic position, applying in the absence of any exceptional circumstances such as those in *Patel v Ali* (1984), is that a court will use the equitable remedy of specific performance of the contract to ensure that, if B wishes, A completes the promised transfer of A's legal estate in the land to B.

5.84    What happens, however, if A, rather than refusing to sell the land to B, instead trans-fers it to a third party, C? If C is registered as the new holder of A's legal estate, it is clear that C has a good legal title to the land. In contrast, B has no legal property right. The courts of equity, however, developed a means of protecting B. As noted by Lord Collins in *Southern Pacific Mortgages Ltd v Scott* (2015), there is a 'long line of authority that following exchange of contract the seller holds the property on trust for the buyer'. As a result, B has more than just a personal right against A: B has an equitable interest in the land. Such a right is therefore prima facie binding on C: it will bind C unless C has a defence to it (for an example of C's having such a defence, see *Lloyds Bank v Carrick* (1996)). The trust arising in such a case is not an express trust: although A promised to transfer A's estate to B, A never declared a trust of that estate. It is another example of a constructive trust, often known as the 'vendor–purchaser constructive trust'.

**5.85** There are some uncertainties as to the operation of the vendor–purchaser constructive trust: they are helpfully discussed by Turner (2012). One question is as to exactly when B's equitable interest arises; another is as to whether that equitable interest, when it first arises, is best described as arising under a trust. In *Southern Pacific Mortgages Ltd v Scott* (2015), the Supreme Court tackled another tricky question, and held that, even where such a trust arises, B is not yet in a position to give a third party, B2, a legal or equitable property right in the land. So if, for example, B attempts to make a lease of the land to B2, B2 will acquire a property right in the land only if and when the promised transfer of A's estate to B is completed. A further question is as to whether the trust can arise only where a court would grant specific performance of A's promise to B (**5.90**).

**5.86** For our present purposes, however, the key feature of the vendor–purchaser constructive trust is simply that the existence of a contract binding A to make a transfer of a property right in land to B is another means by which B can acquire an equitable property right in land. The important point is that the contract imposes a duty on A, and that duty relates to a specific property right of A. The vendor–purchaser constructive trust thus shares the same basic qualities as other means of acquiring equitable interests that we have considered in this chapter. As we will now see, the principle behind that form of constructive trust is of wider application, and can give also rise to equitable interests that do not arise under a trust, and do not depend on a contract.

## The Wider Principle: The Doctrine of Anticipation

**5.87** The vendor–purchaser constructive trust can be seen as depending on a principle that has a wider application, and can be referred to as the 'doctrine of anticipation'.

---

*Walsh v Lonsdale* **(1882):** Lonsdale made a contract with Walsh, promising to grant Walsh a seven-year lease of a mill, with rent payable yearly in advance. No lease was granted, but Walsh took possession of the mill, paying rent in arrears at the end of each quarter. Lonsdale demanded payment in advance, relying on the terms of the promised lease and, when Walsh failed to pay, Lonsdale levied distress (ie took possession of Walsh's goods as a remedy for non-payment of rent). Walsh argued that, as the promised lease had not been granted, its terms did not apply. He sought to rely on the common law analysis of his position: he had a yearly periodic tenancy, arising as a result of his possession of the land, and Lonsdale's acceptance of rent (see **7.63**). The Court of Appeal, invoking the Judicature Acts of 1873–5, found instead that the equitable rules governed: Lord Jessel MR explained that, as there was a contract to grant the lease, which could be enforced by specific performance, Walsh 'holds,

> therefore, under the same terms in equity as if a lease had been granted'. He was therefore under a duty to pay rent yearly in advance.

**5.88**  The key idea in *Walsh v Lonsdale* is that, as Lonsdale was under a duty to Walsh, and that duty was to give Walsh a property right in particular land, Walsh had an equitable interest in that land. Of course, on the facts of the case, the existence of that equitable lease worked to Walsh's disadvantage. As Lord Jessel MR pointed out, however, Walsh was also 'protected in the same way as if a lease had been granted; he cannot be turned out by six months' notice as a tenant from year to year'. In other words, whilst the common law position was that Walsh only had a periodic tenancy, the equitable position, which prevailed, was that Walsh had an equitable lease.

**5.89**  The principle in *Walsh v Lonsdale* can be referred to as the *doctrine of anticipation*: where A is under a duty to grant B a recognized property right, such as a lease, equity can 'anticipate' that grant by regarding B as *already* having that right. As we saw when considering the vendor–purchaser constructive trust, the doctrine of anticipation can give rise to a trust; in *Walsh v Lonsdale*, it gave rise instead to an equitable lease. It depends simply on the content of A's duty: what type of property right must A grant to B? For example, if A is under a duty to grant B an easement, then B acquires an equitable easement (see **9.41**). Note too that A's duty may arise from a contract, or it may not. If, for example, a court order made in divorce proceedings imposes a duty on A to transfer a property right in particular land to B, that court order gives B an immediate equitable interest in that land (*Mountney v Treharne* (2003)).

**5.90**  The idea behind the doctrine of anticipation is often associated with the maxim that: 'equity looks on as done that which ought to be done'. The generality of that maxim has been convincingly criticized (Swadling (2011)), but it is still possible to defend the doctrine of anticipation. It depends on the same basic idea as all means of acquiring an equitable interest: A is under a duty to B, and that duty relates to a specific right of A. In *Walsh v Lonsdale* itself, Lord Jessel MR emphasized that a court would grant specific performance of A's duty to B. This is often said to be a requirement of the doctrine of anticipation, but some care must be taken, as it would be odd if the question of whether B acquires an equitable interest (which is capable of binding a third party) were to depend on the wide factors (such as the personal circumstances of A) that can affect a court's willingness to order specific performance. It may be, as suggested by Turner (2012) in relation to the vendor–purchaser constructive trust, that the key question is not whether, in fact, specific performance would have been ordered at a particular point in time, but rather whether A's duty is in general of a type where specific performance might be ordered.

**5.91**  It is important to be aware of the limits of the doctrine of anticipation. First, it applies only where A's duty is to give B a *recognized property right in specific land* (see McFarlane (2003a). For example, A's contractual promise to allow B to share occupation of A's land will not give B an equitable interest: as we saw in **Chapter 3**, such a contractual licence gives B only a personal right against A. This is because, whilst A is under a duty to B, and it may well be that a court would order specific performance of that duty against A, A's duty does not relate to a specific property right of A: it is not a duty to transfer a property right to B, nor is it a duty to grant B a recognized property right. It is instead only a duty not to exercise A's power to terminate the licence and have B removed from the land.

5.92   Secondly, the doctrine of anticipation applies only where A is indeed under a duty to B. If, for example, A makes an oral promise to transfer land to B, there will be no *contractual* duty on A, as any contract for the sale or other disposition of an interest in land must be made in writing signed by both parties: see section 2 of the Law of Property (Miscellaneous Provisions) Act 1989 (4.5–4.31). It would, therefore, be a mistake to think that the doctrine of anticipation removes the need to comply with any formality rules. The 1989 Act, however, applies only to contracts and so it is possible, in such a case, for A to be under a non-contractual duty to B. One possible means by which a non-contractual duty can be imposed on an owner of land is the doctrine of proprietary estoppel.

## Proprietary Estoppel

5.93   Proprietary estoppel is another means by which a party can acquire an equitable interest in land. It is true that, in some cases relating to land, B may be content to use an estoppel only as a defence, to prevent A asserting A's property right against B (see eg *Inwards v Baker* (1965)). In such cases, the estoppel can be said to operate as a 'shield', giving B a defence, and is thus no different in its effect from other estoppel doctrines, such as promissory estoppel. It is clear, however, that the doctrine of proprietary estoppel can also operate as a 'sword' and so give B a positive right. Like the doctrine of anticipation, proprietary estoppel sometimes gives rise to a trust, and sometimes gives rise to a different type of interest: it depends on the content of the particular duty that the doctrine imposes on A, a party with a property right in land. It is important to note that proprietary estoppel does not always give B an equitable interest in A's land. In some cases, the doctrine of proprietary estoppel will apply, but A's duty will simply be to pay a sum of money to B, or to allow B a licence to make some use of land. In such cases, as A's duty is not a duty to transfer any land to B, nor a duty to give B a property right in land, A's duty does not relate to any specific property right of A, and so B does not acquire an equitable interest.

5.94   It has been said that the 'classic case' of proprietary estoppel is one in which B builds on A's land, mistakenly believing it to be B's own land and A, knowing of B's mistake, fails to intervene and instead allows B to build. As A had a legal estate in the land on which B built, and the building then becomes part of the land (1.84–1.88), the position at common law was that A could prevent B from making any use of the building, and so would benefit from B's work. Courts of equity would not, however, accept that result, and would intervene to prevent the particular type of unconscionable conduct which consists of A doing nothing and then claiming the benefits of B's hard work. This long-established principle, depending on A's acquiescence in B's mistake, is now seen as part of the doctrine of proprietary estoppel. In the last 50 or so years, however, the doctrine has developed in very significant ways, and now recognizes further principles.

---

**Thorner v Major (2009):** Peter Thorner owned a farm. David, whose father was a cousin of Peter's, had worked on the farm for 30 years. David was not paid by Peter for that work. David believed that, on Peter's death, he would inherit the farm. Both David and Peter were taciturn farmers, and there had been no explicit promise by Peter, but David's belief developed over 15 years and was encouraged by Peter's conduct. For example, Peter once gave David some paperwork relating to two assurance policies on Peter's life and said 'That's for my death duties.' As a result of his belief, David worked on the farm and did not pursue other opportunities. Peter died without having made a valid will, and the farm passed, under intestacy legislation, to other relatives of Peter's. David, invoking proprietary estoppel, claimed that those relatives should transfer the farm to him. The House of Lords agreed and found that the farm and related assets (together worth around £3 million) should be transferred to David. It supported the finding of the first instance judge that Peter had made promises or assurances to David that were intended to be taken seriously and to be relied on, and that, because of his reliance on those promises or assurances, David would now suffer a detriment if the farm and related assets were not transferred to him.

---

5.95   *Thorner v Major* provides a memorable demonstration of the power of proprietary estoppel. Peter had not made a valid will in David's favour, nor had he made any contract with David. Yet the combination of Peter's implied promises, David's reliance on them, and the detriment that David would suffer if the promises were not honoured, meant that it would 'shock the conscience' of the court if David were left with no claim. It seems that, in such a case, equity intervenes to deal with a particular type of unconscionable conduct by A, a party with a property right in land: leaving B to suffer a detriment as a result of B's reasonable reliance on A's promise that B would acquire a right in the land, where it was reasonable for B to regard A's promise as seriously intended by A

5.96   In *Thorner v Major*, Lord Hoffmann stated that David was 'entitled to the beneficial interest in the farm and farming business as they were at Peter's death'. Certainly, proprietary estoppel is one means by which B can acquire an equitable interest in A's land; in some cases, that equitable interest will consist of a beneficial interest under a trust. Everything depends on the nature of the duty imposed on A. In *Thorner*, Peter's duty had been to honour his promise and to transfer the farm (the land and business) to David. David therefore acquired an equitable interest in the land, as Peter was under a duty to David (arising through proprietary estoppel) and that duty related to a specific piece of land (it was a duty to transfer that land to David).

## The Requirements of Proprietary Estoppel

5.97   In *Thorner v Major*, Lord Walker noted that most scholars see proprietary estoppel as based on three main elements: 'a representation or assurance made to the claimant;

reliance on it by the claimant; and detriment to the claimant in consequence of his (reasonable) reliance'.

5.98　As noted at 5.94, those three elements were present in *Thorner* itself. The principle applied in *Thorner*, however, looks different from that at work in the 'classic case' of proprietary estoppel, also discussed at 5.94, which does not require any promise or assurance by A to B, but instead depends on A's acquiescence and thus on A's failure to communicate to B. As a result, some scholars have, more recently, argued that it would instead be better to separate out the different strands of proprietary estoppel (see eg Mee (2011), Low (2012), McFarlane (2014)) and to distinguish, for example, between the acquiescence-based strand and the promise-based strand that applied in *Thorner*.

5.99　In any case, the most significant type of proprietary estoppel claim in practice is one that is based not on B's belief that B *already* has a right in particular land, but, as in *Thorner*, on B's belief that he or she will acquire such a right *in the future*. It is these cases that we will focus on when considering the requirements of proprietary estoppel, and in the remainder of this chapter. It is clear that, unlike other doctrines referred to as estoppel (such as promissory estoppel), proprietary estoppel can be used as source of rights by B: it is a sword and not just a shield. In *Thorner*, Lord Walker linked this to the fact that a proprietary estoppel claim necessarily relates to identified land (or, possibly, other property) of A. It can be argued, however, that the principle behind proprietary estoppel should apply more generally, and also be capable of assisting B where B relies on a promise unrelated to A's property (McFarlane and Sales (2015)). That question need not detain us, however, as our focus is land law and it is clear that the doctrine can apply in relation to land.

## Requirement 1: Promise or Assurance by A

5.100　It is clear that if A simply tells B that he or she intends to transfer land to B, no proprietary estoppel claim can arise: if B relies on A's current intention, B does so at his or her own risk as, of course, A's intention may change. Equally, as demonstrated by *Thorner*, if A instead makes an express or implied promise, which B reasonably understands as seriously intended by A as capable of being relied on, this first requirement of proprietary estoppel will be met.

> *Walton v Walton* (1994): Alfie Walton had for many years worked long hours for low pay on the family farm owned by his mother. His relationship with her had broken down by the time of her death, and her will required that the farm be sold, and the proceeds divided amongst various parties, not including Alfie. He claimed that, on many occasions, his mother had promised to leave the farm to him, and he had relied on this by continuing to live and work there. The first instance judge said that, although Mrs Walton had made promises, they were never intended to create a legal obligation, and so could not give rise to a claim. In the Court of Appeal, Hoffmann LJ accepted that Mrs Walton had never intended to come under an immediate duty to Alfie, but held that this did not prevent a proprietary estoppel claim,

as the question was 'whether a person in the position of [B] would reasonably have regarded the promises which the judge found to have been made as serious statements upon which he could rely'. On the facts of the case, the answer to that question was Yes, and Alfie's claim succeeded.

**5.101**  *Walton v Walton* demonstrates an important aspect of proprietary estoppel: it may be based on a promise of A, even if there is no contract between A and B. In that case, Hoffmann LJ distinguished proprietary estoppel from contract on the basis that it does not impose an immediately binding duty on A to perform A's promise but, instead, it 'looks backwards from the moment when the promise falls due to be performed and asks whether, in the circumstances which have actually happened, it would be unconscionable for the promise not to be kept'. This aspect of proprietary estoppel meets a concern expressed by Lord Scott in *Thorner v Major*. If, for example, A makes a promise to leave certain land to B on A's death, but A's circumstances then change in a significant and unexpected way—so that, for example, A needs to sell the land to pay for medical care—then the doctrine of proprietary estoppel has sufficient flexibility to recognize that it may no longer be unconscionable for A to refuse to honour the promise to B. As we will see, such differences between proprietary estoppel and contract are also important when considering the impact of formality rules on proprietary estoppel (**5.114–5.116**) and when considering the extent of any right acquired by B through proprietary estoppel (**5.117–5.123**).

**5.102**  The idea that a proprietary estoppel claim can arise where A merely *encourages* B to believe that A will confer a right relating to land on B (without making an express or implied promise to do so) is supported by some Court of Appeal decisions (see eg *Inwards v Baker* (1965), *Crabb v Arun DC* (1976), *Hoyl Group v Cromer Town Council* (2015)). Certainly, if a court is trying to find a single overarching test for proprietary estoppel, which also includes the 'classic' acquiescence-based form of proprietary estoppel, then it has to use a neutral term such as 'encouragement', as there is clearly no promise by A where A simply stands by and allows B to act. There is a strong case, however, for saying that where B is not acting under a mistake as to B's *current* rights, but is instead acting on a belief that A will give B a right in the future, then B's reliance will be reasonable only if A made a promise to B. Certainly, the following case is one in which the House of Lords denied B's proprietary estoppel claim, even though A clearly encouraged B to believe that B would acquire an interest in A's land.

*Cobbe v Yeoman's Row Management Ltd* **(2008):** Mrs Lisle-Mainwaring was the sole director of YRML, a company that held the registered freehold of land in Knightsbridge. She hoped to develop the land and agreed with Mr Cobbe, a property developer, that he would prepare an application for planning permission. They came to an oral agreement that, if planning permission were granted, the freehold would be sold to Mr Cobbe, or a company nominated by him, for £12 million, subject to a duty to pay to YRML 50 per cent of the amount, if any, by which the gross proceeds of sale of the developed property exceeded £24 million. When Mr Cobbe succeeded in obtaining planning permission, YRML, acting

> through Mrs Lisle-Mainwaring, refused to honour the oral agreement. Mr Cobbe's propri-
> etary estoppel claim succeeded at first instance, and YRML was ordered to pay him £2 mil-
> lion. That award was upheld by the Court of Appeal, but overturned in the House of Lords,
> where it was found that the requirements of proprietary estoppel had not been made out. It
> was acknowledged though that YRML had to pay Mr Cobbe a reasonable sum (estimated at
> around £150,000) for his work in preparing the planning application, as he had performed
> those services at the request of, and for the benefit of, YRML.

**5.103**   The simplest explanation for the denial of the proprietary estoppel claim in *Cobbe* is that
A had not made a sufficiently certain promise to B. Whilst an agreement in principle
had been reached, important points were still outstanding: for example, would the land
be sold to Mr Cobbe, or to a company nominated by him?; How would YRML take security for the duty of the buyer to pay 50 per cent of any proceeds over £24 million? As a
result, it can be said that Mr Cobbe could not reasonably regard YRML as having made
a promise seriously intended as capable of being relied on. The same basic point can be
made in a different way: it could equally be said that Mr Cobbe did not reasonably rely
on YRML, as such reliance occurred even in the absence of a sufficiently clear commit-
ment by YRML; or that Mr Cobbe was relying simply on the hope, or the chance, of the
sale going ahead, not on any promise by YRML. This possibility of making the same
point in different ways provides support for the idea that the individual requirements of
proprietary estoppel are all closely linked.

**5.104**   Other explanations for the decision in *Cobbe* have, however, been given. In the case itself, each of Lord Scott and Lord Walker suggested that no proprietary estoppel claim
could arise as B knew that A's promise was not contractually binding. Yet this is hard
to square with cases, such as the pre-*Cobbe* decision in *Walton v Walton* (**5.100**) or the
post-*Cobbe* decision in *Thorner v Major* (**5.94**), in which a claim was successfully based
on A's promise to leave land to B in a will: it would be very hard for B to show, in such
cases, that he or she thought that A's promise was immediately legally binding. It might
then be said that there is a difference between commercial cases such as *Cobbe* and domestic cases such as *Walton* or *Thorner*. It is, of course, important to bear in mind the
factual context when applying the requirements of any doctrine, but, as pointed out by
Hopkins (2011), it is difficult to justify having different legal tests for the commercial
and domestic spheres. Certainly, there is no shortage of commercial cases in which proprietary estoppel claims have succeeded (*Herbert v Doyle* (2010), *Hoyl Group v Cromer
Town Council* (2015)).

## Requirement 2: Reliance by B

**5.105**   Reliance by B is necessary in order to provide the link between A's conduct in the past (eg
A's promise to B) and the detriment that B will suffer if A behaves in a certain way in the
future (eg if A does not honour the promise). In *Thorner v Major*, for example, David's
reliance consisted of his deciding to continue working on Peter's farm for low pay, rather
than taking up other opportunities. The question of whether reliance has been established should be primarily factual, requiring a comparison between B's actual behaviour

and how B would have behaved in the absence of A's past conduct (eg if A's promise had not been made). In some cases, however, judges have departed from that position, and made it easier for B to establish reliance.

5.106    In *Greasley v Cooke* (1980), for example, Lord Denning MR stated that, where A makes a representation (or, presumably, a promise) intending B to rely on it, then reliance should be presumed, so that it becomes A's job to show that B did not rely on that representation or promise. That is an unusual test, as of course the general position is that it is for B to prove the elements of B's claim. It is true that where A has made a *fraudulent* misrepresentation, reliance may be presumed, but that rule is based on the courts' understandably harsh approach to fraud, and it seems out of place where A has simply made a promise and then changed his or her mind. In *Wayling v Jones* (1993), for example, the Court of Appeal stated that Mr Wayling only needed to show that he would have acted differently if Mr Jones, after having made the promise to him, had then told Mr Wayling that he had changed his mind and would not fulfil the promise. As noted by Cooke (1995), this is an 'unusually generous' test as it allows B's claim to succeed even if B would have acted in exactly the same way if no initial promise had been made.

5.107    It is worth noting that the High Court of Australia, in *van Dyke v Sidhu* (2014) has rejected Lord Denning MR's view that there is a presumption of reliance in proprietary estoppel, and that, in English law, the presumption does not apply in any other form of estoppel (*Steria Ltd v Hutchison* (2007)). Similarly, when discussing the requirement of reliance in *Campbell v Griffin* (2001), Robert Walker LJ did not refer to the *Wayling v Jones* test.

5.108    It may be that the better approach is simply to apply the standard legal test for reliance, without the modifications in either *Greasley* or *Wayling*, but for the courts to continue to be sensitive to the fact that reliance is a matter that must be looked at 'in the round', so that it can be established by a pattern of overall conduct, without B necessarily having to prove definitively that a specific decision was made on the basis of a belief that B would acquire a right in A's land.

## Requirement 3: The Prospect of Detriment to B

5.109    It is often said that 'detrimental reliance' is a requirement of proprietary estoppel, but care must be taken. B's reliance need not be immediately detrimental: the question is rather whether, having acted in that way, B would *now* suffer a detriment if, for example, A refuses to honour A's promise to B. In *Crabb v Arun DC* (1976), for example, B relied on his belief that he would acquire a right of way over A's land by failing to reserve an easement when selling off part of his own land. As a result of not reserving such an easement, B no doubt sold that part of his land for a higher price than would otherwise have been the case. The reliance was thus not immediately detrimental. When A later refused to grant B the expected easement, however, the prospect of detriment was realized: with no easement over the part of the land sold off, nor over A's land, B would have no means of accessing his retained land.

5.110   It is clear that the concept of detriment should not be approached in a narrow, purely financial way. In *Gillett v Holt* (2001), for example, the Court of Appeal looked at matters 'in the round', taking account of the different ways in which, over a period of 30 years, B had based his life on A's promises that he would acquire farmland on A's death. It was stated there that the requirement of detriment 'must be approached as part of a broad inquiry as to whether repudiation of an assurance is or is not unconscionable in all the circumstances'.

5.111   In considering B's potential detriment, a court must also take account of any counter-vailing benefits acquired by B, either directly from A or as a result of B's reliance on A (see eg *Henry v Henry* (2010)). So if, for example, A has allowed B rent-free occupation of land that may reduce, or even wholly remove, the prospect of detriment. As we will see at **5.117–5.123**, the courts are interested not only in the presence of any detriment, but also in its *extent*, as that may be relevant when calculating what right B should acquire as a result of a successful proprietary estoppel claim.

## Requirement 4: Unconscionability?

5.112   There is a debate as to the proper role of unconscionability in proprietary estoppel (see eg Dixon (2002, 2010), Hopkins (2004)). As was made clear in *Cobbe v Yeoman's Row Management Ltd* (2008), B cannot appeal to unconscionability as a way to bypass the three requirements of a promise or assurance, reliance, and detriment. It seems that unconscionability instead has a limiting role to play. In *Thorner v Major*, Lord Walker referred to those three requirements as the *main* elements of proprietary estoppel; his Lordship had previously referred to unconscionability as another element, stating in *Cobbe v Yeoman's Row Management Ltd* that if the three main elements 'appear to be present but the result does not shock the conscience of the court, the analysis needs to be looked at again'.

5.113   It can be suggested that unconscionability is relevant in both a general way, and in two specific ways. The general way is simply that, as an equitable doctrine, proprietary es-toppel depends, at an abstract level, on the goal of preventing A from acting unconscion-ably: this goal has been linked to the general aim of preventing A acting opportunistically, by exploiting the strict legal rules that deny B a claim (Smith (2014)). The first specific way is that the general notion of unconscionability may help a court when interpreting one of the three main requirements of the doctrine, for example in assessing if B's detri-ment is sufficiently substantial to merit a claim (*Gillett v Holt* (2001)). The second spe-cific way it may help is when dealing with questions such as the effect of an unexpected change of circumstances on A (see **5.101**), or the impact of any misconduct of B (as if, eg, B put undue pressure on A to make a promise to give B a right in A's land). This ana-lysis is consistent with the view taken by Tomlinson LJ in *Southwell v Blackburn* (2014) that unconscionability is 'not a watertight element in the estoppel but rather a feature which permeates all of its elements'.

## Proprietary Estoppel and Formality Rules

**5.114**  Part of the importance of proprietary estoppel lies in its ability to give rise to rights even in the absence of any formal, written dealings between the parties. In *Cobbe v Yeoman's Row Management Ltd* (2008), however, Lord Scott suggested that B should not be able to base a proprietary estoppel claim on A's oral promise to give B a right in land, as that would be inconsistent with the need for a written document, signed by both parties, imposed by section 2 of the Law of Property (Miscellaneous Provisions) Act 1989.

**5.115**  Lord Scott's doubts are misplaced. The simple point is that the 1989 Act regulates when a *contract* has arisen between the parties and, as noted at **5.101**, a proprietary estoppel claim, even if based on a promise, is distinct from a contractual claim. As Lord Neuberger, writing extra-judicially, has put it: 'the fact that, if there was a contract, it would be void is irrelevant: indeed, the very reason for mounting the proprietary estoppel claim is that there is no enforceable contract' (Neuberger (2009)).

**5.116**  It is true that, in some cases, courts have met concerns about the possible effect of the 1989 Act by finding that B's right arises under a constructive trust, and then relying on section 2(5) of the 1989 Act, which creates an exception for resulting, implied, or constructive trusts. Such an approach is, however, unnecessary: if a proprietary estoppel claim is seen as distinct from a contractual claim, then there is no need to rely on an exception to the basic rule in section 2(1), as that rule simply does not apply in the first place (McFarlane (2005)).

## The Effect of Proprietary Estoppel

**5.117**  If B can establish a proprietary estoppel claim, how will the court determine the specific right acquired by B? In some cases where B's claim is based on a promise of A, that promise will be enforced: in *Thorner v Major* (2009), for example, B's successful claim led to B's acquisition of the farm, including both the land and other farm assets. Certainly, in such a case, B cannot receive *more* than was promised by A, as it cannot be unconscionable for A simply to honour that promise, even if B decided to rely in such a way that B will suffer some detriment even once the promise is honoured.

**5.118**  It is, however, possible for the court to decide that B should acquire *less* than was promised, as shown by the following example.

---

*Jennings v Rice* **(2002):** Mrs Royle owned a home in Somerset, and died without leaving a will. Mr Jennings had initially worked for her as a part-time gardener but, by the end of her life, he did a lot of unpaid work for her (running errands etc) and also cared for her, often staying overnight at her home to do so. He claimed that Mrs Royle had assured him that she would 'see him right' in her will (or words to that effect) and that he had relied on those assurances by working for her without payment. He claimed to be entitled to the value of Mrs Royle's house and furniture (valued at £435,000). The first instance judge found that the requirements of proprietary estoppel were made out, and that Mr Jennings should receive £200,000. The Court of Appeal upheld that judgment, rejecting Mr Jennings's argument that his expectation of receiving the house and its furniture should necessarily be protected.

**5.119**   In *Jennings v Rice*, the principal judgment was given by Aldous LJ, who emphasized that the 'award must be proportionate' and that it would be very odd if B were always entitled to the enforcement of A's promise, no matter how little detriment B might otherwise incur. In doing so, he invoked the concept of unconscionability: '[i]f the conscience of the court is involved, it would be odd if the amount of the award should be set rigidly at the sum expected by the claimant'. Similarly, in *Henry v Henry* (2010), the Privy Council emphasized that it is important to establish the extent of B's detriment when deciding what right B should acquire through proprietary estoppel. In that case, compensating benefits received by B reduced the extent of that detriment, and so reduced the right acquired by B.

**5.120**   In *Jennings v Rice*, A's promises to B were somewhat unclear, but the Court of Appeal has refused to enforce even a very clear promise, if that result would be disproportionate given the limited nature of B's potential detriment (*Ottey v Grundy* (2003)). Such an approach makes good sense, given that a proprietary estoppel claim is different from a contractual claim, and so does not impose an immediate duty on A to perform a promise. Rather, the court, as noted by Hoffmann LJ in *Walton v Walton* (1994) (**5.100**) looks backwards to see what is required to prevent A acting unconscionably.

**5.121**   Whilst it is therefore clear that B's expectation will not always be protected, there is still some uncertainty (or, as Lewison LJ put it in *Davies v Davies* (2016), a 'lively controversy') as to the correct approach. On one view, proportionality has a positive role to play. The aim of the doctrine is to prevent the particular form of unconscionable conduct that consists of A leaving B to suffer a detriment as a result of B's reasonable reliance on A's promise. This view gains support from the idea that, if, before any dispute came to court, A had given B a countervailing benefit that removed any prospect of detriment to B, B would have no claim against A; therefore, if the court now orders A to do the same, B can have no complaint. As noted by Lewison LJ in *Davies*: 'Logically, there is much to be said' for such an approach. It also provides some guidance to a court in a case where it decides not to enforce A's promise, as the aim of removing B's detriment can then determine the extent of B's right.

**5.122**   A second view is that the starting point is that A's promise should be enforced, and this will be departed from only if A can show that such a result would be disproportionate, given, for example, the limited nature of the detriment that B would suffer. On this approach, proportionality instead has only a negative role to play—it is a reason for departing from the basic position of enforcing A's promise. So, for example, if B's only reliance on A's promise to leave a house to B is that B spent £5,000 on repairs to that house, it would be out of all proportion for B to acquire the house itself, and a money award would suffice to prevent any unconscionable conduct. On this view, however, there may be cases where the extent of B's detriment is clearly lower than the value of A's promise, but A's promise is still enforced.

5.123    It is possible to find support in the cases for each of the first view (see eg *Sledmore v Dalby* (1996)) and the second view (see eg *Suggitt v Suggitt* (2012)). It is also possible, of course, to take neither view, or to adopt a mixture of the two—in his judgment in *Jennings v Rice* (2002), for example, Robert Walker LJ suggested that protecting B's expectation would be particularly suitable in a case where B's reliance consists of performing B's side of a bargain with A. There is certainly no academic agreement on the best approach to take (contrast, eg, Gardner (2006) with Mee (2009)); and looking overseas is of limited assistance as, for example, there is a similar inconsistency in the approach of Australian courts. The uncertainty is likely to continue until the courts reach a clear view as to the particular nature and function of the promise-based form of proprietary estoppel: is its aim to prevent A leaving B to suffer a detriment as a result of reasonable reliance on A's promise; or is it instead concerned with establishing when, in general, A's promise should be enforced?

## Proprietary Estoppel and Third Parties

5.124    In *Thorner v Major* (2009), the House of Lords was essentially concerned only with the rights of David Thorner against Peter Thorner: any such rights would be binding on Peter's administrators when dealing with his property on his death. It therefore did not matter if David's rights were personal rights or, instead, property rights. If, however, Peter (A) had fallen out with David (B) and, before his death, had sold the farmland to a third party (C), it would be important to know if David could have any claim against that third party.

5.125    One useful starting point might be to consider the position where B's rights against A arise under a contract. As we saw in **Chapter 3**, it is necessary to look at the *content* of B's right. If A's contractual duty is simply to pay B a sum of money, or to let B share occupation of A's land, then B has only a personal right, which cannot, in itself, bind C. If, however, A's contractual duty is to grant B a recognized property right then, as a result of the doctrine of anticipation (see **5.87–5.92**), B will acquire an immediate equitable property right.

5.126    We might expect the same analysis to apply to proprietary estoppel: like contract, it is simply a means of acquiring rights, and so we have to look to the content of the specific right acquired by B to tell if it can, or cannot, bind C. So, in our hypothetical twist on *Thorner*, if Peter had sold the land to C shortly before Peter's death, and at that point Peter was under a duty to transfer the farmland to David, then David would have had an equitable property right, which is capable of binding C. If, however, Peter had sold the land to C much earlier, after David had undertaken only limited reliance on Peter's promise, then at that point Peter might well have been under a duty only to pay David a sum of money, and so David would only have had a personal right against Peter, which cannot bind C.

**5.127**   That basic picture may well be not very far from the truth. Things are complicated, however, by the way in which first the courts, and then Parliament, have dealt with proprietary estoppel. As a result, it is necessary to distinguish between two types of situation.

### Situation 1: C Acquires a Right After a Court Order in B's Favour

**5.128**   The position here is reasonably clear: the court order sets the content of B's right, and so we simply need to ask if the order gave B a property right in the land, or instead only a personal right against A. Only in the former case can C be bound by B's right. So if, for example, the court ordered A to transfer land to B, the doctrine of anticipation can operate to give B, from the time of the court order at least (*Mountney v Treharne* (2003)), an equitable interest in the land, which is capable of binding C (although, of course, C may have a defence to that right). If the court instead ordered A to pay B a sum of money, then clearly B has only a personal right against A, which cannot bind C.

**5.129**   An apparent complication in relation to licences can easily be dealt with. There are cases in which a court has assumed that a licence arising by proprietary estoppel can bind a third party (see eg *Williams v Staite* (1979)). Those cases, however, were decided at a point when it was also thought that a contractual licence could bind a third party. Now that it is clear that a contractual licence gives B only a personal right against A, the same must be true of a licence arising by proprietary estoppel (3.81–3.82). The effect of a right on a third party depends on its content, not on the means by which it was acquired.

### Situation 2: C Acquires a Right Before a Court Order in B's Favour

**5.130**   The general view taken by the courts is that, before any court order is made in B's favour, B has only an 'equity by estoppel' or an 'inchoate equity': a right to go to court and seek relief. This is the case even if all the requirements of proprietary estoppel have been met. It means that, if C acquires a right in the relevant land before any court order in B's favour, then the crucial question is whether B's 'equity by estoppel' is a personal right or a property right.

**5.131**   The concept of the 'equity by estoppel' fits well with the idea, discussed at 5.101, that proprietary estoppel is a backward-looking doctrine, which does not impose an immediate duty on A, but instead allows a court to look at the facts which have occurred and decide what is necessary to prevent unconscionable conduct by A. On this view, before such a court order, A is not under a duty to B, but is rather under a liability (McFarlane (2016)). The difference between a duty and a liability can be seen by considering, for example, a rule that says that there is a £50 fine for smoking on a railway platform. If we saw someone breaching that rule, we might say that he or she is *liable* to pay a fine: their conduct means that someone (eg a member of the transport police) now has the power to impose the fine. It would, however, be odd to say, when we see the smoker, that he or she is under a duty to pay the fine: that duty will arise only at a later point, if the official does indeed exercise the power to impose the fine (S Smith (2012)). So, if proprietary estoppel does not impose an immediate duty on A, and that duty arises instead only at the time of a possible court order against A, it can be said that, before any such court order, A is under a liability to B. This analysis may help to explain the idea of an 'equity by estoppel', as it fits with other situations in which B is said to have a 'mere equity'. For example, if B transfers a right to A as a result of A's misrepresentation, and B therefore has a power to rescind the transfer and regain the right, it is not true to say that A is under an immediate duty to B: after all, B may decide to let the transfer stand. That does not mean, however, that A's position is secure: as B may choose to rescind the transfer and regain the right, A is subject to a liability.

5.132   The idea of A being under a liability, and not a duty to B, makes it difficult to say that, before any court order is made, B already has an equitable interest in A's land. That is because, as we have seen in this chapter, such rights arise where A is under a *duty* to B in relation to specific property held by A. Equally, however, it does not mean that, before a court order is made, B has only a personal right against A. The crucial question is as to the content of A's liability. If, at a particular time, a court hearing a dispute between A and B would satisfy A's liability by ordering A to transfer land to B, or to give B a recognized property right in the land, then it makes sense to say that B's claim relates to A's land, and so gives B a right capable of binding C. If, however, at that time, a court would instead satisfy A's liability by ordering A to pay a sum of money to B, or to allow B a licence to make some use of the land, then it would be odd to say that B has anything other than a personal right against A. In such a case, the eventual court order would only give B a personal right against A, so it cannot be the case that B is in a better position *before* such a court order.

5.133   On this view, the notion of an 'equity by estoppel' reflects the fact that, before a court order is made, A is under no duty to B, but is instead under a liability. To know if that 'equity by estoppel' is capable of binding C, we must ask how, immediately before the moment when C acquired C's right, a court would have satisfied that liability of A. If it would have ordered A to transfer the land to B, or to grant B a recognized property right in the land, then B's equity by estoppel can bind C (subject to defences). If, however, a court would not have made such an order, but would instead have ordered A to pay a sum of money to B, or to give B a licence, then B's equity by estoppel cannot bind C.

5.134   There is, however, an obstacle in the way of this view. Section 116 of the Land Registration Act 2002 states that each of an 'equity by estoppel' and a 'mere equity' 'has effect from the time the equity arises as an interest capable of binding successors in title (subject to the rules about the effect of dispositions on priority)'. This suggests that, even if a court would only have ordered A to pay a sum of money to B, or to give B a licence, B's equity by estoppel is still capable of binding C. It has been pointed out that such a result is unsatisfactory (McFarlane (2003b)) as it means that B's position is stronger simply because no court order has been made, and also that the 2002 Act, which generally aims to protect the position of C when acquiring a right in registered land, instead imposes an additional burden on C. It may be, then, that the term 'equity by estoppel' in section 116(a) should be interpreted to refer only to those cases in which, had a court heard the dispute at that time, A's liability would have been satisfied by ordering A to transfer A's land to B, or to grant B a recognized property right in that land.

## Proprietary Estoppel and Constructive Trusts

5.135 We have seen in this chapter that proprietary estoppel is a means by which B can acquire an equitable interest in A's land, even if there have been no written dealings between A and B. The same is true of the different constructive trusts principles we have examined (**5.22–5.86**). There is certainly an overlap between proprietary estoppel and constructive trusts. This is because, in some cases, proprietary estoppel may lead to a court's imposing a duty on A to transfer land to B, or to hold land for the benefit of each of A and B. In such cases, the content of A's duty is such that B has a beneficial interest under a trust. In *Thorner v Major*, for example, Lord Hoffmann referred to David as having the beneficial interest in Peter's farm. Of course, however, a proprietary estoppel claim need not lead to a trust: in *Jennings v Rice*, for example, A's estate was instead ordered to pay a sum of money to B. So, whilst proprietary estoppel may sometimes give rise to a constructive trust, it does not always do so: everything depends on the content of A's duty (and, in the period before a court order in B's favour, on the content of A's liability).

5.136 Equally, a constructive trust may arise even if B has no proprietary estoppel claim. In *Pallant v Morgan* (1953) itself, for example, B acted on his agreement with A by failing to bid for particular land. That did not cause B a detriment as A would in any case have outbid B for the land. B would therefore have no proprietary estoppel claim, as the detriment element had not been met. However, B's failure to bid meant that A acquired the land more cheaply (as he did not have to outbid B) and so A had acquired an advantage in relation to the acquisition of the land. As noted at **5.79**, the *Pallant v Morgan* trust can arise if there is *either* a disadvantage to B *or* a benefit to A as a result of B's action. Moreover, it seems that the *Pallant v Morgan* principle necessarily leads to the enforcement of the bargain between A and B: in contrast, we saw at **5.117–5.123** that a successful proprietary estoppel claim based on A's promise to B does not always lead to the protection of B's expectation.

5.137 It therefore seems that, whilst the promise-based strand of proprietary estoppel is similar in some ways to the principle behind the *Pallant v Morgan* trust, it is distinct from it. The same can be said of the common intention constructive trust. First, such a common intention can be inferred from particular conduct of B, such as making a direct contribution to the purchase price or mortgage payments, whereas there is no rule that such conduct means that a court will necessarily find that A made any promise or assurance to B. Secondly, even where a common intention is instead based on express discussions between A and B, there seems to be a difference when it comes to calculating the nature of the right acquired by B. Under a common intention constructive trust, it seems that the parties' arrangement or understanding will be enforced, irrespective of the extent of B's detriment: B acquires an immediate beneficial interest in the land, as A and B had planned. In contrast, as we noted at **5.101**, proprietary estoppel instead looks back over the dealings between A and B to decide what is now necessary to prevent unconscionable conduct by A, and that need not involve enforcing any promise of A. As Lord Walker put it in *Stack v Dowden* (2007), a proprietary estoppel claim 'is a "mere equity"'. It is to be satisfied by the minimum award necessary to do injustice, which may sometimes lead to no more than a monetary award. A "common intention" constructive trust, by contrast, is identifying the true beneficial owner or owners, and the size of their beneficial interests.'

5.138  The following case provides a useful example of the differences between a proprietary estoppel claim and a common intention constructive trust.

---

**Southwell v Blackburn (2014):** Ms Blackburn and Mr Southwell, an unmarried couple, had set up home together in a house registered in the sole name of Mr Southwell. When their relationship broke down nine years later, Ms Blackburn claimed that he held his legal title on trust for the benefit of each of them in equal shares. The first instance judge found that no common intention constructive trust had arisen as Ms Blackburn had made no direct financial contribution to the purchase price or mortgage payments, and Mr Southwell had made no clear promise to her that she would become an equal owner of the house. However, this did not mean that Mr Southwell had made no assurance at all: it was likely that he had instead assured Ms Blackburn that she would have some security as to her rights to occupy the home, and this promise of security was not conditional on the parties' relationship continuing. As a result, Ms Blackburn had given up her own secure rented accommodation, in which she had invested money, as well as leaving her job and moving with her children to be with Mr Southwell. The first instance judge, finding that it would therefore be unconscionable if Mr Southwell did 'anything other than seek to put her back in the same position as she was before she gave up her own house', ordered him to pay Ms Blackburn £28,500. The Court of Appeal dismissed his appeal, finding that there was no inconsistency in rejecting the common intention constructive trust claim, but finding that a proprietary estoppel claim had arisen.

---

# FURTHER READING

Allan, G, 'Once a Fraud, Forever a Fraud: The Time Honoured Doctrine of Parol Agreement Trusts' (2014) 34 LS 419.

Fox O'Mahony, L, 'Property Outsiders and the Hidden Politics of Doctrinalism' (2014) 67 CLP 409.

Gardner, S, 'Reliance-Based Constructive Trusts' in C Mitchell (ed), *Resulting and Constructive Trusts* (Oxford: Hart Publishing, 2009).

Gardner, S, 'Problems in Family Property' (2013) 72 CLJ 301.

Hayward, A, '*Stack v Dowden* (2007); *Jones v Kernott* (2009): Finding a Home for "Family Property"' in N Gravells (ed), *Landmark Cases in Land Law* (Oxford: Hart Publishing, 2013).

Hopkins, N, 'Regulating Trusts of the Home: Private Law and Social Policy (2009) 125 LQR 310.

McFarlane, B, 'Constructive Trusts Arising on Receipt of Property *Sub Conditione*' (2004) 120 LQR 667.

McFarlane, B and Sales, P, 'Promises, Detriment, and Liability: Lessons from Proprietary Estoppel' (2015) 131 LQR 610.

Mee, J, 'Expectation and Proprietary Estoppel Remedies' in M Dixon (ed), *Modern Studies in Property Law: Vol V* (Oxford: Hart Publishing, 2009).

Sloan, B, 'Keeping up with the *Jones* Case: Establishing Constructive Trusts in "Sole Legal Owner" Scenarios' (2015) 35 LS 226.

Turner, P, 'Understanding the Constructive Trust between Vendor and Purchaser' (2012) 128 LQR 582.

Yip, M, 'The *Pallant v Morgan* Equity Reconsidered' (2013) 33 LS 459.

## SELF-TEST QUESTIONS

1  What do you understand to be the difference between express, resulting, and constructive trusts? What role does the settlor's intention play in the creation of each of these types of trust?

2  Explain the operation of: (i) the presumption of resulting trust; and (ii) the presumption of advancement. In what circumstances does each apply?

3  What initial presumption of ownership is drawn in the following cases and, in each, in what circumstances and for what purpose might a common intention constructive trust be claimed by B?

   a  A is the sole legal owner of a home where she lives with her cohabitee B.

   b  A and B are joint legal owners of the home in which they cohabit.

4  What do you understand to be the difference between an inferred and imputed common intention and what role does each of them have in relation to the common intention constructive trust?

5  What result does the doctrine of *Rochefoucauld v Boustead* provide when T reneges on the oral agreement in the following transactions?

   a  A transfer of land from B to T on T's oral agreement to hold the land on trust for B.

   b  A transfer of land from X to T on T's oral agreement to hold the land on trust for B.

6  In what circumstances does a constructive trust arise under the *Pallant v Morgan* equity? What do you consider to be the distinctive feature or features of this form of constructive trust?

7  What is the 'doctrine of anticipation'? Can you explain when it can give rise to a constructive trust?

8  What are the three main elements of proprietary estoppel? Can you explain how each was present in *Thorner v Major*?

9  In what ways does a proprietary estoppel claim, even if based on a promise, differ from a contractual claim?

10  What are the differences between a common intention constructive trust and a proprietary estoppel claim?

# 6

# Trusts of Land

## SUMMARY

This chapter considers the legal regulation of trusts of land, focusing on co-ownership trusts. The chapter explains the two forms of co-ownership that exist in English law—the joint tenancy and tenancy in common—and the 'severance' rules that enable a joint tenant to become a tenant in common. The chapter then considers the trustees' powers, beneficiaries' rights, and the role of the court in relation to co-ownership trusts as provided by the Trusts of Land and Appointment of Trustees Act 1996. Finally, the chapter explores how the courts resolve disputes as to whether co-owned land should be sold.

Key topics explored in this chapter are:

- Joint tenants and tenants in common (6.6–6.20)

- Severance (6.21–6.58)

- Termination of co-ownership (6.59–6.61)

- Co-ownership and trusts (6.62–6.84)

- Applications to court, including applications for sale (6.85–6.126)

## Introduction

6.1 In Chapter 5 we considered the 'acquisition question' in relation to trusts. We have seen how trusts of land come into existence. We have seen in Chapter 5 that trusts can be created expressly or arise informally. In this chapter we consider the 'content question' in relation to trusts. Once a trust has come into existence, the law needs to explain the rights and responsibilities of the parties to the trust—the trustees and beneficiaries—and provide a mechanism to resolve disputes between them. What should happen, for example, if one of the beneficiaries wants to sell the land and another beneficiary wishes to keep the land for his or her sole occupation? What is the effect on the beneficiaries if one of them has debts that he or she has not paid, or becomes bankrupt as a result? In this chapter we consider how the law regulates trusts of land. By doing so, we learn what it means to be a beneficiary under a trust: what rights beneficiaries have and the law that governs the relationships that exist between (i) the beneficiaries; (ii) the beneficiaries and the trustees; and (iii) the beneficiaries and their creditors who wish to sell the land against the beneficiaries' wishes in order to secure repayment of a debt. We leave aside the 'defences question'—the enforcement of beneficial interests against third parties who purchase legal title from the trustees or lend money on security of the legal title. The defences question is addressed in **Chapter 11**.

6.2 Our focus in this chapter, as in **Chapter 5**, is on co-ownership trusts. Co-ownership describes the situation in which two or more people are concurrently entitled to legal and/or beneficial title to an estate in land. Co-ownership may arise either in relation to a freehold or leasehold estate, and is of particular relevance in understanding the legal regulation of the home. For example, co-ownership describes the common situation where spouses or cohabitees (H and W) jointly own their home, whether legal title is vested (and, in registered land, registered) in the names of one or both of the parties, as shown in **Figure 6.1**.

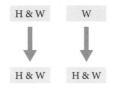

**Figure 6.1**  Co-ownership

6.3 Co-ownership also arises where legal title is held by two or more trustees on behalf of a single beneficiary (who may or may not be one of the trustees), as shown in **Figure 6.2**. Where the beneficiary is of full age and capacity, this form of legal co-ownership is a type of 'bare trust'. A bare trust can be brought to an end by the beneficiary directing the trustee(s) to transfer legal title to him or her under the rule in *Saunders v Vautier* (1841). Similarly, under the Trusts of Land and Appointment of Trustees Act 1996 (TOLATA), s 6(2) the trustees can bring an end to a bare trust by conveying legal title to the beneficiary, who is required (and may be ordered by the court) to 'do whatever is necessary to secure that it vests in them' (TOLATA, s 6(2)(a) and (b))—for example, by securing registration of title. However, the trustees' power to bring an end to a trust extends beyond bare trusts (**6.74**).

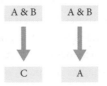

**Figure 6.2**  Co-ownership of legal title

**6.4** The defining characteristic of co-ownership is that the parties have 'unity of possession'; that is, they are each entitled to possession of the whole of the land. No co-owner can point to part of the land and claim that it represents his or her 'share' of the land. For example, if two people are co-owners of a house divided into two flats, then each of them is entitled to occupy both of the flats. Neither can point to one of the flats and say 'that flat is my share of the land'. The beneficiaries may agree between themselves that for convenience or out of preference they will each occupy one of the flats, but their agreement as to *occupation* does not detract from their entitlement to *possession* of the whole. It is unity of possession that distinguishes co-ownership from 'successive owner-ship', in which possession is enjoyed consecutively, as shown in **Figure 6.3**. Historically, the regulation of successive ownership was a central concern of land law. Successive ownership was used, through a type of trust known as a 'strict settlement' (governed most recently by the Settled Land Act 1925), to keep land within a family, passing down from generation to generation, in order to perpetuate wealth and power and keep estates intact. Co-ownership has now replaced successive ownership in economic and social importance. The creation of new strict settlements under the Settled Land Act 1925 is prohibited (TOLATA, s 2). While successive ownership arrangements remain possible, subject to compliance with the rule against perpetuities (which places a limit on the period of time within which a future interest in property may vest or take effect), they are fiscally unattractive as they are subject to unfavourable treatment under the inherit-ance tax regime.

**Figure 6.3**  Successive ownership

**6.5** It is a particular feature of English law that a trust exists in all cases of co-ownership. Many people who own their home with their spouse or partner may be surprised to be told that they hold the legal title of their home on trust for themselves as benefi-ciaries. Where the trustees and beneficiaries are the same people, the existence of the trust will not be a practical concern to them on a day-to-day basis. However, as a matter of law, the existence of the trust is significant. The trust is best understood as a device through which the powers of management and disposition of the land are sep-arated from the enjoyment of the land, whether 'enjoyment' takes the form of occupa-tion or receipt of profits and the proceeds of sale. Through the imposition of the trust, the powers of management and disposition are vested in the legal owner or co-owners as trustee(s), while enjoyment of the land vests in the beneficial or equitable owners. Even when the same people are both trustees and beneficiaries, it is important to differentiate the capacity in which a person is exercising his or her rights and duties in relation to the land. That will become practically important to the parties on the happening of key events; such as the death of one of the parties or the intervention of a third party or creditor claiming entitlement to one beneficiary's share. The existence of a trust in all cases of co-ownership means that the rules discussed in this chapter play a particularly important role in understanding the rights and responsibilities that people have in relation to land that they own. The rules discussed in this chapter apply to all land except:

- land that is in sole ownership, where there is only one legal owner and no party has a claim to a beneficial interest through the rules on the acquisition of a trust discussed in **Chapter 5**—this is the only land in respect of which there will not be a trust; and

- land that is subject to historic Settled Land Act trusts, created before TOLATA came into force—this land is held on trust, but the rights and responsibilities of the parties is governed by the Settled Land Act, rather than by the rules discussed in this chapter.

## Joint Tenants and Tenants in Common

6.6    The relationship between co-owners takes the form either of a 'joint tenancy' or a 'tenancy in common'. The essence of a joint tenancy is that each joint tenant is wholly entitled to the land when acting collectively, but that, individually, no single joint tenant has any 'share' in the land with which he or she can separately deal. In Coke's (1832) classic description, '[E]ach joint tenant holds the whole and holds nothing, that is, he holds the whole jointly and nothing separately'. The practical consequence of each joint tenant holding 'the whole' is felt when a joint tenant dies. As a joint tenant does not own a 'share' when a joint tenant dies he or she has no interest in the property to pass by will or intestacy. Title simply 'survives' in the remaining joint tenants through the process of survivorship (**6.19-6.20**). Hence, for example, if spouses or cohabitees are joint tenants of their home, on the death of the first of them, title remains in the survivor. There is no passing or vesting of title in the surviving spouse or cohabitee because he or she was already 'wholly entitled' to the home. The operation of survivorship is the key practical difference between the joint tenancy and the tenancy in common.

6.7    A joint tenancy is characterized by what are known as the 'four unities'. The presence of the four unities is a precondition of a joint tenancy, but is not determinative that the co-owners are joint tenants (**6.14**). The four unities consist of unity of possession (**6.4**), unity of interest (the joint tenants have the same interest in the land), unity of title (the joint tenants must derive their title from the same act, eg, of adverse possession, or document), and unity of time (joint tenants derive their title at the same time).

6.8    Tenants in common hold what are described as 'undivided shares' in the land. Each tenant in common may deal with his or her share individually during his or her lifetime (eg by selling the share to another co-owner or to a third party). On the death of a tenant in common, his or her share passes through his or her will or under the rules of intestacy. The shares are 'undivided' in the sense that the land is not divided into distinct 'shares'. The tenants in common still enjoy unity of possession (6.4). The fact the parties have undivided shares does not enable any one of them to point to a particular part of the land and claim it as representing his or her 'share'.

6.9    In sum, it may be said that while joint tenants can act only *collectively* and their acts necessarily affect the whole of the co-owned estate, tenants in common can also act *individually* in relation to their own undivided shares in the estate.

6.10   Where co-owners are joint tenants, one or more of the co-owners may subsequently become a tenant in common through the process of severance (6.21–6.58). Severance is irreversible and there is no process through which co-owners who are tenants in common (either from the outset or by virtue of severance) can become joint tenants.

## Co-ownership of a Legal Estate

6.11   The rules that govern co-ownership of a legal estate are unhelpfully spread across the Law of Property Act 1925 (LPA 1925) and the Trustee Act 1925. The rules are difficult to construe by the standards of more modern legislation. But each rule is part of a jigsaw puzzle intended to ensure that legal ownership of land operates in a particular way. The aim of the different rules contained in the legislation is to ensure that there is always a single and indivisible legal title, held by a maximum of four co-owners as trustees. The existence of a single and indivisible legal title facilitates transactions carried out in relation to land, as it means that at the most four signatures will be required on any transaction affecting the legal estate. It does not mean that only four people can benefit from a piece of land. There is no limit on the number of beneficiaries for whom the legal owners may hold the land on trust.

6.12   To achieve the objective of a single and indivisible legal title, it is necessary to ensure that co-ownership of a legal title is always held as a joint tenancy. That ensures that purchasers and others can deal confidently with the legal owners as collective managers of the legal title (6.6 and 6.9). Section 1(6) of the LPA 1925 provides that '[a] legal estate is not capable of subsisting or of being created in an undivided share in land'—that is, as a tenancy in common. This provision therefore confines co-ownership of a legal estate to a joint tenancy. If legal title is purported to be transferred to co-owners as tenants in common, the co-owners become legal joint tenants and hold title on trust for themselves as equitable tenants in common (LPA 1925, s 34(2)). The reference to 'subsisting' (alongside 'created') in section 1(6) of the LPA 1925 implies that severance of a legal joint tenancy is prohibited, and this prohibition is put beyond doubt by section 36(2) of the Act. The objective of a single and indivisible legal title would be defeated if, once transferred to joint tenants, a co-owner could sever his or her legal ownership, so provision against severance is essential.

6.13    The limit on the number of joint tenants of a legal title is contained in section 34(2) of the Trustee Act 1925. That provision imposes a limit of four trustees or co-owners of legal title to land—and therefore, in registered land, a limit of four registered proprietors. Where an attempt is made to transfer legal title to land to more than four people as joint tenants, the first four named who are able and willing to act become trustees (Trustee Act 1925, s 34(2)). If legal title is purported to be transferred to more than four people as tenants in common, the first four who are able and willing to act take the title as joint tenants and hold the land on trust for all of the intended transferees as tenants in common (LPA 1925, s 36(2)). There is no magic reason why four has been chosen as the limit on the number of legal co-owners, through it provides a balance between facilitating dealings with land, on the one hand, whilst providing a degree of flexibility and a safeguard against fraudulent dealings by trustees, on the other (as all of the joint tenants would need to collude to undertake unauthorized dealings).

## Co-ownership in Equity: Joint Tenants or Tenants in Common?

6.14    While legal title is confined to a joint tenancy (6.12), beneficiaries who are co-owners in equity can be joint tenants or tenants in common. Equitable co-owners can be joint tenants only where the four unities are present (6.7). However, the existence of the four unities is not determinative as they may be present (but are not required) in a tenancy in common (Smith (2005)). Assuming the presence of the four unities, whether the co-owners are equitable joint tenants or tenants in common will be determined by either: (i) the terms of any express declaration of trust; or (ii) the application of presumptions.

6.15    In an express trust, the parties may declare the capacity in which beneficial entitlement is held. In *Goodman v Gallant* (1986) the court held that such a declaration is conclusive. In *Cowcher v Cowcher* (1972) Bagnell J considered that 'A trust for A and B without further definition creates an equitable joint interest'. However, in *Robertson v Fraser* (1870–1) Lord Hatherley LC noted: 'I cannot doubt, having regard to the authorities respecting the effect of such words as 'amongst' and 'respectively' that anything which in the slightest degree indicates an intention to divide the property must be held to abrogate the idea of a joint tenancy, and to create a tenancy in common.'

**6.16**   It has consistently been held that a mere declaration that a survivor can give a valid receipt for capital monies is insufficient to establish an express joint tenancy (*Harwood v Harwood* (1991), *Huntingford v Hobbs* (1993), *Stack v Dowden* (2007)).

**6.17**   In registered land, joint transferees have the opportunity to state whether equitable title is to be held as a joint tenancy, but there is no requirement to do so and therefore issues of interpretation continue to arise as to whether the terms of a trust are sufficient to declare a joint tenancy (*Stack v Dowden* (2007), Pawlowski and Brown (2013b)).

**6.18**   In the absence of an express declaration of joint tenancy or tenancy in common, the status of equitable co-owners is determined by the application of the following presumptions.

- As a general maxim, equity follows the law. Legal title can only be held as a joint tenancy (**6.12**), so where the legal title is co-owned, equitable title will also be held by the parties as joint tenants.

- Where parties contribute to the purchase of land unequally, the general maxim supporting an equitable joint tenancy continues to apply if the land is bought 'in joint names for joint occupation by a married or unmarried couple, where both are responsible for any mortgage' (*Jones v Kernott* (2011)). Notably, this statement by the Supreme Court, which is provided by way of 'clarification' of the House of Lords' decision in *Stack v Dowden* (2007), appears narrower than that earlier decision. In *Stack v Dowden* the majority of the House of Lords suggested that the presumption equity follows the law would apply (even in the event of unequal contributions) to cases in the 'domestic consumer context'. The presumption may be displaced by the application of a common intention constructive trust, but only where the circumstances are 'very unusual' (see further **Chapter 5**).

- In other cases where parties contribute unequally, the initial presumption of an equitable joint tenancy is displaced (by a presumption of resulting trust, see further **Chapter 5**) in favour of an equitable tenancy in common so that each party's beneficial share reflects his or her contribution to the purchase. An equitable tenancy in common will therefore arise in the commercial context where, for example, two companies share premises (*Malayan Credit v Jack Chia* (1986)). Following the 'clarification' of *Stack v Dowden* by *Jones v Kernott*, an equitable tenancy in common will also arise in the domestic consumer context in respect of homes bought in the joint names of parties who are not in an intimate relationship; for example, those bought jointly by parents and children, siblings, or friends.

- Where legal title is solely owned and co-ownership arises only in respect of the equitable interest, there is no initial presumption of a joint tenancy. The general rules that operated prior to *Stack v Dowden* and *Jones v Kernott* (and supported by Lord Neuberger in his minority judgment in the former case) may continue to apply. If so, then equitable co-owners who contributed equally to the purchase will be joint tenants, while unequal contributions will give rise to a tenancy in common so that each party's share reflects his or her contribution to the purchase. However, the ethos underpinning the judgments in *Stack v Dowden* and *Jones v*

*Kernott* is to move away from reliance on financial contributions to determine entitlement to the home. It is consistent with this ethos to suggest, at least as regards parties in an intimate relationship, that even in a case of sole legal ownership the parties should be equitable joint tenants where the court concludes that the parties share beneficial ownership equally.

## Survivorship

6.19   Survivorship operates only in respect of a joint tenancy (**6.6**). The effect of survivorship is that on the death of a joint tenant, title remains (or 'survives') in the other joint tenants. As joint tenants do not hold 'shares' (in contrast to the 'undivided shares' held by tenants in common) there is no share to pass under the deceased's will or the intestacy rules. Survivorship does not operate in a tenancy in common where, upon death, a tenant in common's undivided share passes under his or her will or through intestacy rules.

*Example*: A and B are joint tenants at law and in equity. When A dies, legal and equitable title remains or survives in B. A has no 'share' to pass under his or her will or under intestacy rules (**Figure 6.4**).

*Example*: A and B are joint tenants at law, but tenants in common in equity. When A dies, legal title remains or survives in B. However, survivorship does not operate in respect of the equitable tenancy in common. A's equitable share passes under his or her will or under intestacy rules (**Figure 6.5**).

**Figure 6.4**   Survivorship—legal and equitable joint tenants

**Figure 6.5**   Survivorship—legal joint tenants

6.20   As the examples at **6.19** illustrate, through survivorship the longest surviving joint tenant will become the sole owner. Where the joint tenants die simultaneously, practical difficulties are avoided by an arbitrary presumption that they die in order of seniority, so that survivorship operates in favour of the youngest (LPA 1925, s 184).

*Example*: A and B are joint tenants in law and in equity. B is younger than A. A and B are killed together in a car crash. A presumption is drawn that A died first so that survivorship operates in favour of B. B therefore died as sole owner and the land passes under B's will or under intestacy rules applicable to B's estate (**Figure 6.6**).

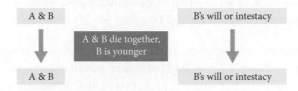

**Figure 6.6** Survivorship—presumption on simultaneous death

## Severance

6.21   Severance is the process through which a beneficial joint tenant may become a tenant in common. By doing so, the severing joint tenant obtains an undivided share in the land that can be separately dealt with and which, on his or her death, will pass under the terms of their will or through statutory rules on intestacy. The severing joint tenant is invariably credited with an equal share (*Goodman v Gallant* (1986)). The severing joint tenant is no longer affected by survivorship, which continues to operate as between any remaining joint tenants. Severance is irreversible.

*Example*: A, B, C, and D are joint tenants at law and in equity. A severs his or her equitable joint tenancy. A, B, C, and D remain joint tenants at law. In equity, A is a tenant in common with a 25 per cent share, while B, C, and D are joint tenants of the remaining 75 per cent. If B and C then die, survivorship operates at law leaving A and D as joint tenants. In equity, survivorship operates in respect of the joint tenancy, so that D survives to the 75 per cent share. A (with 25 per cent) and D with (75 per cent) are now tenants in common in equity (**Figure 6.7**).

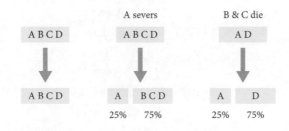

**Figure 6.7** Severance by a joint tenant

**6.22**    Because survivorship operates immediately upon the joint tenants' death, severance must take place during his or her lifetime. In particular, this carries the consequence that severance cannot take place by will. For example, if A and B are joint tenants in law and equity of a home and B dies leaving a will in which her share of the home is passed to C, the will has no effect in relation to the home. Survivorship operated immediately upon B's death, with the result that from that moment legal and equitable title to the home survived to A.

**6.23**    Severance can take place only in respect of an equitable joint tenancy. A legal joint tenancy cannot be severed (LPA 1925, s 36(2)) (**6.12**).

**6.24**    There are four methods of severance. Three methods developed through case law and are known as the *Williams v Hensman* (1861) methods of severance: an act of a joint tenant operating on his or her share (**6.32–6.41**); mutual agreement (**6.42–6.44**); and severance by a course of dealing (**6.45–6.49**). The fourth method is statutory and enables severance through a written notice served on the other joint tenants (LPA 1925, s 36(2)) (**6.26–6.31**). In addition to these methods of severance, severance may arise as a result of the unlawful killing of one joint tenant by another (**6.50–6.51**).

**6.25**    Of the four methods of severance, two may be used *unilaterally* by one joint tenant; an act operating on a share and statutory severance through written notice. Where unilateral severance takes place, as long as there are two or more remaining joint tenants, the joint tenancy remains intact between them and exists alongside the severed tenancy in common. Severance by mutual agreement or through a course of dealing requires the participation of all joint tenants. As all of the joint tenants are involved, the effect of severance by mutual agreement is necessarily to turn all of the equitable joint tenants into tenants in common.

*Example*: A, B, C, and D are joint tenants at law and in equity. A severs through written notice. A, B, C, and D remain joint tenants at law, but in equity A is a tenant in common with a 25 per cent share, while B, C, and D are joint tenants of the remaining 75 per cent (**Figure 6.8**).

*Example*: A, B, C, and D are joint tenants at law and in equity. The parties sever the equitable joint tenancy by mutual agreement. They remain joint tenants at law, but in equity they are now tenants in common, each holding a 25 per cent undivided share (**Figure 6.9**).

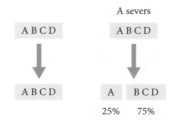

**Figure 6.8**  Unilateral severance

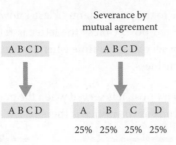

Figure 6.9  Mutual severance

## Statutory Severance

6.26  By statute, a joint tenant can sever by serving written notice on the other joint tenants (LPA 1925, s 36(2)). There is no particular form that the notice must take. However, the notice must express an immediate severance and denote that ownership of the land (or of the proceeds of sale of the land) is to be held in a manner inconsistent with a joint tenancy. A direction merely as to how the proceeds of sale of land is to be used is insufficient to constitute statutory severance (*Nielson-Jones v Fedden* (1975)). In *Re Draper's Conveyance* (1969), the issue of a summons and affidavit asking the court to order the sale of a former matrimonial home and equal distribution of the proceeds between a former husband and wife was held to constitute severance by written notice. In contrast, no severance was effected by a petition to the court in *Harris v Goddard* (1983) 'that such order may be made by way of transfer of property and/or settlement in respect of the former matrimonial home . . . and otherwise as may be just'. The petition did not evince an immediate desire to sever, but merely invited the court to exercise a discretion which, when exercised, may or may not result in severance.

6.27  For written notice to effect a severance it must be validly served on all other joint tenants. In the light of the ways in which the LPA 1925 enables notice to be served (6.29), there is no requirement that the notice has actually been received by the joint tenants (*Kinch v Bullard* (1999)). Severance takes effect at the moment of service, regardless of if or when the joint tenants received the notice.

6.28  In the usual course of events, written notice is sent and received and the matter is beyond doubt. Where the notice is connected to judicial proceedings it will be served in the context of those proceedings assuming the joint tenants are all party to the proceedings (cf *Quigley v Masterson* (2011) as a case in which the joint tenant was not a party). Questions over the timing of service may typically arise where a death occurs in close proximity to a written notice being sent, or where a joint tenant, having issued notice, seeks to intercept it following a change of mind—possibly to take advantage of another joint tenant's sudden death.

6.29  General guidelines on service of notice contained in section 196 of the LPA 1925 apply to section 36(2) (*Re 88 Berkeley Road* (1971)). Applying section 196, there are two ways in which notice can be served:

- by being left at the joint tenant(s)' last-known place of abode or business in the UK;

- by posting the notice to the joint tenant(s)' last-known place of abode or business in the UK by registered post. Unless the letter is retuned undelivered, notice is deemed to have been served at the time when the letter would have arrived in the ordinary course of business.

6.30    If notice is sent by the ordinary post, it is served when the postman or postwoman pushes the letter through the letterbox as the notice is thereby 'left' in the premises.

---

**Kinch v Bullard (1999):** Mr and Mrs Johnson were beneficial joint tenants of their matrimonial home. The parties were divorcing and Mrs Johnson, who was terminally ill and expected to pre-decease her husband, sent a notice of severance to Mr Johnson by ordinary first-class post. The letter was duly delivered but, before seeing it, Mr Johnson suffered a serious heart attack. Realizing that she was now likely to outlive her husband, Mrs Johnson destroyed the letter. Mr Johnson died a couple of weeks later, followed, in a matter of months, by Mrs Johnson. An action was brought by the parties' respective executors to determine whether the notice—delivered, but then destroyed—had operated to sever the joint tenancy. If it had, then each party had a 50 per cent share to pass under the terms of their respective wills; if not, survivorship would have operated on Mr Johnson's death, leaving the entire property to pass under Mrs Johnson's will. It was held that the notice was served when delivered in the post and could not be 'un-served'. Therefore the joint tenancy had been severed. Neuberger J suggested—albeit tentatively—that it would be possible to withdraw notice after a letter had been sent but before it was delivered if the withdrawal is communicated prior to the letter being delivered.

---

6.31    Severance by registered post is illustrated by *Re 88 Berkeley Road* (1971). Written notice was sent by registered post and signed for on delivery by the joint tenant who had sent the letter without, it seems, the letter ever being passed on to the other joint tenant to whom it was addressed. Severance was still held to have taken place; receipt was not required.

## Severance by an Act of a Joint Tenant Operating on His or Her Share

6.32    An act of a joint tenant operating on his or her share causes severance by destroying one or more of the unities of title, time, and interest which are a precondition for the subsistence of a joint tenancy (6.7). There is a logical difficulty in talking of an act operating on a share; we have emphasized in this chapter that joint tenants—in contradistinction to tenants in common—do not have shares (6.6). In what way, can it then be said that a joint tenant has acted on his or her share in order to effect severance? The analytical difficulty with this method of severance is effectively sidestepped by treating the act itself as causing severance and so freeing up the share to be the subject of the act in question (Crown (2001)).

6.33    There is no set form that the 'act' must take. The clearest example of an act operating on a share is a disposition (referred to in *Williams v Hensman* (1861)). Other acts that have been accepted as sufficient include entering a contract for sale (*Brown v Raindle* (1796)) or acquiring a greater share in the land than the other joint tenants (Megarry and Wade (2008)). Conversely, it is established that a mere unilateral declaration of intent is not an 'act' and cannot constitute severance (*Nielson-Jones v Fedden* (1975), *Burgess v Rawnsley* (1975)). In the absence of an 'act', unilateral severance must be effected through the statutory method of written notice (6.26–6.31). These examples suggest that an act requires a share to be divested, or for there to be a legal obligation to divest a share.

6.34    A disposition may be voluntary—for example, the transfer of a share (by sale or gift) to another one of the joint tenants or to a third party—or involuntary. The most important example of an involuntary disposition is bankruptcy. The effect of a joint tenant being declared bankrupt is that his or her share vests in the trustee in bankruptcy.

6.35    Where the act operating on a share takes the form of a sale or other disposition of one joint tenant's share to another joint tenant, the joint tenant who receives the share is left in a particular position. The recipient of the share is a tenant in common as regards the newly acquired share, but remains a joint tenant in relation to his or her original interest. Hence, just as the joint tenancy and tenancy in common can subsist side by side (6.21), the same beneficiary may be a joint tenant in relation to his or her initial interest and a tenant in common as regards a subsequently acquired interest.

*Example*: A, B, C, and D are joint tenants at law and in equity. A sells his or her share to B. A, B, C, and D remain joint tenants at law and hold on trust for B as tenant in common of the severed 25 per cent share and for B, C, and D as joint tenants of the remaining 75 per cent (Figure 6.10).

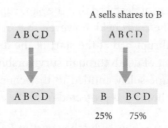

A sells shares to B

ABCD → ABCD

ABCD → B  BCD
         25%   75%

Figure 6.10    Severance by sale to another joint tenant

6.36    The clearest instance of a voluntary act operating on a share is an outright transfer of a share by a joint tenant by sale or gift, whether to another joint tenant or a third party. A joint tenant may also do an act that constitutes a partial transfer of his or her interest, whilst retaining an interest him or herself. A partial transfer arises where a joint tenant declares a trust of his or her share. The effect of such a declaration of trust is that the joint tenant's severed share is held on a sub-trust for the beneficiary. The joint tenant retains his or her beneficial interest, which is now subject to the trust. A partial transfer also arises on the grant of a mortgage or charge by a joint tenant. Such mortgages may be unlikely to be granted expressly, because the security of a beneficial share may not be commercially attractive, but they arise, not infrequently, as the result of a failed attempt by a single joint tenant to mortgage the legal title through, for example, forgery or undue influence committed against the other co-owners (Nield (2001)). For example, in *First National Securities v Hegerty* (1965) a husband forged his wife's signature on a legal charge to use the property as security for a loan. Bingham J considered this to constitute a disposition of the husband's beneficial share, which severed the beneficial joint tenancy and created a valid equitable charge over the husband's share. However, the matter was not argued in the case as it was unclear whether the parties were in fact equitable joint tenants or tenants in common.

6.37    An involuntary act operating on a share is most likely to arise through the interception of a debt affecting one of the joint tenants. Bankruptcy has provided the focus of attention, although the grant of a charging order also operates to sever a joint tenancy as the debt becomes secured against the debtor's share (*C Putnam & Sons v Taylor* (2009)). While bankruptcy undoubtedly causes severance, debate continues as to the time at which severance occurs. This can be significant where the bankrupt (or another joint tenant) dies during the course of the bankruptcy. If death predates the time of severance, then survivorship operates, taking the beneficial interest beyond the reach of the creditors.

6.38    Courts have adopted conflicting approaches to identifying the date on which severance occurs in the event of bankruptcy. In *Re Palmer* (1994), a decision on the current legislation (Insolvency Act 1986), it was held that severance occurs at the time of the declaration of bankruptcy. This date was chosen because, from the time of the declaration, the bankrupt's estate is held in trust by the Official Receiver—vesting in the trustee in bankruptcy immediately upon appointment. Mr Palmer was declared bankrupt after his death. Where that occurs, through the doctrine of 'relation back' the declaration of bankruptcy dates from the day of death, so that the bankrupt's estate on that day vests in the trustee in bankruptcy. The court held, however, that 'relation back' did not include a joint tenancy that the bankrupt had at the start of the day of their death, but which ceased to exist at the moment of death through survivorship (6.22). Through survivorship, Mr Palmer's wife became solely entitled to that couple's home on her husband's death, which meant that the home was protected from the effect of the bankruptcy.

6.39    A different date of severance was chosen by the court in *Re Dennis* (1996)—a later case than *Re Palmer*, but decided under previous legislation (Bankruptcy Act 1914). In that case, the bankrupt and his wife were joint tenants of their home. Between the date of the act of bankruptcy (by failing to comply with a bankruptcy notice) and the declaration of bankruptcy, the wife died. The court held that severance occurred at the date of the act of bankruptcy. This meant that, on her death, the wife was a tenant in common of a 50 per cent share, which passed to the couple's children. If the date of the declaration of bankruptcy had been chosen (the date adopted in *Re Palmer*), survivorship would have operated on the wife's death, leaving the bankrupt as sole owner and the entire house therefore available to his creditors.

6.40    Notably, in *Re Palmer* and *Re Dennis* the courts' interpretation of the timing of severance produces results that are sympathetic to the bankrupt's family. The courts' choice as to the date of severance conflicts and, while factually distinct, there is no logical reason for treating the date of severance as different, according to whether bankruptcy occurs during the bankrupt's lifetime, or after his or her death. The analysis in *Re Palmer* should now be followed in all cases, because it applies the current legislation. If applied to the facts of *Re Dennis*, it would appear to reverse the decision in that case.

6.41    Subsequent to the decision in *Re Palmer*, a new provision (s 421A) has been inserted into the Insolvency Act 1986 (IA 1986). The effect of section 421A is that where a joint tenant is declared bankrupt after his or her death (so that survivorship operates in favour of the remaining joint tenants), the survivors may be required by the court, on an application by the trustee in bankruptcy, to compensate the bankrupt's estate by payment of a sum not exceeding the value lost through survivorship. Hence, while the operation of severance remains governed by *Re Palmer*, the financial consequences of the decision may be reversed by an application under section 421A.

## Severance Through Mutual Agreement

6.42    The second category of severance identified in *Williams v Hensman* (1861) (6.24) is severance through mutual agreement. Unlike the previous methods of severance considered—statutory severance (6.26-6.31) and an act operating on a share (6.32-6.41)—mutual severance requires the participation of all of the joint tenants. Its effect, when applied, is to turn all the joint tenants into equitable tenants in common (6.25).

6.43    The rationale for severance through mutual agreement lies in the common intention of the parties. For example, in *Davis v Smith* (2011) the Court of Appeal held severance to have taken place where correspondence between the joint tenants evidenced a common intention that a house should be sold and the proceeds divided equally. This stands in contrast to the rationale for severance by an act operating on a share. Such an act effects severance by the destruction of one or more of the unities of title, time, and interest (6.7). In mutual agreement, destruction of a unity is the *result* of the severance, not the *cause* of it.

6.44    The scope of severance through mutual agreement is difficult to pinpoint in the abstract: it is sandwiched between the stricter requirement of an 'act' (6.33) which permits unilateral severance (6.25) and the more liberal third category of a course of dealings (6.45-6.49), which also requires the participation of all joint tenants. Hence, mutual agreement applies where there is no valid contract to constitute an act, but (unlike severance by a course of dealings) it appears to require an informal agreement. However, that 'agreement' may be inferred by the parties' conduct.

*Burgess v Rawnsley* (1975): Mr Honick and Mrs Rawnsley were joint tenants of a house occupied by Mr Honick alone. The property had been purchased in the expectation that the parties would both live there, but while Mr Honick anticipated marriage, Mrs Rawnsley intended to live alone in the upstairs flat. The parties' mismatched expectations came to light after the purchase. Mrs Rawnsley did not move in, but reached an oral agreement to sell her share to Mr Honick for £750. She then changed her mind and sought a higher price. Matters stood this way at Mr Honick's death, whereupon the house was sold and Mrs Burgess, his administratrix, sought to establish that severance had occurred, leaving his estate entitled to 50 per cent of the proceeds of sale. The Court of Appeal unanimously held that severance had occurred through mutual agreement. The oral agreement to sell for £750 was sufficient to effect severance even though there was no enforceable contract and despite the fact that Mrs Rawnsley had repudiated the agreement.

## Severance by Course of Dealings

6.45    In common with severance by mutual agreement, severance through a course of dealings requires the participation of all of the joint tenants and is founded on the common intention of the parties (6.43).

6.46    Unlike severance through mutual agreement, a course of dealings does not require there to be an agreement—even inferred—between the parties. Instead, it 'includes cases where what is to be inferred is that the parties have mutually treated their interests as a tenancy in common in ignorance that they were really joint tenants' (*Hunter v Babbage* (1995)). This form of severance is therefore focused on the conduct of the parties and is sometimes described as severance by mutual conduct. Hence, for example, the execution of mutual wills by joint tenants may constitute severance through mutual conduct as joint tenants have no share to dispose of through a will (6.19).

6.47    The key issue that arises in understanding the scope of severance by a course of dealings is determining when negotiations that fall short of an agreement are able to effect severance. In *Burgess v Rawnsley* (1975), where severance was held to have taken place through mutual agreement (6.44), the Court of Appeal were divided as to the scope of a course of dealings as a method of severance and as to its application to the facts of the case. Pennycuick LJ commented that '[o]ne could not ascribe to joint tenants an intention to sever merely because one offers to buy out the other for £X and the other makes a counter-offer of £Y'. In contrast, Lord Denning MR suggested that '[e]ven if there was not any firm agreement but only a course of dealing, it clearly evinced an intention by both parties that the property should henceforth be held in common and not jointly'.

6.48    In *Burgess v Rawnsley* Lord Denning MR also suggested that severance through a course of dealings should have been applied on the facts of *Nielson-Jones v Fedden* (1975). There, a memorandum agreed between the parties directed the husband to 'use his entire discretion and free will' to decide whether to sell the parties' former matrimonial home to purchase a home for himself. The husband died having entered a contract for sale and a deposit having been paid. The memorandum was held not to constitute statutory severance because it concerned only use of the proceeds of sale, not their ownership (6.26). Walton J rejected an alternative argument that there had been severance by mutual conduct through the parties' discussions as regards their financial arrangements and the distribution of the deposit. Lord Denning MR considered that '[t]he husband and wife entered on a course of dealing sufficient to sever the joint tenancy. They entered into negotiations that the property should be sold. Each received £200 out of the deposit paid by the purchaser. That was sufficient.'

**6.49**  To the extent that reliance is placed on negotiations to establish a course of dealings, these should be accepted only where the agreement, if reached, would have been sufficient to sever within the category of mutual conduct. If the agreement would have been insufficient to effect severance, it necessarily follows that negotiations for the agreement cannot do so (*Hunter v Babbage* (1995)). Whether negotiations will be sufficient to constitute a course of dealings is heavily dependent on the facts. An agreement in principle by a divorcing couple who were joint tenants of two properties to transfer one of the properties to each of them was held not to constitute a course of dealings, where it was clear that the wife had not committed to becoming a tenant in common prior to the division of the parties' property in their divorce proceedings (*Gore and Snell v Carpenter* (1990)). In the same case the court accepted, as a matter of principle, that even failed negotiations can constitute a course of dealings on appropriate facts.

## Severance Through Unlawful Killing

**6.50**  Public policy prevents a person responsible for the unlawful death of another from benefiting from his or her death. Such benefit could arise through the operation of survivorship where one joint tenant is responsible for the death of another. The public policy rule is achieved through forfeiture under the Forfeiture Act 1982, which also provides for the possibility of relief against forfeiture.

**6.51**  In *Re K* (1985), Vinelott J accepted the view of counsel that 'the forfeiture rule unless modified under the Act of 1982 applies in effect to sever the joint tenancy in the proceeds of sale and in the rents and profits until sale'. This implies that, where relief is awarded, the correct analysis is that severance does not occur, leaving survivorship to operate. Hence, it is the availability of relief that determines whether severance occurs (Bridge (1998)). In *Re K*, relief was awarded where a wife, who was the victim of domestic abuse, had been convicted for manslaughter after she had unintentionally shot and killed her husband (she had intended to threaten him). The culpability of the defendant is the principal factor in determining relief (contrast the outcome in *Dunbar v Plant* (1998) with that in *Chadwick v Collinson* (2014)).

## Severance and the Common Intention Constructive Trust

**6.52**  The effect of *Stack v Dowden* (2007) and *Jones v Kernott* (2011) is to impose a presumption of joint tenancy in respect of particular properties that are purchased as homes. The presumption can be rebutted through a common intention constructive trust (**6.18**). The common intention constructive trust is 'ambulatory' meaning that the parties' intentions (and therefore their beneficial shares) can change over time. In *Stack v Dowden* and *Jones v Kernott* the parties' shares were ultimately quantified as being unequal: respectively

65/35 per cent and 90/10 per cent. There are unresolved doctrinal issues as to how the outcome in these cases can be rationalized with the rules of severance. If parties begin (as they did in those cases) as equitable joint tenants, but end with unequal shares, then severance must have taken place. But on what basis? Further, severance credits the parties with equal shares (6.21). Hence, it appears that severance alone cannot explain the outcome in the cases. If the parties severed in equal shares and a transfer of a beneficial interest was then made to leave the parties with the correct proportions, that transfer appears to constitute a disposition of an equitable interest—which is required to be made in writing (LPA 1925, s 53(1)(c)).

6.53   Neither the method of severance applied nor the application of section 53(1)(c) of the LPA 1925 are addressed by the House of Lords in *Stack v Dowden* or the Supreme Court in *Jones v Kernott*. The ambulatory nature of the trust has been replied upon to explain both the severance and alteration of the parties' beneficial shares (Mee (2012)). But it remains unclear which head of severance—if any—would thereby apply. A change in the parties' common intention could constitute severance through mutual agreement (6.42-6.44). Alternatively, there could be an act operating on a share (6.32-4.41), see Pawlowski and Brown (2013a)). Mee (2012) suggests that section 53(1)(c) does not apply 'because each new division of the beneficial ownership occurs under a new, or (to put it a different way) newly refreshed, constructive trust'. The creation and operation of constructive trusts is exempt from the formality requirement by section 53(2). Pawlowski and Brown (2013a) suggest that section 53(2) applies to exempt the (notional) transfer if that transfer takes place under the existing constructive trust. If each new common intention gives rise to a new trust, then the authors suggest that there is no reason in principle why the parties should not be able to agree to sever in unequal shares. On that basis, no question of the application of section 53(1)(c) arises.

### A Critique of the Severance Rules and of the Beneficial Joint Tenancy

6.54   The Law Commission (1985) considered two radical reforms of severance: first, limiting severance to the statutory method of written notice; secondly, enabling severance by will. Reform of severance was not carried over into the Commission's subsequent final report on Trusts of Land, on the basis that the issue is also relevant to personal property. The Law Commission instead anticipated returning to the topic of severance in future work on severance, though this has not materialized.

6.55   The reforms considered by the Law Commission represent polarized responses to dissatisfaction with the operation of the current rules. The first possibility, of confining severance to the statutory method of notice, would require the abolition of the *Williams v Hensman* (1861) methods and, inevitably, increase the incidence of survivorship. The *Williams v Hensman* method of severance by an act operating on a share is currently relied upon by creditors to make a joint tenant's share available to discharge debts on bankruptcy. Legislation and case law reflects a general public policy concern to ensure that debts are paid. In view of this policy, it appears unlikely that a change to the rules of severance would be countenanced without any potential difficulties that would arise in relation to bankruptcy being resolved. In that respect, the abolition of severance by an act operating on a share appears problematic. While the other *Williams v Hensman* methods have generated few cases, it is possible that they are relied upon by practitioners, making the impact of abolition difficult to predict (Tee (1995)).

**6.56**   The second possibility, of extending severance to permit severance by will, appears to strike at the heart of a joint tenancy as a gamble on survivorship. As Tee (1995) notes, it would enable a 'rogue' joint tenant to 'have his cake and eat it' by placing words of severance in a will and enjoying the possibility of the right of survivorship without any risk to his or her estate in the event of pre-deceasing the other joint tenant(s). Additionally, questions of construction are likely to arise as to whether the wording of a will constitutes severance.

**6.57**   Any reform of the severance rules necessarily impacts on the operation of survivorship: a liberalization of severance makes survivorship less likely to occur, while restrictions on severance increase the likelihood of the joint tenancy remaining intact on the death of the parties. Survivorship is the key difference between the joint tenancy and tenancy in common (**6.19**). Therefore, the question underlying reform of severance is the desirability of the beneficial tenancy in common. Difficulties and uncertainties in the application of severance rules would be removed at a stroke by confining equitable ownership to the tenancy in common. But because this would come at the expense of survivorship, is it a price worth paying?

**6.58**   The operation of survivorship is most obviously consistent with the likely intentions of parties embarking on what they anticipate will be a lifelong relationship. As Smith (2005) notes, the 'great majority' of severance cases appear to arise as a consequence of relationship breakdown, following which survivorship ceases to match the parties' intentions. The joint tenancy remains apt to give effect to the likely intentions of parties where a relationship ends on death, while the imposition of a tenancy in common places an onus on the parties, in all cases, to ensure that their intentions are reflected in an up-to-date will. But intestacy is common: it is estimated that between half and two-thirds of adults in England and Wales have not made a will, many of whom will die before having done so (Law Commission (2011)). In the light of the incidence of intestacy, it must be doubted whether the imposition of a joint tenancy in all cases would better ensure that the parties' intentions are fulfilled than does the current law.

## Termination of Co-ownership

**6.59**   Co-ownership comes to an end once there is a sole legal and equitable owner. For example, in a joint tenancy where the operation of survivorship leaves a single owner entitled in law and in equity (**6.19-6.20**). Where the same person is entitled in law and equity, this also marks the end of the trust. Where the legal and equitable owners are different (eg if T is the sole legal owner and B the sole beneficial owner), a bare trust remains. A sole beneficiary who is of full age and capacity may insist that legal co-owners transfer legal title to him or her through the rule in *Saunders v Vautier* (1841).

6.60    Co-ownership is not terminated, however, merely by the sale of co-owned land to a single purchaser. Even assuming the purchaser has a defence against the enforcement of the beneficial interests against him or her (Chapter 11) so that the land is no longer co-owned, the co-owner's interests in the land (whether as joint tenants or tenants in common) shift from the land into the proceeds of sale.

6.61    Co-ownership may also be brought to an end through partition. Partition is a process through which the trustees physically divide the land and transfer separate plots into the sole ownership of the beneficiaries. The beneficiaries thus cease to be co-owners, with unity of possession over the land, and become sole owners of their separate parcels of land. Trustees have power to partition land where it is held on trust for beneficiaries as tenants in common who are absolutely entitled (TOLATA, s 7). That is, the power exists where T1 and T2 hold land on trust for B1 and B2 as tenants in common, but not where T1 and T2 hold land on trust for B1 and B2 as joint tenants, or for B1 for life, and thereafter to B2. Confining the power to a tenancy in common ensures that partition does not interfere with the operation of survivorship (6.19–6.20). Where the power exists, it is exercisable only where all of the beneficiaries consent (TOLATA, s 7(3)). Partition may also be ordered by the court (TOLATA, s 14). See *Atkinson v Atkinson* (2010), *Ellison v Cleghorn* (2013).

## Co-ownership and Trusts

6.62    Whenever land is co-owned, whether co-ownership arises in relation to the legal title, the beneficial interests, or both, the land is held on trust. All co-ownership trusts now constitute 'trusts of land' and are governed by TOLATA. The scope of the Act extends to apply to co-ownership trusts that were in existence on 1 January 1997 when the Act came into force (TOLATA, s 1). The Act also applies equally whether a trust is expressly created or implied. Hence, for example, common intention constructive trusts (the creation of which is discussed in Chapter 5) are trusts of land.

6.63    While our discussion of TOLATA is focused on its application to co-ownership trusts, it should be noted that the Act applies beyond this. In addition to co-ownership trusts, the following are also 'trusts of land' governed by the Act (TOLATA, s 1):

- successive interest trusts (6.4) with the exception of those in existence and governed by the Settled Land Act 1925 on 1 January 1997;
- bare trusts.

6.64    TOLATA originated in proposals by the Law Commission (1989). Of its time, and in terms of its effect on the conceptual scheme of land law, the Act was described by

Harpum (1998) as 'the most significant measure of property law reform since the legislation of 1925'.

6.65    Prior to the 1996 Act, co-ownership trusts were almost invariably classified as 'trusts for sale'—a form of trust regulated by the LPA 1925. The trust for sale reflected the prevailing expectation at the time of the 1925 legislation that co-ownership trusts would most likely arise in connection with land held as an investment. Hence, for example, the trustees had a duty to sell the land from the moment the trust was created, and a power to postpone sale. The investment ethos of the 1925 legislation reflected prevailing patterns of land ownership.

6.66    In the second half of the 20th century, Britain became 'A Nation of Home Owners' (Saunders (1980)) in which the majority of households (at its peak, over 70 per cent) were owner-occupied. Moreover, home ownership has increasingly taken the form of co-ownership, as social changes have made it common for both partners in a relationship to be economically active. The spread of co-ownership has been assisted by the development of equitable doctrines, particularly the common intention constructive trust, through which contributions to the acquisition of the home by non-legal title-owning spouses and cohabitees have been recognized through conferring beneficial ownership (Chapter 5). Land was therefore being held for 'use'—as a home—rather than merely as an investment and the trust for sale was not a suitable legal basis for governing such trusts. In particular, it was nonsense to say that spouses or cohabitees who co-owned their home were under a duty to sell the home from the moment of its purchase.

6.67    The introduction of the 'trust of land' as a replacement for the trust for sale represents a shift to a form of regulation that is more suited to the use of land as a home, reflecting modern trends of home ownership. This shift is marked, in particular, by:

- the removal of the duty to sell, which had been the defining characteristic of the trust for sale (6.65);

- the abolition of a doctrine, known as the doctrine of conversion, through which beneficial interests under a trust of sale were artificiality interpreted as being interests in the proceeds of sale (not in the land) from the inception of the trust (TOLATA, s 3); and

- the creation of a statutory right to occupy land held on trust by certain beneficiaries (6.77–6.83).

These changes take place within a comprehensive statutory scheme that identifies the powers of trustees and the rights of the beneficiaries and makes provision for oversight of the exercise of the trustees' powers by an application to the court.

## A Non-Exclusive Jurisdiction

6.68    Although TOLATA is a comprehensive scheme of regulation, it is not an exclusive regime. Trustees remain subject to general principles of trust law—a matter acknowledged within the terms of the Act (**6.70**). Similarly, beneficiaries may derive rights otherwise than through TOLATA. For example, beneficiaries who have a right to occupy under TOLATA (**6.77-6.83**) may also have a right to occupy through a 'home right' under the Family Law Act 1996 (FLA 1996). Such rights may arise in favour of a spouse or civil partner who is a beneficial co-owner but does not own legal title (FLA 1996, s 33). Similarly, applications to court involving trusts of land may arise under other legislation. Where a beneficiary has a 'home right' under the FLA 1996, questions relating to occupation may be brought to court under that Act (FLA 1996, s 33) rather than under TOLATA.

**6.69**    Questions relating to the sale of land held on trust may arise under a myriad of legislation, depending on the circumstances in which sale is sought. For example, where a beneficiary is bankrupt, an application for sale is considered under the IA 1986 (TOLATA, s 15(4), see **6.111-6.120**); where legal title to co-owned land is mortgaged, sale by the mortgagee in the exercise of their power of sale is governed outside TOLATA (**Chapter 8**); where co-owners are divorcing, an application for sale may be made under the Married Women's Property Act 1882.

## Trustees' Powers

**6.70**    Trustees are given 'all the powers of an absolute owner' (TOLATA, s 6). However, it is important to bear in mind that these powers are conferred on the trustees in their capacity as trustees. Trustees have the powers of an absolute owner, but they are *not* absolute owners and their powers must be exercised with reference to their obligations as trustees. Trustees are directed to exercise their powers with regard to the rights of the beneficiaries (TOLATA, s 6(5)) and in a manner consistent with any other enactment or rule of law or equity (TOLATA, s 6(6)). In effect, what section 6 means is that trustees must exercise the powers with which they are conferred in a manner that does not constitute a breach of trust.

**6.71**    Where a trust is expressly created, the settlor may exclude or restrict the trustees' powers, or make their exercise subject to obtaining consent (eg of the beneficiaries) (TOLATA, s 8).

**6.72**    One effect of section 6 is to remove the duty to sell that characterized the trust for sale. As the Law Commission (1989) noted, the powers of an absolute owner include a power to sell or to retain the land. While these are equally weighted, TOLATA is, in fact, biased against sale (Hopkins (1996)). The settlor of an express trust could conceivably exclude the power of sale under section 8 and therefore make the land inalienable. In contrast, a settlor is unable to compel trustees to sell. While a duty to sell can be expressly imposed, where this is done the trustees are given a power to postpone the sale and indefinite protection against liability for so doing (TOLATA, s 4).

**6.73**    Trustees who act contrary to limitations on their powers—both general limitations arising under section 6 and any expressly imposed under section 8—may be held personally liable to the beneficiaries for breach of trust. However, purchasers of land enjoy a degree of protection. The protection provided to purchasers of unregistered land is detailed in section 16 of TOLATA. In registered land, under the general operation of the Land Registration Act 2002, a purchaser would be affected only by a limitation on the trustees' powers entered as a restriction on the register (see **Chapter 11**).

**6.74**  Where the beneficiaries are all absolutely entitled to the land and of full age and capacity, the trustees have power to convey the land to them (TOLATA, s 16(2)). The beneficiaries are required to do whatever is necessary to secure that the title vests in them (TOLATA, s 16(2)(a))—for example, in registered land apply for registration. In such a case, the beneficiaries would be entitled to bring an end to the trust by requiring a transfer of title to them through the rule in *Saunders v Vautier* (1841). The power conferred on trustees thus provides them with an analogous ability to act and, by doing so, to relieve themselves of any future duties towards the beneficiaries. Where the beneficiaries are co-owners, the effect of the exercise of the trustees' power (or of the beneficiaries acting under *Saunders v Vautier* (1841)) is the creation of a new trust in which the beneficiaries hold title on trust for themselves, as co-ownership necessarily takes effect under a trust (**6.62**).

## Beneficiaries' Rights

**6.75**  TOLATA 1996 confers two key rights on beneficiaries:

- a right to be consulted by the trustees as to the exercise of their powers (s 11);

- a right to occupy (s 12).

**6.76**  Trustees are directed 'so far as practicable' to consult with beneficiaries of full age who are beneficially entitled to an interest in land and to give effect to the wishes of the majority (in terms of the parties' beneficial shares) 'so far as consistent with the general interest of the trust' (TOLATA, s 11(1)). The right to be consulted is particularly significant to a beneficiary who is not also a legal owner and who does not therefore play a direct role in the management of the trust: for example, where A holds the parties' home on trust for A and B, section 11(1)(a) requires A to consult B in the exercise of his or her powers as trustee. The right to be consulted may be excluded in express trusts (TOLATA, s 22(2)(b)). It does not apply to trusts arising under a will made before the commencement of the Act (TOLATA, s 11(2)(b)) or to express trusts created before commencement (TOLATA, s 11(3)). These limitations are designed to ensure that the intentions of settlors who relied on the previous law (under which no duty to consult arose unless expressly imposed) are respected.

**6.77**  A beneficiary who is entitled to an interest in possession has a right to occupy where one of two conditions are satisfied: either the purposes of the trust include making the land available for occupation by the beneficiary; or the land is held by the trustees to be available for occupation by the beneficiary (TOLATA, s 12(1)). No right to occupy arises, however, where the land is 'unsuitable' for occupation by the beneficiary (TOLATA, s 12(2)). This qualification enables the subjective characteristics of the beneficiaries to be taken into account: for example, no right to occupy will arise if the land is a farm and the beneficiary is not a farmer (Smith (1989), Pascoe (2006)).

6.78    The purpose of the trust may be derived from the declaration of an express trust, or be ascertained by the circumstances. The alternative criterion of availability enables the right to be claimed where the land is available for occupation, even if this is not within the purposes of the trust. For the trustees to make land available for occupation contrary to the express wishes of the settlor would, however, constitute a breach of trust and therefore would be outside the trustees' powers within section 6(6) (Hopkins (1996), Pascoe (2006)).

6.79    The trustees may impose 'reasonable conditions' on beneficiaries in occupation by virtue of their entitlement under section 12 (TOLATA, s 13(3) and (5)). The conditions may include paying outgoings or expenses in respect of the land.

6.80    Where two or more beneficiaries are entitled to occupy, the trustees may exclude or restrict one or more of those entitled, but at least one qualifying beneficiary must be allowed to occupy (TOLATA, s 13(1)). Where a beneficiary's occupation has been excluded or restricted by the trustees, the beneficiary or beneficiaries in occupation may be required by the trustees to pay compensation to those excluded from occupation (TOLATA, s 13(6)). Gardner (2014) suggests that a general jurisdiction conferred on trustees to impose 'reasonable conditions' on occupation (TOLATA, s 13(3)) may also be used to require payments to be made to non-occupying beneficiaries. If so, trustees will be able to require payments to be made to non-occupying beneficiaries even where they have not been excluded by the trustees.

6.81    Where section 13 applies, it is an exclusive regime for enabling payments to be made to non-occupying beneficiaries (*Stack v Dowden* (2007), *Murphy v Gooch* (2007)). In cases outside the scope of the provision, occupying beneficiaries may be required to make payments to non-occupying beneficiaries through equitable accounting (*French v Barcham* (2009)). Hence, for example, equitable accounting is available where the non-occupying beneficiary has no right to occupy within section 12. It may also apply where a non-occupying beneficiary has a right to occupy, but has not been excluded from occupation, but only if Gardner's interpretation of section 13 (6.80) is rejected.

6.82    Whether payments are ordered under section 13 or through equitable accounting is practically significant as the quantification of awards may differ. Equitable accounting is generally confined to the rental value of the property whereas, under TOLATA, trustees are directed to have regard to a number of 'wider non-property concerns' (Bright (2009)). These non-property concerns include the intentions of the settlor(s), the purposes for which the land is held, and the circumstances and wishes of beneficiaries who have a right to occupy (TOLATA, s 13(4)).

6.83    The difference in quantum between equitable accounting and TOLATA is described by Bright (2009) as a shift from 'property to welfare'. However, she notes that this shift does not in fact appear to have impacted on the quantum of awards made by the court under the statutory scheme. Rental value remains attractive to the court as it is 'a relatively objective value on which evidence can easily be supplied'. An alternative and equally objective basis on which compensation may be quantified is the cost incurred by an excluded beneficiary in obtaining alternative accommodation (*Stack v Dowden* (2007)).

6.84   Where land held on trust lends itself to a physical division, the trustees may use their powers under section 13 of TOLATA to restrict each beneficiary to occupying part of the trust land. Hence, in *Rodway v Landy* (2001), following the termination of a business partnership between two GPs, the court ordered that business premises that the GPs held on trust for themselves in equal shares should be divided to provide each of them with a self-contained surgery. There was no partition here, which would have required a division of the title to the surgery so that each GP held legal title to their separate business premises (6.61).

## Applications to Court

6.85   An application can be made to the court by a trustee or a person with an interest in the trust property (TOLATA, s 14). A person with an interest in the property includes, in particular, the beneficiaries and their secured creditors. A wide range of matters may be referred to the court: for example, the exercise of the trustees' powers in respect of beneficiaries' rights to occupy (6.77–6.83; *Rodway v Landy* (2001)) or a decision to bring an end to the trust through partition (6.61). However, most significantly, an application to the court will be made where there is a dispute as to whether the land should be sold (6.97–6.110).

6.86   On an application under section 14, the court has discretion to make 'any such order…as the court thinks fit' relating to the exercise by the trustees of their functions or declaring the nature or extent of a person's interest in the property. In exercising its powers, the court has held that it is not constrained by rules of equity that limit how the trustees can exercise their powers themselves. Hence, for example, the court can order the trustees to exercise their powers in a manner that could constitute a breach of trust if exercised by the trustees themselves in the same way (*Bagum v Hafiz* (2016)).

6.87   Where an application to court is made, the court is directed to take into account a number of factors (TOLATA, s 15):

- the intentions of the person(s) who created the trust (s 15(1)(a), see 6.89);
- the purposes for which the property subject to the trust is held (s 15(1)(b), see 6.90–6.91);
- the welfare of any minor who occupies or might reasonably be expected to occupy any land subject to the trust as his home (s 15(a)(c), see 6.92–6.94);
- the interests of secured creditors (s 15(1)(d), see 6.95);

- in applications relating to occupation, the circumstances and wishes of beneficiaries who are entitled to occupy, or would be so entitled apart from an exercise of the trustees' powers to exclude or restrict their occupation (s 15(2), see (6.96);

- the circumstances and wishes of all the beneficiaries (s 15(3), see (6.96)—but this factor is excluded where the application concerns the exercise of the trustees of their power to bring the trust to an end by transferring the property to the beneficiaries (6.74).

6.88 The list of factors referred to in section 15 is non-exhaustive—the court may take other matters into account. For example, in *White v White* (2003) the court ordered sale of a home following the breakdown of the parties' relationship. In doing so, the court had regard to the need of the beneficiary who made the application for sale to raise money to provide a home for herself. Further, TOLATA does not provide any weighting of factors. The responsibility lies with the judge to determine how much weight to afford to all relevant factors, including those not specifically referred to in TOLATA (*White v White*).

6.89 Intentions are fixed at the time the trust is created, to the exclusion of intentions subsequently generated (*White v White*). Where more than one person created the trust, it is the parties' common intention that is relevant (*White v White*).

6.90 In contrast to intentions, the purposes for which property is held on trust may change over time. However, a change of purpose requires the consent of all of the trustees. In *White v White*, following breakdown of the parties' relationship, it was held that the provision of a home for their children was not within the purposes of the trust of their home. There was no evidence that such a purpose had been put to, and therefore agreed by, the mother. However, the welfare of the children fell to be considered under section 15(1)(c).

6.91 Where property is acquired as a family or matrimonial home, courts have taken divergent views as to whether the purpose survives the departure of one of the parties. In *First National Bank plc v Achampong* (2003) and *Bank of Ireland Home Mortgages v Bell* (2011) the Court of Appeal considered that the purpose of providing a family home had ended following the departure (in both cases) of the husband, despite the continued occupation of the wife. In contrast, in *Edwards v Lloyds TSB* (2004) the purpose of the trust was considered to continue after the husband's departure in the light of the continued occupation of the wife and the couple's two children. In relation to the purposes of the trusts, the only apparent difference between the cases was that in neither *Achampong* nor *Bell* were there children present to whose interests the courts were prepared to give weight under section 15(1)(c). But as the welfare of children falls to be considered separately it is unsatisfactory for their presence or absence to be a determining factor in the courts' approach to defining the purpose of the trust. Such an approach leaves vulnerable those who are not in occupation with minor children: in the absence of an ongoing purpose, there is nothing for the beneficiary to have weighed against the interest of the creditors (Probert (2001)). In contrast, those in occupation with children have both an ongoing purpose (s 15(1)(b)) and the welfare of the children (s 15(1)(c)) to weigh against the creditors.

**6.92**   Prior to the enactment of TOLATA, significant doubt existed as to the extent to which the interests of children could be taken into account in a dispute as to sale of a home held on trust for sale. In a trust for sale, the primary purpose of the trust was necessarily sale, reflecting the fact that the trustees were under a duty to sell (**6.65**). This *duty* to sell took precedence over the trustees' *power* to postpone sale, resulting in a basic rule that the land would be sold unless all of the trustees agreed to exercise the power to postpone (*Re Buchanan-Wollaston's Conveyance* (1939)). This basic rule was mitigated by the recognition that trusts could have secondary or collateral purposes other than sale, and that in a dispute between beneficiaries, sale would not be ordered for as long as a collateral purpose could be achieved (*Jones v Challenger* (1960)). In reality, the 'secondary' purpose was in fact the primary purpose of the trust—in the shadow of the statutorily imposed primary duty to sell. In this context, the question for the court was whether the collateral purpose of a trust for sale could include the provision of a home for children. This is a question which gave rise to different answers. Conflicting Court of Appeal case law suggested that the purposes of a trust for sale could include the provision of a home for children (*Browne v Pritchard* (1975), *Williams v Williams* (1976), *Re Evers' Trust* (1980)) or that the interests of children were 'only incidentally to be taken into consideration...so far as they affect the matter between the two persons entitled to the beneficial interests' (*Burke v Burke* (1974)).

**6.93**   The express reference to the welfare of minors as a factor for the court to take into account (TOLATA, s 15(1)(c)) therefore resolves the debate prevailing at the time of the enactment of TOLATA. It is also consistent with the underlying ethos of the Act to provide a scheme of regulation that reflects the fact that much co-owned land is the parties' home. However, there is no weighting of factors (**6.88**). Other factors may therefore favour sale despite the occupation of children. In *White v White* (2003), the Court of Appeal confirmed an order of sale by the judge at first instance. The court noted that the judge had correctly taken into account both the interests of the children in remaining in their home and their mother's need to realize her only capital asset. In that case, the judge was also satisfied that, following the sale, cheaper suitable accommodation would be available.

**6.94**   *White v White* may indicate that in practice the weight afforded to occupying children is no different under TOLATA than it was under the previous scheme of the trust for sale. Although, as noted (**6.92**), there were conflicting decisions on the relevance of children, the balance of the authorities suggested that where a house was occupied by one of the beneficiaries with minor children, sale would not be ordered unless alternative (cheaper) accommodation could then be provided (*Williams v Williams* (1976); a rule of thumb echoed in the decision in *White v White*).

**6.95**   The interests of secured creditors (TOLATA, s 15(1)(d)) may be relevant in any application to the court, not merely those made by the creditors. Hence in *Anneveld v Robinson* (2005), in a dispute over sale between co-owners on the breakdown of their relationship, the practical impossibility of a large mortgage being paid by one of the parties, if allowed to remain in occupation, was a significant factor in the court's decision to order sale.

**6.96**  The court is specifically directed to take into account the circumstances and wishes of beneficiaries who are or would be entitled to occupy only where the application relates to the trustees' powers to exclude or restrict occupation, or to impose conditions on occupying beneficiaries (TOLATA, s 15(2), on the trustees' powers see 6.79–6.83). However, the beneficiaries' right to occupy may implicitly be relevant—and therefore be taken into account—in other applications. For example, an effective order of sale requires vacant possession, which necessarily impacts on the beneficiaries' right to occupy (*Miller Smith v Miller Smith* (2010)).

## Applications for Sale

**6.97**  Applications for sale of co-owned land may arise under TOLATA or other legislation, depending on the identity of the applicant and the basis upon which sale is sought (6.69). Applications for sale by a co-owner or by a secured creditor of a beneficiary are considered under TOLATA, while those by a trustee in bankruptcy are governed by the IA 1986 (TOLATA, s 15(4)).

## Applications by Co-owners

**6.98**  Cases arising from disputes as to sale between the co-owners are relatively infrequent. Typically such cases arise following the breakdown of the relationship between a couple who have co-owned their home. One party wishes to remain in the home (either alone or with children), while the other wants the house to be sold. Such cases raise a tension between the 'use' of land as a home and its 'investment' function. The question that arises is in what circumstances one party's desire to remain in the home takes precedence over the other's wish to realize the investment and 'move on' (Gardner (2014)).

**6.99**  In *White v White* (2003), *Anneveld v Robinson* (2005), and *Miller Smith v Miller Smith* (2010) sale was ordered in a dispute between co-owners. In each case, the reasons for ordering sale differ. In *White v White* a mother's need to realize her only capital asset weighed against the welfare of the children who remained in occupation with their father, where cheaper, suitable alternative accommodation would be available. In *Miller Smith v Miller Smith* the court based its decision on the likely outcome of pending proceedings for ancillary relief on the couple's divorce. In *Anneveld v Robinson* the inability of either of the parties alone to discharge the mortgage appeared key. The infrequency of the case law makes it difficult to draw general conclusions about the courts' approach (Hopkins (2009)). As these cases illustrate, the courts' approach to applications for sale by co-owners is 'highly flexible, circumstance dependent' (Dixon (2011)).

**6.100**  In *Finch v Hall* (2013) a dispute between co-owners arose as to the sale of a house held as an investment. The house had been inherited by four siblings following the death of their parents. After a period of renting the house, it was marketed for sale on an express agreement that sale required the unanimous agreement of the co-owners. In the event, an offer was made which three of the four co-owners wished to accept. On an application under TOLATA, the court refused to set aside the parties' express agreement and therefore declined to order sale.

**6.101** It has been held that the court does not have discretion under TOLATA to order one beneficiary to sell his or her share under the trust to another beneficiary. In *Bagum v Hafiz* (2016) a mother and two sons were beneficiaries of the home that they shared. Following a dispute, one of the sons moved out. The mother asked the court to make an order under section 14 of TOLATA for him to sell his share in the home to the other son, who remained in residence. The court held that it had no jurisdiction to do so. However, the court deferred an order for sale for six weeks, during which time the resident son was given the right to purchase the share at a price determined by the court.

## Applications by Creditors

**6.102** In order to bring an application to court under TOLATA, a claimant must have 'an interest in [the trust] property' (TOLATA, s 14, see **6.85**). With respect to creditors, this is met in two circumstances. First, where the debt is secured over land from the outset. Secondly, where a charging order is obtained over land in respect of an unsecured debt. The effect of a charging order is to turn an unsecured debt into a secured one. While the fact that the debt was initially unsecured has been acknowledged by the courts, in practice it has not had an impact on decisions (*Close Invoice Ltd v Pile* (2008), *Forrester Ketley & Co v Brent* (2009), *C Putnam & Sons v Taylor* (2009), *National Westminster Bank plc v Rushmer* (2010)). Hence, for practical purposes regarding applications for sale under TOLATA, no distinction need be drawn between creditors whose debt was secured from the outset and those whose debt became secured as a result of a charging order.

**6.103** It is possible for a beneficial tenant in common to grant an equitable charge (or mortgage) over his or her share, but such arrangements are not necessarily commercially attractive to lenders. Such interests are more likely to arise because a purported grant of a legal mortgage over the entire estate fails: for example, because one co-owner (A) has exerted undue influence over the other (B) (*First National Bank plc v Achampong* (2003)), or has forged B's signature to procure a mortgage (*Mortgage Corporation v Shaire* (2001)). The result of the undue influence or forgery is that the charge takes effect only against A's beneficial share. A, whose conduct is likely to exert opprobrium rather than sympathy— is unlikely to contest the sale. Disputes therefore typically arise between the creditor and B, who are both 'innocent' victims of A's conduct.

**6.104** Applications for sale by creditors bring to the fore the disparities in the meanings and functions attached to the land for the parties—particularly where the land in question is the beneficiary's home. For the creditor, the house represents purely an economic interest. The creditor has a legitimate expectation of being able to call on the security to ensure payment of the debt. This expectation is reinforced by public policy concerns to ensure the continued availability of capital, which would be diminished by a legal environment in which debts are not paid. For the beneficiary, the home represents both a tangible investment interest and non-financial or 'x-factor' (Fox (2006)) values. As Fox

(2006) explains, 'an occupier's desire to retain the property for use and occupation as a home is not merely sentimental but may also encompass multi-emotional, psychological, social and cultural matters. These meanings can operate to intensify the occupier's attachment to their home, and to exacerbate the experience of losing the home through actions at the hands of a creditor.' Despite the ethos of TOLATA of recognizing that many co-ownership trusts relate to the home (**6.66–6.67**) and the apparently broad-based nature of the discretion conferred on courts (TOLATA, s 14, **6.86**), incommensurable 'x-factor' values have struggled to be afforded weight when pitted against the quantifiable claims of creditors.

**6.105** Where a creditor succeeds in obtaining an application for sale, the proceeds of sale are divided proportionately between the beneficiaries in accordance with their respective beneficial shares. Only those proceeds representing the debtor's share are used to discharge the debt (but cf *Bank of Ireland v Bell* (2001)). If the co-owners were joint tenants, then the creation of the equitable charge by one co-owner, or the grant of a charging order, constitutes an act operating on the joint tenant's share to sever the joint tenancy (**6.32–6.41**).

**6.106** Prior to TOLATA, applications for sale by creditors and trustees in bankruptcy were heard under the same jurisdiction (LPA 1925, s 30—repealed by TOLATA). Under that jurisdiction, the courts' practice was to order sale unless there were 'exceptional circumstances' (**6.118–6.120**) (*Re Citro* (1991), *Lloyds Bank v Byrne* (1993)). The provision of separate jurisdictions for these applications, alongside the broad-based discretion in TOLATA that applies to applications for sale by creditors, led to an initial suggestion that TOLATA has 'changed the law' (*Mortgage Corporation v Shaire* (2001)).

***Mortgage Corporation v Shaire* (2001):** Mr Fox forged Mrs Shaire's signature to obtain a mortgage over the couple's co-owned home, with the effect that the mortgage took effect against his 25 per cent beneficial share. Following Mr Fox's death, the mortgagee made an application for sale of the home. If the case had arisen under the LPA 1925 it is likely that sale would have been ordered as the facts do not reveal 'exceptional circumstances'. Neuberger J, however, considered that TOLATA had 'changed the law'. Applying section 15 of the 1996 Act, Neuberger J noted that the intentions of Mrs Shaire and Mr Fox when the house was acquired (within s 15(1)(a)) were to provide a home for themselves and for Mrs Shaire's son from a previous relationship. The property was now held (within s 15(1)(b)) both as a home and an asset for Mrs Shaire, with 75 per cent of the beneficial interest, and as security for the loan as regards Mr Fox's 25 per cent share. The interest of the creditor fell to be considered under section 15(1)(d), while Mrs Fox's son was now an adult and therefore his position could not be taken into account. Under section 15(3), it was also relevant that Mrs Shaire had the majority of the beneficial interest. Weighing up these factors, Neuberger J noted, on the one hand, that for Mrs Shaire to leave her home of nearly 25 years 'would be a real and significant hardship, but not an enormous one'; on the other hand, for the mortgagee to be 'locked into a quarter of the equity of a property would be a significant disadvantage unless they had a proper return and a proper protection as far as insurance and repair is concerned'. He therefore

> proposed a solution under which the mortgage would be converted into a loan, on which Mrs Shaire would pay interest pending any future sale. Failing agreement on this (or Mrs Shaire's ability to pay), sale would be ordered.

**6.107**  The suggestion that TOLATA had changed the law is not without controversy. The Law Commission had envisaged that section 15 would consolidate and rationalize the approach adopted in the case law and therefore develop an approach along the lines of the doctrine of collateral purposes (**6.92**; Law Commission (1989)). Pascoe (2000) suggested that Neuberger J's approach was tantamount to 'wiping the slate clean and starting afresh with secured creditors the likely casualties'. In fact, the extent of any such change appears minimal—and *Shaire* (2001) may stand alone as a decision in which TOLATA has led to a different outcome, although the matter is not beyond doubt (Hopkins (2009)). It is clear from subsequent case law (**6.109-6.110**) that courts have continued to defer to the interests of creditors in a manner that reflects the prevailing approach under the previous law (illustrated by *Re Holliday* (1981)). In *Fred Perry Holdings v Genis* (2014) Master Price noted that while *Shaire* (2001) suggested that 'a different approach in favour of families might be appropriate following on the reform of the law by [TOLATA]' the cases showed that 'the upshot has been to give precedence to commercial interests rather than to the residential security of the family. Whilst it may be argued that precedence to such commercial interest fails to take adequate account of the public interest in maintaining a stable family unit, bearing in mind the attendant social costs of eviction and family breakup, this does not seem to be the current state of the authorities in relation to sections 14 and 15 of [TOLATA].'

**6.108**  It was predicted when TOLATA was enacted that section 15 would operate as an incentive for creditors to obtain an order of bankruptcy, enabling them to rely on the more favourable provision in section 335A of the IA 1986 (Hopkins (1996), **6.111-6.120**). The point is illustrated by *Alliance and Leicester plc v Slayford* (2001). There, a wife's beneficial interest was not binding on a mortgagee as the transaction had been entered through her husband's undue influence. The court held that it was not an abuse of process for the mortgagee to sue the husband on his personal covenant to pay the debt, with a view to bankrupting him and bringing an application for sale under the IA 1986, rather than proceeding under TOLATA. Hence, even if a more flexible approach had been developed under TOLATA, it would have been 'a paper tiger, easily undercut by recourse to the insolvency regime' (Radley-Gardner (2003)).

**6.109**  To the extent that *Shaire* (2001) indicates a more sympathetic approach to beneficiaries in actions by creditors, the decision may have been a false dawn. It is notable that despite Mrs Shaire's 75 per cent beneficial interest and long-term occupation of the house as her home, sale would only be prevented if the mortgagee's interest could satisfactorily be protected. Subsequently, in *Edwards v Lloyds TSB* (2004), the court agreed to postpone sale for five years while the children completed their education. Mr and Mrs Edwards co-owned their home. Mr Edwards' 50 per cent beneficial share was subject to a mortgage, which did not affect Mrs Edwards as her signature had been forged. Mr Edwards could not be traced and the bank applied for sale. Although other factors were mentioned in support of postponing sale, it was clear that the interests of the secured creditor would not be adversely affected. There was sufficient equity in Mr Edwards' share for the court to be confident that the debt would be discharged by sale even after the postponement.

6.110   The weight generally attached to the position of creditors is illustrated by two cases decided subsequent to *Shaire* (2001).

---

**First National Bank v Achampong (2003):** Mr and Mrs Achampong co-owned their home. Mr Achampong's 50 per cent beneficial share was subject to a mortgage which did not affect Mrs Achampong following a successful claim based on undue influence. Mr Achampong returned to Ghana leaving his wife in occupation with the parties' adult children—one of whom was mentally disabled—and three infant grandchildren. Blackburne J considered it 'plain that an order for sale should be made'. The intention of the trust (s 15(1)(a)) of providing a home for the couple was at an end through the husband's absence and Blackburne J was not persuaded that he should give much if any weight to any wider 'purpose' (s 15(1)(b)). There was an absence of evidence as to the impact on the grandchildren's welfare (s 15(1)(c)). Against this, without an order for sale the bank would be kept waiting indefinitely for any payment (s 15(1)(d)).

---

**Bank of Ireland v Bell (2001):** Mr and Mrs Bell co-owned their home. Mr Bell's 90 per cent share was subject to a mortgage which did not affect Mrs Bell as a result of forgery of her signature. Mr Bell had left the property and the couple had divorced. Mrs Bell, who was in poor health, remained in occupation together with the couple's son. Any intention (s 15(1)(a)) or purpose (s 15(1)(b)) that the property was to provide a family home was considered to have come to an end on Mr Bell's departure, or when possession proceedings commenced. The son's occupation was only a 'slight consideration' (s 15(1)(c)) as he was nearly 18 years old. Mrs Bell's interest was 10 per cent (s 15(3)) and there was no equity in the property that would be realized for her on a sale. Against this, the debt (at the time, £300,000) was increasing daily in the absence of any payment of capital or interest (s 15(1)(d)).

---

## Applications by Trustees in Bankruptcy

6.111   Where an individual becomes bankrupt, his or her property vests in a trustee in bankruptcy who is required to realize the bankrupt's assets and distribute them in accordance with a statutory scheme in order to discharge the debts (IA 1986, s 305). Where the bankrupt co-owns land, his or her equitable share vests in the trustee in bankruptcy. If the bankrupt was an equitable joint tenant, his or her bankruptcy causes severance as an involuntary act operating on the share (6.37).

6.112   Applications for sale by a trustee in bankruptcy of land held on trust for sale are governed by section 335A of the IA 1986 (TOLATA, s 15(4); IA 1986, s 335A(1)), which directs the court to 'make such order as it thinks just and reasonable' taking into account specified factors (listed in 6.116). The factors the court is directed to consider under section 335A are different to those referred to in TOLATA. Moreover, section 335A provides a presumption that where the application is made more than a year after the bankrupt's estate vests in the trustee in bankruptcy, sale shall be ordered unless there are exceptional circumstances.

**6.113**  Section 335A of the IA 1986 must be read in conjunction with other provisions of the Act (inserted into the Act by the Enterprise Act 2002) that represent a policy of providing a 'fresh start' for bankrupts. Two provisions are made in respect of a dwelling-house which, at the time of the bankruptcy, was the sole or principal home of the bankrupt and/or his or her current or former spouse or civil partner. In respect of such property:

- sale will not be ordered if the bankrupt's share is below a prescribed level and therefore of marginal benefit to creditors (IA 1986, s 313A). The prescribed level is currently £1,000 (Insolvency Proceedings (Monetary Limits) (Amendment) Order (SI 2004/547));

- the beneficiary's share is returned unless, within three years (IA 1986, s 283A), the property is 'realized' (6.114) or the trustee in bankruptcy has made one of a number of specified applications—including an application for sale.

**6.114**  Realization requires a transaction that involves the trustee in bankruptcy 'getting in the full cash consideration for the deal' (*Lewis v Metropolitan Properties Realisations Ltd* (2010)). Hence, property is realized, for example, where it has been sold or where the bankrupt's share is bought out by one of the other co-owners.

**6.115**  The collective effect of the provisions of the IA 1986 is as follows. From the time the bankrupt's share under a trust of land vests in the trustee in bankruptcy:

- there is a one-year 'adjustment period' during which the court has discretion to order sale, exercisable by reference to the factors in section 335A (listed in 6.116);

- after that adjustment period, sale will be ordered unless there are exceptional circumstances;

- however, if the property falls within section 283A then, following the adjustment period, the trustee in bankruptcy has two years during which sale will be ordered unless there are exceptional circumstances. A total of three years will then have passed and the property will be returned to the bankrupt unless it has been realized or a specified application has been made.

**6.116**  In all applications under section 335A, the court is directed to take into account the interests of the bankrupt's creditors (s 335A(2)(a)). Where the application relates to a dwelling-house which is or has been the home of the bankrupt or the bankrupt's current or former spouse or civil partner, the court is, additionally, directed to consider the following factors:

- the conduct of the current or former spouse or civil partner so far as contributing to the bankruptcy (s 335A(2)(b)(i));

- the needs and financial resources of the current or former spouse or civil partner (s 335A(2)(b)(ii));
- the needs of any children (s 335A(2)(b)(iii));
- all the circumstances of the case other than the needs of the bankrupt (s 335A(3)).

**6.117**  References to 'needs' in section 335A are interpreted broadly to incorporate not only financial needs, but also medical and psychological needs. As a result, while the financial, medical, and psychological needs of a current or former spouse or civil partner and children are taken into account, the medical and psychological needs of the bankrupt, as well as his or her financial needs, are excluded from consideration (*Everitt v Budhram* (2009)).

**6.118**  The test of exceptional circumstances has its origins in case law decided under the previous legislation, in which the courts had signalled a narrow approach to its definition, requiring matters to be present that fall beyond 'the melancholy consequence of debt and improvidence with which every civilised society has been familiar' (*Re Citro* (1991)). To be exceptional, therefore, the factors must be 'out of the ordinary course, or unusual, or special, or uncommon' (*Hosking v Michaelides* (2004)). The need to move home and neighbourhood, together with the consequential disruption of such a move, including to children's education, are not, therefore, 'exceptional' however distressing they may be (*Re Citro*).

**6.119**  The following provide examples of exceptional circumstances.

- *Claughton v Charalambous* (1999): the poor health and reduced life expectancy of the bankrupt's spouse. The couple's home had been adapted to meet her mobility needs. Sale was postponed for as long as the wife lived in the property.
- *Re Bremner* (1999): the need for the bankrupt's wife, who was also his carer, to care for him in their home. The bankrupt was elderly and terminally ill with cancer, though his own 'needs' were excluded from consideration (**6.116**).
- *Martin-Sklan v White* (2007): the 'web of support' provided by neighbours, relatives, and schools to help the bankrupt's children when his partner, an alcoholic, left the home on drinking bouts. Sale was postponed for seven years, until the youngest child reached 18.
- *Nicholls v Lan* (2007): the needs of the bankrupt's spouse, who was a chronic schizophrenic, whose medical circumstances meant that a forced sale could have specific psychiatric effects. Sale was postponed for 18 months to enable her to realize funds from the sale of another property to buy out the trustee in bankruptcy's share.
- *Everitt v Budhram* (2010): the mental and physical needs of the bankrupt's spouse, including those related to a stroke and diabetes. The bankrupt's spouse had also been declared bankrupt, but proceedings against him had been temporarily stayed following his loss of capacity. Notably, if those proceedings had continued,

his needs would have been excluded from consideration (**6.116**). Sale was post-poned for a year, or until three months after a possession order was made against the bankrupt's spouse.

- *Foenander v Allan* (2006): sale was postponed pending an insurance claim for subsistence which, if agreed, would significantly increase the value of the home. The case is unusual as the exceptional circumstances were therefore financial.

**6.120**  The fact that creditors will not be prejudiced by sale does not, alone, constitute exceptional circumstances (*Donohoe v Ingram* (2006)). However, where exceptional circumstances are present, the impact on the creditors of a postponement of sale is clearly taken into account by the court in determining whether, and for how long, to postpone sale. Hence, in *Foenander v Allan* (2006) and *Martin-Sklan v White* (2007) the postponement of sale was not expected to prejudice the creditors as the sum realized on sale would still be sufficient to repay the debt. In *Re Bremner* (1999), the court noted that it would not necessarily have postponed sale if the bankrupt had been younger, or less ill or had a longer life expectancy. In *Grant v Baker* (2016), the court overturned an indefinite postponement of sale awarded by the judge at first instance and explained that the need for the property to be sold in a reasonable period was 'a nettle that had to be grasped'. The strong weight the courts afford to the interests of creditors mirrors the approach taken on applications for sale by a creditor (**6.102–6.110**). *Nicholls v Lan* (2007) appears an unusual case in which the court postponed sale despite the fact that the proceeds realized by sale would be insufficient to pay the outstanding debt.

## Applications for Sale and Human Rights

**6.121**  An application for sale of the home under TOLATA or the IA 1986 engages Article 8 of the European Convention on Human Rights (the right to respect for private and family life) in respect of those who will be affected by the sale and thus these two pieces of legislation need to demonstrate human rights compliance under section 3 of the Human Rights Act 1998 (see **2.31**). 'Home' has an autonomous meaning under Article 8 (**2.68–2.70**) and all those with 'sufficient continuing' links to the home must be taken into account, not only those with property rights (*Gillow v UK* (1989), Buyse (2006)). Hence, for example, children have a right to respect for their home under Article 8, even though children are unlikely to be co-owners of the home. Against this, however, the applicant for sale—as a person with 'an interest' in the land—has a right to peaceful enjoyment of their possessions under Article 1 Protocol 1, which may be infringed if they are unable to realize their interest.

**6.122**  The human rights contained in Article 8 and Article 1 Protocol 1 are qualified, rather than absolute (**2.4**). This means that an interference with those rights is permitted where there is a legitimate aim and the interference is proportionate to that aim. Where the application for sale is governed by TOLATA, the discretion conferred on the court (ss 14–15) ensures that the proportionality of the application can be considered. The human rights compliance with applications for sale under TOLATA was confirmed in the context of an application for sale by a creditor in *National Westminster Bank plc v Rushmer* (2010). There, Arnold J considered that the balance required for proportionality would necessarily be drawn by the court taking into account the factors the court is directed to take into account by the Act (**6.87**). He explained:

> *[I]n my judgment, it will ordinarily be sufficient . . . for the court to give due consideration to the factors specified in section 15 of TOLATA. That will ordinarily enable the court to balance the creditor's rights, which include its rights under Article 1 of the First Protocol, with the Article 8 rights of those affected by an order for sale. I would not rule out the possibility that there may be circumstances in which it is necessary for the court explicitly to consider whether an order for sale is a proportionate interference with the Article 8 rights of those affected, but I do not consider that this will always be necessary.*

**6.123**  The question of human rights compliance is more contentious in respect of applications for sale governed by the IA 1986. In order for courts to consider the proportionality between sale and the interference with human rights, it is necessary for the courts to have discretion. Where a trustee in bankruptcy makes an application for sale more than a year after the bankruptcy, discretion exists only where the court is satisfied that there are exceptional circumstances. If such circumstances are present, then it has been suggested that the balancing exercise the court is directed to undertake under the IA 1986, 'precisely captures what is required' to ensure human rights compliance (*Nicholls v Lan* (2007)). But in the absence of exceptional circumstances, there is no discretion—instead, there is a presumption in favour of sale (**6.112**). Further, the courts have defined exceptional circumstances narrowly, as meaning circumstances outside the usual range of those expected to arise on a bankruptcy (**6.118**). The courts' narrow approach makes the likely incidence of cases in which there is no discretion greater.

**6.124**  Concerns over the compatibility of the IA 1986 with human rights have led to two suggestions. In *Barca v Mears* (2004) the court held that there should be 'a shift in emphasis' to the interpretation of the IA 1986 so that exceptional circumstances would be found where 'the consequences of the bankruptcy are of the usual kind, but exceptionally severe'. This change in approach will ensure that discretion exists in a wider range of cases. In *Ford v Alexander* (2012) the court rejected a more radical argument that a proportionality test should be read into section 335A so that exceptional circumstances were present whenever sale would be disproportionate. In rejecting the argument, the court appeared to treat proportionality and exceptionality as 'coterminous' (Cowan and Hunter (2012)) so that the statutory reference to 'exceptional' already ensured the proportionality balance required by Article 8.

**6.125**  There is no doubt that situations in which human rights considerations dictate against sale will be rare. Furthermore, the courts have shown considerable reluctance to interfere with the policy laid down by Parliament when interpreting legislation conferring rights to possession by private parties and, by the same token, sale of the home

(*McDonald v McDonald* (2016)). This is particularly the case in applications by creditors and trustees in bankruptcy, as the need to ensure the repayment of debts will invariably carry significant weight. Indeed, there is no reported case in which the wide interpretation of exceptional circumstances advocated in *Barca v Mears* (2004) has led to sale being postponed to protect an occupier's Article 8 rights. It has been said that the subsequent case law 'evidences only a variety of alluring yet ultimately unpersuasive defences of the status quo, intended to keep the *Barca* objection at bay' (Baker (2010)).

**6.126**   Where, even on the wide interpretation of the term proposed in *Barca v Mears*, there are no exceptional circumstances, it may be presumed that sale is a proportionate interference with Article 8 rights. In this respect, the existence of the one-year adjustment period before the creditor's interests prevail may be significant. Even in such cases, however, the absence of discretion remains problematic as it excludes any consideration of the parties' human rights. Further, the difference in treatment between applications by creditors, on the one hand, and trustees in bankruptcy, on the other, may raise a question of compliance with Article 14 (non-discrimination) unless the difference in treatment can be justified.

## FURTHER READING

Baker, A, 'The Judicial Approach to "Exceptional Circumstances" in Bankruptcy: The Impact of the Human Rights Act 1998' [2010] Conv 352.

Bright, S, 'Occupation Rents and the Trusts of Land and Appointment of Trustees Act 1996: From Property to Welfare' [2009] Conv 378.

Cooke, E, *Land Law* (2nd edn, Oxford: Oxford University Press, 2012), ch 5.

Dixon, M, 'To Sell or Not to Sell: That is the Question. The Irony of the Trusts of Land and Appointment of Trustees Act 1996' (2011) 70 CLJ 579.

Fox, L, 'Creditors and the Concept of a "Family Home": A Functional Analysis' (2005) 25 LS 201.

Fox, L, *Conceptualising Home: Theories, Laws and Policies* (Oxford: Hart Publishing, 2006).

Hopkins, N, 'Regulating Trusts of the Home: Private Law and Social Policy' (2009) 125 LQR 310.

Law Commission Report No 181, *Transfer of Land: Trusts of Land* (1989).

Pawlowski, M and Brown, J, 'Joint Purchasers and the Presumption of Joint Beneficial Ownership—A Matter of Informed Choice?' (2013b) 27 Tru LI 3.

Smith, RJ, *Plural Ownership* (Oxford: Oxford University Press, 2005).

## SELF-TEST QUESTIONS

1   What are the key differences between a joint tenancy and a tenancy in common?

2   How may joint tenants sever the joint tenancy: (i) unilaterally; and (ii) mutually? What is the effect of severance?

3    What are the main ways in which a co-ownership trust can come to an end?

4    In what ways does the Trusts of Land and Appointment of Trustees Act 1996 reflect the fact that co-ownership trusts commonly exist in respect of the beneficiaries' home?

5    Where a dispute arises as to whether co-owned land should be sold, on what basis will the court resolve the dispute on an application by: (i) one of the co-owners; (ii) the creditor of one of the co-owners; and (iii) the trustee in bankruptcy of one of the co-owners?

# 7 Leases

## SUMMARY

This chapter considers leases. Leases can count as legal estates in land and can thus provide ownership of land for a period. They are very important in practice: many people have leases of their homes, and most businesses have leases of their commercial premises. We will see how the content, acquisition, and defences questions apply to leases, and will also see that there are often both contractual and proprietary aspects to the operation of a lease. This chapter will also consider leasehold covenants. A leasehold covenant is essentially an express or implied promise made by a landlord to a tenant, or by a tenant to a landlord. The importance of such covenants is that they may, in certain circumstances, bind not only the original landlord or tenant who made the promise, but also a future party who steps into the shoes of that landlord or tenant by acquiring the rights of the landlord or of the tenant. Leasehold covenants must be carefully distinguished from general covenants (which we will examine in Chapter 10): special rules apply to leasehold covenants as they form part of the special relationship that binds a landlord and a tenant. Indeed, those special rules provide the main reason why a purchaser of a flat will almost always acquire a lease, rather than a freehold, of that flat.

Key topics explored in this chapter are:

- The distinction between a lease and a licence (7.1–7.4)
- The content question: the requirement of exclusive possession (7.8–7.27)
- The content question: the requirement of a certain term (7.28–7.39)
- The content question: the nature of a 'Bruton lease' (7.49–7.58)
- The acquisition question: how leases may be created or transferred (7.59–7.72)
- Priority and the defences question: when may C have a defence to a lease (7.73–7.76)
- The contractual and proprietary aspects of a lease (7.83–7.86)
- The nature and operation of leasehold covenants (7.87–7.113)
- Remedies for breach of leasehold covenants (7.114–7.129)
- Flat ownership and commonhold (7.130–7.137)

## Introduction

**7.1**  In this chapter, we are looking at a particular *type of right* that one person (B) might have in the land of another (A). Where B is in occupation of A's land with A's permission, it is likely that B's right will be either a lease or a licence. The distinction between the two types of right is very important. A lease can count as a property right in land. In fact, along with the freehold, it makes up the two types of right that can count as a legal estate in land. As we saw in **Chapters 1** and **3**, the lease is, therefore, very close to the top of the hierarchy of rights in relation to land. The licence, in contrast, is at the bottom. A licence consists simply of a permission to make some use of another's land and does not count as a legal estate or interest in land, nor as an equitable interest. As we saw in **Chapter 3**, even if A is under a contractual duty not to revoke a licence, that licence still gives B only a personal right against A.

**7.2**  The distinction between a lease and a licence therefore reflects the most fundamental distinction in land law: between a property right and a personal right. A lease is almost always a property right. So, if B has a lease of A's land, and A then sells that land to C, B's lease is capable of binding C. In contrast, if B instead only has a licence to make some use of A's land, and A then sells that land to C, B's licence is not capable of binding C (see **3.70** and **Figure 7.1**).

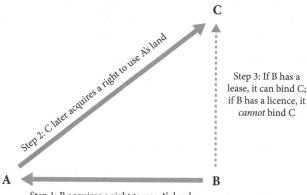

**Figure 7.1**  Leases, licences, and third parties

Similarly, if B has a lease of A's land and a stranger, X, then interferes with B's reasonable enjoyment of the land, X may well have committed the tort of nuisance against B. If, however, B has only a licence of A's land, then B cannot bring a claim in nuisance against X (see *Hunter v Canary Wharf* (1997)).

**7.3**  Some care is needed, however. As we will see at **7.49–7.58**, it was said in the House of Lords that, in some cases, B can have a lease without having a property right. In those rare cases, B's lease will not be capable of binding C. Conversely, as we saw at **3.83–3.86**, there may be cases in which B has only a licence, but can assert a right against C. Those cases, however, do *not* mean that the *licence itself* binds C. For, in those cases, the right that B asserts against C is not the licence, but is rather a *different* right, arising as a result of C's conduct.

**7.4** Impact on third parties is therefore one reason for distinguishing the lease from the licence. It is not, however, the only one. Many of the most important cases do not involve third parties at all. Instead, in those cases B wanted a lease in order to qualify for statutory protection against A. There was once very important statutory protection for B if B had a lease of his or her home. That protection used to apply even if A was just a private landlord. In the private sector, however, there is now very little meaningful statutory protection for B, even if B has a lease. The statutory protection given to a party with a lease continues to be important if A is a local authority or a provider of social housing. Even in those cases, however, B does not qualify for protection if B has only a licence. So it can be very important, in working out B's rights against A, to know if B has a lease or a licence. Indeed, as we noted at **3.87–3.89**, and as we will see again at **7.42–7.43**, it seems that a judge's approach both to the definition of a lease, and to the impact of a licence on third parties, may well depend on the willingness of that judge to accord B the statutory protection that comes with having a lease rather than a licence.

## Terminology

**7.5** In a case where B is occupying A's land with A's permission, various terms can be used to describe the parties. Unless given a particular meaning by a statute, these terms do not have precise technical definitions. For example, if B is occupying under a short-term agreement then, whether B has a lease or a licence, A is often described as a landlord. In such a case, if B has a licence, B is often called a lodger; if B has a lease, B will instead be a tenant. Where A grants B a long lease, A's estate will often be called a reversion (as the right to possess the land will go back, or revert to, A when B's lease ends). The term 'tenancy' is often used by statute and it is generally interpreted to refer to the relationship between A and B if, and only if, B has a lease. So if B has only a licence, there will be no tenancy.

**7.6** The word 'tenancy', like the French 'tenir', literally refers to holding. When we talk of a tenancy in the context of a lease, we are referring to the *type* of right held by B. This use of the word should be distinguished from the terms 'joint tenancy' and 'tenancy in common', which we examined in **Chapter 6**. Those terms instead refer to *ways* of holding a right. They are used only in cases of co-ownership: where two or more parties hold a right together. So if A simply grants a lease to B, then B has a tenancy, but there is no co-ownership: each of A and B has a separate, individual right. Conversely, if A and B are co-owners of a freehold, there will be a joint tenancy at law, and either a joint tenancy or tenancy in common in equity, even though there is no lease. And if A and B are co-owners of a lease (eg where A and B buy a flat together) then there is a tenancy in the sense both of the type of right held by A and B (a lease) and of the way in which they hold that right (as joint tenants of that lease at law, and either as joint tenants or tenants in common of that lease in equity).

**7.7**    Different terms can also be used to distinguish between different types of lease. Again, unless used in a particular way by a statute, these terms do not have precise technical definitions. So, for example, we could differentiate between a residential lease (a lease to B of land that B occupies as his or her home), a commercial lease (a lease of business premises), and an agricultural lease (a lease of a farm). In relation to residential leases, we might also distinguish between long leases (eg when B has a 999-year lease of a flat) and short leases (eg when B has a tenancy for one year only). When looking at short residential leases, there are also different statutory terms used to mark out the different levels of statutory protection available to B. For example, if a private landlord grants a short lease of residential property, the default position in England is that the tenant has an assured shorthold tenancy: a type of lease which provides only very limited statutory protection (under the Renting Homes (Wales) Act 2016, new residential leases of land in Wales no longer give rise to an assured shorthold tenancy, with the default position instead being that the parties have a 'standard occupation contract'; but, again, the statutory protection available to the tenant in such a case is only limited). In contrast, where a local authority in England grants a lease to B, B may have a secure tenancy: such a lease, in general, provides significant statutory protection, as the grounds on which the local authority can regain possession of the land are limited, even if the agreed period of the lease has ended (under the Renting Homes (Wales) Act 2016, the default position is that a residential lease granted by a 'community landlord', such as a local authority, will be a 'secure contract' and will similarly give B significant statutory protection).

## The Content Question: Exclusive Possession

### The Concept of Exclusive Possession

**7.8**    Section 1(1) of the Law of Property Act 1925 (LPA 1925) states that only two types of right can count as a legal estate in land: (a) 'An estate in fee simple absolute in possession'; and (b) 'A term of years absolute'. The phrase 'term of years absolute' refers to a lease. As clarified by the further definition of the phrase given by section 205(1)(xxvii) of the LPA 1925, it excludes a term defined by reference to the life of one or more people (under s 149(6), if A attempts to grant B a lease for B's life, it takes effect as a lease for 90 years determinable on B's death) and it also excludes any lease granted after 1925 in which the tenant's right to possession of the land begins more than 21 years after the grant.

**7.9**    The simplest way to understand the content of a lease is consistent with section 1(1) of the LPA 1925 and was set out by Lord Templeman in the following case, which is the most important decision on leases.

***Street v Mountford* (1985):** Mr Street, a solicitor, gave Mrs Mountford a right to exclusive possession of two rooms of a house which he owned. The parties' signed written agreement described Mrs Mountford as having a licence and so made clear that Mr Street did not intend to grant her a lease. The rent set was £37 a week. Under the terms of the Rent Act 1977, if Mrs Mountford had a lease, Mr Street would, however, be obliged to accept whatever level of rent was determined as fair by an independent officer or tribunal. The House of Lords, reversing the view of the Court of Appeal, found that Mrs Mountford did indeed have a lease. The crucial point was that, whatever language the parties had used to describe her right, Mrs Mountford did have a right to exclusive possession of the land, and so could be seen as free, in the words of Lord Templeman, to 'exercise the rights of an owner of land which is in the real sense [her] land, albeit temporarily and subject to certain restrictions'.

**7.10** There are two key parts to Lord Templeman's explanation of a lease. First, a lease gives B rights of ownership. This is consistent with the fact that a lease can count as a legal estate in land: a lease, like a freehold, confers rights of ownership of land. Secondly, the ownership held by B is temporary as it is limited in time: we will examine this second requirement at **7.38–7.39**.

**7.11** Our focus now is on the first part of Lord Templeman's analysis: the point that a lease involves ownership. We need to focus on the legal position during the operation of the lease. For example, if A has a freehold and grants B a lease of the land for six months, if we were asked the general question of whether A or B owns the land, we would almost certainly say that A does. But if we were to look specifically at the six-month period covered by the lease, there is a crucial sense in which B, rather than A, has ownership *during that time*.

**7.12** The point is that, for the duration of the lease, it is B, rather than A, who has the *right to exclusive possession* of the land. This means that it is B, rather than A, who has the general power to decide, for example, if X can visit the property and stay for dinner. It means that if Z comes on to the property without any legal authority or permission from B, B can then sue Z. This is true even if Z had permission from A to enter the property. This right to exclude others is a key part of what it means to own property (Gray (1991), Harris (1996), Merrill (1998)). Indeed, Lord Hoffmann once stated that exclusive possession is the 'bedrock of English land law' (*Hunter v Canary Wharf* (1997)).

**7.13** When considering if the agreement between A and B confers a right to exclusive possession on B, it is important to note Lord Templeman's observation that B may have such a right, even if his temporary ownership of the land is 'subject to certain restrictions' (**7.9**). So, for example, the terms of the lease might stipulate that B is not allowed to keep a pet in the property, or that B must allow A, or A's authorized agents, to enter the property if major repairs are required. Such restrictions are consistent with B's having a right to exclusive possession. They are contractual limits, specifically agreed in advance, on the exercise of that right, but they do not prevent the right existing. For example, if you have a freehold of land, you clearly have a right to exclusive possession of that land. You might then grant your neighbour a right of way across part of the land, or you might, when buying the land, have promised the vendor that you would not use the land for commercial purposes. These restrictions limit the way in which you can exercise your rights as owner of the land, but they do not deny that ownership. The point is that a *specific, limited* restriction is not inconsistent with ownership.

**7.14**  Indeed, in *Street v Mountford*, Lord Templeman pointed out that the presence in A and B's agreement of terms such as those preventing B from keeping pets, or allowing A to enter to carry out major repairs, may in fact *support* B's claim to have a right to exclusive possession. The argument runs as follows. For the duration of the parties' agreement, it must be either A or B who has ownership of the land, and with it the right to exclusive possession. A key feature of ownership is that it is *open-ended*: it is impossible to spell out all the different uses an owner may make of his or her land (Harris (1996)). So, if the rights held by A during the agreement are spelt out by specific terms, this suggests that the *general* right to the land is held by B. After all, if A had kept the right to exclusive posses-sion, why would A need to rely on a specific term allowing A to enter the premises only for limited purposes? Conversely, if the agreement defines the specific, limited uses that B can make of the land, then it must be A who has kept the general right to the land, and so B will have only a licence. An example of this is provided by *Hunts Refuse Disposals v Norfolk Environmental Waste Services Ltd* (1997): A had a freehold of a quarry and gave B a right to use the site 'for depositing waste' for 21 years. The Court of Appeal held that B had a licence rather than a lease, as B had been given permission only to use the land for a limited purpose, and so did not have the open-ended rights that characterize ownership.

**7.15**  The logic behind Lord Templeman's approach can be shown in the figures below. In **Figure 7.2**, A has given B only specific, limited rights to make use of the land and has retained the right to exclusive possession. It is A, rather than B, who therefore has the basic authority to decide if strangers such as X, Y, and Z can enter the land: B has only a licence. In contrast, in **Figure 7.3**, A has transferred his or her ownership, for a period, to B and any rights that A has in relation to the land are specific, limited rights arising as a result of the agreement with B. In that case, B has a lease: in Lord Templeman's words (**7.9**), B is 'able to exercise the rights of an owner of land which is in the real sense his land, albeit temporarily and subject to certain restrictions'. It is therefore B who has the basic authority to decide if strangers such as X, Y, and Z can enter the land.

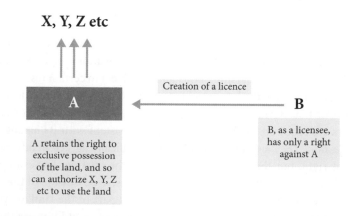

**Figure 7.2**  The effect of a licence

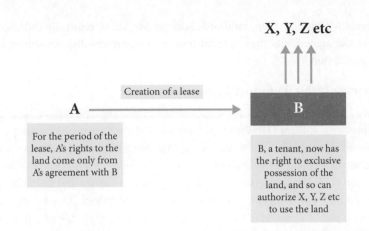

**Figure 7.3** The effect of a lease

## Exclusive Possession in Practice

**7.16** In *Street v Mountford* itself, the exclusive possession test was very easy to apply, as A conceded that the agreement gave B a right to exclusive possession of the property for the period of the agreement. Lord Templeman was also confident, more generally, that: 'In the case of residential accommodation there is no difficulty in deciding whether the grant confers exclusive possession.' So, B would have only a licence (and therefore be a lodger) if 'the landlord provides attendance or services which require the landlord or his servants to exercise unrestricted access to and use of the premises. A lodger is entitled to live in the premises but cannot call the place his own.' For example, a later House of Lords' decision, *Westminster CC v Clarke* (1992), confirmed that B had no right to exclusive possession, and hence no lease, where A, a council, housed B in accommodation made available to vulnerable homeless persons on the following terms: B was not entitled to any particular room; B had to have the prior approval of the council staff for any visitors; B was obliged to comply with any instructions from the warden in charge of the hostel; and B was told he might have to share accommodation. In Lord Templeman's words in that case: 'These limitations confirmed that the council retained possession of all the rooms of the hostel in order to supervise and control the activities of the occupiers.'

**7.17** Lord Templeman was, however, unduly optimistic in thinking that it would *always* be simple to apply the exclusive possession test in residential cases. The crucial point is that significant statutory protection, such as security of tenure and rent control, used to be available to a residential tenant of a private landlord (**7.4**). In *Street v Mountford*, therefore, Mr Street, when allowing Mrs Mountford to take occupation, had been very keen not to grant her a lease, as the statutory protection was available only to parties with a lease. He had been happy to give her a right to exclusive possession as, at that time, it had generally been thought—as a result of decisions of a Court of Appeal led by Lord Denning MR—that, if A made clear that he had no intention to give B a lease, no lease would arise. *Street v Mountford* changed that, by affirming the traditional rule that it is exclusive possession, rather than intention to create a lease, that is decisive (**7.42-7.45**).

After *Street v Mountford*, then, landlords such as Mr Street naturally did their best to ensure that the agreements they entered into with occupiers did *not* confer a right to exclusive possession.

**7.18**    A good example of this is provided by the following case.

---

***Antoniades v Villiers* (1990):** Mr Antoniades held a long lease of a small top-floor flat and rented it out to a couple, Mr Villiers and Miss Bridger. They had moved in together and signed identical, but separate, documents, each containing a clause that: 'The licensor shall be entitled at any time to use the rooms together with the licensee and permit other persons to use all of the rooms together with the licensee.' Mr Antoniades argued that neither occupier had exclusive possession: they each had to share with the other and, potentially, with further occupiers. The House of Lords rejected this argument. First, it made no difference that the two occupiers signed separate documents: it was clear that the documents were interdependent parts of a single transaction with the landlord and that they were moving in together as a couple. Secondly, the term purporting to allow the landlord to insert further occupiers was not a genuine part of the agreement: given the small size of the flat: 'Mr Antoniades did not genuinely intend to exercise the powers save possibly to bring pressure to bear to obtain possession.'

---

**7.19**    It is easy to understand the policy behind the House of Lords' decision in *Antoniades v Villiers*. If the availability of important statutory protection turns on the question of whether B has a right to exclusive possession, that protection would be fatally undermined if A could deny it to B by simply including a term allowing for the insertion of further occupiers, even if there was no genuine intention to rely on that term in practice. One way to give effect to such a policy would be to say that, when interpreting the term 'lease' or 'tenancy' as used in the relevant statute, the courts should take a purposive approach and so can find a lease even if, technically, the terms of the agreement appear to deny B exclusive possession. That was not the route adopted in *Antoniades v Villiers*, however. Lord Templeman instead suggested that the term denying exclusive possession could be disregarded as it was inserted by A with the purpose of ensuring that B did not qualify for the protection provided by the Rent Acts. That reasoning is, however, difficult to accept.

**7.20**    It is certainly true that *once* it is found that B has a lease, then any relevant statutory protection will apply even if the agreement between A and B attempts to exclude the statute: in that sense, 'you cannot contract out of the Rent Acts'. But it is clearly permissible for A to choose to give B a licence rather than a lease, and thus to prevent statutory protection such as the Rent Acts from applying in the first place. The fact that A's purpose in doing so is to ensure that the Rent Acts do not apply should not be relevant: after all, my purpose in putting savings into a tax-free savings account is to avoid paying tax, but that is perfectly permissible.

**7.21**    In *Street v Mountford*, Lord Templeman said that, in considering occupation agreements, the court should 'be astute to detect and frustrate sham devices and artificial transactions whose only object is to disguise the grant of a tenancy and to evade the Rent Acts'. It is true that there is a generally applicable sham doctrine, which allows a court to disregard apparent contractual terms if those terms were in fact intended by A and B 'to give to third parties or to the court the appearance of creating between the parties legal rights and obligations different from the actual legal rights and obligations (if any) which the parties intended to create' (to use the formulation suggested by Diplock LJ in *Snook v London and West Riding Investments Ltd* (1967)). This doctrine might apply if, for example, A and B execute documents making it appear that A has sold land to B when, in fact, the parties intend that A will keep ownership of the land, and that no rights will be acquired by B (see eg *Miles v Bull* (1969)). In a case such as *Antoniades*, however, the sham doctrine clearly does not apply, as it is not the case that A and B intended to create a lease, and then to pretend that it was only a licence; rather, A actively *did* want to give B only a licence.

7.22   The limited nature of the sham doctrine explains why Lord Templeman, in *Antoniades*, refined his earlier comment and stated that, in *Street v Mountford*: 'It would have been more accurate and less liable to give rise to misunderstandings if I had substituted the word "pretence" for the references to "sham devices" and "artificial transactions". There is, however, no generally established test for ascertaining a 'pretence'. All we can do, therefore, is note that terms seem to have been stigmatized as 'pretences' when, as in *Antoniades*, it has been found that the parties did not genuinely intend that the term would be relied on in practice (Bright (2002)). This does not, however, answer the prior question of *why* a court should be able to disregard such terms, as there is no general rule of contract law that a term is only binding if the parties intend that it be enforced in practice.

7.23   It should finally be noted that, whilst the rationale of the courts' approach to 'pretences' remains unclear, the question has been stripped of much of its practical importance by the dramatic reduction in the statutory protection available to a residential tenant of a private landlord. The modern day Mr Street or Mr Antoniades will have no qualms in granting a lease, as it will be an assured shorthold tenancy and will thus provide the occupier with no security of tenure and no rent controls. Of course, the political pendulum may swing again, and a future Parliament may decide to reinstate some of the protection formerly available. If so, it is important to note the very sensible recommendation of the Law Commission that the scope of any future protective legislation should *not* be limited to those occupying under a lease (see Law Commission (2006a)). That proposal has not been followed in England, but was implemented by the Welsh Assembly in the Renting Homes (Wales) Act 2016. Future residential leases and licences in Wales are, under the Act, 'occupation contracts' and may be 'secure contracts' (as will usually be the case where the landlord is a 'community landlord' such as a local authority) or 'standard contracts' (as will usually be the case where the landlord is a private person or body). Whilst the distinction between a lease and a licence is crucial in determining the effect of an occupier's rights on a third party, it is very difficult to see why it should make a difference to any statutory rights of the occupier against the landlord, and so the Welsh approach on this point has much to recommend it.

## Exclusive Possession and Multiple Occupation

**7.24**  The decision in *Antoniades v Villiers* shows that it is possible for two or more parties, acting together, to acquire a lease (**7.18**). Another appeal, decided by the House of Lords along with *Antoniades*, demonstrates some of the difficulties that can arise in such a case.

---

*AG Securities v Vaughan* **(1990):** AG Securities had a long lease of a London flat. The flat had four bedrooms, as well as communal areas, and was rented out to four students, one of whom was Mr Vaughan. The four had not moved in as a group: instead, each had moved in as and when a former occupier left and a room became available. The four occupiers, acting together, argued that they held a lease and so qualified for statutory protection, which would prevent AG Securities from ending the lease. The House of Lords rejected that argument. It was clear that, when an individual occupier had left, it had been AG Securities, as landlord, which had the final say on who replaced that occupier. It was clear therefore that the arrangement between the occupiers and the landlord was designed to 'provide accommodation for a shifting population of individuals who were genuinely prepared to share the flat with others introduced from time to time who would, at least initially, be strangers to them'. It therefore could not be said that any current set of occupiers had a joint right to exclusive possession.

---

It might perhaps have been possible for each individual occupier to argue, instead, that he or she had exclusive possession of his or her specific bedroom, but the House of Lords was clearly correct to find that the occupiers had no joint right to exclusive possession of the whole house.

**7.25**  In *AG Securities v Vaughan*, however, the House of Lords went further than was strictly necessary for its decision, and held that, in any case where two or more occupiers attempt to establish a joint lease, it is necessary to show that they acquired their right to exclusive possession as *joint tenants*, rather than as tenants in common. As we saw in **Chapter 6**, a joint tenancy is harder to establish than a tenancy in common, as it involves not only unity of possession (ie a joint right to possession) but also unity of time, of title, and of interest. If two parties attempt to acquire a freehold as tenants in common, as when A conveys a freehold to B1 and B2 in equal shares, then, as we saw at **6.12**, B1 and B2 take the legal estate as joint tenants by force of statute (as the LPA 1925, s 1(6) prevents there being a legal tenancy in common of land) but hold as tenants in common in equity. In contrast, it seems that if B1 and B2 attempt to acquire a new lease as tenants in common, they will simply fail to acquire *any* lease.

**7.26**  The requirement that the parties genuinely take the lease as joint tenants has therefore been subject to some academic criticism (eg Sparkes (1989)). It can, however, be defended. The point is that, in a case such as *AG Securities*, B1 and B2 claim that their contract with A has given rise to a lease, and thus claim that, together, they hold a particular contractual right against A. Co-ownership of a contractual right can occur only by means of a joint tenancy, as it can arise only where A makes a joint promise to B1 and B2 (see eg *Re McKerrell* (1912)). If, instead, A makes separate promises to B1 and B2, then B1 and B2, by definition, are not claiming the same right.

**7.27** The practical impact of the approach in *AG Securities* can be seen by considering *Mikeover v Brady* (1989). B1 and B2, a couple, moved into the premises together. So far, so like *Antoniades*. After B1 moved out, however, B2 remained in occupation and paid only half of the rent. If B1 and B2 had been joint parties to a single contract with A, each would then have been liable to A for the *whole* of the rent. B2's payment of only half of the rent therefore suggested that B1 and B2 in fact had separate rights to occupation, and so B2 could not show that, jointly with B1, she had a right to exclusive possession of the premises. Instead, B1 and B2 each had separate licences from A.

## The Content Question: Certainty of Term

**7.28** Lord Templeman's classic analysis of a lease is that, if B has a lease, B is 'able to exercise the rights of an owner of land which is in the real sense his land, albeit temporarily and subject to certain restrictions' (see **7.9**). The temporary nature of B's rights is reflected in the requirement that B's right to exclusive possession must be for a *limited time* only. It may be for a very long period, such as 3,000 years, but, even in such a case, there is a definite temporal limit to B's right to exclusive possession.

**7.29** This requirement that a lease must have a certain term is simple to state, and can be simply explained. It is necessary to maintain the distinction between a lease and a freehold. Each of those two rights can count as a legal estate in land, and each confers ownership. There is, however, no time limit imposed on a freehold. In contrast, a lease is, from the moment of its creation, doomed to end. This is why a lease is described by section 1(1) of the LPA 1925 as a 'term of years absolute': a terminus is where buses stop, and a university term, even if it feels very long, does end at some point. A related way of thinking of this point is that, if B has a lease, there must be another party, A, the grantor of the lease, with a prior estate, either a freehold or a longer lease. It is possible for A, by granting the lease to B, to suspend his or her right to exclusive possession for a period, but it would be inconsistent with A's ownership of the land if there were no certain point when A would be able to regain the right to exclusive possession. A further explanation (Williams (2015)) is that, given that a freehold does not technically consist of ownership forever (**3.56**), and that a freehold owner cannot give a right that he or she does not have, it is simply not possible for A to give B a right to exclusive possession which might possibly last forever.

**7.30** The requirement that a lease be for a limited period has, nonetheless, caused some problems in practice. It can frustrate parties' intentions and thereby lay a trap for them, as shown by the following example.

---

*Prudential Assurance v London Residuary Body* **(1992):** In 1930, the London City Council (A) bought from Mr Nathan (B), a strip of land adjoining a public road, as it thought it might later need to widen the road. A agreed with B that, in return for an annual rent of £30, B could have exclusive possession of the strip, which also adjoined B's shop, until the road-widening took place. The LRB, A's successor in title, was bound by any lease granted by A to B, but attempted to regain possession of the land from Prudential Assurance, B's successor in title, which equally had the benefit of any lease granted by A to B. The land was not, however, needed for road-widening. The LRB was successful as it is impossible to create a lease for a period that does not have a certain end date but instead ends only if and when a particular event occurs. B did acquire a lease by means of B's payment, and A's acceptance, of annual rent (**7.63–7.64**), but that lease was only a yearly tenancy, and so the LRB could end it by giving the appropriate period of notice. As a result, the LRB was able to regain possession even though the land was not required for road-widening.

The result in *Prudential Assurance* was thus clearly inconsistent with the terms of the original agreement, and so can be seen as frustrating the intentions of A and B (although, as noted by Bright (1993), it is equally unlikely that A and B had foreseen that the agreement would still be in place even 60 years later, when the relative value of the £30 rent would of course be far lower). The requirement of a certain term may also seem arbitrary in its effect. In the *Prudential Assurance* case, if A and B had simply agreed instead that B was to have a right to exclusive possession for 3,000 years, such right to end if the land was needed for road-widening, B would have had a valid 3,000-year lease.

**7.31**  It is certainly interesting to note that, although Lord Browne-Wilkinson applied the requirement for a certain term in *Prudential Assurance*, thereby allowing the LRB to succeed, he was unhappy with the rule. He said that it led to a 'bizarre outcome' and was an 'ancient and technical rule of law' for which '[n]o one has produced any satisfactory rationale'. His decision to apply the rule was therefore based only on the need to avoid a *judicial* change to the rule, which would be retrospective and so potentially unsettle existing titles to land. He therefore urged the Law Commission to see if legislation could be introduced to reform a rule which 'operates to defeat contractually agreed arrangements'.

**7.32**  What should we make of these criticisms of the requirement that a lease must be for a certain term? First, the requirement clearly does place a limit on the freedom of A and B. But that should be no surprise. The key feature of property rights is that they can bind third parties. The interests of third parties must therefore be borne in mind when considering if A and B have successfully created a property right. The law gives effect to the interests of third parties by placing limits on the freedom of A and B to create property rights: a right created by A and B can count as a property right in land only if it is on the list of permitted estates or interests in land (**3.17–3.24**). It is therefore to be expected that a rule about the required content of a lease may operate to defeat the intentions of the parties. After all, it is important to remember that, in a case such as *Prudential Assurance*, the question was not whether A could breach the terms of its contract with B, it was rather whether a stranger to that contract (the LRB) could act contrary to the terms of that contract between A and B. Indeed, whilst the law on this point is not entirely clear, obiter opinions expressed by members of the Supreme Court suggest quite strongly that if it had been A, the original landlord, which had sought to terminate the lease against the original tenant, B, then B could have prevented this by simply relying on the terms of the contract (*Berrisford v Mexfield* (2012)). Secondly, it is true that A and B could easily avoid the rule by specifying that B is to have a lease for 3,000 years that can be terminated when the land is needed for road-widening. But, in that case, the rationale for the requirement of a certain term would be met, as it would then be clear that the lease would necessarily come to an end. Indeed, the fact that a rule can easily be complied with may be seen as a reason in favour of, rather than against, that rule.

7.33   A further potential criticism of the requirement of a term arises from Lord Browne-Wilkinson's description of the rule as one which 'requires the maximum duration of a term of years to be ascertainable from the outset'. It can then be suggested, as Baroness Hale did in the *Berrisford* case, that: 'Periodic tenancies obviously pose something of a puzzle if the law insists that the maximum term of any leasehold estate be certain.' This is because, if B has, say, a yearly tenancy of A's land, and B continues to pay the rent, and A continues to accept that rent, B's right to exclusive possession will automatically continue until either A or B gives at least six months' notice that, at the end of the current annual term, the tenancy will not be continued. The operation of a periodic tenancy is, however, entirely consistent with the rationale of the requirement for a certain term. This is because A always has the power to end the tenancy by giving the appropriate period of notice and so it is clear that A can, if A wishes, regain the right to exclusive possession of the land. In fact, as Lord Neuberger explained in *Berrisford*: 'the law in this area is the same for all types of tenancy, whether or not periodic in nature'. So if, for example, B has a yearly periodic tenancy but A and B agree that A can only give notice if and when the land is needed for road-widening, then, whilst that restriction may bind A as a matter of contract law, it will *not* be a part of B's lease and so will not be capable of binding a successor in title of A.

7.34   It can therefore be argued that the requirement for a certain term is justifiable. As noted at **7.32**, it must nonetheless be admitted that, like many other rules of the land law system, it may be a trap for parties who act without proper legal advice. For individuals, however, the potential danger of the rule has been mitigated by the Supreme Court's decision in the following case.

*Berrisford v Mexfield Housing Co-operative Ltd* (2012): Mrs Berrisford found herself in a similar position to that of Mrs Scott (see *Scott v Southern Pacific Mortgages Ltd* (2014), discussed at **12.38–12.43**): she owned a property, was having difficulty keeping up with the mortgage payments, but did not want to move out. Adopting a slightly different solution to that of Mrs Scott, Mrs Berrisford sold the property to Mexfield, a fully mutual housing co-operative, on the basis that, as a member of the cooperative, she could continue to have sole possession of the property. Her agreement with Mexfield stated that she would have possession 'from month to month' but that Mexfield could terminate her right to possession only in certain circumstances, which included her being 21 days or more late in paying the rent, and her ceasing to be a member of the cooperative. None of those events set out in the agreement had occurred, but Mexfield argued that it nonetheless had the power to give notice that it would not renew Mrs Berrisford's monthly periodic tenancy. Its argument was that Mrs Berrisford had a simple monthly lease, that it could refuse to renew, as it is impossible to have a valid lease that will automatically continue unless certain events occur: as in *Prudential Assurance*, such an arrangement does not give B exclusive possession for a term as if the events do not occur, there will be no end to B's right to exclusive possession. The Supreme Court accepted that it is not possible to have such an open-ended lease, but nonetheless found in favour of Mrs Berrisford, on the basis that the effect of the parties' agreement was that she had, in fact, a 90-year lease of the property, which could be determined early only if Mrs Berrisford died or if one of the events set out in the agreement (eg sufficiently late payment of rent) occurred.

**7.35** The first point to note in *Berrisford* is that statutory protection is generally available, under the Housing Act 1988, to a tenant of social housing so that, even if such a tenant has only a monthly lease, the landlord will be prevented from retaking possession unless it can show that one of the specific grounds of possession permitted by the statute has arisen (**7.7**). Mrs Berrisford did not, however, have such a secure tenancy, as the statutory protection does not apply to housing cooperatives. As Lord Hope explained, this exception was made on the overly optimistic assumption that, in a cooperative, the interests of the landlord and tenant would coincide and there would be no need for statutory protection. So, on one view, the real problem in *Berrisford* lay with the scope of the Housing Act 1988, and not with the requirement for a certain term.

**7.36** The second point to note in *Berrisford* is that it was Mexfield itself, rather than any successor in title, that wished to terminate the lease. As noted at **7.32**, all the members of the Supreme Court who expressed a view on this issue thought that Mrs Berrisford could, therefore, have prevented Mexfield from terminating the lease by simply relying on the terms of the agreement which, after all, clearly bound Mexfield as a matter of contract law.

**7.37** The Supreme Court's discussion of the contract law point was, however, obiter, as it was decided that, despite appearances, the agreement between Mexfield and Mrs Berrisford *did* give rise to a valid lease, as it was consistent with the requirement for a certain term. It was held that the agreement had in fact created a *90-year lease, determinable by Mexfield only on Mrs Berrisford's death or according to the terms of the agreement*. Two stages of reasoning were applied to reach this conclusion:

Step 1: at common law, before the coming into effect of the LPA 1925 on 1 January 1926, an agreement like that between Mexfield and Mrs Berrisford would give rise to a lease for Mrs Berrisford's life, determinable according to the terms of the agreement.

Step 2: a lease for life created on or after 1 January 1926 is converted by section 149(6) of the LPA 1925 into a 90-year lease, determinable on the tenant's death or according to the terms of the lease.

**7.38** On the facts of *Berrisford* itself, it may perhaps be reasonable to argue that, as the parties clearly intended that Mrs Berrisford's right to exclusive possession would end on her death, the lease, whilst expressed to be a monthly tenancy, could charitably be interpreted as a lease for life, so that section 149(6) of the LPA 1925, which applies to a lease for life, could then operate to turn the lease into a 90-year lease determinable on the death of the tenant. A contrast can be drawn with the following case.

---

**Southward Housing Co-operative Ltd v Walker (2015):** This case again involved the apparent grant of a lease by A, a housing cooperative, to B, an individual. In contrast to *Berrisford*, the apparent lease was not made as part of a mortgage rescue scheme, and it was clear that neither A nor B had intended that B would have a legal right to remain in the premises for life. Hildyard J rejected B's argument that, whenever there is an uncertain term, a tenancy for life arises, holding instead that, where A and B clearly do not intend such a result, there is no rule of law that requires a court to find that B has a tenancy for life.

---

Whilst there is thus a limit to the applicability of the Supreme Court's reasoning in *Berrisford*, there may still be a problem with that reasoning. It relies on a particular view, which may well be incorrect, of how the common law operated prior to the LPA 1925. For example, Lord Dyson relied on a textbook from 1920 which stated that where land is given for a 'definite period of time of uncertain duration, a freehold estate is conferred, as in the case of a gift for life'. This accords with *Bracton*, an important 13th-century account, which contrasts a gift for life with a term of years. So it seems that, prior to the LPA 1925, a grant of exclusive possession like that in *Berrisford* would give rise to a *freehold* life interest, not to a lease. If that is right, then section 149(6) is of no relevance, as it applies only to a *lease* for life. Moreover, as a result of section 1 of the LPA 1925, a freehold limited to B's life can no longer exist as a legal estate, so is it permissible today to make use of a rule which gave rise to a freehold life interest?

**7.39** Whilst these concerns about the reasoning in *Berrisford* are significant, it is also important to note that the Supreme Court's decision, in one way, takes some of the sting out of the requirement for a certain term. It ensures that B can rely on the limits on the landlord's right to possession, not only against the original landlord, but also against a successor in title. The decision, of course, provides no assistance if B is a company, as a company does not have a natural life and so the two steps of reasoning set out at **7.37** cannot apply. This does bring some inconsistency into the law: precisely the same arrangement for the possession of land can have a different legal effect according to whether B is a natural person or a company. So, whilst reducing the potential danger of the certain term requirement for an individual, and thus lessening one argument for statutory reform, the decision in *Berrisford* provides a different motive for legislation: to equalize the position of individuals and companies.

## The Content Question: No Need for Rent

**7.40** At some points in *Street v Mountford*, Lord Templeman refers to the 'grant of land for a term at a rent with exclusive possession' as the hallmark of a lease. On the facts of *Street v Mountford*, of course, rent was paid and so nothing turned on this reference to rent. It is important to note that, despite Lord Templeman's formulation, the payment of rent is *not* a requirement of a lease. This is made clear, for example, by section 205(1)(xxvii) of the LPA 1925, where the definition of a 'term of years absolute' starts thus: 'a term of years (taking effect either in possession or in reversion whether or not at a rent) …' and by the decision of the Court of Appeal in *Ashburn Anstalt v Arnold* (1989). In some cases, for example where B acquires a long lease, it may be that B will make a one-off, up-front payment (known as a 'premium') rather than paying rent; in other cases, as in *Ashburn*, it may be that A simply does not require payment at all. Just as A may transfer a freehold to B by way of gift, without requiring payment, so may A grant B a lease for free. As long as the transaction between A and B was intended to create legal relations, there is no need for payment. Contractual consideration may be provided by B by means other than the payment of money and, in any case, whilst a lease almost always involves a contract between A and B, there is no requirement that it must: a lease can arise simply by way of grant, without any need for a contract, as confirmed by Millett LJ in *Ingram v IRC* (1997).

## The Content Question: The Role of Intention

### Intention to Create Legal Relations is Required

**7.41**  The grant of a lease by A to B involves the creation of legal rights and so, as noted at **7.40**, it depends on the parties having an intention to create legal relations. As in other areas of law, that requirement can potentially be manipulated by a court which, for particular policy reasons, does not wish to find that B has acquired legal rights. For example, in *Burrows v Brent LBC* (1996), the House of Lords held that no lease was created when A, a local authority with the benefit of a possession order allowing it to remove B, a tenant, agreed with B that B could nonetheless remain in occupation if it complied with certain conditions. B then breached one of those conditions and A, relying on its earlier possession order, wished to remove B. B argued that, whilst its initial tenancy had ended on the date set out in the possession order, its later agreement with A then gave rise to a *new* lease, which was protected under statute as a secure tenancy. If that was correct, then A could take possession only on one of the grounds for possession provided by statute, and not simply as a result of B's breach of the condition imposed by the later agreement. Such a result would have been unwelcome as a matter of broader policy, as it would have made it difficult for local authorities, in the future, to make agreements not to enforce possession orders, and so would have worked against the broader interests of tenants. The House of Lords avoided that result by finding that the later agreement between A and B had not been intended to create legal relations, so that B did not have a lease but was merely a 'tolerated trespasser'. It is difficult, however, to accept that A did not intend the new agreement to create legal rights, given that it carefully set out the conditions on which B was to be allowed to continue to occupy the land. The case may, therefore, be an example of a court manipulating the concept of intention to create legal relations in order to reach a particular result.

## Intention to Create a Lease, or to Give B a 'Stake in the Land', is Not Required

7.42  We noted at 7.17 that Mr Street, although he did not wish to grant a lease to Mrs Mountford, had nonetheless been perfectly happy to give her a right to exclusive possession. That was because, as the law appeared to be when the parties made their agreement in 1983, a lease could arise only if A intended to give B a lease, or at least a 'stake in the land', rather than a mere licence. So if, as in *Street v Mountford*, A made clear his intention that B should only have a licence, that was regarded as determinative, even if the rights given to B by the agreement amounted to exclusive possession. That was the position taken in a number of Court of Appeal decisions, and championed by Lord Denning MR (see eg *Errington v Errington* (1952), *Marchant v Charters* (1977)). As Lord Denning readily admitted, this was a departure from the traditional view that a right to exclusive possession for a term was a lease, even if the parties intended it to be a licence. His view was that, given the statutory protection available to a party with a lease, the courts had to redraw the distinction between a lease and a licence in order to permit A, if he or she wished, to avoid being subject to that statutory regulation. A consequence of this approach was that parties who, under the traditional approach, would be regarded as having a lease (a property right capable of binding third parties) would instead be seen as having only a contractual licence. This led the Court of Appeal, in the same period, and again at Lord Denning's urging, to allow contractual licences to be capable of binding third parties. This was another departure from orthodoxy as the House of Lords in *King v David Allan* (1916, see 3.78) had previously made clear that a contractual licence cannot bind a third party.

7.43  Both parts of Lord Denning's 'revolution' (to use a term he himself employed in *Marchant v Charters* (1977)) were later rejected. As we saw at 3.78–3.82, it has instead been confirmed that a contractual licence is not, in itself, capable of binding a third party. And, in *Street v Mountford* (1985), the House of Lords confirmed the traditional position that if the agreement between A and B in fact gives B a right to exclusive possession for a term, B has a lease, even if the agreement was intended to give B only a licence. A lease can therefore arise even in the absence of an intention to give B a property right, or a 'stake in the land'. The parties are judged not by the rights they may have wished to produce, but by what they have actually created in their agreement, a point captured in Lord Templeman's homely observation in *Street v Mountford* that: 'The manufacture of a five-pronged implement for manual digging results in a fork even if the manufacturer, unfamiliar with the English language, insists that he intended to make and has made a spade.'

7.44  There is no controversy as to one part of the House of Lords' approach in *Street v Mountford*. The mere fact that the parties' agreement refers to B's right as a licence rather than as a lease cannot be decisive. It is for the court to decide whether the rights produced by the agreement do or do not fall within the definition of a lease. Similarly, if A makes a promise to give B a gift of £50, there is no contract (because no consideration) even if A and B each refers to the promise as a contract. A second aspect of the approach has, however, been queried. It is often the case that a right can count as a property right only if A and B intend that it should have that effect. For example, imagine that A gives B, her neighbour, a right to walk across a specific part of A's land. Such a right is capable of counting as an easement. As we will see in **Chapter 9**, however, it is equally possible for A to give B a mere licence to walk across A's land. So, in establishing if an easement has been granted, we need to ask if A and B intended that B's right would be capable of binding third parties, and not just A. It has been argued that a similar approach should be adopted in relation to leases (see Hill (1996)). There is, however, an important difference between a lease and an easement. The former, like a freehold, consists of a right to exclusive possession. It is not possible for B to have a right to exclusive possession that is binding only on A. So, if the parties' agreement gives B such a right, there is no need to ask if A and B intended it to be a property right: a right to exclusive possession of specific property for a limited period is *necessarily* a property right.

7.45  This does not mean, however, that the intention of A and B is irrelevant. First, as noted at **7.41**, A and B's agreement can give B a lease only if the parties intended to create legal relations. Secondly, and crucially, it is the parties who choose the content of the agreement and thus control the nature of the rights acquired by B. It is at this stage that the parties, by limiting B's rights to use the land, or by maintaining A's general right to control of the land, can ensure that B does not acquire a right to exclusive possession and so does not acquire a lease. What the parties cannot do is to make an agreement that gives B rights amounting to a right to exclusive possession, and at the same time insist that B has only a personal right against A. To provide another domestic analogy to go with Lord Templeman's fork, if you are cooking, your intention is crucial as you can choose what ingredients to use. But if you mix eggs, flour, butter, and sugar before baking it in the oven, you have not made a casserole, even if that was your intention. You chose the ingredients but, whether you like it or not, you have made a cake.

## The Content Question: Other Legal Relationships?

7.46  Our discussion so far suggests a simple test for the content of a lease: does B have a right to exclusive possession of land for a term? In *Street v Mountford*, however, Lord Templeman also set out a number of exceptions: cases in which B can have such a right without having a lease. He stated that: 'There can be no tenancy unless the occupier enjoys exclusive possession; but an occupier who enjoys exclusive possession is not necessarily a tenant.' It might therefore be said that if B's right can be explained as depending on a different legal relationship, B does not have a lease. It is difficult to see, however, why the lease should thus have to give way to other possible relationships, particularly if B wants access to particular advantages (such as statutory protection) that depend on B's having a lease.

7.47  The first point to make is that some of the 'exceptions' outlined by Lord Templeman are not true exceptions to the general test for a lease. First, there are cases where the parties lacked intention to create legal relations: in those cases, as noted at **7.41**, A has not granted B a right to exclusive possession. Lord Templeman also gave the example of a 'service occupier': a caretaker, for example, who has exclusive possession of a house next to the property he or she is employed to look after. In such a case, the possession of the employee is attributed to the employer (just as, for the purpose of vicarious liability in tort, the actions of an employee may be attributed to an employer) and so, technically, the employee has no independent right to possession. Secondly, some cases can be explained on the basis that B does not have a right to exclusive possession *for a term*: this is the case, for example, where B takes possession of land as a squatter. In such a case, B, as soon as he or she takes possession, acquires a freehold (see **4.84**), not a lease, as there is no time limit on the right to exclusive possession acquired by B. Thirdly, there are cases in which it is difficult, in principle, to deny B a lease. For example, Lord Templeman suggests that 'an object of charity' does not have a lease; but, as long as there is an intention to create legal relations, it is hard to see why the motive of A in giving B a particular right should affect the nature of that right.

7.48    Lord Templeman also suggested that a lease will not arise in a case where A has 'no power to grant a tenancy'. This must be true if, for example, A is a body set up by statute and the statute denies A the power to grant a lease. A more difficult issue is where A has no estate in land, but then attempts to grant B a lease of that land. The obvious answer in such a case is that B has no lease; but, as we will now see, that obvious answer has been rejected by the House of Lords.

## The Content Question: The *Bruton* Lease

### The Decision in *Bruton v London and Quadrant Housing Trust*

7.49    Can you, the reader of this book, give me a lease of Buckingham Palace? Of course, lacking any rights in the Palace yourself, you cannot give me an estate in the land, nor can you give me a property right in it. We would therefore expect that it is impossible for you to give me a lease: as we have seen, a key feature of a lease is that it confers a property right. According to the reasoning of the House of Lords in the following case, however, it *is* possible for you to give me a lease of the Palace.

*Bruton v London and Quadrant Housing Trust* (2000): The London Borough of Lambeth owned a block of flats. It planned to demolish the block and to build new flats but, whilst it was waiting to start on that work, it gave the Housing Trust permission to use the flats to provide temporary accommodation to the homeless and others in need of housing. Mr Bruton was one such person, and the Trust entered an agreement with him for the occupation of one of the flats in the block. The agreement described his right as a licence, but it appeared to give him, in substance, a right to exclusive possession and therefore, by the application of *Street v Mountford* (**7.9**), a lease. Mr Bruton was keen to have a lease, as section 11 of the Landlord and Tenant Act 1985 would then operate to impose on the Trust a duty to carry out certain types of repairs to the property. The problem for Mr Bruton was, of course, that his agreement was with the Trust, and not with Lambeth. The Trust had only a licence: in fact, Lambeth had no statutory power, in those circumstances, to give the Trust a lease. The question considered by the House of Lords, therefore, was whether the Trust, a party seemingly without its own right to exclusive possession, could give Mr Bruton a lease. The answer it gave was Yes: Mr Bruton did have a lease and the Trust was under the statutory repairing duty.

7.50  **Figure 7.4** may help to clarify the background to *Bruton*.

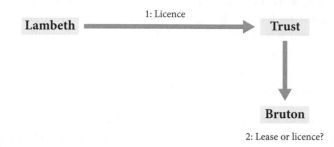

Lambeth — 1: Licence → Trust → Bruton — 2: Lease or licence?

**Figure 7.4** *Bruton v London and Quadrant Housing Trust*

7.51  It is clear that a '*Bruton* lease' does *not* give B an estate in land (eg Lord Scott in *Kay v Lambeth LBC* (2006) referred to a *Bruton* lease as a 'non-estate tenancy'). It is also clear that such a lease does *not* give B a property right (as noted by, eg, Lord Hobhouse in *Bruton* itself). This was of no concern to Mr Bruton: like Mrs Mountford (see **7.9**), his concern was not with third parties; instead, he wanted to take advantage of statutory protection available against A, the Trust. So, as Lord Hoffmann put it in *Bruton*, the crucial question for the House of Lords was: 'Did this agreement create a "lease" or a "tenancy" within the meaning of the Landlord and Tenant Act 1985 or any other legislation which refers to a lease or tenancy?'

7.52  The House of Lords approached the question in the following way. First, it looked solely to the terms of the agreement between the Trust and Mr Bruton. Although the agreement consistently referred to Mr Bruton as a licensee, we know of course that the label used by the parties is not decisive (**7.44–7.45**) and it was found that, overall, the rights given to Mr Bruton in the agreement *did* amount to exclusive possession. So, in the normal case where the Trust itself had a freehold or a lease, Mr Bruton would have had a lease and so would have qualified for the statutory protection under the 1985 Act. The second question was whether the Trust's lack of an estate prevented the agreement from giving Mr Bruton a lease. The House of Lords held that it did not. Lord Hoffmann stated that: 'the term "lease" or "tenancy" describes a relationship between two parties who are designated landlord and tenant. It is not concerned with the question of whether an agreement created an estate or other proprietary interest which may be binding on third parties.' So, it is the nature of the contract between A and B which determines if B has a lease. *If* A has an estate in the land, that lease will also give B an estate in the land and hence a property right. But, if A does *not* have such an estate, B still has a lease. As a result, Mr Bruton had a lease, the Trust was under a statutory duty to carry out repairs, and you can grant me a lease of Buckingham Palace.

## Explaining the Decision

**7.53**   When an unexpected decision is made by our top court, commentators usually greet it with a number of different explanations. The first explanation to consider must be the one given by the court itself. The basic effect of *Bruton* is to split leases into two types: the well-known standard lease, which gives B an estate in land and a property right capable of binding third parties; and the newly recognized *Bruton* lease, which gives B only contractual rights against A. The difference between the *Bruton* lease and a licence is that, in the former case, the terms of the agreement between A and B would give B a standard lease, *if* A had an estate in the land.

**7.54**   The essential difficulty with this explanation of *Bruton* is that it requires us to do three things: first, to recognize a wholly new type of lease; secondly, to provide answers to tricky questions (such as what formal requirements, if any, govern the acquisition of a *Bruton* lease?); and, thirdly, to reconsider the meaning of exclusive possession. After all, the point in *Street v Mountford* (1985) is that the right to exclusive possession is fundamental to a lease. Clearly, Mr Bruton did *not* have such a right, as he did not have a right good against the rest of the world to control access to the property. To say that Mr Bruton had a right to exclusive possession binding only on the Trust makes no sense: it is an inherent part of such a right that it is capable of binding third parties (**7.44**). Given this, it is difficult, as a matter of principle, to see why it is relevant that he *would* have had a right to exclusive possession *if* the Trust had been in a position to confer it: the Trust was not in such a position, so Mr Bruton did not have a right to exclusive possession, so he should not have a lease.

**7.55**   A second explanation is to invoke the concept of a tenancy by estoppel (Routley (2000)). This concept (which needs to be carefully distinguished from the broader doctrine of proprietary estoppel discussed at **5.93–5.138**) depends on the idea that, if A purports to give B a lease, then A cannot rely on his or her own lack of title to deny that a lease exists between A and B. Its application to the facts of *Bruton* was rejected by a majority of the Court of Appeal, on the basis that, as the agreement between the Trust and Mr Bruton was described throughout as a licence, the Trust had made no representation that Mr Bruton had a lease, and so no estoppel could arise. As Routley rightly argues, however, that reasoning seems to confuse a tenancy by estoppel (which does not require a representation, but instead requires A to give B rights which would create a lease if A had title) with the different doctrine of estoppel by representation. The more important difficulty for this explanation, however, is that it was expressly rejected by the House of Lords in *Bruton*. Lord Hoffmann stated that 'the question of tenancy by estoppel does not arise in this case. The issue is simply whether the agreement is a tenancy. It is not whether either party is entitled to deny some obligation or incident of the tenancy on the ground that the trust had no title.'

**7.56**   A third explanation of the decision in *Bruton* makes use of the concept of relativity of title (Roberts (2012)). The point is that, even if its agreement with Lambeth only amounted to a licence, if the Trust then in fact took possession of the land, it could thereby independently acquire a freehold, just as a squatter taking possession acquires such an estate.

And then, just as a squatter can grant a lease (albeit one that does not bind any parties, such as the paper owner, with a better title to the land), so can the Trust grant Mr Bruton a lease (albeit one that does not bind any parties, such as Lambeth, with a better title to the land). This analogy between a lease granted by a squatter and a *Bruton* lease was made by Lord Scott (*Kay v Lambeth LBC* (2006)). In principle, it provides a neat explanation of how a licensee, if it also has possession in fact, may grant a lease. In practice, the difficulty lies in showing that the Trust did act in such a way as to acquire its own, independent freehold. Further, this third explanation makes the position of Mr Bruton depend on the rights of the Trust, and so differs in its requirements from each of the first and second explanations.

7.57   A fourth explanation would be to admit that, as he had no right to exclusive possession, Mr Bruton did not have a lease in the usual sense of that word. But the question in the case itself was whether he had a lease or a tenancy *within the meaning of the 1985 Act*. The question of statutory interpretation, then, is whether the Trust should be able to escape a repairing duty simply because it did not have an estate in the land. This takes us to the purpose of the statute. The most likely reason for imposing a repairing duty is that it is unfair for a party with only a short-term right to occupy to have to bear the cost of work which is necessary to enable him or her to occupy comfortably and which will, in the long term, benefit someone else. That reason obtains even if the landlord does not itself have an estate in the land. On this view, the decision in *Bruton* does not require us to rethink our general view of the lease, it just means that we have to interpret the 1985 Act in a particular way. This view has much to recommend it: as we saw at **7.23**, the Law Commission (2006a) sensibly recommended that future legislation protecting residential occupiers should apply whether or not the occupier has a property right capable of binding third parties, and that very approach has now been adopted by the Welsh Assembly. The difficulty with this explanation, however, is that one of the key points of *Street v Mountford* is that, when interpreting protective legislation, the courts should simply apply the traditional, orthodox definition of a lease and should not allow that definition to be influenced by the statutory consequences of B having a lease. That is, after all, why the House of Lords rejected Lord Denning's attempts to *limit* the scope of the protective legislation by *narrowing* the definition of a lease. So, it could be said that, as the relevant legislation in *Bruton* did not make clear that even a party without a property right qualifies for statutory protection, but instead used the familiar concept of a tenancy to describe qualifying occupiers, the judges should simply have adopted the conventional meaning of that word, and found against Mr Bruton.

## The Impact of the Decision

7.58   As we have seen, the decision of the House of Lords in *Bruton*, with its recognition of a purely contractual lease, gives rise to an interesting conceptual question. Care must be taken, however, not to exaggerate its impact. First, the decision does not cast into doubt the fundamental divide between a lease, on the one hand, and a licence, on the other. At its highest, the *Bruton* decision simply means that a very limited class of agreements—where the rights given to B would amount to a right to exclusive possession, if

A had such a right to give—will be regarded as leases rather than licences, even though it is accepted that such an agreement gives B only a personal right against A. Secondly, the chief practical impact of the decision rests in the application of statutory protection. The controversy surrounding *Bruton* provides a further reason to undertake reform of the statutory protection available to occupiers, as has occurred in the Renting Homes (Wales) Act 2016, so that the scope of such protection does not depend on the question of whether B has a lease in the land. The distinction between a property right and a personal right is fundamental to the structure of land law, as it determines whether or not B's right is capable of binding a third party, but it should not determine the nature of the statutory duties owed by A to B.

# The Acquisition Question

**7.59**  In considering the application of the acquisition question to leases, we need to keep in mind two key distinctions. First, between the *creation* of a new lease and the *transfer* of an existing lease. Secondly, between *legal* leases and *equitable* leases.

## Creating a Legal Lease

**7.60**  Formality rules may determine whether A has successfully exercised A's power to grant B a legal lease. First, section 52 of the LPA 1925 (**4.33**) imposes a general requirement that a deed must be used to create a legal estate or interest in land. Secondly, sections 4 and 27 of the Land Registration Act 2002 (LRA 2002, **4.52**) impose a requirement that, if B's lease is for more than seven years, it must be registered if it is to be a legal lease. In addition, certain unusual types of lease, which are otherwise particularly hard for a third party to discover, must also be registered even if granted for seven years or less (eg a lease where B's right to exclusive possession is to start more than three months after the grant of a lease; or a 'time-share' lease, whereby B does not have a continuous right to exclusive possession but, eg, has that right only for certain weeks of the year: see further LRA 2002, s 4(1)(d)–(g) and s 27(2)(b)(ii)–(v)).

**7.61**  There is, however, an important exception to the general requirement imposed by section 52 of the LPA 1925. As a result of section 54(2) of the LPA 1925, a legal lease can be created without a deed, in fact *without any writing at all*, if three conditions are met. First, the lease must be for three years or less. Secondly, it must give B an immediate right to exclusive possession (see *Long v Tower Hamlets LBC* (1998), interpreting the words of s 54(2) that the lease must 'take effect in possession'). Thirdly, it must be at a reasonable market rent (see *Fitzkriston LLP v Panayi* (2008), interpreting the words of s 54(2) that the lease must be 'at the best rent which can be reasonably obtained without taking a fine'). The main aim of the section is to allow relatively short leases to be created informally, hence the first condition. The purpose of the second and third conditions is to protect C, a third party who might acquire land from A after A has granted an oral lease of that land to B. The second condition increases the chances of C's being able to discover B's lease; the third means that, even if C is bound by the lease, C will at least receive a reasonable rent as compensation. The second condition may cause problems to B in practice, however, as it is not uncommon for A to grant B a lease under which B's right to exclusive possession begins a few weeks in the future: in such a case, section 54(2) will not apply, and a deed must be used if the lease is to be a legal lease. Similarly, if the rent agreed by A and B is *below* the market rent, the third condition of section 54(2) is not met, and, again, a deed must be used if the lease is to be a legal lease.

**7.62**  The formality requirements for the creation of a legal lease, set out at **7.60–7.61**, can also be presented as shown in **Table 7.1**.

| Nature of B's lease | Is a deed required under LPA 1925, s 52? | Is registration required? |
|---|---|---|
| 3 years or less | Yes: unless the lease takes effect immediately in possession and is at a reasonable market rent: LPA 1925, s 54(2) | No: unless the lease is in one of the exceptional categories: LRA 2002, s 4(1)(d)–(g) and s 27(2)(b)(ii)–(v) |
| More than 3 but not more than 7 years | Yes | |
| More than 7 years | Yes | Yes |
| Implied periodic tenancy | No | No |

Table 7.1  The formality requirements for the creation of a legal lease

**7.63**  **Table 7.1** shows that no formality requirements apply to the *implied periodic tenancy*. This is because such a lease is implied from the conduct of the parties where B offers, and A accepts, payments of rent. For example, we saw at **7.30** that, in *Prudential Assurance v London Residuary Body* (1992), an agreement giving B exclusive possession of A's land until that land was needed for road-widening did not, in itself, create a lease, as it was for an uncertain term. B nonetheless had a lease as B's payment and A's acceptance of rent gave rise to an implied periodic tenancy. As the rent was calculated by reference to a yearly sum, B had a yearly periodic tenancy. On the facts of the *Prudential Assurance* case, the yearly periodic tenancy was of little real use to B. B had a succession of individual yearly leases, and A could terminate B's right to exclusive possession by simply giving the required six months' notice that A would refuse to enter into a new yearly lease. Where, instead, B pays rent calculated on a monthly basis, B then has a monthly tenancy, and the notice period is one month. Similarly, if rent is calculated on a weekly basis, B has a weekly tenancy, with a notice period of one week.

**7.64**  There is an important rule in cases where two or more parties jointly hold a periodic tenancy. Even if the parties' right to exclusive possession has lasted for a number of years, it depends technically on a series of individual periodic tenancies. The consent of each of the parties is therefore necessary for each renewal of the tenancy. So, if one of the joint tenants decides to move, and gives a notice to quit to the landlord, the joint periodic tenancy can end, once the notice period expires, even if another joint tenant wants the tenancy to continue. This rule, as explained by the House of Lords in *Hammersmith & Fulham LBC v Monk* (1992) makes perfect conceptual sense: each renewal of the periodic tenancy involves a contract between the tenants and the landlord, and all the tenants have to agree if such a contract is to exist. In practice, however, it operates harshly on a joint tenant who does not wish the tenancy to end, as he or she may then have to leave their home without their consent. As a result, its compatibility with the European Convention on Human Rights has been challenged: certainly, if the landlord is a public body such as a local authority, it will have to bear in mind the Article 8 right of a joint tenant wishing to remain in their home when deciding whether to seek possession of the property (*Sims v Dacorum BC* (2015), discussed at **2.45**).

## Transferring a Legal Lease

**7.65** In a case where a legal lease has previously been granted to A, B can acquire that lease by means of a transfer from A. It is important to note that the terms of A's lease may well include a covenant preventing, or limiting, such an assignment. If A makes a transfer in breach of such a covenant, the landlord will then have a power to terminate the lease, leaving B with nothing (**7.115**). It is therefore important for B to check that any restrictions on A's power to assign the lease have been complied with. Where A has an existing legal lease, A may instead grant B a sub-lease, by giving B a right to exclusive possession for a period shorter than that remaining on A's lease. As such a sub-lease consists of the creation of a new lease, the formality rules discussed at **7.59–7.64** are relevant. Again, B must be careful to check that the terms of A's lease do not contain a relevant prohibition on such sub-leases.

**7.66** Where A attempts to transfer an existing legal lease to B, a deed must be used: section 52 of the LPA 1925. There is, in particular, a trap for B in the case where A's original lease was created orally under section 54(2) of the LPA 1925 (**7.61**). Even though that legal lease was created orally, a deed is necessary for its *transfer* (see eg *Crago v Julian* (1992)). The general requirement in section 52 of the LPA 1925 applies, as the exception in section 54(2) is expressly limited to the 'creation' of leases. Where A's lease is registered, any transfer of that legal lease to B will also of course require B to be registered in place of A (LRA 2002, s 27(2)(a)).

## Acquiring a New Equitable Lease

**7.67** If A has an estate in land, it is *not* the case that A can simply choose whether to grant B a legal lease or an equitable lease: 'a landlord does not elect to grant an equitable tenancy; such a tenancy arises in certain specified circumstances recognized by equity' (*Alexander-David v Hammersmith & Fulham LBC* (2010)). Those circumstances involve A's coming under a duty to grant B a legal lease. So if B's right does not count as a legal lease because it does not have the required *content* (eg because it is not a right to exclusive possession; or it is not a right to exclusive possession for a certain term), then it cannot be an equitable lease. If, however, B's planned right does have the required content, but B has not met the requirements for the *acquisition* of a legal lease, it may be possible for B to show that, instead, he or she has an equitable lease.

**7.68**   A well-known example of this point is *Walsh v Lonsdale* (1882, **5.87**). In that case, Lonsdale was under a contractual duty to give Walsh a right to exclusive possession of a mill for seven years. The content of Walsh's right therefore met the requirements of a lease. Lonsdale had not yet performed its contractual duty by granting Walsh a lease, but Walsh took possession nonetheless and paid rent, which Lonsdale accepted. There were two possible ways of characterizing the parties' relationship. The first was that an implied periodic tenancy had arisen (**7.63**). Such a lease would arise simply from the payment and acceptance of rent, and so would not include the specific further duties agreed by the parties, such as a duty of Walsh to pay rent in advance if Lonsdale demanded it. The second was that, as Lonsdale was under a contractual duty to grant Walsh a lease, Walsh had an equitable lease. Such a lease, arising as a result of the parties' contract, *would* include the specific further duties agreed by the parties, including Walsh's duty to pay rent in advance. The court adopted the second view: this meant that Walsh had been under a duty to pay rent in advance, and Lonsdale had acted lawfully by seeking to recover that rent.

**7.69**   In *Walsh v Lonsdale*, then, the absence of any formal grant of a lease did not prevent the creation of an equitable lease. But we must be careful: this does *not* mean that formality rules are irrelevant when considering equitable leases. Such rules may be relevant if B bases the claim for an equitable lease on A's being under a *contractual* duty to grant B a lease. Section 2 of the Law of Property (Miscellaneous Provisions) Act 1989 states that a contract for the sale or other disposition of an interest in land must be in writing signed by both parties and must contain all the terms expressly agreed by the parties (**4.5–4.31**). An exception is made for a lease that meets the conditions imposed by section 54(2) of the LPA 1925 (**7.61**). After all, since such a lease can be granted without any writing, it would be odd if a contract to grant it could not also be oral. A contract to grant any lease outside the scope of section 54(2) of the LPA 1925 is, however, caught by section 2 of the 1989 Act and so must be in writing. In such a case, then, if the dealings between A and B are purely oral, B cannot claim that A is under a contractual duty to grant B a lease.

**7.70**   It is important to note, however, that if B can show that A is under a *non-contractual* duty to grant B a lease, an equitable lease can arise, even in the absence of writing. First, section 2 of the 1989 Act applies only to *contracts*: it does not prevent B from arguing that A's duty arises from some other source, such as proprietary estoppel (see eg *Whittaker v Kinnear* (2011), disagreeing with Lord Scott's expressly obiter view on this point in *Cobbe v Yeoman's Row Management Ltd* (2008)). Secondly, whilst section 53(1)(a) of the LPA 1925 states a general rule that writing is required for the creation or disposal of an interest in land, it also allows for such creation or disposal to occur by operation of law, and it seems clear that if A's duty to B is non-contractual, it does indeed arise by operation of law. Certainly, it has been accepted that a proprietary estoppel claim can, even in the absence of writing, lead to A's being under a duty to grant B a lease (see eg *Yaxley v Gotts* (2000), *Herbert v Doyle* (2010)). It is true that, in those cases, the Court of Appeal relied on section 2(5) of the 1989 Act and found that, as B's right arose under a constructive trust, it fell within a statutory exception to the need for writing. In such cases, it is however very hard to find any genuine trust, as A was simply under a duty to grant B a lease. The better analysis, therefore, is that section 2 of the 1989 Act never applied in the first place as B's claim was not based on a contract: 'the fact that, if there was a contract, it would be void is irrelevant: indeed the very reason for mounting the proprietary estoppel claim is that there is no enforceable contract' (Neuberger (2009), **5.114–5.116**).

7.71   When B does rely on a contract with A as the source of A's duty to grant B a lease, and thus as the source of B's equitable lease, it is often said that an equitable lease will arise only if a court would order specific performance of A's contractual duty (see eg *Coatsworth v Johnson* (1866)). A careful historical analysis has shown, however, that there is no sound foundation for this supposed requirement (Gardner (1987)). The point may instead be that the key question is not whether, in fact, specific performance would have been ordered at a particular point in time, but rather whether A's duty is in general of a type where specific performance might be ordered (**5.90**).

### Transferring an Equitable Lease

7.72   In a case where A already holds an equitable lease, it may be possible for A to transfer that equitable lease to B. As we noted at **7.65**, B must take care that A's agreement with A's landlord does not impose any relevant restriction on A's power to assign the lease. As for formality requirements, it seems that, even if A's lease arose purely orally (perhaps as a result of proprietary estoppel), the transfer of that lease to B must be made in writing, as it is caught by both section 53(1)(a) and section 53(1)(c) of the LPA 1925.

## Priority and the Defences Question

7.73   The key difference between a lease and a licence is that a lease (with the exception of the *Bruton* lease: **7.49–7.58**) is a property right and so is capable of binding third parties. As we saw in **Chapter 3**, however, property rights do not *always* bind third parties: it may be possible for a third party to take priority, either by relying on an earlier property right or by establishing a defence to B's pre-existing property right. In considering the possible defences available to C against B's pre-existing lease, it is again vital to distinguish between legal leases and equitable leases.

### Defences for C Where B has a Pre-Existing Legal Lease

7.74   The general position, of course, is that it is very difficult for C to have a defence against a pre-existing legal property right. This is certainly true of legal leases. In particular, if B has a legal lease of registered land, it will be *impossible* for C to use the lack of registration defence (provided by the LRA 2002, s 29) against B's legal lease. This is for two reasons. First, if B's lease is for more than seven years, or is one of the exceptional shorter leases which requires registration (**7.59**), then it can only be a legal lease if it has been registered: by definition, then, C will not be able to rely on the lack of registration defence. Secondly, if B's lease is for seven years or less, it can be a legal lease in the absence of registration. Such a legal lease counts as an *overriding interest* under paragraph 1 of Schedule 3 to the LRA 2002 and so is immune to the lack of registration defence.

### Defences for C Where B has a Pre-Existing Equitable Lease

7.75   If B has an equitable lease, B may protect that right by the entry of a notice on the register. This will serve to ensure that C, if later acquiring a competing right in the land, will not be able to use the lack of registration defence against B's equitable lease. If there is nothing on the register recording B's equitable lease, and C meets the requirements of section 29 of the LRA 2002 (**11.9**), then C will be able to take free from B's right, *unless* B is in actual occupation of the land at the relevant time (**11.37–11.59**). It is important to note that, unlike a legal lease, an equitable lease can be an overriding interest *only* if it is protected by B's actual occupation of the land. Paragraph 1 of Schedule 3 to the LRA 2002 protects only legal leases, and not equitable leases, as it refers to a lease *granted* to B, and that word has been interpreted as applying only to legal leases (see *City and Permanent Building Society v Miller* (1952)).

7.76   As a result, there is a crucial difference between legal leases and equitable leases when it comes to defences. A legal lease can bind C, a party later acquiring a registered right in the land for value, even if B is not in actual occupation of the land; an equitable lease can bind such a third party only if it was either protected by a notice on the register or was protected by B's actual occupation of the land at the relevant time.

## The Ending of a Lease

7.77   A lease may be a good thing, but it must come to an end. After all, the key difference between a lease and a freehold is that a lease is a right to exclusive possession for a *term*. The most natural way for a lease to end is the expiry of its period: for example, a five-year lease granted on 31 December 2014 will not last into 2020. A lease will also end if one of the parties exercises a power to terminate the lease early. It is, for example, common for a business lease to include a 'break clause': a term giving the tenant a power to end the lease early, which is useful to the tenant if the premises prove to be unsuitable, or a lower rent is available elsewhere.

7.78   We also saw that, in *Berrisford v Mexfield* (2012, **7.34**), the terms of the lease gave the landlord the power to terminate if certain events occurred. Where a landlord attempts to exercise such a power, it is said to *forfeit* the lease. As such forfeiture can have severe consequences for a tenant, particularly in a residential context, both equity and statute impose limits on the landlord's power to forfeit the lease. Forfeiture is almost always a response to a breach by B of one of the covenants contained in the lease, and so we will consider it when examining leasehold covenants (**7.115–7.129**).

7.79   The existence of a lease depends on there being a relationship between two parties: the landlord and the tenant. So, if B, the tenant, also acquires the estate of A, the landlord, the lease will end, as B cannot be both landlord and tenant. In such a case, B's lease is said to *merge* into the greater estate acquired by B. Such merger can cause something of a trap for B: if B, as tenant, had an easement over some other land, it would seem that the merger should also cause the easement to end, as the easement was an incident of B's lease, which no longer exists. This point, and the Court of Appeal's controversial view of it in *Wall v Collins* (2007), is discussed at **9.14**.

7.80  It is also possible for a lease to end as a result of the doctrine of frustration, if a change in circumstances means that the tenant will no longer receive the essential benefit for which he or she bargained. It had previously been thought that, as long as B had the right to exclusive possession for the agreed term, B would necessarily have that essential benefit, and so the doctrine of frustration could not apply to leases. In *National Carriers Ltd v Panalpina (Northern) Ltd* (1981), however, the House of Lords took a different view, and held that a sufficiently radical change in circumstances could, in theory, lead to a lease's being discharged by frustration. The case involved a lease of a warehouse by a warehousing company, and a road closure prevented the company from making its planned use of the warehouse. On the facts, there was no frustration, as the closure lasted for only 20 months of the ten-year lease, but the House of Lords did accept that frustration of a lease was, in theory, possible.

7.81  Similarly, it was also once thought that a serious breach by a landlord of its duties under a lease could not give the tenant a power to terminate the lease: such a breach would not interfere with B's right to exclusive possession and so would not deprive B of the essential benefit of the lease. Again, however, the modern approach is different: it has been recognized that the continuation of B's right to exclusive possession may not always suffice to give B the essential benefit of his or her bargain. So if, for example, A's serious breaches of his or her duty to repair residential premises render them unfit for B to live in, the 'central purpose' of the parties' bargain will be jeopardized and B may then choose to terminate the lease and thus be free to move out and cease paying rent (see *Hussein v Mehlman* (1992), the reasoning in which was approved by the Court of Appeal in *Chartered Trust plc v Davies* (1997)).

7.82  The courts' willingness to contemplate applying the doctrines of frustration and of termination of breach to leases rests on a sensible recognition that B's central purpose in acquiring a lease may not be the simple acquisition of an estate in the land. It has also led to some speculation as to whether, in the modern law, the lease is now seen as primarily a creature of contract rather than of property. We will now examine that issue.

## Contract or Property?

7.83  The first point to note is that asking if a particular type of right, such as a lease, is contract or property is like asking if a tree is large or evergreen: it can be both. In the usual case, a lease consists both of a contract between A and B *and* the grant of a property right by A to B. There are exceptions. We have seen both that it is possible to grant a lease without making a contract (**7.40**) and, in the case of the *Bruton* lease, it is possible to have a purely contractual lease that does not give B a property right (**7.49–7.58**). The point is that contract relates to the *acquisition* question, as a contract is a means of acquiring rights, whereas property relates to the *content* question, as a property right is a type of right.

7.84   How then should we understand an analysis such as that of Lord Browne-Wilkinson in *Hammersmith & Fulham LBC v Monk* (1992), which contrasts the 'contractual' and the 'proprietary' approaches to leases? The question in that case was whether the consent of both tenants was necessary for the continuation of a joint periodic tenancy. The answer was Yes: see 7.64. This was simply a result of the fact that occupation of land under a periodic tenancy, even if it continues for a long time, occurs under a succession of periodic tenancies. Each new periodic tenancy requires the consent of all the parties to it. This does not mean, however, that a lease is better seen as contract rather than property. Consent is crucial in the transfer and creation of property rights even if no contract is involved: this is the case, for example, when A makes a gift of land to B or when A declares a trust of land in B's favour.

7.85   The same analysis can explain the application to leases of the doctrines of frustration and of termination for breach (7.80–7.82). The key point again is that those doctrines reflect the fact that, where an arrangement takes effect because of the parties' consent, that consent may be given on a particular shared basis. If that basis fails, the arrangement may cease to bind. The important modern development lies not in seeing the lease as about contract rather than property, but rather in recognizing that the basis of the arrangement does not consist solely of B's acquiring a right to exclusive possession of land. As Bright has noted, the courts have instead recognized that the fundamental shared basis of the lease agreement may be possession *plus* provision of land fit for use, for example as a warehouse or as a home (Bright (2007)).

7.86   The remaining significant case said to contribute to the 'contractualization' of the lease is *Bruton v London and Quadrant Housing Trust* (2000). As noted at 7.58, it is important not to exaggerate the impact of that decision. Whilst it does recognize that, in exceptional circumstances, B may have a purely contractual lease, it does not alter the fact that, in the vast majority of cases, where A does herself have an estate in land, the creation of a lease will involve *both* a contract between the parties *and* B's acquisition of a property right in land.

# Leasehold Covenants

## Introduction to Leasehold Covenants

7.87   We have seen that as a minimum a lease must grant exclusive possession for a term of years. However, the parties will invariably wish to define their relationship in more detail by agreeing their respective obligations through leasehold covenants. For instance, if nothing else the landlord will want the tenant to covenant to pay the rent and the tenant will want the landlord to covenant to give him or her quiet possession. The parties will also generally agree who is obliged to repair and insure the premises, as well as who is to pay for that insurance and repair. Controls on the way in which the tenant can use the premises are also common as are restrictions on the tenant's ability to dispose of their lease without the landlord's consent. Certain of these covenants may be implied, for instance in a lease of a dwelling for less than seven years the landlord is required to keep the exterior, structure, and utility services in repair (see the Landlord and Tenant Act 1985, s 11(1)). However, many covenants will be express. Indeed, a good portion of a written lease is devoted to covenants given by the tenant to the landlord (the tenant's covenants) and by the landlord to the tenant (the landlord's covenants).

7.88  As the content of these covenants can vary widely depending upon the type of lease, the question which we will consider is how these obligations affect those who subsequently became interested in the premises. Our primary focus will be upon the parties who take an assignment (meaning transfer) of either the landlord's entire reversionary interest or an assignment of the tenant's entire lease. Throughout we will refer to the original parties to the lease as LO (original landlord) and TO (original tenant) and the assignees of the reversion as LA (landlord's assignee) and of the lease TA (tenant's assignee). **Figure 7.5** sets out this web of relationships.

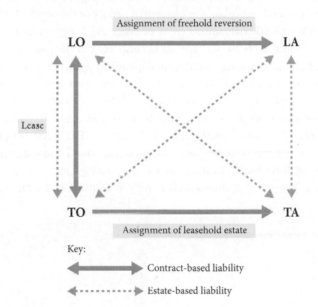

Figure 7.5  Leasehold covenant relationships

We will also briefly consider how a party who is granted a lesser interest out of the lease, for instance a sub-tenant (ST) or a mortgagee, may be affected by the tenant's covenants.

7.89  This is essentially a defences question because we will be asking when these parties have a defence to an action for breach of a leasehold covenant. The answer is dependent upon two principal factors. First, is the dual character of the lease as both a contract and a property interest so that liability may be derived either from the contractual relationship of LO and TO (privity of contract) or the estate-based relationship of the parties to the lease at the relevant time (privity of estate). Secondly, there is a temporal factor— remember leases can be granted for 999 years or even longer. It is vital to know whether the lease was granted before or after 1 January 1996 because the law was amended as from that date by the Landlord and Tenant (Covenants) Act 1995 (LTCA 1995).

**7.90**  We also need to consider the remedies available to the parties should a breach of covenant against a liable party be proven. We will concentrate, in particular, on the right of a landlord to forfeit the lease for a breach of a tenant's covenant. This draconian remedy is tempered by the tenant's right to apply for relief from forfeiture.

**7.91**  Lastly, we will place the significance of leasehold covenants in the context of the ownership of flats when the lease is employed to overcome the difficulties of passing liability for positive obligations relating to land. This use of the lease in flat ownership is contrasted with the purpose-designed, but little used, commonhold title.

## Privity of Estate

**7.92**  Students will be familiar from their study of contract law with the concept of privity of contract which will exist between LO and TO as the original parties to the lease contract. However, we need to explain the concept of privity of estate which is central to the enforcement of leasehold covenants. Privity of estate exists between the current parties to the leasehold estate. Initially, this will be LO and TO but the parties within privity of estate may change during the leasehold term depending upon in whom the lease and the reversion are respectively vested. Thus, if LO assigns the reversion to LA, privity of estate will exist between TO and LA as the current parties to the leasehold estate and, because LO is no longer a party to the leasehold estate, he or she ceases to come within privity of estate. Likewise, if TO assigns the leasehold estate to TA, privity of estate will exist between LO, or if the reversion has been assigned, LA, and TA and again TO (like LO) will cease to be within privity of estate (see *City of London Corp v Fell* (1994) at 464 per Lord Templeman). **Figure 7.6** shows these privity of contract and estate relationships.

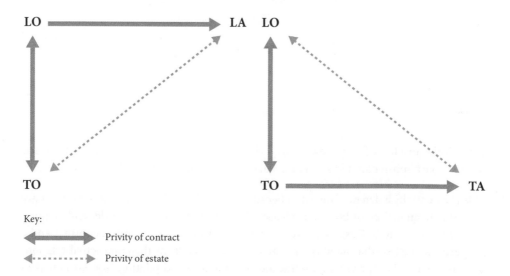

Figure 7.6 Privity of contract and estate relationships

**7.93**  Privity of estate operates to effectively annex the right to sue and be sued upon those covenants, which are very closely associated with the lease, to the leasehold estate itself. Nourse LJ, in the Court of Appeal decision in *Fell* ((1993) at 604), explained that privity of estate operates because '[t]he contractual obligations which touch and concern the land having become imprinted on the estate, the tenancy is capable of existence as a species of property independently of the contract'. The distinct strength of privity of estate lies in the fact that it encompasses both positive and negative covenants that form part of the leasehold estate. We will see that this provides an advantage over freehold covenants (see Chapter 10) and it is this feature which led to the use of the lease to facilitate flat ownership (see 7.130-7.136).

## Pre-1996 Contractual Enforceability (LO and TO)

**7.94**  Privity of contract does not fluctuate. LO and TO remain liable in contract upon all their covenants, both personal and those that relate to the leasehold land, throughout the lease term even though they may assign their respective estates. The parties need to look at how their liabilities are framed by the lease contract. For instance, the parties might expressly agree that they are liable only whilst they are parties to the leasehold estate. However, it is unusual for a landlord to agree to limit a tenant's contractual liability in this manner. A more common possibility, particularly in commercial leases, is that the parties agree that the landlord can increase the rent after a stated number of years to reflect current market rents in what is generally called a rent review. In these circumstances, TO will continue to be bound by privity of contract by the agreed rent review provisions even though they have assigned the lease by the time the rent review takes effect (*Centrovincial Estates plc v Bulk Storage Ltd* (1983), *Selous Street Properties Ltd v Oronel Fabrics Ltd* (1984)). It is only where the rent is varied pursuant to a separate agreement, to which TO is not a contractual party, that he or she will not be bound (*Friends Provident Life Office v British Railways Board* (1997), see also LTCA 1995, s 18).

**7.95**  The continued contractual liability of LO and TO can operate particularly harshly against TO (see Law Commission (1988), paras 3.1-3.3). TO could be sued, for instance on a covenant to pay rent or service charge, long after they have assigned their lease. A possibility that many tenants do not appreciate, as Lord Nicholls described in *Hindcastle Ltd v Barbara Attenborough & Associates Ltd* (1997) at 83:

> *a person of modest means is understandably shocked when out of the blue he receives a rent demand from the landlord of property he once leased. Unlike the landlord, he had no control over the identity of the assignees down the line and had no opportunity to reject them as financially unsound.*

TO does have two possible means of redress. First, they will have a restitutionary cause of action against the defaulting assignee (*Moule v Garrett* (1872)). Secondly, TO may recover from TA by relying on an express or implied indemnity covenant from TA (see LPA 1925, s 77). TA in turn may sue the next assignee by relying upon a similar indemnity covenant and so on down the chain of assignees until the real culprit is called upon to fulfil his or her obligations. However, the efficacy of this chain of indemnity covenants is limited by the strength of each link, for instance a link may be broken by an assignee's death or insolvency (*RPH Ltd v Mirror Group Newspapers and Mirror Group Holdings* (1992)).

**7.96**   The unenviable position of TO is improved marginally by the LTCA 1995. A landlord who wishes to recover a fixed sum from TO (eg in respect of unpaid rent, service charge, or liquidated damages for breach of covenant) must give notice to TO within six months of the sum becoming due (s 17). If TO pays this sum, they can claim an overriding lease to secure the sum paid (s 19). This overriding lease is interposed between the current landlord and tenant so that TO becomes the immediate tenant of the landlord and the immediate landlord of the defaulting current tenant. TO is then able to claim the rental due against the defaulting current tenant and take appropriate enforcement action, for instance by forfeiting the lease and finding a new, hopefully financially sound, tenant.

**7.97**   TO's liability will cease if the original leasehold term comes to an end and is replaced by a new lease. For instance, TA may surrender the original lease and obtain a re-grant of a new lease. A similar termination of contractual liability will occur where TA extends the lease by statute, for instance under the Landlord and Tenant Act 1954 (applicable to certain commercial leases, see *City of London Corp v Fell* (1994)).

## Post-1996 Contractual Enforceability (LO and TO)

**7.98**   One of the primary drivers behind the passing of the LTCA 1995 was to address the unfairness (particularly to TO) of the contractual liability already described. It is intended to provide the tenant or the landlord, notwithstanding the terms of the lease, with 'an exit route from his future liabilities' (*London Diocesan Fund v Phithwa* (2005) at [16] per Lord Nicholls).

### Release of TO

**7.99**   Section 5 of the LTCA 1995 operates to release TO, under a lease entered into on or after 1 January 1996, from contractual liability on the tenant's covenants when they assign their lease to TA. There is an important qualification, however. Where TO requires the consent of his or her current landlord to assign the lease, the landlord may withhold consent unless TO enters into an authorized guarantee agreement (AGA) under which TO guarantees TA's future performance of the tenant's covenants including the payment of rent and service charge (s 16). If TA in turns assigns the lease, he or she too may be required to enter into an AGA to guarantee the next assignee's performance of the tenant's covenants (see s 16 and *K/S Victoria Street v House of Fraser (Stores Management) Ltd* (2012)). Devices to try and circumvent the release of TO (or their guarantor), or arrangements that would have that effect, are rendered void by section 25 of the LTCA 1995. For instance, TO's AGA can only guarantee TA's performance and not the performance of any future assignees of the lease and an assignment by a tenant to their guarantor is prohibited (*K/S Victoria Street v House of Fraser (Stores*

*Management) Ltd* (2012), *Tindall Cobham 1 Ltd v Adda Hotels* (2014), *EMI Group Ltd v O&H Q1 Ltd* (2016)).

### Release of LO

**7.100**  The release of LO from contractual liability is not automatic upon the assignment of the reversion on a lease entered into on or after 1 January 1996. LO may request a release by serving notice upon TO not less than four weeks before the assignment of the reversion (s 6). If TO refuses to agree to the release, the court may grant the release where it is satisfied that it is reasonable to do so (s 8).

**7.101**  A potential way around this process has emerged from the decision in *London Diocesan Fund v Phithwa* (2005)). Although the LTCA 1995 cannot be excluded or varied (s 25), the majority of the House of Lords in *Phithwa* decided that a limitation of liability contained within the original covenant and thus, at least technically agreed to by TO, did not offend this prohibition. The majority construed the LTCA 1996 as providing an additional route, rather than an exclusive route, by which contractual liability could be limited. However Lord Walker, alive to the possibility that landlords could so simply bypass the tenant's approval of a release, provided a robust dissent (at [35]).

## The Position of Assignees LA and TA

**7.102**  We now turn to look, on the one hand, at the ability of assignees of the reversion (LA) to enforce the tenant's covenants and assignees of the lease (TA) to enforce the landlord's covenants. Here we talk of passing *the benefit* of leasehold covenants because the issue is whether LA or TA *can sue* upon the leasehold covenants. On the other hand, we also need to consider the liability of assignees of the reversion (LA) to observe and perform the landlord's covenants and of assignees of the lease (TA) to observe and perform the tenant's covenants. Here we talk of the passing of *the burden* of the leasehold covenants because the issue is whether LA or TA *can be sued* upon the leasehold covenants. We will refer to LA and TA but the same principles apply to subsequent assignees of both the reversion from LA and subsequent assignees of the lease from TA. However, remember that these principles apply only to assignees of the whole reversion or leasehold estate where privity of estate exists. We will look at the position of persons taking a lesser interest, for instance a sub-lessee or a mortgagee, in **7.112**. Again, the principles differ according to whether the lease was created before or after 1 January 1996, although when the assignment itself takes place is of no consequence.

### The Landlord's Covenants in Pre-1996 Leases

**7.103**  The passing of the benefit and the burden of the landlord's covenants given by LO to TO is governed by section 142 of the LPA 1925. Upon an assignment of the reversion, the section enables TO to sue LA because the burden of the landlord's covenants passes. Upon an assignment of the lease from TO to TA, the section passes the benefit of the landlord's covenants so TA can sue the current landlord; that is, either LO or LA—see **Figure 7.7**.

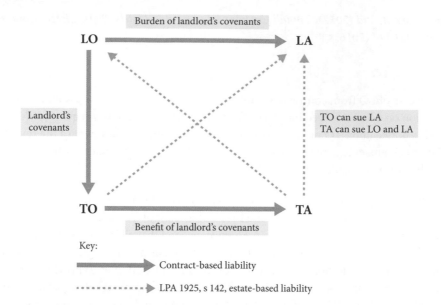

Key:

———————▶ Contract-based liability

┄┄┄┄┄┄┄▶ LPA 1925, s 142, estate-based liability

**Figure 7.7** Law of Property Act 1925, s 142: benefit (who can sue) and burden (who can be sued) of landlord's covenants

The section does not necessarily pass the burden and benefit of all the landlord's covenants as the section operates only in relation to those covenants that have 'reference to the subject matter of the lease'. This is a concept we will examine in **7.105**.

### The Tenant's Covenants in Pre-1996 Leases

7.104    The passing of the benefit of the tenant's covenants is governed by section 141 of the LPA 1925. This section thus enables LA to sue TO (or TA) for the rent or the other tenant's covenants given by TO to LO; for instance, governing the use of the premises or restricting the tenant's ability to dispose of the lease—see **Figure 7.8**. Again, these covenants must have 'reference to the subject matter of the lease'.

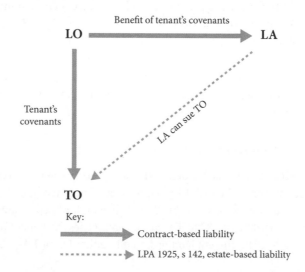

Key:

———————▶ Contract-based liability

┄┄┄┄┄┄┄▶ LPA 1925, s 142, estate-based liability

**Figure 7.8** Law of Property Act, s 141: benefit of tenant's covenants (who can sue)

The passing of the burden of the tenant's covenants is governed not by statute but by the common law provided there is privity of estate: see *Spencer's Case* (1583). This case has for centuries provided the basis upon which TA is bound to observe and perform the tenant's covenants given by TO that 'touch and concern the land' (see **Figure 7.9**).

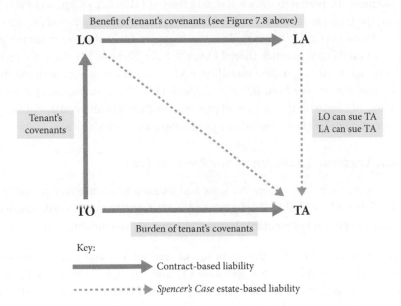

Figure 7.9 *Spencer's Case*: burden of tenant's covenants (who can be sued)

### Qualifying Covenants in Pre-1996 Leases

**7.105** We have noted that sections 141 and 142 apply to covenants that have 'reference to the subject matter of the lease' and that *Spencer's Case* applies only to covenants that 'touch and concern the land'. The two expressions have the same meaning (*Caern Motor Services Ltd v Texaco* (1994)). They operate to exclude those leasehold covenants which are in essence personal to the identity of a specific landlord or tenant rather than affecting the premises themselves. Both concepts have proved rather elusive to definitely pin down but the clearest criteria are found in the judgment of Lord Oliver in *P&A Swift Investments v Combined English Stores Group plc* ((1989) at 640)—remember that the reference to 'reversioner' refers to LA:

> ... the following provides a satisfactory working test of whether, in any given case, a covenant touches and concerns the land: (1) the covenant benefits only the reversioner for the time being, and if separated from the reversion ceases to be of benefit to the covenantee; (2) the covenant affects the nature, quality, mode of user or value of the land of the reversioner; (3) the covenant is not expressed to be personal ...; (4) the fact that a covenant to pay a sum of money will not prevent it from touching and concerning the land so long as the three foregoing conditions are satisfied and the covenant is connected with something to be done on to or in relation to the land.

The vast majority of covenants commonly found in leases will satisfy this test but there are one or two tricky common areas where inconsistent outcomes have resulted. A surety's covenant, which was in issue in *Swift*, was held to satisfy the test but a covenant to repay a tenant's deposit does not even though it serves a similar surety function (*Hua Chiao Commercial Bank Ltd v Chiap Hua Industries Ltd* (1987)). An option for a tenant to purchase the reversion does not satisfy the test (*Woodall v Clifton* (1905)) but an option for the tenant to renew his or her lease does so (*Beesly v Hallwood Estates* (1961), *Phillips v Mobil Oil Co Ltd* (1989)). The court accepted that this latter anomaly arose purely from established practice (*Mobil Oil* at 891 per Nicholls LJ). Nevertheless, to be enforceable against third parties (including LA) the covenant to renew should be protected by registration (see both *Beesly* and *Mobil Oil*). This result appears inconsistent with section 142 and with the concept of privity of estate but is retained in statutory form where an option to renew is granted in a post-1996 lease (see s 3(6)(b)).

### Equitable Leases and Assignments of Pre-1996 Leases

7.106   Privity of estate exists only where the lease and its assignment are recognized at law—questions that we looked at in **7.60–7.62** and **7.66**, respectively. Accordingly, we need to consider the position of equitable leases and equitable assignments (see **7.67–7.72**).

7.107   There is a distinction between the operation of sections 141 and 142 of the LPA 1925 and *Spencer's Case* in this respect. Sections 141 and 142 operate whether the original lease, or the assignment of the reversion, is legal or equitable. LA of an equitable lease is thus able to sue and be sued upon the leasehold covenants but he or she will only be able to sue TO because to pass the burden of the tenant's covenants *Spencer's Case* requires that the lease (and its assignment) must be legal in form (*Purchase v Lichfield Brewery* (1915)). This distinction is inconvenient and one-sided when TO may expressly assign the benefit of the landlord's covenants under an equitable lease to TA to enable TA to sue upon these covenants.

7.108   Various ways around this problem have been devised and suggested. Denning LJ in *Boyer v Warbey* (1953) offered a simple, but unsatisfactory, solution by suggesting that the fusion of law and equity by the Judicature Act 1873 overcame the distinction. A direct link between LO (or LA) and TA might be created through a separate express contractual nexus or as a result of an implied legal periodic tenancy arising from LO's (or LA's) acceptance of rent from TA. Negative tenant's covenants may be enforced against TA through the doctrine in *Tulk v Moxhay* (1848)—see **Chapter 10**. However, perhaps the most effective route lies in the threat that LA may exercise a right of re-entry to forfeit the equitable lease if TA does not perform the tenant's covenants. We consider forfeiture in **7.115–7.129**. At this point it is sufficient to appreciate three features. First, the landlord's right to re-enter and forfeit a lease for breach of covenant will terminate the equitable lease. Secondly, this right to re-enter, as a separate interest in land, is independent of the landlord's right to sue upon the covenant and will be effective against TA. Thirdly, a leasehold covenant that 'touches and concerns' the land is regarded as part of the land, or to use Nourse LJ's expression, 'imprinted' on the land. Employing these three features, a landlord can rely on a breach of a leasehold covenant to exercise a right of re-entry and forfeit the equitable lease even though he or she is unable to sue TA directly on the covenant to recover damages or obtain an injunction.

## Post-1996 Leases and the Landlord and Tenant (Covenants) Act 1995

7.109  The LTCA 1995 attempts to overcome the principal difficulties of the pre-1996 law governing the enforcement of leasehold covenants. We have already seen how it addresses the continuing contractual liability of TO and LO. We now need to consider how the LTCA 1995 operates to pass the benefit and burden of leasehold covenants to LA and TA. The Act by section 3 does so by providing a statutory framework of enforceability in relation to leases entered into on or after 1 January 1996. Thus, TA is entitled to enforce the landlord's covenants and is bound by the tenant's covenants (s 3(2)) and LA is likewise entitled to enforce the tenant's covenants and is bound by the landlord's covenants (s 3(3)).

7.110  The LTCA 1995 dispenses with the need for the covenant to 'touch and concern' the land or 'to have reference to the subject matter' of the lease. The statutory framework of enforceability applies to all express or implied leasehold covenants unless the covenant is expressed to be personal to a particular person (s 2 and s 28). There is thus a shift in emphasis from having to prove that the covenant is transmissible to a presumption that it is so unless the parties have expressly provided that the covenant is personal. In *BHP Petroleum Great Britain Ltd v Chesterfield Properties Ltd* (2002) the covenant in question was for the landlord to carry out repairs and thus was a covenant that clearly would have touched and concerned the land or had reference to the subject matter of the lease. Nevertheless, because the covenant was expressed to be personal to Chesterfield, it did not qualify as a landlord's covenant for the purposes of the Act and Chesterfield could not seek a release from contractual liability (see 7.101). Whilst the result seems correct, the decision presents the danger that TO also may be unable to obtain a release from contractual liability where a tenant's covenant is expressed to be personal.

7.111  The issue then is to determine when a covenant is expressed to be personal. We can see from *Chesterfield* that the parties can expressly state in the written terms of the lease that a covenant is personal. However, in *First Penthouse Ltd v Channel Hotels and Properties (UK) Ltd* (2003) the court decided that the personal character of a covenant may also be expressed through the nature of the obligation imposed. This possibility just seems to hark back to the previous 'touch and concern' test (see 7.105). The statutory framework of enforceability established by the LTCA 1995 also removes the distinction between legal and equitable leases. Both landlord's and tenant's covenants in post-1996 leases will be enforceable regardless of whether the lease or related assignment is legal or equitable.

## The Position of Sub-Tenants

7.112  Where a tenant grants a lease for a shorter period than his or her own lease, even if that period is just one day, a sub-lease is granted. This sub-lease creates a new estate in the land with contractual liability and privity of estate between the tenant (as landlord under the sub-lease) and the sub-tenant (ST). Privity of estate will also exist between the tenant (as landlord under the sub-lease) and an assignee of the sub-lease (SA). However, there is no privity of estate between the landlord under the head lease and ST. ST thus is not bound by, nor can he or she enforce, the leasehold covenants in the head lease.

7.113    Nevertheless, it is unwise for ST to ignore the head lease covenants. First, the sub-lease is likely to include a covenant requiring ST to observe the covenants in the head lease. The benefit of this covenant may be expressly conferred upon the head landlord so that he or she can also enforce this covenant (*Amsprop Trading Ltd v Harris Distribution Ltd* (1997)). The second reason why ST cannot ignore the head lease covenants arises because the sub-lease is created out of the head lease and will fail if the head lease is brought to an early end. For instance, if ST breaches a covenant in the head lease, the head landlord may exercise their right of re-entry and forfeit the head lease so that both the head tenant and ST will face eviction. Lastly, the negative covenants in the head lease (ie covenants that do not necessitate incurring expense) will be directly enforceable by the head landlord against ST under the doctrine of *Tulk v Moxhay* which we will consider in **Chapter 9** (see *Hemingway Securities Ltd v Dunraven Ltd* (1996)).

## Remedies for Breach of Covenant

7.114    The usual contractual remedy of common law damages, and the equitable discretionary remedies of specific performance and injunction, are available to remedy a breach of either the landlord's or tenant's covenants. There is in addition a statutory right for a tenant to obtain specific performance of a landlord's covenant to repair a dwelling-house (Landlord and Tenant Act 1985, s 17). By contrast, only in exceptional circumstances is a court likely to grant a landlord specific performance of a tenant's covenant to repair (*Rainbow Estates Ltd v Tokenhold* (1999)). A landlord's right to claim damages from a tenant for breach of a repairing covenant is also subject to a limited measure of statutory control. First, the damages recoverable are limited to the amount by which the value of the landlord's reversion is diminished (Landlord and Tenant Act 1927, s 17) and, secondly, where the lease is over seven years (with at least three years remaining) the landlord must follow the stipulated notice procedure (see Leasehold Property (Repairs) Act 1938). Where the breach is a failure to pay rent, the landlord may decide to sue the tenant in debt as the rent becomes due for payment. There is also the possibility, where the lease is of commercial premises, of the landlord recovering rent by seizing and selling the tenant's goods under the Commercial Rent Arrears Recovery scheme (see Tribunals, Courts and Enforcement Act 2007, Part 3).

### Forfeiture

7.115    However, the primary route by which a landlord obtains redress for breach of a tenant's covenant is through the process of forfeiture; accordingly, we will concentrate our attention on this remedy. Forfeiture is a powerful remedy since it will operate to extinguish the tenant's lease by the exercise of a landlord's right to re-entry the premises. Although forfeiture is an effective weapon for the landlord, it can produce a heavy-handed response. It is possible for a tenant of a long-term lease to lose his or her whole interest because of a comparatively minor breach. In addition, any derivative interest granted out of that lease—for example, a sub-lease or mortgage—will also be lost. Accordingly, forfeiture is strictly controlled. First, a right of re-entry must be expressly granted by the lease—it will usually be stated to be exercisable upon a failure to pay rent or for the breach of any other tenant's covenant. Secondly, a landlord may waive a right of re-entry comparatively easily (see **7.117**). Thirdly, a landlord must follow a prescribed process which is intended to warn the tenant of the impending threat of forfeiture and afford them the opportunity to remedy the breach (**7.118-7.122**). Fourthly, the court may grant a tenant relief from forfeiture (**7.123-7.129**). Lastly, certain residential leases either cannot be forfeited or are subject to additional protection (see **7.134**).

### The Twilight Period

**7.116** To forfeit the lease the landlord must exercise the re-entry either by physically (but peacefully) re-entering the premises or by bringing proceedings for possession. The latter course is required in the case of residential premises (see the Protection from Eviction Act 1977, s 2) and is also the more usual course. Rather strangely, it is the landlord's service of possession proceedings which forfeits the lease and not the court's order for possession. Thereafter the tenant is a trespasser and no longer liable to pay rent. Instead, the landlord may claim mesne profits—being damages for the tenant's use of the land—which is calculated according to the current rental value of the land. The artificiality of this process has been criticized (see eg Law Commission (2006b) at **1.9**). Not only is the relationship of the parties one of landowner and trespasser but there is the possibility that if the court does not order possession the lease will magically revive. There is thus what is sometimes referred to as a 'twilight period' during which the parties' relationship is far from unsatisfactory (see Bignell (2007)).

### Waiver

**7.117** A landlord may not rely upon a right of re-entry to forfeit a lease where he or she has waived their right. This may happen intentionally where the landlord decides to ignore the breach of covenant and allow the lease to continue or unintentionally where the landlord with knowledge of the breach nevertheless does some act which recognizes the continued existence of the lease (*Matthews v Smallwood* (1910), *Central Estates (Belgravia) Ltd v Woolgar (No 2)* (1972), *Cornillie v Saha* (1996), *Greenwood Reversions Ltd v World Environment Foundations Ltd* (2008)). The most common example of such an act is the demand and acceptance of rent due after the breach. Waiver is, however, less of an issue where a breach of covenant is continuing, for instance when the disrepair or unauthorized user continues, because the landlord can merely rely on a later breach (*Segal Securities Ltd v Thoseby* (1963)).

### Notice

**7.118**   Although the common law rule is that rent should be formally demanded before a right to re-enter is exercised, leases will frequently expressly exclude this requirement.

**7.119**   Covenants other than for the payment of rent are governed by section 146(1) of the LPA 1925 which requires notice to be given to the tenant before the exercise of a right of re-entry. An attempt to forfeit without service of a notice is void (*Billson v Residential Apartments Ltd* (1992)). The notice is intended to warn the tenant that the landlord intends to rely on a breach and to let him or her know what they must do to avoid forfeiture.

**7.120**   The notice must specify the breach in adequate detail (*Akici v LR Butlin Ltd* (2006)) and call upon the tenant to remedy the breach (if it is capable of remedy) and request compensation (if desired). In addition, where the lease is of dwelling-houses a notice relating to a breach of a repairing covenant will have to advise the tenant of their rights under the Leasehold Property (Repairs) Act 1938 to serve a counter-notice to prevent the forfeiture proceeding unless a court orders otherwise.

**7.121**   The most problematic aspect of section 146 notices relates to the question of whether or not a breach is capable of remedy and, if it is, how long the tenant needs to be given to remedy the breach and thus avoid forfeiture. The first issue is relatively easy for landlords to overcome by merely stating that the breach should be remedied if it is capable of remedy. However, if a landlord does not use this convenient wording it is necessary to determine if the breach is capable of remedy. It could be argued that no breach can be remedied, in the sense that it is impossible to put the clock back to before the breach, but the courts have taken a wider approach by asking whether or not the harm occasioned by the breach can be remedied (*Savva v Hussein* (1997)). Positive covenants, for instance to repair, are generally considered capable of remedy (*Expert Clothing & Services & Sales Co Ltd v Hillgate House Ltd* (1986)). By contrast, the ability to remedy a negative covenant has proved more controversial. A breach of a negative user covenant may be incapable of remedy where a stigma generated by the prohibited user continues to blight the premises (*Dunraven Securities v Holloway* (1982)). In *Scala House & District Property Co Ltd v Forbes* (1974) a once-and-for-all breach of a negative covenant against subletting also was found incapable of remedy. Subsequently, the courts have backtracked from sweeping statements that all negative covenants are incapable of remedy. In *Expert Clothing*, the decision in *Scala* was doubted and limited to covenants against subletting. This change in approach has gone hand in hand with an appreciation of the wider meaning of remediability in *Savva* and Neuberger LJ (in dicta) in *Akici v LR Butlin Ltd*, went so far as to suggest that all breaches of positive or negative covenants should be capable of remedy although he was bound to acknowledge the authority of *Scala* and the stigma cases. Subsequently, the Supreme Court has expressed support for these views (*Telchadder v Wickland Holdings Ltd* (2014)).

**7.122**   The time afforded to a tenant to remedy a breach must be reasonable which will inevitably depend on the nature of the breach, the course of the dispute, and the remainder of the term (*Expert Clothing & Services & Sales Co Ltd v Hillgate House Ltd* (1986)).

## Relief from Forfeiture

**7.123**  Relief operates to recharacterize forfeiture from a tool of expropriation of the tenant's term to a security for the tenant's performance of the covenants contained in the lease. The rules governing relief are, however, complicated by the interplay between the courts' original equitable jurisdiction to grant relief and subsequent statutory measures. Furthermore, there is a difference between the rules governing relief from a failure to pay rent and breaches of other covenants. Where relief is granted, the lease is restored as if there had been no suspension of the parties' landlord and tenant relationship.

### Relief from Non-Payment of Rent

**7.124**  Relief from forfeiture for non-payment of rent has long been granted upon payment of the arrears and any costs. The original jurisdiction is equitable but is now overlain by various statutory measures. The result is a maze of absolute and discretionary rights that differ according to whether the application is made before or after possession is ordered or the landlord has re-entered (whether peacefully or otherwise), and also depends upon whether proceedings are brought in the High Court or county courts. The details of the county court jurisdiction are found in section 138 of the County Courts Act 1984 and of the High Court jurisdiction in sections 210 and 212 of the Common Law Procedure Act 1852. If the tenant does not qualify for relief under the relevant statutory jurisdiction, relief may be granted under equity's jurisdiction.

**7.125**  Reflecting the security function of forfeiture, the principle underlying the grant of relief under both the statutory and equitable jurisdictions is that the relief will be granted where the tenant pays the full arrears even if the tenant has a poor payment record (*Gill v Lewis* (1956)). Indeed, in some instances of the relevant statutory jurisdiction the tenant will enjoy an absolute right to relief in these circumstances.

### Relief from Breaches of Other Covenants

**7.126**  A tenant's right to relief from the breach of other covenants is governed by section 146(2) of the LPA 1925. The time by which a tenant must apply for relief differs according to whether the landlord is re-entering by taking proceedings for possession or whether he or she has re-entered peacefully. It will be recalled that the latter route is only feasible in respect of vacant commercial premises (see **7.115**). Where the landlord is taking proceedings for possession, the tenant must apply for relief either during the proceedings themselves or at the latest before the possession order is executed by the physical recovery of possession. Where the landlord has entered peacefully, the tenant may apply for relief within a reasonable time of the event. This position was reached by the House of Lords in the important case of *Billson v Residential Apartments Ltd* (1992). A contrary conclusion would have left the tenant with no effective right to relief, since he or she had already been evicted, and an incentive for landlords to shortcut relief by re-entering without a court order.

**7.127**  It will be recalled that the forfeiture of a lease will also terminate the interests derived out of the lease, for instance a sub-tenant or a mortgagee (**7.113**). Their right to apply for relief is rather more complicated. The primary jurisdiction is found in section 146(4) which operates to grant a new lease between the landlord and the holder of the derivative interest. It is also possible that relief might be sought under section 146(2) (see the definition of lessee in s 146(5)(b)). In this instance, the head lease is revived and the links within the chain of landlord and tenant/mortgage relationships are restored. The difficulty, particularly for a mortgagee, is that the holder of a derivative interest may be unaware of the landlord's re-entry and will lose their right to apply for relief if they do not apply in time. It is in these circumstances that resort to equity's jurisdiction to grant relief could assist, but it remains unclear whether this jurisdiction is overtaken by section 146 (see *Shiloh Spinners Ltd v Harding, Abbey National Building Society v Maybeech Ltd* (1985), *Smith v Metropolitan City Properties* (1986)). Unfortunately *Billson* did not provide an answer.

7.128   The court's discretion to grant relief is wide and unfettered and all the circumstances of the case will be taken into account (*Rose v Hyman* (1912)). Of particular significance are the gravity of the breach, the conduct of the parties, the question of whether or not the breach can be remedied, and the disparity between the loss caused to the landlord by the breach and the loss caused to the tenant should the lease be forfeited (*Shiloh Spinners Ltd v Harding* (1973)). Relief will rarely be granted where the breach is intentional or cannot be remedied, unless the breach is trivial and the damage to the landlord's reversion insignificant or the potential windfall to the landlord is disproportionate (*Central Estates (Belgravia) Ltd v Woolgar (No 2)* (1972), *Van Haarlam v Kasner* (1992), *Greenwood Reversions Ltd v World Environment Foundations Ltd* (2008), *Patel v K&J Restaurants Ltd* (2010), *Magnic Ltd v Ul-Hassan* (2015), *Freifeld v West Kensington Court Ltd* (2015)).

## Reform of Forfeiture

7.129   It should come as no surprise that there have long been calls for reform of forfeiture. The latest proposals are found in the Law Commission's report, *Termination of Tenancies for Tenant Default* (Law Commission (2006b)) in which the Law Commission called for the abolition of forfeiture and its replacement by a statutory scheme. In essence, what is proposed is that termination for breach of any covenant should be based upon a common process, to be known as a termination action, and triggered by a landlord's notice rather than the need for a right of re-entry. Within a termination action, which could take a quicker summary form, opportunities would exist for a tenant to remedy the breach or claim relief. The court would be given wide discretion, based upon statutory criteria, to decide the termination action as it considers fit by granting or refusing the termination order or alternatively ordering sale, the grant of a new tenancy, or the transfer of the existing tenancy. Whilst these proposals have been welcomed, they have not been enacted.

## Flat Ownership: Residential Long Leases and Commonhold

7.130   Leases play many roles. Shorter term tenancies provide residential accommodation for a significant number of people who cannot afford to buy a home or require the flexibility provided by short leasehold terms. Such tenancies are found in both the public sector, by social housing landlords, and the private sector, where there has been a growth in the number of private landlords. Commercial premises, both of offices and shops, are often leased for terms of varying length with some security of tenure offered by the right of the tenant to renew their lease provided they can pay the current market rent (see the Landlord and Tenant Act 1954, Part II). A further important role of leases is their use in the ownership of flats and other premises where there are common facilities which require a legal framework that enables the sharing of rights and obligations, particularly repairing and maintenance responsibilities. We will see in **Chapter 10** that such frameworks are difficult to achieve within freehold ownership, because generally positive obligations between freehold owners are not enforceable against subsequent owners. By contrast, we have seen in this chapter that, through privity of estate, positive obligations within a lease are enforceable between subsequent assignees of both the landlord's reversion and the lease itself. Accordingly, lawyers have adopted the leasehold framework to cater for the ownership of flats and other developments where there are shared facilities. We will explore in outline this leasehold framework, highlighting some of the tensions and problems that result, before looking at the alternative commonhold framework introduced by the Commonhold and Leasehold Reform Act 2002.

## The Long Leasehold Ownership of Flats

**7.131**  The vast majority of purchasers of flats will buy a long lease of their flat for a term in excess of 99 years. This lease will include the grant of a number of other rights and obligations on the part of both the lessor and lessee. There will be easements granted for the flat-owner to use the common parts including the entrance, stairs, any gardens or other recreational facilities, as well as to receive rights of support and shelter from the rest of the building and to use essential services like water, gas, and electricity that may flow through the common parts or indeed the structure of other flats. Each flat will also be subject to similar reservations in favour of other flats in the development. There will be negative leasehold covenants which control what the flat-owners can and cannot do within their 'owned' flat. Positive covenants will impose obligations on the flat-owner to keep their flat in repair and to pay a proportion of the costs of maintaining and repairing the common parts and structure of the building through a service charge. This service charge may often be a significant sum although, by contrast, the rent payable under long flat leases is generally small and known as ground rent. It will generally be the landlord who bears the positive obligation of actually making sure that the building and common parts are repaired and maintained, again through a positive leasehold covenant. The performance of the flat-owner's negative and positive covenants will be backed up by a right of re-entry granted to the landlord to forfeit the lease in the event of breach by the flat-owner. In order to create this complex network of rights and obligations, each lease of a flat within the development will be granted on the same terms and often result in leases of considerable length and complexity.

**7.132**  Using this leasehold structure to ensure the performance of essential positive obligations means that we have the ownership of two estates—the freehold reversion held by the lessor (or landlord) and the long lease held by the flat-owner as lessee. It is important thus to understand who the landlord will be. There are generally two possibilities. The freehold reversion may be transferred by the developer of the flats to a management company owned and controlled by the flat-owners collectively. A flat-owner will thus buy the lease of his or her flat and a share in the management company. Effectively freehold ownership is replicated by a long lease of the individual flats within the development and collectively ownership of the common parts and collectively responsibility for the management, maintenance, and repair of the whole development. The alternative is that the developer will retain the freehold with the responsibility to the flat-owners collectively for the management, maintenance, and repair of the whole development, the cost of which will be met by the flat-owners collectively through their payment of the service charge. Of course, the original developer may decide to sell their investment in the development together with their responsibilities, as lessor, to another property investment company. The essential feature of this latter framework is that the leasehold reversion and attendant rights and obligations are held by an outside investor and not the flat-owners collectively.

7.133   The issues presented by these two frameworks thus differ. Where the leasehold reversion is held by a management company owner collectively by the flat-owners, the issue is coping with the difficulties surrounding communal ownership. The flat-owners, as shareholders of the management company, need to collectively make decisions about the management, maintenance, and repair of the development as well as decisions about the future of the flat leases themselves, including decisions about renewal of the flat leases as they near the end of the leasehold term and the possibility of forfeiting a lease where an individual flat-owner is in serious default. The essential question is thus not so concerned with the split in ownership between the freehold and the lease, but just how effectively the flat-owners are able to cooperate. Where the leasehold reversion is held by an outside investor (whether the original developer or another), the issues revolve around the need to balance the interests of the split in ownership between the lessor, as an investor, and the flat lessee's, as home-owners. As the lessor will invariably be the more experienced and better resourced party, who originally crafted the framework of rights and responsibilities found in the lease, these issues centre upon trying to ensure that the flat-owners are not exploited. The elements of this balancing exercise revolve around two broad areas. First, the vulnerability of flat-owners as lessees for a term certain rather than as freehold owners and, secondly, the challenge of communal living particularly the risk of inadequate and/or exploitative management. These are difficult, delicate, and complex balances to strike. Indeed, the initial jurisdiction (and the expertise) to deal with most of the flat ownership and management disputes under discussion is entrusted to a specialist court—the First-tier Tribunal (Property Chamber).

7.134   The purchasers of flats think of themselves as becoming owners rather than tenants. Indeed, they are owners but of a leasehold estate. The clock is always counting down under a lease even if it is initially granted for a long term. By the time the lease has less than about 60 years to run, it will start to become labelled as 'a wasting asset' which purchasers will be less willing to buy and lenders less willing to accept as security for a loan. The solution is to grant flat-owners (as lessees) rights either individually to extend their leasehold term or collectively to acquire the leasehold reversion, using a corporate vehicle, in a process known as enfranchisement. The flat-owners must pay the lessor for these rights but for a consideration which is generally below market value. Both these rights are now contained in the Commonhold and Leasehold Reform Act 2002.

**7.135** We have already explored the right of a landlord to bring a lease to an early end, if a tenant fails to pay the rent or breaches any other of the tenant's covenants, by re-entering and forfeiting the lease, and noted the measures that temper this extreme right (see **7.115–7.128**). There are additional safeguards where there is a long lease of residential premises. A landlord must serve a written demand where rent is due under a long lease exceeding 21 years of a dwelling (see the Commonhold and Leasehold Reform Act 2002, s 166). To avoid notices being used to harass rather than help tenants of dwelling-houses, a landlord cannot forfeit unless the amount owed is above the prescribed minimum or the tenant has been in arrears for a prescribed period (s 167) and the amount of any disputed services charge has been determined by the court or the Property Chamber of the First-tier Tribunal (Housing Act 1996, s 81). Rent under long leases of dwellings is often low but these safeguards are important because they also apply to outstanding service charges which are frequently treated in the same way as rent. In addition, the landlord cannot serve a section 146 notice, for the alleged breach of other tenant's covenants, unless the tenant has admitted the breach or a court or tribunal has determined that there is a breach (Commonhold and Leasehold Reform Act 2002, s 168). Nevertheless, in this context the concept of forfeiture itself seems inimical to the expectations of ownership held by flat owners.

**7.136** The ability for investor lessors to make unfettered decisions about which repairs to carry out and in what way, by whom, and for what cost clearly can lead to exploitation of flat-owners by investor landlords. Service charges could be inflated by carrying out unnecessary work or employing (often associated) workers at higher than market cost. Alternatively, investor landlords receiving little return on their investment might fail to adequately fulfil their management obligations. Requests for maintenance and repair could go unheeded or performance standards could be poor, late, or inadequate. The solutions offered to these sometimes intractable problems are to try and control excessive service charges (see Landlord and Tenant Act 1985) and to grant flat-owners a collective right to take over the management through a company established for that purpose under their control (see Commonhold and Leasehold Reform Act 2002). These measures, however, are of limited utility if the lease itself is defective in establishing coherent and effective responsibilities for repair and maintenance. The possibility of applying to court to rectify the lease helps to overcome the practical difficulties of doing so where there are many owners (together with their mortgagees) who would otherwise need to agree, and participate in, a variation of the lease.

## Commonhold

**7.137** The effectiveness of all these measures is constrained by the inherent hurdles presented by communal living which require joint decision making and the reconciliation of different views, expectations, and lifestyles between people living in close proximity yet legally dependent on each other. Solutions to these issues are likewise inherently complex. The long leasehold structure has been the solution developed in this jurisdiction. Other jurisdictions have developed other legal structures including condominium title in North America and strata title in Australasia and Singapore which seek to resolve these issues through a freehold conception of title. The introduction of commonhold title in this jurisdiction has sought to emulate these other structures. In practical terms, commonhold title resembles the long leasehold structure where the flat-owners hold the reversion through a communally owned management company. However, commonhold is fundamentally distinct by providing the flat-owners with a freehold title to their flats with the freehold title to the common parts held by a communal corporate body, in which the flat-owners are all members, called the commonhold association. The commonhold association is also responsible for the management of, and joint decision making within, the development. The detailed legal rights and obligations of the freehold flat-owners are contained in a commonhold community statement (rather than in a common form of lease), which is enforceable between the flat-owners for the time being of the development. Despite its closer association with freehold ownership, commonhold has so far failed to capture the imagination of developers and their financiers who have preferred to stay with the familiar and tested long lease structure. Also there has been no real support or demand from aspirant flat-owners to adopt the commonhold structure.

# FURTHER READING

Bignell, J, 'Forfeiture: A Long Overdue Reform?' [2007] L&T Rev 140.

Blandy, S, Dupuis, A, and Dixon, J, *Multi-Owned Housing: Law, Power and Practice* (Aldershot: Ashgate, 2010).

Bridge, S, 'Former Tenants, Future Liabilities and the Privity of Contract Principle' (1996) 55 CLJ 313.

Bridge, S, 'Leases: Contract, Property and Status' in L Tee (ed), *Land Law: Issues, Debates, Policy* (Cullompton: Willan, 2002).

Bridge, S, '*Street v Mountford* (1985); *AG Securities v Vaughan; Antoniades v Villiers* (1988): Tenancies and Licences: Halting the Revolution' in N Gravells (ed), *Landmark Cases in Land Law* (Oxford: Hart Publishing, 2013).

Bright, S, 'Avoiding Tenancy Legislation: Sham and Contracting Out Revisited' (2002) 61 CLJ 146.

Davey, M, 'The Regulation of Long Residential Leases' in E Cooke (ed), *Modern Studies in Property Law: Vol 3* (Oxford: Hart Publishing, 2005), ch 10.

Dixon, M, 'The Non-Proprietary Lease: The Rise of the Feudal Phoenix' (2000) 59 CLJ 25.

Gravells, N, 'Forfeiture of Leases for Breach of Covenant' [2006] JBL 830.

Hill, J, 'Intention and the Creation of Proprietary Rights: Are Leases Different?' (1996) 16 LS 200.

Law Commission Report No 297, *Renting Homes* (2006a), esp Parts 1 and 2.

Law Commission Report No 303, *Termination of Tenancies for Tenant Default* (2006b).

McFarlane, B and Simpson, E, 'Tackling Avoidance' in J Getzler (ed), *Rationalizing Property, Equity and Trusts: Essays in Honour of Edward Burn* (Oxford: Oxford University Press, 2003).

Van der Merwe, C and Smith, P, 'Commonhold—A Critical Appraisal' in E Cooke (ed), *Modern Studies in Property Law* (Oxford: Hart Publishing, 2005), vol 3.

## SELF-TEST QUESTIONS

1    What are the key differences between a lease and a licence?

2    What are the two key requirements of a lease?

3    How, in practice, can a court tell if an agreement gives an occupier a right to exclusive possession?

4    Does the Supreme Court's decision in *Berrisford v Mexfield* mean that there is no longer a rule that a lease must be for a certain term?

5    Does the House of Lords' decision in *Bruton v London and Quadrant Housing Trust* mean that a lease is not an estate in land?

6    What are the key differences between a legal lease and an equitable lease?

7    Explain what we mean by 'privity of estate' making reference to which parties fall within privity of estate.

8    How has the contractual liability of the original parties to a lease been affected by the Landlord and Tenant (Covenants) Act 1995?

9    When does a covenant 'touch and concern' the land? Does this concept continue to have relevance after the Landlord and Tenant (Covenants) Act 1995?

10    When is a leasehold covenant capable of remedy?

11    How draconian a remedy is forfeiture?

12    Is there a pressing need for commonhold?

# 8 Mortgages and Security Interests in Land

## SUMMARY

This chapter examines the law governing security interests that can exist in land, taking the legal charge by way of mortgage in the social setting of home ownership as its primary focus. It looks first at the different types of security interest that can exist in land and considers the nature of the lender's and the borrower's respective proprietary interests under each form. The chapter moves on to consider the rights and powers of the lender on the enforcement of the security. The chapter then turns to concentrate on the position of the borrower and the ways in which the law seeks to protect the borrower as the more vulnerable party during the course of the mortgage transaction.

Key topics explored in this chapter are:

- Forms of legal and equitable security interests in land (8.9–8.22)
- Equity of redemption (8.29–8.30)
- Lender's right to possession (8.31–8.54)
- Lender's power of sale and to appoint a receiver (8.55–8.67)
- Market regulation (8.73–8.93)
- Surety transactions and procedural fairness (8.94–8.107)
- Control of mortgage terms (8.108–8.123)

## Introduction

8.1 Our modern way of life is dependent on credit. Government's housing policy since the end of the Second World War has promoted home ownership, made possible by lenders willing to advance the purchase price provided repayment is supported by the borrower's regular income and secured by a mortgage over the home. The financial crisis of 2007 and 2008 led to a fall in home ownership largely as a result of more restrictive lending criteria that lenders are required to adopt. Even though the government has introduced financial incentives to support home ownership, particularly for first-time buyers, many people who would like to become home owners have been unable to take that first step on the housing ladder and are forced to rent a home from a private landlord. The knock-on effect has been a growth in Buy to Let mortgages entered into by individuals who wish to fund an investment in the housing market as private landlords. The private rental sector is becoming more important as successive governments wish to reduce the cost and responsibility of supporting social housing whether rented (at below market rent) by local authorities, housing associations, and other social landlords.

8.2   Consumer spending is also supported by credit. Whilst much consumer credit is unsecured, for instance through credit and store cards, lenders may only be prepared to advance the money for larger purchases if the borrower can offer security. Furthermore, borrowers, who accumulate sizeable amounts of unsecured debt from a range of lenders, may find it advantageous to consolidate the debt in one lender and obtain better repayment terms if the consolidated debt is then secured by way of a second mortgage on the borrower's home. In later life, the accumulated value in an individual's home may be tapped to provide income to meet living and care costs through what are commonly referred to as equity release schemes. The providers of such schemes will advance the necessary funds against taking security over the home to be realized once the borrower eventually moves or passes away.

8.3   Much commercial activity is also dependent on companies being able to borrow from financial institutions, who are more willing to lend and to offer better terms, if the company can offer security over the company's assets or a guarantee from the company's shareholders or directors. Such a guarantee may in turn be secured upon the guarantor's assets including their home. In this way, companies can utilize their fixed assets, such as their premises, to raise money to promote (or save) their business. This loan finance (as it is called) is particularly important for small and medium-sized businesses that cannot raise funds from investors through a public stock exchange. The level of borrowing is often seen as a barometer of economic activity and the encouragement that security affords a marker of a mature and stable economy.

8.4   So why do lenders want the security that a mortgage offers? A mortgage confers upon the lender a distinct legal or equitable property right in the borrower's land (or other asset) which confers upon the lender a number of rights to which it can resort if the borrower fails to repay the loan. The lender then has not just a contractual right to sue the borrower for non-payment of his or her debt but can also rely upon the legal or equitable right conferred by the security to obtain repayment. For instance, the lender may be able to obtain possession and sell the property to repay the debt. There are thus two elements to the grant of a security interest. First, the loan agreement, which gives rise to contractual obligations on the borrower to repay the loan and a corresponding contractual right for the lender to sue if the borrower defaults. Secondly, the legal or equitable proprietary interest conferred upon the lender by the borrower to secure repayment. We commonly call this security interest a 'mortgage' and the lender 'a mortgagee' and the borrower, 'a mortgagor.' However, as we will see this is a rather loose use of terminology as a mortgage is just one form of security interest. Nevertheless, in accordance with common parlance, we will use the term mortgage generically but we will refer to 'lender' and 'borrower' rather than 'mortgagee' and 'mortgagor' as it is easy to confuse the two expressions.

8.5 The rights conferred by the mortgage are called a right of recourse over the asset. These rights of recourse are important upon the borrower's insolvency when the borrower is unable to repay all their debts. The lender's right of recourse in effect removes the mortgaged asset from the borrower's insolvency. The lender is in control of the realization of the mortgaged asset rather than the trustee in bankruptcy (if the borrower is an individual) or liquidator (if the borrower is a company) and, what is more, is entitled to do so with minimal court oversight. The lender's obligation is to ensure the sale is properly conducted and, after deducting the sums owed to them, to hand over the balance to the borrower's trustee in bankruptcy/liquidator or to the borrower if he or she is solvent. The significance of the mortgage is thus felt most keenly upon default in loan repayment. Indeed, Clarke (1997) suggests that the proprietary quality of mortgages is marginal since they confer on the lender no more than conditional rights of management which are dependent upon the likelihood of default, an event which is within the control of the borrower.

8.6 Nevertheless, as a proprietary interest a mortgage is entitled to priority against others claiming an interest in the mortgaged asset. Indeed, we have seen throughout this book that many classic property disputes arise out of the competition between the lender as mortgagee and third parties including family members living with the borrower (*National Provincial Bank v Ainsworth* (1965), *Williams & Glyn's Bank v Boland* (1981), *City of London Building Society v Flegg* (1988), *Lloyds Bank plc v Rosset* (1991), *Abbey National Building Society v Cann* (1991), *Southern Pacific Mortgages Ltd v Scott* (2015)).

8.7 The benefits provided to the lender by a mortgage are not just proprietary. Because of the potency of the lender's rights, a borrower will often be keen to pay off the debt owed to the lender before other credit commitments. Many borrowers are prepared to pay interest on their credit card balances than miss mortgage repayments and run the risk of losing their homes. Likewise, a business will not want to risk losing its premises. It may make more sense to delay paying a supplier. This persuasive effect of security is known as the 'hostage function' of mortgage credit. A lender can also use the loan agreement and mortgage to monitor and control the borrower by imposing terms which call upon the borrower to provide credit information, to minimize other credit commitments, or maintain the value of the security; for instance, through covenants to insure, repair, or not to create competing proprietary interests.

8.8 Security interests, including mortgages, are not without controversy particularly in the commercial sphere. They can sideline unsecured creditors' chances of recovery where the lender obtains security over all, or virtually all, the borrowing company's assets leaving little from which the unsecured creditors can seek repayment. These criticisms have been the target of legislative reform (see the Insolvency Act 1986 particularly the introduction of administration (see Sch B1) and the prescribed part for unsecured creditors (s 176A)). However, the company's main banker or financier still retains a dominant position by virtue of their security. The efficiency of secured credit has also been questioned.

It is argued that although secured creditors may charge lower rates of interest in the light of their reduced risk, unsecured creditors may charge higher rates for any credit to compensate for their increased credit exposure. There is thus no overall economic advantage to secured credit—indeed, it is argued that the cost of setting up security arrangements creates an economic disadvantage. These insights are more theoretical than real given that unsecured creditors rarely insist that the borrower pays higher rates of interest (see Mokal (2002) for a summary of the debate).

## Forms of Security

**8.9** There are four forms of security interest known to English law—the pledge, the lien, the mortgage, and the equitable charge (see *Re Cosslett Contractors Ltd* (1998) at 508 per Millett LJ). The pledge and the contractual and common law forms of the lien are possessory securities because they entitle the lender to take (in the case of a pledge) or retain (in the case of a lien) possession of the borrower's assets until the debt is repaid. Pledges remain important in international trade since certain forms of documents are recognized as evidence of ownership of goods. Pledges also have a residuary role at the lower end of the consumer credit market when pawnbrokers take possession of a borrower's goods generally in return for small cash advances. One of the forms of lien recognized at common law, meanwhile, is a repairer's lien which entitles a repairer of goods to keep the goods that have been repaired until the repair costs are paid. Given their essential possessory nature, neither a pledge nor a contractual or common law lien can be taken over land. It is the non-possessory equitable mortgage and charge, and the statutory hybrid of the legal charge by way of mortgage, which are the focus of our attention in examining security interests over land. We will also have a word to say about equitable liens which, despite their name, are more akin to equitable charges. It is important to be clear about the different forms of these security interests as, unfortunately, given the colloquial use of the term 'mortgage' in a generic sense to cover all forms of security interest, it is easy to confuse the different forms.

### The Mortgage

**8.10** The legal nature of a mortgage comprises the transfer by the borrower to the lender of a proprietary interest in the borrower's land subject to the agreement of the lender to re-transfer that interest back to the borrower upon repayment of the debt (see *Swiss Bank Group v Lloyds Bank Ltd* (1982) at 594 per Buckley LJ). This agreement gives rise to the borrower's right to redeem the mortgage and with it the right to recover his or her property unencumbered by the mortgage. At law the borrower's right to redeem must be exercised in accordance with the strict terms governing the time, place, and form of repayment set out in the loan agreement. It could thus easily be lost where the borrower failed to observe these terms with the result that the lender would become entitled to the property free from the borrower's right to redeem. The inequity of this possibility is evident where the value of the property exceeds the amount of the loan. It is thus no surprise to find that equity will recognize the borrower's continued equitable right to redeem, and the consequent duty of the lender to return the property to the borrower, even though the strict repayment terms have not been observed. Indeed, the borrower's right to recover his or her property upon repayment of the loan is recognized as an equitable property right, capable of binding third parties, known as the borrower's equity of redemption representing the value of the property less the amount required to redeem the mortgage. In this manner, a mortgage is distinguished from an outright sale of the borrower's property with the lender's inherent security rights in the property represented first by their right to take possession and, secondly, by their right to extinguish the borrower's equity of redemption by a process known as foreclosure.

## The Charge

8.11   A charge creates a new property interest that encumbers or burdens the borrower's proprietary interest. In contrast to a mortgage, there is no transfer of the borrower's existing proprietary interest. The new interest created by the charge grants the lender the right to apply the charged property to repay the borrower's debt (*Re Cosslett Contractors Ltd* (1998) at 508 per Millett LJ). A charge is thus said to appropriate the borrower's property to the satisfaction of the borrower's debt. In the absence of express or implied powers in the charge itself, the lender must seek a court order for the sale of the property. Upon repayment of the debt the charge is discharged because there is simply no debt to be appropriated to the borrower's property. The charge is a creation of equity although, as we shall see, the Law of Property Act 1925 (LPA 1925) introduced the legal charge by way of mortgage as a unique security interest over land. Equitable charges may take one of two forms. There is the fixed equitable charge which can be taken over specific property and the floating charge which can be taken over a changing fund of assets and entitles the borrower to deal with the assets within that fund until a specified event when the floating charge crystallizes into a fixed charge. It is not possible to create a floating charge over an individual's assets but the floating charge has proved a popular form of commercial security interest when taken over all the present and future company's assets. It enables the company to continue to operate by dealing with their assets in the ordinary course of business yet at the same time offers the lender a comprehensive form of security which can be easily activated should the company fall into financial difficulty. The distinguishing feature between a fixed and floating charge is one of control over the charged property. If the borrower is entitled to deal with the property without the consent of the lender, the charge is floating but, if the lender's consent is required to enable the borrower to pass title to the charged property to a purchaser, the charge is fixed (see *Re Spectrum Plus Ltd* (2005)).

## The Equitable Lien

8.12   The equitable lien confers an equitable property right upon the lender which is similar in content to an equitable charge but as a matter of acquisition can only arise by operation of law rather than consensually. The most significant equitable lien relating to land is the 'unpaid vendor's lien'. A seller who has already transferred his or her ownership to a purchaser but has not yet been fully paid, is entitled to an equitable lien over the purchaser's freehold or leasehold title (as appropriate) to secure the unpaid portion. A similar lien can be claimed by a purchaser of land where the purchaser has paid, or partly paid, the purchase price but has not yet received the seller's title to the land to be purchased.

## Legal Charge by Way of Mortgage of Land

**8.13**  The predominant form of security over land recognized by English law has been described as a 'work of fiction' and 'a confusion of things' (Watt (2007)). That fiction arises as a result of the historical development of security interests in land to which we must briefly turn to unpack the confusion. Mortgages have a very long history—landowners have always needed money. However, in times gone by the Christian church frowned upon the charging of interest both because it gave rise to profit without risk or honest labour and also preyed upon the misfortune of others. The original forms of mortgage avoided this displeasure by taking a possessory form—possession of the land was handed to the lender until repayment. As these possessory forms developed, either the borrower's fee simple was conveyed to the lender or a lease granted to the lender subject, either to an agreement to reconvey or to surrender the lease, on repayment. Alternatively, the fee simple or leasehold grants were automatically defeasible upon repayment of the loan. The physical passing of possession was not really convenient for either party—the lender (as a financier) preferred to concentrate on lending money and not property management, whilst the borrower did not want to lose the use of their land. It thus became common practice for the borrower to remain in possession as a tenant at will or sufferance of the lender. The 'fiction' lies in the fact that the lender was either the freehold owner, or a tenant, of the land and so entitled to the incidents of ownership in particular possession. The borrower's legal rights were confined to a precarious right to de facto possession and a right to recover unencumbered ownership upon repayment of the debt. The social and religious acceptance of interest earning debt made this fiction increasingly anomalous. It was only the intervention of equity that cast a degree of reality into the mortgage as a security interest through the equitable right to redeem, and its recognition of the borrower as an equitable owner, through the equity of redemption.

**8.14**  The LPA 1925 provided an opportunity to cast off this historical baggage but it failed to do so. It retained the mortgage by sub-demise but abolished the mortgage by conveyance and, more importantly, introduced a hybrid form of security—the legal charge by way of mortgage (LPA 1925, ss 85 and 86). The mortgage by sub-demise became obsolete during the 20th century as the legal charge by way of mortgage gained pre-eminence and the Land Registration Act 2002 (LRA 2002) finished the job by effectively abolishing the mortgage by sub-demise (LRA 2002, ss 4(1), 23, and 51). The legal charge by way of mortgage is described as a hybrid form of security for although it introduced the charge as the lender's proprietary interest, it retained the possessory nature of that interest by providing that a legal chargee would retain the rights and powers as if they held a mortgage by sub-demise for 3,000 years (LPA 1925, s 87(1)). Thus, the old fiction remains in a different but just as complicated form. The parties' relationship is conceived of as a lease with the lender as tenant, entitled to but not in possession (*Grand Junction Co Ltd v Bates* (1954), *Weg Motors Ltd v Hales* (1962), *Cumberland Court (Brighton) Ltd v Taylor* (1964), *Regent Oil Co Ltd v JA Gregory (Hatch End) Ltd* (1966)). The borrower is the legal owner and a notional landlord but their right to possession is poorly articulated (see *Figgins Holdings Pty Ltd v SEAA Enterprises Ltd* (1999)).

## Equitable Mortgages and Charges of Land

8.15 Although the legal charge by way of mortgage is the predominant security interest, we need to distinguish three forms of equitable security interest over land. First, the equitable charge of the legal estate, secondly, the equitable mortgage of the equitable estate and, lastly, the equitable charge.

### An Equitable Charge of the Legal Estate

8.16 An equitable charge of the legal estate arises from an incomplete acquisition of a legal security interest. For instance, an equitable charge of the legal estate will arise where a borrower holding a legal estate in land agrees to grant the lender a legal charge. An agreement to create a legal charge under the doctrine of anticipation will give rise to a duty in equity on the borrower to grant the lender a legal charge (see **Chapter 5**). The agreement must be in writing and comply with section 2(1) of the Law of Property (Miscellaneous Provisions) Act 1989 to be enforceable. Thus, the old practice of creating an equitable charge of the legal estate merely by depositing the title documents of the land with the lender is no longer effective (*United Bank of Kuwait plc v Sahib* (1997)). It may be possible for an equitable charge of the legal estate to arise where the borrower has made a non-contractual promise to grant a legal charge upon which the lender has reasonably relied to their detriment, thus imposing a duty upon the borrower by way of estoppel (*Kinane v Mackie-Conteh* (2005) but see *United Bank of Kuwait plc v Sahib* (1997)). The challenge is to prove reasonable reliance upon the borrower's promise where the parties are in a commercial relationship (compare *Cobbe v Yeoman's Row Management Ltd* (2008) and *Thorner v Major* (2009)).

8.17 A borrower will also come under a duty in equity to grant the lender a legal charge where he or she purports to grant a legal charge but has not completed the required formalities; for instance, because a deed has not been used or the purported legal charge has not been registered (*Bank of Scotland v Waugh* (2014)).

8.18 The content of the parties' relationship under an equitable charge of the legal estate is treated as if the promise had been performed and the legal charge granted at least so far as the parties' rights and responsibilities are consistent with the equitable nature of the security. For example, an equitable chargee of the legal estate cannot normally sell the legal estate unless the equitable charge has been granted by deed or its equitable status results from non-registration (see LPA 1925, s 88(6) and *Swift 1st Ltd v Colin* (2011), see also LRA 2002, ss 23 and 24 and *Skelwith (Leisure) Ltd v Armstrong* (2015)). Alternatively, the equitable chargee of the legal estate may derive their authority to deal with the borrower's legal estate from another source, for instance a power of attorney.

## Equitable Mortgage of an Equitable Interest

8.19   An equitable mortgage of an equitable estate will arise where the borrower only holds an equitable estate in the land. It thus flows from the content of the property constituting the security. For example, a beneficiary's equitable interest under a trust of land may prove acceptable security although by no means as common as the security offered by the legal estate.

8.20   An equitable mortgage of an equitable interest will be created in the traditional fashion by transferring the equitable interest to the lender subject to their agreement to retransfer the property when the loan is repaid.

## Equitable Charge

8.21   An equitable charge may be created over either the legal estate or an equitable estate or interest of the borrower where there is an intention that these proprietary interests are to be made available for the satisfaction of the debt. The intention that the borrower has a duty to apply his or her property to repay the debt must be evidenced in writing although no particular form of wording is required (LPA 1925, s 53(1)(a)). Examples of such an intention are found in cases where one co-owner has purported to charge the co-owner's joint legal estate but has either forged their fellow co-owner's signature or has exerted undue influence (or other legal wrong) to persuade their fellow co-owner 'to agree' to the charge. In these circumstances, the charge cannot take effect as a legal charge against both co-owners' jointly held legal estate. However, the lender may claim an equitable charge over the 'guilty' co-owner's equitable interest. The entry into the purported charge evinces an intention that at least their own interest in the property is to stand charged with repayment of the lender's loan (*First National Securities Ltd v Hegarty* (1985), *Thames Guaranty Ltd v Campbell* (1985), *Ahmed v Kendrick* (1988)).

8.22   This form of equitable charge is conceptually different to the equitable charge over the legal estate considered at **8.15–8.18**. The lender under this form of equitable charge has no right to call upon the borrower to create a legal charge by way of mortgage. Indeed, we have seen that the borrower may have no capacity to do so. The lender's inherent rights and powers are confined to a right to apply to court to force a sale of the charged property or to appoint a receiver to collect the income derived from the property. To avoid confusion between the two types of equitable charge, McFarlane (2008) suggests that we reserve the label 'equitable charge' to equitable charges of the legal estate and that we use the label 'purely equitable charge' to refer to the interests considered in this paragraph.

## Charging Orders

8.23    Charging orders are a creation of statute, namely the Charging Orders Act 1979 (COA 1979). They provide an important means by which an unsecured creditor can enforce a judgment debt by becoming a secured creditor and forcing the sale of their judgment debtor's property. Charging orders have 'the like effect and shall be enforceable ... in the same manner as an equitable charge created by the debtor under his hand' (COA 1979, s 3(4)). Charging orders can be used to place pressure on judgment debtors to pay even comparatively small judgment debts.

8.24    There are two stages to the charging order enforcement process. First, the charging order must be obtained. Upon making the charging order the judgment creditor becomes a secured creditor and entitled, subject to registration, to claim priority over subsequent purchasers of the land. Once the charging order is obtained, the second step is for the judgment debtor to enforce the charge by applying to court for an order for sale or to appoint a receiver.

8.25    In order to obtain a charging order, the judgment creditor must apply to court. The initial application for a charging order nisi is often made without informing the judgment debtor (ie ex parte). The judgment debtor is then given time either to challenge the making of the order or to pay the judgment debt. Failing which, the charging order nisi is made absolute. The court, in deciding whether or not a charging order should be made, must consider all the circumstances of the case, including the personal circumstances of the judgment debtor and whether any other creditors would be prejudiced by the charging order (COA 1979, s 1(5)). The court will usually decline to make a charging order if the judgment debtor is on the brink of insolvency (*Roberts Petroleum Ltd v Bernard Kenny Ltd* (1983), *Nationwide BS v Wright* (2010)). To do so would simply enable the judgment creditor to jump the priority queue to the prejudice of other unsecured debtors. If the debtor is not insolvent, there is an expectation that a charging order will be granted. If relevant circumstances subsequently come to light, the judgment debtor or any other person with an interest in the property may apply to vary or discharge the order (COA 1979, s 3(5)).

8.26    Common circumstances that fall to be considered include the property rights of a co-owner of the property or the competing financial claims of the judgment debtor's family since, sadly, marriage break-up and financial difficulties often go hand in hand. For instance, a spouse, usually the wife, may have a claim for ancillary financial relief to provide for herself and/or any children's maintenance in divorce proceedings against her husband, the judgment debtor. The difficult question is then the balance the courts should strike between the financial claims of the husband's judgment creditors, on the one hand, and his wife and children, on the other hand. Both have legitimate claims over the husband's insufficient resources. The usual practice is for the application to be transferred to the Family Division so that the claims can be considered together. In striking a balance between the two claims, the court will take all the circumstances into account and strive to ensure that the paramount interests of the judgment debtor's children in securing suitable accommodation are met whilst minimizing delay in discharging the judgment debt (see *Harman v Glencross* (1986), *Kremen v Agrest* (2013)).

**8.27** The court's wide discretion will once again be called into consideration when the creditor holding the benefit of a charging order applies to court to enforce the charge. Where the charging order is made over one co-owner's interest in jointly held property, the application for sale will be made under section 14 of the Trusts of Land and Appointment of Trustees Act 1996 (TOLATA) which is considered in Chapter 6. In *Close Invoice Financing Ltd v Pile* (2009) the court indicated that similar considerations will influence their discretion to order sale where the judgment debtor is the sole owner of the property.

## Reform

**8.28** The Law Commission has long advocated reform to bring the law into step with reality and to reduce the confusing array of security interests over land (see Law Commission (1991)). Its proposals advocate a statutorily constructed form of security for both legal and equitable security interests with clearly defined rights and responsibilities. Unfortunately, its proposals have fallen on deaf ears. Financiers are familiar with the existing forms even if they do not fully understand them. Instead, as we shall see, various statutory provisions and the impact of the regulation of consumer lending has to some extent helped to reflect reality. Nevertheless, it remains important to be clear about the distinctions between the different forms of security interest over land and to guard against the loose use of terminology which unfortunately continues to be all too common.

## Equity of Redemption

**8.29** We have seen that under the traditional form of mortgage by conveyance the borrower's proprietary interest in the land is cast as the equity of redemption, encapsulating the borrower's equitable right to repay the loan even after the legal date for repayment has passed and the lender's duty to re-convey the land back to the borrower. The equity of redemption played a critical role in converting what would otherwise be an outright conveyance of ownership into a security interest to help redress the fiction that lies within the mortgage relationship. The historical origins of this concept are not clear, although by the 17th century the courts of equity appear to have routinely allowed borrowers to redeem their land despite a failure to comply with the legal conditions for repayment. They may have done so either by awarding specific performance of the lender's agreement to re-convey the land upon repayment or by granting the borrower relief from the forfeiture of their land to the lender (see Watt (2007)). The development of the equity of redemption provides an important and interesting insight into the development of equitable doctrine and the relationship between the courts of law and the courts of equity. It provides an example of the influence of a number of Lord Chancellors of the time in shaping their emerging Chancery jurisdiction which, although on its face was in direct conflict with the common law courts, proved a convenient route to achieve the desired outcome of the mortgage as a security interest (Sugarman and Warrington (1997)).

8.30   The equity of redemption remains an influential concept today but we need to translate its significance into the realm of the legal charge by way of mortgage. In particular, it is argued that under a legal charge the equity of redemption as a proprietary concept is outmoded (Nield (2005), Watt (2007)). Under a legal charge the borrower retains the legal estate in his or her land and creates a charge out of that estate to confer upon the lender a right to look to the land to support recovery of the debt. Where the loan is used by the borrower to purchase the land, we will see that the courts characterize the transaction as the borrower acquiring ownership (confusingly referred to as the equity of redemption) already subject to the legal charge (see **Chapter 11** and *Abbey National BS v Cann* (1991), *Southern Pacific Mortgages Ltd v Scott* (2015)). Upon repayment of the loan, there is no redemption in the sense of any land to be re-conveyed back to the borrower. The charge is simply discharged because there is no longer any debt to be recovered from the earmarked land. The borrower does need equity's assistance to be able to repay the debt even though he or she may not have met the contractual terms of the loan agreement. The equitable right of redemption (or rather repayment) remains crucial to the operation of the legal charge as a security interest. What also remains influential is the symbolism of the equity of redemption as a reflection of the economic value of the borrower's interest in the land. This value is reflected in monetary terms (ie the value of the property less the loan) and in investment value from potential increases in the land's market value which generally accrues to the borrower.

## Lender's Rights and Remedies

8.31   A lender has a contractual right to sue the borrower for recovery of the mortgage debt but the real value in taking security is to take direct action to recover the mortgage debt from the mortgaged property by exercising the rights and powers the security confers. We will concentrate upon the rights and remedies granted by the legal charge by way of mortgage as the most common form of security over land. The most sought-after rights and remedies are the power to sell the mortgaged property to recover the debt from the sale proceeds with any balance, representing the borrower's equity, being paid back to the borrower. However, for the lender to sell the land most advantageously, the lender will usually wish to obtain vacant possession. Occasionally, particularly in relation to commercial property or a Buy to Let mortgage, a lender may wish to take over the management of the property to claim the income it produces. In these circumstances, a lender may appoint a receiver who is usually not only granted power to receive the income from the property but wider powers of management including the power of sale. It is thus the right to take possession and the powers to sell and appoint a receiver that will be our primary focus.

8.32   At one time the power of a mortgagee to foreclose was an important right. Foreclosure operates to extinguish the borrower's property rights leaving the lender the full legal and beneficial owner (LPA 1925, ss 88(2) and 89(2)). It is thus a drastic remedy, particularly where the debt represents only a small portion of the value of the property and the lender reaps a windfall profit. As a result, foreclosure is strictly controlled by the court. The lender must apply to court which will direct accounts to be taken to determine the amount owed to the lender; the borrower has then one last chance to repay this sum before the foreclosure order absolute is granted. Even so, the court may exercise its discretion to order sale rather than foreclosure and the foreclosure order itself may be reopened where the circumstances upon which it was made are subsequently challenged (*Campbell v Holyland* (1877), see also the more recent Hong Kong examples in *Hang Seng Bank v Mee Ching Development Ltd* (1970), *Frencher Ltd (in liquidation) v Bank of East Asia* (1995)). Given this time, expense, and uncertainty, foreclosure is effectively obsolete where security is taken over land. It remains significant, under the label of appropriation, where security is taken over shares or other financial collateral (see the Financial Collateral Arrangements (No 2) Regulations 2003 (SI 2003/3226) and *Cukurova Finance International Ltd v Alfa Telecom Turkey Ltd* (2015)).

## Source of the Lender's Rights and Powers

8.33 A lender's rights and powers may flow from the inherent nature of the security, be implied by statute, or expressly conferred or varied by the mortgage. A classic mortgage by conveyance or sub-demise in its conferral of a legal estate upon the mortgagee gave an inherent right to possession and also a right to foreclose. A charge, by contrast, gives no inherent right to possession or to foreclose. A chargee must apply to court for an order for sale or to appoint a receiver unless within the charge itself these rights are expressly conferred or may be otherwise implied.

8.34 A legal charge by way of mortgage as a hybrid security grants an implied statutory right to take possession. Section 87(1) of the LPA 1925 provides that the lender under a legal charge by way of mortgage enjoys the same rights and remedies as if they held a mortgage by sub-demise for a term of 3,000 years. Thus, the lender under a legal charge of land enjoys a right to possession. A lender, whose security is created by deed including a legal charge of land, also benefits from the implied powers conferred by section 101 of the LPA 1925 including the power of sale and to appoint a receiver. A second legal chargee may also claim these powers since their security must be created by deed, although they will only be able to sell subject to any property interests that can claim priority; for instance, the first legal charge. An equitable mortgagee or chargee may also benefit from the statutory powers implied by section 101 of the LPA 1925 but only if the mortgage/charge is made by deed. Furthermore, the ambit, for instance of a power of sale, will depend upon the content of the equitable security right (see 8.15–8.21). An equitable charge of the legal estate, arising because of some failure in acquisition, may claim the section 101 implied powers in relation to both the equitable and legal estate (*Swift 1st Ltd v Colin* (2011)). An equitable mortgagee or a purely equitable chargee may only exercise the implied powers in relation to the equitable proprietary right that constitutes their security. Some other device, for instance a power of attorney from the borrower, is necessary to enable the lender to deal with the legal estate.

8.35    An inherent or implied power may be expressly supplemented or varied by the terms of the security interest. Institutional lenders usually adopt standard form documentation which they pay their lawyers to prepare. They think carefully about the terms of the rights and powers they desire. It is thus equally important for a borrower, or their advisers, to carefully read the mortgage to gain a full understanding of their lender's rights and powers.

## Regulation of the Lender's Rights and Remedies

8.36    The lender's rights and powers have long been constrained to ensure that they are exercised only to facilitate recovery of the lender's debt and that they are employed with due care and probity. These constraints operate on a number of fronts. We will see that equity imposes fiduciary-type duties particularly over the way in which a lender exercises their power of sale and the manner in which a receiver manages the mortgaged property (see eg *Palk v Mortgage Services Funding plc* (1993) at 337–8 per Sir Donald Nicholls V-C).

8.37    The enforcement of mortgages over the home are subject to particular statutory and regulatory controls which try and ensure that the mortgage is only enforced after the continued viability of the borrower's quest for home ownership has been explored. The most common causes of mortgage repayment difficulties arise from the disruption caused by job loss, illness, or relationship breakdown all of which may be short-lived. We will explore how these regulatory controls operate a little later when considering the protection of the borrower (see **8.68-8.72**). For the time being, it is sufficient to note that these controls set out the steps that a regulated mortgage provider is required to take if a borrower cannot meet their repayment commitments (see the Financial Services and Markets Act 2000 (FSMA 2000) and the Financial Conduct Authority's (FCA) Handbook, MCOB 13). MCOB 13 requires a mortgage provider to explore ways in which the mortgage debt might be rescheduled to enable the borrower to get back on track in fulfilling their repayment obligations, for instance by granting a payment holiday, extending the mortgage term, capitalizing the arrears, or changing the repayment method. Other sources of financial help may be available, for instance through social security payments or other government schemes, and a lender is required to tell the borrower of these possibilities. All in all, a regulated mortgage provider is expected 'not to repossess the property unless all other reasonable attempts to resolve the position have failed' (MCOB 13.3.2A). Similar calls for forbearance are found in the Consumer Credit Sourcebook (CONC) when the mortgage is subject to the Consumer Credit Act 1974 (CCA 1974). However, the FCA acknowledges that lenders' compliance with these rules is mixed (FCA (2014)).

8.38    If a lender does seek possession of a home, judicial scrutiny of forbearance operates (whether the mortgage is regulated or not), first, through the Pre-action Protocol on Repossession based upon Mortgage Arrears which calls for lenders to demonstrate to the court that they have explored forbearance before possession proceedings can be issued and, secondly, through the court's discretion to adjourn or delay the execution of a possession order against a dwelling-house conferred by section 36 of the Administration of

Justice Act 1970. All these measures seek to promote a change in culture triggered by the spectre of raising repossessions following the financial crisis of 2007–8 from 'pay and possess' to 'managed forbearance' (Wallace and Ford (2010), Wallace (2012)).

8.39 It is often not until a borrower faces the threat of enforcement proceedings that they resort to the protections available to them, for instance against unfair terms or credit relationships, which we will explore further at 8.91–8.93 and 8.111 (see eg *Commercial First Business v Atkins* (2012), *Graves v Capital Homes Loans Ltd* (2014)).

## Possession

8.40 The starting point is that the lender under a legal charge by way of mortgage is entitled to an immediate right to possession that is not dependent upon the borrower's default (*Four-Maids Ltd v Dudley Marshall (Properties) Ltd* (1957)). Thus, the fact that the borrower has a counterclaim or a right of set-off against the lender does not detract from the lender's right to immediately claim possession (*Mobil Oil Co Ltd v Rawlinson* (1982), *Citibank Trust v Ayivor* (1987), *National Westminster Bank plc v Skelton* (1993)). Even equity will not assist to grant the borrower time to remedy the breach of their loan obligations (*Birmingham Citizens Permanent BS v Caunt* (1962)). This stark starting point, however, is overlain by a number of mechanisms that cast a remedial gloss, particularly where possession is sought over the home. The first and most obvious is that the mortgage may expressly vary the lender's inherent right to possession and provide that it is only exercisable upon default.

### The Purpose

8.41 The lender cannot claim possession because they would like to live in the borrower's home. A lender can only exercise their right to facilitate the recovery of their debt.

> **Quennel v Maltby (1979):** A student house had been let without the consent of the landlord's mortgagees and thus did not bind them. The landlord wished to evict the students but did not have grounds to do so. He struck on a scheme to try and solve his problem. His wife took a transfer of the mortgage from the existing mortgagee and then took proceedings for possession based upon the fact the letting was unauthorized. The court refused to grant the order for possession when the purpose was to evict the students rather than recover the loan.

It is thus a little surprising to find that seeking possession may be justified as a means of putting pressure on the borrower to repay even though there is little or no prospect of recovery (*Co-operative Bank plc v Phillips* (2014) but see *Albany Home Loans Ltd v Massey* (1997) and the Protection from Eviction Act 1977 at 8.44).

### Equitable Duty to Account

8.42 Equity will not interfere with the lender's right to take possession but it will control its exercise. When a lender goes into possession, equity places upon them a duty to take due care of the property and to account strictly not only for what is received but for what ought to have been received. Thus, if the property is rented the lender must account for the rental they receive and take due steps when the tenants leave to rent the property for a market rent (*White v City of London Brewery* (1889)). The origin and exact extent of the duty is a little obscure (see Frisby (2000)). However, it is perceived as sufficiently onerous by lenders to dissuade them from taking possession unless absolutely necessary, for instance as a prelude to sale.

### Process

8.43  We have already noted that where a mortgage is taken over someone's home, regulatory business conduct rules expect lenders to show forbearance and that the Pre-action Protocol on Repossession based on Mortgage Arrears backs up this call (8.37–8.38). If a lender fails to take adequate forbearance steps, the borrower may complain to the FCA (as the regulator) or the Financial Ombudsman Service (as the designated alternative dispute resolution body). If enforcement action is taken by the lender the court, in accordance with the Pre-action Protocol, should not allow the lender to issue proceedings without checking that the lender has considered forbearance with the borrower but they have been unable to agree how the loan repayment can be put back on track (but see the criticism of Whitehouse (2009)). But will the court refuse an order for possession? It appears not (*Thakker v Northern Rock plc* (2014)). The Irish courts, after initial sympathy for the borrower, have taken a similar line (*Irish Life & Permanent Plc v Dunne and Dunphy* (2015) overturning *Stepstone Mortgage Funding Ltd v Frizzel* (2012)).

8.44  An important question is whether or not the lender must seek the court's assistance in obtaining possession. Lenders do accept the keys from a borrower who voluntarily gives up possession of his or her home, but what if a borrower wants to stay if he or she can? A lender must obtain a court order for possession where the mortgage is regulated by the CCA 1974 (s 125). The same clear prohibition does not apply to other mortgages over residential property although mooted by the Ministry of Justice (2009). However, again there are a number of ways in which a lender is 'persuaded' to seek the assistance of the court. There are two statutory provisions which impose criminal liability. First, it is an offence to use violence to gain access to occupied premises (Criminal Law Act 1977, s 6) and, secondly it is also an offence to harass an occupier of residential premises to give up occupation (Protection from Eviction Act 1977, s 1(3), *Roberts v Bank of Scotland* (2014)). There is also regulatory pressure for a lender to seek possession of residential premises by way of a court order. For instance, one might expect the FCA to take a dim view of lenders who do not seek a court order for possession in pursuit of their obligation to treat their customers fairly. The Council of Mortgage Lenders, as the trade body of mortgage providers, certainly believes its members should seek a court order and has issued guidance to that effect.

### Court's Discretion Under Section 36 of the Administration of Justice Act 1970 (as amended)

8.45  This section provides for final court adjudicated forbearance. It was enacted when it became clear that the court has no equitable jurisdiction to delay possession (see Payne

(1969)). The section does not limit the lender's right to take possession but it does control its exercise by conferring upon the court power to adjourn proceedings, or stay or postpone the execution of the possession order they are bound to make where they are satisfied that 'the mortgagor is likely to be able within a reasonable period to pay any sums due under the mortgage or to remedy a default'. The section provides an important jurisdiction to allow a borrower a final chance to clear the amount he or she owes (or at least any arrears) as well as independent oversight of the regulatory pressures upon lenders to show forbearance (Haley (1997), McMurtry (2007)). However, this discretion is narrowly defined which stands in contrast to the court's wider discretion when sanctioning sale or repossession of a home under alternative, but contextually similar, statutory provisions—for example, when making an order where the mortgage is regulated by the CCA 1974 (McMurtry (2010)) and an order under TOLATA 1996, see Chapter 6.

8.46  The section applies to land which includes a dwelling-house even though the house may not be the borrower's home (*Bank of Scotland v Miller* (2001)). It can thus apply to possession proceedings where a dwelling-house is subject to a commercial mortgage.

8.47  However, the jurisdiction is only available where the lender is seeking possession by way of a court order (*Ropaigealach v Barclays Bank plc* (2000)). It is thus possible, if a purchaser can be found, for a lender to avoid the jurisdiction simply by selling the property themselves or through a receiver (*Horsham Properties Group Ltd v Clark* (2009)). This sale will overreach the borrower's proprietary right in the house and enable the purchaser to claim possession as against the borrower as a trespasser and against any other occupier depending upon the property rights that occupier enjoys (LPA 1925, ss 88(1) and 89(1) but see *National & Provincial BS v Ahmed* (1995)). This is a serious flaw in the legislation that is controversial (Clarke (1983), Dixon (1999)). It could conceivably be challenged as incompatible with the human right to respect for the home enshrined in Article 8 of the European Convention on Human Rights (see the Human Rights Act 1998, s 3 and Sch 1, and Nield and Hopkins (2013) but see *McDonald v McDonald* (2016)). We saw at 8.44 that a lender will usually be persuaded to seek possession by way of a court order but it is regrettable that the legal position does not necessitate this practice.

8.48  Possession proceedings will be issued against the borrowers (as mortgagors) and notice of the proceedings must also be sent to the house itself so as to inform any occupier. Such an occupier may be a spouse or partner of the borrower, who enjoys equitable co-ownership with the borrower, or has a statutory right of occupation (see Chapter 11). If they learn of the possession proceedings either as a result of this notice or otherwise, they can apply to court to be joined as a party and seek the protection of section 36. Alternatively, a tenant may be in occupation. Where the tenancy has been authorized by the lender, it is binding upon them according to the terms of the tenancy and by claiming possession the lender can direct the rental to be paid to them. Invariably in these circumstances the lender will do so through a receiver (see 8.64-8.67). Where the tenancy is unauthorized by the lender, the tenancy is not binding on the lender and the tenant may be evicted. The unauthorized tenant cannot apply under section 36 but is afforded limited respite by applying to court to exercise the court's discretion to stay execution of the possession order for a period of up to two months (Mortgage Repossession (Protection of Tenant etc) Act 2010, O'Neill (2011)).

**8.49**   The court's discretion may be exercised where it is satisfied that the borrower is likely to be able to pay any sums due under the mortgage or remedy any other default within a reasonable time. The majority of cases concern mortgage arrears when the court is solely concerned with how and when the borrower is able to meet their financial commitments. The terms of the mortgage will define the borrower's repayment commitments but will often provide that upon default the full amount of capital and interest due under the mortgage becomes immediately repayable. However, when the court is considering the sums due where mortgage payments are paid in instalments, they are entitled to look only to the arrears rather than the full amount outstanding (Administration of Justice Act 1973, s 8, *Central Trustees v Ross* (1979), *Bank of Scotland v Grimes* (1986)). By contrast, a mortgage repayable on demand, which is common in much commercial borrowing, means just that and the sums due following a demand are the full amount of the capital and interest that is owed (*Habib Bank Ltd v Tailor* (1982)). We do, however, need to differentiate two circumstances. The first is where the borrower decides that the only way in which they can meet their mortgage commitments is by selling the house and downsizing, by buying a cheaper house, or exiting home ownership altogether and finding a new home on the rental market. Secondly, there is the situation where the borrower has suffered an interruption in income, perhaps because of illness, job loss, or relationship breakdown, but hopes to be able to get their mortgage payments commitments back on track by clearing the arrears that have accumulated.

**8.50**   In the first situation, the court will only exercise its discretion if there is a foreseeable prospect that the borrower will sell their home (eg *LBI HF v Stanford* (2015)). Perhaps an offer from a prospective purchaser has been received but the mere fact that the property is being advertised for sale or may be sold in the future is unlikely to be enough.

> **Bristol & West BS v Ellis (1997):** Mrs Ellis had fallen into arrears after her husband had left her. She asked the court to suspend the warrant to enforce repossession so that she could sell the house in three to five years' time when her children had finished their full-time education. She produced estate agents' opinions showing that the likely sale price of £80,000–£85,000 would be sufficient to discharge the mortgage of £70,000. However, the court refused her application given the uncertainty of the housing market and the consequent risk that the projected sale proceeds would be insufficient to meet the mortgage debt.

**8.51**   A borrower may force a sale, in the face of his or her lender's opposition, by an application to court under section 91 of the LPA 1925. An unusual example of this jurisdiction is found in the following case.

> **Palk v Mortgage Services Funding plc (1993):** The Palks' house was valued at less than the amount the Palks owed their lender as a result of the housing recession of the late 1980s and early 1990s. Their lender wanted to gain possession but delay the sale of the Palks' house until the property market recovered. They wanted to let out the property in the meantime and apply the rent in meeting part of the ongoing mortgage repayments. The Palks were concerned that this strategy would merely increase the level of their arrears and successfully applied to court to force the sale of their house.

However, the court is only likely to order sale if the sale price will exceed the mortgage debt but only exceptionally, as in the Palks' case, where there is negative equity (ie the house is worth less than the mortgage debt). The real issue is who should control the sale.

---

*Cheltenham & Gloucester plc v Krausz* **(1997):** The Krauszs were in mortgage arrears totalling about £83,000 and their lender had obtained a possession order which the court had suspended on several occasions. The Krauszs hoped to clear their arrears from the sale of their house and they found a purchaser who was prepared to pay £65,000. However, their lender refused to agree to the sale believing that the property was worth nearer £90,000— they wanted to obtain possession and sell the property themselves in exercise of their power of sale. The Krauszs applied for an order for sale under section 91 but the court refused. The court distinguished the unusual circumstances in *Palk*. They held that if there is negative equity the lender should be entitled in the normal course to control the sale to minimize their exposure to risk since there is a danger that the borrower will try and delay the sale so that they can stay in their home.

---

**8.52** In the second situation, the court will take a more measured look. At the time the Administration of Justice Act 1970 (AJA 1970) was enacted it was intended to provide assistance to borrowers who suffered a temporary interruption to their ability to meet their mortgage commitments, for instance because they had lost their job or had become ill. It was thus anticipated that 'a reasonable time' would be relatively short. However, during the prolonged housing recession of the late 1980s and early 1990s, when many borrowers fell into mortgage arrears and were in negative equity, the Court of Appeal developed a rather more long-term view. They did so in the important case of *Cheltenham & Gloucester BS v Norgan* (1996) with a view partly to reduce the time, trauma, and expense of repeated applications to adjourn or stay the proceedings. The question to be asked is whether, taking into account the whole of the remaining mortgage term, it is likely that the borrower will be able to repay all that is owed to the lender. In answering this question, the court needs to consider such matters as what is the reason for the arrears, how long any temporary difficulty is likely to last, how much the borrower can reasonably afford to pay both now and in the future, the agreed mortgage terms including the length of the anticipated repayment term, and the anticipated repayment schedule. The borrower's financial resources may be bolstered by the limited state assistance available through Support for Mortgage Interest (SMI) although the government is keen to reduce this funding by encouraging borrowers to take out payment protection insurance to cover the risk of job loss or illness. In the light of these facts, it is then possible for the court to ask whether it is reasonable for the lender to recoup the arrears of interest over the whole term, to extend the repayment term, or to add the arrears to the capital (at 356 per Evans LJ). To answer these questions, the parties will need to produce the necessary evidence including detailed financial statements. Although these questions should already have been explored privately by the parties as part of the forbearance exercise expected pursuant to MCOB 13 and the Pre-action Protocol, *Norgan* remains an important decision. The court's role under the AJA 1970 provides a final opportunity for an independent evaluation of a mortgage's sustainability before a borrower finally loses their home.

8.53  It is difficult to gain a clear idea of how the courts actually exercise their discretion under the AJA 1970 as the proceedings largely take place in the county court whose decisions are not reported. It is only rarely that a case finds its way on appeal to a higher court whose judgments are reported. Bright and Whitehouse (2013) have conducted empirical research which reveals that unfortunately all too often borrowers fail to take advantage of section 36, judges lack the necessary evidence upon which to exercise their discretion, and borrowers lack access to advisers who could help them negotiate the daunting process of saving their home.

8.54  Where a court decides to adjourn proceedings or grant a stay, suspension, or postponement of execution of the possession order, they may only do so for a definite period although the borrower may apply to have that period extended (*Royal Trust Co of Canada v Markham* (1975), *Bank of Scotland plc v Zinda* (2012)). The court has unfettered discretion to attach conditions to the stay as it thinks fit (*Bank of Scotland plc v Zinda* (2012)). For instance, they may impose conditions dictating the amounts the borrower must continue to pay which need not be confined to the arrears.

## The Power of Sale

8.55  The power of sale may be conferred either expressly, by the terms of the mortgage or charge, or impliedly, by section 101(1)(i) of the LPA 1925, where the mortgage or charge is created by deed. It is a powerful remedy because it entitles the lender to sell without having to go to court. It thus enables the lender to take control of the sale and deduct the outstanding loan, including any arrears, from the sale proceeds and account to the borrower (or a subsequent mortgagee or chargee) for any balance. The court's intervention is limited to oversight of how the sale is conducted to safeguard the interests of the borrower. Nevertheless, as the power of sale is effectively agreed to by the borrower it is not thought that the power can be challenged as a disproportionate deprivation (or control) of the borrower's possessions which would be incompatible with Article 1 Protocol 1 of the European Convention on Human Rights (see the Human Rights Act 1998, s 3 and Sch 1, and *Horsham Properties Group Ltd v Clarke* (2009)).

### The Mechanics of Sale

8.56  Under section 101(1)(i) of the LPA 1925 the power of sale *arises* when the loan becomes due for repayment—that is, upon the legal date for redemption (*Twentieth Century Banking Corp v Wilkinson* (1977)) or where the mortgage is repayable by instalments, when an instalment payment is due. Thus, the power of sale *arises* soon after the creation of the mortgage. However, the power will not become *exercisable* until the borrower defaults. The events of default are often expressly stated in the mortgage but there is a fall-back position in section 103 of the LPA 1925 which specifies three events of default. First, when notice is given requiring repayment which the borrower fails to comply with within three months, secondly, when interest is in arrear for two months or more and, lastly, when there has been some other breach of the mortgage or charge. Where the mortgage is regulated by the FSMA 2000 or the CCA 1974 the lender should also comply with the forbearance requirements of the relevant conduct of business rules.

**8.57**   To enable the lender to pass title to a purchaser free of the borrower's interest in the mortgaged property, section 88(1) of the LPA 1925 provides that the borrower's interests are effectively overreached and vest instead in the proceeds of sale. Accordingly, the lender is under a duty to apply the proceeds in first paying the costs of the sale, secondly in satisfying the mortgage debt and, lastly, in paying any balance to the person next entitled; namely, the borrower or a subsequent mortgagee (LPA 1925, s 105). A purchaser from a mortgagee must check that the power of sale has arisen but is not required to check that an event of default has occurred—the receipt of the lender for the sale proceeds is sufficient (LPA 1925, ss 105 and 107).

### Duties of the Lender

**8.58**   The lender owes duties in equity (not tort) to exercise the power of sale in good faith to recover the mortgage debt and to take reasonable care in the conduct of sale with a view to obtaining a proper market price for the property.

> **Cuckmere Brick Co v Mutual Finance (1971):** The lender's mortgage was secured on land with planning permission to build 100 flats and 35 houses. Following default, the lenders in exercise of their power of sale put the land up for auction. The auction details referred only to the planning permission for the houses and it was only at the auction itself that they gave details of the planning permission for the flats. The land was sold for £44,000 but the borrowers maintained that the land, if it had been properly advertised, could have been sold for £75,000. They successfully brought an action for an account from the lenders to reflect the price that should have been obtained.

> **Tse Kwok Lam v Wong Chit Sen (1983):** Following default, the lender exercised his power of sale by putting the mortgaged property up for sale by auction. The auction was only advertised with limited details shortly before it took place. A reserve price was fixed without the advice of a qualified valuer and at the auction only one bid for the reserve price was made by the lender's wife, representing a company in which the lender was interested as a shareholder. Although there was no rule against a lender selling to a company in which they were interested, the circumstances of this sale demonstrated a lack of reasonable care and called into question the good faith of the lender. Given the time it had taken for the borrower to object to the sale, it would not be set aside but damages would be awarded to reflect the price that should have been obtained.

**8.59**   The duty arises in equity from the relationship between the lender and borrower which confers upon the lender a power of sale over the property in which they are both interested (*Silven Properties Ltd v Royal Bank of Scotland plc* (2004)). As a result, the duty is owed to the borrower (or a subsequent mortgagee or chargee or guarantor) but not to everyone who might foreseeably suffer loss, for instance an unsecured creditor of the mortgagor (*Alpstream v PK Airfinance Sari* (2016)). Thus, in *Parker-Tweedale v Dunbar Bank (No 1)* (1991) a beneficial co-owner of the mortgaged house was unable to bring a direct claim against the lender. His claim was against his wife, as trustee of the legal estate, who in turn had a right of action against the lender, although on the facts of the case no breach of duty was proved.

8.60    Although the lender's duty arises in equity, the lender is not a trustee of their power of sale. The power is granted to the lender to protect their own interests in recovery of their debt. The lender can thus choose the time of sale and is not required to take steps to maximize the value of the property. The extent of the lender's obligations is illustrated by the following cases.

> **China and South Seas Bank Ltd v Tan (1990):** The mortgaged property was the shares of a company which formed part of a property group owned by the guarantor, Tan. The property group ran into financial difficulties and the shares dropped dramatically in value. When Tan, as guarantor, was called upon to personally meet the balance of the debt, he alleged that the bank was in breach of its duties by not selling the shares before they had fallen in value. The Privy Council rejected his claim—the lender was not obliged to act and could choose the time when it did so.

> **Silven Properties Ltd v Royal Bank of Scotland (2004):** In preparing to sell the mortgaged property, the lender's receiver had explored the possibility of trying to increase its return by obtaining planning permission and letting some of the vacant units that formed part of the property. In fact, these plans did not proceed but the borrower maintained that the lender's receiver was in breach of duty in not maximizing the return from the property. The Court of Appeal rejected this claim. Whilst the lender was under a duty upon going into possession to take reasonable steps to ensure that the property did not deteriorate in value, it was entitled to sell it in its present state and was not obliged to maximize its value by undertaking further work.

8.61    The nature of the lender's duty is not to obtain the highest price for the property but to take reasonable steps to try and achieve a proper market price at the time that it chooses to sell. The focus is thus not directly on the price but on the lender's conduct. The cases we referred to at **8.58** demonstrate that the court's attention looks to the marketing activity—how was the property advertised, was the advice of expert valuers sought and followed, how did the lender decide what offer to accept, if the property was auctioned how was the reserve price (if any) set? The court accepts that deciding a market price for property is not an exact science but looks rather to a range of prices that allows for a margin of judgment. It is only once a breach of duty is proved that the court must fix the price that should have been obtained to calculate the amount due to the borrower in pursuance of the lender's duty to account (*Michael v Miller* (2004), *Alpstream v PK Airfinance Sari* (2016)).

8.62    The duty of good faith looks both at and beyond the lender's actions or inactions in trying to obtain a proper market price. It is concerned with the lender's motives which (at least in part) must be directed at recovery of the mortgage debt and not some other purpose (*Quennel v Maltby* (1979), *Downsview Nominees Ltd v First City Corp Ltd* (1993), *Meretz Investments NV v ACP Ltd* (2008)). Those motives will be tainted where a conflict of interest is evident. A lender cannot sell to itself (*Farrars v Farrars Ltd* (1889)). It may sell to a related party but, as we saw in *Tse Kwok Lam* (**8.58**), the sale will be carefully scrutinized to check that the lender has obtained a proper price given the evident conflict of interest (*Mortgage Express v Mardner* (2004), *Bradford & Bingley plc v Ross* (2005), *Alpstream v PK Airfinance Sari* (2016)).

8.63 If a breach of duty is proved, a borrower's primary remedy will be to seek an account from the lender to recover damages reflecting the difference in price between what the lender obtained from the sale and what it ought to have received. Where there is no such differential in the price, there will be no duty to account even if there are questions over whether the lender's conduct of the sale met the required standards (*Alpstream v PK Airfinance Sari* (2016)). An order setting aside the sale will only be possible where there is some impropriety which demonstrated a lack of good faith—an undervalue is insufficient (*Corbett v Halifax BS* (2003)). Even so, the court will not set aside a sale where there is an unwarranted delay or to do so would cause unnecessary hardship. Furthermore, the purchaser should be adequately protected. A purchaser must check that the lender has a power of sale that has arisen but is not concerned to check that the power has become exercisable following an event of default (LPA 1925, s 104 and LRA 2002, s 52). Where the land is registered, a registered chargee has the power of disposal and any limitation must be recorded on the register in order to affect a purchaser (LRA 2002, s 52). A purchaser is vulnerable to a sale being set aside against them if they have notice of, or are implicated in, the lender's impropriety (*Lord Waring v Manchester Assurance Co Ltd* (1935), *Property and Bloodstock Ltd v Emerton* (1968), *Corbett v Halifax BS* (2003)). However, they will not be affected if the sale is merely at an undervalue unless the undervalue itself raises the prospect of impropriety rather than just a lack of care (*Corbett v Halifax BS* (2003), *Southern Pacific Mortgages Ltd v Scott* (2015)).

## The Power to Appoint a Receiver

8.64 Appointment of a receiver is an attractive option for a lender where the mortgaged property requires a degree of management either to generate sufficient income to clear the mortgage arrears or before it is sold. It is thus a common enforcement strategy for commercial mortgages, including Buy to Let mortgages. A power to appoint a receiver is implied into mortgages created by deed (LPA 1925, s 101(1)(iii)) but it is common for an express power to be contained in the mortgage deed to detail the powers of management of the receiver.

8.65 A receiver is appointed by giving notice to the borrower after the power has become exercisable following an event of default (LPA 1925, s 109). The receiver will then enter into possession of the property and take over its management to apply the income in satisfaction of the mortgage debt after its own costs and expenses have been met. The mortgage will frequently grant the receiver a power of sale so that by appointing a receiver the lender can indirectly sell the property to recover the mortgage debt. The reason why a lender may choose this indirect route is to avoid liability as a mortgagee in possession (see 8.42).

8.66 Although appointed by, and acting upon the directions of, the lender, a receiver is expressed to be the agent of the borrower and liable to the borrower in the event of a breach of his or her agency responsibilities (LPA 1925, s 105(2)). This is rather an unusual form of agency given that the borrower has no say in the identity of the receiver and is unable to give instructions as to how the receiver should act. The relationship between the lender, borrower, and receiver is tripartite. The mortgage provides the borrower's authority for the lender to appoint and give directions to the receiver. The receiver so appointed owes duties both to the lender and the borrower in equity arising from the receiver's management of the mortgaged property (*Gaskell v Gosling* (1896), *Medforth v Blake* (2000), *Silven Properties Ltd v Royal Bank of Scotland* (2004)).

8.67   The standard of care expected of a receiver is similar to, but slightly different from, that of the lender when exercising its power of sale. When selling the mortgaged property, a lender's role and duties tend to coincide (*Downsview Nominees v First City Corp* (1993), *Silven Properties Ltd v Royal Bank of Scotland* (2004)). However, a receiver's role is also that of management and thus, on occasions, it has a duty to act to protect the mortgaged property in a similar way to a lender who enters into possession (Loi (2010)).

> **Medforth v Blake (2000):** Medforth ran a pig farm. When he ran into financial difficulties his lenders appointed Blake as a receiver. In running the pig business, Blake incurred losses and Medforth successfully claimed that Blake had contributed to those losses by failing to obtain discounts on the bulk purchase of pig feed.

## Protection of the Borrower

8.68   Within credit transactions, the borrower is often perceived as the more vulnerable party. This may be true where the borrower is in need of funds to live, lacks the knowledge or experience in financial affairs to fully understand their repayment commitments, or where the security is an important asset such as their home. Certainly, when credit did not form such a central part of everyday life, the courts of equity were prepared to sometimes challenge the basic tenet of freedom of contract because they recognized that 'necessitous men are not, truly speaking, free men, but, to answer a present exigency, will submit to any terms the crafty may impose upon them' (*Vernon v Bethell* (1762)). To some extent times have changed.

8.69   There are still unfortunately 'crafty' lenders but these usually fall outside the mainstream lenders, namely banks and building societies, who must be regulated to operate in credit markets and value their reputation to maintain their competitive position. Nevertheless, recent financial scandals from the mis-selling of Payment Protection Insurance to the fixing of LIBOR, as well as the irresponsibility of the banks in precipitating the economic crisis of 2007/2008, has shaken the reputation of banks and highlighted the need for more effective national and global regulation of financial institutions.

8.70   In modern commercial lending, the borrower may be a profitable company which wishes to fund the expansion of its flourishing business or maintain its liquidity with an overdraft facility from its bankers. Such companies can source competitive loan terms and afford the services of lawyers and other advisers to protect their interests. Other companies may not be so fortunate if they are struggling to start a business or maintain competitiveness in a difficult marketplace. These companies, in order to persuade a lender to provide loan facilities, may additionally have to look to their shareholders and directors to offer their personal assets, in particular their homes, as security.

8.71 The same divergence in types of borrowers is also evident within domestic lending. Borrowers range from those who wish to use their earning power to buy a home, to those who are in financial difficulties and wish to raise money or consolidate their immediate liabilities. The former should be able to choose from a number of mainstream banks and building societies who are prepared to offer competitive loan terms because the risk of default is low. The borrower's earnings should cover his or her repayments and the loan will be secured against property which it is hoped will increase (or at least maintain) its value. The latter more closely resemble those who were equity's traditional concern. They are unlikely to have the luxury of choice or to be able to afford the guidance of professional advisers. However, in both cases domestic borrowers are likely to lack the experience of credit markets that are the domain of the financial institutions that earn their profits from credit and can dictate, rather than have to negotiate, loan terms. Furthermore, within loan contracts the risk of non-performance is with the borrower. A borrower must maintain a steady income stream to meet his or her extended debt obligations in the face of possible disruptions caused by unemployment, sickness, or relationship breakdown, which are the primary causes of domestic mortgage default, yet are largely beyond the control of the borrower.

8.72 We have already considered how borrowers may be protected when a lender seeks possession (by requiring the lender to first show forbearance) or the lender actually enters into possession and/or exercises their power of sale (by imposing equitable duties to account). We now need to explore the complex web of other protections that are available to this spectrum of different types of borrower. We will divide our examination into three broad areas:

- first, we will look at the regulation of the market for certain credit products, including first and second mortgages secured on the home, that operates through the FSMA 2000 and the CCA 1974;

- secondly, we will look at the operation of contractual vitiating factors that guard against exploitation in the creation of mortgages—we will concentrate by way of example on the effect of undue influence or misrepresentation on the creation of mortgages over the family home to secure credit advanced for a borrower's business;

- lastly, we will look at the common law, equitable and statutory consumer controls over loan terms particularly those terms that govern redemption, interest rates, and collateral advantages.

## Market Regulation

**8.73**  Within credit market regulation, protection is offered by controlling who can lend within those markets and by setting standards of market conduct to which they must adhere. The secured credits market with which we are primarily concerned is the market for regulated mortgage contracts, which are defined as loan contracts secured by a mortgage over land, at least 40 per cent of which is used as a dwelling (see the FSMA 2000 (Regulated Activities) Order 2001 (SI 2001/544), arts 61 and 61A, as amended). Other forms of secured credit are also subject to regulation including home purchase plans (ie Sharia-compliant mortgages), home revision plans (ie equity release products), sale and rent-back products (see *Southern Pacific Mortgages Ltd v Scott* (2015)), and certain forms of Buy to Let mortgages. There is thus a close connection between market regulation and the delivery of housing policy. Regulated lenders are the gatekeepers of mortgage-funded home ownership, important funders to the private rental sector, and to the utilization of housing wealth in later life.

**8.74**  The evolution of mortgage market regulation has been relatively recent but has proceeded at a rapid pace. Initial regulation operated through the CCA 1974. However, there has been, and continues to be, a steady advance towards regulation by the FCA, as the primary regulator of financial services, under the FSMA 2000. Regulated mortgages contracts became subject to FSMA regulation in 2004. Home purchase plans and home revision plans followed in 2007, sale and lease-back transactions in 2009, and lending secured by a second charge as well as certain Buy to Let mortgages in 2016. This regulatory reordering has been influenced by European legislation in the form of the Mortgage Credit Directive (2014/17/EU) and Mortgage Credit Directive Order 2015 (SI 2015/910; MCD).

**8.75**  The impetus for this regulatory march is not just the socio-economic importance of secured credit and the evident vulnerability of consumer borrowers already referred to, but also the need to ensure the stability of the financial system as a whole (see the FCA's statutory strategic objective in the FSMA 2000, s 1B(2)). The financial crisis of 2007–8 was not dubbed 'the credit crunch' without reason. Irresponsible mortgage lending, coupled with the adverse effect of funding mechanisms that lenders employed, including their reliance on funds raised from international financial markets and mortgage-backed securities, contributed to financial instability that necessitating government intervention to rescue ailing banks: see generally the Turner Review (FSA (2009)).

**8.76**  The FSMA 2000 regulatory approach seeks to move away from the strict command and control rules evident in the CCA 1974 to a more nuanced principle-based approach to regulation. By setting out broad standards of conduct, known as Principles of Market Conduct (see FCA PRIN Handbook), the expectation is that lenders will embed these standards into their business in a manner which best suits their particular modes of operation. The FCA, as regulator, monitors the lenders' compliance with these market standards initially through guidance and persuasion. This 'soft' approach to regulation does have a harder edge. The Principles are backed up by more detailed conduct of business rules found in the Mortgage Conduct of Business Handbook (FCA, MCOB Handbook), which since the financial crisis have become more prescriptive. The FCA also enjoys wide-ranging investigatory and disciplinary powers so that if persuasion is ineffective the FCA can resort to coercion.

**8.77**  The standards of conduct expected in the mortgage market have been founded upon neo-liberal contractual principles. The expectation is that borrowers and lenders will make rational and self-interested decisions in agreeing respectively to lend and borrow, provided that differences in their knowledge and experience of credit markets is to some extent 'corrected' by first requiring the more experienced/knowledgeable lenders to disclose key information to the less experienced/knowledgeable borrower about the credit terms that are being offered. And, secondly, in the case of consumers, education to understand those credit terms and the financial contractual commitments they are entering into (see Money Advice Service (previously the Consumer Financial Education Body) established by the Financial Services Act 2010). Thus, lenders are expected to make responsible lending decisions, supported by regulatory benchmarks of prudent business conduct within the MCOB. Whilst borrowers are expected to make responsible borrowing decisions provided they have the information upon which they can make a rational choice from a selection of loan terms on offer. The regulatory focus is thus upon trying to ensure a competitive credit market, to provide a choice of suitable mortgages, and transactional equality in the decision to contract based upon comparative information disclosure of the salient mortgages' terms (see eg Ramsay (2006)). The financial crisis exposed the weakness of neo-liberal theory in demonstrating that lenders, driven by their fight for market share, do not always make responsible lending decisions. They relied too heavily on the protection against default provided by their security and also failed to protect their interests by conducting adequate checks of the borrower's ability to afford loan terms in the light of their income and liabilities (see FCA, Mortgage Market Review (2009–12) (MMR). It is also now appreciated that borrowers find it difficult to make responsible borrowing decisions given their drive to step onto and up the housing ladder, coupled with the behavioural nuances that influence their financial judgments. As a result, amendments to the MCOB have inched away from strict neo-liberalism, for instance towards greater lender responsibility in the decision to contract (see Nield (2010, 2015)).

**8.78**  The FSMA 2000 seeks to control lenders' business conduct through a number of mechanisms by:

- licensing of lenders, mortgage brokers, and key personnel who conduct regulated mortgage business;

- setting standards of business behaviour, through overarching principles and detailed rules and guidance, to which lenders are expected to adhere;

- conferring extensive monitoring, investigatory, and disciplinary powers upon the FCA to seek to ensure that lenders comply with the required business standards; and

- providing borrowers with access to informal, quick, and cheap resolution of complaints through alternative dispute resolution by the Financial Ombudsman's Service (FOS).

## Licensing

8.79 The FCA controls those who can conduct mortgage business; for instance, banks, buildings societies, as well as mortgage brokers through whom lenders sell their mortgages. The FCA does so by licensing to signal the regulatory reputation of the lender or broker (FSMA 2000, s 19). An unlicensed mortgage provider who conducts regulated mortgage business is guilty of a criminal offence (FSMA 2000, s 23) and any mortgage they have taken is unenforceable except to the extent that the court is satisfied that it is just and equitable to order enforcement (FSMA 2000, ss 19 and 26–28A and *Helden v Strathmore Ltd* (2011)). A licensed mortgage provider who acts in breach of their licence is not criminally liable nor is any mortgage they have taken unenforceable but they may be held accountable for any damage they have caused pursuant to an action for breach of statutory duty (FSMA 2000, s 20). The FCA also controls those individuals who play a significant role in an authorized mortgage provider's business, for instance senior management and sales personnel who have direct contact with potential borrowers. The FCA must approve such personnel as 'fit and proper persons' and also may prohibit certain persons from being involved in selling mortgages (FSMA 200, ss 56–59A). A borrower may recover damages pursuant to an action for breach of statutory duty where he or she has suffered loss from the actions of either an unauthorized 'fit and proper person' or a prohibited person but the enforceability of any mortgage is unaffected (FSMA 2000, s 71).

## The Principles and Rules

8.80 Authorized lenders are subject to a three-tier strata of regulation of their day-to-day business. These strata are found in the statements of principles, codes of practice, and rules that the FCA may make having consulted both mortgage lenders (through their practitioner panel) and consumers (through their consumer panel) (FSMA 2000, ss 1M–1R and Part IXA). The principles set out overarching expectations of the standards of behaviour to which lenders are expected to adhere. They reflect the principles-based regulation already referred to. Perhaps the most significant principle is that lenders should 'pay regard to its customers and treat them fairly' (FCA PRIN Handbook, Prin 6). This principle (often referred to as TCF) provides a central theme of the FCA's regulatory activity including their compliance action. The codes of practice provide guidance on the types of activity which comply with or breach the relevant principles. Their role is thus illustrative. The rules set out the detailed regulations that govern the conduct of mortgage business and are found in the MCOB Handbook. These rules provide a 'cradle to grave' statement of what lenders should and should not do in selling mortgages, during the life of the mortgage and in the event of mortgage default—we have already considered MCOB 13 which sets the standards expected of lenders in the exercise of their powers (see 8.37). They assist but do not satisfy compliance with the principles (*R (on the application of British Bankers Association) v FSA* (2011)).

8.81 The most significant rules are found in MCOB 4, 5, 6, 7, and 11. MCOB 4A, 5A, 6A, 7A, 7B, and 11A provide additional rules necessitated by the implementation of the MCD which largely reflect the ethos of the existing rules but supplement their detail. MCOB 5, 5A, 6, 6A, 7, 7A, and 7B require information disclosure of the important loan terms in a standard format and are intended to allow borrowers to compare these terms and choose the loan that best suits their needs. MCOB 11 and 11A require lenders to conduct afford-ability checks and MCOB 4 and 4A require lenders to provide advice on the suitability of a loan to the needs of the particular borrower. Changes to these rules, implemented as a result of the MMR, demonstrate a shift from neo-liberal responsibility of the borrower to make an independent rational borrowing decision to greater lender responsibility to try and ensure that the borrower can afford the mortgage loan in order to try and minimize the risk of future default (Nield (2010)). The result has been to make it more difficult for some aspirant home owners to obtain mortgage finance. Particular casualties have been first-time buyers, who must save a larger deposit from their own funds, older borrowers who cannot demonstrate adequate income beyond their retirement, and borrowers who have a poor credit record (Nield (2015)). Certain government initiatives seek to provide some help particularly to first-time buyers (see Help to Buy at http://www.helptobuy. org.uk/).

## Compliance and Redress

8.82 We must differentiate measures available to the FCA, as the primary regulator, to try and ensure regulatory compliance by lenders and the routes by which a borrower may seek redress; for instance, for a failure by their lender to observe the MCOB rules or to treat them fairly.

8.83 The FCA seeks to exert influence upon lenders to persuade them to comply with regu-latory standards but it does have extensive disciplinary powers which can lead to the imposition of a fine upon the offending lender or *in extremis* modification or withdrawal of FCA authorization (FSMA 2000, Part XIV). For instance, certain lenders were dis-ciplined after the financial crisis for irresponsible lending. Prior to resorting to discip-linary proceedings there is a halfway house in obtaining a formal undertaking from the lender to mend their ways. In order to gather evidence of lenders' conduct, the FCA also enjoys wide monitoring and investigatory powers targeted at individual lenders. In addition, it conducts thematic reviews of particular aspects of lenders' behaviour within the mortgage market. Certain other bodies, for instance the FOS, also may bring to the attention of the FCA evidence of consistent breaches of the principles or rules and are furthermore empowered to make a formal complaint to the FCA to which the FCA is required to respond (FSMA 2000, Part XVIA).

8.84 If a borrower has a complaint against their lender they are expected to try and resolve it initially through the customer complaint process which each regulated mortgage provider must provide. If their complaint is not satisfactorily resolved informally, there are two options. The first, and the most common route, is for the borrower to ask the FOS to assist. We consider this route further in the next paragraph. Secondly, an individual borrower may bring an action for breach of statutory duty if they have suffered damage because their lender has not complied with the FCA's rules (FSMA 2000, s 150, eg *Figurasin v Central Capital Ltd* (2014), *Saville v Central Capital Ltd* (2014) but see *Green v Royal Bank of Scotland plc* (2013), *Nexis Property Ltd v Royal Bank of Scotland plc* (2013)). If their lender cannot meet the claim, for instance because it is insolvent, the borrower can recover compensation from the Financial Services Compensation Scheme (eg *Emptage v Financial Services Compensation Scheme Ltd* (2013)).

## Financial Ombudsman's Service

8.85   The FOS is established by Part XVI of the FSMA 2000. It is independent of the FCA and is empowered to consider complaints made by borrowers, whether regulated by the FSMA 2000 or the CCA 1974, as well as other financial services consumers. The FOS in resolving complaints provides an alternative dispute resolution service which is not bound by strict legal rules. It will resolve a complaint in a way it considers 'fair and reasonable', primarily either by rejecting the complaint, by ordering the offending lender to pay 'fair' compensation up to a statutory cap of £150,000, or by directing the lender to take 'just and appropriate' steps (FSMA 2000, s 29, and see *Bunney v Burns Anderson Group plc* (2007)). The borrower is not required to pay any 'costs'. An FOS decision is binding on the lender in the same way as a county court judgment but a borrower may decline to accept an award and pursue their complaint through the courts (*Clarke v In Focus Asset Management & Tax Solutions Ltd* (2014)). The FOS thus provides a convenient, accessible, and cost-effective means by which borrowers' complaints can be resolved by an independent but experienced body. It has played a major role, for instance, in resolving disputes over the mis-selling of endowment mortgages and payment protection insurance. The FOS has attracted criticism, largely from financial services providers, that its decisions can be arbitrary, inconsistent, and opaque. These criticisms are to an extent being addressed by measures to try and ensure that the way in which the FOS exercises its 'fair and reasonable' judgment is more transparent and follows known guidelines (see FSMA 2000, Sch 17, para 8). For instance, it now publishes some details of its decisions and information and advice as to how it will resolve disputes, including a monthly newsletter and subject-specific technical guidance: for example, on how it handles complaints concerning mortgage arrears and early repayment charges.

## Regulation under the Consumer Credit Act 1974

8.86   The CCA 1974's primary focus is on unsecured credit provided, for instance, by credit and store cards, hire-purchase, and payday loans. Despite its focus on unsecured credit, the CCA 1974 continues to affect certain forms of secured credit although it appears that the government's intention is to transfer the regulation of all secure credit to the FSMA 2000 regulatory regime. Already, responsibility for overseeing the regulation of consumer credit under the CCA 1974 has passed to the FCA from its initial regulator the Office of Fair Trading. We will thus concentrate on the differences between the two regimes.

8.87  The CCA 1974 originally regulated secured credit under £25,000. Regulated mortgage contracts (subject to FSMA 2000 regulation) ceased to come within the CCA 1974 in 2004 and the £25,000 cap was removed by amendments introduced by the Consumer Credit Act 2006. It is thus mainly lending secured by a second charge which continues to be subject to the CCA 1974, although subject to the distinct regulatory approach of the FCA (see 8.73–8.85).

8.88  Lending secured by a second charge is often targeted at debt consolidation. This arises where a borrower wishes to consolidate a number of unsecured debts, often carrying high rates of interest, into one debt at a lower rate of interest but secured against their home. Alternatively, a second charge may be taken to secure a loan made for sizeable capital expenditure, for instance home improvements. As the risk of default is high, the lender will charge high rates of interest over a short loan period and often impose more onerous terms: for example, high default charges. One thus might expect the level of consumer protection to be higher and regulation more rigorous. This is indeed the case. The CCA 1974 is also based upon neo-liberal principles with transactional fairness at its core but its scrutiny is more invasive and extensive and the courts have a more prominent role to play.

8.89  Credit providers must be licensed by the FCA. An unlicensed lender, or a lender who acts outside their permission, is subject to criminal sanctions with any loan agreement and supporting mortgage unenforceable save by the direction of the FCA (CCA 1974, ss 26–28A). Credit providers should adhere to the overarching FSMA 2000 principles (eg PRIN 6—to treat their customer fairly) and the detailed rules found in the CONC handbook which detail such generic matters as advertising, information disclosure, responsible lending (including affordability assessments), required action on default, as well as specific standards for second charge lending. Borrowers with a mortgage subject to CCA 1974 regulation may also seek the assistance of the FOS already explored (see 8.85).

8.90  In addition, the CCA 1974 lays down its own statutory requirements which are formalistic in their approach (see generally the CCA 1974, Parts V–VIII). There are prescribed forms and procedures with compliance driven by the threat of unenforceability of the loan and mortgage save with permission of the court (CCA 1974, ss 55, 65, 106, and 127 and see eg *London North Securities Ltd v Meadows* (2005), *Phoenix Recoveries (UK) Ltd v Kotecha* (2011), *Consolidated Finance Ltd v Collins* (2013), *Grace v Black Horse Ltd* (2014), *Re London Scottish Finance Ltd* (2014)). The disclosure of pre-loan information, the form, the process of completion (including a cooling-off period), and execution of both the credit agreement and the charge must all comply with the detailed requirements of the CCA 1974 (ss 55, 60–64, and 105). In addition, during the course of the loan the CCA 1974 requires credit providers to supply copies of the relevant documentation to the borrower (ss 55C, 58, 61A–64, 77–78A, and 107–111) and dictates the process of enforcement, including the need for court proceedings in the event of default (Part VII, ss 76 and 126 but see *Waterside Finance Ltd v Karim* (2013)). The courts are also granted some latitude to alter the credit relationship by varying the loan terms both when confirming the enforceability of the loan or controlling enforcement following default; for example, through Time Orders (ss 127, 129, 135, and 136, see eg *Carey v HSBC plc* (2009)).

8.91   However, perhaps the most distinctive feature of the CCA 1974 armoury is the court's jurisdiction, under sections 140A–140C of the CCA 1974, to reopen a regulated consumer credit transaction where it decides the credit relationship is unfair to the borrower—because of the terms of the agreement, the way in which the creditor has exercised or enforced any of his or her rights, or because of any other thing done (or not done) by the creditor whether before or after the making of the agreement. Unfairness under sections 140A–140C is for the courts to define. They have shown some reluctance to engage with this task until the Supreme Court case of *Plevin v Paragon Personal Finance Ltd*.

> **Plevin v Paragon Personal Finance Ltd (2014):** Mrs Plevin had been sold payment protection insurance but had not been told that almost 72 per cent of the premium she had paid was in fact commission paid to the broker. In a previous case (*Harrison v Black Horse Ltd* (2011)) the Court of Appeal had decided that this non-disclosure was not unfair because it did not offend the relevant FSMA 2000 conduct of business rules. The Supreme Court disagreed and held the relationship to be unfair because Mrs Plevin may well have declined to rely on the advice to take up the insurance if she had known about the level of commission.

The Supreme Court said it was not possible to give a precise and universal test of unfairness but they have provided some very general pointers. First, the relationship that is unfair must be between the creditor and the debtor and not, for instance, the relationship between a debtor and a broker, unless that broker is the agent of the creditor. Secondly, the court is generally concerned with hardship to the debtor but, although a term may operate harshly against a particular debtor, it may not be unfair where its purpose is to protect the legitimate interests of the creditor. Thirdly, the unfairness must arise from the statutory grounds. Fourthly, although there is inevitably a disparity in the knowledge and experience between the creditor and debtor, that disparity does not necessarily render the relationship unfair.

8.92   Also of considerable interest are the Supreme Court's thoughts on the guidance provided by the FCA's conduct of business rules to the concept of fairness under sections 140A–140C. Presumably, published guidance from other regulators (eg the FOS) would be treated in a similar way. The Supreme Court accepted that this guidance might be influential but sounded notes of caution given the different role which conduct of business rules play. These conduct rules are generic and generally only provide threshold standards for a wide variety of circumstances. Furthermore, their formulation has compensation for loss in mind. Their Lordships also noted the different standards formulated by the conduct rules and sections 140A–140C. The conduct rules provide prospective hard-edged guidance whilst sections 140A–140C are concerned with the inherently more fluid concept of fairness at the time of resolution of a dispute which results from past conduct.

8.93   It is unclear whether the sections 140A–140C jurisdiction, or indeed other CCA 1974 provisions enabling the court to intervene, will be retained when the regulation of secured lending becomes more integrated into the FSMA 2000. Although the courts have not shown themselves to be particularly consumer-friendly in exercising their powers under the CCA 1974, their jurisdiction does have the potential to offer a powerful route to direct borrower redress through judicial oversight rather than regulatory control. It surely would thus be a retrograde step not to carry over this jurisdiction to regulation under the FSMA 2000.

## Surety Mortgages and Procedural Fairness

8.94   Students of contract will be well aware that it is a fundamental principle that parties freely enter into their contractual obligations. In upholding this principle the law has developed a number of doctrines that enable a party to set aside transactions where he or she can prove that their consent has not been freely given. These doctrines come under the umbrella of vitiating factors and include duress, undue influence, misrepresentation, unconscionable bargains, and *non est factum*. We turn now to examine how these factors may affect a mortgage transaction. In particular, we are concerned with surety mortgages where commercial and domestic borrowing comes together. For example, a spouse wishes to raise finance for his or her business but the lender will only advance the money if the loan can be secured by a mortgage over the family home to which the borrower's spouse must consent when the home is jointly owned, whether at law or in equity. The following leading cases illustrate the situation and the insights they provide will dominate our consideration of the legal issues involved.

***Barclays Bank plc v O'Brien* (1994):** Mr O'Brien needed money for his business. He negotiated a loan from Barclays, a term of which was that the bank would take a mortgage over the family home that Mr and Mrs O'Brien jointly owned. To 'persuade' his wife to grant the mortgage to Barclays Mr O'Brien misrepresented the amount that would be secured under the mortgage and was over-optimistic about the future profitability of the business. When the business failed and the bank tried to enforce their mortgage, Mrs O'Brien successfully argued that the mortgage should be set aside against her share in the home because of her husband's misrepresentations. The bank should have suspected that the husband might misrepresent the situation and thus should have taken steps to ensure that Mrs O'Brien had freely entered into the mortgage.

***CIBC v Pitt* (1994):** Mr Pitt wished to obtain a loan secured on the home he owned jointly with his wife. He told the bank that they wanted to buy a second home but in fact he used the loan to invest in the stock market. Mrs Pitt was reluctant to agree to the mortgage but Mr Pitt wore her down by constant badgering and finally she agreed. When Mr Pitt's investments failed and he could not repay the loan, CIBC wanted to enforce the mortgage. Mrs Pitt argued that the mortgage should be set aside against her interest in the home because of the actual under influence of her husband. The House of Lords refused to do so because, although Mr Pitt had unduly influenced his wife, the circumstances were such that the bank could not be expected to have notice of the husband's behaviour.

---

*Royal Bank of Scotland v Etridge (No 2)* **(2001):** Mr and Mrs Etridge bought an expensive new home which was purchased in Mrs Etridge's name. Mr Etridge arranged the finances which included funds from the sale of their existing home and two mortgages—one from the Royal Bank of Scotland and another from a trust. Mrs Etridge went with her husband to the bank's solicitors and she signed the mortgage documentation without reading them or having them explained to her—she trusted her husband that all was in order. When the Etridges could not repay their loans, the Royal Bank of Scotland sought possession of the Etridges' home. Mrs Etridge unsuccessfully argued that she was not bound by the mortgage because it should be presumed that her husband had unduly influenced her to enter into it. The House of Lords decided that there was no undue influence but, even if there had been and the Royal Bank of Scotland knew of this risk, the bank was entitled to assume that Mrs Etridge had been properly advised by their solicitors and thus had freely entered into the mortgage aware of its contents and implications.

---

**8.95** The decision in *O'Brien* paved the way for a wave of cases in which surety mortgages were challenged, usually by a wife asserting that the mortgage should be set aside against her interest in the home because she had been unduly influenced by pressure from her husband to enter into the mortgage. It was argued that the bank should have known of this likelihood in the circumstances and taken steps to ensure that her consent had been freely given. The House of Lords responded to the popularity of the *O'Brien* defence in its subsequent decision in *Etridge* when it took the opportunity to refine and constrain the application of undue influence to surety mortgages. The challenge usually has been made by wives claiming undue influence by their husbands and in our discussion we will refer to husband and wife. However, the same argument may be made where there is some other close personal relationship between the borrower and mortgagor/surety whether within a heterosexual or homosexual relationship or between family members or even close friends (see eg *Abbey National Bank Plc v Stringer* (2006), *Credit Lyonnais v Burch* (1997)).

## Undue Influence

**8.96** Undue influence is a difficult concept to pin down. Lord Clyde in *Etridge* (at [92]) observed that '[i]t is something which can be more easily recognised when found than exhaustively analysed in the abstract'. At its core, undue influence is the improper use of pressure or influence to effectively deprive a party of his or her free and independent will. The victim may perfectly understand his or her actions but nevertheless their judgment has been overborne so that the decision they make cannot be truly said to be their own. Inevitably, it is difficult to determine when influence crosses the line to become undue. In *Daniel v Drew* ((2005) at [36]) Ward LJ described the critical distinction— '[t]he [wife] may be led but she must not be driven and her will must be the offspring of her own volition, not a record of someone else's'.

**8.97**  Undue influence in its legal categorization takes two broad forms. First, there is actual undue influence where overt acts exert the improper pressure and thus it is similar to duress to which it has been compared. For instance, actual undue influence was found in *Pitt* when Mr Pitt continuingly nagged his wife to grant the mortgage. Actual undue influence is a legal wrong and without more can provide the basis for setting aside a transaction. Secondly, evidence of undue influence may be presumed from the relationship between the parties. Within presumed or relational undue influence, certain types of relationship are accepted in themselves as giving rise to a presumption that the trust inherent in these relationships has been abused. Examples of these relationships are solicitor and client, doctor and patient, parent and child, religious leader and follower but they do not include husband and wife. The essential trust and confidence or dependency that characterizes presumed undue influence may also be established within a particular relationship that falls outside these established categories. It is this basis of presumed undue influence that has been asserted within the family context as sometimes existing in a particular close relationship—for instance, that a wife places trust and confidence or depends upon the financial judgment of her husband. In this second category, proof of trust and confidence is not of itself sufficient to establish presumed undue influence. The relationship must be viewed in the context of the particular transaction under scrutiny when undue influence may be evidentially presumed because the wife's agreement to the transaction can only be explained by the likelihood that the husband exerted improper pressure. Presumed undue influence is thus an evidentiary presumption which shifts the balance of proof to the alleged perpetrator to demonstrate that he or she dealt fairly with the victim who was thus able to exercise their own judgment. The fact that the victim has been independently advised by a person with the relevant facts and expertise is often employed to demonstrate that a presumption of influence has been rebutted.

**8.98**  Undue influence has often been associated with gifts that a donee has pressurized a donor to make. Its role in the surety mortgages exemplified by *O'Brien*, *Pitt*, and *Etridge* is a novel application of the doctrine because the allegation of undue influence is made in relation to the husband's undue influence over his wife but the mortgage is granted to the lender. There is no suggestion that the lender has exerted undue pressure. The argument is that the mortgage should nevertheless be set aside because the lender should have known that undue influence was a foreseeable risk in transactions of this nature and thus should have taken steps to ensure that the wife freely consented to the mortgage, for instance by receiving independent advice. There are thus three stages:

(i)  that the wife was unduly influenced by the husband;

(ii)  that the bank has actual or constructive notice of this risk;

(iii) that the bank did not take adequate steps to satisfy itself that the wife freely entered into the mortgage.

(*Etridge* at [101] per Lord Hobhouse.)

### The First Stage: Proof of Undue Influence

8.99   The wife must prove that she was unduly influenced by her husband. If there is no proof of actual or presumed undue influence, there is no basis upon which the mortgage can be set aside and there is no purpose in moving on to the other two stages. Following *Etridge*, the evidentiary hurdle to raise a presumption of undue influence has become significantly higher and more difficult for the wife to clear.

8.100   To raise a presumption of undue influence between spouses it is necessary to look first at the relationship of the parties and, secondly, at the nature of the transaction in question. The wife must establish, first, that she placed trust and confidence in her husband in financial matters, rather than exercised her own judgment and, secondly, that the mortgage was a transaction that called for an explanation because a person in her situation would not ordinarily enter into such a mortgage (*Etridge* at [13]–[14] per Lord Nicholls).

8.101   Relevant factors in establishing a relationship of trust and confidence might be the spouses' relative ages, education and experience, the length of their relationship, their respective characters, and the role each has assumed—when religious or social norms emanating from their respective cultural backgrounds may be influential. Lords Scott and Nicholls in *Etridge* suggested that, whilst trust and confidence is to be expected between spouses, what is unacceptable is the abuse of that trust. Such abuse may arise where the husband fails to fully explain or misrepresents, whether intentionally or otherwise, the purpose of the loan or the extent of the security (*Etridge* at [159]–[160] per Lord Scott and [33] and [36] per Lord Nicholls).

8.102   In characterizing the types of transactions which, when coupled with a relationship of trust and confidence, can raise a presumption of undue influence, the House of Lords in *Etridge* looked to the test established in *Allcard v Skinner* (1885) which asks whether the mortgage is explicable by the parties' relationship or calls for further explanation. Although acknowledging that a mortgage over the home to secure a loan for the benefit of the husband's business provided scope for abuse, their Lordships suggested that a surety mortgage might readily be explicable without further explanation (*Etridge* at [29]–[33] and [36] per Lord Nicholls).

8.103   If a wife is able to raise a presumption of undue influence the burden of proof shifts to the bank to provide evidence that the wife did in fact enter into the mortgage of her own independent will. The most common means employed is to demonstrate that independent advice has broken the husband's presumed influence. It is, of course, important that the advice is independent, adequate, and timely. In *Etridge* the House of Lords underlined the need for professional capability and impartiality from the solicitor advising the wife who might, if there was no conflict of interest, also be the husband's solicitor. The risks attendant on the mortgage, particularly the risk of losing her home, must be explained to the wife and it must be made clear to her that '[t]he decision to enter into the mortgage is hers and hers alone' (*Etridge* at [64]–[68] per Lord Nicholls).

## The Second Stage: Notice to the Bank

**8.104**  In *O'Brien* the first and second stages tended to coalesce with similar evidence satisfying both stages. However, in *Etridge* the House of Lords clearly differentiated the two stages. Whilst they required more stringent proof of undue influence, they set a simple and relatively low-level test to put the bank on notice of the risk of undue influence which it is straightforward for the bank to identify. Whenever a wife stands surety for her husband's debts (whether directly or through a company which he owns) the bank should be aware of the risk of undue influence (*Etridge* at [46]–[49] per Lord Nicholls). Indeed, whenever the relationship between the debtor and surety is non-commercial the bank will be on notice of the risk of undue influence (*Etridge* at [87] per Lord Nicholls).

## The Third Stage: The Steps the Bank Should Take

**8.105**  In a non-commercial surety mortgage, where the bank is on notice of the risk that the surety's consent may have been procured by undue influence, the bank must 'take reasonable steps to bring home to the individual guarantor the risks [s]he is running by standing as surety' (*Etridge* at [87] per Lord Nicholls). These steps are not directed at discovering whether there has been undue influence but are to minimize the risks that the mortgage is tainted by undue influence or misrepresentation by checking that it has been brought home to the wife the risks she is running (*Etridge* at [54] per Lord Nicholls). The House of Lords in *Etridge* (at [79] per Lord Nicholls) gave specific guidance to banks of what they must do.

**8.106**  First, the bank should find out from the wife the name of the solicitor who is acting for her. They must inform her that they will require written confirmation from her solicitor that she has received advice concerning the mortgage, its implications, and the reason why they are requesting this confirmation. They must not proceed with the mortgage until they have a satisfactory response from the wife. Secondly, the bank must provide the wife's solicitor with the relevant financial details to enable them to advise the wife. The bank must also warn the solicitors if they suspect that the husband has misled the wife. Lastly, the bank should not proceed until they have received written confirmation from her solicitors that the wife has received the necessary advice. It is important to note that the bank do not need to know either that the wife was actually advised or what she was told. The bank is only concerned with its own perspective. If the wife is inadequately advised, her right of redress is against her solicitor (see *Padden v Bevin Ashford* (2012)).

**8.107**  These undue influence cases are interesting on a number of levels. First, they demonstrate the significance of the wealth located in the family home and the socio-economic concerns evident in balancing the interests of the banks against family residential security. In *O'Brien* (at 188) Lord Browne-Wilkinson, against a background of the increase in family home ownership, noted the 'need to ensure that the wealth currently tied up in the matrimonial home does not become economically sterile'. Much commercial activity is centred on small and medium-sized businesses which are owned and run through family companies. Financing such a business is often dependent on employing the wealth tied up in the family home as security but doing so inevitably places the home at risk if the business falters. The final guidance that emerges from *Etridge* takes a significant shift in favour of the bank's interests. It raises the evidentiary bar of undue influence and it formulates procedural steps which banks can conveniently follow. Secondly, the cases touch on sensitive gender issues at the heart of the concept of presumed undue influence between spouses and cohabitees. In trying to explore this question between husband and wife, Lord Browne-Wilkinson in *O'Brien* (at 188) makes a wide gender-laden judgment in observing that, despite greater gender equality, it is often the husband who continues to be the primary financial decision maker (Kaye (1997)). Lastly, the conceptual basis for undue influence within the range of vitiating factors has drawn interesting academic comment. Here, the principal question is whether or not undue influence is claimant-based because the consent of the wife is impaired, or defendant-based because of the wrongful conduct of the husband in pressurizing the wife to agree to the mortgage. This foundational distinction has implications upon the wider issue of how we categorize the spectrum of vitiating factors flowing through duress to actual and presumed undue influence and then unconscionable bargains. A claimant-based approach draws a clear line between undue influence and unconscionable bargains but the distinction becomes illusory if a defendant-based approach is adopted and, it is suggested, undue influence and unconscionable bargains could be assimilated into one doctrine (Birks and Chin (1995), Bigwood (1996), Chen-Wishart (1997), Capper (1998), Devenney and Chandler (2007)).

## Control of Mortgage Terms

**8.108** There has always been a concern that freedom of contract within loan transactions may need to be constrained to protect the borrower's more vulnerable position. Initially there were laws against usury (the practice of charging interest), the courts of equity then cast their protective eye over the borrower through their creation and protection of the equity of redemption and readiness to strike down oppressive and unconscionable terms. More recently, there have been consumer protection measures operating both through specific legislation and the regulation of certain credit markets.

**8.109** The object and degree of protection has varied with the distinct roles that loan finance has played and the consequent changing character of borrowers to which we alluded at the start of this chapter (see **8.1**). A clear distinction can presently be drawn between commercial borrowing and consumer borrowing. In commercial borrowing, where businesses are expected to be able to protect their own interests (or pay others to do so) freedom of contract generally still prevails save where oppression and unconscionability provides a base line for equity's protection (see **8.121**). Certain small business proprietors under financial pressure also may reflect the vulnerability more usually associated with consumers. Such businesses may qualify for the protection afforded by the CCA 1974 (Brown (2007)) and, where a business loan is secured by a first charge upon a dwelling-house occupied by the proprietor, it will qualify as a regulated mortgage contract within the FSMA 2000. Interestingly amongst regulators, notably the FCA, there is a growing awareness that some protection may be justified for small and medium-sized businesses: for instance, against lenders peddling complex and inappropriate financial products (see the FCA's action on interest rate hedging products at http://www.fca.org.uk/consumers/financial-services-products/banking/interest-rate-hedging-products).

**8.110** In consumer borrowing, the range of measures to protect consumers is diverse (depending on the type of finance) but consistent in adopting fairness as its expected standard. We have already considered market regulation through the FSMA 2000 and the CCA 1974 which requires lenders to treat their customers fairly and the work of the FOS in resolving borrower complaints including those relating to onerous terms—see 8.73–8.85.

**8.111** In addition, there is control over the substance, operation, and clarity of contractual terms—previously imposed by the Unfair Terms in Consumer Contract Regulations 1999 (SI 1999/2083) but now found in the Consumer Rights Act 2015 (CRA 2015). This general consumer protection legislation applies to consumer mortgage contracts as much as any other consumer contract (*Newham LBC v Khatun* (2004)). Pursuant to this legislation, an individual term (save for the all important interest rate) may be struck down if 'contrary to the requirement of good faith, it causes a significant imbalance in the parties' rights and obligations under the [loan] contract, to the detriment of the consumer' (CRA 2015, s 62(4), *Director General of Fair Trading v First National Bank plc* (2002)). Relevant within this inquiry is whether a lender, dealing fairly and equitably with the borrower, could reasonably have assumed that the borrower would have agreed to the term if it had been the subject of individual contractual negotiation (*Aziz v Caixa d'Estalvis de Catalunya, Tarragona i Manresa (Catalunyacaixa)* (2013)). A non-exhaustive 'grey list' of terms that may be regarded as unfair are listed in Schedule 2, Part 1 to the CRA 2015 (CRA 2015, s 63). The FCA, as mortgage regulator, plays an important part in monitoring and ensuring compliance with the standards of fairness laid down in the CRA 2015 (Unfair Terms Regulatory Guide—UNFCOG). Furthermore, the Consumer Protection and Markets Authority issued guidance in July 2015 on the type of terms they consider to be unfair. We will concentrate our attention upon the measures that protect the equitable right to redeem, collateral advantages, excessive interest rates, and penalties imposed in the event of default.

## Redemption

**8.112** Within equity's development of the equity of redemption and the attendant equitable right to redeem, the courts of Chancery were alert to confine mortgages solely to their security function and thus to strike down any measures which might restrict the borrower's ability to recover their property upon repayment of the loan. The clogs and fetters doctrine was the result. The significance of this doctrine is now marginal and has been described as 'an appendix to our law which no longer serves a useful purpose and would be better excised' (*Jones v Morgan* (2001) at [72] per Lord Phillips). It tends to impact solely upon commercial borrowing in three main respects. As we will see, protection in consumer borrowing is more effectively addressed through statutory and regulatory measures.

**8.113** First, is the prohibition upon options to purchase the mortgaged property granted to the lender as part of the mortgage transaction (*Samuel v Jarrah Timber & Wood Paving Corp Ltd* (1904), *Reeve v Lisle* (1902)). The prohibition is absolute and it is no matter that the option is neither regarded as unconscionable nor obtained as a result of economic duress (*Jones v Morgan* (2001)). The courts have managed, in the main, to restrict the significance of this ban on options to purchase by requiring the option to be part of the mortgage transaction both in time and purpose (*Lewis v Frank Love* (1961), *Warnborough Ltd v Garmite Ltd* (2003), *Brighton & Hove CC v Audus* (2009) but note *Jones v Morgan* (2001)).

**8.114** Secondly, a postponement of the right to redeem for a period is not per se an unacceptable clog on the equity of redemption but it may be struck down where the right becomes illusory or is oppressive and unconscionable (*Fairclough v Swan Brewery Co* (1912), *Knightsbridge Estates Ltd v Byrne* (1939)). The test is high because it is not equity's role to alter commercial parties' bargains. Thus, it is insufficient if the prohibition is merely unreasonable.

---

**Knightsbridge Estates Ltd v Byrne (1939):** Knightsbridge had mortgaged a number of properties to secure a loan of £300,000 at an interest rate of 6.5 per cent. They were subsequently able to renegotiate a more favourable interest rate of 5.25 per cent but only if they agreed to repay the loan by half-yearly instalments over a 40-year period. Interest rates continued to fall and Knightsbridge tried to repay the loan and redeem their mortgage before the 40-year period had expired. They argued that it was unreasonable to insist upon this postponement of their right to redeem. The Court of Appeal agreed that to delay redemption for 40 years might be thought unreasonable but that was not the test. The court would not interfere to rewrite a bargain agreed by two commercial parties unless the bargain was oppressive or unconscionable.

---

**8.115** Lastly, charges for early redemption are common but unpopular. Lenders may offer advantageous rates to borrowers who agree that they will not redeem for a fixed period. It is beneficial to a lender to have the certainty of a known return during that period. The price to be paid for these advantageous interest rates is the payment of an agreed sum to the lender should the borrower wish to redeem early. In commercial borrowing such charges will only be struck down if they are oppressive and unconscionable but in consumer borrowing both the FSMA 2000 and the CCA 1974 require such charges to be explained to the borrower before they borrow and dictate that they are not excessive but represent a genuine pre-estimation of the lender's loss. Furthermore, an early redemption charge runs the risk of a challenge of unfairness under the CRA 2015 or where section 140A of the CCA 1974 applies.

## Collateral Advantages

**8.116**  A collateral advantage is an added benefit that a lender imposes as a condition of the mortgage. The most common examples occur within the commercial context when a lender, for example a brewery or petrol company, may advance money to enable the borrower to purchase or develop their business on the condition that the borrower purchases products solely from the lender through a tied or solus agreement. In these circumstances, the common law doctrine against restraint of trade or the equitable protection from oppressive and unconscionable terms may operate, although competition legislation is more likely to provide effective control (*Alec Lobb (Garages) Ltd v Total Oil Great Britain Ltd* (1985), *Esso Petroleum Co Ltd v Harpers Garage (Stourport) Ltd* (1968)). Although collateral advantages are less common in consumer borrowing, market regulation and the fairness standards demanded by section 140A of the CCA 1974 and the CRA 2015 may be applied. For instance, these controls have helped to provide redress against the mis-selling of payment protection insurance (see *Plevin v Paragon Personal Finance Ltd* (2014)).

**8.117**  Equity's interest in collateral advantages declined along with the clogs and fetters doctrine. At one time, equity viewed all collateral advantages as a clog upon the equity of redemption particularly where the borrower remained subject to the advantage after they had paid off their loan (*Biggs v Hodinott* (1898), *Noakes v Rice* (1902), *Bradley v Carrit* (1903)). A sea change occurred as a result of the following important decision.

---

*G&K Kreglinger v New Patagonia Meat and Cold Storage Co Ltd* **(1914):** When advancing money to New Patagonia, Kreglinger negotiated a right to purchase at the market price for a period of five years all sheepskins resulting as a by-product of New Patagonia's operations. When New Patagonia redeemed their loan within the five-year period they unsuccessfully claimed that they should be released from the obligation to sell Kreglinger the sheepskins. The House of Lords decided that the sheepskin contract was an independent, although connected, transaction which would only be struck down if it could be characterized as oppressive and unconscionable. Given the payment of market consideration for the skins, and the commercial status of the parties, it could not be so characterized.

---

**8.118**  The importance of *Kreglinger* lies in its move away from a black-and-white approach to terms that might impact upon redemption (in this instance a collateral advantage) to a respect for freedom of contract between commercial parties, who can negotiate on equal terms. Such freedom will only be overturned if terms fall foul of equity's wider abhorrence of oppressive and unconscionable conduct developed from their oversight of unconscionable bargains (*Alec Lobb Garages Ltd v Total Oil (GB) Ltd* (1985)). Similar developments are evident in *Knightsbridge Estates Ltd v Byrne* (1939) (see **8.114** for postponement of the right to redeem) and *Multiservice Bookbinding Ltd v Marden* (1979) (see **8.119–8.122** for excessive interest rates) but not yet in options to purchase (see **8.113** and *Jones v Morgan* (2001) above). It is thus oppression and unconscionability that remain equity's most potent contribution to protection of the commercial borrower.

## Interest Rates

**8.119**  The cost of borrowing is of central concern to any borrower. Concern is centred upon excessive rates and the possibility that rates may be varied upwards during the loan term. The control of unfair terms exerted by the CRA 2015 is of little assistance, both because pricing falls outside its brief and fluctuating interest rates are not generally regarded as unfair if notice of the variation is given to the borrower. Rather unrealistically, it is reasoned that at this point the borrower can repay or seek finance elsewhere if the cost proves unaffordable. The source of protection thus largely must rest with equitable and regulatory controls. In a market economy it is believed that interest rates should reflect market conditions with pricing generally reflecting the degree of risk. Secured lending attracts a lower rate of interest than unsecured lending given the lower degree of risk. Nevertheless, certain market benchmarks seek to set interest rates at a realistic level to support economic activity, including business growth and consumer spending. These benchmarks also take some cognizance of the role of mortgage finance within housing policy. The benchmark for consumer mortgages is set by the Bank of England with mortgage providers setting their interest rates in line with this rate. Commercial borrowing may also follow the Bank of England base rate but may also use other international interest rate benchmarks, for instance LIBOR (London Interbank Offer Rate).

**8.120**  Economists argue against setting interest rate ceilings (eg Department of Trade and Industry (2003)) although payday loans have proved an exception (FCA (2014)). Compound interest is a different matter. It can lead to a sharp increase in the amount of the debt because interest is capitalized and added to the debt with interest then charged on the increased capital debt. Whilst compound interest is common in commercial borrowing, it is frowned upon in consumer borrowing and may contribute to the unfairness of a section 140A relationship where borrowing is governed by the CCA 1974 (*Patel v Patel* (2009), *Barons Finance Ltd v Olubisi* (2010)).

**8.121**  Where statutory and market controls do not bite, equity's control of oppressive and unconscionable terms provides a final (although fragile) safety net. The test of oppression and unconscionability is strict. It looks not only at the substantive fairness of the terms themselves, but also at the procedural fairness with which they are agreed. Abuse by the lender of their dominant position, which operates to take advantage of the vulnerability of the borrower, is required (*Alec Lobb Garages Ltd v Total Oils (GB) Ltd* (1985)). Consideration of the financial expertise of the parties and their respective bargaining positions is thus key (*Cityland & Property (Holdings) Ltd v Dabrah* (1968)). An unsuccessful attempt was made to challenge high rates of interest in the following case.

---

*Multiservice Bookbinding Ltd v Marden* **(1979):** Multiservice borrowed £36,000 from Marden to fund the purchase of new premises. The loan could not be redeemed for ten years; interest was calculated at 2 per cent above the bank rate on the entire amount of the loan over that term (regardless of capital repayment) and interest was compounded after 21 days. In addition, any repayments of capital and interest were linked to the Swiss Franc to protect the lender against currency fluctuations—sterling did indeed devalue against the Swiss Franc.

> When Multiservice came to redeem, they owed in excess of £133,000 but they failed to prove that these terms were oppressive and unconscionable.

The weakness of Multiservice's claim lay in the fact that, although the terms were unreasonable, they were not oppressive and unconscionable. Multiservice were a small but profitable company who wished to expand—they were not trying to stave off insolvency. Furthermore, they had retained professional advisers to act for them. On the other hand, no abuse by Marden could be proved.

**8.122**  A claim in *Multiservice* that the fluctuation in interest rates consequent upon the tie to the Swiss Franc was against public policy also failed. However, *Paragon Finance Ltd v Nash* (2002) has recognized some legal (as opposed to market) restraint upon the ability of a lender to vary interest rates. It does so by implying a term that rates should not be varied improperly, arbitrarily, or capriciously and further that in exercising a contractual discretion to vary rates the lender must not do so unreasonably—in the sense that no lender acting reasonably would act in a similar way.

## Penalties

**8.123**  A loan agreement may impose default charges or a higher rate of interest if the borrower defaults in prompt payment. Ostensibly these payments are characterized as an estimation of a lender's loss whether through lost income or increased administration charges. However, they may come under scrutiny under the court's equitable jurisdiction as a penalty, because the charge imposed is out of all proportion to the lender's legitimate interest; for instance, in compensating them for their loss as opposed to punishing the defaulter for their breach (*Makdessi v Cavendish Square Holdings BV; ParkingEye Ltd v Beavis* (2015)). Additionally, in consumer borrowing such default charges or penalties may be challenged under consumer protection legislation, because the term fails to meet the required standards of fairness. Certain default charges were held to fall short of the standards of fairness required by section 140A of the CCA 1974 in *County Leasing Ltd v East* (2007) and the Unfair Terms in Consumer Contracts Regulations 1999 (SI 1999/2083, the predecessor of the CRA 2015) in *Falco Finance Ltd v Gough* (1999) (see also *Director General of Fair Trading v First National Bank plc* (2002), *Aziz v Caixa d'Estalvis de Catalunya, Tarragona i Manresa (Catalunyacaixa)* (2013) but note *Makdessi v Cavendish Square Holdings BV; ParkingEye Ltd v Beavis* (2015)).

# FURTHER READING

Bright, S and Whitehouse, L, 'Information, Advice and Representation in Housing Possession Cases' (Universities of Oxford and Hull, 2014).

Clark, A, 'Security Interest in Property' in JW Harris (ed), *Property Problems: From Genes to Pension Funds* (London: Kluwer, 1997).

Haley, M, 'Mortgage Default: Possession, Relief and Judicial Discretion' (1997) 17 LS 483.

Law Commission Report No 204, *Land Mortgages* (1991).

Loi, KCF, 'Receiver's Power of Sale and Duty of Care' [2010] Conv 369.

McMurtry, L, 'Mortgage Default and Repossession: Procedure and Policy in the Post-*Norgan* Era' (2007) 58 NILQ 194.

Nield, S, 'Mortgage Market Review: "Hard-Wired Commonsense?"' (2015) 38 J Consumer Policy 139.

Wallace, A, 'Feels like I am doing it on my own: Examining the Synchronicity between Policy Responses and the Circumstances and Experiences of Borrowers in Arrears' (2012) 11 Social Policy and Society 117.

Wallace, A and Ford, J, 'Limiting Possessions? Managing Mortgage Arrears in a New Era' [2010] IJHP 133.

Watt, G, 'Mortgage Law as Legal Fiction' in E Cooke (ed), *Modern Studies in Property Law: Vol 3* (Oxford: Hart Publishing, 2007).

## SELF-TEST QUESTIONS

1   Why is the legal charge by way of mortgage described as a hybrid security?

2   What advantages would there be if the Law Commission's recommendation to reform the forms of security of land was enacted?

3   What do we mean by an equity of redemption?

4   Is it now true to say that a lender enjoys an immediate right to possession?

5   To what extent does the court's discretion under section 36 of the AJA 1970 dovetail (if at all) with the standards of forbearance required by MCOB 13?

6   A lender can sell the mortgaged property without the consent of the court but what controls are there over how they do so?

7   Contrast the duties in the enforcement of the mortgage security owed by a lender and a receiver.

8   How does the FSMA 2000 'protect' borrowers?

9   What impact does the FOS have upon the resolution of mortgage disputes?

10   In commenting upon undue influence and misrepresentation in the context of surety mortgages over the home, why were the House of Lords keen to ensure that 'a law designed to protect the vulnerable does not render the matrimonial home unacceptable security to financial institutions'?

11   Explain the distinction between the tests of 'oppression and unconscionability' and 'unfairness' in the control of mortgage terms.

# Easements

## SUMMARY

The next two chapters consider the property relationships that may exist between neighbours. This chapter is concerned with rights to make limited use of the land of another which are known as easements. The chapter explains the content characteristics of an easement before moving on to the acquisition question by exploring the rules that govern when an easement is created. Finally, the chapter briefly considers the defences that can defeat an easement either when a purchaser can claim priority over a pre-existing easement whether of registered land or unregistered land, or when an easement is terminated.

Key topics explored in this chapter are:

- The four defining characteristics of an easement (**9.7–9.28**)
- The express creation of an easement (**9.30**)
- The implied creation of an easement (**9.31–9.50**)
- Prescription (**9.51–9.59**)
- Defences to a pre-existing easement (**9.61–9.64**)

## Introduction

**9.1** An easement is the right of a landowner to enjoy a limited use of neighbouring land. An essential feature of an easement is thus the need for two pieces of land: the dominant land to which the benefit of the easement is attached and the servient land over which the easement is exercised. Easements are usually positive in nature by allowing the dominant landowner to go onto the servient land to use some facility. The most common positive easements are rights of way to use a road or path on the servient land or to use the drains running under the servient land. However, easements may also be negative in nature. Negative easements create a right for the dominant owner to receive something from the servient land. They are negative because they do not actually allow the dominant owner to go onto the servient land although they do to prevent the servient owner from using his or her land as freely as they might otherwise be able to do. Established negative easements include rights to receive light or air flowing from the servient land so that a servient owner may be prevented from building on his or her land in a manner which interferes with that right. Rights of support which prevent a servient owner from removing an existing structure or feature on the servient land are also an established form of negative easement.

9.2   Easements are common with many adjoining properties, both enjoying and being burdened by an easement. Although easements have a long history, the agricultural and industrial revolutions provided an incentive to their development and popularity. The enclosure movement, that was a feature of the agricultural revolution, saw an end to communal systems of agricultural ownership and the spread of individually owned farms. A little later the industrial revolution was characterized by the more intensive development of privately owned land and the growth of industrialized towns and cities. Although the sole ownership of smaller areas of land proved economically efficient, it also required closer cooperation between adjoining landowners to maximize their individual resources. For instance, a landowner may grant a right of way over their land to their neighbour to avoid their neighbour's land becoming inaccessible. Likewise, a landowner who has the benefit of water from a river or spring may be persuaded to grant his or her neighbour, who does not enjoy such a naturally occurring resource, a right to water particularly where the supply is plentiful. These trends have not diminished as our modern way of life sees ever more intensive development of land both for housing and commercial uses. For instance, individual flat ownership is only possible if easements can be utilized to provide common rights of access over shared gardens, hallways, and lifts.

9.3   Easements are proprietary rights that exist for a defined estate. They are thus capable of accruing for the benefit of purchasers of the dominant land and of binding a purchaser of the servient land. In this respect, they differ from a mere gratuitous or contractual permission to use the land of another, which operate only as a personal obligation. We have already noted that to avoid land ownership becoming unduly burdened and to facilitate the marketability of land, the list of proprietary rights is limited and the boundary between proprietary and personal rights is strictly controlled (**Chapter 3**). It is only those rights over neighbouring land which fulfil certain characteristics that can operate as easements.

9.4   Whilst we will confine our consideration to easements in this chapter, there are a range of other rights over the land of another. Foremost amongst private rights are profits à prendre which are rights to take the natural produce from another's land including rights to fish and to shoot game. Profits are very similar to easements save that they do not have to be connected to dominant land but can be taken to benefit an individual.

9.5   Rights of a public nature are rights to use public facilities, for instance the public roads, which are enjoyed by all individuals. To enable public utility companies to supply essential services to people's homes and businesses, these companies enjoy statutory way-leaves over private land to create a national network of gas, electricity, water, and sewage services.

**9.6**   Access to and the use of open spaces is a matter of increasing concern particularly for those who wish to enjoy our diminishing natural resources. The Countryside and Rights of Way Act 2000 goes some way to acknowledging that there are certain areas of both state-owned and privately-owned land (named access land) which all members of the public should be able to enjoy subject to controls to protect the natural environment. The Supreme Court has also considered, although declined to determine, whether there exists a common law right for the public to have access to the sea (*R (on the application of Newhaven Port and Properties Ltd) v SS for Environment, Food and Rural Affairs* (2015)). Some rights to use communal facilities may also be enjoyed by the members of a particular locality, for instance a right to use a village green may be enjoyed by the inhabitants of the village.

## The Content Question

**9.7**   We need to be able to identify those rights over the land of another which are capable of being easements and thus, as a proprietary right, can affect future purchasers of both the dominant land (who can legitimately exercise the right) and purchasers of the servient land (who must submit to the exercise of the right as a burden on their ownership). The Court of Appeal in the leading case of *Re Ellenborough Park* (1956) summarized the four essential characteristics of an easement:

(i)   there must be two distinct areas of land—dominant land and servient land (**9.8–9.12**);

(ii)   the dominant and servient land must be owned by different people (**9.13–9.14**);

(iii)   the easement must 'accommodate' the dominant land (**9.15–9.19**); and

(iv)   the right must be capable of forming the subject matter of a grant (**9.20**).

We will use this classic statement to explore the content question as it applies to easements. Where one or more of these requirements are not met, the right cannot be an easement and thus qualify as a proprietary right. However, the right may operate merely as a personal licence between the parties (**3.68–3.84**).

### There Must Be Dominant Land and Servient Land

**9.8**   The proprietary status of easements is presently dependent upon the right to use the land of another being attached or appurtenant to a piece of land—the dominant land—rather than being for the benefit of a particular person. We thus say that an easement cannot exist 'in gross'. Some have argued that this requirement is unnecessary (see Sturley (1980)). English law accepts vboth profits and way-leaves as rights over the land of another that can exist in gross and other jurisdictions have dispensed with this requirement. The argument turns on two main policy factors. First, the danger of the possible excessive use of the servient land and, secondly, the drawbacks of encouraging a proliferation of property interests which might affect the marketability of land and the ease of its transfer. After all, it could be difficult to trace those individuals who have the benefit of an easement where they have no association with nearby land. The Law Commission has re-examined the debate but decided that as a matter of policy the requirement for dominant and servient land should remain (Law Commission (2011), para 2.24).

**9.9**    Given the requirement for two pieces of land, it is important to be able to physically identify that part of the servient land subject to the right and the extent of the dominant land entitled to exercise the right. The facility on the servient land will need to be identified in the grant and thus details of the servient land will not generally give rise to difficulty but identifying the dominant land raises more issues. It is necessary to be able to identify the dominant land at the time the easement is created, thus it is not possible for a dominant owner to obtain a grant of an easement to benefit additional land that he or she may acquire in the future (*London & Blenheim Estates Ltd v Ladbrooke Retail Parks Ltd* (1994)).

**9.10**    Where the dominant owner already owns or subsequently acquires additional land adjacent to the dominant land, he or she cannot claim the benefit of the right for that additional land. This is known as the 'rule in *Harris v Flower*' (1904) in which Romer LJ (at 127) stated 'if a right of way be granted for the enjoyment of Close A, the grantee because he owns or acquires Close B cannot use the way in substance for passage over Close A to Close B'. For instance, in *Peacock v Custins* (2002) Mr Peacock was prohibited from using a right of way that he enjoyed for the benefit of one field in order to access an adjacent field that he also owned (see also *Das v Linden Mews* (2003)). The rule can raise some difficult questions surrounding the intention with which an easement is exercised (see Paton and Seabourne (2003)). For instance, Mr Peacock could have quite legitimately used the right of way to access the dominant land and then, once there and in exercise his ownership, again quite legitimately have decided to enter and use his adjacent field. The problem he faced was that he could not use the right of way leading to his dominant land with the intention to go and access his adjacent field. It thus becomes important, but somewhat artificial, to determine if and when the dominant owner forms the intention to access the adjacent land.

---

*Giles v Tarry* **(2012):** Mr Tarry had a right to use Mr Giles' driveway to access fields on either side of the driveway (Field A). However, Mr Tarry also rented an adjacent field (Field B) that could only be accessed through Field A. Knowing that he did not have a right of way along the driveway to access Field B, Mr Tarry drove his sheep into Field A and then onto the public road before doubling back and driving the sheep through Field A and into Field B. The Court of Appeal, reversing the decision of the High Court, held that the High Court should have looked at the intention with which Mr Tarry drove the sheep along the driveway and not the physical and somewhat artificial route he used. This intention was plainly to allow the sheep to graze both Fields A and B as a single agricultural unit. The use of Mr Giles' driveway to access both Fields A and B was thus a breach of the rule in *Harris v Flower* so far as it was used to access Field B.

---

**9.11**  It has been acknowledged in applying the rule in *Harris v Flower* that a degree of latitude is necessary when the use of the adjacent land is merely ancillary to the use of the dominant land. In *Peacock v Custins* the court acknowledged that there would be no objection to the use of the right of way if Mr Peacock merely went onto his adjacent field for a picnic. Likewise, in *Massey v Boulden* (2003) it was legitimate to use a right of way to access a house, including a modest extension to the house, which had been built on a small area of land adjacent to the dominant land. In determining whether a use is ancillary to enjoyment of the dominant land, it is necessary to show that the right is not 'in substance' used for the benefit of the adjacent land either because the adjacent land derives no benefit or because any benefit is insubstantial.

---

*Macepark (Whittleberry) Ltd v Sargeant (No 2)* (2003): A hotel close to Silverstone race circuit was leased to Macepark with the benefit of a right of way across adjoining land. Macepark wanted to create a direct link to Silverstone for use by its guests by utilizing the right of way and also obtaining the agreement of the owners of intervening woods to pass through the woods that lay between the hotel and Silverstone. However, Sargeant, as servient owner of the right of way, objected. The High Court agreed that utilizing the right of way to create the direct link to Silverstone was not insubstantial as it would also benefit the owners of the wood, who could charge for this use of their land, as well as the owners of Silverstone who would benefit from this direct link to their circuit.

---

**9.12**  The rationale for the rule in *Harris v Flower* lies in the simple fact that the original terms of the grant are solely for the benefit of the dominant land. However, perhaps a more convincing justification is found in minimizing the risk of excessive use of the servient land (Paton and Seabourne (2003)).

## The Dominant and Servient Land Must Be Owned and Occupied by Different Persons

**9.13**  A landowner who owns both the dominant and servient land has no need of an easement. His or her ownership provides the right to use the servient land. The Law Commission has recommended a small relaxation of this requirement where the dominant and servient land are registered under separate titles but in the name of the same registered owner (Law Commission (2011), para 3.255). This relaxation is intended to assist the sale of a housing development where the development company has divided their ownership of the development into different plots under separate registered titles between which easements are necessary or desirable.

**9.14**  We have noted that an easement is attached to an estate in the land (9.3). Thus, a tenant may enjoy an easement over their landlord's servient land because the easement is attached to their leasehold estate (*Wright v Macadam* (1949)). Accordingly, where the lease to which an easement is attached is brought to an early end by forfeiture, the easement will also cease. However, in *Wall v Collins* (2007) this orthodoxy was challenged where a lease merged with the freehold reversion of the dominant land upon the tenant's purchase of the freehold reversionary estate. The court held that the leasehold right of way that the tenant enjoyed over adjoining servient land did not also merge with the freehold reversion. It continued to be attached to the dominant land for the period for which it was granted. Although the decision is convenient, the Law Commission has suggested that orthodoxy should be restored by reversing this decision by statute but that convenience can be maintained by allowing the dominant owner to elect to retain the benefit of the easement upon the merger of a lease with the freehold reversion either upon the tenant's acquisition of the freehold reversion or the tenant's surrender of their lease to their landlord (Law Commission (2011), para 4.44).

## An Easement Must Accommodate the Dominant Land

**9.15**   To afford a right over the land of another proprietary status, the right must benefit the dominant land rather than an individual owner. The idea of land itself enjoying the benefit of a right is somewhat strained but the import of this requirement is that the benefit should accrue to the owner for the time being of the dominant land rather than confer a personal advantage upon a particular owner. The distinction is illustrated by the case of *Hill v Tupper*.

> **Hill v Tupper (1863):** A canal company leased land beside a canal to Mr Hill and granted him an exclusive right to put and use boats on the canal. Mr Tupper owned a pub beside the canal and started renting out boats to be used on the canal. Mr Hill objected claiming he had an exclusive easement to use the canal in this way. The court characterized Mr Hill's right as a personal commercial advantage rather than a property right attached to his land.

It could be argued that land with a right to use a canal is more attractive than land without such a benefit (see *Platt v Crouch* (2004)), but the court in *Hill v Tupper* was satisfied that Mr Hill was claiming a monopolistic commercial advantage which had no particular connection to his land as opposed to his business. He was not just exercising a positive right to put boats on the canal but also asserting a negative right to prevent any other boats from using the canal.

**9.16**   Accommodation refers to the need for the easement to benefit the dominant land in some way. That benefit may enhance the economic value of the dominant land but that is not the defining yardstick. The issue is whether the normal enjoyment of the land is enhanced. This is a question of fact to be determined by considering both the nature of the dominant land and the right itself. The issue of accommodation was one of the central questions raised in *Re Ellenborough Park* (1956) in which the particular right was a right to use a communal garden granted to the houses that surrounded the garden. It was accepted that this facility would enhance the use of the houses as residential accommodation by providing attractive outside space in which to relax and enjoy the amenity the gardens afforded. The Court of Appeal contrasted rights to gain free admittance to a zoo or Lord's Cricket

Ground by pointing out that, whilst both might be economically valuable, each were independent of the use of the dominant land as a home and thus did not sufficiently enhance its residential use. Similarly, it might be argued that a communal garden would not be sufficiently connected to benefit the use of the dominant land for other purposes, for instance as a factory or farm.

**9.17** Where the dominant land is used for commercial purposes it can be difficult to distinguish between the commercial enhancement of the dominant owner's particular business and the general commercial use of the land. *Hill v Tupper* (**9.15**) presents an example of a right which was too closely associated with Mr Hill's business. He was, after all claiming an exclusive right. By contrast, in *Moody v Steggles* (1879) a right to erect a sign on the servient land to indicate and advertise the dominant owner's business (a pub) was held to be an easement. The court refused to distinguish between the use of the land and the business conducted on it. It might be argued that the sign could have indicated, and thus benefited, any commercial enterprise conducted on the dominant land.

**9.18** Although accommodation is said to be a question of fact, it is clear that there are value judgments to be made that may vary along with changing social conditions, technical advances, and accepted modes of property use. For instance, in *Re Ellenborough Park* (1956) it was doubted that mere rights of recreation and amusement could command the necessary utility that lies at the heart of accommodation (**9.16**). This view may not be so readily accepted in our more heath conscious and pleasure-seeking times when rights to use swimming pools, gyms, and spas are marketed as attractive communal features of some residential developments (*Regency Villas Title Ltd v Diamond Resorts (Europe) Ltd* (2016)).

**9.19** One clear feature of accommodation is the need for close proximity between the dominant and servient land. The two pieces of land need not be adjacent but they do need to be sufficiently close to connect the benefit of the right to the dominant land itself.

## The Right Must Be Capable of Forming the Subject Matter of a Grant

**9.20** It was acknowledged in *Re Ellenborough Park* (1956) that the significance of this last condition is 'not entirely clear' (at 164 per Lord Evershed MR). It could reflect the simple requirement that, as a legal interest in land, an easement must be granted by deed by a grantor to grantee whom both enjoy the necessary capacity. However, the requirement has more far-reaching implications which focus upon how the easement affects the servient land. The common purpose of its various elements is to prevent too onerous a burden being placed upon the servient land. To understand this requirement, we will analyse its features under the following interconnected elements:

    (i)   the requirement for certainty in the scope of the grant (**9.21**);

    (ii)  the requirement that the right places no positive burden on the servient owner (**9.22**);

(iii)  the limitation on new easements (9.23); and

(iv)  the 'ouster' principle, which prohibits rights which exclude the servient owner or amount to a claim to joint ownership (9.24-9.28).

### Certainty in the Scope of the Grant

9.21   Proprietary rights must be clearly defined and in the case of easements it must be clear to what burden the servient land is subject and to what rights the servient owner must submit. For this reason, there is no general right to a view (*Harris v De Pinna* (1886)) or to uninterrupted television reception (*Hunter v Canary Wharf Ltd* (1997)). Nevertheless, the Supreme Court has contemplated the possibility of a right to make a noise that would otherwise constitute a nuisance (*Coventry (t/a RDC Promotions) v Lawrence* (2014)). It may be possible to provide certainty by confining rights, which would otherwise be too amorphous, within clear parameters. For instance, there is no general right to light and air but when these rights are received through a defined channel they become sufficiently certain to qualify as easements (*Harris v De Pinna* (1886)). Likewise, in *Re Ellenborough Park* (1956) the right to use the spatially defined garden was sufficiently certain in contrast to a general liberty to wander over a large and ill-defined area.

### No Positive Burden on the Servient Owner

9.22   An easement does not normally require the servient owner to do anything. He or she is only required to allow the dominant owner to exercise his or her right without interference. Furthermore, the servient owner is not required to keep the subject matter of the easement in repair. For instance, a right of way or drainage does not require the servient owner to keep the road or drains in repair (*Duke of Westminster v Guild* (1985)). Nor does a right to the supply of water or electricity require the servient owner to maintain a continuous supply of that utility. He or she is only prohibited from interrupting the natural supply of water (*Schwann v Cotton* (1916), *Rance v Elvin* (1985)) or the existing supply of electricity (*Duffy v Lamb* (1998), *William Old International Ltd v Arya* (2009)). The ancient obligation to maintain stock-proof fences to keep out a neighbour's cattle from adjacent common land presents a limited exception which can oblige a neighbour to maintain a boundary fence (*Jones v Price* (1965)). An obligation to repair the subject matter of an easement also can arise from some other source of liability, for instance as a result of an express or implied contractual term (see eg *Liverpool CC v Irwin* (1977)) or to avoid tortious liability whether for negligence, nuisance, or breach of statutory duty under the Occupiers Liability Act 1984 (see eg *Rees v Sherrett* (2001)).

### Caution in Recognizing New Easements

9.23   We have noted that developments in our lifestyle may call for the recognition of new forms of easements, thus it has been said that the class of easements is never closed (*Re Ellenborough Park* (1956) at 140 per Danckwerts J). Nevertheless, the courts are cautious in recognizing new forms of easements that materially differ from the type of rights that have already been accepted. There is a particular reluctance to accept new negative easements. For instance, in *Phipps v Pears* (1965) the Court of Appeal refused to accept that a right of protection from the weather could constitute an easement where the demolition of a house had left the wall of the adjacent house exposed. The alleged right was negative in both the sense that the dominant owner was not claiming any right to do something on the servient land and in the sense that the servient owner would have been prohibited from acting as he would otherwise be entitled to do. The owner could have protected his property by seeking the agreement of his neighbour not to demolish the wall—an agreement which could have bound any subsequent owner of his neighbour's land as a restrictive covenant (see Chapter 10).

### The Ouster Principle

9.24 An easement is a *limited* right over the land of another. Thus a claim to exclusive or joint possession of the servient land cannot be an easement. Instead it might be a lease or occupational licence, if granted with the consent of the servient owner (see Chapter 7), or a claim to adverse possession, if no such consent has been forthcoming (see Chapter 4).

9.25 The distinction is easier to state than it is to apply. For instance, in *Re Ellenborough Park* (1956) the Court of Appeal was unimpressed by suggestions that the right to use the communal garden constituted a claim to joint ownership although the servient owners were effectively prevented from using the land in any other way. By contrast, in *Copeland v Greenhalf* (1952) a claim to a right to park and store cars failed because the court was of the view that it constituted a claim to exclusive or, at least, joint ownership.

9.26 To some extent easements inevitably affect the manner in which the servient owner can utilize their land. A right of way cannot be obstructed and thus a servient owner will be unable to build on the servient land so as to interfere with the right. The challenge is to establish how much user is too much and furthermore to formulate a reliable test to capture when that line has been crossed. In recent years, the issue has centred upon when a right to park a car on servient land can qualify as an easement. *Copeland v Greenhalf* provides an example where a claim failed on the facts but, equally, there are instances where a right to storage has been upheld (see *Wright v Macadam* (1949)).

9.27 In *London & Blenheim Estates Ltd v Ladbrooke Retail Parks Ltd* (1992) the court suggested that the test is one of degree and the line crossed when the right is so extensive that the servient owner is left with no reasonable enjoyment of his or her land. For instance, in *Batchelor v Marlow* (2003) the Court of Appeal held that an exclusive right to park between the hours of 9.30 am and 6.00 pm rendered the servient owner's use of the land illusory. However, in *Virdi v Chana* (2008), whilst accepting the *Batchelor* test, the Court of Appeal held that the servient owner retained sufficient reasonable enjoyment of her land, that formed part of a car park space, where she could continue to alter its surface (if desired) and maintain her adjacent fencing and planting. The *Batchelor* test suggests that it is necessary to look at the relative areas of the car park space and the overall size of the servient land as well as the exclusivity of the right to park and any other temporal or spatial restrictions by which the right is defined. Although the test has been followed, it is not without its critics—both judicial and academic. In the Scottish case of *Moncrieff v Jamieson* (2007) Lord Scott suggested that the test should not turn on the relative area of the car park space to the whole of the servient land but should focus upon whether the servient owner retains sufficient possession and control over that part of the servient land over which the right is claimed, namely the car parking or storage space. These tests look at the situation from the position of the servient owner and what use he or she retains. However, Luther has suggested the question should be approached from the point of view of the dominant owner. The focus would then be upon the nature of the right claimed by the dominant owner and the extent to which that use underpins a claim to possessory entitlement rather than a limited use which characterizes an easement. Where the claim is not possessory in nature, Luther suggests that the defining test should be one of certainty and not degree of use (Luther (1996)).

9.28  There is no doubt that rights to park present a fundamental challenge to the ouster principle and the Law Commission has recommended that the principle be abolished (Law Commission (2011), para 3.028). Given our love affair with the car, there is a clear social utility, as well as an economic incentive, in recognizing rights to park but, given their exclusive nature, such rights are of a rather different nature than other accepted types of easement. We should thus be cautious in abandoning a principle which underpins the distinction between easements and possessory rights to which other rules and principles apply (see Xu (2012)).

## The Acquisition Question

9.29  Having answered the content question of what rights over the land of another are capable of being recognized as easements, it is important to next consider the manner in which an easement can be acquired by the dominant owner. There are four main routes:

(i)  express grant;

(ii)  implied grant;

(iii)  presumed grant established by long user;

(iv)  statute, for instance both the Access to Neighbouring Land Act 1992 and the Party Walls Act 1996 grant rights to enter neighbouring land to carry out certain repair and buildings works.

We will concentrate our attention on the first three routes.

## Express Grant

9.30  The formality rules considered in **Chapters 4** and **5** apply equally to easements. Thus, a legal easement must be created by deed and, where an easement over registered land is created after 13 October 2003, the deed must be registered (Land Registration Act 2002

(LRA 2002), s 27). The benefit of the easement will be recorded in the property register of the dominant land and the burden of the easement will be entered upon the charges register of the servient land. An equitable easement may arise by virtue of the doctrine of anticipation or by an estoppel (see eg *Crabb v Arun DC* (1976)).

## Implied Grant

9.31 An easement can be acquired by implication usually where the land is subdivided by the sale of one or more plots. There are four routes by which an easement may be implied:

(i) easements of necessity (**9.34–9.35**);

(ii) intended easements (**9.36–9.39**);

(iii) under the rule in *Wheeldon v Burrows* (**9.40–9.44**); and

(iv) by the operation of section 62 of the Law of Property Act 1925 (LPA 1925, **9.45–9.50**).

9.32 The underlying rationale for the first three of these routes lies in the maxim that a grantor should not be allowed to derogate from their grant. Accordingly, where a landowner disposes of part of their land they cannot use their retained land in a way that frustrates the use of the disposed portion by the grantee. Although this rationale may be clear, the basis for the rules themselves is less clear. Candidates include presumed intention and utility. On the one hand, implication is said to lie in the presumed intention of the parties with each rule formulating that presumed intention from a different evidentiary source. Indeed, each rule gives way to a contrary intention and the rule in *Wheeldon v Burrows* and the operation of section 62 are often excluded by express contractual terms adopted in the sale and purchase of land. However, on the other hand, there is also an underlying hint of public policy in optimizing land usage. The Law Commission has described the result as a 'complex matrix of overlapping rules' and has recommended that presumed intention be sidelined in favour of a single utilitarian rule (see Law Commission (2008), para 4.019). It suggests that the sole basis for implication should look to whether the easement is 'necessary for the reasonable use of the land' at the time of the disposition taking into account a number of factors including the use of the land, any intended future use of the land, and the physical characteristics of the land (Law Commission (2011), para 3.45). However, it is these same factors that provide the different evidentiary sources against which the grant is to be read and the presumed intention extracted under the existing rules. Accordingly, Douglas (2015b) argues that any complexity arises not from the different rules of presumed intention but from the different evidentiary demands upon which they are based. Hence, he questions the need or advantage of the Law Commission's recommendations.

9.33 Before looking at each of the rules we need to clarify the distinction between the grant of an easement and the reservation of an easement. Both lead to the creation of an easement but differ according to whether it is the dominant or servient land which is being sold. Where the grantor is disposing of the dominant land but retaining the servient land, we talk of the grant of an easement. The grantor is not only disposing of the dominant land itself but is also presumed to be granting an easement over the servient land that is retained (see **Figure 9.1**).

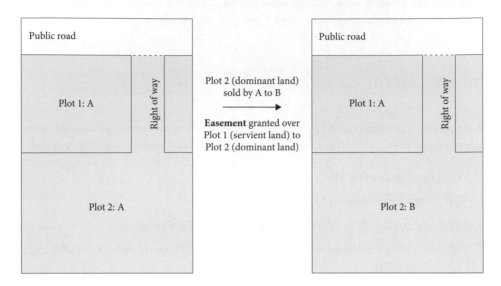

**Figure 9.1** Easement by implied grant

However, where the grantor is disposing of the servient land but retaining the dominant land, we talk of reserving an easement to create a reservation. In effect the grantor is reserving a limited continued use of the servient land. He or she is keeping back that right to benefit the dominant land retained (see **Figure 9.2**). The distinction is important because the law is less inclined to support the implication of a reservation than the implication of an easement. The expectation is that a landowner should be explicit if he or she wishes to reserve an interest.

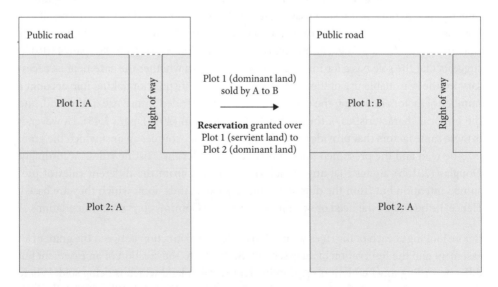

**Figure 9.2** Easements by implied reservation

## Easements and Reservations of Necessity

**9.34**  Easements of necessity arise in limited circumstances where land becomes landlocked upon the disposal by an owner of part of their land. Thus, for instance, if an owner sells his back garden leaving that land with no express right to access the public road, a presumed easement of necessity will arise to enable the new owner to pass over the seller's retained land to reach the public road. A high degree of necessity is required and thus generally easements of necessity arise to provide rights of access (but see *Walby v Walby* (2012)). If there is some other means of access, even if that route is most inconvenient, no easement of necessity will be implied (eg by water in *Manjang v Drammeh* (1991)). The scope of an implied grant of necessity will depend upon what is essential for the use of the dominant land at the time of the grant. For instance, the right may be limited to pedestrian rather than vehicular access (see *MRA Engineering Ltd v Trimster* (1988)).

**9.35**  At first sight it seems that easements of necessity are justified on the grounds of public policy to prevent land becoming economically sterile. But it is clear that the rationale for the implication rests on the presumed intention of the parties and as such may be excluded by a contrary intention (*Nickerson v Barraclough* (1981)).

## Intended Easements and Reservations

**9.36**  Intended easements fall into at least two, possibly three, categories. The first arises where the implication is intended from the right in question because it is necessary for the enjoyment of an expressly conferred easement. The right to water from a defined source, for example a river or spring, requires an intended easement to access that source by entering the servient owner's land even if that access is not expressly granted (see *Pwllbach Colliery Co Ltd v Woodman* (1915)).

**9.37**  The second arises from the circumstances of a grant where it is necessary to give effect to the common intention of the parties that an easement should be implied. An example of this second category is found in the case of *Wong v Beaumont Property Trust Ltd*.

---

*Wong v Beaumont Property Trust Ltd* **(1965):** Mr Wong rented the basement of a building to open a Chinese restaurant. The lease defined this use and furthermore required Mr Wong to eliminate all smells and other nuisances caused by his business and to comply with all health regulations. It emerged that, if Mr Wong was to perform these leasehold covenants, he would need to erect a larger extractor system but his landlord refused consent. An intended easement was implied for Mr Wong to erect the necessary flue to give effect to the intention of the parties as expressed in the lease.

---

It was clear that neither Mr Wong nor his landlord had an intention that there should be a right to erect the flue. Their intention related to the manner in which both the parties intended the premises should be used which it transpired could only be achieved by granting the right sought. The process is thus to establish the parties' intended use of the land and then to consider what rights are necessary to give effect to that use. In *Wong* the parties stated the permitted use of the property in the express terms of their lease but an intention may be gleaned from other circumstances (see *Stafford v Lee* (1993)).

9.38 The third possible category arises from the parties' intention that the right itself should be granted as a matter of necessary inference. *Re Webb's Lease* provides an example of circumstances where a claimant was unable to prove the necessary inference.

---

*Re Webb's Lease* **(1951):** Mr Webb ran a butcher's shop and leased out the upper floors upon the external walls of which advertisements were displayed. Although the tenant of the upper floors initially raised no objection to the advertisements, they subsequently demanded some recompense for this use of the external walls. Mr Webb claimed he had a reservation to display the advertisements and so did not need to pay for the privilege. The court did not agree and declined to recognize the right that Mr Webb claimed.

---

The fact that the tenant had not previously raised any objection to the advertisements was insufficient evidence that the right Mr Webb claimed was intended. There were other reasonable explanations for the tenant's conduct. It should be noted that the case concerned an implied reservation because Mr Webb was trying to argue he had retained the right to advertise on the external walls when he let the upper floors. The courts are hesitant to imply a reservation and will require very clear evidence of the necessary intention.

9.39 The interface between easements of necessity and intended easements is not always easy to divine, although it is clear that intended easements give rise to a wider range of rights than the access rights that dominate easements of necessity. Lawson (2002) suggests that it is more logical to place the first two categories within an expanded view of easements of necessity. Thus, intended easements would solely relate to the third category where the required intention relates to the grant of the right itself rather than the necessity of giving effect to an intention concerning some other grant.

## Implying Easements (But Not Reservations) by the Rule in *Wheeldon v Burrows*

9.40 The rule in *Wheeldon v Burrows* (1879) may give rise to an implied easement, but not an implied reservation. The rule states that:

> ... on the grant by the owner of a tenement or part of that tenement as it is then used and enjoyed, there will pass to the grantee all those continuous and apparent easements (by which, of course, I mean quasi easements) or in other words, all those easements which are necessary for the reasonable enjoyment of the property granted, and which have been at the time of the grant used by the owner of the entirety for the benefit of the part granted. (At 49 per Thesiger LJ.)

The rule operates upon the disposal of part of land when certain rights enjoyed by the part sold or leased (which becomes the dominant land) over the land retained (which becomes the servient land) mature into easements. Whilst the land is in common ownership, the rights cannot be classified as easements in view of the common ownership of the dominant and servient land. At this stage, the rights are sometimes referred to as quasi-easements. It is clear that the rule will not create an implied reservation (*Wheeldon v Burrows*) but may give rise to an implied easement where the servient land and dominant land are disposed of simultaneously (*Schwann v Cotton* (1916)). Only certain rights are capable of becoming easements under the rule in *Wheeldon v Burrows*:

(i)    the right must be enjoyed at the time of the disposal of the dominant land;

(ii)   the right claimed must be 'continuous and apparent';

(iii)  the right claimed must be reasonably necessary for the reasonable enjoyment of the dominant land.

**9.41**  First, the right must be enjoyed by the common owner of the servient and dominant land at the time of the disposal of the dominant land. Where the disposal is of legal effect (eg because a legal estate/interest in the dominant land has been disposed by deed and registration), a legal easement is created but where the disposal is of only equitable effect (eg as a result of the doctrine of anticipation) the easement is equitable (see *Borman v Griffith* (1930)).

**9.42**  Secondly, the exercise of the right must be 'continuous and apparent'. The meaning of 'continuous' does not mean that the right must be continuously exercised but rather invokes a sense of permanence so that the right may be exercised whenever required. 'Apparent' calls for the right to be discoverable by a reasonable careful inspection of the land and thus requires some physical evidence on the servient land that would signal the existence of the right—for instance, a road or pathway in the case of a right of way. In the case of *Ward v Kirkland* (1967) the claim of a right to enter to carry out repairs to the dominant land failed on this score because there was no feature on the adjoining servient land which indicated the existence of the right.

**9.43**  Thirdly, the right must be necessary for the reasonable enjoyment of the land. This test is clearly wider than the strict requirements of easements of necessity and could encompass, for instance, an alternative route of access (*Borman v Griffith* (1930) and *Millman v Ellis* (1995)). The difficulty is in establishing just how much wider. The mere convenience of an alternative access is by itself insufficient. The access should meet some requisite need for the reasonable use of the dominant land. In *Millman v Ellis* the right recognized was to use a lay-by which provided safer access to a busy road and in *Borman v Griffith* (1930) the alternative right of way was wider to allow access for the lorries that served the grantee's business.

**9.44**  The wording of the rule in *Wheeldon v Burrows* suggests that the last two requirements are alternative but there is a view that they are in fact cumulative so both limbs should be satisfied. The authorities are equivocal often because both requirements are satisfied on the particular facts. An intention to create an easement is not lightly implied which suggests that both elements should be met and, indeed, the Court of Appeal has distinguished the rule in *Wheeldon v Burrows* and rights implied by virtue of section 62 of the LPA 1925 on this basis (*Wood v Waddington* (2015)—see 9.48).

## Section 62 of the Law of Property Act 1925

9.45   This section was enacted as a word-saving provision so that it is unnecessary in a conveyance of land to expressly refer to any physical features forming part of the land, including buildings, or to any 'liberties, privileges, easements, rights and advantages whatsoever' which are appurtenant or attached (or reputed to be appurtenant or attached) to the land at the time of the conveyance. When expressly stated in a conveyance or transfer, this provision is known as the 'general words clause'.

9.46   The effect of the section has proved controversial because it has been interpreted to operate in particular circumstances to pass not just existing easements but to effectively upgrade a mere personal permission to a proprietary interest in the form of a fully-fledged easement. An example of this effect is found in the case of *Wright v Macadam* (1949); see also *International Tea Stores v Hobbs* (1903).

> *Wright v Macadam* (1949): Ms Wright was a weekly tenant of two rooms on the top floor of Mr Macadam's house. He gave Ms Wright permission to use a coal shed at the bottom of the garden to store her coal. Ms Wright subsequently entered into a new tenancy from Mr Macadam when Mr Macadam asked Ms Wright to pay for the privilege of using the coal shed. She refused and claimed that this right had become an easement upon the grant of her new lease. The courts upheld her claim by the operation of section 62.

9.47   Commentators differ on whether this uplift effect of section 62 was intended. Tee (1998) maintains that it was not but arises because of a misinterpretation of the word 'right' in the section which she argues was intended to refer to proprietary rights and not mere permissions which confer a personal right (or protection) not to be sued in trespass. Douglas disagrees. In his view (2015a), the width of the wording of the section demonstrates that 'right' was to be given a wider meaning to include both established property rights and rights of a personal nature which reflect the past usage of the land. What is clear is that the section can have unintended and unexpected consequences and the Law Commission has recommended that the uplift effect of the section should be removed (Law Commission (2011), para 3.64).

9.48   Despite this controversial effect of section 62, the section has operated to create an easement only in limited circumstances. This is primarily because of the view that the section calls for diversity of occupation between the dominant and servient land. Diversity of occupation is said to be required to demonstrate that the right is appurtenant to the dominant land rather than merely exercised because of the ownership or legitimate occupation of the servient land (*Long v Gowlett* (1923), *Sovmots Investment*

*Ltd v SS for the Environment* (1979), *Kent v Kavanagh* (2007)). For instance, in *Wright v Macadam* (1949) Ms Wright was in occupation of the dominant land comprising the rooms she rented and Mr Macadam was in occupation of the servient coal shed. The rule has thus largely been confined to the landlord and tenant situation or where diversity of occupation occurs when a seller of land allows a purchaser of the dominant land into occupation before the registration of the legal title. However, the need for diversity of occupation has been questioned more recently in the Court of Appeal cases of *P&S Platt Ltd v Crouch* (2004) and *Wood v Waddington* (2015) where a right is 'continuous and apparent'. In *P&S Platt Ltd v Crouch* the issue was whether the sale of a hotel also conveyed the right to use the river moorings that had previously been used exclusively for the benefit of the hotel guests. The seller of the hotel had thus owned and occupied the hotel and the right to use and occupy the moorings. The diversity of occupation point, however, was not fully argued. There is support from 19th-century case law to suggest diversity of occupation is not required where there is physical evidence on the servient land demonstrating the 'continuous and apparent' nature of the right in the sense already explored in the context of the rule in *Wheeldon v Burrows* (see **9.42** and *Watts v Kelson* (1870), *Bayley v Great Western Railway* (1884), *Broomfield v Williams* (1897)). These cases were called into question by the recent case law referred to above that supports the need for diversity of occupation. The fact that there is a clear feature on the servient land, which signals the right claimed, does not alter the fact that the grantor's use of his or her land explains their enjoyment of the right and does not provide cogent evidence of any particular easement or other permission attached to that ownership. Nevertheless, *Platt* has been followed by the Court of Appeal in *Wood v Waddington* (2015), in which the court considered *Long v Gowlett* (1923), but preferred to follow the earlier statements in the 19th-century cases referred to which recognized that rights could fall within section 62 where their exercise by the common owner or occupier of the servient and dominant land was 'continuous and apparent'.

**9.49** *Platt* and *Wood* also add to the challenge of distinguishing between section 62 and the rule in *Wheeldon v Burrows*. A diversity of occupation requirement marks the rules as mutually exclusive (see *Kent v Kavanagh* (2007)). *Wheeldon v Burrows* operates where the dominant land is disposed of following common ownership of the quasi-dominant and quasi-servient land but, if section 62 requires diversity of occupation between the dominant and servient land, it does not operate in these circumstances but only in the limited landlord and tenant or purchase situations described in **9.48**. If diversity of occupation is not required under section 62 but merely that the exercise of the right is 'continuous and apparent', the distinguishing trait between rights granted under *Wheeldon v Burrows* and section 62 turns on whether or not the right is necessary for the reasonable enjoyment of the land (see **9.43**). Thus, a degree of necessity is required under *Wheeldon v Burrows* but not section 62 with the result that section 62 is potentially wider in its operation.

**9.50** There are other distinctions between the two rules. Section 62 requires a conveyance of the legal estate in order to operate but *Wheeldon v Burrows* can operate upon the creation/transfer of an equitable interest. *Wheeldon v Burrows* can only imply easements that are 'continuous and apparent' and/or 'necessary for the reasonable enjoyment of the land'. Section 62 is not so constrained unless there is no diversity of occupation when, following *Platt* and *Wood*, the right should be 'continuous and apparent'. Where there is diversity of occupation, section 62 can operate in respect of any right that is capable of being an easement provided that in the circumstances the right is not personal to a particular individual or otherwise temporary or precarious (*Phipps v Pears* (1965), *Goldberg v Edwards* (1950)).

## Presumed Grant Prescription

**9.51**  A grant of an easement may be presumed as a result of long user through the doctrine of prescription. Prescription recognizes that long-established de facto enjoyment of the limited use of the land of another should be accorded legal status. Whilst the Law Commission accepts the prevailing view that the current rules of prescription are in urgent need of reform, it acknowledges that prescription should not be abolished because of the valuable role it plays in 'bringing the legal position into line with practical reality' and thus facilitating the transfer and marketability of land (Law Commission (2011), paras 3.75–3.80, see also the comments of Lord Hoffmann in *R v Oxfordshire CC, ex p Sunningwell Parish Council* (2000) at 349).

**9.52**  In this respect, prescription plays a similar role to adverse possession but it operates in a different manner. We have seen in **Chapter 4** that adverse possession operates as an independent means of acquiring ownership through the unilateral possession of the squatter, which in time operates to extinguishing the paper owner's title. As a result, a squatter acquires a new title which cannot be disputed by the paper owner. By contrast, prescription operates by creating a fiction that long user establishes the requisite evidence that the servient owner at one time created a grant of the right claimed. Prescription thus is presented as a form of dependent acquisition even though it arises as a result of the dominant owner's unilateral user and the almost certainly erroneous presumption that the servient owner granted the right.

### The Prescription Periods

**9.53**  Presently in English law there are three possible routes to claim a right by prescription.

(i)  First, at common law a prescriptive right can be claimed on proof of user of a right since time immemorial, which is accepted as 1189. A rebuttable presumption also arises at common law if 20 years' user can be proved. However, this presumption is easily rebutted if factually the user could not have commenced by 1189, for example because of the age of the building upon the dominant land.

(ii) Secondly, the Prescription Act 1832 provides two alternative routes to claim an easement by prescription which try to overcome some of the problems arising from common law prescription. The first route prevents a servient owner from disputing common law prescription where long user can be proved for a period of at least 20 years. The second route provides that a positive claim to a prescriptive right can be made after an extended period of 40 years' user (or 20 years' user of a right to light). In each case, the user must immediately precede the commencement of the action claiming the right.

(iii) Thirdly, at common law the doctrine of lost modern grant requires proof of user for a period of 20 years to establish a fiction that a grant was made but has been lost.

9.54   Common law prescription based upon user since 1189 is plainly almost impossible to prove. The Prescription Act 1832 provides little assistance given its reputation of 'one of the worst drafted Acts on the Statute book'. Its principal difficulty is the requirement that the period of uninterrupted user must immediately precede the action. As a result, the doctrine of lost modern grant remains the most convenient route to prescription. The Law Commission has recommended that this confusing and overlapping array of periods should be rationalized with the adoption of a single prescription period of 20 years' long use for all easements including rights to light (Law Commission (2011), para 3.123).

## User as of Right

9.55   The nature of the user required for prescription must be without force or in the face of objection by the servient owner (*nec vi*, see *Smith v Brudenell-Bruce* (2002), *Winterburn v Bennett* (2016)), without secrecy in the sense of the user being open and discoverable (*nec clam*, see *Union Lighterage Co v London Graving Dock Co* (1902)), and without the permission of the servient owner (*nec precario*). It is described as user 'as of right'. In other words, it must appear that the dominant owner used the right because of the fiction of the grant by the servient owner reinforced by the continued acquiescence of the user by the servient owner (*Dalton v Angus & Co* (1881), *R v Oxfordshire CC, ex p Sunningwell Parish Council* (2000), *Winterburn v Bennett* (2016)).

9.56   'As of right' is to be contrasted with 'by right' which indicates that the servient owner has consented to the user and thus the user is no longer without permission (*nec precario*). That consent or permission may be express. Alternatively, consent can be derived from another source, for instance from a statute or local byelaws (*R (Barkas) v North Yorkshire CC* (2014), *R (on the application of Newhaven Port & Properties Ltd v SS for the Environment, Food & Rural Affairs* (2015)). 'As of right' does not, however, require the use to be lawful—provided that any illegality could be overcome by the servient owner's consent to the use which (of course) is presumed. Indeed, underlying prescription is the presumption of a grant that is evidentially derived from a user that constitutes a trespass (*Bakewell Management Ltd v Brandwood* (2004)).

**9.57** Prescription operates in the realm of freehold ownership because the presumed grant is deemed to be a permanent grant made by a servient owner to a dominant owner for a freehold estate. Accordingly, both the servient and dominant owners must hold freehold estates. It is thus not possible for a lessee to acquire a prescriptive easement over adjoining land, whether held by his or her landlord or another third party. Nor can a prescriptive easement be normally claimed over leasehold land, at least when the lease was in existence at the inception of the long use—the user must be against a freehold owner of the servient land (*Williams v Sandy Lane (Chester) Ltd* (2006), *Llewellyn v Lorey* (2011)).

## Acquiescence and the Rationale for Prescription

**9.58** Why should the long user of the land of another give rise to a fiction that the grant should be presumed? The answer is said to lie in the acquiescence of the servient owner to a sufficiently open user to which the servient owner would have been expected to object (see *Coventry (t/a RDC Promotions) v Lawrence* (2014)). Accordingly, the fact the servient owner did not voice their objection leads to the fictional presumption that they agreed to the use by making a grant (*Dalton v Angus* (1881)). Continued user in the face of a sufficient objection by the servient owner will lead to the user being construed as no longer without force (*nec vi*). A sufficient objection by the servient owner will depend on the circumstances of the case but does not require the servient owner to confront the trespasser or to use physical means or to take legal proceedings to actually prevent the user. It is sufficient for the servient owner to demonstrate their continued objection to the user, for instance by erecting clearly visible signs to demonstrate that they do not acquiesce to the user (*Betterment Properties (Weymouth) Ltd v Dorset CC* (2012), *Winterburn v Bennett* (2016)).

**9.59** The rational of acquiescence is far from satisfactory and has been much criticized. Goymour (2007), for instance, has identified a number of problems. First, the requirement that the user be without permission is internally inconsistent with the concept that prescription is based upon a presumed grant, itself of course a permission. Secondly, the requirement that the user be without permission introduces an element of adversity which also appears inconsistent with the idea of acquiescence. Thirdly, the servient owner's acquiescence is as equally fictitious as the presumption of a grant. Fourthly, there is the confusion between prescription presented as a form of dependent acquisition when in reality it springs from the dominant owner's independent actions. Lastly, this focus upon the technicalities of prescription masks the more relevant questions of utility and the policy underpinning long use rights. These criticisms are particularly pertinent when a servient owner claims a negative, rather than a positive, easement. In these circumstances, the dominant owner will not have made any use of the servient owner's land. He or she is merely claiming that the servient owner should be restrained from acting in a way he or she would otherwise be entitled to do; for instance, by building to interfere with a claimed prescriptive right to light, air, or support (*Hunter v Canary Wharf* (1997)). The Law Commission has accordingly recommended that, whilst the requirement that the user be open, without force, and without permission should be retained, the concept of acquiescence should be abandoned (Law Commission (2011), para 3.121).

## Prescription and Human Rights

**9.60**  In Chapter 4 we saw that the acquisition of title by adverse possession has been challenged as an interference with a right to the protection of possession under Article 1 Protocol 1 of the European Convention on Human Rights. Is prescription a similar interference? Although a servient owner is not deprived of his or her ownership of the servient land by prescription, his or her ownership will be subject to a new burden or 'control'. The issue then becomes whether that new control can be justified because it is in the public interest and is proportionate in its effect. We have noted that prescription does play an important role in recognizing the factual reality of long user. Furthermore, given the nature of the qualifying user, the servient owner is expected to know of that user and have the relatively long period of 20 years in which to do something about it. These are similar justifications to those found in *JR Pye (Oxford) Ltd v UK* (2008) when the European Court of Human Rights found the rules governing the adverse possession of land under the Land Registration Act 1925 to be human rights compatible. One might expect a similar reaction to a challenge to the human rights compatibility of prescription.

# The Defences Question

## Registered Land

**9.61**  Easements, particularly implied and presumed easements, present a challenge to a complete and accurate register. Under the Land Registration Act 1925 all legal easements took effect against a purchaser of registered land as overriding interests even though their existence was not apparent from the register. Equitable easements could also take effect as overriding interests under the Land Registration Act 1925 provided they were openly enjoyed (*Celsteel Ltd v Alton House Holdings Ltd* (1985))).

**9.62**  The Land Registration Act 2002 (LRA 2002) seeks to bring as many easements as is feasible onto the register. The operation of the LRA 2002 is fully considered in Chapter 12, thus for the time being we provide the following summary of its operation in relation to easements.

(i)   Easements that are protected by registration will bind a purchaser (LRA 2002, s 29(2)(a)). There is thus an incentive to register an easement.

(ii)   Easements (whether legal or equitable) created before 13 October 2003 (the date the LRA 2002 came into force) which are overriding interests, although not registered, will continue to override (LRA 2002, Sch 12, para 9). Thus, a dominant owner (as at 13 October 2003) will continue to be able to assert his or her easement against a subsequent owner of the servient land.

(iii) An express easement created after 13 October 2003 must be created by deed and registered to take effect as a legal easement (LRA 2002, ss 25 and 27 and Sch 2).

(iv) An equitable easement created after 13 October 2003 can no longer take effect as an overriding interest in its own right. An equitable easement might conceivably qualify as an overriding interest under Schedule 3, paragraph 2 of the LRA 2002 when the dominant owner can establish actual occupation as opposed to mere use (*Chaudhary v Yavuz* (2013) discussed at **11.40**). However, such proof may be an uphill struggle and thus the dominant owner of an equitable easement is well advised to register to avoid a lack of registration defence.

(v) An implied or presumed easement arising after 13 October 2003 will override *unless*:

- the right is not within the actual knowledge of a purchaser or other disponee *and* the right would not have been obvious on a reasonably careful inspection of the servient land; *or*

- the dominant owner can prove that the easement has been exercised during the period of one year ending with the day of the sale or other disposition (LRA 2002, Sch 3, para 3).

The emphasis is thus upon the discoverability of the implied or presumed easement. Whilst the rules are intended to assist the transparency of the register, they are controversial in removing the proprietary status of legal rights. A dominant owner claiming the benefit of an implied or presumed easement is thus well advised to register their easement (Kenny (2003)).

## Unregistered Land

**9.63**  The rules governing unregistered land are found in the common law doctrine of notice as affected by the Land Charges Act 1972. A legal easement, whether created expressly, by implied grant, or presumed grant, will bind a purchaser or other disponee of the servient land by virtue of its legal status. An equitable easement arising under the doctrine of anticipation will only bind a purchaser or other disponee if the easement is protected by an entry in the Land Charges Register as a Class D(iii) land charge.

**9.64**  These rules relating to unregistered land are of declining importance given the fact that a disposal of the servient land by way of transfer, a lease for more than seven years, or a first mortgage will trigger first registration (LRA 2002, s 4). Existing legal easements, whether arising from express, implied, or presumed grant, will qualify as overriding interests on first registration but equitable easements will not do so and will be defeated by the disponee unless a caution against first registration has been lodged by the dominant owner against the servient land (LRA 2002, Sch 1, para 3 and Part 2).

## Extinguishment of Easements

**9.65**  It is not easy to lose an easement. As a legal interest in land it enjoys the permanence of property.

**9.66**  The common ownership of servient and freehold dominant land will bring an easement enjoyed by the dominant land over the servient land to an end, although a subsequent disposal of the dominant land may trigger the implication of a new easement following the rule in *Wheeldon v Burrows* (**9.40-9.44**). Where the easement is attached to a dominant leasehold estate, the common occupation of the dominant and servient land will operate to suspend the easement until diversity of occupation is restored.

**9.67**  The dominant owner may expressly agree with the servient owner to release an easement. However, it is only in the very clearest circumstances that a dominant owner will be held to have abandoned an easement. It must be possible to demonstrate that the dominant owner has acted, or failed to act, in such a way as to prove an intention to relinquish the easement. Mere non-use for a period of time is insufficient.

## FURTHER READING

Douglas, S, 'How to Reform Section 62 of the Law of Property Act 1925' [2015a] Conv 13.

Douglas, S, 'Reforming Implied Easements' (2015b) 115 LQR 251.

Goymour, A, 'Rights in Property and the Effluxion of Time' in E Cooke (ed), *Modern Studies in Property Law: Vol 4* (Oxford: Hart Publishing, 2007).

Law Commission Report No 327, *Making Land Work: Easements, Covenants and Profits à Prendre* (2011).

Lawson, A, 'Easements' in L Tee (ed), *Land Law: Issues, Debates, Policy* (Cullompton: Willan, 2002).

Luther, P, 'Easements and Exclusive Possession' (1996) 16 LS 51.

Paton, EW and Seabourne, GC, 'Can't Get There From Here? Permissible Use of Easements After *Das*' [2003] Conv 127.

Sturley, M, 'Easements in Gross' (1980) 96 LQR 557.

Tee, L, 'Metamorphoses and Section 62 of the Law of Property Act 1925' [1998] Conv 115.

## SELF-TEST QUESTIONS

1   When does an easement 'accommodate' the dominant land?

2   What does the requirement that to qualify as an easement a right over the land of another 'must be capable of being the subject matter of a grant' encompass?

3   Explain the difference between a positive easement, a negative easement, and a profit à prendre.

4   Why, as a matter of policy, is it important to be able in particular circumstances to imply or presume the grant of an easement?

5   How do the operation of section 62 of the LPA 1925 and the rule in *Wheeldon v Burrows* fit together?

6   In prescription, what is the distinction between 'user as of right' and 'of right'?

# 10

# Freehold Covenants

## SUMMARY

This chapter considers freehold covenants which play an important role in controlling land use and supplement public planning control. They do so by controlling the activities conducted on one piece of land (the servient land) for the benefit of adjacent land (the dominant land). The chapter focuses upon the proprietary effect of covenants relating to freehold land as agreements that can be enforced against subsequent owners of the servient land by subsequent owners of the dominant land. At the present time, only covenants that operate negatively to restrict land use can be enforced against subsequent owners of the servient land. Nevertheless, the chapter goes on to explain a number of devices that conveyancers employ to enforce positive obligations. Leasehold covenants that were considered in Chapter 7 are also employed to overcome this limitation. Finally, the chapter considers in outline the common remedies for breach of a freehold covenant and the statutory jurisdiction to alter outdated covenants before concluding by looking at current reform proposals

Key topics explored in this chapter are:

- The enforceability of the burden of freehold covenants to define who can sue for breach of the covenant (10.6–10.15)

- The indirect enforcement of positive obligations (10.16–10.21)

- Freehold covenants and the acquisition and defences questions (10.22–10.25)

- The entitlement to the benefit of freehold covenants to define who can sue for breach of covenant (10.26–10.46)

- Remedies for breach of freehold covenants (10.47–10.52)

- Statutory modification of freehold covenants (10.53–10.55)

- Reform proposals (10.56–10.59)

## Introduction

10.1 A covenant is an agreement entered into by deed and is contractually binding upon the parties to the covenant without the need for further consideration. We saw in Chapter 7 that covenants in leases may also be enforceable by and against a landlord's assignee of the reversion on the lease and by and against a tenant's assignee of the lease itself. In this chapter we will examine how certain covenants between neighbouring freehold owners may overcome privity of contract to become enforceable by and against subsequent owners of neighbouring property.

10.2 This is an important issue. For instance, a covenant between adjoining freehold owners not to build on their respective pieces of land will be of limited utility should one of them sell their land and their purchaser plead privity of contract to ignore the covenant and build on their property. The issue came to prominence in the 19th century when major cities, like London, grew rapidly as a result of changing economic and social conditions precipitated by the agricultural and industrial revolutions and the expansion of trade. At that time, planning and public health controls were few but more and more people, particularly in the emerging middle class, wanted to improve their living environments. They could do so by creating physically pleasant neighbourhoods, like the leafy squares built in London at that time, and by imposing legal obligations upon the owners for the time being within these neighbourhoods not to change their use and character. We will see that the courts of equity supported these aspirations by developing the proprietary nature of such obligations through restrictive covenants. Although there is now extensive planning and public health regulation, the attraction of creating private enclaves through what is, in effect, private planning control has not diminished. The uniform character of housing estates and gated communities depends upon the enforceability of covenants between their current owners. An owner of land may often wish to control what goes on on neighbouring land, particularly if he or she sells part of their land. Covenants are also employed to this end. Indeed, most residential neighbourhoods are subject to covenants which restrict what home owners within the neighbourhood can do on their land. These covenants may encompass a whole range of obligations. Common restrictions prohibit commercial or industrial use within a residential area, restrict the number of dwellings that can be built or the alterations to existing buildings that can be carried out, covenants may even dictate that the external look of the house must not be altered or that caravans, and such like, cannot be parked so they are visible from the road. One might ask why a landowner would be prepared to submit to these private law impositions upon their freedom to exercise their rights of ownership. The answer lies in the environmental, aesthetic, and financial benefits (reflected in higher house prices) of having direct private control over the development of neighbouring land beyond the controls imposed by local planning authorities through planning and environmental legislation.

## Land Covenant Terminology and Structure

10.3 Before we consider the detailed and sometimes complex rules governing the enforceability of freehold covenants relating to land, we need to be clear about the terminology used and the structure employed to create this local private planning law. A, the freehold owner of Plot 1, may agree with his or her neighbour, B, the freehold owner of Plot 2 not to build on Plot 1 without B's consent. A is known as the *covenantor* because he or she has agreed to perform the obligation (or come under a duty) to B—if A builds on Plot 1 without B's consent, B can sue A. We say A has the burden of the covenant because of

this duty. B is referred to as the *covenantee* and we say B has the benefit of
because he or she can sue A if A breaches the covenant by building on Plot
consent. If A sells Plot 1 to C, B will only be able to sue C, should C breach
if B can establish that the burden of A's duty passes to C—see **Figure 10.1**.
the running of the burden of the covenant with the land, meaning that the
time being of the land subject to the burden of a covenant—Plot 1 in our example—is
under a duty to observe the covenant even though they are not a party to it and thus
under a direct contractual obligation to observe the covenant.

If it is B who sells Plot 2 to D, D will only be able to sue A (or C) if he or she can prove
that they have acquired the benefit of B's covenant with A—see **Figure 10.1**. Likewise,
we talk of the running of the benefit of the covenant with the land to denote the ability of
the owner for the time being of the land with the benefit of the covenant—Plot 2 in our
example—to enforce the covenant.

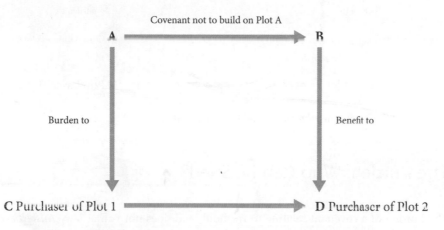

Figure 10.1 The transmission of the benefit and burden of land covenants

10.4 Covenants are generally not restricted in time and thus it can be necessary to follow the
running of the benefit and burden of the covenant for many years through the successive purchasers of Plot 1 and Plot 2 respectively. We call such purchasers of the freehold
of Plot 1 or Plot 2 *successors in title* to A or B as they acquire the entire freehold estate.
By contrast where A or B, or a successor in title to A or B, create a lesser interest out of
their freehold estate, for instance a lease or mortgage, we describe such interest holders
as *deriving title* from A and B. We are equally concerned that they also have the burden
by coming under a duty to perform the covenants or have the benefit and can thus take
action if a covenant is breached on the neighbouring land.

10.5 These situations are relatively straightforward but the picture becomes more complicated if A and B enter into mutual covenants by agreeing with each other that A will not
build on Plot 1 without B's consent and B will not build on Plot 2 without A's consent.
In this situation, A and B are both covenantors, they both have the burden of their respective covenants by being under a duty not to build on their respective plots without
the required consent. They are also both covenantees because they both have the benefit

of a covenant which entitles A to sue B, if B builds on Plot 2 without consent, and B to sue A, if A builds on Plot 1 without consent. If A then sells Plot 1 to C and B sells Plot 2 to D, it is necessary to ask the questions: who has breached the covenant and thus can be sued and who wants to sue? If C has breached the covenant by building on Plot 1 without consent, then it is necessary to show that C is under a duty to observe A's original covenant (ie C is subject to the burden) and can be sued and that D has the benefit of B's original covenant and thus is able to sue C—see **Figure 10.2**.

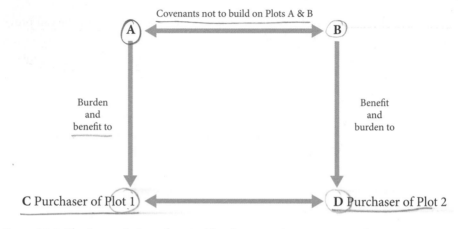

**Figure 10.2** The transmission of mutual land covenants

## The Burden: Who Can Be Sued?

**10.6** The burden of a covenant relating to freehold land does not run at law (*Austerberry v Oldham Corp* (1995)). The courts of law have stood steadfastly by privity of contract by finding that only the original covenantor is under a duty to observe the covenant and can be sued should he or she fail to do so. However, the courts of equity in the mid-19th century began to recognize that a purchaser of land should not be free to ignore the obligations contained in a covenant relating to land of which they have notice. They signalled this developing approach in the landmark case of *Tulk v Moxhay*.

---

*Tulk v Moxhay* (1848): In 1808 Tulk had sold part of land that he owned in what is now Leicester Square to Elms, who covenanted with Tulk that he would 'at all times thereafter at his own cost keep and maintain the piece of ground in sufficient and proper repair, and in an open state, uncovered with any buildings, in neat and ornamental order'. The land sold to Elms came into the ownership of Moxhay. Although Moxhay knew of the covenant that Elms had given to Tulk, he made plans to develop the land. Tulk was able to stop these plans when the court granted him an injunction against Moxhay.

---

Lord Cottenham, the then Lord Chancellor, explained that it would be inequitable for the court to allow a purchaser to ignore a covenant relating to land of which he or she is well aware. There would be little point in the original parties entering into the covenant in the first place if its observance could be so easily avoided. Furthermore, a purchaser could obtain a windfall by selling the land for a higher price if their purchaser were permitted to ignore a covenant which had an impact on the land's value.

**10.7** Lord Cottenham's reasoning in *Tulk v Moxhay* was primarily based upon Moxhay's notice of the covenant to create a direct and independent duty on Moxhay to observe the covenant rather than an explicit acknowledgement of the proprietary nature of the covenant. It was only subsequently that the courts recognized the covenant itself as a pre-existing equitable interest and as such potentially enforceable against a third party. In doing so, the courts developed the characteristics that a covenant would have to display to qualify as a covenant that could affect third parties and thus claim proprietary status. These content requirements of an enforceable freehold covenant may be summarized as:

- the burden of the covenant must relate to the servient land and be intended to run with the land in the sense that the covenant is not solely personal;

- there must be adjoining (or dominant) land that is capable of benefiting from the covenant affecting the (servient) land; and

- the covenant must be negative in nature.

## The Covenant Must Relate to the Servient Land

**10.8** The covenant must relate in some way to the covenantor's land, for instance by controlling the way in which it is used. A covenant, which only creates a personal obligation upon the covenantor in his or her individual capacity, is insufficient. The vast majority of common covenants relate to the way in which the land is used, for instance that 'the land should be used only for residential purposes' or that 'no caravans should be parked on the front driveway'. We sometimes use the expression that the covenant should 'touch and concern the land'—a concept we previously encountered in relation to leasehold covenants (see **7.105**). Covenants that do not qualify would impose only a personal obligation upon the covenantor, for instance 'to send the covenantee red roses on Valentine's day' or 'not to play at the same golf club as the covenantee'. Clearly, these covenants have nothing whatsoever to do with the land although they may say something about the personal relationship between the parties.

**10.9** The obligation, even if it relates to land, must also be intended to affect subsequent owners of the land. There is a statutory presumption that a covenant relating to land is made by a covenantor and his (or her) successors in title and persons deriving title under him (or her) unless a contrary intention is expressed (Law of Property Act 1925 (LPA 1925), s 79). Section 79 will not itself pass the burden of a covenant, it merely provides a convenient means of expressing an intention that a covenant is made by 'the covenantor on behalf of him/herself and his/her successors in title and persons deriving title from him/her or them' and is thus intended to affect subsequent owners (*Morrells of Oxford Ltd v Oxford United Football Club Ltd* (2001)).

## The Covenant Must Benefit Adjoining Dominant Land

**10.10** There must be land that is capable of benefiting from the covenant. The benefit must be attached to the dominant land rather than the covenantee personally, in the sense that it too touches and concerns the dominant land and is intended to benefit the owner for the time being of that land. Once the original covenantee disposes of the land, he or she is unable to enforce the covenant unless he or she retains a contractual right to do so (*London CC v Allen* (1914)). As we shall see the right to enforce the covenant may pass to the owner for the time being of the dominant land (see **10.26–10.46**). It is thus not possible for a covenant to exist in gross for the benefit solely of a person. We can see, for instance, in the classic case of *Tulk v Moxhay*, that Tulk owned land that would benefit from retaining the open character of the land Moxhay had bought. It is the benefit afforded to adjoining land that justifies the imposition of the covenant as a proprietary burden upon the servient land.

**10.11** In satisfying this requirement, there are a number of elements to consider. First, it must be possible to identify the land to be benefited. A properly drafted covenant will do so but, if the conveyancing lawyers have not done their job as well as they should have done, the court may look to the surrounding circumstances to identify the land benefited. This is what happened in the case of *Newton Abbot Co-operative Society v Williamson & Treadgold Ltd*.

---

**Newton Abbot Co-operative Society v Williamson & Treadgold Ltd (1952):** Mrs Mardon owned premises known as Devonia from which she carried on her business as an ironmonger. She also owned property across the street which she sold taking a covenant from the purchaser that he or she would not carry on an ironmonger's business. The covenant did not actually say that it was for the benefit of Devonia. Some years later the Co-op bought Devonia, and the land across the street subject to the covenant came into the ownership of Williamson & Treadgold who began to sell items of ironmongery. The Co-op successfully obtained an injunction for breach of the covenant originally given to Mrs Mardon.

---

The Court of Appeal found from the surrounding circumstances, in particular the close proximity and the nature of the business conducted at Devonia, that it was evident with 'reasonable certainty' that the covenant had been taken for the benefit of Devonia rather than Mrs Mardon personally (see also *Marten v Flight Refuelling Ltd* (1962), *Earl of Leicester v Wells-next-the-Sea UDC* (1973)).

**10.12** Secondly, the covenant must benefit (or accommodate) the dominant land in the sense that it 'affects the value of the land or the method of its occupation or enjoyment' (*Re Gadds Land Transfer* (1966) at 66 per Buckley LJ). In the *Newton Abbot* case, it was argued that the covenant granted to Mrs Mardon was merely a personal non-competition covenant to protect Mrs Mardon's business and not Devonia. The Court of Appeal rejected this argument on the ground that it was Devonia, as the land itself, rather than solely the business conducted upon it, which was intended to benefit. Indeed, it seems that the courts have been relatively relaxed in finding the necessary benefit to the dominant land. In *Wrotham Park Estate Co Ltd v Parkside Homes Ltd* ((1974) at 808) Brightman J recognized that there were clear cases where there was or was not benefit but there were other situations where 'responsible persons can have divergent views sincerely and reasonably held'. In these instances, the court will not pick and choose between particular views provided the opinion advanced can be reasonably held. What can be more problematic is if the area purported to benefit is large but it is stretching the imagination to accept that the whole area derives a benefit even though at least part of the land clearly does so. We will return to this issue when considering the rules governing the running of the benefit (see **10.33**).

10.13    The need for servient and dominant land and the requirement for benefit (or accommodation) draw close parallels between easements and covenants. Indeed, in *London & South Western Rly Co v Gomm* ((1882) at 583) Sir George Jessel suggested that *Tulk v Moxhay* demonstrated 'an extension of the doctrine of negative easements'. Covenants do differ from positive easements because a positive easement grants a right to use the land of another but covenants control the use of the covenantor's land by the covenantee. The analogy is, as Sir George Jessel observed, with negative easements (such as rights to light or support) which prevent the servient owner from using their land in a way which would interfere with the right. We have seen that the courts are reluctant to recognize new categories of negative easements because the same or a similar goal can be achieved through a land covenant (see **9.23**). The threshold for accommodation to the dominant land is approached in rather a more relaxed fashion when a covenant is afforded proprietary effect than when a right qualifies as an easement because it accommodates the dominant land. A further key difference between easements and covenants lies in the manner in which they can be acquired. Covenants are invariably created expressly but, by contrast, we have seen that easements may arise also by implication and presumption based upon long user (see **9.31-9.69**).

## The Covenant Must Be Negative

10.14    A negative or restrictive covenant restrains the owner of the servient land from acting in some way whilst a positive covenant requires a servient owner to fund or perform some activity; for instance, by carrying out repairs or paying someone else to do so. The covenant in *Tulk v Moxhay* had both positive and negative aspects. It called for the land to be kept in an open state, that is, it should not built upon, and it required the land to be maintained. However, as the doctrine developed it was confined to negative obligations (see *Hayward v Brunswick PBS* (1881), *London & South Western Rly v Gomm* (1882)). The reason for rejecting the enforceability of positive covenants appeared to lie in the weight of the obligation that would be placed on the servient owner. However, in this respect the doctrine parted ways with leasehold covenants which, as we have seen, have long been enforced regardless of whether they are positive or negative (see **7.93**). Gardner and Mackenzie (2012) doubt a solely economic justification for this divergence and instead suggest that the distinction displays a discriminatory bias based upon class. The incursion that positive obligations present to the liberty (or dominium) of the freehold ownership, enjoyed predominately by upper sections of society in the 19th century, was considered unacceptable but the same concern was not shown to tenants many of whom came from lower social classes.

10.15    The question of the enforceability of positive covenants came before the House of Lords in the case of *Rhone v Stephens*.

---

*Rhone v Stephens* **(1994):** A house had been divided into two dwellings (a house and adjoining cottage) in such a way that one of the cottage bedrooms lay beneath the roof of the house. Upon the sale of the cottage, the owner of the house covenanted with the purchaser to keep the roof in repair. Some years later, after both the house and the cottage had been sold by the original parties to the repairing covenant, the roof fell into disrepair. The owner of the cottage unsuccessfully tried to rely on the positive covenant to sue the owner of the house for a failure to repair. The House of Lords reaffirmed that it was only the burden of negative covenants that could be enforceable against subsequent owners.

---

Lord Templeman, giving the leading judgment, drew a distinction between negative and positive covenants. He suggested that a negative covenant withdraws from the bundle of rights enjoyed by an owner the right to act in a way that would breach a covenant. A purchaser thus never receives that right when they purchase the land. By contrast, a positive covenant imposes an additional obligation upon the owner of the land that equity will not enforce because to do so would contradict the common law's refusal to enforce covenants against those who are not a party to the covenant. This explanation is not wholly unconvincing (see Gardner (1995)). Rather more understandable is their Lordships' reluctance to overturn orthodoxy by embarking on judicial legislation which would affect the basis upon which land had been bought, sold, and mortgaged for decades. If the enforcement of positive covenants was necessary or desirable as a matter of policy then it was for Parliament to intervene.

## Indirect Enforcement of Positive Obligations

10.16    There is no doubt that the inability to enforce positive freehold covenants as proprietary interests is inconvenient, particularly when it is necessary to regulate the management, maintenance, and repair of shared facilities between landowners. It is to overcome this inconvenience that conveyancers have adopted the lease to facilitate flat ownership (see 7.131–7.136). The issue has attracted the attention of Parliament in the introduction of commonhold title (see 7.137) and the Law Commission has long advocated further legislative reform (see mostly recently Law Commission (2011)). We will look at its proposals at 10.56–10.59. In the meantime, there are other ways in which conveyancers try to address the problem.

### Mutual Benefit and Burden

10.17    The principle of mutual benefit and burden is expressed in the maxim that 'he who takes the benefit of a right must bear the burden upon which it is dependent'. The principle is illustrated by the case of *Halsall v Brizell*.

---

*Halsall v Brizell* **(1957):** Purchasers of an estate of houses in Liverpool were granted a right to use the private roads, drains, and a promenade and sea wall that all lay within the estate. The rights were expressed to be subject to an obligation to contribute to the cost of the repair of these facilities. When Brizell, a successor in title to one of the original purchasers, questioned his contribution the court held that he could not claim the benefit of his right to use the estate facilities without the attendant burden to pay for their upkeep.

The House of Lords in *Rhone v Stephens* approved *Halsall v Brizell* and the principle to the extent that the benefit and burden are reciprocal in the sense that a purchaser's acceptance of the benefit is conditional upon whether he or she also accepts the burden. They refused to accept any wider principle. For instance, Megarry V-C in *Tito v Waddell (No 2)* (1977) had tried to extend *Halsall v Brizell* to include situations where it was evident from the conveyance that a successor in title could not claim the benefit of the right without accepting the burden even if, as originally expressed, the grant of the benefit of the right was not clearly conditional on acceptance of the burden.

**10.18**    The Court of Appeal in *Thamesmead Town Ltd v Allotey* (2000) formulated a two-stage test to establish whether a covenant falls within the principle. The first stage looks to prove that the benefit of a right is only conferred conditionally upon acceptance of the burden. The second stage looks to ask whether the successor in title has a choice as to whether he or she will accept the benefit of the right and its attendant burden. In *Thamesmead* these requirements were not fully satisfied.

> **Thamesmead Town Ltd v Allotey (2000):** Upon a tenant's purchase of his freehold reversion under the Right to Buy he was granted a right to use the estate roads, footpaths, and service utilities and entered into an obligation to contribute to the repair and maintenance of those facilities at Thamesmead as well as the landscaped areas of the estate. When Mr Allotey subsequently purchased the house, he successfully questioned the amount of these charges he was asked to pay. The court held that he was not required to pay that portion of the charges that related to the upkeep of the landscaped grounds as he had no right to use those areas (see also *Elwood v Goodman* (2014)).

In *Thamesmead* the charges could be apportioned but where they cannot the successor in title must accept the whole charges (*Wilkinson v Kerdene Ltd* (2012)).

**10.19**    The mutual benefit and burden test has been conveniently summarized in *Davies v Jones* (2010) at [27] by Sir Andrew Morritt C as follows.

(i)    The benefit and burden must be conferred in or by the same transaction—for example, in a sale and purchase of the whole or part of the land.

(ii)    It must be evident from the construction of the conveyancing documents (whether expressly or by implication) that the enjoyment of the benefit must be relevant to the imposition of the burden, in the sense that the benefit must be conditional on or reciprocal to the burden—for instance, that a right of way over a private road is conditional on paying a contribution to the upkeep of the road.

(iii)    The person upon whom the burden is alleged to have been imposed must have, or have had, the opportunity of rejecting or disclaiming the benefit and not merely a right to receive the benefit. This choice may be more theoretical than real where the successor in title may require the benefit to make his or her required use of the property, for instance a right of way may be essential. Thus effectively he or she must also accept the burden, for instance of the cost of maintenance of the right of way.

## Chain of Indemnity Covenants

10.20   It is common practice for conveyancers to try and build up a chain of personal covenants between successors in title of the covenantor by which direct contractual liability can be imposed through each link in the chain from the original covenantor to the current owner of the servient land. Thus, if A, the owner of Plot 1 has agreed with B, the owner of Plot 2, that he will repair the party wall between Plots 1 and 2, A on selling Plot 1 to C may require C to agree to maintain the party wall and to indemnify A if C fails to do so. B cannot sue C directly but he can sue A who in turn may rely on his personal contractual right from C to indemnify A for any damages B has successfully recovered from A. The same contractual obligations may be imposed when C sells and so on. The chain is only as strong as each link and will break down as a means of passing on the burden of a positive obligation if a link breaks, for instance on the death of one of the parties in the chain. Furthermore, an indemnity covenant will only give a right to claim common law damages in the event of breach.

## Estate Rentcharges

10.21   An estate rentcharge is a legal interest in land that requires the owner of the land subject to the rentcharge to pay a periodic sum which may be supported by a right of re-entry in the event of a failure to pay the agreed sum. As a legal interest in land, a rentcharge is enforceable against a third party. An estate rentcharge may be employed to recover charges for the management, maintenance, and repair of communal facilities by imposing a positive burden on the servient land to meet the costs as defined by the rentcharge. However, the right to re-enter the servient land if the rentcharge is not paid is often viewed as a rather draconian response to a failure to pay what might be a sum which is considerably less than the value of the land.

## The Acquisition Question

10.22   Covenants are invariably created by deed and will often be made pursuant to an agreement to create a covenant contained in the contract for the sale of that land. However, because restrictive covenants operate only in equity it is possible that a restrictive covenant could be created by signed writing (see LPA 1925, s 53(1)(c)) or could arise as a result of proprietary estoppel (see Chapter 5). Usually covenants will arise where a landowner sells part of their land and wishes to continue to control the use of the land they sell. In the case of the development of a housing estate, the developer in order to enhance the marketability of the development, will often wish to promote a uniform and attractive character for the estate. They will thus impose the same restrictive covenants on each of the houses they sell with the intention that the covenants will enhance, or benefit, the whole of the estate. In these circumstances, we refer to the covenants being created as part of a building scheme. We will see the significance of such a label at **10.39–10.43**.

# The Defences Question

**10.23**  We saw in *Tulk v Moxhay* that Moxhay's lack of a defence against Tulk's action to enforce the restrictive covenant was based upon Moxhay's knowledge of the covenant which it would be unconscionable to allow him to ignore. As the courts of equity developed the characteristics of covenants that could be enforced against third parties (see **10.7–10.15**), restrictive covenants came to be recognized as having proprietary effect as equitable interests in the land itself. Notice remained important but in the context of the priority rule that only purchasers for value of a legal estate without notice would have a defence against a pre-existing equitable restrictive covenant. Other persons acquiring a right to the land would be bound as a result of the proprietary status of the restrictive covenant. This approach applied even where the person acquired their right by involuntary acquisition through adverse possession (see *Re Nisbet & Potts Contract* (1906)). This result is doctrinally difficult, if not impossible, to explain. The proprietary effect of a restrictive covenant rests upon the notion that it operates as a burden upon the freehold title of the servient land when the servient owner comes under a duty to observe its terms. Adverse possession will extinguish that freehold title and, one might expect, the restrictive covenant too. However, this result would place in jeopardy the role of restrictive covenants as a local private planning tool that we explained at **10.2**. The Court of Appeal in *Re Nisbet & Potts Contract* thus made what was in effect a policy decision that squatters should come under a duty to observe restrictive covenants affecting the land they possess. They explained that the restrictive covenant was 'a burden imposed upon the land' itself (at 402).

**10.24**  The priority of restrictive covenants created before 1925 continued to be governed by notice but the priority of covenants created after 1925 has been assimilated into the appropriate registration regime under which they fall (see **Chapter 11**). If the restrictive covenant affects unregistered land, it must be registered as a Class D(ii) land charge (Land Charges Acts 1925, s 101, and 1972, s 2(5)). If the restrictive covenants affect registered land they must be protected by the entry of a notice on the Charges Register (Land Registration Act 2002, ss 29 and 32–34). The purpose of requiring such registration is to ensure that a purchaser can discover whether the land is affected by restrictive covenants and decide whether the use they wish to make of the land is consistent with the restrictions the covenants impose.

**10.25**  Where a positive covenant is enforceable under the principle of benefit and burden, notice or registration is not necessary. The principle is contractually based and the obligation to perform the positive covenant is personal to the particular purchaser who has decided to accept the burden in order to enjoy the benefit of the right offered (*Elwood v Goodman* (2014)).

## The Benefit: Who Can Sue?

**10.26**  Those entitled to the benefit of a covenant define who is able to enforce the obligation by taking action on the covenant to obtain an injunction to prevent the breach or claim damages for the loss suffered as a result of the breach. We will look further at these remedies at 10.47–10.52 but, first, we need to examine who can take action beyond the original covenantee. There are three routes by which the benefit of a covenant may pass to a successor in title of the original covenantee or a person deriving title from the covenantee. These are:

(i)   by assignment of the benefit of the covenant;

(ii)  by annexation of the benefit of the covenant to the land, either by express words, implication, or by the operation of section 78 of the LPA 1925; or

(iii) under a building scheme.

These three methods, particularly annexation, have been the subject of highly technical rules. Wade ((1972) at 162) describes these rules as 'producing a body of law of notorious and unnecessary difficulty'. These rules are concerned both with a search for an intention that the benefit of the covenant should pass to subsequent owners of the land and clarity in identifying the physical extent of the land to which the benefit is attached. Wade goes on to explain that the case law displays a tension between 'the conveyancers' view' in searching for certainty from precise words and 'the judicial view' which, whilst at times supporting this technicality, tended to take a more relaxed approach, in searching for the all-important intention that the benefit should run (at 162–5). This more relaxed approach signals a closer similarity between freehold covenants and easements as rights appurtenant to the dominant land which may be enjoyed by subsequent owners without additional formality. The Law Commission's proposals for reform, which we will consider at 10.56–10.59, also advocate closer assimilation.

### Passing the Benefit at Law and in Equity

**10.27**  We noted that law and equity take a distinctly different view when determining who is subject to the burden of a covenant and thus can be sued for breach of a freehold covenant (see 10.6). By contrast, the different approaches of law and equity to who can take the benefit of a covenant, and can thus sue for breach of a freehold covenant, are less marked. For instance, the law recognizes both assignment of the benefit of a covenant and the annexation of the benefit of a freehold covenant to the land itself. By contrast, a building scheme is recognized only in equity. However, the passing of the benefit of a covenant at law is of limited utility because a subsequent owner of the dominant land, who can claim the benefit of the covenant at law, will only be able to sue the original covenantor bearing in mind that the burden of a freehold covenant cannot pass at law—save under the principle of mutual benefit and burden (see 10.17–10.19). The reason flows from the simple fact that you cannot mix and match the legal and equitable routes of passing the benefit and burden of a freehold covenant relating to land. A freehold covenant is either enforced at law or in equity—see Figure 10.3.

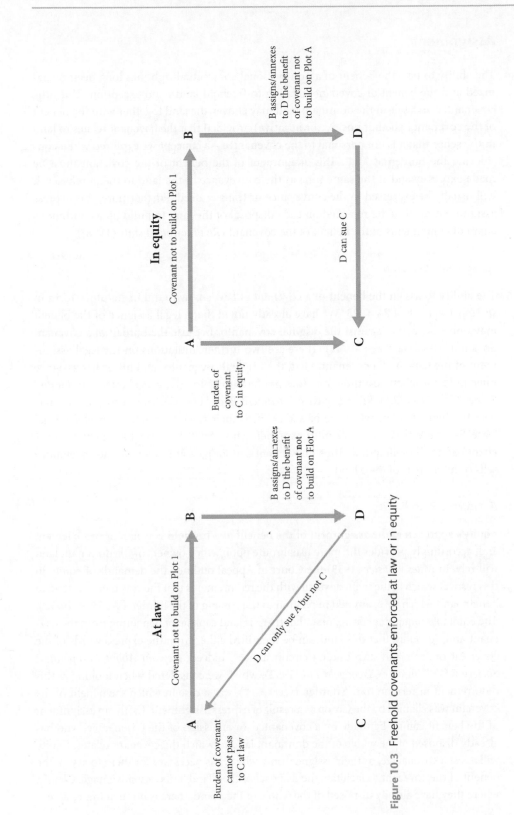

**Figure 10.3** Freehold covenants enforced at law or in equity

## Assignment

10.28    The ability to pass the benefit of a non-personal contractual right has long been recognized and the benefit of covenants relating to freehold land is no exception. Thus, the covenantee on a sale of the dominant land may convey the land together with the benefit of the covenant (whether positive or negative) provided that the covenant relates to land in the sense that it is not personal to the covenantee—a concept we explored when considering the burden at 10.8. This assignment of the benefit of the covenant must be made expressly and at the same time as the conveyance of the land to the purchaser. It will usually be expressed in the conveyance or transfer deed. Furthermore, this express assignment needs to be repeated on each disposal of the land to build up a continuous chain of assignments of the benefit of the covenant (*Re Pinewood Estate* (1958)).

### Assignment at Law

10.29    The ability to assign the benefit of a covenant at law is now found in statutory form in section 136 of the LPA 1925. We have already noted that a legal assignee of the benefit may only take action against the original covenantor because the burden of a covenant does not pass at law (see 10.27). There are two further limitations on the legal assignment of the benefit of a covenant. First, the original covenantee and his or her assignee must hold a legal estate although it does not to be the same legal estate (*Smith and Snipes Hall Farm Ltd v River Douglas Catchment Board* (1949)). Thus a covenantee may pass the benefit at law where he or she conveys their freehold estate or creates a legal lease. Secondly, the covenantee must pass their whole estate because the benefit of a covenant cannot be split at law. Thus, the benefit cannot pass at law where the covenantee sells or leases part of their land.

### Assignment in Equity

10.30    Equity's approach to the assignment of the benefit of a freehold covenant is more lenient and, accordingly, provides the more usual route upon which owners of the dominant land will rely. In *Miles v Easter* (1933) the Court of Appeal outlined the demands of equity in this respect which in the main dovetail with the requirements that the covenant is intend to benefit land which we examined in relation to the passing of the burden (see 10.8–10.13). The equitable requirements are, first, that there is land capable of benefiting from the covenant and, secondly, that this land can be identified either from the express words of the covenant or from the surrounding circumstances. Indeed, *Newton Abbot Co-operative Society v Williamson & Treadgold Ltd* (1952), which we considered when looking at this requirement in relation to the burden (see 10.11), was a case in which the benefit of the covenant was claimed by the Co-op as a result of express assignment. Lastly, an assignment of the benefit cannot be made by a covenantee, or an assign of the covenantee, who has already disposed of the whole of the dominant land to which the covenant relates. Equity will assist a covenantee, or their assignee, only where it is necessary for them to assign the benefit of the covenant to facilitate the disposal of their land to its best advantage. Clearly, where they have already disposed of the whole of their land, there is no such imperative.

## Annexation

**10.31**   Annexation is a once-and-for-all process by which the benefit of the covenant becomes part of the land and will thus pass automatically upon each disposal of the land. Accordingly, annexation offers a distinct advantage over assignment of the benefit on each disposal of the land. Annexation is recognized both at law and in equity. The process might be likened to 'gluing' the benefit of the covenant to the land so that it is bonded to the land. There are two central concerns to effect this process. First, there must be an intention that the benefit of the covenant is to become part of the land and, secondly, it is necessary to determine the physical area of the land to which the covenant becomes part; that is, is annexed or glued. Annexation is thus the flip side of the requirements of accommodation that we discussed in relation to the passing of the burden of covenant at **10.8–10.13**. The clarity of the evidence required to prove these two elements reflects the tension between the 'conveyancers' view' and the 'judicial view'. Conveyancers like the certainty of knowing for sure that the covenant has been annexed by express words of annexation and express identification of the land contained in the covenant itself. A dispute is then unlikely to arise. Remember that there may be large sums of money at stake where a covenant might impede the redevelopment of land because it restricts the type and number of buildings that can be erected on the land. If a dispute does result, judges may be prepared to accept lower standards of evidence provided that they can divine the intention of the parties with sufficient clarity.

### Express Annexation

**10.32**   The starting point is to look at the covenant to see if it contains adequate words of express annexation. We are looking for words that demonstrate an intention that the covenant is taken for the benefit of the owners for the time being of identifiable land rather than merely the original covenantee. We can see this intention in the wording of the covenant in *Rogers v Hosegood* (1900)—note that the land was conveyed by the freehold owner and his mortgagees to the purchaser, who entered into the covenant as covenantor:

> *With the intent that the covenant might as far as possible bind the premises … conveyed and every part thereof, into whosoever hands the same might come, and might enure to the benefit of the mortgagee, their heirs and assigns and others claiming under them to all or any of their lands adjoining or near the premises.*

Thus, it is clear that the covenant is to be glued to the covenantee's land which could be established by evidence of what land they owned nearby at the time. By contrast, the covenant in the case of *Renals v Cowlishaw* (1878) failed the test. It provided merely that the covenant was taken for the benefit of: '*the vendors, their heirs, executors, administrators and assigns*'. No land is mentioned nor is it evident that the covenant is to benefit the covenantee as an owner of the dominant land or his or her successors in title to the land as opposed to any other of their assets. There is only limited support for the possibility that the land intended to be benefited may be gleaned from circumstances surrounding the making of the conveyance (see *Marten v Flight Refuelling Ltd* (1962) at 133).

10.33   The technicalities of the 'conveyancers' view' are illustrated by the following two cases which both involved large estates, as the intended dominant land. It was clear in both cases that the whole of each estate could not claim to benefit from the covenant. The issue thus was whether the benefit was annexed to that part of the land that could benefit.

> **Re Ballard's Conveyance (1937):** Land forming part of the Childwickbury estate was sold and the purchaser entered into covenants with '[the seller,] her heirs and assigns and successors in title owners for the time being of the Childwickbury Estate' which restricted what could built on the land sold. A subsequent purchaser of the land sold asked for a declaration that the covenants were no longer enforceable. The judge held that the wording of the covenants had purported to annex the benefit of the covenant to the whole of the rest of the Childwickbury estate, which amounted to 1,700 acres, but that it was impossible to establish that the whole of this area was intended to benefit from the covenant. Parts of the Childwickbury estate which were closest to the land sold may have benefited from the building controls imposed but it was not possible to sever (ie break up) the covenant and annex it only to these parts.

> **Marquess of Zetland v Driver (1939):** A conveyance of premises in Redcar made by the Marquess's estate contained a covenant by the purchaser not to commit any nuisance to the vendor or occupiers of adjoining property in the neighbourhood. The covenant was expressed to be made for the benefit of such parts of the Marquess's estate as should remain unsold or be sold with the benefit of the covenant. This estate included land close to the premises and other land about a mile away. The premises came to be used as a fish and chip shop and an injunction was sought by the then Marquess to restrain this use. The court awarded the injunction and in so doing distinguished *Re Ballard's Conveyance* because the words of annexation attached the covenant to every part of the Marquess's unsold estate. The estate owned land close to the fish and chip shop and thus there was clearly land that could benefit from the covenant even if the whole of the estate did not.

The fine distinction drawn between these two cases has been doubted by Brightman LJ, taking the 'judicial view' in the case of *Federated Homes Ltd v Mill Lodge Properties Ltd* (1980). He was of the opinion that where it was evident that a covenant was annexed to a particular area of land, it was inherent that it was annexed to each and every part of that land. His views have subsequently been followed in the first instance decision of *Small v Oliver & Saunders* (2006) at [29].

### Statutory Annexation

10.34   The technicalities of express annexation have been sidestepped by judicial recognition that section 78(1) of the LPA 1925 enables automatic annexation of the benefit of freehold covenants relating to land entered into after 1925. This section provides that:

> *A covenant relating to any land of the covenantee shall be deemed to be made with the covenantee and his successors in title and the person deriving title under him or them, and shall have effect as if such successors and other persons were expressed.*

> *For the purposes of this subsection in connection with covenants restrictive of the user of the land 'successors in title' shall be deemed to include the owners and occupiers for the time being of the land of the covenantee intended to be benefited.*

Express annexation remains necessary for covenants entered into before 1925 (see the LPA 1925, s 78(2), the Conveyancing and Law of Property Act 1881, s 58, and *J Sainsbury plc v Enfield LBC* (1989) and *Seymour Road (Southampton) Ltd v Williams* (2010)).

10.35  It was in the case of *Federated Homes Ltd v Mill Lodge Properties Ltd* (1980) that the courts recognized the annexing effect of section 78. The case centred upon a covenant given by Mill Lodge (as covenantor) when they acquired development land from a seller (and covenantee) who retained adjacent land. The covenant provided that Mill Lodge would not develop the land they acquired in excess of a stated density. Subsequently, the seller (and covenantee) sold off two further plots of his adjacent land (the red land and the green land) both of which came into the ownership of Federated Homes. When Mill Lodge threatened to breach the covenant, Federated Homes sought an injunction. There were no express words of annexation in the Mill Lodge covenant but Federated Homes could prove express assignment of the benefit when they acquired the green land but not when they acquired the red land. Nevertheless, the court held that the benefit of the Mill Lodge covenant was also annexed to the red land by section 78. They rejected the submission that section 78 solely provided a convenient drafting device as a word-saving provision. Instead, they decided that the benefit would pass under section 78 either when the dominant land is identified by express words in the conveyance or if the covenant in fact benefits the land of the covenantee in the sense that it touches and concerns the dominant land of the covenantee (see **10.8** and **7.105**).

10.36  The decision in *Federated Homes* sparked considerable controversy by those advocates of the 'conveyancers' view.' The controversy has centred on two main arguments. First, it was argued that this interpretation of section 78 did not accord with the court's interpretation of its sister provision, relating to the passing of the burden of land covenants, found in section 79 (see **10.9**). The wording of the two sections is different and thus it is relatively easy to dismiss this first objection. Secondly, it has been argued that whilst section 79 is subject to a contrary intention, section 78 is not so expressly limited and thus the annexing effect of the section would be mandatory even though it was clear that the original parties to the covenant intended the covenant to impose only personal obligations. The mandatory nature of section 78 was rejected both in *Roake v Chadha* (1984) and in *Crest Nicholson Residential (South) Ltd v McAllister* (2004) when the covenant was expressed to be personal to the parties. In *Crest Nicholson* the court, taking the less stringent 'judicial view' referred both to policy reasons for admitting a contrary intention and to its own interpretation of the section. It focused upon the interpretation of the expression 'successors in title' to encompass only 'those successors to the land of the covenantee intended to be benefited' which permits certain successors in title to be excluded, for instance where the covenant is expressed to be personal.

10.37  Statutory annexation addresses the first evidential concern—namely, an intention that the benefit is to be annexed (or glued) to the land for the benefit of the covenantee's successors in title. But there is still the need to satisfy the second evidential requirement, namely adequate identification of the dominant land as the area of land to which the benefit is annexed. In *Crest Nicholson Residential (South) Ltd v McAllister* (2004) the Court of Appeal decided that the dominant land should be identifiable from the express words of the covenant, although it is permissible to consider extrinsic evidence to explain the meaning of those words. For instance, the covenant might refer to the covenantee's retained land and extrinsic evidence could be brought to explain what neighbouring land the covenantee actually owned at the time the covenant was made. This view reflects the more restrictive approach identified in *Federated Homes* and provides for greater certainty. Even so, it can still be difficult, after many years and many sales of parts of the dominant land, to identify the present owners entitled to the benefit of a covenant (see Howell (2004)).

10.38 From time to time there have been suggestions that, like an easement, the benefit of a freehold covenant is a right appurtenant to land which should pass, unless a contrary intention is expressed, under section 62 or 63 of the LPA 1925 (see eg Wade (1972)). The courts have been unimpressed by such arguments and have either declined to consider them (see *Federated Homes Ltd v Mill Lodge Properties Ltd* (1980), *Shropshire CC v Edwards* (1982)) or rejected them (see *Roake v Chadha* (1984), *Sugarman v Porter* (2006)).

## Building Scheme

10.39 The Chancery courts recognized that the enforcement of common covenants within a particular residential or other development merited special consideration. Equity thus developed the idea of a building scheme to enable the reciprocal enforcement of common covenants by and against all owners of the development to create, in effect, a local private law governing the user of the land within the development. A building scheme thus permits both the burden and benefit of a covenant to pass to all owners for the time being within the scheme but it is in the context of who can sue (ie the benefit) that the rules governing building schemes are most frequently employed. Building schemes have their own technicalities but they do have a distinct advantage in overcoming a timing problem that can occur with the other ways of passing the benefit of freehold covenants within a building development.

### The Timing Problem

10.40 If we have a small development of ten plots, on the sale of Plot 1 the purchaser (as covenantor) will agree to observe certain restrictive covenants with the developer (as covenantee) and the owner of Plots 2–10. The benefit of these covenants can be annexed to Plots 2–10 either by express words or statutory implication. When Plot 2 is sold, the purchaser (as covenantor) will agree to observe the same restrictive covenants with the developer (as covenantee) and the owner of Plots 3–10. The benefit of the Plot 2 covenants cannot be annexed to enable the owner of Plot 1 to sue because Plot 1, having been sold before Plot 2, does not form part of the developer's dominant land. Indeed, the problem is magnified as each plot is sold, and the same covenants imposed. For instance, by the time Plot 9 is sold the benefit cannot be annexed to Plots 1–8 and only Plot 10 remains as the developer's dominant land to which the covenant can be annexed. Once Plot 10 is sold, the developer retains no dominant land that is capable of benefiting from the covenant and thus neither the benefit nor the burden can pass in equity. Within a building scheme, this timing problem is overcome. All the current owners of land within the scheme may sue (by claiming the benefit) and be sued (by being subject to the burden) upon the common covenants that they have all individually given regardless of when the covenants were imposed or when they acquired ownership.

### The Requirements of a Building Scheme

10.41  The classic statement of the requirements for a building scheme is found in Parker J's statement in *Elliston v Reacher* ((1908) at 384). These requirements are that:

  (i)   the parties derive their ownership from a common seller;

  (ii)  prior to sale the seller laid out the estate, or at least part of the estate, in plots subject to covenants which were intended to be imposed on all the plots;

  (iii) these covenants were intended by the common seller to be, and were, for the benefit of all the plots to be sold; and

  (iv)  the purchasers of the plots purchased them from the common seller on the understanding that the common restrictions would be for the benefit of the other plots within the estate.

These requirements may be satisfied by many housing estates but in other cases they have proved too prescriptive. Accordingly the courts, taking the 'judicial view' in more recent times, have taken a less prescriptive approach (see eg *Baxter v Four Oaks Properties Ltd* (1965), *Re Dolphin's Conveyance* (1970), *Birdlip v Hunter* (2015)). They have taken their guidance from the two essential elements of a building scheme set out in the case of *Reid v Bickerstaff* (1909) (see also the earlier authorities of *Renals v Cowlishaw* (1876) and *Spicer v Martin* (1888)). First, there must be a defined area of land that is subject to the scheme so that each purchaser knows the extent of their obligations. Secondly, there must be an intention that all owners of plots within that area are subject to, and take the benefit of, the covenants that are imposed upon each plot. These requirements flow from the reciprocity of obligations that are the foundation of a building scheme.

10.42  In satisfying the first element, it is not essential that the area of the building scheme is defined in the conveyances themselves, provided that it can be established with reasonable certainty from other sources (*Re Dolphin's Conveyance* (1970) at 659, *Stocks v Whitgift Homes Ltd* (2001)). The second element of intention requires more than the imposition of similar covenants on each plot. Indeed, it is acceptable that the exact content of the covenants differ depending on the different types of property within the estate (*Elliston v Reacher* (1908) at 387). What is required is an understanding that the covenants are for the benefit of all purchasers of land within the estate and not just the common seller. That intention is frequently evident from the conveyances of the plots within the estate. For instance, in *Re Dolphin's Conveyance* the seller undertook with each purchaser that he would impose the same covenants on the sale of every plot within the estate. The intention may also be gleaned from the surrounding circumstances although the courts are then likely to look for the more demanding evidence described in *Elliston v Reacher* (*Lund v Taylor* (1975), *Jamaica Mutual Life Assurance Society v Hillsborough Ltd* (1989), *Emile Elias & Co Ltd v Pine Groves Ltd* (1993)).

### 'A Local Law'

10.43   The effect of a building scheme is sometimes referred to as a 'local law' founded upon a community of interests that is enforceable in equity rather than through a maze of contractual obligations. All current owners within the estate are subject to and may enforce the local law. The effect of the local law applies with equal force even where the original plots have been further subdivided into smaller units (*Brunner v Greenslade* (1972)). It also may be found within a leasehold development to enable lessees of individual units (eg flat owners) to enforce the common covenants found in their leases directly against each other, although no direct contractual or property relationship exists between them (*Williams v Kiley t/a CK Supermarkets Ltd* (2003)). This horizontal enforcement between the flat owners themselves is to be contrasted with the vertical enforcement of leasehold covenants between the parties to the lease itself that we consider in Chapter 7 (*Williams v Kiley t/a CK Supermarkets Ltd*).

## Statutory Contractual Solutions

10.44   Both section 56 of the LPA 1925 and section 1 of the Contracts (Rights of Third Parties) Act 1999 can assist the enforcement of freehold covenants by enabling a person, who is not a party to the covenant, to take action for breach of the covenant. For instance, the timing problem referred to at 10.40 can be addressed by relying on these provisions.

10.45   The sections differ in their scope. Section 56 of the LPA 1925 enables a person who is named in a covenant as entitled to the benefit to take action although he or she is not a party to the covenant. For instance, if a covenant is expressed to be given by A (as purchaser/covenantor) to B (as seller/covenantee) and also with C (as an adjoining landowner/covenantee), C obtains a direct right to enforce the covenant against A because he or she is a named covenantee. So if we look at the example considered at 10.40, the purchaser of Plot 2 could expressly covenant both with the developer, as the owner of Plots 3–10, and with the owner for the time being of Plot 1.

10.46   Section 1 of the Contracts (Rights of Third Parties) Act 1999 will also provide C with a direct right to enforce the covenant but it is wider in its scope. It will operate also where A covenants with B *for the benefit* of C, as opposed to with C as a named covenantee, and also where C can either be identified by name or by reference to a defined class but is not actually in existence at the time the covenant is made; for example, 'the future owners of the dominant land'. Thus, again, given our example at 10.40, the purchaser of Plot 2 could expressly covenant with the developer, as owner of Plots 3–10, and for the benefit of the owner for the time being of Plot 1.

## Covenant Remedies

**10.47**  Damages and an injunction are the usual remedies available to a dominant owner for breach of a restrictive covenant by the servient owner. Damages are available at law where the action is against the original servient owner, as the original covenantor. Equitable damages may be awarded under Lord Cairns' Act 1858 where it is a subsequent servient owner who has breached the covenant since the burden of the covenant only runs in equity. A prohibitory injunction is available where the dominant owner is seeking an injunction to restrain a threatened or continuing breach of covenant: for instance, where the servient owner is about to build on the servient land in breach of a restrictive covenant. A mandatory injunction is necessary if a dominant owner is seeking the court's assistance in ordering the servient owner to remedy a breach that has already occurred: for instance, where the servient owner has already built in breach of covenant and an injunction is required to force him or her to demolish the building.

**10.48**  The grant of an injunction has been considered a natural remedy for breach of a restrictive covenant raising an expectation that injunctive relief will be available (*Doherty v Allmand* (1878)). Merely granting damages would allow the wrong to continue and inevitably reduces the effectiveness of restrictive covenants as a control over land use. However, there is growing judicial hesitation in supporting a general expectation of injunctive relief particularly where the dominant owner may not have suffered any real monetary damage and it would cause undue hardship to the servient owner. The courts have always been more cautious in awarding a mandatory injunction, given the costs imposed upon the servient owner and the difficulty of the court monitoring compliance with the action it demands of the servient owner (see eg *Shephard Homes Ltd v Sandham* (1971), *Wrotham Park Estate Co Ltd v Parkside Homes Ltd* (1974), *Wakeham v Wood* (1982)).

**10.49**  The principles upon which injunctive relief might be refused were articulated in the case of *Shelfer v City of London Electric Light Co Ltd* (1895) in which AL Smith LJ (at 322–3) set out the following four guidelines when damages would be awarded in place of an injunction—where, on the one hand, the damage suffered by the dominant owner was small, could be calculated in monetary terms, and would adequately compensate the dominant owner whilst, on the other hand, it would oppressive to the servient owner to grant an injunction rather than damages. These guidelines have provided useful working rules but there were signs that they were being rather mechanically applied and a concern that the court's discretion should not be constrained (see eg *Jaggard v Sawyer* (1995), *Gafford v Graham* (1999)). The Supreme Court revisited the *Shelfer* guidelines in *Coventry t/a RDC Promotions v Lawrence* (2014) which concerned the noise nuisance caused from a motorcycle speedway track rather than a breach of covenant. Nevertheless, their guidance to the grant of injunctive relief is instructive. The Supreme Court emphasized that the *Shelfer* guidelines should not be mechanically applied to constrain judicial discretion and Lord Neuberger offered the following modification:

> *First, the application of the four tests must not be such as 'to be a fetter on the exercise of the court's discretion'. Second, it would, in the absence of additional relevant*

*circumstances pointing the other way, normally be right to refuse an injunction if those four tests were satisfied. Thirdly, the fact that those tests are not all satisfied does not mean that an injunction should be granted (At [123].)*

**10.50** The question is whether *Coventry* will herald a more restrictive approach to the grant of injunctive relief. Gray and Gray have noted the trend towards 'a new social ethic of reasonableness between neighbours' that calls upon neighbours to show some give and take rather than stand on their strict rights in expecting the grant of an injunction (Gray and Gray (2009) at 3.4.78–3.4.79). The Supreme Court in *Coventry* also addressed the public interest inherent in enforcing private rights between neighbours. They referred to the grant of planning permission, which as a matter of public policy might approve an activity which breaches private neighbour obligations, as a possible factor which could influence the grant of an injunction; although they did so in the context of nuisance rather than a breach of restrictive covenant. It seems inappropriate, however, to take into consideration the quite different public policy considerations inherent in the grant of planning permission in the enforcement of privately agreed restrictive covenants. For instance, we will see that the interface between public and private controls in the statutory modification of restrictive covenants has been downplayed (see **10.55**).

**10.51** To ensure effective relief and avoid a defence plea of waiver or estoppel, a dominant owner needs to act quickly if he or she wishes to seek an injunction and an interlocutory injunction can be sought pending a full hearing (see eg *Gafford v Graham* (1999)). However, if an interlocutory injunction is granted, the dominant owner will be required to give an undertaking to indemnify the servient owner if the case is not ultimately decided in their favour even though, as we have seen, there may be complex points of law involved. Yet if an interlocutory injunction is not sought or granted, the dominant owner runs the risk that by the time the case comes to be finally heard, the court will be less inclined to grant an injunction because to do so will cause hardship to the servient owner by disrupting what has become, in the intervening period, the status quo (see eg *Shaw v Applegate* (1977) and *Gafford v Graham* (1999) where the case was first heard in 1996 some seven years after the breach and the appeal heard some two years later).

**10.52** Where an injunction is refused, damages will be awarded to compensate for the monetary loss suffered by the dominant owner as a result of the servient owner's breach. Damages at law generally reflect the loss in terms of value suffered by the dominant owner flowing from the servient owner's breach of covenant. Equitable damages under Lord Cairns' Act 1858 also may be awarded even though there is little (if any) monetary loss to the dominant owner's land. Damages in these circumstances reflect the market cost to obtain a release from the covenant, sometimes referred to as the 'lost opportunity to bargain' (*Wrotham Park Estate Co Ltd v Parkside Homes Ltd* (1974), *Jaggard v Sawyer* (1995), *Gafford v Graham* (1999)). Thus damages are compensatory rather than restitutionary. Even damages representing a lost opportunity to bargain were classified as compensatory in *WWF Worldwide Fund for Nature v World Wrestling Federation* (2008). A servient owner who has increased the value of their land as a result of the breach, perhaps by building a larger or more houses than the covenant stipulates, generally will not be required to disgorge that profit—such damages may be available in principle in exceptional cases. It is only the loss to the dominant owner of the opportunity to bargain for the release from the covenant that is recoverable. The Supreme Court in *Coventry* unfortunately declined to provide any further insight into how damages should be assessed.

## Modification of Covenants

10.53 Covenants as interests in freehold land with proprietary effect are enduring. There are covenants that were created in the 19th century which are still enforceable today. Yet the character of neighbourhoods changes and so the covenants affecting a piece of land or an estate may have outlived their use and exert an impediment on future redevelopment. A court may be persuaded that a covenant is obsolete and should no longer be enforced but these instances are rare (see eg *Sobey v Sainsbury* (1913), *Chatsworth Estates Co v Fewell* (1931)). A more significant jurisdiction is that found in section 84 of the LPA 1925 which enables the Lands Chamber of the Upper Tribunal to discharge or modify a restrictive covenant in certain circumstances.

10.54 These circumstances are where it can be established that the covenant is obsolete as a result of changes to the servient land, the neighbourhood, or other circumstances (s 84(1)(a)), the covenant impedes some reasonable user of the land (s 84(1)(aa)), or where those persons entitled to the benefit of the covenant agree (s 84(1)(b)) or a proposed discharge or modification would not injure those persons entitled to the benefit of the covenant (s 84(1)(c)).

10.55 The second ground, namely that the covenant impedes the reasonable user, was added in 1970 to provide an additional basis for modification or discharge. The issue of 'reasonable user' is measured against the criteria set out in section 84(1A) and (1B) which looks to either the practical benefits of the substantial value that continue to be afforded to the dominant owner by the covenant or to whether continued enforcement of the covenant is contrary to the public interest, bearing in mind the public planning history and proposals for the neighbourhood. In this inquiry the tribunal must also consider whether compensation would provide adequate redress to the dominant owner against any loss they may suffer if the covenant was discharged or modified. It is thus under this ground that there is some interface between the effect of private obligations and public planning considerations. Nevertheless, the fact that planning permission may have been granted for redevelopment that would breach the covenant is merely a consideration but is not decisive. Indeed, Gray and Gray (1999) have observed that the tribunal in refusing to permit modification or discharge despite the grant of planning permission provides an important degree of protection over and above that afforded by the public planning process.

## Reform

10.56 The law governing land covenants has long been mooted for reform. The main targets for reform are the enforceability of positive obligations, the undue complexity of the rules for the running of the benefit of covenants relating to land, including the difficulties associated with identifying the dominant land to which the benefit of a covenant is attached, and the continuing contractual liability of the original parties to the covenant. We saw in **Chapter 7** that where a number of owners share common facilities, legislation has tried to address some of these issues through the introduction of commonhold tenure. However, commonhold has not proved a panacea and, in any event, where facilities are shared by only a few adjoining owners the commonhold structure is overly complex and costly to administer.

10.57　The most recent proposals for reform are found in the Law Commission Report No 327 (2011). It advocates the introduction of a new legal proprietary interest—the land obligation—which would gradually replace restrictive covenants over both registered and unregistered land. The land obligation would encompass negative and positive obligations, including the payment of money, over servient land for the benefit of dominant land. The burden and benefit of a land obligation would be binding on parties acquiring all or any part of the servient and dominant land without the need to rely on the rules that we have examined in this chapter. This new legal interest would be created by deed and registration in the appropriate register with, in the case of registered land, a plan providing certainty in identifying the servient and dominant land.

10.58　The introduction of a new legal interest to the limited roll call of property rights that can affect third parties would be a radical development and it is important that there are safeguards in place. The current proposals first confine the new form of land obligation to covenants that touch and concern the dominant land to provide upfront and familiar parameters. Secondly, the registration requirements should provide accessible information of land obligations to potential purchasers of either the servient or dominant land. Lastly, the jurisdiction of the Upper Tribunal to discharge or modify a land obligation is intended as a final safeguard against outdated and onerous obligations.

10.59　The Law Commission has also proposed a limited inroad into the principle that a covenant cannot exist in gross but must benefit dominant land. Following the example of other jurisdictions, it has recommended the introduction of conservation covenants (see Law Commission (2014)). These obligations would be for the public benefit to promote the conservation of the natural and built environment rather than the benefit of adjoining land. The Law Commission's proposals are based upon a statutory regime rather than the creation of a new proprietary interest. A landowner would enter into a covenant with a conservation body, for instance a charity, a local authority, or other public entity, which would impose obligations with a conservation objective upon the owner for the time being of the land in question with the identified conservation body responsible for the enforcement of the obligations.

## FURTHER READING

Cowan, D, Fox O'Mahony, L, and Cobb N, 'Third-Party Interests in the Use and Control of Land' in *Great Debates in Property Law* (Basingstoke: Palgrave Macmillan 2012), ch 7.

Gardner, S, 'Two Maxims of Equity' (1995) 54 CLJ 60.

Gravells, N, 'Federated Homes Ltd v Mill Lodge Properties Ltd (1979) Annexation and Intention' in Landmark Cases in Property Law (Oxford: Hart Publishing, 2013), ch 5.

Howell, J, 'The Annexation of the Benefit of Covenants to Land' [2004] Conv 507.

Law Commission Report No 327, Making Land Work: Easements, Covenants and Profits à Prendre (2011).

MacFarlane, B, 'The Numerous Clausus Principle and Covenants Relating to Land' in S Bright (ed), Modern Studies in Property Law: Vol 6 (Oxford: Hart Publishing, 2011), ch 15.

O'Connor, P, 'Careful What You Wish for: Positive Freehold Covenants' [2011] Conv 19.

Wade, HWR, 'Covenants: "A Broad and Reasonable View"' (1967) 31 CLJ 157.

## SELF-TEST QUESTIONS

1    Is there a continuing role for land covenants as a form of private planning control?

2    Are restrictive covenants genuine property interests or a peculiar species of personal contract?

3    Restrictive covenants and easements share some common characteristics. What are their similarities and differences?

4    What is meant by annexation? Do you think automatic annexation is justified?

5    A building scheme is said to be based upon a community of interests. How are those interests identified?

6    When should an injunction be granted to remedy the breach of a restrictive covenant?

7    Should the land obligation, as proposed by the Law Commission, be introduced?

# 11

# The Defences Question

## SUMMARY

In this chapter we consider land law's priority rules, which we conceptualize as the defences question. Priority rules is the name given to a set of rules that determine the circumstances in which a property right held by one party (B) against another party's title (A) can be enforced when A transfers the title to a third party (C) or grants a mortgage over the title to C as security for a loan. In the language of property law, the question raised by this scenario is whether C's property right has priority over B's right—or, in other words, whether C has a defence against B enforcing his or her property right against C. We note the general 'first in time' rule, under which where B and C's property rights conflict, priority is determined by their order of creation. We then consider the circumstances in which C has a defence against B's claim to priority. We focus on the priority rules that apply in registered land. We examine the specific rules provided in the Land Registration Act 2002 for registered dispositions of registered estates for valuable consideration and two defences that operate outside the provisions of the Act; the defence of consent and overreaching. Finally, we consider the relationship between priority rules and provisions of the general law under which B may have a personal or proprietary claim against C.

Key topics explored in this chapter are:

- Introduction to the priority triangle (11.1–11.7)
- Priorities and the Land Registration Act 2002 (11.8–11.33)
- Overriding interests (11.34–11.62)
- The defence of consent (11.66–11.69)
- Overreaching (11.70–11.89)
- Alternative causes of action (11.90–11.94)

## Introduction to the Priority Triangle

11.1   Many disputes that arise in land law cases can be distilled into a fairly simple set of facts, which run as follows.

- One party, who we call A in this chapter, holds a legal title to land (freehold or leasehold).

- A second party, who we call B, acquires a property right in A's land. For example, B may have a beneficial interest under a trust (Chapter 5), a lease (Chapter 7), or an easement (Chapter 9).

- A third party, who we call C, then acquires title to A's land or obtains a security interest in relation to A's land. For example, C purchases A's legal title, or A grants C a lease (or sub-lease) or A grants C a mortgage as security for a loan.

The question that arises from this set of facts is whether B is able to enforce his or her property right against C. In property law, this question is generally referred to as one of 'priorities' and the rules used to determine whether B can enforce his or her right against C are known as 'priority rules'. As Figure 11.1 shows, we can consequently think of the factual scenario that has been described as involving a *priority triangle* between A, B, and C. Each of B and C has property rights and property rights are, in principle, enforceable against everyone. Priority rules determine whose property right—B or C's—takes priority or precedence over the other. It is important to emphasize two points about B's position: first, that B has property rights in A's land, not merely a personal right to use A's land; and, secondly, that B's property rights already exist when C acquires title. Priority rules are needed only where these two factors are present. Personal rights, by their nature, are binding (if at all) only against the person who granted the rights. B would not be able to enforce property rights against C if those rights arose only after C acquired title.

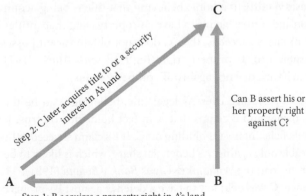

Figure 11.1   The priority triangle

11.2   Two points should be borne in mind about the terminology adopted in this chapter. First, we have conceptualized the priority rules as involving a question of defences. Defence is a more familiar term than priorities, and captures the essence of the question from the point of view of C, whose acquisition of the title triggers the dispute. As B's rights—being property rights—are, in principle, enforceable against C, the question can be seen as one of whether C has a defence against B's rights. Secondly, we have described B as the second party and C as the third party in priority cases. In some explanations of the priority rules, the identity of these parties is transposed, and B is described as the third party, on the basis that he or she is not a party to the transaction between A and C.

11.3   The priority rules through which the defences question is answered differ between unregistered and registered land. In this book, we consider only the priority rules that operate in registered land. Due to the prevalence of registered titles, these rules are by far the most practically important. The priority rules that operate in unregistered land are discussed in McFarlane, Hopkins, and Nield (2015).

11.4   The fact that A grants property rights to B and then C acquires title does not necessarily mean that a dispute between B and C will arise. The categories of estates and interests in land that we have considered in **Chapter 3** are designed to be able to coexist to maximize the use of land. For example, if A grants B an easement and then mortgages the land to C, disputes are unlikely to arise. B's exercise of his or her easement does not interfere with C's security interest and so C is likely to be content for B to continue to exercise his or her easement. C will, however, want to know about the existence of B's interest before granting the mortgage, as it may impact on the value of the security being offered. Similarly, if C is purchasing the land, C may be content for B to continue to exercise an easement, but will want to know that the easement exists before committing to the purchase. Disputes arise where B's property right conflicts with the later right acquired by C or where, even though B and C's property rights could coexist, C objects to B's exercise of their right. Examples include the following.

- C purchases A's title to a home believing that title is being acquired with vacant possession and B then claims to have a property right that entitles B to live in the home. If B's claim succeeds, then C does not obtain vacant possession, but takes the title subject to B's property right (eg *Hodgson v Marks* (1971) where C was held not to have a defence against B's property rights).

- C acquires a mortgage over A's legal title, believing A to be the sole legal and equitable owner and B claims that A in fact holds title on trust for A and B and that B's beneficial interest is binding on C. If B's claim succeeds, then C's mortgage is enforceable only against A's beneficial share, which is likely to be inadequate security for the loan (eg *Williams & Glyn's Bank v Boland* (1981), **11.17** and **11.44–11.45**) where C was held not to have a defence against B's property rights).

- C purchases A's title, but B claims to have an option to purchase the land. If B's claim succeeds, B can exercise the option and require C to sell the land to B under the terms of the option to purchase. C may therefore be required to sell land that he or she does not wish to sell, while the sale price in the option may be below the market value and perhaps below the sum that C has paid (most famously in the unregistered land case *Midland Bank Trust Co v Green* (1981, **11.6–11.7**). But there, C was A's wife and had purchased A's title for £500 with the purpose of defeating an option to purchase held by their son, B. The son had not registered his option on a register of land charges that exists in unregistered land. As a result of the non-registration of the option, it was held that C had a defence against B's option.

* A grants an easement to B and then sells his or her title to C. C wants to stop B from exercising the easement (*Chaudhary v Yavuz* (2013) where C was held to have a defence against B's easement. B was therefore prevented from exercising his easement).

**11.5** It is difficult to overemphasize the importance of priority rules in land law. While the rules are brought into sharp focus when a dispute arises between B and C (as in the examples outlined at **11.4**), it would be wrong to think of their operation as confined to such instances. Where C is purchasing legal title from A, or accepting A's title as security for a loan, C will use priority rules to investigate A's title *before* going ahead with the purchase. Through an investigation of title, C will seek to discover whether there are any pre-existing property rights affecting A's title and, if so, whether C will have a defence against these if he or she goes ahead with the purchase or accepts the land as security for a loan. In this way, priority rules serve a dual purpose. As well as being used to determine whether C has a *defence* against B's property right, they also inform C of the *content* of A's title. Land law's priority rules are therefore considered and applied each time a transaction takes place in relation to land.

**11.6** Priority disputes have provided the context for some of the most legally and socially important land law cases. If the examples at **11.4** are borne in mind, it will be apparent that tens or hundreds of thousands of pounds of value can depend on whether C has a defence against a property right claimed by B. The answer to that question may determine whether C can take possession of land that he or she has purchased, whether C will be able to recover the full value of a mortgage loan for which A has used his or her title to land as security, or whether C will be required to sell land to B at an undervalue. The financial implications are starkly illustrated by *Midland Bank Trust Co v Green* (1981). There, B's option would enable him to purchase the land for around £22,000. At the time of the sale of the land to C, the land was valued at £40,000. By the time of the judgment, the value had risen to £450,000. If C had not had a defence against B's property right arising from his failure to register the option, then she would have been compelled to sell the land to B for £22,000.

**11.7** Beyond the financial consequences of a decision, other matters arise in priorities cases. *Green* (1981) is an unusual case because the land had been transferred from A to C with the intention of defeating B's option to purchase. A and C knew that C would have a defence against B's option and relied on the existence of a defence to defeat B's property right following a breakdown of relations within the family. The priority rules in issue in the case were those of unregistered land. The case, however, illustrates a much broader point that modern statutory priority rules leave no scope for moral judgment. In the Land Registration Act 2002 (LRA 2002) there is no requirement for C to act in good faith in order to rely on the priority rules contained in the Act. For some commentators, the absence of an ethical dimension in priority rules is a potential source of injustice (Wade (1956)). But moral judgments are complex and even in the context of *Green* it is far from clear that the House of Lords considered the application of statutory priority rules to produce an outcome that was unethical or immoral. As Lord Wilberforce explained, A and C may have been motivated not only by a desire to prevent their son (B) from obtaining the land, but also by a desire to enable the land to be distributed to all of their children, rather than being acquired by one son, to the exclusion of his siblings. The provision of certainty in land law, such as that provided by priority rules, as in any branch of law or administration, carries an inevitable trade-off with justice in individual 'hard' cases. Certainty and justice are not diametrically opposed, but how the balance between the two is drawn is a matter on which views will differ. Priority rules take an economic perspective of the business of property dealings, which ultimately favours security and stability in property transactions.

## Priorities and the Land Registration Act 2002

**11.8** The starting point in understanding the approach of registered land to priorities is section 28 of the LRA 2002. That section provides that except as provided by sections 29 and 30 of the Act, 'the priority of an interest affecting a registered estate or charge is not affected by a disposition of the estate or charge'. Section 28 means that except as provided by sections 29 and 30, the LRA 2002 does not alter how questions of priority are determined under the general law. Under the general law, the basic priority rule is one of 'first in time'. In other words, priorities are determined by the order of creation, and so the first interest created prevails over any later property rights. This basic rule is illustrated in the following example:

- A has a freehold or leasehold title to land;
- B then acquires an easement in relation to A's land;
- A then transfers his or her title to C.

On these facts, the starting point is that B's easement will take priority over C's property right simply because B's right was first in time.

**11.9** The exception contained in section 29 is highly significant. As a result of section 29, the basic first in time rule does not apply to a specific category of transactions, which are provided with their own priority rules. This category of transactions is an important one, including within its scope the most common transactions undertaken in relation to land. In short, the effect of section 29 is to provide a distinct scheme of priorities that applies on the ordinary sale or mortgage of registered land. The language used in the statute is, necessarily, more complex.

- Section 29 of the LRA 2002 applies to 'registrable dispositions' of registered estates (s 29) made for 'valuable consideration'.

- Registered estates are legal freehold estates and legal leases created for a term of more than seven years. These are the estates that, as we have seen in Chapter 4, are registered with a unique title number.

- A 'registrable disposition' of a registered estate includes the transfer of a registered estate, the creation out of a registered estate of a new lease of more than seven years' duration, and the creation of a legal mortgage. The creation of a lease of seven years or less is *not* a registrable disposition, but it is placed in the same position as a registrable disposition for the purposes of the application of priority rules (LRA 2002, s 29(4)).

- The requirement of 'valuable consideration' excludes from this scheme of priorities transfers by gift, for nominal consideration (LRA 2002, s 132(1)), or through adverse possession.

Hence, in the language of the LRA 2002, a transfer of an existing registered freehold or leasehold, or the creation of a legal mortgage over a registered estate—as takes place in the ordinary sale or mortgage of land—is a registrable disposition of a registered estate for valuable consideration. As such, these transactions are subject to the priority rules contained in section 29. Section 30 provides the same scheme of priorities for registered dispositions of registered charges (mortgages), but for simplicity references in this chapter are confined to section 29.

11.10  Section 29 provides as follows: on a disposition of a registered estate for valuable consideration, C has a defence against the enforcement of pre-existing property rights held by B except in two situations.

- First, where B's right is protected by entry on the register. The means by which B protects his or her right by entry on the register is the entry of a 'notice' (LRA 2002, ss 32–39, see 11.27–11.33).

- Secondly, where B's interest is an overriding interest within Schedule 3 to the LRA 2002. The category of overriding interests provides 'a very significant impediment' to the accuracy of the register (Law Commission (2001)). By definition, these are interests that do not appear on the register, but against which C is not afforded any defence. They are considered at 11.34–11.62.

11.11  In order to apply section 29, one further requirement must be met. As the registered proprietor, A is conferred with 'owner's powers' (LRA 2002, s 23). These include the 'power to make a disposition of any kind permitted by the general law in relation to an interest of that description'. Hence, for example, A's owner's powers include the power to sell the title, to create a lease or sub-lease, and to use the title as security by granting a mortgage. C is entitled to assume that A's owner's powers are free from any limitations, except those reflected by an entry on the register (LRA 2002, s 26). In order to rely on section 29, however, C must have complied with any limitations on A's owner's powers that are reflected by an entry on the register. That is because, in the absence of compliance, C will not be able to complete the disposition by registration (11.26). The means of registering a limitation is through entry of a restriction (LRA 2002, ss 40–47, discussed at 11.23–11.26). As we will see, entry of a restriction is of particular relevance to priorities where B holds a beneficial interest under a trust.

11.12   The defences afforded to C under section 29 apply 'at the time of registration' against pre-existing rights held by B 'immediately before the disposition' (completion of the sale or mortgage). That is the time at which C will accept A's title. C is not afforded protection against property rights arising in favour of B in the gap between disposition and registration. We have explored this 'registration gap' in Chapter 4. C's vulnerability in this period will be cured only by the introduction of e-conveyancing; a development which we have seen in Chapter 4 is currently on hold.

11.13   Where C has a statutory defence against B's property right, what happens to that right? This is a matter on which the language of section 29 is open to interpretation. The generally accepted view, endorsed by Norris J in *Halifax plc v Curry Popeck (a firm)* (2008) is that section 29 operates to 'destroy the subsistence of those interests as interests in land, leaving them capable of enforcement as personal rights'. As such, B is confined to personal remedies that may be available against A. However, on its terms section 29 merely 'postpones' B's property right in favour of C. As such, it may be argued that B's right remains as an interest in land and is able to take priority against any rights that are not derived under the disposition to C (Dixon (2009)).

11.14   The cumulative effect of the provisions of the LRA 2002 governing owner's powers and the effect of a registered disposition can be summarized as follows. C has a defence against B's pre-existing legal rights where C has provided valuable consideration and:

- the disposition complies with any limitations on A's owner's powers entered on the register as a restriction; and
- B's interest is not protected on the register by entry of a notice; and
- B's interest is not within the category of overriding interests.

In addition to these provisions in section 29, C will have a defence against B's pre-existing property right in two further circumstances:

- where B has expressly or impliedly consented to C having priority;
- where the disposition operates to overreach B's property right.

A roadmap of priorities in registered land is provided in Figure 11.2.

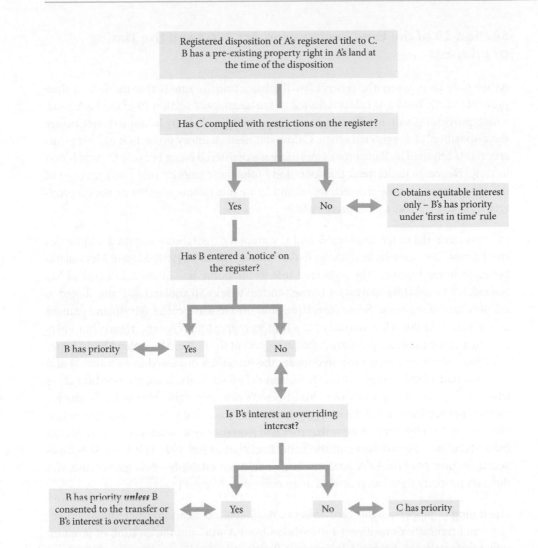

**Figure 11.2** Roadmap of priorities for registered dispositions under the LRA 2002

11.15   Hence, to understand the scheme of priorities that operates in registered land, this chapter addresses the following five topics:

- restrictions on owners powers (**11.23–11.26**);
- entry of a notice (**11.27–11.33**);
- the categories of overriding interests (**11.34–11.62**);
- consent to priority (**11.66–11.69**)
- overreaching (**11.70–11.89**).

Before embarking on that analysis, a specific point of interpretation that arises under section 29 in relation to the timing of interests must be discussed.

## Section 29 of the Land Registration Act 2002 and the Timing of Interests

11.16   As we have seen, under the general law the basic priority rule is that the first in time prevails (11.8). This basic rule is reflected in the language of section 29 of the LRA 2002, which provides C with a defence against property rights held by B 'immediately before the disposition' of a registered estate. C does not need statutory protection against property rights acquired by B *after* the disposition of a registered estate because C's title is first in time. Hence, to understand the operation of the basic priority rule and the scope of the exception to the rule provided by section 29 we must know whether or not B's property right arose before C's property right.

11.17   In most cases the order in which B and C's property rights were acquired will be beyond doubt. For example, in *Williams & Glyn's Bank v Boland* (1981) Mr and Mrs Boland bought a home together. The registered title to the home was in the sole name of Mr Boland, but he held title on trust for himself and his wife as Mrs Boland had contributed to the purchase of the home. Some years later, unknown to Mrs Boland, Mr Boland granted a mortgage over the title as security for a loan to support his business. Hence, both Mrs Boland and the bank had property rights in respect of the home. Mrs Boland had a beneficial interest under a trust (acquired under the principles discussed in Chapter 5) and the bank had a legal charge. When Mr Boland defaulted on the loan, the question arose whether the bank had priority over Mrs Boland's property right. Mrs Boland's interest clearly predated the grant of the mortgage and so the basic first in time rule favoured her. The onus was on the bank to show that they had a defence against her property right. On the facts, under the provisions of the Land Registration Act 1925 (LRA 1925) equivalent to section 29 of the LRA 2002, the bank could not establish a defence because Mrs Boland's property right was protected as an overriding interest (11.44–11.45).

11.18   The timing of property rights can, however, be difficult to ascertain where there is a sequence of transactions involving a disposition from A to C and the creation of property rights against the title held by A in favour of B. Priority rules do not allow for a 'dead heat' (*Hardy v Fowle* (2007)). The classic case is where A buys property using funds provided by a mortgagee C (an acquisition mortgage) and B has equitable property rights in the property. Such facts may most commonly arise on the purchase of a family home, where B is A's spouse or cohabitee. These facts differ from *Boland* (1981) outlined above (11.17) where the mortgage was granted some years after the home had already been acquired and so Mrs Boland's beneficial interest had arisen several years before the mortgage was granted. In the case of an acquisition mortgage, B's rights are acquired at the time A purchases title, and A is using funds provided by C, the mortgagee, to fund the purchase. On these facts, do B's property rights exist immediately before the disposition (the mortgage) from A to C?

11.19   Conveyancing logic may suggest that B's interest arises before A grants a mortgage to C. The mortgage lender, C, acquires its charge from A and A can only give C a right in relation to the land if A already has the freehold or leasehold estate that is being acquired. On that view, A must acquire a property right before C and logically, therefore, there must be a *scintilla temporis*—a tiny spark of time—during which A holds his or her right free from C's charge. Where B has contributed to the purchase, B's right comes into existence during that *scintilla temporis*, with the result that B's property right is first in time to C. On this analysis, C is therefore bound by B's property right unless C can claim a defence. In other words, a logical analysis holds that there is no difference in principle between cases involving mortgages granted to acquire a title and the *Boland* case, in which the mortgage was granted many years after the title had been obtained.

**11.20**  Despite the logic of the analysis provided by *scintilla temporis*, courts have shown a willingness to 'have regard to the substance, rather than the form, of the transaction or transactions which give rise to the competing interests; and in particular that conveyancing technicalities must give way to considerations of commercial and practical reality' (*Whale v Viasystems* (2002)). In doing so, the courts have drawn a clear distinction between cases involving acquisition mortgages and those (like *Boland*) in which the question of priorities arises in respect of a mortgage granted subsequent to the acquisition of title. The analysis to adopt in respect of acquisition mortgages was explained by the House of Lords in *Abbey National Building Society v Cann*.

---

**Abbey National Building Society v Cann (1991):** Mr Cann was the sole registered proprietor of a home in Island Road that he lived in with his mother, Mrs Cann. Mrs Cann had contributed to the cost of the home and so Mr Cann held the title on trust for himself and his mother under the principles of trust discussed in **Chapter 5**. Mother and son decided to move to a smaller home in South Lodge Avenue. They sold their Island Road home and moved to South Lodge Avenue. All of the proceeds of sale of Island Road were used towards the purchase of the South Lodge Avenue home, with additional purchase money obtained through a mortgage granted to the Abbey National. Mr Cann became sole registered proprietor of the South Lodge Avenue home, which he held on trust for himself and his mother—Mrs Cann's beneficial interest in the Island Road home continuing into the proceeds of sale of that home and then into the title to the South Lodge Avenue home. Mrs Cann knew that additional funds would be needed for the purchase, but she was not a party to the loan which was also in Mr Cann's sole name. Further, unknown to his mother Mr Cann had taken out a mortgage of £25,000 even though only £4,000 was required to fund the purchase. Mr Cann defaulted on the repayments and the question arose whether Mrs Cann's beneficial interest had priority over the acquisition mortgage that had been granted to the bank. Mrs Cann argued that her beneficial interest was first in time to the mortgage, so that she had priority over the mortgage unless the bank could claim a defence. She argued that there was a *scintilla temporis* during which Mr Cann held legal title unencumbered by the mortgage, during which her beneficial interest took effect. This argument was rejected by the House of Lords. Lord Oliver noted the 'attractive legal logic' in the argument in view of the fact that Mr Cann could not grant the mortgage until he acquired legal title. However, Lord Oliver said that the *scintilla temporis* analysis 'flies in the face of reality'. The acquisition of the estate is dependent on the provision of funds, to the extent that the acquisition of the estate and the grant of the mortgage 'are not only precisely simultaneous but indissolubly bound together'. In reality, therefore, Mr Cann acquired the legal title encumbered with the mortgage and that was the interest against which Mrs Cann's beneficial interest took effect. Crucially, on the House of Lords' analysis, the mortgage was first in time to Mrs Cann's beneficial interest. This meant that the mortgage necessarily had priority over Mrs Cann's beneficial interest and the Abbey National did not therefore have to establish a defence. As we will see below, the House of Lords went on to hold that, in any event, even if Mrs Cann's mortgage had been first in time, the Abbey National would have had a defence against her claim to priority (**11.41** and **11.69**).

**11.21** The effect of *Abbey National Building Society v Cann* is that beneficial interests—or any other property rights—obtained by B on the acquisition of title by A cannot have priority over a mortgage granted by A to C to fund the purchase of title. The transfer of legal title to A and the grant of the mortgage by A to C are seen as indivisible transactions, so that C's mortgage ranks first in time to B's property rights. In the language of section 29 of the LRA 2002, B does not have a property right 'immediately before the disposition' (the mortgage from A to C).

**11.22** In *Scott v Southern Pacific Mortgages Ltd* (2014) a different question was raised in the Supreme Court in respect of the timing of interests in a sequence of transactions. The case involved a transaction known as a 'sale and lease back'. Such transactions gave homeowners in financial difficulties the possibility of remaining in their homes as tenants by selling the home to a property investment firm, generally at a discounted price. The firm would promise the homeowner that they could remain in occupation for as long as they wished as a tenant. The firm would usually finance the purchase of the home by the grant of a mortgage, though the mortgage lender may have been unaware of the parties' agreement, which may be contrary to the terms of the mortgage. The transactions created significant risks for homeowners which were not necessarily understood. The market for sale and lease-back transactions was effectively shut down after it was subject to regulation in 2009 by the Financial Services Authority (now Financial Conduct Authority). However, this left the courts to decide who should bear losses arising under existing transactions.

> *Scott v Southern Pacific Mortgages Ltd* (2014): Mrs Scott (B in the priority triangle) was the sole registered proprietor of title to her home. She had fallen into financial difficulties following the breakdown of her marriage and had put her home on the market. She was approached by a person connected to a company, North East Property Buyers (NEPB), with whom she reached agreement for a sale and lease back of her home. Under the agreement, Mrs Scott sold her home to a Ms Wilkinson (A in the priority triangle and a nominee of NEPB). Mrs Scott had £65,000 equity in her home, of which she would receive only £24,000 with the remainder being paid to NEPB. In return, NEPB granted Mrs Scott a lease so that she could remain living in her home and promised to pay her a 'loyalty payment' of £15,000 if she continued to rent the home for ten years. Unknown to Mrs Scott, however, the purchase of her home was being funded from a loan obtained from Southern Pacific Mortgage Ltd (SPML, C in the priority triangle) to whom Ms Wilkinson (A) granted a mortgage. Mrs Scott learnt of the mortgage some three years later when, following default on the loan, SPML obtained a possession order against Ms Wilkinson. The question therefore arose whether Mrs Scott had any property rights against Ms Wilkinson's title that had priority over the mortgage granted to SPML. It was clear, following *Cann* (1991), that if Mrs Scott's property rights arose only from the time that Ms Wilkinson obtained title, then she had no claim to priority over SPML. *Cann* dictates that the acquisition of title by Ms Wilkinson and the grant of the mortgage by

her to SPML are indivisible transactions and that any property right Mrs Scott obtained on the acquisition of title by Ms Wilkinson did not exist 'immediately before the disposition' for the purposes of section 29 of the LRA 2002. Instead, Mrs Scott argued that she had property rights from an earlier time—the date of her contract to sell her home to Ms Wilkinson. From the time of the contract for sale Ms Wilkinson had a property right in Mrs Scott's home under the so-called vendor–purchaser trust (see **Chapter 5**). However, the Supreme Court unanimously held that the nature of this right is not such as to enable Ms Wilkinson to grant property rights to third parties, including Mrs Scott. Hence, the Supreme Court unanimously held that any property right acquired by Mrs Scott dated only from the time that Ms Wilkinson obtained title to the home and as such was within the ratio of *Cann*. However, in an obiter discussion the Supreme Court considered whether, if Mrs Scott's argument as to the timing of her interest had succeeded, she would have had a property right in the land 'immediately before the disposition' so that she could claim priority over SPML's mortgage. A majority of the Supreme Court (3:2) held that Mrs Scott would have succeeded on this point. Baroness Hale, leading the majority, rejected an argument that the contract for sale between Mrs Scott and Ms Wilkinson was 'indivisible' from the subsequent transfer of legal title and grant of the mortgage. Hopkins (2015) suggests that the majority view is preferable. Even though for the parties, contract, completion, and mortgage are practically composite stages of a single transaction, the specific legal effects of the contract lean towards keeping it separate and distinct. The majority's obiter finding on this point would have meant that Mrs Scott had an interest 'immediately before the disposition' (the grant of the mortgage to SPML) and therefore her property rights would have priority over the mortgage unless SPML could establish a defence. However, in view of the unanimous finding of the court that the interest obtained under the vendor–purchaser trust is not such as to enable property rights to be granted to third parties, the discussion of the point is otiose. Indeed, the Supreme Court acknowledged that the point is unlikely ever to have practical import.

## Restrictions on Owner's Powers

**11.23** As we have seen, in order to benefit from the priority rules in sections 29 and 30 of the LRA 2002, the disposition to C must comply with any limitations on A's owner's powers that are recorded on the register (**11.11**). The means by which limitations on owner's powers are recorded on the register is by the entry of a 'restriction'. A restriction may be entered by or with the consent of the registered proprietor, or a person entitled to be entered as registered proprietor (LRA 2002, s 43(1)(a) and (b)), or by any other person who has 'sufficient interest' in entering the restriction (LRA 2002, s 43(1)(c)). Restrictions may also be entered by the Registrar (LRA 2002, s 42) who is also required to enter a restriction in specified circumstances (LRA 2002, s 44 on which see **11.25**).

**11.24** A restriction is defined in section 40 of the LRA 2002 as 'an entry in the register regulating the circumstances in which a disposition of a registered estate or charge may be the subject of an entry in the register'. A restriction may prevent the entry of any disposition or disposition(s) of a particular type or may make the entry of a disposition subject to conditions. The restriction may last indefinitely or for a specified period of time. A restriction could therefore prevent the registered proprietors from transferring title, or granting a mortgage or a lease of more than seven years (although the grant of a shorter lease would not be a 'disposition' (LRA 2002, s 27(2)(b)). Or a restriction could make any of those dispositions subject to the registered proprietor obtaining the consent of a named individual or individuals (LRA 2002, s 40(3)(b)). For example, where the registered proprietors hold land on trust, a restriction may require the trustees to obtain the consent of the beneficiaries to a disposition, reflecting a requirement in a deed of trust.

11.25 In relation to priorities, the most significant use of a restriction is in relation to beneficial interests. On a transfer of land, the overreaching mechanism (11.70-11.89) enables C to take the land free from B's beneficial interest. For overreaching to take place, C must pay any purchase money to a minimum of two trustees or a trust corporation. Where land is held on trust, a restriction may be entered on the register to ensure that overreaching occurs on a disposition. Where there are two or more registered proprietors, title is necessarily held on trust and so the Registrar is required to enter a restriction in a form prescribed by the Land Registration Rules 2003 designed to ensure that overreaching takes place (LRA 2002, s 44(1)). The restriction provides that '[n]o disposition by a sole proprietor of the registered estate (except a trust corporation) under which capital money arises is to be registered unless authorised by an order of the court'.

11.26 The general effect of a restriction is that 'no entry in respect of a disposition to which the restriction applies may be made in the register otherwise than in accordance with the terms of the restriction' (LRA 2002, s 41). On analysis of this provision, it is apparent that the effect of failing to comply with a restriction is potentially devastating. In a registered disposition, legal title vests only on registration (LRA 2002, s 27, Chapter 4). Hence, the effect of prohibiting an entry being made in respect of the disposition is that legal title does not pass. For example, if A, a registered proprietor, purports to sell title to C or grant a legal mortgage to C, but C does not comply with a restriction, then the disposition cannot be registered and C does not obtain legal title or a legal mortgage. Without obtaining legal title, C is unable to overreach any beneficial interests or invoke the distinct priority rules applied to registered dispositions. C is left with an equitable title and, under the general law, will be bound by all pre-existing property rights held by any third parties (B). This is because the general rule governing equitable interests is that priority is determined by the order in which the interests are created. Given these consequences, a purchaser would not proceed with completion without ensuring compliance with restrictions: for example, ensuring purchase money is paid to two trustees.

## Entry of a Notice

11.27 As we have seen under the priority rules contained in sections 29 and 30 of the LRA 2002, C does not have a defence against B's interest if B's interest is protected by the entry of a notice on the register (11.10). Section 32 of the LRA 2002 explains '[a] notice is an entry in the register in respect of the burden of an interest affecting a registered estate or charge'. A notice plays a distinct role from a restriction. As we have seen, entry of a restriction tells C something about A's owner's powers: specifically, it informs C of limitations on those powers (11.23). In contrast, entry of a *notice* tells C about property rights—a burden—claimed by B. It informs C of rights that—if, in fact, they exist—will be enforceable against him or her.

11.28    An application for entry of a notice may be made by the registered proprietor or a person claiming an interest in the land (LRA 2002, s 34). The Registrar has the power to enter a notice in respect of a number of interests that would be enforceable against the transferee as overriding interests on first registration of title (LRA 2002, s 37). This power brings those property rights against which C has no defence onto the register. The Registrar also has a duty to enter a notice on the estate that has the burden of an interest created by various dispositions (LRA 2002, s 38). For example, on the registration of a legal lease, the Registrar enters a notice of the lease on the freehold title out of which the lease has been created and on the registration of a legal easement, the Registrar will enter a notice on the estate with the burden of the easement (LRA 2002, s 38).

11.29    Notices are subdivided into 'agreed' and 'unilateral', though each type of notice serves the same function: each ensures that B's property right binds C on a registrable disposition.

- Agreed notices may be entered where the applicant is the registered proprietor, or consents to the entry, or the registrar is satisfied as to the applicant's claim (LRA 2002, s 34(3).

- Unilateral notices may be entered in any case where the applicant claims to be entitled to the benefit of an interest affecting an estate. Entry of the notice instigates a procedure through which the registered proprietor has an opportunity to apply to have the notice cancelled.

Provision for entry of a unilateral notice serves an important purpose. Because the applicant does not need the consent of the registered proprietor, or to satisfy the Registrar as to his or her claim, the notice can be entered without providing evidence of the right claimed. The ability to do so can be significant where, for example, the applicant for the notice discovers that a transfer of the land is imminent and needs to protect his or her interest to secure priority on the sale. Unilateral notices may also be used to protect interests without sending commercially sensitive information—such as the terms of an option to purchase—to Land Registry. However, the ease of entry of the notice also gives rise to concerns of abuse (Justice Committee (2015)) and in its consultation on the LRA 2002 the Law Commission has provisionally recommended changes to the procedure to strengthen the protection afforded to registered proprietors (Law Commission (2016)). The Law Commission (2016) has also provisionally proposed changes to the names of the two different forms of notice to 'summary notice' (unilateral) and 'full notice' (agreed). This change is intended more accurately to reflect the differences between the two forms of notice in respect of what appears on the register. The current terminology of agreed notice is also considered misleading as an agreed notice need not in fact have the consent of the registered proprietor.

**11.30**  The effect of a notice is explained in section 32(3) of the LRA 2002. That subsection provides '[t]he fact that an interest is the subject of a notice does not necessarily mean that the interest is valid, but does mean that the priority of the interest, if valid, is protected for the purposes of sections 29 and 30'. Hence, entry of a notice does not guarantee the validity of the property right claimed. This is in contrast to the effect of registration of title. Registration of A as proprietor of a legal estate operates to vest A with legal title even if, as a matter of general law, A is not entitled to the title (LRA 2002, s 58). In contrast, entry of a notice by B to the effect (for example) that B has a restrictive covenant over A's land does not vest B with a restrictive covenant; instead, it ensures only that *if B in fact has a restrictive covenant*, that restrictive covenant will be enforceable against C. Cooke (2003) suggests terminology to reflect this difference. She describes the entry of a notice as 'recording' an interest, in contradistinction to 'registration' of title.

**11.31**  The description of a notice as entry of a 'burden' (LRA 2002, s 33, see **11.27**) encapsulates the idea that the entry informs C of a third party's property right, subject to which he or she will take title to the land. This idea has a direct impact on the types of right in respect of which it is appropriate to enter a notice. Entry of a notice is confined to property rights that it is anticipated will bind C. The LRA 2002 does not attempt to provide an exhaustive list of property interests in respect of which entry of a notice is possible; instead, the Act defines interests that cannot be protected by the entry of a notice. Of particular importance, section 33 of the LRA 2002 prohibits the entry of a notice in respect of the following property rights: beneficial interests under a trust of land; leases granted for a term of three years or less; and restrictive covenants made between a lessor and lessee in respect of the leased premises.

**11.32**  The rationale for each of the exclusions in section 33 of the LRA 2002 is different. Entry of a notice in respect of a trust of land is prohibited, because beneficial interests under a trust are not intended to bind C. The overreaching mechanism (**11.70–11.89**) supported by entry of a restriction (**11.25**) should ensure that C takes free from beneficial interests. Preventing entry of a notice in relation to a trust is therefore consistent with the curtain principle under which a curtain is drawn across the register against any trusts (**Chapter 4**). Short leases, excluded from entry as a notice, are enforceable against C as overriding interests (LRA 2002, Sch 3, para 1, see **11.60**). Leasehold covenants are excluded, because their enforcement is subject to a separate statutory scheme contained in the Landlord and Tenant (Covenants) Act 1995 (**Chapter 7**).

**11.33**  With these exclusions in mind, the category of interests in respect of which notice may be entered remains very broad. It is an appropriate means of protection for any property right that is not specifically excluded. This includes, for example, equitable mortgages, restrictive covenants, legal and equitable easements, legal leases of more than three years to a maximum of seven years (a lease granted for more than seven years is a registrable estate (LRA 2002, ss 4 and 27)), estate contracts, rights to occupy conferred by the Family Law Act 1996 (**Chapter 6**), and an inchoate equity arising from a claim to proprietary estoppel (**Chapter 5**).

## Overriding Interests

**11.34** As we have seen under the priority rules contained in sections 29 and 3(
2002, C does not have a defence against B's property right if B's right is pro
overriding interest (11.10). Overriding interests are a category of property ri
not appear on the register, but against which transferees under a registered disposition
have no defence. Overriding interests have been described as the 'crack in the mirror' of
title (Hayton (1981)) and as making the idea of a perfect register a 'myth' (Cooke (2003)).
The Law Commission's (1998) rationale for their continued existence is simple: the category acknowledges that there are circumstances in which it is unreasonable to expect B
to register his or her property right to secure its enforcement. The necessary breadth of
the category in the light of this rationale is more contentious. The LRA 2002 has reduced
the number of overriding interests from the previous legislation. The policy adopted by
the Act (as explained by the Law Commission (2001)) is that 'interests should only have
overriding status where protection against buyers was needed, but where it was neither
reasonable to expect nor sensible to require any entry on the register'.

**11.35** The LRA 2002 provides two distinct lists of overriding interests: interests that override at first
registration (listed in Sch 1); and those that override on a disposition of a registered estate
(listed in Sch 3). First registration is treated separately, because the intention is to reflect
the state of the title at that time. Whether C is bound by any overriding interests will have
been determined prior to registration. Our discussion focuses on interests overriding on a
disposition of a registered estate—that is, those transfers that are subject to the distinct priority rules contained in sections 29 and 30 of the LRA 2002. The terminology of 'overriding
interests' is not in fact used in the LRA 2002; it is the language of the previous legislation, the
LRA 1925. Notwithstanding, overriding interests remains a useful and accepted term of reference for what the LRA 2002 describes as 'interests which override registered dispositions'.

**11.36** The full list of these overriding interests is contained in Schedule 3 to the 2002 Act. Our
discussion is confined to the three most important categories, which are contained in
paragraphs 1–3 of the Schedule: short leases; property rights held by those in actual occupation; and legal easements and profits à prendre. Our discussion of these overriding
interests does not follow the order in which they appear in the legislation. We first of all
consider the broadest category of overriding interests and the category that has given
rise to most of the case law; the property rights of those who are in actual occupation.

### Property Rights Held by Persons in Actual Occupation

**11.37** Property rights held by persons in actual occupation are given the status of overriding
interests in Schedule 3, paragraph 2. The scope of this category of overriding interest is
specified in the following terms:

> *An interest belonging at the time of the disposition to a person in actual occupation, so
> far as relating to land of which he is in actual occupation, except for …*

(b) an interest of a person of whom inquiry was made before the disposition and who failed to disclose the right when he could reasonably have been expected to do so;

(c) an interest—

(i) which belongs to a person whose occupation would not have been obvious on a reasonably careful inspection of the land at the time of the disposition, and

(ii) of which the person to whom the disposition is made does not have actual knowledge at that time ...

11.38 Schedule 3, paragraph 2 is the broadest and most notorious category of overriding interests. It is different in its scope from all other categories. Those categories confer the status of overriding interest on a particular property right. This paragraph, instead, confers the status of overriding interest on *any* property right held by a person in occupation. Its focus is therefore on the factual position of the holder of the right, not the type of property right held (Cooke (2003)).

11.39 It is important to note that occupation is the *trigger* for protection, but not the *subject* of protection. The subject of protection is B's property rights. If B is in occupation, but is not entitled to any property rights (eg where B is a licensee), then B has nothing capable of binding C under Schedule 3, paragraph 2. In most cases, property rights that are the subject of protection under that paragraph will have some connection to B's occupation, but it is not necessary for that to be the case. For example, in *Webb v Pollmount Ltd* (1966) an option to purchase freehold title was protected as an overriding interest because the holder of the option was in actual occupation of the premises under a lease (for discussion of the arguments for and against the decision, see Law Commission (2016)). Protection is confined to the geographical extent of B's occupation. This reverses the decision under the LRA 1925 in *Ferrishurst Ltd v Wallcite Ltd* (1999) in which a property right (an option to purchase) extending over offices and a garage was protected even though B was in occupation of the offices only.

11.40 In principle, any property right is capable of being protected by occupation. A specific question arises in respect of equitable easements. In *Chaudhary v Yavuz* (2013) Mr Chaudhary argued that he was in actual occupation of land over which he had an equitable easement. Lloyd LJ suggested that '[at] first sight it seems counter-intuitive, to say the least, to assert that the owner of dominant land ... is in occupation of other land ... over which he asserts an easement'. On the facts Mr Chaudhary's claim failed as he was unable to establish actual occupation (this aspect of the case is discussed at **11.52** and **11.55**). However, McFarlane (2013) has suggested that while an easement cannot constitute exclusive possession, its exercise could constitute occupation for the purposes of Schedule 3, paragraph 2. For example, where there is an easement to store goods or to park a car, the presence of the goods or car could constitute occupation. Possession and occupation are not synonymous and there is no reason in principle why an equitable easement should not be protected under that paragraph where occupation consistent with the exercise of an easement can be established.

## Timing of Occupation

**11.41**   Schedule 3, paragraph 2 protects as overriding interests only those property rights that are held by B 'at the time of the disposition'. As B's occupation is the trigger for protection it is clear that B must be in occupation at the time of disposition. This requirement in respect of the timing of occupation—which was the same under the LRA 1925—provided a further basis on which Mrs Cann's claim to priority over a mortgage granted to fund the acquisition of title by her son failed in *Abbey National Building Society v Cann* (1991). As we have seen (**11.20**), in that case Mr Cann was registered proprietor of legal title to a home which he held on trust for himself and his mother, Mrs Cann. Mr Cann defaulted on a mortgage that had been granted to raise funds for the purchase and so the question arose whether Mrs Cann's beneficial interest had priority over the Abbey National's mortgage. The House of Lords held that Mrs Cann had no possible claim to priority because the mortgage was first in time. In an obiter discussion, the House of Lords considered whether, if Mrs Cann's interest had been first in time, the Abbey National would have had a defence against its enforcement against them. Mrs Cann argued that her beneficial interest would have been binding on the Abbey National as an overriding interest because she was in actual occupation. The House of Lords held that to have an overriding interest, Mrs Cann would need to have been in actual occupation at the date of the disposition—the grant of the mortgage by Mr Cann to the Abbey National. In the normal course of events, it is only at the time of disposition (commonly referred to as completion) that a purchaser moves into property. Mrs Cann had in fact moved some furniture and belongings into the property a few minutes before the disposition took place, but as we will see below (**11.49**), these acts were considered insufficient to constitute occupation.

**11.42**   *Cann* concerned the interpretation of the provisions of the LRA 1925 governing overriding interests. The effect of the decision was that third parties (B) with property rights against a purchaser's (A's) title would never be able to claim an overriding interest against the holder of a mortgage (C) granted by A to fund the purchase of the title because B would not be able to establish occupation at the relevant time. The House of Lords' obiter decision on the point meant that even if Mrs Cann's beneficial interest had been first in time to the mortgage, the Abbey National would have had a defence against her claim to priority. Under the provisions of the LRA 1925 equivalent to section 29 of the LRA 2002, Mrs Cann's interest would have been postponed to the Abbey National as it was neither registered (a beneficial interest is not capable of being protected by entry of a notice, **11.31–11.32**) nor binding as an overriding interest. The same conclusion would be reached today under Schedule 3, paragraph 2 of the LRA 2002.

**11.43**   It is clear therefore that to establish that a property right is an overriding interest under Schedule 3, paragraph 2, B must be in actual occupation at the time of the disposition. There is, however, a curious juxtaposition between the wording adopted in that paragraph, on the one hand, and section 29 of the LRA 2002, on the other. Schedule 3, paragraph 2 refers to '[a]n interest belonging at the time of the disposition to a person in actual occupation'. Under section 29, however, C has a defence at the time of *registration* against interests belonging to B at the time of *disposition* that are not otherwise protected (**11.12**). In *Thompson v Foy* (2010) the juxtaposition between section 29 and Schedule 3, paragraph 2 led Lewison J to suggest that B must be in occupation at the time of registration as well as the time of disposition. He suggested that if B must only be in occupation at the time of registration, then the opening phrase of that paragraph should read 'An interest belonging to a person in actual occupation at the time of the disposition'. Lewison J's comments are obiter and, he acknowledged, against the prevailing commentary.

## Beneficial Interests as Overriding Interests

**11.44**   Both in legal and social respects the most significant use of this category of overriding interests has been to determine the circumstances in which a beneficial interest held by B against a legal title vested in A has priority over a mortgage granted by A to C. In a landmark decision in *Williams & Glyn's Bank v Boland* (1981, **11.17**) the House of Lords held that a beneficial interest was a property right in land for the purposes of the equivalent provision to Schedule 3, paragraph 2 contained in the LRA 1925, so that Mrs Boland's (B's) beneficial interest was binding against the bank (C) that had been granted a mortgage by Mr Boland (A). Mrs Boland's beneficial interest was an overriding interest because she was in actual occupation of the home at the time of the disposition. In many cases, including *Boland*, the beneficial interest acquired by B has arisen informally under the doctrine of common intention constructive trusts discussed in **Chapter 5**. Enabling the holders of such rights to claim priority under Schedule 3, paragraph 2 is consistent with how such rights are acquired. A person who has obtained their rights informally is unlikely to seek to protect those rights by entry on the register, even if it were possible to do so. The provision also accords with the expectations of those in occupation. As Lord Denning explained in *Strand Securities v Caswell* (1965), commenting on the provision in the LRA 1925, '[f]undamentally its object is to protect a person in actual occupation of land from having his rights lost in the welter of registration. He can stay there and do nothing. Yet he will be protected. No one can buy the land over his head and thereby take away or diminish his rights.'

**11.45**   Developments since *Williams & Glyn's Bank v Boland* have, however, had the effect of confining the decision to its facts. As we have noted (**11.17**), in that case Mr Boland was sole registered proprietor of title to a property but he held the title on trust for himself and his wife because of contributions Mrs Boland had made to the purchase. Some years after the property had been purchased, Mr Boland granted a mortgage over the home to the bank. He had granted the mortgage to raise fund to support his business. Mrs Boland was unaware of the mortgage. Subsequent developments have established the following:

- If the mortgage had been granted to fund the cost of purchasing the home, then the mortgage would have ranked first in time to Mrs Boland's beneficial interest and there could have been no argument that she had priority over the bank (*Abbey National Building Society v Cann* (1991), **11.21**).

- In any event, if the mortgage had been granted to fund the purchase of the home, then Mrs Boland would not have been in actual occupation at the time of the disposition to enable her to protect her beneficial interest as an overriding interest (*Abbey National Building Society v Cann*, **11.42**).

- If Mrs Boland had known about the mortgage, then the bank may have been able to claim a defence on the basis that she had implicitly consented to the mortgage (*Abbey National Building Society v Cann*, **11.69**).

- Mr Boland was the sole registered proprietor and therefore the sole trustee. If there had been two or more registered proprietors (and therefore two or more trustees), then Mrs Boland's beneficial interest would have been overreached on the sale and would no longer have been a property right 'relating to land' for the purposes of Schedule 3, paragraph 2 but would vest instead in the proceeds of the mortgage (*City of London Building Society v Flegg* (1988), **11.80**).

## Defining Actual Occupation

11.46 For a property right to be protected as an overriding interest under Schedule 3, paragraph 2 the holder of the right (B) must be in 'actual occupation' of the land. The requirement of occupation was contained in the previous legislation (LRA 1925, s 70(1)(g)) and decisions under that Act remain relevant to its interpretation (*Link Lending v Bustard* (2010)). However, this general principle is subject to the provision in Schedule 3, paragraph 2. Under that provision, a transferee is not bound by property rights held by a person in actual occupation where two conditions are met: first, B's occupation is not obvious on a reasonably careful inspection; secondly, C did not actually know of the existence of B's property right at the time of the disposition. That provision was new in the LRA 2002 and decisions under the earlier legislation must be read in the light of the need for occupation to be discoverable on a reasonably careful inspection.

11.47 While it is no doubt anticipated that purchasers and mortgage lenders will carry out a physical inspection of the land, no actual inspection is required (*Thomson v Foy* (2010)). Where C conducts a reasonable inspection and this does not reveal B's occupation, it may be expected that the inspection will be considered conclusive in terms of the operation of the qualification in Schedule 3, paragraph 2(c)(i) on B's ability to claim an overriding interest. Where C does not inspect, or C's inspection falls short of being reasonable, then the court may address the qualification by asking a hypothetical question, 'whether [B's] occupation would have been obvious on a reasonably careful inspection' (*Thompson v Foy* (2010)). If not, then C's failure to inspect will not deprive C of invoking the qualification in paragraph 2(c)(i).

**11.48**  Although courts have been reluctant to lay down a test for determining whether a person is in actual occupation, in *Link Lending v Bustard* (2010) Mummery LJ set out a number of factors that courts have taken into account. Bogusz (2014) suggests that his judgment 'forms the foundation of the definitional attributes of occupation'.

---

**Link Lending v Bustard (2010):** Ms Bustard had been the sole registered proprietor of her home. She suffered from severe mental illness which was compounded by alcohol abuse. She was swindled into transferring the property to Mrs Hussein who then used the property as security for a loan from Link Lending. Ms Bustard had an equity to set aside the transaction against Mrs Hussein based on her lack of capacity. The question arose whether Ms Bustard was in actual occupation of the property so that the equity was also binding against Link Lending. At the date of the disposition, Ms Bustard had been absent from the property for over a year having been sectioned under the Mental Health Act and admitted to hospital. Her furniture and personal possessions remained at the property and she made brief but regular supervised visits. She had continued to discharge the outgoings and always intended to return home. The Court of Appeal confirmed the finding of the judge at first instance that Ms Bustard had remained in actual occupation. Mummery LJ identified a number of factors that have to be weighed in determining whether a person is in actual occupation. He explained, '[t]he degree of permanence and continuity of presence of the person concerned, the intentions and wishes of that person, the length of absence from the property and the reason for it and the nature of the property and personal circumstances of the person are among the relevant factors'. On the facts, the evidence demonstrated that Ms Bustard had 'a sufficient degree of continuity and permanence of occupation'. Her absence from the property was involuntary and explained by objective reasons, while her intention to return was manifested by her regular visits.

---

**11.49**  The requirement for a degree of permanence and continuity has its origins in *Abbey National Building Society v Cann* (1991). In that case, as we have seen the House of Lords held that for a property right to be protected as an overriding interest through actual occupation, the holder of the right (B) must be in occupation at the time of the disposition (**11.41**). At that time, Mrs Cann had moved some furniture into the home that she was going to live in with her son. These acts were preparatory to commencing occupation, rather than evidence of actual occupation. Lord Oliver explained that occupation requires 'some degree of permanence and continuity which would rule out mere fleeting presence'. In *Lloyds Bank v Rosset* (1989) the Court of Appeal acknowledged that occupation should be assessed by reference to the state of the property. Mrs Rosset's daily visits to a property whilst it was being renovated were sufficient to show occupation of a semi-derelict house. Similarly, in *Thomas v Clydesdale Bank* (2010) the court considered there was an arguable case that Ms Thomas' occupation was established by her almost daily presence while the property was being renovated. There, Ramsey J also noted 'the intention and wishes' of Ms Thomas and her partner that they would both reside in the property once the renovations were complete.

**11.50** The need for permanence and continuity does not create difficulties where B is temporarily absent. In *Chhokar v Chhokar* (1984), a wife in hospital to have a baby was considered to remain in actual occupation of her home despite her physical absence. Her possessions evidenced her occupation. Longer absences present a greater challenge for demonstrating that occupation has been maintained. In *Link Lending v Bustard* (2010) we have seen that Ms Bustard was considered to remain in actual occupation of her home despite her absence from the property for more than a year whilst in hospital (**11.48**). In reaching its decision, the Court of Appeal distinguished the facts of the case from *Stockholm Finance Ltd v Garden Holdings Inc* (1984). There, a Saudi princess who had not 'set foot' in her London home for a year was held not to be in actual occupation. Princess Madawi owned a house in London where there was furniture and clothing and caretaking arrangements were in place. However, she was absent from the property because she was living with her mother in Riyadh. Walker LJ acknowledged that where a person is intermittently present in a home, it is a matter of 'perception which defies deep analysis' whether there is continuous occupation with occasional absences or alternating periods of presence and absence. He considered that both the length and the reason for the absence may be relevant, but that 'there must come a point at which a person's absence from his house is so prolonged that the notion of his continuing to be in actual occupation of it becomes insupportable'.

**11.51** More controversial is the extent to which B's intentions and wishes should be used to determine whether he or she is in occupation. Taking into account intent as well as physical acts has resonance with how 'possession' is understood—for example, in a claim to adverse possession discussed in **Chapter 4**. The analogy is not, however, a perfect one: occupation and possession are not synonyms. Further, in the priority context, reference to B's intent is problematic as it is not something that C can discover through an inspection of the land. Bogusz (2014) suggests that despite the difficulties, B's intentions and wishes are being relied upon by the court both increasingly and strategically. She warns of 'occupation creep' where 'the existence of actual occupation may be extended to a person in circumstances where the facts alone are vague with regard to whether Sch 3 para 2 is satisfied'.

**11.52** In *Chaudhary v Yavuz* (2013) the Court of Appeal held that 'occupation' must be distinguished from 'use' of the land. There, Mr Chaudhary unsuccessfully sought to establish actual occupation in respect of an equitable easement to enable his tenants to use a metal staircase and 'balcony' (or access way) that provided the only means of access to and from two flats. The staircase had been erected on land belonging to Mr Yavuz, pursuant to an agreement between Mr Chaudhary and Mr Yavuz's predecessor in title. One of the basis on which occupation was claimed was the use of the structure by the tenants to get to and from their flats. The court held that this use did not constitute occupation. The distinction between use and possession appears to be one of degree. It might be suggested that however often the staircase and balcony were used, each use consisted only of a fleeting presence.

### Occupation by Proxy

**11.53** It is possible for B's actual occupation to be established by the presence of another person as his or her proxy. In *Lloyds Bank plc v Rosset* (1989) the Court of Appeal accepted that builders who were renovating a semi-derelict house were in actual occupation on behalf of Mrs Rosset. Nicholls LJ suggested that whether occupation by an employee or agent sufficed depended on the 'function which the employee or agent is discharging'. The difficulty with this test is that it shifts focus away from the nature of the occupation: B's resident housekeeper occupies on B's behalf (*Strand Securities v Caswell* (1965)); B's licensee or tenant probably occupies on his or her own behalf, rather than as a proxy for B (*Strand Securities v Caswell*) although in *Chaudhary v Yavuz* (2013) the Court of Appeal left open the question whether tenants were in occupation on behalf of their landlord. But the evidence of occupation in each case may be indistinguishable. In *Lloyd v Dugdale* (2002) Mr Dugdale used business premises in his capacity as managing director of a company in which he was also the majority shareholder. He was considered to be in occupation solely on behalf of the company and therefore a property right that he acquired in his personal capacity was not binding as an overriding interest when the premises were sold. But that case raises a separate issue, because courts do not generally look behind the corporate veil.

**11.54** It is unclear what impact the reasonable inspection qualification (**11.46**) may have on cases involving occupation by proxy. Is it necessary to consider, in each case, whether occupation by B is reasonably obvious on an inspection of the land that reveals the physical presence of an agent or employee, or is it sufficient that the presence of the agent or employee is reasonably obvious? The former interpretation may produce a result analogous to that suggested by *Rosset* (1989) while the latter has the advantage of focusing solely on the nature of the occupation. *Thomas v Clydesdale Bank plc* (2010) may suggest that the latter is sufficient, but the case concerned a preliminary application and the specific interpretation of the reasonable inspection qualification in the context of proxies is not considered.

**11.55** We have seen that a person's possessions have been used as evidence of their occupation during a period of absence from living in a property (**11.50**). A separate question is whether occupation can be established by proxy through the presence of chattels where that is the only use made of the land. In *Chaudhary v Yavuz* (2013) Lloyd LJ suggested that '[o]ccupation must be, or be referable to, personal physical activity by some one or more individuals'. This comment suggests that the presence of chattels alone would not constitute occupation. However, Lloyd LJ's consideration of the point is obiter. In that case, Mr Chaudhary argued that he was in occupation of land through the presence of the metal staircase and balcony. Although not expressed in these terms, Mr Chaudhary's argument appears essentially to be that he was in occupation by proxy through the presence of the structure. Rejecting this argument, Lloyd LJ explained, '[t]he metal structure became part of the land on any basis, regardless of whether any part of it, as a chattel, belonged [to Mr Chaudhary] ... It thus became part of what could be used or occupied'. This leaves open the position where occupation is claimed on the basis of the presence of chattels which are not part of the land in respect of which a person seeks to establish occupation; for example, where goods are stored on the land or a car is parked on the land.

## Occupation by Children

**11.56**  In *Hypo Mortgage Services Ltd v Robinson* (1997) the Court of Appeal held that children under 18 years old are not in actual occupation for the purposes of statutory provisions governing overriding interests, but are present 'as shadows of occupation of their parent'. This approach was considered to be justified by difficulties of making inquiries of children. It has been argued that other means of circumventing this difficulty are available (Cooke (1998)). Ultimately, however, the likelihood of children having property rights is arguably too slim to justify changes in conveyancing practice.

## The Relevance of Inquiry

**11.57**  A property right held by B will not be protected as an overriding interest under Schedule 3, paragraph 2 where inquiries are made of B prior to the disposition and B fails to disclose his or her property right 'when he could reasonably have been expected to do so' (Sch 3, para 2(b)). It is essential that inquiries have been made directly of B (*Hodgson v Marks* (1971)). B is not prevented from relying on Schedule 3, paragraph 2 where inquiries are not made of him or her regardless of whether such inquiries would have revealed the existence of B's interest (*Thompson v Foy* (2010)).

**11.58**  B is only denied protection if disclosure could reasonably have been expected. The practical impact of this limitation is yet to become apparent. As we have noted, protecting the rights of occupiers as overriding interests is consistent with the policy underlying the recognition of informal rights (**11.44**). These rights are particularly significant in the context of the home, and often arise on the basis of the parties' intention and conduct during the course of their relationship. B may be unaware of the existence of a claim until the relationship is subjected to legal analysis at a time of crisis—including a priority dispute with C. If B does not know that he or she has a property right, then will non-disclosure prevent reliance on Schedule 3, paragraph 2? The answer is not apparent on the face of the provision. On the one hand, by making inquiries, C has done all that the provision requires and B should therefore be prevented from asserting an undisclosed claim; on the other hand, it is inherent in the provision that making inquiries will not necessarily protect C against B's property rights. Dixon (2003) suggests that ignorance of the existence of a property right may excuse non-disclosure so that B's property right will still be protected as an overriding interest.

**11.59**  It is uncertain whether the Law Commission (2001) intended the effect of inquiries to be limited to situations in which B could reasonably have been expected to disclose his or her property rights. The Law Commission did not describe the effect of inquiries as limited to B's reasonable disclosure, but instead referred to limiting C's obligation to that of making reasonable inquiries. The Law Commission may have intended the latter, but the former has been enacted. A limitation based on reasonable disclosure by B is substantively different from one based on reasonable inquiries by C.

## Short Leases

**11.60** With some exceptions (LRA 2002, Sch 3, para 1(a) and (b)) legal leases created for seven years or less are overriding interests within Schedule 3, paragraph 1 of the LRA 2002. This provision therefore covers legal leases that fall below the duration at which a lease becomes a registered estate. The combined effect of this paragraph and section 33 of the Act (concerned with entry of a notice, **11.27–11.33**) is to give a dual means of protection to legal leases of more than three years, but not greater than seven years. These leases may be protected by entry of a notice and are overriding interests in the absence of such an entry. Legal leases of three years' duration or less are protected only as overriding interests. Equitable leases fall outside the scope of paragraph 1 (which is confined to 'leases *granted*'). An equitable lease that is not protected by entry of notice may be an overriding interest under paragraph 2, where the tenant is in actual occupation.

## Easements and Profits à Prendre

**11.61** Legal easements and profits are overriding interests under Schedule 3, paragraph 3 of the LRA 2002. An exception is made, however, where the easement or profit is not within the actual knowledge of C at the time of the disposition and would not have been obvious on a reasonably careful inspection of the servient tenement. The exception does not apply, however, if the easement or profit has been exercised in the previous year ending on the date of the disposition. This limitation on the exception is designed to ensure the protection of practically important, but 'invisible' easements, including drainage in an underground pipe. The provision has been tightly drawn and is intended to dovetail with inquiries made by C. The underlying goal is that C should become aware of binding easements prior to completion of the disposition.

**11.62** The scope of Schedule 3, paragraph 3 needs to be understood in the light of the general treatment of easements within the 2002 Act. The express grant of a legal easement is a registered disposition and such easements necessarily appear on the register (LRA 2002, s 27(2)(e)). Paragraph 3 is therefore directed at legal easements that arise from an implied grant under the rules discussed in **Chapter 9**. The limitation of the provision to legal easements is significant: the equivalent provision in the LRA 1925 had controversially been interpreted in *Celsteel Ltd v Alton House Holdings Ltd* (1985) as including some equitable easements. Equitable easements will now bind B only if protected by entry of a notice on the register (**11.27–11.33**) or as overriding interests under Schedule 3, paragraph 2 where actual occupation is established. However, as we have seen the Court of Appeal decision in *Chaudhary v Yavuz* has cast some doubt on whether it is possible to be in actual occupation of an easement (**11.40**).

## Summary: Priority and Registered Dispositions

11.63 The effect of section 29 of the LRA 2002 is that on a registered disposition from A to C, C has a defence against priority claims by B, who held property rights against A's title immediately before the disposition where:

- C complies with any limitations on A's owner's powers that are recorded on the register as restrictions and; and

- B's property right is not entered on the register by a Land Registry notice; and

- B's property right is not protected as an overriding interest.

11.64 C's defence against the enforcement of B's pre-existing rights (other than those entered on the register or binding as overriding interests) provided by section 29 of the LRA 2002 applies at the time of registration against interests held by B at the time of the disposition. In order to find out about the entry of restrictions and notices C will search the register. There is a risk of property rights arising after the search has been made and before the disposition is completed. To offset this risk, provision is made for C to obtain an official search with priority protection. The official search prevents new entries being made on the register with priority over C for 30 working days (LRA 2002, ss 70 and 72, and Land Registration Rules 2003 (SI 2003/1417), rr 147–54).

11.65 To discover the existence of overriding interests, against which C has no defence, C will also need to undertake a physical inspection of the land. The inspection will indicate, for example, whether any other parties are in occupation and whose property rights will therefore take priority over C's title.

### The Defence of Consent

11.66 Where C would otherwise be bound by B's property right, for example because B is in actual occupation and so his or her right is protected as an overriding interest, C may still claim a defence if B consents to C's later property right taking priority. B's consent may be express or implied.

11.67 Express consent typically arises where A, the sole registered proprietor, approaches a bank, C, to raise money using the property as security for a mortgage loan. Following the decision in *Boland* (1981, 11.44) it became apparent that banks in such cases were vulnerable to claims by occupiers that they have property rights in the property that have priority over the mortgage as overriding interests by virtue of actual occupation. The practical response of banks has been to ask those in occupation who are 18 years of age or older to sign a consent form, to undertake not to assert priority over the bank of any property right that the occupier in fact holds (the consent of younger occupiers is not needed because of the application of the shadow doctrine, 11.56). B's consent then provides C with a defence against the enforcement of any property right B holds against C.

11.68   Where C obtains B's express consent, there remains a risk that B will argue that his or her consent is vitiated as having been obtained by misrepresentation, duress, or undue influence. In a series of cases culminating in *Royal Bank of Scotland v Etridge (No 2)* (2001) the courts have identified the circumstances in which C will be able to rely on the defence of consent where such a vitiating factor is present. The steps that C is required to take are considered in Chapter 8. If those steps have not been followed, then B will be able to claim priority over C despite B's apparent consent.

11.69   In *Abbey National Building Society v Cann* (1991), Mrs Cann had not been asked to give her express consent to the mortgage. Her son, Mr Cann, the sole registered proprietor, had lied to the Abbey National and had told them that he did not plan to share occupation of the home. We have seen that the House of Lords decided that Mrs Cann's beneficial interest under a trust did not have priority over the mortgage. The House of Lords held that the mortgage was first in time to Mrs Cann's beneficial interest and so no claim to priority on her part could be made (11.20). We have also seen that the House of Lords considered, in any event, that even if Mrs Cann's beneficial interest had been first in time the Abbey National would have had a defence against her claim to priority. Mrs Cann's beneficial interest would not have been an overriding interest because she was not in actual occupation at the relevant time (11.41). There was one further ground on which the House of Lords held that Mrs Cann could not claim priority over the Abbey National's mortgage. Mrs Cann knew that a mortgage loan would be required to purchase the new home as there was a shortfall of £4,000 from the proceeds of the sale of the previous home. The House of Lords therefore considered that Mrs Cann had impliedly given her consent to the mortgage and on that basis she would have been unable to claim priority over the Abbey National. Lord Oliver explained that Mrs Cann's knowledge meant that Mr Cann was 'permitted by her to raise money on the security of the property'. While Mr Cann had raised £25,000 rather than the £4,000 required, this difference did not affect Mrs Cann's consent because no limitation on Mr Cann's authority had been communicated to the building society. Implied consent to a mortgage had previously been found in *Bristol & West Building Society v Henning* (1985) and *Paddington Building Society v Mendelsohn* (1985) although it remains a controversial proposition (Smith (1990); see further *Credit and Mercantile Plc v Kaymuu Ltd* (2015); Televantos (2016)).

## Overreaching

11.70   Overreaching is a mechanism enabling purchasers to take title free from certain property interests, particularly beneficial interests under a trust. In other words, overreaching provides the purchaser or mortgagee with a defence against the enforcement of those interests. The interests are removed from the land and attach to the proceeds of sale. The purchaser or mortgagee thus obtains title to the land unencumbered by the interest. The holder of the overreached interest no longer has any proprietary claim in the land, but has a beneficial interest in the monies received by the trustees. His or her interest can be said to have been 'shifted' from an interest in land to an interest in money. In this way, overreaching draws a clear distinction between the beneficiaries' rights against purchasers, on the one hand, and their rights against their trustees, on the other (**Figure 11.3**).

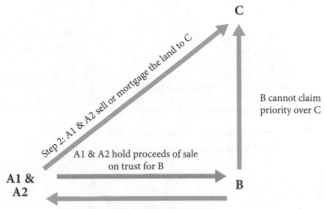

Figure 11.3 Overreaching

11.71   Overreaching applies in relation to both personal property and land, although we are concerned only with its application to land. It applies as long as two conditions are met: first, the interest must be capable of being overreached; and, secondly, the transaction must be one that has overreaching effect (LPA 1925, s 2). In this chapter, we will focus on the particular form of overreaching that applies where a purchaser or mortgagee deals with land held on trust. In such cases, a key element of the requirement that a transaction has overreaching effect is that any capital money is paid to a minimum of two trustees (LPA 1925, s 27(2)). The practical effect of overreaching is thus to draw a division between transactions undertaken by a single trustee and those executed by two or more trustees (see **Figure 11.4**).

- Where A1 and A2, joint registered proprietors, execute a registered disposition of the title in favour of C, the beneficial interests of B are overreached because there are two trustees. C has a defence against any claim to priority that B would otherwise have. B's beneficial interests have shifted from the land to the proceeds of sale of the land, which A1 and A2 hold on trust for B (*City of London Building Society v Flegg* (1988, **11.80**).

- Where A, a sole registered proprietor executes a registered disposition in favour of C, the beneficial interests of B are not overreached because A is a sole trustee. B can therefore claim priority over C if B is in actual occupation, so that B's beneficial interest is an overriding interest (*Williams & Glyn's Bank v Boland* (1981), **11.44–11.45**; see further *Haque v Raja and Khan* (2016)) unless C has a defence. In the absence of a defence, C's title to the land will be subject to B's beneficial interest. Hence, for example, if A had held the land on trust for A and B in equal shares, C will hold title on trust for himself or herself and B, each of whom will be entitled to a 50 per cent beneficial share.

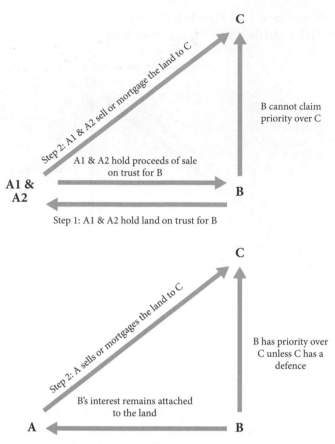

Figure 11.4 Transactions by one and two trustees compared

## Which Interests are Capable of Being Overreached?

**11.72** The interests that are capable of being overreached are specified in section 2 of the LPA 1925. The broad effect of this provision is to draw a distinction between 'family' and 'commercial' interests. Family interests, such as a beneficial interest in a trust, can in theory be readily represented by money. Hence, a 50 per cent share in a house sold for £100,000 can readily be represented by a 50 per cent share in the £100,000 purchase money. Of course, for the beneficiaries, the use of the property as a home may have more practical value than a share in the proceeds of sale (**11.81**). In contrast, commercial interests—such as an easement—'cannot sensibly shift from the land'. Such interests are theoretically as well as practically inseparable from the land over which they are intended to be exercised (*Birmingham Midshires Mortgage Services Ltd v Sabherwal* (2000)).

**11.73** The most significant interests that are capable of being overreached are beneficial interests under a trust of land. Overreaching is most frequently invoked where A1 and A2 are registered proprietors of land which they hold on trust for themselves alone, or for themselves and other beneficiaries, and transfer or mortgage the land to C. The over-reaching mechanism ensures that the beneficial interests are shifted from the land and attach to the proceeds of sale, so that C has a defence against any beneficiaries who claim priority against him or her. Notwithstanding, one of the curious features of overreaching is that section 2 of the LPA 1925 does not in fact provide for overreaching of beneficial interests under a trust of land.

11.74   Section 2 of the LPA 1925 provides that beneficial interests under a trust of land are 'capable of being overreached' on a conveyance by trustees where overreaching is provided for by section 2(2) or 'independently of that subsection'. Section 2(2) provides for overreaching of interests already in existence at the time the trust was created. This is a concept of extended overreaching that may be invoked only by a trust corporation, or by trustees approved or appointed by the court for the purpose. Section 2(2) does not, however, provide for over-reaching of the beneficial interests under the trust. The basis for overreaching beneficial interests under a trust of land must therefore be found 'independently of' section 2(2). The most commonly accepted view is that the ability to overreach beneficial interests under a trust of land is derived from trustees' powers of disposition (Harpum (1990)).

11.75   In addition to the interests for which overreaching is provided in section 2 of the LPA 1925, it was suggested in *Birmingham Midshires Mortgage Services Ltd v Sabherwal* (2000) that 'family' interests (11.72) claimed under proprietary estoppel (Chapter 5) must also be capable of being overreached. In that case, Mrs Sabherwal lived in a house with her two sons and their families. Legal title to the house was vested in the sons, who defaulted on charges granted to BMMS to raise money to support their business ventures. Mrs Sabherwal argued that she had a property right in the home binding on BMMS. As there were two trustees, it was clear that if Mrs Sabherwal had a beneficial interest under a trust her interest would have been overreached. Therefore, she argued that she had prop-erty rights under the doctrine of proprietary estoppel and that these rights were not cap-able of being overreached. The Court of Appeal considered that it would be remarkable if beneficial interests under a trust can be overreached, while more precarious family inter-ests claimed through proprietary estoppel were not subject to the mechanism. Therefore the court considered that family interests under proprietary estoppel are also capable of being overreached. To have decided otherwise would have created a significant lacuna in the operation of overreaching: the mechanism could be avoided simply by claiming an interest through proprietary estoppel rather than constructive trust. To that extent, the decision seems correct—but it is not without difficulty or controversy. In particular, it is unclear on what basis interests claimed under proprietary estoppel are capable of being overreached. There is no statutory basis of such overreaching in section 2 of the LPA 1925 and in the absence of a finding of trust, overreaching cannot be based on trustees' powers of disposition (11.74).

## Transactions with Overreaching Effect

11.76   For beneficial interests under a trust of land to be overreached, statutory requirements as regards the payment of capital money must be complied with (LPA 1925, s 2(1)(i) and (ii)). The statutory requirement, provided in section 27 of the LPA 1925, is that capital money must be paid to two trustees or a trust corporation.

**11.77**  Neither section 2 nor 27 state in their terms that there must be capital money for overreaching to take place. They impose requirements to be met when such money does arise. It has been held that capital money is not in fact required for overreaching to take place.

*[handwritten margin note: A creation of equity allowing for equitable interest in the asset being secured.]*

---

***State Bank of India v Sood* (1997):** Mr and Mrs Sood were registered proprietors of their home. They granted a charge over the home for existing and future liabilities of themselves and their business. No capital money was advanced contemporaneously with this disposition, but, over a period of time, Mr and Mrs Sood accrued debts of over £1 million and the State Bank of India sought to enforce the charge. The five children of the couple argued that they were beneficiaries under a trust of land and that their beneficial interests had not been overreached. The Court of Appeal held that even though no capital money was paid, the charge overreached the beneficial interests claimed by the children. Peter Gibson LJ noted the 'surprising and illogical' results that would otherwise arise. For example, he explained 'if a £1m facility was secured by a mortgage and in the course of time was fully drawn on but at the time of the mortgage only £100 was advanced, there would nevertheless be overreaching in respect of the whole £1m thereby secured, whereas if the £100 had not been advanced at the time of the mortgage, there would have been no overreaching'. We have noted that overreaching operates to shift the beneficial interests from the land into the proceeds of sale (**11.70**). In *Sood*, the absence of capital money did not prevent the beneficial interests being shifted from the land. The court explained that the interests were shifted into the equity of redemption.

---

**11.78**  In *Sood* two trustees executed the charge. However, if the requirement of receipt of capital money in section 27(2) of the LPA 1925 applies only to dispositions in which capital money is paid, it seems that a sole trustee can overreach beneficial interests through dispositions that do not involve payment of capital money. There is no independent statutory requirement that the transaction must be undertaken by at least two trustees. In *Shami v Shami* (2012) a first instance judge assumed without discussion that overreaching within *Sood* could take place by the execution of a charge by a single trustee, but his comment on the point was obiter. It is, however, worth noting that if the third party provides *nothing* in return for the right received from the trustees, overreaching will not occur, because the third party has not acquired a right 'for valuable consideration'. Section 2(1) limits overreaching to a 'purchaser', which is defined as a purchaser for valuable consideration (LPA 1925, s 205(1)(xxi)).

**11.79**  But if *Shami v Shami* is correct, then illogical distinctions between different types of mortgage that the court sought to avoid in *Sood* will still arise. Hence, for example, a mortgage by a sole trustee, with £100 advanced at the outset and debts of £1 million subsequently accrued, would not overreach (because the application of s 27(2) would be triggered by the initial payment of capital money), while a mortgage in which the level of borrowing reached the same amount, but with no initial advanced payment, *would* overreach, because the absence of capital money precludes the application of section 27(2).

While it must be doubted that such results are intended, there is no statutory basis for limiting overreaching to transactions undertaken by at least two trustees unless section 27(2) is applied.

## Overreaching and Overriding Interests

**11.80**  We have seen that the most significant use of overreaching is in respect of beneficial interests under a trust of land (**11.73**). We have also seen that in *Williams & Glyn's Bank v Boland* (1981) the House of Lords held that a beneficial interest held by a person in actual occupation of land is an overriding interest, against which a purchaser or mortgagee (C) has no defence (**11.44**). In *Boland*, Mr Boland was the sole registered proprietor and therefore the sole trustee of title to a home which he held on trust for himself and his wife. As the mortgage was granted by a single trustee, the transaction did not have overreaching effect because section 27(2) of the LPA 1925 was not complied with. The decision in the case gave rise to the question whether it would make a difference if there are two trustees. In other words, does overreaching take precedence over the operation of overriding interests, or can a beneficiary in occupation enforce his or her property right against a mortgagee, even if mortgage monies are paid to two trustees? This question arose for decision in the House of Lords in *City of London Building Society v Flegg* (1988).

---

*City of London Building Society v Flegg* (1988): Mr and Mrs Flegg sold their home of 28 years and, in 1982, contributed the £18,000 proceeds to the purchase of Bleak House as a new home for themselves, and their daughter and son-in-law, Mrs and Mrs Maxwell-Brown. The balance of the £34,000 purchase price was funded by a mortgage. Despite their solicitor's advice that Bleak House should be registered in the names of all four parties, it was, in fact, registered in the joint names of Mr and Mrs Maxwell-Brown who, given the Fleggs' contribution to the purchase price, held the house as joint tenants on resulting trust for themselves and Mr and Mrs Flegg (the resulting trust is considered in **Chapter 5**). Bleak House was occupied and became the home of all four parties. The Maxwell-Browns ran into financial difficulties and, without the knowledge or consent of the Fleggs, they remortgaged the house to the City of London Building Society to raise £37,500. Unfortunately, the Maxwell-Browns were unable to meet the repayments under the mortgage, and the building society sought a declaration that the mortgage bound and could be enforced against the Fleggs' interest, and an order for possession. The Fleggs argued, relying on *Boland* (1981) that their beneficial interests bound the mortgagees as an overriding interest, and that an overriding beneficial interest should not be overreached. This argument was rejected by the House of Lords. Overreaching operated, provided that the statutory conditions were satisfied. At that point, the Fleggs' beneficial interest in their home was transferred to the proceeds of sale so that the couple no longer had an interest in the land that their occupation could protect as an overriding interest. The Fleggs were entitled to a share of the proceeds of the mortgage reflecting their beneficial share in the land—but that was of no practical value as the Maxwell-Browns had used the money towards the discharge of their debts and had subsequently been declared bankrupt.

---

**11.81** Underlying the decision in *Flegg* is a tension between the 'use value' of land—for example, as a home—and its investment value. The shifting of beneficial interests from land to money in the overreaching mechanism views land as an investment and assumes that the physical identity of the property in which the investment is held is less significant than the wealth it represents. At the time of the 1925 legislation when provision was made to overreach beneficial interests, an association between land and investment was a reasonable one to make. At that time it was relatively uncommon for people to own their homes or for trusts to arise in the context of homes. Only around 25 per cent of homes were owner-occupied. During the 20th century, owner-occupation grew significantly to become the majority form of housing. At its peak, over 70 per cent of homes were owner-occupied, although the number has fallen back. Concomitantly, it became increasingly common for homes to be co-owned and therefore held on trust, in part through the development of informal trusts discussed in Chapter 5. The shift in the use of trusts of land from a means of holding an investment to co-ownership of the home was reflected in the introduction of the Trusts of Land and Appointment of Trustees Act 1996 (TOLATA) (Chapter 6). The investment ethos that underpins overreaching conflicts with developments in the use of trusts in connection with the home. Overreaching sees homes only as wealth—the use of the land is invisible to the law (Hopkins (2013a)).

**11.82** The tension between use and investment comes to the fore in cases like *Flegg* (1988) where there are beneficiaries who are not also legal owners. That is most likely to arise where (as in that case) a home is purchased for occupation by multiple generations of a family or extended family members. The operation of overreaching is not problematic in the more usual case where co-owners (typically spouses or cohabitees) are joint registered proprietors of their home and are legal and beneficial co-owners. Both parties will be involved in a disposition of the legal title and the operation of overreaching will accord with their intentions. For example, overreaching will ensure that if the couple move home, then their beneficial interests shift from the home being sold into the proceeds of sale, ready to attach to the new home purchased with the proceeds.

**11.83** Following the decision in *Flegg* (1988) the Law Commission (1989) recommended reform of overreaching to align the operation of the mechanism with changing patterns of land ownership. The Law Commission's central proposal was that the beneficial interest of anyone of full age and capacity in actual occupation of land should not be overreached unless the beneficiary consents. This proposal would provide consistently between overreaching and the ethos underlying TOLATA of giving due regard to the use value of land. However, the government announced that the proposals would not be implemented.

## Overreaching and Breach of Trust

**11.84** As we have seen, the ability to overreach beneficial interests under a trust is considered to lie in the trustees' powers of disposition (11.74). This basis for the mechanism raises the question whether overreaching takes place if the trustees act beyond their powers. Two different scenarios must be considered.

- Trustees may act in breach of trust by executing a transaction that they have no authority to undertake. For example, trustees may execute a mortgage over trust property when the instrument creating the trust provides that they do not have the power to grant mortgages. This type of breach of trust is referred to as an ultra vires breach. An ultra vires breach of trust will not overreach beneficial interests. However, that is not the end of the matter. As we have seen, in registered land purchasers are not affected by limitations on registered proprietor's owner's powers that are not entered on the register by a restriction (**11.11**). Hence, in the absence of a restriction on the register, the purchaser will be able to rely on the priority rules contained in section 29 (**11.10**) to claim a defence against the beneficial interests.

- Trustees may have power to effect a transaction, but the manner in which they exercise that power constitutes a breach of trust. This is referred to as an intra vires breach of trust. For example, in *Flegg* (1988) the Maxwell-Browns as trustees had the power to mortgage Bleak House but they acted in breach of trust by granting a mortgage to raise funds for their own personal use rather than in pursuance of their duty to act for the benefit of the trust. *Flegg* implicitly demonstrates that overreaching is unaffected by an intra vires breach of trust. The trustees may be personally liable to the beneficiaries for breach of trust, though such liability will be of no practical value if the trustees do not have resources.

**11.85** Ferris and Battersby (2002) have suggested that *Flegg* may have been reversed by TOLATA. They suggest that TOLATA has the effect that any transaction by trustees in contravention of any rule of law or equity—including the transfer in *Flegg*—is an ultra vires breach. Their argument appeared implicitly to be endorsed in *HSBC v Dyche* (2009). There, the judge doubted that a transfer by trustees that was made in breach of trust could overreach a beneficial interest. However, the effect of a transfer made in breach of trust is not fully discussed and the judge did not refer to the decision in *Flegg*. On the facts, there are other grounds on which overreaching would not have taken place; in particular, the capital money was not paid to two trustees (**11.76**). In its review on the LRA 2002, the Law Commission (2016) has provisionally proposed that the matter is put beyond doubt, so that registered proprietor's owner's powers under the LRA 2002 (**11.11**) are not subject to any limitations imposed by the common law, equity, or by other legislation (which would include TOLATA).

## Overreaching and Human Rights

**11.86** The question whether the operation of overreaching is compatible with human rights was raised in *Sabherwal* (2000) and *National Westminster Bank plc v Malhan* (2004), but in neither case was the issue determined. In both cases submissions based on human rights were rejected on the simple ground that the mortgages had been entered into before the Human Rights Act 1998 came into force and the Act does not have retrospective effect. However, in *Malhan*, Morritt V-C appeared indisposed to the arguments advanced on behalf of the beneficiary.

11.87   Human rights jurisprudence has, however, moved on since the compatibility of the over-reaching mechanism was raised. In *Malhan* counsel conceded that overreaching could not be challenged on the basis of Article 8 (the right to respect for the home) or Article 1 Protocol 1 (peaceful enjoyment of possession) alone. Instead, the argument in *Malhan* was based upon the discriminatory effect of overreaching where there are two trustees in comparison with the failure of overreaching where there is only one trustee. In the light of subsequent domestic case law concerning Article 8 and Article 1 Protocol 1, counsel's concession may have been correct. Although it seems relatively clear that overreaching engages Article 8 and Article 1 Protocol 1 that interference can be justified in accordance with the process we considered in Chapter 2.

11.88   Whether the courts will be inclined to question the policy of overreaching, under Article 8 and/or Article 1 Protocol 1, is a most difficult issue. It seems likely that our domestic courts would find justification under both Article 1 Protocol 1 and Article 8 since we have seen in *McDonald v McDonald* (2016, see further Chapter 2) that the courts are resistant to accepting the horizontal effect of human rights between parties within private property relationships, or to interfere with the policy laid down by Parliament. The courts have shown deference to the policy choices of Parliament in shaping property law, which has evolved over many centuries and which, in the case of statutory rules, have been considered by Parliament. Both TOLATA and the LRA 2002 have provided opportunities for an appraisal of overreaching both by the Law Commission and Parliament. Further, as we have seen the Law Commission's (1989) recommendations for reform of overreaching following *Flegg* (1988) were rejected by government (11.83). Thus the courts are likely to be particularly cautious in questioning the policy of overreaching. Whether the Strasbourg Court will take the same view is debateable and will depend on whether or not it believes the UK has acted within its margin of appreciation. We should have a clearer view once the appeal in *McDonald* is heard.

11.89   Foremost amongst the compatibility challenges of overreaching is the automatic trigger of overreaching by the payment of any capital monies to two trustees, not only on the basis of discrimination raised in *Malhan* (2004), but also as a process that provides no opportunity for the rights, or the personal circumstances, of a beneficiary occupying the trust property as his or her home to be protected, or to be balanced against the rights of the purchaser or mortgagee. It is this lack of procedural safeguards that represents the most serious grounds for arguing that the interference with human rights under Article 1 Protocol 1 or, particularly Article 8, falls beyond the margin of appreciation enjoyed by Member States and thus that Member States are under a positive duty in this regard.

## Alternative Causes of Action

11.90   In this chapter we have discussed the priority rules that apply to registered land. The effect of the rules can be summarized as follows. On a disposition of land from A to C, property rights held by B immediately before the disposition will have priority over C as being first in time unless C has a defence. C will have a defence where:

- the disposition from A to C is a registered disposition of a registered estate for valuable consideration within section 29 of the LRA; and

- C complies with any limitations on A's owner's powers entered on the register as a restriction; and

- B's interest is not protected by entry on the register of a notice; and

- B's interest is not an overriding interest; or

- B has given consent to C taking priority over B's interest; or

- B's interest has been overreached.

**11.91**  In most cases where C has a defence against B's property right, B will have no legal recourse against C. B's only possible recourse will be against A where, for example, the disposition from A to C is a breach of trust. However, priority rules do not exist in a legal vacuum and in a minority of cases B may have a cause of action against C.

**11.92**  The possibly of alternative courses of action arises, in particular, where the transaction between A and C is tainted by fraud or other wrongdoing. Two situations must be distinguished. The first is where fraud or wrongdoing affects the validity of the transaction between A and C. The question that arises in such cases is whether A can recover his or her title from C under the rules in the LRA 2002 concerned with rectification, alteration, and indemnity. Those rules are discussed in **Chapter 4**. The second situation is where the fraud or wrongdoing does not affect the validity of the transaction between A and C. In such a case should C, whose registered title is unimpeachable, be able to rely on statutory priority rules to claim a defence against the enforcement of property rights held by B?

**11.93**  There is no requirement in the LRA 2002 that C must act in good faith in order to rely on the priority provisions contained in the Act. On the face of it, therefore, C's ability to invoke a defence against B is unaffected by the fraud. However, in making the recommendations that led to the LRA 2002 the Law Commission (1998) emphasized the possibility of B being able to impose liability on C under the general law. Although the Law Commission referred to the possibility of 'personal liability', in fact liability may be personal or proprietary, as the two following examples illustrate.

- *Example of personal liability*: if A holds land on trust and transfers the land to C in breach of trust, then C may be personally liable to the beneficiary, B for knowing receipt of trust property (see eg *Haque v Raja and Khan* (2016), though the claim failed on the facts). The interplay between C's statutory defence against B's property right and the imposition on C of personal liability is contentious. In *Farah Constructions Pty Ltd v Say-Dee Pty Ltd* (2007) the High Court of Australia refused to impose personal liability on the recipient of trust property who had a statutory defence against the enforcement of B's beneficial interest. Conaglen and Goymour (2009) have argued that the same outcome should be reached in the context of the LRA 2002. Their argument is based on the view that the imposition of personal liability for knowing receipt of trust property is not based solely on wrongdoing by C, but is fundamentally concerned with the vindication of B's title. The personal claim is therefore 'parasitic' on the property right and cannot arise where C enjoys statutory protection against the proprietary claim. Their argument is ultimately unconvincing, however, as wrongdoing in the form of 'knowing' receipt is central to the imposition of liability (Hopkins (2013b)).

- *Example of proprietary liability*: if A transfers land to C 'subject to' a property right held by B and C, who has a defence against B's property right under priority rules, seeks to renege on the 'subject to' agreement, a constructive trust may be imposed under which B acquires new property rights against C. The imposition of a trust in such circumstances is illustrated by *Binions v Evans* (1972). There, Mrs Evans (B), a widow, lived in a cottage provided to her and her late husband by her husband's employers (A). The cottage was sold by the employers to the Binions (C) 'subject to' Mrs Evans' right to live there for the rest of her life. The Binions then brought proceedings to remove Mrs Evans from the cottage. On the facts, the court considered that Mrs Evans had property rights in the cottage at the time of the sale to the Binions against which the Binions did not have a defence under the applicable priority rules. However, the nature of Mrs Evans' rights, and whether she had property rights, were contentious. In the alternative, Lord Denning MR held that, on the assumption Mrs Evans did not have property rights at the time of the sale, a constructive trust would be imposed on the Binions to prevent them from reneging on the 'subject to' agreement pursuant to which the land was transferred. Hence, regardless of the position prior to the sale, Mrs Evans would acquire new property rights binding the Binions when they sought to renege on the agreement. The imposition of a constructive trust in such circumstances has been endorsed in subsequent cases (*Ashburn Anstalt v Arnold* (1989), *Lloyd v Dugdale* (2002)). It is essential to show, however, that C has undertaken a new obligation in respect of B. This requirement ensures that the imposition of a constructive trust is not used to circumvent the operation of priority rules to determine the enforcement of any existing property right held by B. The imposition of proprietary liability has the effect that B obtains new property rights against C. This analysis is conceptually distinct from the situation in which B has an existing property right against A's title at the time of the transfer which is held to be binding on C. The imposition of proprietary liability concerns the *acquisition question* while the enforcement of pre-existing property rights is governed by the *defences question*.

11.94   The general approach of English law is that the operation of priority rules is not affected by fraud or other wrongdoing that does not affect the validity of the transaction between A and C. Instead, reliance is placed on liability being imposed under the general law in appropriate cases. It is useful to note that there is nothing inherent in the nature of priority rules or in a system of registration of title that requires such an approach to be taken. A policy decision has been made in English land law to favour security and stability of property transactions to an extent that is not universally adopted. Torrens systems of title registration operate differently and deny C statutory protection against pre-existing property rights in cases of fraud (for further consideration, see Cooke and O'Connor (2004)). In *Southern Pacific Mortgages Ltd v Scott* (2014) Baroness Hale voiced some reservations at the 'all or nothing' approach displayed by English law. She asked, rhetorically, '[s]hould there not come a point when a vendor [B] who has been tricked out of her property can assert her rights even against a subsequent purchaser or mortgagee [C]' and '[s]hould there not come a point when the claims of lenders [C] who have failed to heed the obvious warning signs that would have told them that this borrower was not a good risk are postponed to those of vendors [B] who have been made promises that the borrowers [A] cannot keep?'

## FURTHER READING

Bogusz, B, 'The Relevance of "Intentions and Wishes" to Determine Actual Occupation: A Sea Change in Judicial Thinking?' [2014] Conv 27.

Cooke, E, *The New Law of Land Registration* (Oxford: Hart Publishing, 2003).

Dixon, M, 'The Reform of Property Law and the Land Registration Act 2002: A Risk Assessment' [2003] Conv 136.

Harpum, C, 'Overreaching, Trustees' Powers and the Reform of the 1925 Legislation' (1990) 49 CLJ 277.

Hopkins, N, '*City of London Building Society v Flegg* (1987): Homes as Wealth' in N Gravells (ed), *Landmark Cases in Land Law* (Oxford: Hart Publishing, 2013a).

Jackson, N, 'Overreaching in Registered Land Law' (1996) 69 MLR 214.

Law Commission Consultation Paper No 227, *Updating the Land Registration Act 2002* (2016).

Law Commission Report No 254, *Land Registration for the Twenty-First Century: A Consultative Document* (1988).

Law Commission Report No 271, *Land Registration for the Twenty-First Century: A Conveyancing Revolution* (2001).

Smith, R, '*Williams and Glyn's Bank Ltd v Boland* (1980): The Development of a System of Title by Registration' in N Gravells (ed), *Landmark Cases in Land Law* (Oxford: Hart Publishing, 2013).

Thompson, MP, '*Midland Bank Trust Co Ltd v Green* (1980): Maintaining the Integrity of Registration Systems' in N Gravells (ed), *Landmark Cases in Land Law* (Oxford: Hart Publishing, 2013).

## SELF-TEST QUESTIONS

1    In what circumstances does section 29 of the LRA 2002 provide a purchaser or mortgagee of registered land with a defence against pre-existing property rights?

2    What do you understand by the doctrine of *scintilla temporis* and what relevance does the doctrine have in relation to priorities?

3   Compare and contrast the role played by entry of a restriction and entry of a notice. Give examples of property rights that each of these forms of entry on the register may be most relevant in respect of.

4   What is an 'overriding interest'? What is the relevance of 'actual occupation' to the category of overriding interests? In what circumstances may a person who is not physically present on land be held to be in actual occupation?

5   What is the effect of overreaching? For what property interests is overreaching of most significance?

6   In each of the following circumstances, would B or C have priority?

   a   A (a single trustee) holds legal title to a home on trust for herself and for B, her husband. A and B are both living in the house when A uses title as security for a loan obtained from a bank, C. A defaults on the loan.

   b   A1 and A2 are joint registered proprietors of a home which they hold on trust for themselves and for B1 and B2. All four parties are living in the house when A1 and A2 use the title as security for a loan obtained from a bank, C. A1 and A2 default on the loan.

7   In relation to 6(a) above, consider the following:

   a   Would it make any difference to your answer if A1 and A2 were not paid any purchase money at the time of the mortgage, but were instead granted an overdraft facility? Over the next year, A1 and A2 became overdrawn to £500,000 at which point C sought to enforce the security?

   b   Would it make any difference to your answer if A1 and A2 did not have power to mortgage, so the grant of the mortgage by them was an ultra vires breach of trust?

   c   What courses of action, if any, might B have against C?

# 12

# Concepts and Contexts

## SUMMARY

In Chapter 1, we explained that the focus of this book is on private rights to use land. In Chapters 2–11, we set out the core rules applying to such rights, using the content, acquisition, and defences questions to provide a structure for those rules. The purpose of this chapter is to take a step back and to consider some of the wider issues raised by those rules, and the nature of the challenges faced by judges and Parliament when deciding how best to develop those rules. After all, in addition to understanding the current rules of land law, it is helpful to be able to evaluate those rules. We hope that the discussion in this final chapter may be particularly useful for anyone writing compulsory essays, or even voluntary dissertations, in land law.

Key topics explored in this chapter are:

- The importance of concepts and of contexts in land law (12.1–12.9)
- The tension between concepts and contexts and the effect of different judicial approaches to land law (12.10–12.16)
- The relative merits of judicial, and of legislative, reform of land law (12.17–12.26)
- The impact of statutory reform, particularly of registration statutes, in land law (12.27–12.32)
- The impact of human rights and of regulation in land law (12.33–12.43)
- The role of non-doctrinal approaches in evaluating land law (12.49–12.50)

## Concepts versus Contexts

### The Importance of Concepts

12.1 As explained in Chapter 1, our focus has been on private rights to use land and, in particular, the *concepts* used by the law to define such rights, and to resolve conflicts between such rights. We have, for example, picked out the *content, acquisition,* and *defences* questions as useful means to understand the structure of land law.

**12.2**  We have also seen that the rules of land law are often quite technical. This technicality can be linked to a preference for concepts over contexts. For example, the difference between the outcomes in *Williams & Glyn's Bank v Boland* (1981) and *City of London Building Society v Flegg* (1988) depended entirely on the fact that, in the former case, the legal estate in the land was held by only one trustee, whereas in the latter case, it was held by two trustees, to whom the lender jointly paid the mortgage loan (1.78–1.79). Whilst the context of each case was otherwise identical, that seemingly trivial difference was crucial to the operation of the *defences* question, as it allowed the lender in *Flegg*, unlike that in *Boland*, to rely on the overreaching defence recognized by section 2 of the Law of Property Act 1925.

**12.3**  We have also seen, for example in Chapters 4 and 11, that formality is very important in land law. As far as *acquisition* is concerned, if B wishes to show, for example, that A has given B a legal property right in particular land, then B will have to show that the transaction has been completed with the right formalities. The transfer from A to B of a legal freehold, for example, requires the use of a deed and registration by B as the holder of the estate. Formality, in the sense of entering a notice on the register, is also very important when considering the *defences* question. For example, consider a case where B claims to have acquired an equitable interest in A's registered land, but B has failed to protect that interest by entering a notice on the register (for an example, see *Chaudhary v Yavuz* (2013)). If A's registered estate is then sold to C, and B was not in actual occupation of A's land at the time of the sale, then C will have a defence against B's pre-existing equitable interest, *even if* C knew or ought to have known about B's right. This is clear from sections 28 and 29 of and Schedule 3 to the Land Registration Act 2002. In such a case, the general concept of registration, and its role in protecting a party such as C, is thus regarded as more important than the specific contextual point that, on the facts, C in fact knew, or ought to have known, about B's right.

**12.4**  The context of disputes such as those in *Boland* and *Flegg* is even sharper, as it pits an innocent occupier of a home against an institutional lender. The technical, formal nature of the land law rules often obscures the social importance of the underlying dispute. It seems that the famous observation of Fitzjames Stephen, whilst made in a different context, can be applied to land law: 'The only thing which prevents English people from seeing that law is really one of the most interesting and instructive studies in the world, is that English lawyers have thrown it into a shape which can only be described as studiously repulsive.' The technical, formal flavour of land law is, however, no accident. As it deals with rights to use a scarce but very important resource, land law often has to deal with very difficult questions. One of the attractions of a carefully structured system of land law is precisely that it can take some of the heat out of such disputes: it can resolve them through clear and settled principles, not by requiring judges to embark on the perhaps impossible task of weighing the merits, on the specific facts, of the competing parties' positions. Indeed, a key function of the concepts is precisely to direct attention away from case-specific issues which may be relevant to the merits, but which may equally make it harder for parties to be certain in their dealings with land. So, in a case such as *Flegg*, for example, we might want to know, when considering the general merits if, for example, the parents' contribution to the purchase price of the house had been crucial for its purchase, and if the building society had been aware of the parents' contributions. Similarly, in a case such as *Yavuz*, we might want to know if C knew about B's right, or could easily have discovered it, and if B's failure to enter a notice on the register was, on the particular facts of the case, excusable. The technical land law rules, however, operate to make such questions irrelevant, by focusing a court's attention on formal questions, such as the number of trustees involved in the mortgage, or whether or not a notice was entered on the register. The task of the courts is, in that way, made easier, and, as a result, there is more chance of the parties and their lawyers being able to work out, in advance of any court order, what rights they have in the land.

12.5   Indeed, although those who say that land law is boring are unlikely to intend a compliment, it is a real virtue of land law that it provides a dispassionate way of handling potentially emotive cases, such as the three we examined in **Chapter 1**, all pitching innocent occupiers of a family home against a bank or building society (see McFarlane (2008)). In *Stack v Dowden* (2007), Lady Hale stated that 'In law, "context is everything"'. On the contrary, however, one of the main aims of law is to provide general rules that can be applied consistently, so that we can have a reasonable idea of the result of a case without knowing all of its particular facts, and thus have a path out of the 'wilderness of single instances'. That aim is particularly important when considering property rights, which have the special quality of being able to bind a party who played no part in their creation. A third party, when deciding whether to deal with particular land, needs to have a reasonable chance to ascertain, without undue cost, the prospects of being bound by a preexisting right relating to the land. It is therefore no surprise that concepts have a crucial role to play in land law (see eg Smith (2014) noting the important role in property law of rules with a formal nature: ie rules with a 'relative invariance to context').

## The Importance of Contexts

12.6   Whilst it may thus be a mistake to say that context is everything, it would equally be an error to think that concepts alone can suffice. However careful we are in defining our rules, the difficult contextual questions cannot be concealed forever: they cannot be simply swept under the conceptual carpet. The risk is that general rules, designed to apply irrespective of context, will be unable to respond adequately to the demands of justice in a particular case.

12.7   For example, one of the content requirements of a lease is well established: it must give B a right to exclusive possession of land. It then seems that, if B deals with a party that does not itself have such a right to exclusive possession, B cannot have a lease of that land. In the context of *Bruton v London and Quadrant Housing Trust* (2000, **7.49–7.58**), however, the application of that rule might seem to have an unfair result: it would mean that the Housing Trust could rely on its own lack of exclusive possession to escape a statutory repairing duty it would otherwise owe to Mr Bruton. Why should Mr Bruton lose out because of the lack of title of the Trust? Similarly, in *Berrisford v Mexfield* (2012, **7.34–7.39**), it seemed that the rule that a lease must be for a certain term, if applied to the particular context of the 'mortgage rescue scheme' in that case, might lead to the unfair result that the housing cooperative (or at least its successor in title) would be free to remove Mrs Berrisford from her home, even if she had not breached any of the terms of her occupation agreement.

12.8 Of course, the House of Lords in *Bruton*, like the Supreme Court in *Berrisford*, found a way to resolve this tension between concept and context: not by giving up on the very idea of applying concepts, but rather by departing from the previous understanding of the operation of those concepts. As we saw in **Chapter 7**, it is far from clear that, as far as the concepts themselves are concerned, the solutions adopted were convincing. Our present interest, however, is in the wider point: the outcome in each of those cases suggests that some sensitivity to context is required when applying the rules of the land law system.

12.9 It is often (although, as shown by *Bruton* and *Berrisford*, not always) recourse to principles of equity that gives the land law system the flexibility to take account of context and of the merits of the particular case. As far as the *acquisition* question is concerned, the doctrine of proprietary estoppel provides a good example. In a case such as *Thorner v Major* (2009, **5.94**), for example, Peter Thorner had not transferred any land to David Thorner, either during his life or in his will, nor had he made any contract to do so. Nonetheless, the detriment that would result to David as a result of his reliance on Peter's implied promise to leave his farm to David meant that it would 'shock the conscience' of the court (to adopt the phrase used by Lord Walker in *Cobbe v Yeoman's Row Management Ltd* (2008)) if David were left without a remedy. The doctrine of proprietary estoppel, developed from rules originally applied by courts of equity, was thus used to prevent an unfair result. The strictness of the acquisition rules regulating the requirements for a transfer of land, or for a contract to make such a transfer, is thus mitigated by the possibility of a proprietary estoppel claim. It has been suggested that equity, in many such cases, provides a 'safety valve' that can prevent parties, such as the administrators of Peter Thorner, from exploiting the strictness of formal legal rules (Smith (2014)). Certainly, at one level, equitable rules provide a means to soften some of the harsher technicalities of common law (as we saw, eg, in **Chapter 6**, when considering how methods of severance recognized in equity can be used to avoid the harshness of the doctrine of survivorship) and so provide some scope for the particular context of the case to be taken into account.

## The Tension

12.10 The problem is that, even taking into account the possibility of recourse to equitable principles, there may be cases where the *concepts* of the land law system are not flexible enough to respond to the perceived demands of fairness in a particular *context*. The limits of the common intention constructive trust provide a good example: although based on equitable principles, the doctrine soon became constrained by its own, specific requirements: see **5.44–5.45**). Indeed, Lord Bridge's idea in *Lloyds Bank v Rosset* (1991)—that, in the absence of express discussions, a common intention to share the beneficial interest can be inferred only where B has made direct contributions to the purchase price or mortgage—itself has the same function as technical land law rules such as the need for registration. It operates to exclude factors (eg non-financial contributions) which may well be relevant to our view of the general merits of B's claim, but which may be harder to establish or test for in practice. Excluding such factors from the resolution of the dispute not only reduces litigation costs but also makes it easier for A, B, and third parties to ascertain their rights in relation to the land.

**12.11**    At this stage, two points are particularly worth noting. First, it would be misleading to describe the tension between concepts and contexts as a clash between certainty and fairness. The point is that certainty itself is an aspect of fairness: it is important, for example, that parties can plan their lives, and having some certainty as to their rights in land may be crucial to such planning. Secondly, even if we were to accept that particular land law rules are in need of reform, that does not mean that we have to challenge the underlying approach of the system as a whole (see eg the discussion of the *numerus clausus* principle at **3.17-3.24**). We can change the operation of a concept without abandoning the system's preference for concepts over context. Nonetheless, it is possible that specific examples, taken together, may be symptomatic of a deeper problem.

**12.12**    The central idea is that, in such cases, the discrepancy between the outcomes to which the concepts lead and the outcomes perceived to be fair may lead us to question the priority given, across the land law system as a whole, to such concepts. There is certainly a general tension, throughout land law, as to the correct balance between upholding general concepts and remaining sensitive to particular contexts. That tension is reflected not only in the different outcomes that judges may reach in a specific case but, more importantly, in the different *approaches* they might apply.

## Differing Approaches

**12.13**    This can be seen by returning to the very first case considered in this book, *National Provincial Bank v Ainsworth* (1965). The Court of Appeal and House of Lords reached different conclusions on the content question, with the former, but not the latter, finding that Mrs Ainsworth's right was capable of binding the bank (**1.61-1.62**).

**12.14**    There was also a deeper, methodological divide between the two courts. In the Court of Appeal, Lord Denning MR argued that, once Mrs Ainsworth's right (a 'deserted wife's equity') bound the bank, this gave the court discretion as to whether, and on what terms, she might remain in occupation. In exercising that discretion the court, in Lord Denning's words, had to combine '[j]ustice to the bank, with mercy to the wife'. His clear preference, then, was that a court should have the freedom to consider all the possibly relevant features of the particular case, and so could weigh up directly the merits of either side's claims. On that approach, context would then be everything. The House of Lords, however, robustly rejected that position, preferring to place weight on the conceptual rules and seeking to avoid, in Lord Wilberforce's words, a 'radical departure from sound principles of real property law'. Those principles demanded that either Mrs

Ainsworth had a property right in the land, which was then prima facie binding on the bank, or she did not: there was no room for the court to exercise the discretion preferred by Lord Denning.

**12.15**  The differing approaches adopted by Lord Denning and by the House of Lords can each be seen as examples of a more general model as to how cases should be decided. For example, building on the analysis of Weber (the influential German sociologist and political economist), Harris (1987) identified two different models that may influence a judge. First, and apparent in Lord Denning's judgment in the Court of Appeal in *Ainsworth*, is the 'utility model of rationality'. This fits closely with a non-expert's expectation of how a dispute should be decided: by weighing up the practical advantages of finding for Mrs Ainsworth, or finding for the bank. Context is, indeed, everything. Secondly, apparent in the House of Lords' approach in the same case, is the 'doctrinal model of rationality'. This can be seen as linked to a preference for formalism, or 'lawyers' law': the dispute should be decided by applying general legal concepts, such as the distinction between a personal right and a property right, even if those concepts might seem technical and remote to a layperson.

**12.16**  Of course, it is unlikely that any judgment could be seen as containing no elements at all of either of the utility or doctrinal models: no judge will wholly favour either contexts or concepts to the exclusion of the other. In *Ainsworth*, for example, Lord Denning tried to show how the concepts developed in the existing case law provided support for his favoured discretionary approach. Nonetheless, it is still possible to place particular approaches at different points on a spectrum, with contexts at one end and concepts at the other.

## Judicial versus Legislative Reform

**12.17**  A particular judge's view as to the appropriate point on the spectrum between contexts and concepts may be heavily influenced by his or her view as to the limits of judicial, as opposed to legislative, development of the law.

**12.18**  In the House of Lords in *Ainsworth*, for example, each of Lord Cohen and Lord Upjohn, whilst favouring a conceptual approach, and deciding in favour of the bank on the basis that Mrs Ainsworth had no property right in the family home, also called on Parliament to consider reforming the law. The point is that a judge may think that, given the particular context (in this case, a spouse in occupation of the family home) the best result is one that is inconsistent with the prevailing conceptual rules. In such circumstances, the judge may feel that he or she lacks the legitimacy to change the law in order to reach that result, but that Parliament should pass reforms. On this view, statutory reform has three key advantages: first, Parliament can consider a wider range of information (eg representations from interested groups; social statistics and expert evidence etc); secondly, a (partly) elected body may be better placed to ascertain the views of the broader public, to which some of its members are accountable; thirdly, any reform will be prospective only, and so will not interfere with any expectations on which the parties may have based their dealings.

**12.19** Indeed, after the decision in *Ainsworth*, Parliament passed the Matrimonial Homes Act 1967. It introduced a new framework for balancing the rights of a non-owning spouse with those of a third party, such as a bank. That basic framework is still in place today, and is now found in the Family Law Act 1996: its protection is not limited to spouses but also extends to civil partners. B is given a basic right of occupation in a home owned by his or her spouse or civil partner; and that right is capable of binding a third party, but *only* if B's right has been entered on the register.

**12.20** In passing this legislation, Parliament came up with a specific solution applying only in the particular context of occupation of a family home by a spouse or civil partner. The general conceptual rules are departed from in two significant ways. First, the right of occupation does not operate like a property right: it is not prima facie binding on C. Rather, it binds C *only* if registered. It is not the case that C can rely on B's lack of registration as part of a defence against B's pre-existing property right. If that were so, B's actual occupation would give B an overriding interest and would thus make B's right of occupation immune from the lack of registration defence (**11.37–11.59**). The spouse or partner's right to occupy, however, cannot count as an overriding interest, even if B is in actual occupation, as it is not a property right in land. On the other hand, it is more than a mere personal right, as it will bind C if registered. Secondly, the statutory right of occupation does not operate like a normal licence: a court has relatively wide powers to exclude or restrict B's right, taking into account, for example, the housing needs and resources of A and B, and of any 'relevant child'. The position of C can also be taken into account, as C can apply for B's right to be terminated on the basis that it would be 'just and reasonable' to do so (*Kaur v Gill* (1988)). The sort of context-specific balancing preferred by Lord Denning can thus take place, without challenging one of Lord Wilberforce's key points in *Ainsworth*: that such uncertainty is inconsistent with the concept of a property right. Necessarily, of course, the discretion given to the court makes it harder for the parties to know, in advance of any decision by a court, how a dispute will be decided: certainty is thus compromised in order to provide some protection to an occupying spouse or civil partner who lacks an interest in the family home.

**12.21** A contrast can be drawn with the current position regarding the acquisition of a beneficial interest in the family home. In such a case, of course, the claim of the cohabiting partner (whether or not married or in a civil partnership) is not simply to occupation: it is to a share, in equity, of the benefits of the other partner's ownership of the land. A crucial point here is that, ever since the common intention constructive trust was acknowledged in *Gissing v Gissing* (1971), the courts have insisted that it depends on a *general*, conceptual rule as to acquisition which applies across different legal contexts. Indeed, the Court of Appeal has, on two occasions, stated that the principles of the common intention constructive trust can also apply, via the *Pallant v Morgan* equity, in a commercial case (*Banner Homes Group plc v Luff Developments Ltd* (2000); and, by a majority, in *Crossco No 4 Unlimited v Jolan* (2012)). This has, no doubt, limited the flexibility and reach of the doctrine. Conceptually, of course, it *should* be difficult for B to show that he or she has acquired a beneficial share of A's property, especially where there is no written record of any declaration of trust or agreement between A and B. Inevitably, in some cases, judges have expressed sympathy for the position of B, but have been unable to stretch the concept of the common intention constructive trust far enough to accommodate B's claim. It is therefore no surprise that judges have sometimes stated that reform can come only from Parliament (see eg *Burns v Burns* (1984)), as Parliament has the legitimacy to introduce a tailored solution, applying only to the specific context of the shared family home.

12.22 In England and Wales at least, no such statutory reform has occurred (5.64–5.69). The response to the Law Commission's (2007) proposals in its report, *The Financial Consequences of Relationship Breakdown*, is instructive. From a conceptual perspective, those proposals had the merit of leaving the rules governing the acquisition of a beneficial interest unchanged: B's protection was instead to come from a claim to financial relief, recognized by a special regime specific to the context of partners who had cohabited for a minimum period, or who have a child together. The main public objection to the proposals, however, was based on the fear that they somehow 'undermined marriage'. The vociferousness with which those objections were expressed may well have played a part in deterring the UK government of the day, and subsequent UK governments, from championing the Law Commission's proposals (note that a separate set of reforms had however already been introduced in Scotland in the Family Law (Scotland) Act 2006).

12.23 The lack of UK parliamentary action on the Law Commission's proposals creates a dilemma for the courts in England and Wales. On the one hand, it can be forcefully argued that, if the legislature, taking into account public reaction, has decided not to act, then any similar judicial reform would face charges of illegitimacy (Mee (2011)). On the other, it might be said that it would now be idle for judges to continue to look to Parliament to change things for B's benefit, and so they should take matters into their own hands. There is some evidence of that view in Lady Hale's judgment in *Stack v Dowden* (2007). That case was decided before the Law Commission's 2007 proposals were published, but Lady Hale did refer to its Discussion Paper (2002), which had concluded that it was not possible to devise a suitable statutory scheme for the ascertainment and quantification of beneficial interests in the shared home. Lady Hale stated that the importance of that conclusion for the judges was that 'the evolution of the law of property to take account of changing social and economic circumstances will have to come from the courts rather than Parliament'.

12.24 One difficulty with judicial reform, even if concerns as to its democratic legitimacy are put to one side, is that it is limited by the accidents of litigation, and constrained by the doctrine of precedent. It seems clear, for example, that the judges in each of *Stack* and *Jones v Kernott* (2012) were keen to change the law as set out in *Lloyds Bank v Rosset* (1991). As noted at 5.57–5.60, however, it is far from clear that they succeeded. The point is that, in each of *Stack* and *Jones*, A and B were jointly registered as holding the legal estate in the land. Technically, then, whatever the intentions of the judges in those cases, it can be said that the decisions do not interfere with the precedent of *Rosset*, which was a case in which B claimed a beneficial interest in land registered in A's sole name.

**12.25** Another problem with judicial reform is its retrospective nature: in English law, judges are not permitted to limit their interpretation of the law, or any changes to the law, to take effect only in the future. The judges' power to interpret or develop the law depends on their power to decide the case before them, and the parties before the court are entitled to be judged on the basis of the law as it was at the time of their actions. This restriction can cause some discomfort in cases where the judges are consciously seeking to develop the law: in *Stack*, for example, Lord Walker stated that the law had 'moved on' since *Rosset*, whereas a more plausible view is that *Stack* itself was attempting to create, not to recognize, a development in the law (Swadling (2007)).

**12.26** The problem of retrospective reform is particularly important in land law. For example, in *Prudential Assurance v London Residuary Body* (1992, 7.30), Lord Browne-Wilkinson expressed strong reservations about the rule that a lease must be for a certain term, regarding it as an 'ancient and technical' rule that lacked a purpose and could lead to a 'bizarre outcome'. He stated that: 'If, by overruling the existing authorities, this House were able to change the law for the future only I would have urged your Lordships to do so. But for this House to depart from a rule relating to land law which has been established for many centuries might upset long established titles. I must therefore confine myself to expressing the hope that the Law Commission might look at the subject …' The concern is a valid one: one of the reasons for having conceptual rules of land law, especially as to the content question, is that parties can then ascertain what property rights burden particular land and can plan their dealings accordingly. A significant judicial change to the content rule for leases (or, eg, a judgment allowing positive freehold covenants to count as equitable interests in land) might therefore cause significant disruption. Indeed, that argument has been used even against a relatively minor development in the courts' approach to interpreting a statutory provision (Newsom (1981, 1982), arguing against the view of s 78 of the Law of Property Act 1925 adopted in *Federated Homes Ltd v Mill Lodge Properties Ltd* (1980), 10.35–10.36).

## The Impact of Statutory Reform

**12.27** The approach of judges who prefer to leave context-specific reform to the legislature may be seen as reflecting a certain attachment to the existing conceptual rules. A similar caution can sometimes be seen at work when judges interpret and apply statutory reforms: even though Parliament has intervened, a desire to protect prior expectations, or to uphold well-established concepts, may influence a judge's interpretation of the legislation.

**12.28** We saw one example of this phenomenon in Chapter 7, when considering the approach taken by the Court of Appeal, under the leadership of Lord Denning, to the content requirements of a lease. Various statutory reforms gave additional protection to B, beyond that available at common law, if B had a lease of his or her home. For example, the grounds on which A could retake possession of the land, even at the end of the contractually agreed period of the lease, were limited: B thus had some 'security of tenure'. It would thus seem that Parliament had considered the particular context of those occupying their home under a lease, and deemed that the general concepts of property law gave insufficient protection to such a party's interest in his or her home. Lord Denning, in contrast, seems to have regarded it as important that A should be able to avoid such additional burdens, and so rejected the orthodox content requirements of a lease (which focus on whether or not B has a right to exclusive possession) to ask instead if A had intended to give B a 'stake in the land'. If A had no such intention, no lease was found, and the statutory protection was not available to B. In *Street v Mountford* (1985), the House of Lords of course rejected that 'revolution' of Lord Denning and reinstated the orthodox test for the content of the lease (**7.43**).

**12.29**  It seems then that, in a desire to limit the effect of legislation protecting those with leases of their home, and to give A the opportunity to avoid the particular contextual solution provided by Parliament, Lord Denning was willing to manipulate the test for a lease, in order to allow A to preserve the general conceptual position that A should be free to take possession of the land at the end of the period agreed with B. This contrasts with the same judge's stance in *Ainsworth*, which showed instead a willingness to depart from the conceptual position in order to provide protection in the particular context of someone occupying a matrimonial home. This shows that a judge's preference for contexts as opposed to concepts may vary in different situations.

## Registration Statutes

**12.30**  The judicial attitude to registration statutes, such as the Land Registration Act 1925 and the Land Registration Act 2002, provides a further example of how a judicial attachment to a pre-existing conceptual position may limit the contextual impact of statutory reforms. First, such statutes may aim to replace pre-existing rules, particularly as to the acquisition and defences questions, with a new regime, focused on the fact of registration. It is possible, however, that judges adopting a cautious attitude to the legislation may prefer to limit the extent to which such pre-existing rules are changed. A classic example is *Peffer v Rigg* (1977): Graham J, adopting a surprising interpretation of the 1925 Act, was prepared to find that, if C acquired a legal estate in registered land with knowledge that it had been held by A on trust for B, and was transferred to C in breach of that trust, C would not be able to use the lack of registration defence against B's equitable interest under the trust. That result accorded with the concept, applying in other areas of property law, that if C acquires trust property with knowledge of the trust, C will not be able to use the general bona fide purchaser defence. The problem was that, in the specific context of dealings with registered land, that defence had been replaced by the scheme under the 1925 Act, under which, it had generally been assumed, the question of C's knowledge was irrelevant. Differing possible approaches to the interpretation of 'actual occupation' (**11.37-11.59**) can be seen as raising a similar issue: should the term be taken literally (as the House of Lords preferred in *Boland* (1981, **1.69**) or should it be interpreted in such a way as to make the operation of the registration statute conform as closely as possible to the general bona fide purchaser defence? A judge's view on that question may well depend on his or her view as to the extent to which general property law concepts should be replaced in particular contexts by different values.

**12.31**  Of course, such questions can arise only where a statute leaves some room for interpretation. The Law Commission was careful to ensure that there was no room for an interpretation such as that in *Peffer v Rigg* to be given to the 2002 Act (2001, paras. 5.16–5.21). The provisions under the Act in relation to rectification are, however, not so clear. In particular, whilst rectification is possible where there is a 'mistake' on the register, the key term 'mistake' is not defined by the Act. Different views can be taken in, for example, a case where X is fraudulently registered in place of B, and C then acquires a right from X (**4.76-4.77**). Does the power to order rectification for a mistake allow a court to order rectification, in favour of B, against C? On one view, the registration of C is not itself a mistake, as C acquired a right from X, who was at that time the registered proprietor, and section 58 of the Land Registration Act 2002 states that X's registration is conclusive as to X's power to grant such rights. A different view, more favourable to B, is that as X's registration was of course mistaken, rectification against C can be seen as part of correcting that initial mistake. A further view, still more favourable to B, is that C's registration is itself mistaken, as the general principle of property law is that C should not be able to acquire a right in B's property without B's consent. A desire to apply general property law concepts, rather than special registration concerns, may lead a judge to prefer that third view.

**12.32**  It is possible to give further examples where the extent of a judge's attachment to general principles of property law has influenced his or her interpretation of a statutory registration scheme (see eg the divergent approaches of the Court of Appeal in *Malory Enterprises Ltd v Cheshire Homes (UK) Ltd* (2002) and *Swift 1st Ltd v Chief Land Registrar* (2015), **4.78 4.83**). The important point for present purposes is a general one. In the report that led to the 2002 Act, the Law Commission emphasized that its ambitious goals for the registration system required not only a new statute but also 'a change in attitude' (Law Commission (2001), para 1.9). This referred primarily to the attitude of parties dealing with land, but it is also true that, if a system is truly to be one of 'title by registration', judges have to adopt a particular stance to applying the rules of the registration regime. The difficulty is that, under the 2002 Act as under the 1925 Act, judges have proved reluctant to depart wholly from general concepts of property law (Jackson (2003), Goymour (2013)). It is noteworthy, for example, that in *Scott v Southern Pacific Mortgages Ltd* (2015), Lady Hale stated that: 'It is important to bear in mind that the system of land registration is merely conveyancing machinery. The underlying law relating to the creation of estates and interests in land remains the same.' Such a view, demonstrating judicial caution in the face of legislative change, shows that not all judges have adopted the attitude urged by the Law Commission in relation to the 2002 Act, according to which it is registration that confers title, not the underlying general principles of property law. Indeed, it is interesting to note that, in its 2016 Consultation Paper, *Updating the Land Registration Act 2002*, the Law Commission has recognized that the tricky three-party case discussed at **12.31**, where an innocent C acquires a registered right from X, and X's registration was procured by a fraud on B, cannot always be resolved by simply applying clear *ex ante* rules: rather, as under the current law, there should be some discretion for a court to consider the impact of the particular facts, and thus of the specific context of the dispute, when deciding which of B and C is to have priority, and which must instead settle for an indemnity (**4.83**). This takes us back to the tension discussed at **12.10**: should the land law rules, especially those relating to registration, aim to have a technical, formal character that excludes many factors that might otherwise seem relevant to the general merits of the case, or should judges instead have a wider discretion to take those merits into account when aiming to strike the right balance between B and C?

## The Impact of Human Rights

**12.33**   In **Chapter 2**, we discussed the important role played by human rights in land law. The judgment of the Supreme Court in *Manchester CC v Pinnock* (2011) is significant as it demonstrates how, partly in response to decisions of the European Court of Human Rights, judges have come to accept that Article 8 of the Convention may require a particular *contextual* examination of a public body's claim to possession of land, even in a case where, conceptually, the public body is not bound by any personal right or property right of the occupier. The fact that it took a long time for English law to reach that conclusion shows that at least some judges preferred to apply the orthodox *conceptual* position that, if not bound by any personal right or property right, an owner of land is simply entitled to possession of that land (see eg the judgment of Lord Scott in *Harrow LBC v Qazi* (2004)). Equally, the refusal of the Supreme Court in *McDonald v McDonald* (2016) to allow Article 8 to have an impact on a claim for possession made by a *private* party (**2.77-2.79**) may be linked to a preference for cases to be decided by the application of general conceptual rules, rather than by the weighing of contextual factors involved in subjecting a claim for possession to a proportionality test.

**12.34**   A preference for concepts over contexts in land law is reflected in rules that focus the attention of the court on a narrow range of often technical issues, and exclude from consideration specific factual aspects of the particular case which might seem relevant to the general merits (**12.10**). Where a party is allowed to invoke a human right, such as Article 8, however, the number of potentially relevant factors is expanded greatly: as confirmed by Lord Hope in *Powell* (2011), for example, context is crucial when assessing the proportionality of a local authority's claim to possession: the 'occupier's personal circumstances and any factual objections she may raise' will be relevant. As Bright (2013) has noted: 'the proportionality question does require a shift towards a contextualised, non-hierarchical way of thinking, in which factors extraneous to property doctrine may come into play, such as the personal or social circumstances of the occupier and the effect that eviction will have on him and his family or community'. Indeed, the approach to proportionality under Article 8, with its focus on the aims of an owner of the land, and the particular circumstances of an occupier, resembles in some respects the balancing of the concerns of a lender and an occupier that Lord Denning called for in the Court of Appeal in *Ainsworth* (**12.14**) but which was rejected in that case by the House of Lords. The point is that, when an occupier is allowed to appeal to Article 8 in seeking to resist a local authority's application for possession, it is of course harder for that local authority, or any interested third party, to know if the application for possession will be successful: the certainty for which land law rules generally aim is thus jeopardized. The contrast between those traditional rules and a human rights approach is starkest when an appeal to human rights may mean that, even though B entered A's land as a trespasser, B's personal circumstances must still be considered before A's right to possession can be asserted (Walsh (2015)).

**12.35** It is no surprise, therefore, that, notwithstanding the landmark *Pinnock* decision, the Supreme Court has limited the impact of human rights in land law in two important ways. First, even where a human right, such as Article 8, can be invoked, the court emphasized in *Pinnock* that it will only be in a rare case that B, an occupier without any personal right against A, or any property right in the land, will be able to show that an order for possession would be disproportionate. Nonetheless, of course, the possibility of such cases has significant consequences for the design of the statutory procedures by which A can claim possession (**2.86–2.92**). Secondly, in *McDonald v McDonald* (2016), the court refused to allow B to invoke Article 8 when resisting an application for possession made by A, a private landlord (see **2.77–2.79**). It is significant that, in doing so, the court referred to the need, recognized in the structure of the Housing Act 1988, for such landlords to have a 'high degree of certainty that, if they follow the correct procedures and comply with their own obligations, they will be able to regain possession of the property'. In considering that legislation, the Supreme Court also emphasized that:

> In the field of proprietary rights between parties neither of whom is a public authority, the state should be allowed to lay down rules which are of general application, with a view to ensuring consistency of application and certainty of outcome. Those are two essential ingredients of the rule of law and [allowing Article 8 to be invoked] would involve diluting those rules in relation to possession actions in the private rented sector.

**12.36** Of course, the Supreme Court in *McDonald* was dealing with a specific statutory scheme which gave effect to a clear legislative policy to encourage private letting by allowing private landlords to control the terms on which property is rented and giving such landlords certainty as to how and when they can recover possession. Nonetheless, there is also a wider value, seen throughout land law, to parties having certainty as to their rights in land. That certainty is necessarily compromised if the exercise of such rights is subjected to a proportionality test. The current position seems to be that, where the property right is held by a public body, such a test may apply, as the European Convention on Human Rights is aimed at controlling the state and its emanations, and as public bodies are in any case subject to public law restraints (such as a disability from acting in a wholly unreasonable way) when exercising their rights. In such cases, then, the court has to look beyond the formal aspects of the content, acquisition, and defences questions and must also ask if the action of the public body is proportionate, given the particular factual circumstances of the case. Where, however, a private individual or body wishes to rely on their contractual or proprietary rights in relation to land, certainty is prioritized: part of the value of such a right to a private party consists precisely in the freedom to assert the right as he or she wishes. The general, formal concepts of land law, like the particular statutory scheme considered in *McDonald*, may exclude many seemingly important contextual factors, but this does at least give parties the ability 'to know exactly where they stand'.

# The Impact of Regulation

12.37    At various points in this book, we have considered how regulatory rules, although not directly conferring any private rights to use land, may be important in controlling how, in particular contexts, a party may act. In relation to mortgages, for example, the regulation of the credit market, by affecting the behaviour of lenders, can influence not only the terms of a mortgage, but also a lender's attitude to its enforcement (**8.36–8.39**). Such regulation is often motivated by contextual demands and, whilst not directly affecting the conceptual legal rules, it clearly has a practical effect on the parties' transactions.

12.38    In considering the operation of the conceptual rules of land law, therefore, it is often important to be aware of the regulatory background. A good example is provided by the decision of the Supreme Court in *Scott v Southern Pacific Mortgages Ltd* (2015), which we have encountered at a number of points in this book. The Supreme Court's approach in that case can be seen as favouring a conceptual approach, as it addressed a number of technical questions as to the content, acquisition, and defences questions. In particular it decided that the right of occupation of Mrs Scott (B) was only a personal right against the nominee of the mortgage rescue company (A), and so it could not bind the lender, Southern Pacific (C), even though B had been in actual occupation of the land throughout. This meant that, whilst B had sold her home to A on the basis of a promise that she could remain in occupation for as long as she wished, B was, through no fault of her own, obliged to leave her home.

12.39    The decision in *Scott*, like the three cases examined in **Chapter 1**, provides a good example not only of the structure of many land law cases, but also of the difference between conceptual and contextual approaches. Lord Collins, for example, noted that: 'It is impossible not to feel great sympathy with Mrs Scott and the former home owners in her position, who may have been not only the victims of a fraud which tricked them out of their homes, but also of unprofessional and dishonest behaviour by the solicitors appointed to act for them.' Nonetheless, he immediately made a point in favour of the conceptual approach, according to which the general merits are secondary to the question of whether or not B had a property right capable of binding C: 'there is also an important public interest in the security of registered transactions'.

**12.40**  Given the discussion in this chapter, it is also worth noting that Lady Hale, whilst agreeing with the result in the case, stated that it was 'harsh' and raised the possibility that its effect might be limited by asking: 'Should there not come a point when a vendor who has been tricked out of her property can assert her rights even against a subsequent purchaser or mortgagee?' and also by considering whether C might be said to have acted 'irresponsibly'. She also stated that: 'There ought to be some middle way between the "all or nothing" approach of the present law.' It may be that such a middle way refers simply to the indemnity provisions of the Land Registration Act 2002, which provide a means for an unsuccessful party, in some cases, to receive compensation from the funds administered by Land Registry. Or Lady Hale's comment could be taken as a broader challenge to one of the conceptual premises of property law, upheld by the House of Lords in *Ainsworth* (1965, **12.14**): that B's right either binds C, or it does not.

**12.41**  The specific harshness to B in *Scott* has, however, now been removed by less far-reaching means. The mortgage rescue deal in that case had taken place in 2005. Such deals, common at the time, were often marketed to B as a means to remain in his or her home despite difficulties in meeting mortgage repayments. B sold his or her home to A, using the proceeds to pay off the existing mortgage, and A then leased the home back to B, promising to allow B to remain in occupation for as long as B wished. The problem for B was that B might be pressured by the circumstances into selling the house for an unnecessarily large discount and, as shown by *Scott*, the supposedly secure right to occupy the home might turn out to be a mirage, especially if A was unable to keep up the payments on the mortgage it used to finance its purchase of the home. Concerns about the transactions were significant enough to trigger a study by the Office of Fair Trading. It found, in 2008, that home owners entering such schemes often failed to understand the risks involved, and that solicitors provided by the mortgage rescue companies to give advice to those home owners were not always independent.

**12.42**  Lord Collins in *Scott* then takes up the story:

> In 2009 the Financial Services Authority recommended that consumer detriment occurring in this market warranted a fast regulatory response, and in the same year sale and rent back transactions became a regulated activity under s 19 of the Financial Services and Markets Act 2000. As a result, in February 2012 the FSA reported that most sale and rent back transactions were unaffordable or unsuitable and should never have been sold, but that in practice the entire market had shut down. They are now very rare.

**12.43**  By controlling the activities of lenders, then, regulation has meant that, although the conceptual rules that led to the harsh result in *Scott* have not been changed, the prospect of those rules working injustice in the specific context of mortgage rescue schemes has been dramatically reduced.

## Context as Alibi?

**12.44** The decision in *Scott* provides a useful way to draw together the main threads of this chapter. The *context* of the case is very similar to that in *Berrisford v Mexfield* (2012, **12.7**): B had sold her home through a mortgage rescue scheme, on the basis that, if certain conditions were met, she would be able to carry on living in that home for as long as she wished. Although B had met those conditions, she was at risk of losing her home (in *Berrisford*, it would have been a case of losing the home to A, the cooperative with which B made the mortgage rescue agreement; in *Scott*, the home would be lost to C, the third party that financed the acquisition of the home by the mortgage rescue company). In *Berrisford*, the Supreme Court was able to manipulate the relevant *concepts* to reach a result that accorded with the contextual demands of justice: B was free to remain in occupation. In *Scott*, despite expressing sympathy for B's plight, the Supreme Court's interpretation of the relevant technical concepts meant that C was free to remove B from her home.

**12.45** In *Scott*, we saw that, at least for the future, the regulation of such mortgage rescue agreements has provided protection for home owners. Regulation can thus allow the concepts to continue unchanged whilst also preventing those concepts from working injustice in a specific context. On one view, this can be a neat way to reconcile the competing concerns noted by Lord Collins in *Scott*: to protect home owners from the risk of disadvantageous mortgage rescue schemes without reforming the doctrinal rules which draw, for good reason, a clear distinction between personal rights and property rights.

**12.46** A similar view, indeed, can be taken of the role of equity, or even of human rights: by mitigating the harshness of conceptual property law rules, such context-focused interventions can allow those conceptual rules to keep their general nature. In the vast majority of cases, then, the conceptual rules can continue to apply, providing certainty and giving parties and the courts a reasonably efficient means of knowing their rights. Part of the justification for the strictness of those conceptual rules is that a 'safety valve' exists in specific contexts where the concepts, left to themselves, would work an injustice. Historically, equity often provided such a safety valve (Smith (2014)); more recently, human rights and regulation have played a similar role. With a registration scheme, the possibility of an indemnity payment can perhaps be seen in the same way: it may provide financial compensation for a party who loses out through the operation of strict registration rules.

**12.47** From a different perspective, however, these varied ways of tempering the strictness of the conceptual rules can be seen as excuses: as *alibis* (to use the term of Rudden (1992)) that prevent us from questioning the validity of those conceptual rules. Indeed, in cases such as *Berrisford* (and also, perhaps, *Bruton*, **12.7**), an unexpected but limited change to the content of those rules can also be seen as a fudge which allows the deeper flaws in the conceptual rules to go unexamined.

**12.48** A more fundamental challenge to the orthodox view of land law consists of going further still and questioning not just specific concepts applied in land law (eg the distinction between personal rights and property rights) but the very notion of relying on concepts, rather than contexts, to decide who gets to use land, and how they get to use it. Such critical approaches have been applied to many different areas of law, and land law is no exception: for a stimulating example, see Fox O'Mahony (2014).

## A Final Thought

**12.49**    As we have seen throughout this book, land law concerns private rights to use land, and so we need answers to questions as to the nature of those rights (the *content* question), as to how people get such rights (the *acquisition* question), and as to what happens when such rights conflict (the *defences* question). The special features of land as a permanent, finite resource mean that certainty as to parties' rights is crucial. As Dixon (2015) has put it:

> in the field of property law, doctrinal analysis which seeks to identify and codify the rules, based on statute and precedent, supports what is seen to be a core function of property law. Doctrinal analysis has a value in property law that almost speaks for itself.

**12.50**    Books such as this one focus on such doctrinal analysis as it provides the best way to learn and understand the current rules of land law. As Dixon rightly notes, this of course does not mean that doctrinal analysis is the *only* way to examine land law. A helpful recent book gives examples of a number of different methods of researching property law, including, for example, theoretical, socio-legal, empirical, comparative, critical, and economic approaches (Bright and Blandy (2015)). Such approaches would, however, be of limited use if not based on a solid foundation as to how land law currently operates. It may be a cliché, but this is a particularly appropriate point to say it: achieving a sound understanding of the current rules need not be the end of your thinking about land law, nor even the beginning of the end, but it is perhaps the end of the beginning.

## FURTHER READING

Bright, S, '*Manchester City Council v Pinnock* (2010): Shifting Ideas of Ownership of Land' in N Gravells (ed), *Landmark Cases in Land Law* (Oxford: Hart Publishing, 2013).

Bright, S and Blandy, S (eds), *Researching Property Law* (Basingstoke: Palgrave Macmillan, 2015) (reviewed by B McFarlane (2017) 133 LQR 166).

Dixon, M, 'A Doctrinal Approach to Property Law Scholarship: Who Cares and Why?' in S Bright and S Blandy (eds), *Researching Property Law* (Basingstoke: Palgrave Macmillan, 2015).

Fitzjames Stephen, Sir J, 'Codification in India and England' (1872) 1 The Law Magazine 963, 980.

Fox O'Mahony, L, 'Property Outsiders and the Hidden Politics of Doctrinalism' (2014) 62 CLP 409.

Goymour, A, 'Mistaken Registration of Land: Exploding the Myth of "Title by Registration"' (2013) 72 CLJ 617.

Harris, J, 'Legal Doctrine and Interests in Land' in J Eekelaar and J Bell (eds), *Oxford Essays in Jurisprudence* (Oxford: Oxford University Press, 1987).

Jackson, N, 'Title by Registration and Concealed Overriding Interests' (2003) 119 LQR 660.

Law Commission Report No 307, *Cohabitation: The Financial Consequences of Relationship Breakdown* (2007).

Law Commission Report No 271, *Land Registration for the Twenty-First Century: A Conveyancing Revolution* (2001).

Law Commission Consultation Paper No 227, *Updating the Land Registration Act 2002* (2016).

McFarlane, B, *The Structure of Property Law* (Oxford: Hart Publishing, 2008), pp 1–14.

Mee, J, 'Burns v Burns: The Villain of the Piece?' in S Gilmore et al (eds), *Landmark Cases in Family Law* (Oxford: Hart Publishing, 2011).

Rudden, B, 'Equity as Alibi' in S Goldstein (ed), *Equity and Contemporary Legal Developments* (Jerusalem: Harry and Michael Sacher Institute for Legislative Research and Comparative Law and Hebrew University of Jerusalem, 1992).

Smith, H, 'Property, Equity, and the Rule of Law' in L Austin and D Klimchuk (eds), *Private Law and the Rule of Law* (Oxford: Oxford University Press, 2014).

Swadling, W, 'The Common Intention Trust in the House of Lords: An Opportunity Missed?' (2007) 123 LQR 511.

Walsh, R, 'Stability and Predictability in English Property Law—The Impact of Article 8 of the European Convention on Human Rights Reassessed' (2015) 131 LQR 585.

# SELF-TEST QUESTIONS

1   Are there good reasons for thinking that certainty is a particularly important concern in land law?

2   What might be the disadvantages of a judicial approach that focuses entirely on applying the relevant legal concepts and pays no heed to the particular context of a dispute?

3   Do you think it is possible to classify the approaches of individual judges according to their place on a spectrum with a focus on concepts at one end, and a focus on contexts at the other?

4   What are the disadvantages of judicial reform of land law? What are the disadvantages of legislative reform of land law?

5   Which area or areas of land law do you think are most in need of reform? How should such reform take place?

# Bibliography

## Chapter 1

Birks, PBH, 'Before We Begin: Five Keys to Land Law' in S Bright and J Dewar (eds), *Land Law: Themes and Perspectives* (Oxford: Oxford University Press, 1998).

Law Commission Report No 271, *Land Registration for the Twenty-First Century: A Conveyancing Revolution* (2001).

McFarlane, B, *The Structure of Property Law* (Oxford: Hart Publishing, 2008), pp 1–14.

O'Connor, P, 'Registration of Title in England and Australia' in E Cooke (ed), *Modern Studies in Property Law: Vol 2* (Oxford: Hart Publishing, 2003).

Smith, L, 'Fusion and Tradition' in S Degeling and J Edelman (eds), *Equity in Commercial Law* (Sydney: Law Company of Australasia, 2005).

## Chapter 2

Allen, T, *Property and the Human Rights Act 1998* (Oxford: Hart Publishing, 2005).

Bright, S, '*Manchester City Council v Pinnock* (2010)' in N Gravells (ed), *Landmark Cases in Land Law* (Oxford: Hart Publishing, 2013), ch 11.

Buyse, A, 'Strings Attached: The Concept of "Home" in the Case Law of the European Court of Human Rights' [2006] 3 EHRLR 294.

Fox, L, *Conceptualising Home: Theories, Law and Policies* (Oxford: Hart Publishing, 2006).

Goymour, A, 'Proprietary Claims and Human Rights—A "Reservoir of Entitlement"?' (2006) 65 CLJ 696.

Goymour, A, 'Property & Housing' in D Hoffman (ed), *The Impact of the UK Human Rights Act 1998 on Private Law* (Cambridge: Cambridge University Press, 2011), ch 12.

Gray, K, 'Land Law and Human Rights' in L Tee (ed), *Land Law: Issues, Debates, Policy* (Cullompton: Willan, 2002), ch 7.

Hickman, T, *Public Law after the Human Rights Act* (Oxford: Hart Publishing, 2010).

Howell, J, 'The Human Rights Act 1998: Land, Private Citizens, and the Common Law' (2007) 123 LQR 618.

Lees, E, 'Actions for Possession in the Context of Political Protest: The Role of Article 1, Protocol 1 and Horizontal Effect' [2013] Conv 211.

Leigh, I, 'Horizontal Rights, the Human Rights Act and Privacy: Lessons from the Commonwealth?' (1999) 48 ICLQ 57.

Nield, S, 'Clash of the Titans: Article 8, Occupiers and their Homes' in S Bright (ed), *Modern Studies in Property Law* (Oxford: Hart Publishing, 2011), vol 6.

Nield, S, 'Article 8 Respect for the Home: A Human Property Right' (2013a) 24 KLJ 147.

Nield, S, 'Strasbourg Triggers Another Article 8 Debate' [2013b] Conv 148.

Nield, S, 'Shutting the Door on Horizontal Effect' [2017] Conv forthcoming.

Nield, S and Hopkins, N, 'Human Rights and Mortgage Repossession: Beyond Property Law Using Article 8' (2013) 33 LS 431.

Peroni, L and Timmer, A, 'Vulnerable Groups: The Promise of an Emerging Concept in European Human Rights Convention Law' (2013) 11 IJCL 1056.

Walsh, R, 'Stability and Predictability in English Property Law—The Impact of Article 8 of the European Convention on Human Rights Reassessed' (2015) 131 LQR 585.

## Chapter 3

Battersby, G, 'Informally Created Interests' in S Bright and J Dewar (eds), *Land Law: Themes and Perspectives* (Oxford, Oxford University Press, 1998).

Birks, PBH, 'Before We Begin: Five Keys to Land Law' in S Bright and J Dewar (eds), *Land Law: Themes and Perspectives* (Oxford: Oxford University Press, 1998).

Briggs, A, 'Contractual Licences: A Reply' [1983] Conv 285, 290–1.

Douglas, S, 'The Content of a Freehold: A "Right to Use" Land' in N Hopkins (ed), *Modern Studies in Property Law: Vol 7* (Oxford: Hart Publishing, 2013).

Edelman, J, 'Two Fundamental Questions for the Law of Trusts' (2013) 129 LQR 66.

Epstein, RA, 'Notice and Freedom of Contract in the Law of Servitudes' (1981–2) 55 S Cal L Rev 1353.

Gardner, S, '"Persistent Rights" Appraised' in N Hopkins (ed), *Modern Studies in Property Law: Vol 7* (Oxford: Hart Publishing, 2013).

Gray, K and Gray, SF, 'The Rhetoric of Realty' in J Getzler (ed), *Rationalizing Property, Equity and Trusts: Essays in Honour of Edward Burn* (Oxford: Oxford University Press, 2003).

Harris, JW, *Property and Justice* (Oxford: Oxford University Press, 1996), pp 68–75.

Hill, J, 'The Termination of Bare Licences' (2001) 60 CLJ 87.

Law Commission Report No 327, *Making Land Work: Easements, Covenants and Profits à Prendre* (2011).

McFarlane, B, 'Constructive Trusts Arising on a Receipt of Property *Sub Conditione*' (2004) 120 LQR 667.

McFarlane, B, 'The *Numerus Clausus* Principle and Covenants Relating to Land' in S Bright (ed), *Modern Studies in Property Law: Vol 6* (Oxford: Hart Publishing, 2011).

McFarlane, B and Stevens, R, 'The Nature of Equitable Property' [2010] 4 J Eq 1.

Merrill, TW and Smith, HE, 'Optimal Standardization in the Law of Property: The *Numerus Clausus* Principle' (2000–1) 110 Yale LJ 3.

Penner, JE, 'The (True) Nature of a Beneficiary's Equitable Proprietary Interest under a Trust' (2014) 27 Can J L Juris 473.

Rudden, B, 'Economic Theory v Property Law: The *Numerus Clausus* Problem' in J Eekelaar and J Bell (eds), *Oxford Essays in Jurisprudence* (Oxford: Oxford University Press, 1987).

Rushworth, A and Scott, A, 'Total Chaos' [2010] LMCLQ 536.

Swadling, W, 'Opening the *Numerus Clausus*' (2000) 116 LQR 358.

Swadling, W, 'Property' in A Burrows (ed), *English Private Law* (3rd edn, Oxford: Oxford University Press, 2013), 4.23.

Turner, PG, 'Consequential Economic Loss and the Trust Beneficiary' (2010) 69 CLJ 445.

Williams, I, 'The Certainty of Term Requirement in Leases: Nothing Lasts Forever' (2015) 74 CLJ 592.

## Chapter 4

Adams, JE, 'You've No Option: More Consequences of Section 2 of the Law of Property (Miscellaneous Provisions) Act 1989' [1990] Conv 9.

Birks, PBH, 'Before We Begin: Five Keys to Land Law' in S Bright and J Dewar (eds), *Land Law: Themes and Perspectives* (Oxford, Oxford University Press, 1998).

Cooke, E, 'Adverse Possession, Problems of Title in Registered Land' (1994) 14 LS 1.

Cooke, E, *The New Law of Land Registration* (Oxford: Hart Publishing, 2003).

Cooke, E, 'Title in Registered Land' (2004) 14 LS 1.

Cooper, S, 'Regulating Fallibility in Registered Land Titles' (2013) 72 CLJ 341.

Cowan, D, Fox O'Mahony, L, and Cobb, N, *Great Debates: Property Law* (Basingstoke: Palgrave Macmillan, 2012).

Dixon, M, 'The Reform of Property Law and the Land Registration Act 2002: A Risk Assessment' [2003] Conv 136.

Dixon, M, 'Invalid Contracts, Estoppel and Constructive Trusts' [2005] Conv 247.

Dixon, M, 'Criminal Squatting and Adverse Possession: The Best Solution?' (2014) 17 JHL 94.

Dockray, M, 'Why Do We Need Adverse Possession?' [1985] Conv 272.

Goymour, A, 'Mistaken Registrations of Land: Exploding the Myth of "Title by Registration"' (2013) 72 CLJ 617.

Griffiths, G, 'Part Performance: Still Trying to Replace the Irreplaceable' [2002] Conv 216.

Land Registry, Annual Report and Accounts 2015/16 (2016).

Law Commission Consultation Paper No 227, *Updating the Land Registration Act 2002* (2016).

Law Commission Report No 164, *Transfer of Land Formalities for Contracts for Sale etc. of Land* (1987).

Law Commission Report No 254, *Land Registration for the Twenty-First Century: A Consultative Document* (1998).

Law Commission Report No 271, *Land Registration for the Twenty-First Century: A Conveyancing Revolution* (2001).

McFarlane, B, *The Law of Proprietary Estoppel* (Oxford, Oxford University Press, 2014).

Milne, P, 'Mistaken Belief and Adverse Possession—Mistaken Interpretation?' [2012] Conv 343.

Neuberger of Abbotsbury, Lord, 'The Stuffing of Minerva's Owl: Taxonomy and Taxidermy in Equity' (2009) 68 CLJ 537.

Oakley, AJ, 'Conveyancing Contracts by Exchange of Letters' (1995) 54 CLJ 502.

Radley-Gardner, O, 'Civilised Squatting' (2005) 25 OJLS 727.

Ruoff, TBF, *An Englishman Looks at the Torrens System* (Sydney: The Law Book Co, 1957).

Ruoff, TBF et al, *The Law and Practice of Registered Conveyancing* (5th edn, London: Stevens, 1986).

Stark, J, 'The Option to Purchase: A Legal Chameleon' [1992] JBL 296.

Swann, SJA, 'Part Performance: Back from the Dead' [1997] Conv 293.

Xu, L, 'What Do We Protect in Land Registration?' (2013) 129 LQR 477.

## Chapter 5

Allan, G, 'Once a Fraud, Forever a Fraud: The Time Honoured Doctrine of Parol Agreement Trusts' (2014) 34 LS 419.

Barlow, A, Duncan, S, James, G, and Park, A, 'Just a Piece of Paper? Marriage and Cohabitation' in A Park et al (eds), *British Social Attitudes: The 18th Report: Public Policy, Social Ties* (London: Sage, 2001).

Chambers, R, *Resulting Trusts* (Oxford: Oxford University Press, 1997).

Cooke, E, 'Estoppel and Reliance' (1995) 111 LQR 389.

Cowan, D, Fox O'Mahony, L, and Cobb, N, *Great Debates in Property Law* (Basingstoke: Palgrave Macmillan, 2012).

Dewar, J, 'Land, Law and the Family Home' in S Bright and J Dewar (eds), *Land Law: Themes and Perspectives* (Oxford: Oxford University Press, 1998).

Dixon, M, 'Proprietary Estoppel and Formalities in Land Law and the Land Registration Act 2002: A Theory of Unconscionability' in E Cooke (ed), *Modern Studies in Property Law: Vol 2* (Oxford: Hart Publishing, 2007).

Dixon, M, 'Confining and Defining Proprietary Estoppel: The Role of Unconscionability' (2010) 30 LS 408.

Dixon, M, 'Editor's Notebook: The Still Not Ended Never-Ending Story' [2012] Conv 83.

Feltham, JD, 'Informal Trusts and Third Parties' [1987] Conv 246.

Flynn, L and Lawson, A, 'Gender, Sexuality and the Doctrine of Detrimental Reliance' [1995] Fem LS 105.

Fox O'Mahony, L, 'Property Outsiders and the Hidden Politics of Doctrinalism' (2014) 67 CLP 409.

Gardner, S, 'Rethinking Family Property' (1993) 109 LQR 263.

Gardner, S, 'The Remedial Discretion in Proprietary Estoppel Again' (2006) 122 LQR 492.

Gardner, S, 'Reliance-Based Constructive Trusts' in C Mitchell (ed), *Resulting and Constructive Trusts* (Oxford: Hart Publishing, 2009).

Gardner, S, 'Problems in Family Property' (2013) 72 CLJ 301.

Gardner, S and Davidson, K, 'The Future of *Stack v Dowden*' (2011) 127 LQR 13.

Glover, N and Todd, P, 'The Myth of Common Intention' (1996) 16 LS 325.

Hayward, A, ' "Family Property" and the Process of Familialisation of Property Law' (2012) 24 CFLQ 284.

Hayward, A, 'Common Intention Constructive Trusts and the Role of Imputation in Theory and Practice' [2016] Conv 233.

Hopkins, N, *The Informal Acquisition of Rights in Land* (London: Sweet & Maxwell, 2000).

Hopkins, N, 'Understanding Unconscionability in Proprietary Estoppel' (2004) 20 JCL 210.

Hopkins, N, 'Conscience, Discretion and the Creation of Property Rights' (2006) 26 LS 475.

Hopkins, N, 'Regulating Trusts of the Home: Private Law and Social Policy' (2009) 125 LQR 310.

Hopkins, N, 'The Relevance of Context in Property Law: A Case for Judicial Restraint?' (2011) 31 LS 175.

Hopkins, N, 'The *Pallant v Morgan* "Equity"— Again: *Crossco No 4 Unlimited v Jolan Ltd*' [2012] Conv 327.

Law Commission Report No 274, *Eighth Programme of Law Reform* (2001).

Law Commission Report No 278, *Sharing Homes: A Discussion Paper* (2002).

Law Commission Report No 307, *Cohabitation: The Financial Consequences of Relationship Breakdown* (2007).

Law Commission Report No 320, *The Illegality Defence* (2010).

Lord Neuberger of Abbotsbury, 'The Stuffing of Minerva's Owl? Taxonomy and Taxidermy in Equity' (2009) 68 CLJ 537.

Low, K, 'Nonfeasance in Equity' (2012) 128 LQR 63.

McFarlane, B, 'Identifying Property Rights—A Reply to Mr Watt' [2003a] Conv 473.

McFarlane, B, 'Proprietary Estoppel and Third Parties After the Land Registration Act 2002' (2003b) 62 CLJ 661.

McFarlane, B, 'Constructive Trusts Arising on Receipt of Property *Sub Conditione*' (2004) 120 LQR 667.

McFarlane, B, 'Proprietary Estoppel and Failed Contractual Negotiations' [2005] Conv 501.

McFarlane, B, *The Structure of Property Law* (Oxford: Hart Publishing, 2008).

McFarlane, B, *The Law of Proprietary Estoppel* (Oxford: Oxford University Press, 2014).

McFarlane, B, 'Equitable Estoppel as a Cause of Action: Neither One Thing nor One Other' in S Degeling and J Edelman (eds), *Contracts in Commercial Law* (Sydney: Thompson Lawbook Co, 2016).

McFarlane, B and Sales, P, 'Promises, Detriment, and Liability: Lessons from Proprietary Estoppel' (2015) 131 LQR 610.

McGhee, J (ed), *Snell's Equity* (33rd edn, London: Sweet & Maxwell, 2014).

Mee, J, *The Property Rights of Cohabitees* (Oxford: Hart Publishing, 1999).

Mee, J, 'Expectation and Proprietary Estoppel Remedies' in M Dixon (ed), *Modern Studies in Property Law* (Oxford: Hart Publishing, 2009), vol 5.

Mee, J, 'Proprietary Estoppel, Promises and Mistaken Belief' in S Bright (ed), *Modern Studies in Property Law* (Oxford: Hart Publishing, 2011), vol 6.

Nield, S, 'Constructive Trusts and Estoppel' (2003) 23 LS 311.

Oakley, AJ, *Constructive Trusts* (3rd edn, London: Sweet & Maxwell, 1996).

Sloan, B, 'Keeping up with the *Jones* Case: Establishing Constructive Trusts in "Sole Legal Owner" Scenarios' (2015) 35 LS 226.

Smith, H, 'Property, Equity, and the Rule of Law' in L Austin and D Klimchuk (eds), *Private Law and the Rule of Law* (Oxford: Oxford University Press, 2014).

Smith, SA, 'Duties, Liabilities, and Damages' (2012) 125 Harv L Rev 1727.

Swadling, W, 'The Nature of the Trust in *Rochefoucauld v Boustead*' in C Mitchell (ed), *Resulting and Constructive Trusts* (Oxford: Hart Publishing, 2009).

Swadling, W, 'The Fiction of the Constructive Trust' (2011) 64 CLP 399.

Turner, P, 'Understanding the Constructive Trust between Vendor and Purchaser' (2012) 128 LQR 582.

Worthington, S, *Equity* (2nd edn, Oxford: Oxford University Press, 2006).

Yip, M, 'The *Pallant v Morgan* Equity Reconsidered' (2013) 33 LS 459.

Youdan, TG, 'Formalities for Trusts of Land and the Doctrine in *Rochefoucauld v Boustead*' (1984) 43 CLJ 306.

Youdan, TG, 'Informal Trusts and Third Parties: A Response' [1988] Conv 267.

## Chapter 6

Baker, A, 'The Judicial Approach to "Exceptional Circumstances" in Bankruptcy: The Impact of the Human Rights Act' [2010] Conv 352.

Bridge, S, 'Assisting Suicide Rendered Financially Painless' (1998) 57 CLJ 31.

Bright, S, 'Occupation Rents and the Trusts of Land and Appointment of Trustees Act 1996: From Property to Welfare' [2009] Conv 378.

Buyse, A, 'Strings Attached: The Concept of Home in the Case Law of the ECHR' [2006] 3 EHRLR 294.

*Coke upon Littleton* (19th edn, 1832).

Cowan, D and Hunter, C, ' "Yeah but, No But", or Just "No"? Life after *Pinnock v Powell*' [2012] JHL 58.

Crown, BC, 'Severance of Joint Tenancy by Partial Alienation' (2001) 117 LQR 477.

Dixon, M, 'To Sell or Not to Sell: That is the Question. The Irony of the Trusts of Land and Appointment of Trustees Act 1996' (2011) 70 CLJ 579.

Fox, L, *Conceptualising Home: Theories, Laws and Policies* (Oxford: Hart Publishing, 2006).

Gardner, S 'Matrimonial Relief between Equitable Co-habitants 1: Liquidating Beneficial Interests Otherwise than by Sale' [2014] Conv 95.

Harpum, C, 'The Law Commission and Land Law' in S Bright and J Dewar (eds), *Land Law Themes and Perspectives* (Oxford: Oxford University Press, 1998).

Harpum, C, et al (eds) *Megarry and Wade: The Law of Real Property*, (7th edn, London: Sweet & Maxwell, 2008).

Hopkins, N, 'The Trusts of Land and Appointment of Trustees Act 1996' [1996] Conv 411.

Hopkins, N, 'Regulating Trusts of the Home: Private Law and Social Policy' (2009) 125 LQR 310.

Law Commission Report No 181, *Transfer of Land: Trusts of Land* (1989).

Law Commission Report No 331, *Intestacy and Family Provisions Claims on Death* (2011).

Law Commission Working Paper No 94, *Trusts of Land* (1985).

Mee, J, 'Ambulation, Severance and the Common Intention Constructive Trust' (2012) 128 LQR 500.

Nield, S, 'To Sever or Not to Sever: The Effect of a Mortgage by One Joint Tenant' [2001] Conv 462, 462–3.

Pascoe, S, 'Section 15 of the Trusts of Land and Appointment of Trustees Act 1996: A Change in the Law?' [2000] Conv 315.

Pascoe, S, 'Right to Occupy Under a Trust of Land: Muddled Legislative Logic' [2006] Conv 54.

Pawlowski, M and Brown, J, 'Co-ownership and Severance After *Stack*' (2013a) 27 Tru LI 59.

Pawlowski, M and Brown, J, 'Joint Purchasers and the Presumption of Joint Beneficial Ownership—A Matter of Informed Choice?' (2013b) 27 Tru LI 3.

Probert, R, 'Creditors and Section 15 of the Trusts of Land and Appointment of Trustees Act 1996: First Among Equals' [2001] Conv 61.

Radley-Gardner, O, 'Section 15 of TOLATA, or, the Importance of Being Earners' [2003] Web JCLI 5.

Saunders, P, *A Nation of Home Owners* (Abingdon: Routledge, 1980).

Smith RJ, 'Trusts of Land Reform' [1989] Conv 12.

Smith, RJ, *Plural Ownership* (Oxford: Oxford University Press, 2005).

Tee, L, 'Severance Revisited' [1995] Conv 105.

## Chapter 7

Bignell, J, 'Forfeiture: A Long Overdue Reform?' [2007] L&T Rev 140.

Blandy, S, Dupuis, A, and Dixon, J, *Multi-Owned Housing: Law, Power and Practice* (Aldershot: Ashgate, 2010).

Bridge, S, 'Former Tenants, Future Liabilities and the Privity of Contract Principle' (1996) 55 CLJ 313.

Bridge, S, 'Leases: Contract, Property and Status' in L Tee (ed), *Land Law: Issues, Debates, Policy* (Cullompton: Willan, 2002).

Bridge, S, '*Street v Mountford* (1985); *AG Securities v Vaughan; Antoniades v Villiers* (1988): Tenancies and Licences: Halting the Revolution' in N Gravells (ed), *Landmark Cases in Land Law* (Oxford: Hart Publishing, 2013).

Bright, S, 'Uncertainty in Leases—Is It a Vice?' (1993) 13 LS 38.

Bright, S, 'Avoiding Tenancy Legislation: Sham and Contracting Out Revisited' (2002) 61 CLJ 146.

Bright, S, *Landlord and Tenant Law in Context* (Oxford: Hart Publishing, 2007), pp 30–3.

Davey, M, 'The Regulation of Long Residential Leases' in E Cooke (ed), *Modern Studies in Property Law: Vol 3* (Oxford: Hart Publishing, 2005), ch 10.

Dixon, M, 'The Non-Proprietary Lease: The Rise of the Feudal Phoenix' (2000) 59 CLJ 25.

Gardner, S, 'Equity, Estate Contracts and the Judicature Acts: *Walsh v Lonsdale* Revisited' (1987) 7 OJLS 60.

Gravells, N, 'Forfeiture of Leases for Breach of Covenant' [2006] JBL 830.

Gray, K, 'Property in Thin Air' (1991) 50 CLJ 252.

Harris, JW, *Property and Justice* (Oxford: Oxford University Press, 1996), pp 68–75.

Hill, J, 'Intention and the Creation of Proprietary Rights: Are Leases Different?' (1996) 16 LS 200.

Law Commission Report No 174, *Landlord and Tenant: Privity of Contract and Estate* (1988).

Law Commission Report No 297, *Renting Homes* (2006a), esp Parts 1 and 2.

Law Commission Report No 303, *Termination of Tenancies for Tenant Default* (2006b).

McFarlane, B, 'Proprietary Estoppel and Failed Contractual Negotiations' [2005] Conv 501.

McFarlane, B and Simpson, E, 'Tackling Avoidance' in J Getzler (ed), *Rationalizing Property, Equity and Trusts: Essays in Honour of Edward Burn* (Oxford: Oxford University Press, 2003).

Merrill, T, 'Property and the Right to Exclude' (1998) 77 Nebraska L Rev 730.

Neuberger of Abbotsbury, Lord, 'The Stuffing of Minerva's Owl: Taxonomy and Taxidermy in Equity' (2009) 68 CLJ 537.

Roberts, N, 'The *Bruton* Tenancy: A Matter of Relativity' [2012] Conv 87.

Routley, P, 'Tenancies and Estoppel: After *Bruton v London & Quadrant Housing Trust*' (2000) 63 MLR 424.

Sparkes, P, 'Co-Tenants, Joint Tenants and Tenants in Common' (1989) 18 Anglo-Am L Rev 151.

Van der Merwe, C and Smith, P, 'Commonhold—A Critical Appraisal' in E Cooke (ed), *Modern Studies in Property Law: Vol 3* (Oxford: Hart Publishing, 2005), ch 11.

Williams, I, 'The Certainty of Term Requirement in Leases: Nothing Lasts Forever' (2015) 74 CLJ 592.

## Chapter 8

Bigwood, R, 'Undue Influence: Impaired Consent or Wicked Exploitation' (1996) 16 OJLS 503.

Birks, PBH and Chin, NY, 'On the Nature of Undue Influence' in J Beatson and D Friedman (eds), *Good Faith and Fault in Contract Law* (Oxford: Oxford University Press, 1995), ch 3.

Bright, S and Whitehouse, L, *Information, Advice and Representation in Housing Possession Cases* (Universities of Oxford and Hull, 2014).

Brown, S, 'The Consumer Credit Act 2006; Real Additional Mortgagor Protection?' [2007] Conv 316.

Capper, D, 'Undue Influence and Unconscionability: A Rationalisation' (1998) 114 LQR 479.

Chen-Wishart, M, 'The *O'Brien* Principle and Substantive Unfairness' (1997) 56 CLJ 60.

Clarke, A, 'Further Implications of Section 36 Administration of Justice Act' [1983] Conv 293.

Clarke, A, 'Security Interests in Property' in JW Harris (ed), *Property Problems from Genes to Pension Funds* (London: Kluwer, 1997).

Department of Trade and Industry, 'Fair, Clear and Competitive: The Consumer Credit Market in the 21st Century' (2003).

Devenney, J and Chandler, A, 'Unconscionability and the Taxonomy of Undue Influence' [2007] JBL 541.

Dixon, M, 'Sorry We've Sold Your Home: Mortgagees and Their Possessory Rights' (1999) 58 CLJ 281.

Financial Conduct Authority, 'The Turner Review: A Regulatory Response to the Global Banking Crisis' (2008).

Financial Conduct Authority, 'Detailed rules for the price cap on high-cost short-term credit', Policy Statement 14/16 (2014).

Frisby, S, 'Making a Silk Purse Out of a Pig's Ear: *Medforth v Blake & Ors*' (2000) 63 MLR 413.

Haley, M, 'Mortgage Default: Possession, Relief and Judicial Discretion' (1997) 17 LS 483.

Kaye, M, 'Equity's Treatment of Sexually Transmitted Debt' [1997] 5 Fem LS 35.

Law Commission Report No 204, *Land Mortgages* (1991).

Loi, KCF, 'Receiver's Power of Sale and Duty of Care' [2010] Conv 369.

McFarlane, B, *The Structure of Property Law* (Oxford: Hart Publishing, 2008).

McMurtry, L, 'Mortgage Default and Repossession: Procedure and Policy in the Post-*Norgan* Era' (2007) 58 NILQ 194.

McMurtry, L, 'Consumer Credit Act Mortgages: Unfair Terms, Time Orders and Judicial Discretion' [2010] JBL 107.

Ministry of Justice, 'Mortgages: Power of Sale and Residential Property', CP55/09 (2009).

Mokal, RJ, 'The Search for Someone to Save: A Defensive Case for the Priority of Secured Credit' (2002) 22 OJLS 687.

Nield, S, 'Charges, Possession and Human Rights: A Reappraisal of S 87(1) of the Law of Property Act 1925' in E Cooke (ed), *Modern Studies in Property Law: Vol 3* (Oxford: Hart Publishing, 2005).

Nield, S, 'Responsible Lending and Borrowing: Whereto Low-Cost Home Ownership?' (2010) 30 LS 610.

Nield, S, 'Mortgage Market Review: "Hard-Wired Commonsense?"' (2015) 38 J Consumer Policy 139.

Nield, S and Hopkins, N, 'Human Rights and Mortgage Repossession: Beyond Property Law Using Article 8' (2013) 33 LS 431.

O'Neill, C, 'The Mortgage Repossession (Protection of Tenants etc) Act 2010—Sufficient Protection for Tenants?' [2011] Conv 380.

Payne Committee Report, *Report of the Committee on the Enforcement of Judgment Debts* (Cmnd 3909, 1969).

Ramsay, I, 'Consumer Law, Regulatory Capitalism and New Learning in Regulation' (2006) 28 Sydney LR 9.

Sugarman, D and Warrington, R, 'Telling Stories: the Rights and Wrongs of the Equity of Redemption' in JW Harris (ed), *Property Problems: From Genes to Pension Funds* (London: Kluwer, 1997).

Wallace, A, 'Feels like I am doing it on my own: Examining the Synchronicity between Policy Responses and the Circumstances and Experiences of Borrowers in Arrears' (2012) 11 Social Policy and Society 117.

Wallace, A and Ford, J, 'Limiting Possessions? Managing Mortgage Arrears in a New Era' [2010] IJHP 133.

Watt, G, 'Mortgage Law as Legal Fiction' in E Cooke (ed), *Modern Studies in Property Law: Vol 3* (Oxford: Hart Publishing, 2007).

Whitehouse, L, 'The Mortgage Arrears Pre-action Protocol: An Opportunity Missed' (2009) 72 MLR 793.

## Chapter 9

Douglas, S, 'How to Reform Section 62 of the Law of Property Act 1925' [2015a] Conv 13.

Douglas, S, 'Reforming Implied Easements' (2015b) 115 LQR 251.

Goymour, A, 'Rights in Property and the Effluxion of Time' in E Cooke (ed), *Modern Studies in Property Law: Vol 4* (Oxford: Hart Publishing, 2007).

Kenny, P, 'Vanishing Easements in Registered Land' [2003] Conv 304.

Law Commission Consultation Paper No 186, *Easements, Covenants and Profits à Prendre* (2008).

Law Commission Report No 327, *Making Land Work: Easements, Covenants and Profits à Prendre* (2011).

Lawson, A, 'Easements' in L Tee (ed), *Land Law: Issues, Debates, Policy* (Cullompton: Willan, 2002).

Luther, P, 'Easements and Exclusive Possession' (1996) 16 LS 51.

Paton, EW and Seabourne, GC, 'Can't Get There From Here? Permissible Use of Easements After *Das*' [2003] Conv 127.

Sturley, M, 'Easements in Gross' (1980) 96 LQR 557.

Tee, L, 'Metamorphoses and Section 62 of the Law of Property Act 1925' [1998] Conv 115.

Xu, L, 'Easement of Car Parking: The Ouster Principle is Out But Problems May Aggravate' [2012] Conv 291.

## Chapter 10

Gardner, S, 'Two Maxims of Equity' (1995) 54 CLJ 60.

Gardner, S with Mackenzie, E, *Introduction to Land Law* (3rd edn, Oxford: Hart Publishing, 2012), pp 312–13.

Gray, K and Gray, SF, 'The Future of Real Burdens in Scots Law' (1999) 3 Edinburgh LR 229.

Gray, K and Gray, SF, *Elements of Land Law* (5th edn, Oxford: Oxford University Press, 2009), 3.4.78–3.4.79.

Howell, J, 'The Annexation of the Benefit of Covenants to Land' [2004] Conv 507.

Law Commission Report No 327, *Making Land Work: Easements, Covenants and Profits à Prendre* (2011).

Law Commission Report No 349, *Conservation Covenants* (2014).

Wade, HWR, 'Covenants: "A Broad and Reasonable View"' (1972) 31 CLJ 157.

## Chapter 11

Bogusz, B, 'The Relevance of "Intentions and Wishes" to Determine Actual Occupation: A Sea Change in Judicial Thinking?' [2014] Conv 27.

Conaglen, M and Goymour, A, 'Knowing Receipt and Registered Land' in C Mitchell (ed), *Constructive and Resulting Trusts* (Oxford: Hart Publishing, 2009).

Cooke, E, 'Children and Real Property: Trusts, Interests and Considerations' [1998] Fam Law 349.

Cooke, E, *The New Law of Land Registration* (Oxford: Hart Publishing, 2003).

Cooke, E and O'Connor, P, 'Purchaser Liability to Third Parties in the English Land Registration System: A Comparative Perspective' (2004) 120 LQR 640.

Dixon, M, 'The Reform of Property Law and the Land Registration Act 2002: A Risk Assessment' [2003] Conv 136.

Dixon, M, 'Priorities Under the Land Registration Act 2002' (2009) 125 LQR 401.

Ferris, G and Battersby, G, 'General Principles of Overreaching and the Reforms of the 1925 Legislation' (2002) 118 LQR 170.

Harpum, C, 'Overreaching, Trustees' Powers and the Reform of the 1925 Legislation' (1990) 49 CLJ 277.

Hayton, DJ, *Registered Land* (3rd edn, London: Sweet & Maxwell, 1981).

Hopkins, N, '*City of London Building Society v Flegg* (1987): Homes as Wealth' in N Gravells (ed), *Landmark Cases in Land Law* (Oxford: Hart Publishing, 2013a).

Hopkins, N, 'Recipient Liability in the Privy Council' [2013b] Conv 61.

Hopkins, N, 'Priorities and Sale and Leaseback: A Wrong Question, Much Ado about Nothing and a Story of Tails and Dogs' [2015] Conv 245.

Justice Committee, 'Manorial Rights', HC 657 (January 2015).

Law Commission Consultation Paper No 227, *Updating the Land Registration Act 2002* (2016).

Law Commission Report No 254, *Land Registration for the Twenty-First Century: A Consultative Document* (1988).

Law Commission Report No 188, *Transfer of Land—Overreaching: Beneficiaries in Actual Occupation* (1989).

Law Commission Report No 271, *Land Registration for the Twenty-First Century: A Conveyancing Revolution* (2001).

McFarlane, B, 'Eastenders, Neighbours and Upstairs Downstairs' [2013] Conv 81.

McFarlane, B, Hopkins, N, and Nield, S, *Land Law: Text, Cases, and Materials* (3rd edn, Oxford: Oxford University Press, 2015).

Smith, R, 'Mortgagees and Trust Beneficiaries' (1990) 109 LQR 545.

Wade, HWR, 'Land Charges Registration Reviewed' (1956) 14 CLJ 216.

## Chapter 12

Bright, S, '*Manchester City Council v Pinnock* (2010): Shifting Ideas of Ownership of Land' in N Gravells (ed), *Landmark Cases in Land Law* (Oxford: Hart Publishing, 2013).

Bright, S and Blandy, S (eds), *Researching Property Law* (Basingstoke: Palgrave Macmillan, 2015).

Dixon, M, 'A Doctrinal Approach to Property Law Scholarship: Who Cares and Why?' in S Bright and S Blandy (eds), *Researching Property Law* (Basingstoke: Palgrave Macmillan, 2015).

Fitzjames Stephen, Sir J, 'Codification in India and England' [1872] 1 The Law Magazine 963, 980.

Fox O'Mahony, L, 'Property Outsiders and the Hidden Politics of Doctrinalism' (2014) 62 CLP 409.

Goymour, A, 'Mistaken Registration of Land: Exploding the Myth of "Title by Registration"' (2013) 72 CLJ 617.

Harris, JW, 'Legal Doctrine and Interests in Land' in J Eekelaar and J Bell (eds), *Oxford Essays in Jurisprudence* (Oxford: Oxford University Press, 1987)

Jackson, N, 'Title by Registration and Concealed Overriding Interests' (2003) 119 LQR 660.

Law Commission Consultation Paper No 227, *Updating the Land Registration Act 2002* (2016).

Law Commission Report No 271, *Land Registration for the Twenty-First Century: A Conveyancing Revolution* (2001).

Law Commission Report No 278, *Sharing Homes: A Discussion Paper* (2002).

Law Commission Report No 307, *Cohabitation: The Financial Consequences of Relationship Breakdown* (2007).

McFarlane, B, *The Structure of Property Law* (Oxford: Hart Publishing, 2008), pp 1–14.

Mee, J, '*Burns v Burns*: The Villain of the Piece?' in S Gilmore et al (eds), *Landmark Cases in Family Law* (Oxford: Hart Publishing, 2011).

Rudden, B, 'Equity as Alibi' in SR Goldstein (ed), *Equity and Contemporary Legal Developments* (Jerusalem: Harry and Michael Sacher Institute for Legislative Research and Comparative Law and Hebrew University of Jerusalem, 1992).

Smith, H, 'Property, Equity, and the Rule of Law' in L Austin and D Klimchuk (eds), *Private Law and the Rule of Law* (Oxford: Oxford University Press, 2014).

Swadling, W, 'The Common Intention Trust in the House of Lords: An Opportunity Missed?' (2007) 123 LQR 511.

Walsh, R, 'Stability and Predictability in English Property Law—The Impact of Article 8 of the European Convention on Human Rights Reassessed' (2015) 131 LQR 585.

# Index

# F